Encyclopedia
of Terrorism

Encyclopedia of Terrorism

Volume 1: A–L

DISCARD

PETER CHALK, EDITOR

ABC-CLIO

Santa Barbara, California • Denver, Colorado • Oxford, England

Library of Congress Cataloging-in-Publication Data

Encyclopedia of terrorism / Peter Chalk, editor.
     p. cm.
  Includes bibliographical references and index.
  ISBN 978-0-313-30895-6 (hardcopy : alk. paper) — ISBN 978-0-313-38535-3 (e-book) 1. Terrorism—Encyclopedias. I. Chalk, Peter.
  HV6431.E534 2013
  363.32503—dc23   2012016710

ISBN: 978-0-313-30895-6
EISBN: 978-0-313-38535-3

17 16 15 14 13   1 2 3 4 5

This book is also available on the World Wide Web as an eBook.
Visit www.abc-clio.com for details.

ABC-CLIO, LLC
130 Cremona Drive, P.O. Box 1911
Santa Barbara, California 93116-1911

This book is printed on acid-free paper ∞

Manufactured in the United States of America

This book is dedicated to the countless thousands
whose lives have been taken or destroyed by
the scourge of modern-day terrorism.
May we never forget their loss.

Contents

Introduction

Since the cataclysmic attacks of September 11, 2001 (9/11), terrorism has emerged as arguably one of the main national and international security concerns in the contemporary era. Whereas in the past militant extremists sought to send an indirect message of fear through the principle of "kill one, frighten a thousand," today the emphasis is on perpetrating attacks with the specific intention of inflicting mass coercive damage. Terrorist groups have also demonstrated a proven ability to operate on a truly transnational basis, employing land, air, sea, and cyber modalities in pursuit of their objectives. At the same time, the underlying drivers for terrorism have become more complex and multifaceted and in many cases have led to the forging of tactical and strategic alliances that have effectively blurred erstwhile distinctions between national and international conflict zones or, more pointedly, the "near" and "far" enemy.

Despite the appearance of the so-called new terrorism, it is important to remember that this form of violence has a long lineage, and many groups that were established well before 9/11 continue to pose discernible threats. In order to appreciate this history and provide a context for understanding the current manifestation of terrorism, this encyclopedia catalogs the most important groups, individuals, and incidents that have been associated with militant violent extremism over the past six decades. Its aim is to offer a comprehensive and easily accessible reference work to inform practitioners, policymakers, academics, students, and interested members of the public.

All of the entries included in this volume were chosen on the basis of their salience to terrorist phenomena—selected in terms of their enduring legacy, threat potential (actual, potential, or latent), or perceived infamy. Each topic is fully cross-referenced and accompanied by a list of relevant readings that can be used to source and expand on the material presented in the text. The names and affiliations of the contributors are listed at the back of the book. The editor would like to acknowledge the exemplary work of these individuals, without whom this project would have been impossible to complete.

Definitional Issues

The encyclopedia does not pretend to offer a fully inclusive, generally accepted definition of terrorism, recognizing the inherently subjective and political nature of the subject. That said, the volume does proceed from the assumption that there are certain specific traits commonly unique to this mode of violence that help to set it apart from other substate security challenges. Seven in particular are worthy of note:

First, terrorism is a *political activity.* Whatever group we are talking about, the presence of underlying political objectives is a common characteristic. Aims can be defined in terms of self-determination, ideology, ethnonationalism, single-issue causes, or religious imperatives and are typically transformed into higher moral imperatives that are then used to justify actions that are taken in their name. For the Al Qaeda suicide operative, it is the jihad fought to cleanse the Muslim world from moral decay, corruption, evil, and unbelievers. For the Red Army Faction (RAF) kidnapper, it was the Marxist notion of world socialism. For the Earth Liberation Front (ELF) environmental militant, it is the struggle to save the planet from the rapacious actions of globalization and the self-interested greed of modern society. For the xenophobe Aryan Nations white supremacist, it is to protect the sanctity of the national status quo from the contaminating influences of Jews and foreign outsiders. And for the Tamil Tiger bomber, it was the establishment of an independent state of Eelam that was no longer subservient to the dictates of Sinhalese rule.

Second, although terrorism is politically motivated, it manifests itself as a *criminal action.* Virtually all forms of terrorist activity, such as bombing, maiming, kidnapping, murdering, and hijacking, are punishable under the penal codes of most states. A major confusion in the debate over terrorism stems from the failure to distinguish between ends and means. Although some militant groups may well pursue objectives that could be regarded as legitimate, it does not necessarily follow that any means, however unjust, are thereby exonerated. Indeed, this dictum constitutes the principal premise of the just war doctrine on which international standards regarding the conduct of violence are based.

Third, terrorism is a form of *psychological warfare.* The immediate objective is not so much to destroy (at least traditionally) but, through the use or threat of violence, to create an atmosphere of anxiety and collapse that is then levered to influence political behavior. The ultimate purpose (rarely achieved) is to destroy the structural supports that give society its strength by reducing the population to pockets of frightened individuals concerned only with their personal safety and thus isolated from their wider community context. The most psychologically damaging factor in this regard is the unpredictability of danger, whereby no one any longer knows what to expect from anybody else.

Fourth, terrorism is inherently an *indiscriminate* form of violence—something that is vital if the practice is to generate the desired psychological state already outlined. Indiscrimination plays an important role in the generation of anxiety responses: the more unpredictable terrorism becomes, the more disorienting its effects tend to be. The utility of the terror weapon is thus rooted in a feeling of helplessness that is based on actual impotence: the attacks appear completely irrational, which precludes the possibility of responding in any rational manner. Only when one knows against whom and from where the terrorist is likely to strike, can one take appropriate countermeasures.

The indiscriminate element of terrorism does not contradict the fact that terrorist groups have a primary target audience they are trying to influence and against which they will concentrate their acts of violence. However, it does affirm the assertion that they will not necessarily restrict their activities to this group alone. Indeed, by their very nature, it is impossible to ensure that bomb attacks, one of the most characteristic forms of terrorism, will result in the deaths of only the selected victims—particularly when they occur in crowded shopping malls or on board aircraft.

Fifth, terrorism is essentially a form of violence that *involves noncombatant victims*. In most cases attacks are carried out against the civilian population with the specific intent of delivering a message that is designed to shock. The midair destruction of Pan Am Flight 103 over Lockerbie in 1988, the Oklahoma City bombing in 1995, 9/11, the 2002 Bali suicide strikes, and the 2004 Madrid commuter-train explosions are all graphic cases in point. Operations conducted against the military can also be said to be terroristic when they are directed against troops not deployed in an active fighting role. When terrorists do target security forces it is almost always done for the psychological rather than the material effect, with the violence occurring in a noncombat context. Soldiers have been killed, for instance, while on leave, eating out in restaurants, traveling on public transport, transiting airports, performing peacekeeping duties, or sleeping in their barracks.

Sixth, terrorism is *a form of political communication* in which violent acts are committed to gain attention and/or a hearing. It is the very essence of terrorism that it be noticed. Advertising not only demonstrates the existence of a group but also serves as a reminder of its political agenda. By staging dramatic acts, terrorists are able to project themselves as a group that must be listened to and taken account of. In this context, the importance of the modern processes of mass communications cannot be overlooked. Former British prime minister Margaret Thatcher once referred to the media as providing the terrorist with the "oxygen of publicity." While this may be somewhat of an exaggeration, there is a definite element of truth in the statement. Maximum exposure via television, radio, satellite communications, and newspapers ensures that the terrorist is able to carry his/her conflict right to the very heart of the audience she/he is trying to influence. Without this publicity it would be impossible for the terrorist to achieve the necessary emotional reaction that is required to induce a general state of fear and collapse.

Finally, terrorism is a tactic that is carried out by *substate* organizations. This is not to deny the phenomenon of state terror itself, merely to argue that as a systematic policy, it demonstrates certain idiosyncratic features that are of sufficient importance to warrant separate study. Not only are the outcomes of the two phenomena completely different (states can inflict damage on a scale that terrorists could never hope to attain), but government-instigated terror tends to be more predictable than that at the substate level (as it is usually directed at specific sectors of society such as minorities, opposition activists, and ethnoreligious groups). Moreover, given the scale of destruction that the state is capable of inflicting, media coverage of its activities will be positively discouraged for fear of international reprisals.

Although this conceptualization excludes the notion of state terror, it needs to be stressed that governments very often play a significant role in sponsoring terrorist organizations that espouse aims compatible with their own foreign policy objectives. However, the militants who benefit from such external support should not be confused with the bureaucratized agents of state coercion. They remain different in that they are organized at a substate level, function according to a chain of command that operates independently from that of the external patron, engage in actions that are defined by their own (rather than the sponsor's) political agenda, and are only very rarely recognized as being part of the official state apparatus.

A Conceptualization of Terrorism

On the basis of the preceding criteria, this volume conceptualizes terrorism as the use or threat of illegitimate violence employed by substate actors as a means to achieve specific political ends (with those objectives differing according to the organization concerned). It is a psychological tactic that seeks to generate widespread fear through the indiscriminate targeting of noncombatant victims. In this sense, terrorism can be regarded as a means of extreme political dialogue that aims to influence behavior through the precipitation of a general state of fear and collapse. In order to fulfill this communicative function effectively, terrorism must aim to maximize publicity, and the perpetrators need to claim responsibility for their actions.

List of Entries

Abbas, Abu
Abdel-Rahman, Omar
Abu Nidal Organization (ANO)
Abu Sayyaf Group (ASG)
Achille Lauro Hijacking
Action Directe (AD)
Adams, Gerry
Adel, Saif al-
Ahmedabad Bombings
Air France Hijacking
Air India Flight 182 Bombing
Al Qaeda
Al Qaeda in the Arabian Peninsula
   (AQAP)
al-Aqsa Martyrs' Brigades
al-Badr
Alex Boncayo Brigade (ABB)
al-Fatah
al-Gama'a al-Islamiyya
Algiers Bombings
Ali Raza Mosque Bombing
al-Ittihad al-Islami (AIAI)
al-Quds Mosque
al-Shabaab
Amal
Amaqim Shopping Mall Bombing
Amir, Yigal
Amman Hotel Bombings
Amman Toxic Chemical Bomb Plot
Angry Brigade
Ansar al-Islam (AaI)
Ansar al-Sunnah (Sunni Army)
Anthrax Attacks (United States)
Arafat, Yasser
Armenian Secret Army for the Liberation
   of Armenia (ASALA)
Aryan Nations (AN)
Asahara, Shoko
Asbat al-Ansar

Ashdod Port Attack
Atef, Mohammed
Atlanta Abortion Clinic Bombings
Atta, Mohamed
Aum Shinrikyo
Australian Embassy (Jakarta) Bombing
Autodefensas Unidas de Colombia (AUC)
Ayyash, Yahya
Azhar, Masood
Azzam, Sheikh Abdullah Yussuf

Baader, Andreas
Baader-Meinhof Gang
Babbar Khalsa (BK)
Baghdad Ministry of Justice and Provincial
   Council Building Bombings
Bahaji, Said
Bali Bombings (2002)
Bali Bombings (2005)
Baltic Exchange Bombing
Banbridge Bombing
Banca de Agricultura Bombing
Bandaranaike International Airport
   Attack
Bangladesh Bombings
Basayev, Shamil
Bashir, Abu Bakar
Beam, Louis
Beersheba Bus Bombings
Beilen Train Siege
Ben Yehuda Shopping Mall Bombing
Beslan School Hostage Crisis
Bhagwan Shree Rajneesh Cult
bin al-Shibh, Ramzi
bin Husin, Azahari
bin Laden, Osama
Birmingham Pub Bombings
Bishopsgate Bombing
Black September Organization (BSO)

A

ABBAS, ABU

Abu Abbas, the nom de guerre of Muhammad Zaidan, was born in Safed, Palestine, on December 10, 1948, and moved with his family to Syria that same year. In 1968 he joined the Popular Front for the Liberation of Palestine–General Command (PFLP-GC), led by Ahmad Jibril. Abbas disagreed with Jibril over the PFLP-GC's strong support for Syria and its failure to criticize Syrian support of the Phalange against the Palestine Liberation Organization (PLO) in Lebanon. In April 1977, Abbas and Talat Yaqub left the PFLP-GC to form the Palestine Liberation Front (PLF).

During the 1980s, Abbas advocated armed struggle against Israel, chiefly in the form of terrorism mounted from southern Lebanon. He was wounded in fighting during the 1982 Israeli invasion of Lebanon. In 1983, when the PLF split into three factions, he led the largest, pro-Iraqi group. In 1984 he became a member of the PLO's executive committee.

On October 7, 1985, Abbas masterminded the PLF's most dramatic terrorist action, the hijacking of the Italian cruise ship *Achille Lauro* that resulted in the death of an American Jew named Leon Klinghoffer. The hijacking team subsequently negotiated safe passage to Tunisia, and although the United States forced the plane transporting them to land at an air base in Sicily, the Italian government let the passengers depart, and Abbas escaped among them. A year later Italy tried the PLF leader in absentia and sentenced him to life imprisonment. However, he was never detained.

In 1990 Abbas was implicated in an attempted terrorist attack on Nizamim Beach near Tel Aviv, that was designed to torpedo the possibility of PLO-Israeli peace talks. Although he was heavily criticized for the strike, the PLF continued to receive regular funding from PLO chairman Yasser Arafat.

In 1996 Abbas publicly embraced the Palestinian peace process, and Israel allowed him to enter Gaza, after which he moved to Iraq. An outstanding U.S. warrant for Abbas's arrest remained in place, and he was eventually taken by American forces in 2003 during the invasion of Iraq. He died while in custody, reportedly of natural causes, on March 8, 2004.

See also: Achille Lauro Hijacking; Palestine Liberation Front (PLF)

Further Reading

Alexander, Yonah. *Palestinian Secular Terrorism.* Ardsley, NY: Transnational, 2003.
Borger, Julian. "Homecoming of a Hijacker; Julian Borger Talks with the *Achille Lauro* Mastermind Abbu Abbas at His Political Party's New Offices in Gaza." *The Guardian* (UK), May 28, 1988.

Cowell, Alan. "Hijacker Defends *Achille Lauro* Killing." *New York Times,* November 14, 1988.
Nassar, Jamal R. *The Palestine Liberation Organization: From Armed Struggle to the Declaration of Independence.* New York: Praeger, 1991.

Spencer C. Tucker

ABDEL-RAHMAN, OMAR

Omar Abdel-Rahman was born in Fayyum, Egypt, on May 3, 1938. He suffered from childhood diabetes, which resulted in blindness when he was 10 months old. By age 11 he had memorized the Koran and devoted himself to preaching the Muslim faith. He graduated in Koranic studies from Al-Azhar University in Cairo. As a professor at the Theological College in Asyut, he gained a large militant following in Cairo's southern slums and villages after speaking out against the government's violations of traditional Islamic sharia laws. Abdel-Rahman became the spiritual leader of the loosely knit, highly militant al-Gama'a al-Islamiyya (Islamic Group) umbrella organization and the Egyptian Islamic Jihad. Both organizations opposed the Egyptian government's policies and preached militant jihad. Islamic Jihad was responsible for the 1981 assassination of Egyptian president Anwar Sadat.

In 1981 Abdel-Rahman and 23 other Islamic militants were arrested in connection with Sadat's assassination. Abdel-Rahman spent three years in Egyptian jails, where he was tortured. Although acquitted of conspiracy in the assassination of Sadat, Abdel-Rahman was expelled from Egypt and went to Afghanistan, where he reportedly made contact with Al Qaeda leader Osama bin Laden. Abdel-Rahman then traveled widely recruiting mujahideen to fight in Afghanistan against the Soviet Union. Returning to Egypt, he was again arrested in 1989 for inciting antigovernment clashes in Fayyum but was again acquitted.

Sheikh Omar Abdel-Rahman is an Egyptian theologian who fled to the United States in 1990 to escape trial in Cairo for his suspected involvement in several terrorist attacks on Coptic Christians in northern Egypt. He is currently incarcerated for his alleged role in the 1993 bombing of the World Trade Center in New York City. (AP/Wide World Photos)

Abdel-Rahman fled Egypt after being linked to further terrorist attacks on Coptic

Christians in northern Egypt and illegally entered the United States in 1990 on a tourist visa obtained in Sudan. He gained permanent U.S. residency as a religious worker in 1991, an action that the U.S. Immigration and Naturalization Service (INS) now says was erroneous. However, Abdel-Rahman's marriage to an American Muslim convert enabled him to avoid deportation despite Egypt's calls for his extradition and his status as a prominent figure on the official U.S. terrorist list.

Abdel-Rahman was discovered in January 1993 to be actively preaching militant Islamic fundamentalist sermons in New York's Muslim mosques to thousands of Egyptian, Yemeni, Sudanese, and other Muslim immigrants. The sheikh's messages, secretly recorded on tape cassettes and funneled to his followers in the Egyptian underground, advocated "the eradication of all those who stand in the way of Islam" because "the laws of God have been usurped by Crusaders' laws. The hand of a thief is not cut off, the drinker of liquor is not whipped, the adulterer is not stoned. Islamic holy law should be followed to the letter."

Abdel-Rahman was arrested in the United States in July 1993 for his suspected involvement in the World Trade Center bombing, but insufficient evidence forced the INS to initially hold him on lesser charges of illegal immigration and polygamy. He was held in a U.S. federal prison while he appealed the deportation order against him and was awarded limited preferential treatment because of his ill health and blindness.

On October 1, 1995, in the largest terrorism trial up to that point in U.S. history, Abdel-Rahman was convicted of 48 of 50 charges, including seditious conspiracy for leading a four-year terrorist campaign of bombings and assassinations intended to destroy the United Nations building and other landmarks in the New York area. He was also convicted of conspiring to assassinate Egyptian president Hosni Mubarak and of solicitation to attack U.S. military installations. Abdel-Rahman was sentenced to life imprisonment on January 17, 1996. He is currently serving his life sentence at the Federal Administrative Maximum Penitentiary hospital in Florence, Colorado. Abdel-Rahman is also believed to have ordered the November 1990 assassination in New York of militant Zionist leader Rabbi Meir Kahane.

See also: World Trade Center (New York) Bombing; Yousef, Ramzi Ahmed

Further Reading

Fried, Joseph P. "Sheik Sentenced to Life in Prison in Bombing Plot." *New York Times*, January 18, 1996.

Lance, P. *1000 Years of Revenge: International Terrorism and the FBI.* New York: HarperCollins, 2003.

Macfarquhar, Neil. "In Jail or Out, Sheik Preaches Views of Islam." *New York Times,* October 2, 1995.

Spencer C. Tucker

ABU NIDAL ORGANIZATION (ANO)

The Abu Nidal Organization (ANO) was established in 1974. The group was founded by Sabri al-Banna (the "Father of the Struggle"), who broke from al-Fatah in rejection of what he perceived to be the latter's preference for political negotiation over armed struggle. The ANO, which viewed the elimination of Israel as vital to the goal of Arab unity, emerged as one of the best-organized and most lethal terrorist networks of the 1980s. At its peak, the group had around 500 members, who were responsible for attacks in more than 20 countries across the Middle East and Europe. During its most active period while based out of Libya in the mid-1980s, the ANO carried out a vicious campaign of assassinations targeting Jordanian ambassadors and Palestine Liberation Organization (PLO) representatives; engaged in hijackings, including the seizure of Pan Am Flight 73 in Karachi, Pakistan, which ended with the deaths of 22 people after negotiations failed; and perpetrated several civilian atrocities, such as the 1982 grenade attack on the Goldenberg Restaurant in Paris (which left 6 dead and 22 injured) and the indiscriminate massacre of 22 worshippers at a Turkish synagogue in Istanbul on September 6, 1986. Arguably its most infamous (and audacious) action was the twin assault on the El Al Airlines counters at the Rome and Vienna airports (December 27, 1985), which resulted in 17 fatalities and over 100 injuries.

ANO activity began to decline toward the latter part of the 1980s, largely due to more effective counterterrorist measures on the part of the Jordanian government, growing internal dissension over the group's alleged willingness to work for the highest payer, and al-Banna's own paranoia that some of his top deputies were plotting to overthrow him. Compounding the group's difficulties was a curtailment of state support in response to the apparent progress being made in bringing peace to the Middle East during the 1990s. In 1999 al-Banna was forced to leave Libya and, suffering from declining health, was granted asylum in Iraq by Saddam Hussein. Three years later he was found in a Baghdad apartment, killed by multiple gunshot wounds. His death, which has never been fully explained, marked the effective dissolution of the ANO even though it continues to exist in name.

See also: Rome Airport Attack (1985); Vienna Airport Attack

Further Reading

Melman, Yossi. *The Master Terrorist: The True Story of Abu-Nidal.* New York: Adama Books, 1986.
Seale, Patrick. *Abu Nidal: A Gun for Hire.* New York: Random House, 1992.
Steinberg, Matti. "The Radical Worldview of the Abu-Nidal Faction." *Jerusalem Quarterly* 48 (1988).

Peter Chalk

ABU SAYYAF GROUP (ASG)

The Abu Sayyaf Group (ASG) was founded on Basilan Island in 1991 under the leadership of *ustadz* (teacher) Abdurajak Janjalani. Originally known as the al Harakat-ul al Islamiya, the group has stated its goals as the eradication of all Christian influence in the southern Philippines and the creation of an Islamic state of Mindanao whose "nature, meaning, emblem and objective are basic to peace" (Surah I-Al Fatiha, undated ASG proclamation).

Although Janjalani originally created his movement as one dedicated to establishing an Islamic state of Mindanao, he quickly tied this objective to the regional and global supremacy of Islam through armed struggle. Toward that end, the ASG paralleled its anti-Christian agenda in Mindanao with an effort to forge and consolidate logistic and operational links with external terrorist groups. Concrete evidence of these transnational ambitions first emerged in 1995 when five ASG cells were directly implicated in Oplan Bojinka (Bonjinka Operation), a multipronged plot aimed at assassinating the pope and President Clinton, bombing Washington's embassies in Manila and Bangkok, and sabotaging U.S. commercial airliners flying trans-Pacific routes from American West Coast cities. The plan was hatched by Ramzi Yousef, the convicted mastermind of the 1993 attack against the World Trade Center in New York, and was foiled only when volatile explosive compounds ignited a fire in the apartment he was renting in Manila.

The fervor of the ASG's Islamist agenda—both domestic and international—began to atrophy in the wake of the discovery of Bojinka, a process that rapidly gathered pace three years later when Janjalani was killed in a shoot-out with Philippine police on the island of Basilan. This particular event proved to be a defining moment in the ASG's evolutionary history, triggering a leadership crisis that was followed by the loss of ideological direction and subsequent factionalization that saw the group degenerate into a loosely configured but highly ruthless kidnap-for-extortion syndicate. A number of subsequent operations proved to be highly profitable. The abductions of Western tourists in the first half of 2000, for instance, are believed to have netted the ASG an estimated $20 million in ransom payments (allegedly arranged through the "good offices" of Libya).

The criminal disaggregation of the ASG proved to be short-lived, however. Beginning in 2003, concerted attempts were made to reenergize the group as an integrated and credible Islamist force. The bulk of these efforts were coordinated under the combined auspices of Khaddafi Janjalani (the younger brother of Abdurajak) and Jainal Antel Sali (also known as Abu Solaiman), a self-proclaimed ASG spokesman, both of whom sought to return the group to its militant jihadist origins following the arrest and killing of several leading bandit commanders. Notably, these included Ghalib Andang (also known as Commander Robot) and Aldam Tilao (also known as Abu Sabaya), two domineering personalities who had orchestrated many of the earlier kidnap-for-extortion operations claimed in the group's name.

Although they are now dead, Khaddafi and Solaiman's influence has been significant in reorienting the tactical and strategic direction of the ASG. The group, though disaggregated, now routinely refers to itself by its original nomenclature—al Harakat-ul al Islamiya—and has steadily scaled back its lucrative kidnap-for-extortion activities in favor of a more directed focus on attacking high-profile civilian and Western targets in major metropolitan areas.

Arguably more important, the ASG has sought to consolidate ties with the pro-bombing bloc of Jemaah Islamiyah (JI), acting as the main vehicle for furthering its operational and logistic activities in Mindanao. Intelligence sources in the Philippines confirm that militants associated with the faction continue to pass through areas under ASG control and that at least two of the most wanted men in Southeast Asia are now based in Patikul under the group's protection: Joko Pitono (also known as Dulmatin), and Zulkifi bin Hir (also known as Marwan).

Despite this reenergized jihadist focus, the ASG is weaker today than at any other time in the past. Ongoing raids by the Philippine military, carried out with U.S. military assistance, have seen the group's numbers dwindle to around 100 hardcore members supplemented by at most 200 part-timers. Most of these militants are split between 18 separate cells scattered across Sulu, Basilana, and Zamboanga. Compounding matters, the ASG has still to identify a universally accepted emir (leader) to replace Khaddafi and reunite the organization under a single command structure.

So long as this remains the case, the ASG's ability to perpetrate long-range, strategically disruptive attacks will be constrained. That said, the organization still has the capacity to pull off limited, localized strikes when opportunities arise. On August 4, 2010, for example, an individual suspected of being tied to ASG staged an attack on the Zamboanga City Airport, killing 2 and injuring 22. Just over two months later, on October 21 the group was tied to the bombing of a passenger bus in Cotabato that left 9 people dead and 13 wounded, 4 critically. Most recently, in November 2011 ASG was connected to an explosion at a budget hotel in Zamboanga that was hosting a wedding. The blast resulted in 3 fatalities and 27 additional casualties.

See also: Jemaah Islamiyah (JI); *SuperFerry 14* Bombing; Valentine's Day Bombings

Further Reading

Bowden, Mark. "Jihadists in Paradise." *The Atlantic* (March 2007).
Chalk, Peter, Angel Rabasa, William Rosenau, and Leanne Piggott. *The Evolving Terrorist Threat to Southeast Asia: A Net Assessment.* Santa Monica, CA: RAND, 2009.
Elegant, Simon. "Asia's Own Osama." *Time,* April 1, 2002.
"The Man Who Wasn't There." *Time,* February 20, 1995.
Maydens, Seth. "Libyan Aid Helps to Free Hostages Held in the Philippines." *New York Times,* October 21, 2001.

Peter Chalk

ACHILLE LAURO HIJACKING

The Italian-flagged cruise liner *Achille Lauro* was seized off Port Said, Egypt, on October 7, 1985. The hijackers, led by Palestine Liberation Front (PLF) commander Abu Abbas, held 400 passengers hostage for two days and demanded the release of 50 Palestinian prisoners held in Israeli jails. Negotiations with Egyptian and Palestine Liberation Organization (PLO) representatives culminated in a deal where, in exchange for the release of the ship and those on board, the attacking team would be granted free passage to Tunis. However, U.S. fighter jets intercepted the plane carrying the men to North Africa and forced it to land in Sicily. Three of the hijackers were arrested, but Italian authorities refused to hand over Abbas and two associates, who fled to what was then Yugoslavia.

Passengers being evacuated from the Italian cruise ship *Achille Lauro*. The ship had been hijacked off the Port of Said, Egypt, by members of the Palestine Liberation Front (PLF) on October 7, 1985. One wheelchair-bound American passenger, Leon Klinghoffer, was killed during the incident. (AP/Wide World Photos)

During the standoff one person was killed, Leon Klinghoffer, an elderly wheelchair-bound passenger from New York, who was shot and dumped overboard. Although the PLO settled a $1.5 billion court case with the Klinghoffer family in 1997, the group has always asserted that the hijackers were working independently and without their support. The attack remains one of the most audacious acts of maritime terrorism in history.

See also: Abbas, Abu; Palestine Liberation Front (PLF)

Further Reading

Bohn, Michael K. *The Achille Lauro Hijacking: Lessons in the Politics and Prejudice of Terrorism.* Dulles, VA: Potomac Books, 2004.

Cassese, Antonio. *Terrorism, Politics and Law: The Achille Lauro Affair.* Princeton, NJ: Princeton University Press, 1989.

"85 *Achille Lauro* Killing 'a Mistake.'" *New York Times,* April 23, 1996.

Peter Chalk

ACTION DIRECTE (AD)

Action Directe (AD, or Action Direct) had its roots in the "new leftism" of late 1960s France and in the violent extreme-left student organizations Groupes d'Action Revolutionnaires Internationalistes and Noyaux Armes Pour l'Autonomie

Populaire, which emerged in the early 1970s. From these groups the activists Jean-Marc Rouillan, Natalie Menigon, Joelle Aubron, and Regis Schleicher formed AD in 1979. The quartet announced their intention "to wreck society through direct action by destroying its institutions and the men who serve it, and by relying on the peoples' forces."

In March 1979 AD began its campaign with a machine-gun strafing of the Ministry of Cooperation in Paris. This was followed by a spate of bombings on public buildings in the city as well as violent robberies and even an antitank rocket fired at the Ministry of Transport. Although attacks declined after Rouillan and Menigon were arrested in September 1980, they intensified again after the two were released, along with Schleicher, in a 1981 amnesty.

In 1982 the AD internationalized its agenda, forging close operational ties with similar "fighting communist organizations" such as the Belgian Cellules Communistes Combattantes and the German Rote Armee Fraktion (RAF). In August 1985 these links were cemented with a joint RAF-AD car bomb attack on the U.S. Air Force base at Ramstein, Germany, which killed 2 and wounded 20. Despite its solidarity with the cause of other fighting communist organizations, AD continued to undertake operations in France. In January 1985 the group shot General Rene Audran, director of international affairs at the French ministry, following this with the assassination of George Besse, the chief executive of Renault, in November 1986.

For several years, Menigon and Rouillan had used a remote farmhouse at Vitry-aux-Loges (Loiret), east of Orleans, as a safe house. However, the location of the site was betrayed by an inside AD informer, and the building was put under active surveillance. In 1987 the special tactical operations wing of the French Gendarmerie Nationale, the Recherche Assistance, Intervention, Dissuasion, stormed the farmhouse and apprehended the entire leadership of AD. The arrests effectively decapitated the organization, creating a void it was never able to recover from.

See also: Cellules Communistes Combattantes (CCC); Rote Armee Fraktion (RAF)

Further Reading

Dartnell, Michael. "Action Directe." In Martha Crenshaw and John Pimlott, eds., *International Encyclopedia of Terrorism*. Chicago: Fitzroy Dearborn, 1997.

Dartnell, Michael. *Action Directe: Ultra-left Terrorism in France 1979–1987*. London: Frank Cass, 1985.

Hamon, Alain, and Jean-Charles Marchand. *Action Directe: Du terrorisme Francais a l'Euroterrorisme*. Paris: Editions Seuil, 1986.

Richard Warnes

ADAMS, GERRY

Gerard (known as Gerry) Adams was born in Belfast on October 6, 1948. He was the eldest of 10 children, born into a family with a strong tradition of Irish Republicanism. His father, also Gerry, had served a long prison sentence for shooting a police officer. Leaving school at 17, Adams was employed as a barman before becoming involved in the unrest that began in Belfast in 1969 and marked the beginning of "the Troubles" in Northern Ireland. Adam's exact role in this period is controversial; he has described himself as being involved in "defense work" in Roman Catholic areas, whereas the British security forces have alleged he was a senior member, if not the leader, of the Provisional Irish Republican Army (PIRA) unit in the Ballymurphy area of West Belfast. Adams has consistently denied the allegations of membership in the PIRA that have dogged him ever since.

In 1971 Adams was arrested and interned on a prison ship but was released in 1972 to participate in secret peace talks between Sinn Féin/PIRA leaders and the British government, as a representative of those Republicans interned by the security forces. However, these talks proved to be fruitless, and Adams returned with the delegation to Belfast. He was rearrested and again interned in 1973 and spent another four years in incarceration, eventually being released in 1977, having tried to escape twice. During these four years Adams began to write articles discussing the need for the Republican movement to develop a political strategy that would work in parallel with the "armed struggle."

In February 1978 Adams was again arrested on charges of membership in the PIRA, but he was acquitted after the judge ruled there was insufficient evidence to convict him. In November 1978 he was elected as vice president of the Republican political party, Sinn Féin. This new role gave Adams the opportunity to promote his view on the need for a new political approach to complement the armed struggle, a strategy that subsequently became known as the "armalite (bullet) and the ballot box" approach. This dual-track strategy was given a significant boost in the wake of the 1981 hunger strikes in which 10 Republican prisoners starved themselves to death in protest at being classed as criminals. The result was an upsurge in support for both the PIRA and Sinn Féin in nationalist areas, and in October 1982, Adams was one of five Sinn Féin candidates who won seats in the inaugural elections for the Northern Ireland Assembly. This marked a reversal of the previous Republican strategy of refusing to participate in elections for any assembly in the United Kingdom or the Irish Republic (known as the abstentionist policy), although the five then boycotted the assembly, refusing to take their seats.

Adams achieved further electoral success in June 1983 when he was returned as the Westminster Member of Parliament for West Belfast, but he again refused to take his seat. In November that same year he became the president of Sinn Féin, securing a key role in controlling the direction of the Republican movement, and he remains in that office at time of writing. However, Adams's career was almost cut short in March 1984 when he was seriously injured in an assassination attempt carried out by the Ulster Defence Association/Ulster Freedom Fighters.

Adams's modernizing agenda within Republicanism received a boost in 1986 when the party formally overturned the abstentionist policy (which led to a schism within Sinn Féin, with former president Ruairi O'Bradaigh leaving to form his own party, Republican Sinn Féin). Adams and his supporters argued it made little sense to mobilize mass political support only to squander its potential by refusing to participate in the elected bodies, notably the Dail in Dublin. This ballot-box element of Republican strategy also led in 1988 to talks between Adams and the leader of the Social Democratic and Liberal Party, Sinn Féin's main political rival, in an attempt to form a coherent nationalist political strategy, a goal finally achieved in 1993.

It has been suggested that it was around this time, and in particular as a response to the widespread revulsion that surrounded the exceptionally lethal bombing of a fish shop in the Protestant Shankill area of Belfast in October 1993, that Adams and his supporters began to perceive that the continuation of violence was preventing Sinn Féin from fully exploiting the potential of the ballot-box strategy. Despite the loss of his Westminster seat in 1992, Adams continued to play a leading role in Republican thinking, and in August 1994 he was integral to the announcement of the first PIRA cease-fire. Adams and Sinn Féin expected that the cessation of PIRA violence would open the way for the party's full participation in the political process. While the British government did not immediately reward Sinn Féin, the electorate did, with an upsurge in support for the party in nationalist areas.

Despite the collapse of the first PIRA cease-fire just under two years later, Adams regained his West Belfast seat in May 1997, and Sinn Féin achieved its best electoral result in Northern Ireland, gaining 16 percent of the vote. The PIRA cease-fire was subsequently renewed in July 1997, and shortly afterward Sinn Féin was invited to participate in all-party peace talks, chaired by George Mitchell. Subsequently Adams succeeded in convincing Sinn Féin members to endorse the 1998 Good Friday Agreement, even though this meant recognizing the partition of Ireland, previously a touchstone of Irish Republicanism.

Having led his party and Republicans more widely into the renewed political structures of Northern Ireland, Adams stepped back to allow his longtime colleague Martin McGuinness (a self-confessed former PIRA member) to take the roles of, first, education minister and then deputy first minister of Northern Ireland. Adams remains president of Sinn Féin. It has been suggested that he was aware that his taking on a ministerial role could have been too much to bear for his Republican compatriots, and so, in order to preserve the political process he had helped build, Adams was forced to take a backseat.

In late 2009 Adams's family history was the subject of intense media scrutiny when it emerged that his brother, Liam, had been accused of sexually abusing his own daughter. Adams was forced to admit publicly that his father, Gerry, a stalwart Republican, had also sexually abused some of his own children.

See also: Good Friday Agreement; Provisional Irish Republican Army (PIRA)

Further Reading

Adams, Gerry. *Before the Dawn: An Autobiography.* New York: HarperCollins, 1997.

Alonso, Rogelio. "The Modernization in Irish Republican Thinking toward the Utility of Violence." *Studies in Conflict and Terrorism* 24 (2001).

Biographies of Prominent People. Conflict Archive on the Internet, 2012. http://cain.ulst.ac.uk/othelem/people/biography/apeople.htm.

Hari, Johann. "Gerry Adams: Unrepentant Irishman." *The Independent* (UK), September 9, 2009. http://www.independent.co.uk/news/people/profiles/gerry-adams-unrepentant-irishman-1783739.html.

McAllister, Ian. "The Armalite and the Ballot Box: Sinn Fein's Electoral Strategy in Northern Ireland." *Electoral Studies* 23 (2004).

Moloney, Ed. *A Secret History of the IRA.* London: Penguin Books, 2007.

Greg Hannah

ADEL, SAIF AL-

Saif al-Adel was born in Egypt on November 11, 1960. He was Osama bin Laden's security and possibly military chief. A 2005 report by Robert Windrem claims that al-Adel moved to Iran after the U.S. invasion of Afghanistan in 2001 and the subsequent death or capture of key Al Qaeda leaders, including Mohammed Atef. While details of his current whereabouts are unclear, it is believed that he may have been involved in planning attacks against Saudi Arabia from Iran.

Al-Adel was thought to have been a colonel in the Egyptian Army; however, this has been disputed by some scholars. In 1987 he was accused of attempting to form a military wing of the al-Jihad group to overthrow the government. To avoid capture, he fled to Afghanistan with his wife (Mohamed Mekawi) and five children. There, he participated in the latter stages of the mujahideen campaign against the Soviet Union.

Al-Adel is thought to have trained the operatives who ambushed American troops in Somalia in 1993 and is suspected of being a key player in organizing the 1998 bombings of the U.S. embassies in Nairobi and Dar es Salaam. Following these attacks, he was placed on the Federal Bureau of Investigation's most wanted terrorist list.

Authorities believe that al-Adel took over the responsibility for Al Qaeda's terrorist operations following Atef's death in a 2001 U.S. air strike. A 2005 article on al-Adel published in the London Arabic daily *Al Sharq al Awsat* similarly asserted that he was organization's military leader.

It was in this guise that al-Adel reportedly introduced Abu Musab al-Zarqawi to the Al Qaeda organization. The two were linked through Abu-Qatada, a Palestinian fundamentalist and terrorist ideologue. They reputedly agreed to set up a central leadership command in Iran from which other terrorist commands could branch off (it remains unclear whether or not this was to take place under the overarching framework of Al Qaeda). Little has been heard of al-Adel since 2005, and while he is still thought to play an active role in Al Qaeda, his current whereabouts are unknown.

See also: Atef, Mohammed; Al Qaeda; bin Laden, Osama

Further Reading

Mohammed, Al Shafey. "Seif Al-Adl: Al-Qaeda's Ghost." *Al Sharq al Awsat,* June 1, 2005. http://aawsat.com/english/news.asp?section=3&id=191.

"Saif al Adel." *Wikipedia.* http://en.wikipedia.org/wiki/Saif_al-Adel.

Windrem, Robert. "Al-Qaida Finds Safe Haven in Iran." *NBC News,* June 24, 2005. http://www.msnbc.msn.com/id/8330976/.

Horacio Trujillo

AHMEDABAD BOMBINGS

On July 26, 2008, a series of improvised explosive devices (IEDs) were detonated in Ahmedabad, a city of 3.5 million considered to be the cultural and commercial heart of the state of Gujarat in western India. The blasts killed 56 people and injured more than 200 others in a span of 70 minutes. Most of the bombs were hidden in lunchboxes or on bicycles.

The explosions occurred in two waves early in the evening. The first series of attacks targeted busy marketplaces, the second an area near the L.G. Hospital and Trauma Center. The latter killed at least 25 people, some of whom were casualties who were being treated from the first explosions. The blasts were considered to be of low intensity and were similar to bombings that took place in Bangalore the previous day—killing 2 and wounding 20. Indian police believed that the IEDs had been deployed across the city by a team of four people working from a car that had been stolen in Mumbai during the second week of July.

Several TV channels reported they had received e-mails from an organization calling itself Indian Mujahideen (IM) claiming responsibility for the attacks. According to the messages, the bombings had been carried out in revenge for a 2002 massacre by Hindu mobs in Gujarat that killed more than 1,000 people, mainly Muslims.

IM is believed to be a shadow amalgam of the Students Islamic Movement of India (SIMI), Lashkar-e-Taiba (LeT), and Harakat ul-Jihad al-Islami (HuJI). It has taken credit for several attacks against targets in India and first received significant attention in May 2008 after stating that it had been behind synchronized blasts in Jaipur that left 56 people dead.

SIMI is an Islamic group that was formed in Aligarh, Uttar Pradesh, in April 1977. The organization's stated mission is to liberate India from Western materialistic cultural influence and to make society conform to a Muslim code of conduct. SIMI has been labeled a terrorist organization by both India and the United States.

LeT, which was co-founded by Hafiz Muhammad Saeed and Zafar Iqbal, is one of the largest and most active Islamist terrorist outfits in South Asia. With its headquarters based in Muridke, near Lahore in the Punjab province of Pakistan, the group operates several training camps in Pakistan-ocuppied Kashmir (POK). LeT's main aim is to introduce an Islamic state in South Asia and to "liberate" Muslims residing in Indian Kashmir.

HuJI is an Islamic fundamentalist militant organization that has been active in Pakistan, Bangladesh, and India since the early 1990s. The group was formed in 1984 by Fazlur Rehman Khalil and Qari Saifullah Akhtar during the Soviet-Afghan War. After Moscow's retreat from Kabul, the movement turned its attention to exporting jihad to the Indian states of Jammu and Kashmir under the patronage of Pakistan. HuJI's footprint was extended to Bangladesh in 1992 with direct assistance from Osama bin Laden.

By August 16, 2008, Indian police had arrested 10 suspects affiliated with SIMI on charges of waging war against the state and murder. Among those arrested was Mufti Abu Bashir, an employee of a software firm who had allegedly masterminded the Ahmedabad attacks in an attempt to provoke violence between Hindus and Muslims.

Shiv Vishvanathan, a well-respected professor of anthropology in India, said the type of attack carried out in Ahmedabad was a very good way to achieve this objective: "This is different, because for the first time it's every day, it's utterly anonymous, it's excessive. The familiar becomes unfamiliar. The apple seller you meet might be carrying a bomb. It creates suspicion. It's a perfect way to destabilize society."

Following the bombings, Indian authorities moved to harden high-profile targets that could be hit in a similar vein, including movie theaters, commuter trains, and prominent temples and mosques. Although these measures have since thwarted some attempted acts of terrorism, they have had only a limited impact on safeguarding the numerous civilian-centric venues that India's congested cities offer.

See also: Harakat ul-Jihad al-Islami (HuJI); Indian Mujahideen (IM); Lashkar-e-Taiba (LeT); New Delhi Bombings; Students Islamic Movement of India (SIMI)

Further Reading

Clarke, Ryan. *Lashkar-i-Taiba: The Fallacy of Subservient Proxies and the Future of Islamist Terrorism in India.* Carlisle, PA: U.S. Army War College, Strategic Studies Institute, March 2010. http://www.strategicstudiesinstitute.army.mil/pdffiles/pub973.pdf, accessed August 1, 2011.

Rabasa, Angel, Peter Chalk, Kim Cragin, Sara A. Daly, Heather S. Gregg, Theodore W. Karasik, Kevin A. O'Brien, and William Rosenau. *Beyond al-Qaeda. Part 1: The Global Jihadist Movement.* Santa Monica, CA: RAND, 2006.

Srivastava, Devyani. *Terrorism and Armed Violence in India: An Analysis of Events in 2008.* IPCS Special Report 71. New Delhi: Institute of Peace and Conflict Studies, May 2008.

"Students Islamic Movement of India (SIMI)." South Asia Terrorism Portal, July 27, 2008. http://www.satp.org/satporgtp/countries/India/terroristoutfits/simi.htm, accessed August 1, 2011.

Donna Bassett

AIR FRANCE HIJACKING

On December 24, 1994, four members of the Groupe Islamique Armeé (GIA), led by Abdul Yahia, hijacked an Air France Airbus at Algiers airport as it was preparing to leave for Paris. Denouncing the Algerian government—which two years previously had annulled elections won by the fundamentalist Fronte Islamique du Salut (FIS, or Islamic Salvation Front)—as illegitimate, the terrorists demanded the release of imprisoned colleagues. When Algerian authorities refused to comply, the terrorists executed three hostages—an Algerian police officer, a Vietnamese diplomat, and a French embassy cook. Despite the killings, they released 63 women and children, who were rapidly debriefed by the Algerian and French authorities for any relevant intelligence.

Under increasing pressure, on December 26, the Algerians allowed the jet to take off, but instead of flying to Paris the plane landed at Marseilles-Marignane airport after the French authorities managed to persuade the terrorists that they needed to take on extra fuel. However, the government had no intention of either servicing the aircraft or, indeed, permitting it to leave Marignane. During the course of interviews with some of the released hostages, intelligence sources had determined that the GIA team was in fact planning on crashing the plane into Paris or exploding it over the city—a foreshadow of the tactics that were to be used in the United States on September 11, 2001. While negotiators on the ground deliberately stalled for time, the Gendarmerie Nationale's elite tactical intervention squad, Groupe d'Intervention de la Gendarmerie (GIGN), was preparing for an assault from a staging post on the island of Majorca in southern Spain. A final deadline was set for 10:00 P.M. on December 26, when the terrorists said they would kill all those remaining on the plane. Six hours prior to this, while sniper cover was provided, several GIGN units deployed to their assault positions.

Just as the rescue team was preparing to storm the plane, the GIA terrorists directed a burst of gunfire at the airport control tower. This forced Major Denis Favier, GIGN's commander, to launch an immediate-action assault. As snipers fired into the cockpit area where two terrorists had been identified, a seven-man GIGN team entered the front of the plane using a mobile stairway, deployed stun grenades, and immediately shot one of the terrorists dead. However, the commandos came under heavy fire from the other three hijackers, who had taken shelter in the flight deck, and several members were seriously injured. The lead GIGN squad was quickly reinforced by a second assault team, who after an intense, 20-minute firefight neutralized the remaining GIA attackers. All 170 passengers on board the plane as well as the crew survived. Even though nine Gendarmes had suffered injuries, some serious, the rescue was widely lauded as a resounding success and testament to France's counterterrorism capabilities.

See also: Groupe Islamique Armeé (GIA)

Further Reading

"4 Hijackers Die as Commandos Storm Jetliner." *Vancouver Sun* (Canada), December 27, 1994.

Fox, Robert. "Militants Bring Their Brutality to Europe." *Daily Telegraph* (UK), December 27, 1994.

Harclerode, Peter. *Secret Soldiers: Special Forces in the War against Terrorism.* London: Cassell, 2002.

Micheletti, E. *Le GIGN en Action.* Paris: Histoire & Collections, 1997.

Micheletti, E. "GIGN French Anti-Terrorist Unit." *RAIDS* 41 (April 1995).

Randall, Colin. "'It Seemed the Time Had Come.'" *Daily Telegraph* (UK), December 27, 1994.

Randall, Colin, and Charles Masters. "All Four Islamic Terrorists Killed in Shoot-Out at Marseilles Airport." *Daily Telegraph* (UK), December 27, 1994.

Richard Warnes

AIR INDIA FLIGHT 182 BOMBING

Air India Flight 182 exploded in midair on June 23, 1985, off the west coast of Ireland. The plane was en route to New Delhi, via London, and had departed from Toronto, Canada. All 329 passengers on board were killed. That same day, a second bomb concealed in a suitcase on a flight from Vancouver to Tokyo exploded at Narita International Airport. Although no group claimed responsibility for the bombings, it is suspected that members of Babbar Khalsa (BK), a Sikh extremist group in India seeking an independent state of Khalistan, were behind both attacks and that the two bombs originated in Vancouver. There, an unidentified man had booked two separate itineraries to New Delhi. The first ran east from Vancouver via Toronto and London; the second west, via Tokyo. In each case, bags were checked through to India, but the accompanying passenger never boarded either flight.

Most of those who died on Flight 182 were Canadian citizens of Indian descent. The failure of the intelligence services and police to prevent the attack or apprehend those behind it was widely criticized and seen by many as an insult to the expatriate community. The controversy gained momentum after it was discovered that the Royal Canadian Mounted Police (RCMP) had advanced warning of the attack (supplied by a Sikh informant) but filed the information as "unconfirmed" and failed to pass it on to the Canadian Security Intelligence Service (CSIS). In late 2000 the Canadian government charged two men from British Columbia in the Flight 182 bombing—cleric Ajaib Singh Bagri and businessman Ripudaman Singh Malik. Both were acquitted on all counts in 2005. A third man, Inderjit Singh Reyat, was arrested in 2001 and subsequently sentenced to five years for manslaughter in a plea bargain. As of 2009, no one had been convicted for actually carrying out the attack, and the case remains open. Prior to 9/11, the bombing of Flight 182 was the most destructive act of aviation sabotage in history.

See also: Babbar Khalsa (BK); Tokyo Airport Attack

Further Reading

Blaise, Clark, and Bharati Mukerjee. *The Sorrow and the Terror: The Haunting Legacy of the Air India Tragedy.* Markham, ON, Canada: Viking Books, 1987.

"Cover Up by Canadian Spy Agency Alleged; Sikh Agent Reputedly Had Advanced Information about 1985 Airline Bombing." *Washington Post,* June 3, 2003.

Jiwa, Salim. *The Death of Air India Flight 182.* London: W. H. Allen, 1986.

Nickerson, Colin. "15-Year Probe of Jet Bombing Brings 2 Arrests: Canada Detains Sikh Militants." *Boston Globe,* October 29, 2000.

"Police Had Hint 11 Days before 1985 Air India Bombing, Inquiry Hears." *CBC News,* May 1, 2007. http://www.cba.ca/canada/story/2007/05/01/air-india.html.

Peter Chalk

AL QAEDA

Al Qaeda is a salafi Sunni organization that was established sometime between 1987 and 1988 by Sheikh Abdullah Azzam, a mentor to Osama bin Laden—the group's former leader. Azzam was a professor at King Abd al-Aziz University in Jeddah, Saudi Arabia. Bin Laden attended that university, where he met and was strongly influenced by Azzam.

Al Qaeda developed from the Mujahideen Services Bureau that Azzam had established in Peshawar, Afghanistan. Bin Laden funded the organization and was considered the deputy director. This organization recruited, trained, and transported Muslim volunteers from any Muslim nation into Afghanistan to fight the jihad (holy war) against the Soviet armies in the 1980s.

Additional elements in Al Qaeda arrived with members of radical groups from other countries, such as a faction of Egyptian Islamic Jihad, some of the members of which had been indicted and fled Egypt. The credo of Al Qaeda came from their beliefs, based on ideas by many radical Islamist thinkers, including the practice of *takfir,* declaring that Muslim leaders who colluded with non-Muslim interests were apostates. Azzam adopted and expanded on these arguments, and bin Laden applied them to the government of Saudi Arabia, which he believed was too closely allied with the West. He proposed armed struggle to combat the far as well as the near enemy in order to create a new Islamic society.

Following the mysterious death of Sheikh Azzam in November 1989, bin Laden took over the leadership of Al Qaeda. He continued to work toward Azzam's goal of creating an international organization comprised of mujahideen who will fight the oppression of Muslims throughout the world. Al Qaeda aims to establish an authentic Islamic form of government, to fight against any government viewed as contrary to the ideals of Islamic law and religion, and to aid Islamic groups trying to establish an Islamic form of government in their countries.

In its original configuration, a *majlis al-shura,* or consultative council, headed Al Qaeda. Bin Laden acted as the *amir al-mu'minin* (commander of the faithful) of the

A video still released by Al Jazeera television shows Osama bin Laden with Egyptian jihad leader Ayman al-Zawahiri at an undisclosed location in 2001. (AP/Wide World Photos)

council, followed by several other generals and then the leaders of related groups (which at the movement's height numbered at least 24). The actual majlis was made up of four main subcommittees: military, religious-legal, finance, and media. Bin Laden personally selected the respective heads of these committees, and each reported directly to him. All levels were highly compartmentalized, and secrecy was considered the key to all operations.

As result of the U.S. invasion of Afghanistan (Operation Enduring Freedom) and the subsequent initiation of the global war on terror, Al Qaeda's organizational structure has become far more fluid and disaggregated in nature. While a residual command core continues to exist in the Federally Administered Tribal Areas along the Pakistani-Afghan border, Al Qaeda has become increasingly reliant on self-funded and self-directed locally based affiliates (and in certain cases individuals) to carry out attacks, which are claimed in its name rather than undertaken at its behest. Indeed, in many ways the group now acts as a segmented and polycentric "movement of movements" whose relevance lies more in its ability to inspire than to command per se.

Al Qaeda's ideology has appealed to both Middle Eastern and non–Middle Eastern Muslim groups. There are also a number of radical Islamic terrorist groups who initiated an association with Al Qaeda via public declarations, such as Tanzom Qa'idat al-Jihadi Bilad al-Rafidyan (Al Qaeda in Iraq) and Al Qaeda fi Jazirat al-Arabiyya (Al Qaeda in the Arabian Peninsula). The central focus of the group's militant message has been the United States, Israel, the West, and what it defines as apostate Arab states. The genesis of this antipathy goes back to the 1991 Persian Gulf War, which was first precipitated by the Iraqi invasion of Kuwait on August 2, 1990. Bin Laden, originally a well-to-do Saudi Arabian, allegedly offered to commit Al Qaeda's mujahideen to help liberate Kuwait and defend Saudi Arabia from possible future Iraqi attacks. The Riyadh government declined the offer and permitted the stationing of hundreds of thousands of U.S. and coalition soldiers in Saudi Arabia during the run-up to the war (Operation Desert Shield). This move enraged bin Laden, who perceived the presence of foreign troops in Saudi Arabia as a blatant acknowledgment of the political linkage between the Saudi government and the United States. He also portrayed this as a religious failing, for Saudi Arabia is home to both Mecca and Medina, the holiest of places in all of Islam, and the members of the Saudi royal family are the guardians of these.

After condemning the stationing of U.S. troops in Saudi Arabia, bin Laden was expelled from the kingdom and had his citizenship revoked. He then took up residence in Sudan, where he began training Al Qaeda fighters and allegedly orchestrated an assassination attempt against Egyptian president Hosni Mubarak in 1994. Under intense international pressure, led by the United States, Sudan expelled bin Laden and the Al Qaeda leadership in late 1996.

From Sudan the Al Qaeda core traveled directly to Afghanistan, where the Islamic fundamentalist Taliban regime had already ensconced itself. Under the leadership of Mullah Omar, the movement not only protected Al Qaeda but also helped arm and bestow its fighters with an air of legitimacy. The provision of safe haven in Afghanistan proved to be a major boon to Al Qaeda, allowing the organization to set up dedicated training terrorist camps and plan for long-range strategic attacks.

In February 1998 bin Laden issued his now-infamous Khost fatwa in which he and the leaders of several other radical organizations—most notably, Ayman al-Zawahiri, the commander of Egyptian Islamic Jihad—vowed to wage a holy war against Israel and its allies. Issued under the banner of the World Islamic Front for Combat against the Jews and Crusaders, the declaration affirmed: "[Killing] Americans and their allies—civilians and military—is an individual duty for every Muslim who can do it in any country in which it is possible to do it, in order to liberate the al-Aqsa Mosque [in Jerusalem] and the holy mosque [in Mecca] from their grip, and in order for their armies to move out of all the lands of Islam, defeated and unable to threaten any Muslim. This is in accordance with the words of Almighty Allah, 'and fight the pagans all together as they fight you all together,' and 'fight them until there is no more tumult or oppression, and there prevail justice and faith in Allah'."

In August of that year, Al Qaeda carried out its first major terrorist operation against the West—the bombings of the U.S. embassies in Kenya and Tanzania, which left more than 200 dead and wounded another 4,000. The incident was followed two years later by the suicide strike on the USS *Cole* while it was refueling at the Yemeni port of Aden; 17 American sailors perished in this attack.

Al Qaeda's most horrific deed was yet to come, however. On September 11, 2001, the organization hijacked four commercial airliners, flying two into the New York World Trade Center and one into the Pentagon in northern Virginia; the fourth, which was probably heading for either the Capitol building or the White House, crashed in a Pennsylvania field before reaching its target, killing all on board. The attacks, now colloquially referred to as 9/11, killed an estimated 2,976 people and remain the most destructive act of terrorism in history. While the vast majority of Muslims condemned 9/11, others celebrated it as a heroic show of force against a repressive and imperialist power. In addition, many disputed that there was any evidence to directly connect bin Laden to the attacks and continue to believe to this day that they were staged either by Israel or the Central Intelligence Agency as a pretext to justify an onslaught against the Islamic world.

Al Qaeda and/or its affiliates have since taken responsibility, either directly or indirectly, for a wave of high-profile destructive attacks around the world. Some of the most notable cases have included the bombing of the M/V *Limburg* in 2002, the Casablanca bombings of 2003 (33 dead, over 100 wounded), the Riyadh housing complex attack in 2003 (26 dead), the Istanbul bombings of 2003 (57 dead, 700 wounded) and 2008 (17 dead, 154 wounded), the Madrid commuter train bombings of 2004 (nearly 200 dead), the London Underground bombings of 2005 (52 dead), the Amman bombings of 2005 (70 people dead), and the Glasgow International Airport attack in 2008. In addition, Al Qaeda has been behind several major plots, perhaps the most infamous (and disruptive) being the preempted 2006 plan to bomb transatlantic commercial airliners using liquid explosives.

Following the 2003 Anglo-American invasion of Iraq (Operation Iraqi Freedom), Al Qaeda also became intimately involved in supporting the growing insurgency in that country. Acting primarily through Abu Musab al-Zarqawi (until his death in 2006), the group took responsibility for numerous suicide strikes against allied forces as well as the bombings of the United Nations headquarters in 2004 and the Jordanian embassy in 2003.

Although Al Qaeda enjoyed initial support in Iraq, the movement fundamentally misread the strategic situation on the ground and incorrectly assumed that indigenous Iraqis would back its effort to create an Islamic caliphate in the country. While the organization retains a residual presence in Iraq, the tempo of its activity has declined markedly since 2007.

As noted, the U.S.-led war on terror has significantly impacted on Al Qaeda's organizational character. The group has also suffered from the loss of its founding emir—Osama Bin Laden (killed May 2, 2011)—as well as many of its most experienced commanders, The group is now dispersed and other than enclaves in Federally Administered Tribal Areas, lacks a concerted safe haven from which to operate. That said, Al Qaeda's influence continues to permeate many religious, social, and economic structures in the Muslim world, and the movement's decentralized configuration has made it increasingly difficult to track, monitor, and predict. Moreover, the group has successfully levered the Internet to comment on current issues, mobilize sympathizers through the process of self-radicalization, and encourage followers to keep up the fight. Through these processes, Al Qaeda has managed to project itself as an entity that exists in all places at all times which has successfully kept the movement and its activities at the forefront of global attention in the ongoing fight against transnational terrorism.

See also: bin Laden, Osama; Casablanca Bombings; Heathrow Liquid Bomb Plot; Istanbul Bombings; *Limburg* Bombing; London Underground Bombings; London-Glasgow Airport Plot; September 11 (2001); United Nations Headquarters (Baghdad) Attack; U.S. Embassy (East Africa) Bombings; USS *Cole* Bombing; Zarqawi, Abu Musab al-

Further Reading

Bergen, Peter L. *Holy War, Inc.: Inside the Secret World of Osama bin Laden.* New York: Touchstone, 2002.

Gunaratna, Rohan. *Inside Al Qaeda.* New York: Columbia University Press, 2002.

Hueston, Harry R., and B. Vizzin. *Terrorism 101.* 2nd ed. Ann Arbor, MI: XanEdu, 2004.

Scheuer, Michael. *Imperial Hubris. Why the West Is Losing the War on Terror.* Dulles, VA: Brassey's, 2004.

Scheuer, Michael. *Through Our Enemies' Eyes: Osama Bin Laden, Radical Islam and the Future of America.* Dulles, VA: Brassey's, 2006.

Zuhur, Sherifa. *A Hundred Osamas: Islamist Threats and the Future of Counterinsurgency.* Carlisle Barracks, PA: Strategic Studies Institute, U.S. Army War College, 2006.

Harry Raymond Hueston II

AL QAEDA IN THE ARABIAN PENINSULA (AQAP)

Plagued with dire economic conditions, porous borders, and weak central government control over provincial regions, Yemen has emerged as an increasingly prominent safe haven for militants and extremists, including Al Qaeda. In January 2009 several of the group's branches in the country merged to form Al Qaeda in the Arabian Peninsula (AQAP). Operating with the suspected aid of tribal leaders, the group shares its parent movement's desire to remove all non-Muslims from Islam's holy land and has carried out numerous attacks in pursuit of this objective—in both Yemen and Saudi Arabia.

While AQAP initially appeared to focus its violent extremism toward targets within the Arabian Peninsula, the group has tried to attack the U.S. homeland on at least two occasions. The first occurred on December 25, 2009, when a Nigerian national attempted to bomb a civilian jet as it was landing at Detroit International Airport. The perpetrator, Umar Farouk Abdulmutallab, had intended to detonate explosives sewn into his underwear but was prevented from doing so by nearby passengers. He was known to have spent time in Yemen, where he met with key AQAP leaders Anwar al-Awlaki and Ibrahim Hassan al-Asiri—both of whom assisted in the planning and financing of the operation.

The second incident took place in October 2010, when AQAP was linked to a plot to blow up commercial passenger and FedEx and United Parcel Service jets destined for the United States. In what experts referred to as a highly sophisticated plan, the planes were going to be destroyed by explosive-rigged ink cartridges inserted into printers bound for Chicago and routed via Dubai and the United Kingdom. The devices were wired to timers and set to detonate as they were being flown over American territory. According to open sources, Saudi intelligence alerted their counterparts in the United States of the shipments, and the ink cartridges were successfully disarmed in Britain before they could go off. Media reports indicated that the bombs were the product of AQAP's chief explosives expert, al-Asiri, and represented a dangerous leap in his technical capability.

These two cases underscored AQAP's determination to plan and conduct complex overseas operations from its haven in Yemen. However, the group's potential international reach extends well beyond terror strikes orchestrated from the Arabian Peninsula. Through Internet publications and jihad chat forums, AQAP has demonstrated a proven ability to inspire homegrown extremists in the United States. Until his death in 2011, al-Awlaki was instrumental to these endeavors—exploiting his ability to speak both Arabic and English and his familiarity with Western society to effectively reach would-be extremists around the globe. Al-Awlaki's primary means for spreading AQAP's extremist ideology was through audio and video recordings posted on the World Wide Web and via an online English-language magazine called *Inspire*. The latter publication, which is edited by another American extremist, Samir Khan, regularly contains articles on weapons (how to make bombs and shoot guns) and the evils committed against the Islamic world.

Perhaps the clearest example of al-Awlaki's ability to reach and influence an American audience was the 2009 shooting at the Fort Hood army base in Texas. The attack, perpetrated by U.S. Army Major Nidal Hasan, left 13 people dead and 32 injured. Before his rampage, Hasan had engaged in correspondence with al-Awlaki that apparently played a significant role in swaying him to violent action.

The massacre received praise in numerous online videos posted by al-Awlaki, who urged others to follow Hasan's path of militant jihadist extremism.

Washington currently considers AQAP one of the main terrorist threats facing the United States and in 2009 initiated a vigorous campaign to root out the group's principal members. Through a combination of covert operations and increased training for Yemeni security forces, this effort has resulted in the elimination of several of the group's leaders. Arguably the most successful was the targeting of al-Awlaki and Khan, both of whom were killed while traveling together in September 2011. Their death marked an important blow to AQAP, not least by reducing its immediate ability to radicalize English-speaking recruits. Exactly what the long-term impact of the pair's demise will be remains to be seen.

Despite increased U.S. counterterrorism activity in Yemen, AQAP has managed to increase its ability to exploit the country as a base for its operations. This is primarily due to the outbreak of widespread pro-democracy protests against the authoritarian rule of President Ali Abdullah Saleh in 2011 (triggered as part of the so-called Arab Spring across the Middle East and North Africa). In an effort to preserve his power base in Yemen, the embattled president refocused the country's military from attacking AQAP in outlying border regions to cracking down on demonstrators in Sanaa. This has enabled the group to induct more members into its ranks—currently estimated at 800 to 1,000—as well as expand its presence in the south of the country.

See also: Al Qaeda; Christmas Day (2009) Airline Terror Plot; UPS/FedEx Bomb Plot

Further Reading

Barfi, Barak. "Yemen on the Brink? The Resurgence of al-Qaeda in Yemen." New American Foundation Counterterrorism Strategy Initiative Policy, January 2010. http://www.newamerica.net/sites/newamerica.net/files/policydocs/Barfi.pdf, accessed February 21, 2011.

"Bomb Plot Cost Just $4,200, Brags al-Qaeda." *South China Morning Post* (Hong Kong), November 22, 2010.

Dozier, Kimberley. "US Officials: US Attack in Yemen Kills al-Awlaki." Associated Press, September 30, 2011.

"Factbox: AQAP, al-Qaeda's Yemen-Based Wing." *Reuters,* March 22, 2011. http://www.reuters.com/article/2011/03/22/us-yemen-president-aqap-idUSTRE72L3QK20110322, accessed February 21, 2012.

Fresco, Richard, and Giles Whittell. "Security Overhaul after al-Qaeda's Bomb Technology Fools the Experts." *The Times* (UK), November 1, 2010.

Griffin, Jennifer, and Justin Fishel. "Two U.S.-Born Terrorists Killed in CIA-Led Drone Strike." *FoxNews.Com,* September 30, 2011. http://www.foxnews.com/politics/2011/09/30/us-born-terror-boss-anwar-al-awlaki-killed/, accessed February 12, 2012.

Johnston, Philip. "Anwar al-Awlaki: The New Osama Bin Laden?" *Daily Telegraph* (UK), September 17, 2010.

Margasak, Larry, Lara Jakes, and Jim Irwin. "Man Cites Orders from al-Qaeda in Failed Bid to Blow Up Plane." *Globe and Mail* (Toronto, Canada), December 26, 2009.

Masters, Jonathan. *Backgrounder: Al-Qaeda in the Arabian Peninsula.* Washington, DC: Council on Foreign Relations, December 7, 2011. http://www.cfr.org/yemen/al-qaeda-arabian-peninsula-aqap/p9369, accessed February 21, 2012.

McElroy, Damien. "US Special Forces Train Yemen Army as Arab State Becomes al-Qaeda 'Reserve Base.'" *Daily Telegraph* (UK), December 13, 2009.

Ross, Brian, and Rhonda Schwartz. "Major Hassan's Email: 'I Can't wait to Join You in the Afterlife.' American Official Says Accused Shooter Asked Radical Cleric When Is Jihad Appropriate?" *ABC News*, November 19, 2009. http://abcnews.go.com/Blotter/major-hasans-mail-wait-join-afterlife/story?id=9130339, accessed February 21, 2012.

Wong, Kristin. "Yemen: 'Major Staging Base' for al-Qaeda." *ABC News*, September 17, 2010. http://abcnews.go.com/Politics/yemen-major-staging-base-al-qaeda/story?id=9478552#.T0QM_JhPaao, accessed February 21, 2012.

"Yemen and al-Qaeda: The Jihadist Threat." *The Economist,* June 18, 2011.

Brandon Aitchison

AL-AQSA MARTYRS' BRIGADES

Militants of the Al-Aqsa Martyrs' Brigades march along the streets of the West Bank town of Jenin on April 2, 2005, during a rally to mark the third anniversary of the assault by the Israeli army on the Jenin refugee camp during their operation Defensive Shield in April 2002. Fifty-two Palestinians and 23 Israeli soldiers were killed, hundreds of homes were reduced to rubble, and 2,000 people were left homeless. The operation was launched after 29 Israelis were killed in a suicide bombing carried out by a Jenin resident. (AP Photo/Mohammed Ballas)

The al-Aqsa Martyrs' Brigades emerged in November 2000 as a dedicated suicide terrorist unit of al-Fatah. During the Second Intifada in the Palestinian Occupied Territories (2000–2002) it rivaled Hamas as the main instigator of suicide operations directed against Israeli targets. Indeed, of the 59 incidents recorded in 2002, 42 percent were attributed to the al-Aqsa Martyrs' Brigades—nearly two-thirds the number that Hamas had staged during the three previous years combined. The emphasis on this particular form of unconventional terrorism reflected three inherent tactical advantages of suicide strikes: They are a cheap and effective way of leveling the battlefield against a stronger opponent, they are a useful means of boosting morale, and they have a proven potential in attracting additional recruits.

Although the al-Aqsa Martyrs' Brigades are known to have a formal relationship with al-Fatah, Yasser Arafat never recognized the group and publicly denounced their actions. However, many people believe that the brigade could not have acted without his implicit endorsement, and certain members have gone on record stating that they received direct orders from him.

The al-Aqsa Martyrs' Brigades operated in both the Occupied Territories and Israel. The group is credited with carrying out the first suicide bombing using a Palestinian woman—a 2002 attack in Jerusalem that left one elderly man dead and injured 114. The perpetrator, subsequently identified as Wafa Idris, was a 28-year-old divorcee who worked a medical secretary for the Palestinian Red Crescent. According to Israeli military sources, the group actively sought to induct women into its ranks in an effort to capitalize on the reluctance of its Islamist rivals, principally Hamas and Palestinian Islamic Jihad, to operate in this manner.

The tempo and intensity of al-Aqsa strikes fell off after 2002 in line with the general improved security climate following the end of the Second Intifada. It reemerged with the outbreak of inter-Palestinian violence in 2006, acting as one of the main forces battling Hamas militias in Gaza.

See also: al-Fatah; Hamas (Islamic Resistance Movement); Palestine Liberation Organization (PLO)

Further Reading

Chalk, Peter, and Bruce Hoffman. *Understanding and Countering Suicide Terrorism.* Santa Monica, CA: RAND, 2004. Chapter 4, "Hamas."

Luft, Gal. "The Palestinian H-Bomb: Terror's Winning Strategy." *Foreign Affairs,* July–August 2002.

"Profile: Al-Aqsa Martyrs' Brigade." *BBC News,* March 5, 2002. http://news.bbc.co.uk/hi/english/world/middle_east/newsid_1760000/1760492.stm.

Wilkinson, Tracy. "Martyrs' Leading War on Israel: Mideast Brigade Linked to Arafat Has Recently Waged More Attacks than Islamic Extremist Groups." *Los Angeles Times,* March 8, 2002.

Williams, Daniel. "A Magnet for Palestinian 'Martyrs': Al-Aqsa Brigades Lead New Wave of Attacks on Israeli Civilians." *Washington Post,* March 7, 2002.

Peter Chalk

AL-BADR

Al-Badr was established in June 1998 with the purported goal of liberating the Indian states of Kashmir and Jammu and merging them with Pakistan. The group was critical of the nationalist stance of Jammu and Kashmir National Liberation Front, which merely sought the independence of the area. As with other Kashmiri *tanzeems* (outfits) such as Lashkar-e-Taiba (Let), Jaish-e-Mohammed (JeM), and Harakat-ul-Mujahideen (HuM), al-Badr has operated with the direct support of Islamabad's InterServices Intelligence (ISI) Directorate.

Although seemingly defunct by the end of the 1990s—with the ISI apparently favoring Harakat-ul-Mujahideen and, especially, Lashkar-e-Taiba —al-Badr resurfaced at the turn of the millennium. During the summer of 2000 it claimed responsibility for several terrorist acts in Jammu and Kashmir. It has since denounced any dialogue between India and Pakistan and continues to violently oppose the Line of Control, the region demarking areas under Pakistani and Indian sovereign authority.

Al-Badr's current leader is Bakht Zameen, a resident of Pakistan's Punjab province. Other senior members include Zahid Bhai (the deputy commander), Irfan (a so-called launching officer), Jasm Bhat (the publicity chief), and Abu Mawai (in charge of communications). The group supposedly has about 200 active participants, including 120 foreign mercenaries, and headquarters in Mansehra, Pakistan. It is active in the Anantnag, Baramulla, Budgam, Srinagar, and Kupwara districts of the Kashmir Valley. There is also some al-Badr presence in the Poonch and Rajouri districts of the Jammu region.

Al-Badr is one of several Pakistani terrorist groups operating under an umbrella group called the United Jehad Council, which has training camps in the Mansehra area. It is believed to have close ties to Jamaat-e-Islami in Pakistan and benefited from the provision of weapons and cross-border haven when the Taliban was in power in Afghanistan. India declared al-Badr a terrorist organization on April 1, 2002. It is also proscribed in the United States.

See also: Harakat-ul-Mujahideen (HuM); Jaish-e-Mohammed (JeM); Lashkar-e-Taiba (LeT); Taliban

Further Reading

"Al-Badr." South Asian Terrorism Portal. http://www.satp.org/satporgtp/countries/india/states/jandk/terrorist_outfits/AL_BADR_tl.htm, accessed November 2, 2011.

Karlekar, Hiranmay. *Bangladesh: The Next Afghanistan?* New Delhi: Sage, 2005.

Rashid, Ahmed. *Descent into Chaos: The United States and the Failure of Nation Building in Pakistan, Afghanistan, and Central Asia.* New York: Viking Books, 2008.

Donna Bassett

ALEX BONCAYO BRIGADE (ABB)

The Alex Boncayo Brigade (ABB) acts as the urban sabotage wing of the New People's Army, the armed component of the Communist Party of the Philippines. The group, named after a labor leader turned guerrilla who was killed by the security forces, was established in 1983 and was highly active in carrying out urban acts of terrorism, perpetrated by so-called Sparrow Squads, throughout the 1980s and 1990s. The ABB was weakened by the arrest of several leading members, including its commanding officer, Felimon Lagman, in 1994. Compounding matters was an ideological split in the New People's Army, which pitted advocates of the ABB's urban-based agenda against those who remained committed to Maoist precepts of rural warfare, including the communist supreme leader, Jose Maria Sisson. Despite these setbacks, the group continued to engage in sporadic assassinations and bombings of telecommunication towers.

The ABB retains a residual presence in Manila and other major metropolitan centers, though its activities today consist mostly of extorting protection money from prominent business interests. This emphasis has cast suspicion on whether the organization exists primarily as a criminal entity, justifying its presence behind the veneer of communist ideology.

See also: New People's Army (NPA)

Further Reading

Branigan, William. "Manila Captures Head of Communist Rebels; Underground Chief Ran Urban Hit Squad." *Washington Post,* May 27, 1994.

Ghosh, Nirmal. "Capture of Head Honcho a Crushing Blow to Manila Reds." *Singapore Straits Times,* July 14, 1997.

Kessler, Richard. *Rebellion and Repression in the Philippines.* New Haven, CT: Yale University Press, 1989.

Liefer, Michael. *Dictionary of the Modern Politics of South-East Asia.* London: Routledge, 1996.

"Philippines: 'Sparrow' Leader Netted." *Pinkerton's Risk Assessment,* October 11, 1996.

Wolf, J. *Anti-terrorist Initiatives.* New York: Plenum, 1989.

Peter Chalk

AL-FATAH

Al-Fatah is a highly influential political, military, and governing faction within the Palestine Liberation Organization (PLO). Al-Fatah, meaning "victory" or "conquest" in Arabic, is a reverse acronym of Harakat al-Tahrir al-Watani al-Falastini (Palestinian National Liberation Movement) and was formally organized on December 31, 1964.

For much of its official history, Yasser Arafat (also chairman of the Palestine Liberation Organization [PLO] from 1969 until his death in 2004) served as the party chief, although the beginnings of al-Fatah date to the late 1950s, when Palestinian groups began fighting the Israelis during their occupation of the Gaza Strip. Al-Fatah's founders include Arafat, Salah Khalaf, Khalil al-Wazir (Abu Jihad), and Khalid Hassan. Al-Fatah was a combination of a political organization (al-Tanzim) and paramilitary cells, the objective of which was the liberation of Palestine, armed resistance to Israel, and the creation of a Palestinian state. From the late 1960s, al-Fatah was larger than many of the other groups under the umbrella of the PLO because it did not avidly espouse their Marxist-Leninist doctrines. Consequently, al-Fatah has experienced a larger Muslim-to-Christian ratio than the small progressive parties. And because al-Fatah controlled much of the monetary resources of the PLO, it wielded considerable influence.

Al-Fatah has undergone many transformations over the years and until very recently hardly resembled a political party in the traditional sense. In its first years, the group eschewed the establishment of a formal organizational structure and indirectly appealed to the Palestinian diaspora in Syria, Jordan, Egypt, Lebanon, Iraq, the Gulf states, and Western countries. Al-Fatah had a following not only in the diaspora but also in important structures such as the General Union of Palestinian Students, the General Union of Palestinian Workers, and the General Union of Palestinian Women. Al-Fatah published an occasional periodical titled *Filastinuna* (Our Palestine).

Early on, and from the 1967 defeat until about 1974, al-Fatah embraced the concept of armed confrontation as the primary means of achieving a unified, independent Palestine. Al-Fatah's pragmatism ensured it a large base of support and also created a de facto ideology that stressed Palestinian unity, with the idea that although Palestinians might have varied approaches to their problems, they could all be united in their three major goals: the destruction of Israel, political freedom from Arab nations, and the creation of a Palestinian state.

Although al-Fatah did not initially maintain an organizational hierarchy (it acted more along the lines of an uncoordinated series of factions, each led by a different head), it did quickly establish a coherent military force capable of harassing the Israelis. Several militant groups based in Jordan were involved in attacks on Israel, among them the Asifah group, and their actions and the Israeli response caused a crackdown and their expulsion by King Hussein of Jordan. That expulsion in 1970, known as Black September, did, however, create fissures between the rightists and leftists within al-Fatah and with the broader Palestinian movement. When al-Fatah reconstituted itself in Lebanon beginning in 1970, it found that resisting involvement in the internal machinations of its host country was impossible. This diminished its effectiveness and made it more prone to pressure from other Arab states. Soon enough, conflict among al-Fatah members surfaced when some in the group began to espouse a two-state solution to the Palestinian-Israeli conflict, which outraged many.

Soon embroiled in the Lebanese Civil War that began in 1975, al-Fatah continued to sponsor attacks against Israeli interests, including two massive assaults on Israeli territory in 1975 that brought the loss of many lives. In 1982 the PLO (and thus al-Fatah) was forced out of Lebanon by the Israeli invasion of that country. From 1982 to 1993 al-Fatah, along with the PLO, was located in Tunisia. In 1983 an anti-Arafatist revolt occurred that was led by Said Muragha (Abu Musa). He created a splinter group known as al-Fatah Uprising, which was backed by Syrian officials. Meanwhile, al-Fatah's Revolutionary Council and the Revolutionary Council Emergency Command both broke with al-Fatah over policy issues. Despite these setbacks, al-Fatah remained the preeminent Palestinian faction, and Arafat maintained an iron grip over al-Fatah.

Many in al-Fatah's leading group had supported a two-state solution ever since the Rabat conference of 1974 and realized this meant tacit recognition of Israel. Al-Fatah's leadership also concluded that armed conflict was not moving the organization any closer to its goal of a Palestinian state. By 1988 Arafat had recognized Israel's right to exist explicitly in meetings and proposed the pursuit of diplomacy and a land-for-peace arrangement.

Arafat backed Saddam Hussein in the 1991 Persian Gulf War because of the assistance (political, economic, and military) that the Iraqi leader had rendered to al-Fatah. This support, however, led to the mass exile of Palestinians from Kuwait after the war and difficult economic times for the Palestinians in general. Consequently, as the effort to reach a comprehensive accord in Madrid was occurring, Arafat had agreed to a secret Palestinian-Israeli track in Oslo, Norway.

The 1993 Oslo Accords and the 1994 creation of the Palestinian Authority (PA) witnessed the relocation of the PLO and al-Fatah to Gaza and the West Bank. This finally centered a permanent Palestinian power base in Palestine after almost 50 years of transience. But by this time the Palestinians were no longer entirely represented by the Tunisian old guard of al-Fatah. Younger leaders were frustrated with the policies of the longtime exiles and with major financial difficulties and corruption. Also, Islamist organizations such as Islamic Jihad of Palestine and especially Hamas had begun to attract far more support from the Palestinian population than al-Fatah. Arafat clung to power, still recognized for his many years of devotion to the Palestinian cause. In January 1996 he was elected as the PA's first president. He now simultaneously held the positions of PLO chairman, PA president, and leader of al-Fatah.

Al-Fatah essentially controlled the PA bureaucracy, although the fissures within the organization began to grow deeper. While al-Fatah attempted to push ahead with the Palestinian-Israeli peace process, certain members who were opposed to it began to sabotage Arafat's agenda. Now the group was divided into hard-liners versus peace proponents, old guard versus youths, and bureaucrats versus revolutionaries. The Second (al-Aqsa) Intifada, which broke out in September 2000, saw the embattled al-Fatah become even more divided against itself. Al-Fatah member Marwan Barghuti organized a militia called al-Tanzim, whose goal was attacking Israeli forces. And in 2002, the al-Aqsa Martyrs' Brigades, another faction consisting of local militias and theoretically aligned with al-Fatah, began launching major attacks against Israeli forces as well. To punish the PA for a particularly heinous suicide bombing in the spring of 2002, the Israelis reoccupied much of the West Bank. Arafat was trapped in his own headquarters, and much of the rebuilding and infrastructure in the West Bank were destroyed. Israeli officials had periodically launched campaigns against Arafat's leadership, and these were now revived.

Now under enormous pressure from Israel and the United States, Arafat reluctantly acquiesced to the creation of a new position within the PA, that of prime minister. In April 2003 he named Mahmoud Abbas to the post. However, after months of infighting, Abbas resigned from office in September 2003. Then in February 2004, 300 al-Fatah members left the group in unison to show their contempt for their leadership. A hasty meeting of al-Fatah's Revolutionary Council was called, but it accomplished nothing and resulted in bitter recriminations from all sides.

Arafat died on November 11, 2004, and this threw al-Fatah and the PA into more turmoil. Days after Arafat's death, al-Fatah's Central Committee named Farouk Qaddumi to replace him. This was in itself problematic because Qaddumi, unlike his predecessor, did not support the peace process. Meanwhile, Abbas was named to succeed Arafat as PLO chairman. For the first time, al-Fatah and the PA were not controlled by the same person. After bitter political machinations, al-Fatah decided to put Abbas up as its presidential candidate in the January 2005 election. Abbas was strongly challenged by Barghuti, who vowed to run as an independent from a jail cell in Israel. Barghuti, who came under intense pressure to bow out, finally did so, opening the way for Abbas's victory in January 2005.

Abbas's victory, however, was not a harbinger of a resurgent and unified al-Fatah. In the December 2004 municipal elections for the PA, Hamas had racked up impressive gains. Then, in December 2005, Barghuti formed a rival political alliance, al-Mustaqbal, vowing to run a new slate of candidates for the January 2006 PA legislative elections. At the last moment, the two factions decided to run a single slate, but this temporary rapprochement was not enough to prevent a stunning victory for Hamas. In fact, Hamas's strength did not rest simply on the divisions within al-Fatah. Indeed, Hamas won 74 seats to al-Fatah's 45, although Hamas had captured only 43 percent of the popular vote. The election allowed Hamas to form its own government and elect a prime minister, Ismail Haniyeh, who assumed the premiership in February 2006. As a result of the Hamas victory, the United States and some European nations cut off funding to the PA in protest of the former's electoral success. This placed the PA in a state of crisis, as no civil servants could be paid, and hospitals and clinics had no supplies. For more than a year, and despite an agreement between Hamas and al-Fatah, the U.S. government continued to state that only if Hamas renounced its violent intentions against Israel in a format satisfactory to Israel and the United States would any funds be allowed into the PA.

On March 17, 2007, Abbas brokered a Palestinian unity government that included both al-Fatah and Hamas, with Hamas leader Haniyeh becoming prime minister. Yet in May violence between Hamas and al-Fatah escalated. Following the Hamas takeover of Gaza on June 14, Abbas dissolved the Hamas-led unity government and declared a state of emergency. On June 18, having been assured of European Union support, Abbas also dissolved the National Security Council and swore in an emergency Palestinian government. That same day, the United States ended its 15-month embargo on the PA and resumed aid in an effort to strengthen Abbas's government, which was now limited to the West Bank. On June 19 Abbas cut off all ties and dialogue with Hamas, pending the return of Gaza. In a further move to strengthen the perceived moderate Abbas, on July 1 Israel restored financial ties to the PA.

Today, al-Fatah is recognized by Palestinians as a full-fledged political party, with the attendant organizational structures that have in fact been in place for several decades. Competition between its four major parties caused problems in the past, but today the competition with Hamas appears more pressing. Al-Fatah can either purge itself of the rampant corruption among its ranks or risk maintaining the status quo and the mass exodus of disaffected party members that will likely follow.

See also: al-Aqsa Martyrs' Brigades; Hamas (Islamic Resistance Movement); Oslo Accords; Palestine Liberation Organization (PLO)

Further Reading

Aburish, Said K. *Arafat: From Defender to Dictator.* New York: Bloomsbury, 1998.

Hart, Alan. *Arafat: A Political Biography.* Rev. ed. London: Sidgwick and Jackson, 1994.

Jamal, Amal. *The Palestinian National Movement: Politics of Contention, 1967–2005.* Bloomington: Indiana University Press, 2005.

Kurz, Anat N. *Fatah and the Politics of Violence: The Institutionalization of a Popular Struggle.* Eastbourne, UK: Sussex Academic, 2006.

Rubin, Barry. *The Transformation of Palestinian Politics: From Revolution to State-Building.* Cambridge, MA: Harvard University Press, 2001.

Said, Edward W. *Peace and Its Discontents: Essays on Palestine in the Middle East Process.* New York: Vintage Books, 1995.

Paul G. Pierpaoli Jr. and Sherifa Zuhur

AL-GAMA'A AL-ISLAMIYYA

Al-Gama'a al-Islamiyya (AGaI) was a militant Islamic group that fought against the Egyptian state for well over a decade. The group began in universities in the early 1970s as an amorphous collection of Islamic students opposed to the Muslim Brotherhood's decision to renounce violence. It soon coalesced, however, and gained strength and local support among impoverished Muslim migrant workers and students. In the late 1980s and early 1990s, AGaI launched a violent campaign against the secular Egyptian government, Coptic Christians, and secular intellectuals. By 1998 the organization's excessive violence had cost it the support of previously sympathetic populations, and disagreements over tactics eventually splintered the group. The United States, the European Union, and the Egyptian government all consider IG a terrorist organization.

At its height AGaI could count on support from several thousand hard-core members and a similar number of more passive supporters. It also controlled Embaba—a poor neighborhood outside of Cairo with a population of around one million—and had strongholds in Upper and Middle Egypt, particularly in Asyut and Minia. AGaI thrived in areas where the state had historically had less of a presence, and it capitalized on this to build arms caches and training camps. Similar to its rival, Egyptian Islamic Jihad (EIJ), AGaI aimed to overthrow the Egyptian government and establish an Islamic state. However, the two organizations differed over tactics on how to achieve this goal. While EIJ focused solely on fighting the state and sought to carry out a coup with only a small band of followers, AGaI emphasized preaching (*da'wa*) to gain adherents at the local level. The group believed this would translate into a base of mass support of sufficient size to overcome the government. Despite these tactical differences, AGaI and EIJ occasionally worked together, and the two were responsible for most of the 1,300 killings that occurred in Egypt in the 1990s. In particular, AGaI's violence was directed against prominent secular personalities, Coptic Christians, tourists, and representatives of the state.

AGaI funded itself primarily from money donated by various outside Islamic nongovernmental organizations, typically from the Arabian Peninsula. In the mid-1990s, however, the Egyptian government cracked down on domestic militants, partly by restricting cash flow into the country from the outside. As a result, AGaI was forced to put more emphasis on petty crime to finance its terrorist operations.

Similar to other Islamist groups in the Arab world, AGaI gained adherents in the 1970s as a result of the Arab defeat in the 1967 war with Israel. The collective shock of that loss led many Egyptians to cast Arab pan-nationalism as a failed ideology, and they looked instead to a return to Islam as the only way to regain their pride. The growing strength of Islamic groups in Egyptian society led the new president, Anwar Sadat, to try to gain their support in an effort to boost his legitimacy. However, when he signed the peace treaty with Israel in 1979, his relationship with Islamist groups was irrevocably shattered. Sadat was eventually assassinated in 1981 by an Islamic extremist who had obtained a fatwa permitting the murder from Sheikh Omar Abdel-Rahman—AGaI's spiritual leader. Sadat's successor to the presidency, Hosni Mubarak, was much less sympathetic to the Islamist groups, and he immediately began jailing them.

Although mass roundups in 1981 disrupted AGaI's networks, it proved to be only a short-term disruption as, like Sadat, Mubarak started to court Islamists in an effort to consolidate his power base. In 1984 the government released most AGaI supporters from prison, which allowed the group to slowly rebuild its local cells. AGaI also found shelter and a receptive audience in Middle and Upper Egypt, where a downturn in global oil prices had forced many migrant workers to return from the Gulf. Educated but unemployed and poor, these youth took offense at the Coptic Christian minority prospering relative to the Muslim majority. AGaI took advantage of this grievance and tailored its message to stir anti-Christian agitation and violence. At the same time, the group worked with local mosques to provide critical public services in poverty-stricken areas where the government's presence was necessary but minimal. This tactic further strengthened AGaI's local support—especially in Embaba, where in 1992 one sheikh famously declared that an Islamic republic based on sharia law had been created. Finally recognizing the threat, the Egyptian government deployed some 14,000 soldiers in an attempt to clear the area of the AGaI presence.

AGaI's peak in popularity in the early 1990s also coincided with the return of a few hundred Egyptian mujahideen from Afghanistan with deadly results. These "Arab Afghans" had spent years learning and honing their battle skills, and they came home ready to continue the jihad against the Egyptian regime. Many joined AGaI, providing it with the necessary trained manpower to significantly elevate the level of violence. The group opened its renewed campaign in June 1992 with the murder of secular intellectual Farag Foda, whom they declared to be guilty of apostasy for his opposition to sharia law. Shortly thereafter, AGaI began attacking tourists—a target selected both for its publicity value and due to its overt symbolism as a consequence of the peace treaty with Israel. The group also started to target state representatives, killing both the speaker of the parliament and the head of the counterterrorism police, and in 1995 even worked with EIJ in a failed assassination attempt on Mubarak in Addis Ababa, Ethiopia.

By 1996, however, AGaI was beginning to weaken as a result of the loss of some of its most skilled militants killed in a draconian counterterrorist response unleashed by the Egyptian government. AGaI was not able to replace these cadres with men of a similar fighting caliber, creating an operational void that was reflected in attacks that were becoming increasingly careless. Adding to the group's difficulties was an increasingly hostile local population, decreasing revenues, and the loss of its spiritual leader, Sheikh Abdel-Rahman, who had been imprisoned in the United States for his role in the 1993 bombing of the New York World Trade Center. This altered strategic environment prompted the emir of Aswan to call for a cease-fire. The majority of AGaI refused to lay down their arms, however, and the following month the group was tied to the murder of 18 Greek tourists (including 14 women) in a Cairo hotel, mistakenly believing they were Israeli.

By July 1997 AGaI's now imprisoned leadership recognized the growing counterproductivity of its violence and appealed for another cease-fire. Though initially supported by Abdel-Rahman (still jailed in the United States), the call was rejected by other exiled clerics. Then, in a show of defiance, AGaI militants brutally murdered 58 foreign tourists and four Egyptians who were visiting the Temple of Hatshepsut in Luxor. Condemned by some in the group but approved by others—particularly the leadership living abroad—the massacre revealed the deep divisions within the organization.

The Luxor attack proved to be the last major operation carried out by AGaI. In the years that followed, the group began to systematically fracture, reflecting schisms in both ideology and tactics. In 2003 the Mubarak government freed over 2,000 jailed AGaI members after the group's imprisoned leadership renounced violence. Many of these former militants joined with Tareq al-Zumour to establish the Building and Development Party, which ran in Egypt's 2011 elections as part of the Islamist Alliance. Other elements from the original AGaI, however, have not foresworn violence and continue to operate from abroad. One faction led by Muhammad al-Hukaymah swore allegiance to Osama bin Laden in 2006 and has since worked in conjunction with Al Qaeda.

See also: Abdel-Rahman, Omar; Al Qaeda; Egyptian Islamic Jihad (EIJ); Hatshepsut (Luxor) Temple Massacre; World Trade Center (New York) Bombing

Further Reading

Abdo, Geneive. *No God but God: Egypt and the Triumph of Islam.* New York: Oxford University Press, 2002.

Brown, Jonathan. "Salafis and Sufis in Egypt." *The Carnegie Papers,* December 2011.

Hafez, Mohammad, and Quintan Wiktorowicz. "Violence as Contention in the Egyptian Islamic Movement." In Quintan Wiktorowicz, *Islamic Activism: A Social Movement Theory Approach,* 61–88. Bloomington: Indiana University Press, 2004.

Kepel, Gilles. *The Roots of Radical Islam.* London: SAQI, 2005.

Kepel, Gilles. "The Threat of Terrorism in Egypt." In Gilles Kepel, ed., *Jihad: The Trail of Political Islam.* London: I. B. Tauris, 2006.

Malthaner, Stefan. *Mobilizing the Faithful: Militant Islamist Groups and Their Constituencies.* Frankfurt, Germany: Campus, 2011.

U.S. Department of State. "Gama'a al-Islamiyya (IG)." *Country Reports on Terrorism 2010,* August 18, 2011. http://www.state.gov/j/ct/rls/crt/2010/170264.htm, accessed January 31, 2012.

Lauren Twenhafel

ALGIERS BOMBINGS

Between February and December 2007, Algeria was plagued by multiple terrorist attacks, including no fewer than18 bombings and attempted bombings. The worst incidents took place on February 13, April 11, and December 12, 2007.

On February 13, a series of seven near-simultaneous explosions rocked several towns east of Algiers. The primary targets were police and security personnel, although the majority of those killed and wounded were civilians. In total, the attack left 6 people dead and 29 injured.

The next major incident attack took place on April 11 in Algiers when two suicide terrorists detonated vehicle-borne improvised explosive devices (VBIEDs) within a few minutes of one another. The first explosion killed 12 and wounded at least 118. The attack was aimed at the Office of the Prime Minister, and the VBIED went off a mere 30 yards from the main door, seriously damaging the six-story building. The second attack took place at a police station in the Bab Ezzouar district of Algiers, leaving 11 dead and another 44 seriously injured. A third VBIED consisting of TNT and gas canisters was successfully disarmed.

The April bombings were followed by a sustained campaign of violence aimed at disrupting national elections planned for May 17. Over a period of three days, a series of attacks were staged across a 500-kilometer (310-mile) zone that extended from Constantine to Algiers. Dozens were killed, and at least 18 soldiers died in bombings and ambushes.

Exactly three months after the April 11 attack, a suicide terrorist detonated a VBIED just outside an army barracks near the village of Lakhdaria, near Bouira. The attack, which coincided with the opening of the All Africa Games in Algiers, killed 8 and wounded between 20 and 30 others. A second bombing took place

Rescue personnel work to clear the rubble from a United Nations (UN) building in Algiers, Algeria, December 11, 2007, after twin truck bombings by an affiliate of Al Qaeda targeted UN offices and a government building, killing at least 62 people. (AP/Wide World Photos)

near a group of gendarmes on patrol near the village of Tigziert, causing two casualties, one of which was fatal.

On September 21, another suicide attack targeting foreigners occurred in the town of Lakhdaria, about 75 kilometers (46 miles) southeast of Algiers. There were no deaths, but nine people were wounded, including five policemen, an Algerian driver, two French workers, and one Italian. Following the incident, Al Qaeda issued a video urging all North African Muslims to rise up and "cleanse" their land of Western infidels, especially those from France and Spain.

The most serious attacks took place in Algiers on December 11, 2007. Involving two VBIEDs that detonated 10 minutes apart, the bombings killed 41—including 17 United Nations (UN) staff members—and injured at least 170. Each of the VBIEDs contained an estimated 1,700 pounds (800 kilograms) of high explosives, later determined to be homemade nitroglycerin.

The first explosion occurred near the Supreme Constitutional Court in the Ben Aknoun district. Several of the victims were students on a school bus that had been passing by when the bomb detonated. The second attack attack took place in the neighborhood of Hydra on the road that runs between the UN and the offices of the United Nations High Commissioner for Refugees (UNHCR). The VBIED leveled the latter building and partially collapsed sections of the former. UN secretary-general Ban Ki-Moon later said this was the worst attack suffered by the organization since 2003, when its headquarters in Baghdad had been bombed, killing 22 people. Algeria's interior minister, Noureddine Yazid Zerhouni, later affirmed that some of the militants arrested after the April 11 bombings had told authorities that the offices of the UN were among the sites targeted for a possible future attack.

The UN bombings generated considerable public anger, particularly with regard to the government's national reconciliation policy. An amnesty for militants who denounced violence had been announced two years prior to the attack. However, many felt that those who had been pardoned were not interested in peace and, far from discouraging terrorism, were actually encouraging it. The attacks on the UN, as well as the earlier incidents during the year, were taken as evidence of this.

Almost all of the bombings were the work of Al Qaeda in the Land of the Islamic Maghreb (AQIM). The group was formerly known as the Groupe Salafiste pour la Prédication et le Combat (GSPC, or Salafist Group for Preaching and Combat), which had itself evolved out of the Groupe Islamique Armeé (GIA, or Armed Islamic Group)—the main militant group in the Algerian civil war of the 1990s. The GSPC formally joined forces with Al Qaeda in September 2006, although the relationship became more robust in January 2007, when the group changed its name to AQIM. Osama bin Laden and Ayman al-Zawahiri heralded this development as "a source of chagrin, frustration, and sadness" for the authorities in Algeria.

The GSPC's name change coincided with a major increase in violence on the part of the organization, with attacks directed against police officials, government authorities, expatriate contract workers (especially those employed in oil and gas extraction), and tourists. The use of VBIEDs also became more common, as did simultaneous suicide attacks. Moreover, whereas the GSPC had formerly limited its activities to Algeria and Morocco (with the exception of occasional GIA forays into

Europe), AQIM expanded its activities to Tunisia and Mauritania and support for its "brothers in Chechnya."

The Saharan faction of AQIM has also become increasingly involved in criminal activities such as arms smuggling, kidnapping, extortion, and drug trafficking. This melding of criminality and terrorism has significantly heightened the overall threat potential of the group as well as complicated efforts at reaching an effective political solution in Algeria through negotiation and compromise.

See also: Al Qaeda; Groupe Islamique Armeé (GIA); Groupe Salafiste pour la Prédication et le Combat (GSPC); United Nations Headquaters (Algiers) Bombing; United Nations Headquaters (Baghdad) Attack

Further Reading

Benhold, Katrin, and Craig Smith. "Tally in Algiers Attacks Uncertain." *New York Times,* December 13, 2007.
Smith, Craig. "At Least 67 Dead in Algiers Bombings." *New York Times,* December 12, 2007.
"UNHCR Chief Condemns Algiers Bombing; Mourns Dead." UNHCR press release, December 11, 2007. http://www.unhcr.org/news/NEWS/475ebc454.html, accessed July 21, 2011.
"UN in Grief at Algeria Bombings." Associated Press, December 12, 2007.

Donna Bassett

ALI RAZA MOSQUE BOMBING

Twenty people were killed and 38 injured when an explosion ripped through the Shiite Ali Raza mosque in Karachi on May 31, 2004. The attack occurred a day after the assassination of prominent pro-Taliban Sunni cleric Mufti Nizamuddin Shamzai in the same area. Investigators said the bombing was staged by a single suicide bomber, who apparently detonated a 10-kilogram (22-pound) device that was sewn into a vest or hidden in a briefcase.

One investigator said there was a strong possibility that the killing of Shamzai (who had been gunned down as he left his home on May 30) was the result of an earlier attack on the Hyderabad mosque (May 7) and that the bombing of Ali Raza was in retaliation for the murder. The incident was the latest in a string of five attacks that had occurred in Karachi that month.

The bombing sparked rioting in the area, with an angry crowd torching two gas stations and a police car while chanting antigovernment slogans and Shiite religious mottos. Some protestors also expressed anger at the United States, which, although a strong ally of Pakistan at the time, was often portrayed by extremist religious elements as deliberately seeking to undermine the Muslim world. While the violence was mostly sectarian in nature, various political analysts speculated that the terrorists were deliberately trying to heighten religious tensions in order to undermine President Pervez Musharraf's rule in the country's main port and financial center.

Musharaf himself promised to take unspecified "major steps" to control the rising violence in the commercial capital, and following a seven-hour cabinet meeting it was decided that key Sindh officials should be removed from their posts for failing to prevent the Ali Raza bombing and the various incidents that preceded it. Two days later, several senior law enforcement officers were fired, including the Karachicity police chief, Asad Ashraf Malik.

On November 25, an antiterrorism court charged a member of the banned Lashkar-e-Jhangvi (LeJ) organization in the Masjid Ali Raza Mosque bombing. The suspect, Gul Hasan, had been arrested on June 13. Although he denied any involvement with the bombing, he was found guilty of masterminding both the Masjid Ali Raza and the Hyderabad Mosque attacks.

See also: Lashkar-e-Jhangvi (LeJ)

Further Reading

Jones, Seth G., and Christine C. Fair. *Counterinsurgency in Pakistan.* Santa Monica, CA: RAND, 2010.

Nasr, Vali. *The Shia Revival: How Conflicts within Islam Will Shape the Future.* New York: W. W. Norton, 2006.

Rabasa, Angel, Peter Chalk, Kim Cragin, Sara A. Daly, Heather S. Gregg, Theodore W. Karasik, Kevin A. O'Brien, and William Rosenau. *Beyond al-Qaeda. Part 1: The Global Jihadist Movement.* Santa Monica, CA: RAND, 2006.

Rashid, Ahmed. *Descent into Chaos: The United States and the Failure of Nation Building in Pakistan, Afghanistan, and Central Asia.* New York: Viking Books, 2008.

Donna Bassett

AL-ITTIHAD AL-ISLAMI (AIAI)

Al-Ittihad al-Islami (AIAI, or Islamic Unity) was the precursor to the later Somali Islamic Courts Union and the current Islamist al-Shabaab movement. Indeed, it has been suggested that AIAI, which was alleged to have had links to Al Qaeda, provided the basis for the wider network of violent Islamists presently active in the Horn of Africa and East Africa.

The AIAI developed during the 1980s as a loose movement of generally educated Somalis, many of whom had worked or studied in the Middle East and who opposed the repression and control of the regime of Siad Barre, then president of Somalia. They believed the only way to rid the country of its endemic corruption and clan factionalism was through the institution of a rigid theocratic order based on a strict interpretation of Islamism.

Following the collapse of the Barre regime in 1991, Osama bin Laden is thought to have funded and supported the AIAI as a conduit through which to gain an operational foothold in the Horn of Africa. Some experts continue to believe that the 1993 killings of Belgian, Pakistani, and U.S. military personnel associated with the United Nations Operation in Somalia (UNOSOM) II mission in Somalia had nothing to do with warlord General Mohammad Farah Aideed but was in fact the work of Al Qaeda and AIAI.

By the mid-1990s, along with a power base in Bosaaso and the Puntland region of Somalia, AIAI had also become active among the Somali population in the Ogaden region of eastern Ethiopia and the wider Somali diaspora in Kenya. At its height, it is believed that the group had around 1,000 active members. Despite attending a February 1995 peace conference for the Somali nation, AIAI was later linked to a number of terrorist attacks including two hotel bombings in Ethiopia and the attempted assassination of Ethiopian minister of transport and communications Abdul Majid Hussein in 1996. In 1999 the group was implicated in the murder of an American aid worker near the Kenyan-Somali border. Perhaps more significantly, U.S. officials have claimed that elements of AIAI cooperated with the Al Qaeda cell responsible for the August 1998 twin suicide bombings of the U.S. embassies in Nairobi, Kenya, and Dar es Salaam, Tanzania. At the time, these attacks were one of the most lethal directed against American interests, leaving 224 people dead and thousands of others wounded.

In the aftermath of 9/11, AIAI's finances together with the group's leaders, Hassan Dahir Aweys and Hassan al-Turki, were sanctioned under presidential executive order 13224. The action was justified on account of the group's suspected links to Al Qaeda, which purportedly included the establishment of joint training camps in various parts of Somalia. Following the onset of Operation Enduring Freedom (OEF) and the so-called U.S.-led global war on terror, many AIAI members dispersed across the Gulf of Aden to the tribal areas of Yemen, and the organization claimed to have dissolved itself. That said, AIAI's legacy has had and continues to have a significant bearing on events in Somalia. One of the main leaders of the Islamic Courts Union, which seized the capital city of Mogadishu in June 2006, was Hassan Aweys. More important was the "career" trajectory of al-Turki, who went on to lead al-Shabaab—then the youth movement of the Islamic Courts Union and currently one of the main terrorist-insurgent threats in the country.

See also: Al Qaeda; al-Shabaab

Further Reading

Gunaratna, Rohan. *Inside Al Qaeda.* New York: Columbia University Press, 2002.
Rabasa, Angel. *Radical Islam in East Africa.* Santa Monica, CA: RAND, 2009.
Rotberg, Robert, ed. *Battling Terrorism in the Horn of Africa.* Washington, DC: Brookings Institution Press, 2005.

Richard Warnes

AL-QUDS MOSQUE

Al-Quds Mosque was the mosque in Hamburg, Germany, where leaders of the September 11 operation worshipped and planned the attack. It was located in a poorer section of Hamburg on Steindamm Street. The mosque was situated above a body-building gym near Hamburg's central railway station. This location, close to cheap transportation, made it attractive to expatriate Muslims. Al-Quds was one of the few Arab Sunni mosques; most of others in Hamburg were Shiite or Turkish Sunni. It was small, holding at most 150 people at prayer time. These small mosques were good places for Islamist extremists to cultivate and recruit members.

Al-Quds was an extremist mosque because of the preaching of its leading cleric, Mohammed al-Fazazi. The founders of the mosque had been Moroccans, and most of its clerics were Moroccans—including al-Fazazi. He preached there constantly. Al-Fazazi believed Western civilization was the enemy of the Muslim world, and he believed in martyrdom. He was quoted in 2000 as saying that "who[ever] participates in the war against Islam with ideas or thoughts or a song or a television show to befoul Islam is an infidel on war footing that shall be killed, no matter if it's a man, a woman, or a child." It was these ideas that attracted Mohamed Atta to Islamist extremism and later to Al Qaeda. Al-Fazazi spent considerable time with the young men in his congregation talking with them about jihad, holy war, and martyrdom. Later, al-Fazazi's involvement in bombings in Morocco and Spain landed him a 30-year prison sentence in Morocco.

The al-Quds Mosque remained a place where it was possible to recruit others susceptible to the appeal of al-Fazazi and, later, Al Qaeda. Atta taught religious classes at al-Quds Mosque, but his hard-line position alienated all but those who thought as he. All of the members of the Hamburg Cell were recruited at the al-Quds Mosque, including Marwan al-Shehhi and Ramzi bin al-Shibh. In August 2010 growing concerns that the site was again serving as a gathering place for Islamic extremists led German security officials to close the mosque.

See also: Atta, Mohamed; bin al-Shibh, Ramzi; Hamburg Cell

Further Reading

Corbin, Jane. *Al-Qaeda: The Terror Network That Threatens the World.* New York: Thunder's Mouth, 2002.
McDermott, Terry. *Perfect Soldiers: The 9/11 Hijackers: Who They Were, Why They Did It.* New York: HarperCollins, 2005.
Vidino, Lorenzo. *Al Qaeda in Europe: The New Battleground of International Jihad.* Amherst, NY: Prometheus Books, 2006.

Stephen E. Atkins

AL-SHABAAB

Originally al-Shabaab (literally "the youth") was the hard-line youth militia of the Islamic Courts Union (ICU), which briefly took control of Mogadishu, Kismayo, and other areas of southern Somalia in June 2006. When a combination of Ethiopian and Somalian transitional federal government (TFG) troops forced the ICU to withdraw from the capital in December 2006, al-Shabaab reconstituted itself as an independent organization and in early 2007 initiated an insurgency in an attempt to gain control of the country. Originally led by Aden Hashi Farah "Ayro," the group has used assassinations, bombings, and more recently suicide attacks to target TFG forces, AMISOM (African Union) peacekeepers, the United Nations, and foreign nationals. The group's declared intention is to establish a caliphate in Somalia based on a strict Wahhabi interpretation of Islam.

Formally called Harakat al-Shabaab al-Mujahideen, or Movement of Warrior Youth, the organization is currently led by Sheikh Ahmed Abdi Godane; he took control after U.S. air strikes killed Farah and several other commanders on May 1, 2008. Al-Shabaab overran Kismayo in August 2008 and by the summer of 2010 had seized most of southern and central Somalia, including much of the capital, Mogadishu.

Numbering around 2,000–3,000 members, al-Shabaab appears to be divided into three commands: the Bay and Bokol, South Central and Mogadishu, and Puntland and Somaliland. An affiliate group also exists in the Juba Valley. The group funds itself mainly through charitable donations raised in areas it controls, although there have been repeated allegations that it has diverted aid in these regions to buttress its war chest.

Some of al-Shabaab's most significant recent attacks have included

- A suicide car attack on an AMISOM base in Mogadishu, killing six peacekeepers (February 22, 2009)
- A suicide car bomb at the Medina Hotel, Beledweyne, killing 35, including TFG security minister Omar Hashi Aden (June 18, 2009)
- The truck bombing of an AMISOM base in Mogadishu, killing 21 peacekeepers (September 17, 2009)
- A suicide attack at Hotel Shamo in Mogadishu, where a ceremony was being held for medical students, killing three TFG ministers

In addition to these domestic attacks there is increasing concern that al-Shabaab has forged close links with foreign extremists, many of whom are thought to be based in Somalia and helping with the training of the group's members. Fears were further heightened in February 2010 when al-Shabaab formally declared its organizational and operational allegiance to Al Qaeda.

Moreover, it now appears that the group has made a conscious strategic decision to export terrorism. Al-Shabaab has been linked to a 2009 plot to attack the Holsworthy Barracks in Australia, efforts aimed at recruiting Americans to carry out bombings on U.S. soil, and the attempted assassination in January 2010 of Danish cartoonist Kurt Westergaard, who created controversy in the Muslim world by drawing pictures depicting Muhammad wearing a bomb in his turban. Most seriously, the group claimed responsibility for the July 11, 2010, suicide bombings in Kampala, which killed 74 people and wounded another 70, as well as an attack against a bus station in Nairobi on November 31 that left 3 people dead and injured 39. Al-Shabaab justified the strikes as retaliation for Ugandan and Kenyan support of the AMISOM mission in Somalia.

See also: Al Qaeda; Holsworthy Barracks Bomb Plot

Further Reading

Landler, Mark. "After Attacks in Uganda, Worry Grows over Group." *New York Times,* July 13, 2010.

Rabasa, Angel. *Radical Islam in East Africa.* Santa Monica, CA: RAND, 2009.

Schmitt, Eric. "Islamic Extremist Group Recruits Americans for Civil War, Not Jihad." *New York Times,* June 6, 2010.

Yusuf, Huma. "Somali Militant Group Al Shabab Aligns with Al-Qaeda." *Christian Science Monitor,* February 4, 2010.

Richard Warnes

AMAL

Afwaj al-Muqawama al-Lubnaniyya (Groups of the Lebanese Resistance), or Amal, is a Lebanese Shia political party founded by Imam Musa al-Sadr in 1974. Prior to its disarmament after the Lebanese Civil War, the group operated as a Syrian-backed militia and vied with Hezbollah for the allegiance of the Lebanese Shia population. Following the end of hostilities, Amal entered politics and has since secured several cabinet positions as well as seats in the Lebanese parliament.

Amal grew out of al-Sadr's Harakat al-Mahrumin (Movement of the Dispossessed), a movement created to advance the interests of the Lebanese Shia community, who in the complex environment of the country's confessional political system felt disenfranchised by rival Christian, Druze, and Muslim populations. In particular, the Shia believed they were underrepresented in the Lebanese political system and received less government funding for social services and education, despite significant demographic growth. Al-Sadr argued that this state of affairs reflected the failure of the traditional Shia leadership in serving its constituency and envisaged Harakat al-Mahrumin as a new vanguard.

Although al-Sadr was initially hesitant to take up arms in pursuit of his objectives, the militarization of rival organizations, particularly Christian groups, prompted him to establish Amal as Harakat al-Mahrumin's military wing in 1974. The group received funding from Syria and would maintain a close relationship with the Assad regime in Damascus throughout its existence.

Organizationally Amal operated under under a loose and decentralized structure, reflecting the geographically dispersed nature of the Lebanese Shia community, which is interspersed among Christian, Sunni, and Druze populations. For this reason, the group depended heavily on regional leaders, overseen by a politburo, to communicate its organization's message and policies.

After its formation, Amal trained with Yasser Arafat's al-Fatah movement and participated in military action against both Israel and the Israeli-backed South Lebanese Army. In keeping with Harakat's staunch opposition to the traditional leadership of the Shia establishment, Amal also adopted antisectarian rhetoric seemingly contrary to the organization's religious orientation. Like other Muslim militias and political parties in Lebanon, Amal viewed Israel as its enemy and expressed solidarity with the Palestinian cause. However, the group's anti-Zionist objectives never received the same emphasis given to its domestic political agenda.

In 1970 Palestinian militants, including the Palestine Liberation Organization, were expelled from Jordan and relocated to Lebanon, amassing in the south and near major cities. Although the country's Shia population initially viewed the arrivals as natural allies, the relationship between the two communities soured as the Palestinian presence elicited Israeli attacks and brought violence to the villages hosting them. In addition, militant and refugee appropriation of property came at the expense of the Lebanese Shia, deepening the latter's resentment. The declining relationship worked to the advantage of Amal, which presented itself as the only force that could guarantee the Shia's security and interests.

The Lebanese Civil War broke out after the founder of the Maronite Christian party, Pierre Gemayel, was the target of an attempted assassination, allegedly perpetrated by Palestinian extremists. Maronite militias responded by attacking a bus of Palestinians, and sectarian war ensued. In the early stages of the conflict, Amal aligned with the Druze-led Lebanese National Movement. It was a party to the

Syrian-backed Tri-Partite Agreement of 1985, which attempted, and ultimately failed, to bring the war to a close.

The mysterious disappearance of al-Sadr in 1978 during a trip to Libya served as a catalyst for the steady mobilization of the Lebanese Shia population. This development was further spurred by the Israeli invasions in 1978 and 1982 as well as by the example of the Iranian Revolution in 1979. Amal benefited from this trajectory and managed to build up a significant base of popular support, especially in the south of the country.

In 1982 the Iranian-backed Hezbollah emerged as a rival militia and competitor for the allegiance of Lebanese Shia. Amal's more moderate character, particularly its willingness to compromise on its stance toward Israel, caused friction with the new movement, and the two groups took opposite sides during the so-called War of the Camps that lasted from 1985 to 1988. During this three-year period Lebanese military elements and Amal launched a combined offensive against the increasingly unwelcome Palestinians, who were themselves supported by Hezbollah and the Druze Progressive Socialist Party. The two organizations also routinely sparred to extend their influence among the Lebanese Shia, a conflict that came to a head in May 1988 when Hezbollah and Amal fought for control of Beirut's southern suburbs. Continuing clashes eventually forced Syria and Iran to intervene directly in the conflict between their respective proxies.

The Lebanese Civil War ended in 1990 with the signing of the Taif Agreement, which stipulated that all militias disarm by 1991. Amal strongly supported the accord, which called for moderate reform of the Lebanese political system. Following its disarmament, Amal continued to exist as a political party in Lebanon. Along with Hezbollah and various Sunni Muslim and Christian groups, it joined the March 8 and Reform and Change bloc in parliament. Amal leader leader Nabih Berri also served in several cabinet positions after the civil war and was elected speaker of the Lebanese parliament in 1992, a post he continues to occupy.

See also: Hezbollah (Party of God); Islamic Jihad Organization (IJO)

Further Reading

Ehteshami, Anoushiran, and Raymond Hinnebusch. *Syria and Iran: Middle Powers in the Penetrated Regional System.* New York: Routledge, 2002.

El Khazen, Farid. "Political Parties in Postwar Lebanon: Parties in Search of Partisans." *Middle East Journal* 57, no. 4 (Autumn 2003).

Norton, Augustus Richard. *Amal and the Shi'a: Struggle for the Soul of Lebanon.* Austin: University of Texas Press, 1987.

Norton, Augustus Richard. *Hezbollah: A Short History.* Princeton, NJ: Princeton University Press, 2007.

Norton, Augustus Richard. "Lebanon after Taif: Is the Civil War Over?" *Middle East Journal* 45, no. 3 (Summer 1991).

Shaery-Eisenlohr, Roschanack. *Shiite Lebanon.* New York: Columbia University Press, 2008.

Shanahan, Rodger. *The Shi'a of Lebanon: Clans, Parties, and Clerics.* New York: Taurus Academic Studies, 2005

Kate Mrkvicka

AMAQIM SHOPPING MALL BOMBING

On May 19, 2003, a female suicide bomber carried out an attack on the Shaarei Amaqim (Amakim) shopping mall in Afula, Israel. She detonated her explosive at 5:14 P.M. after guards stopped her from entering the complex—killing herself and three others and injuring 70. Authorities later said that the mall had conducted a mock terror attack exercise just four days prior to the attack. The exercise is credited with increasing the alertness of security personnel and thus saving lives.

Palestinian Islamic Jihad (PIJ) and the al-Aqsa Martyrs' Brigades both claimed credit for the attack. The latter organization claimed it had video footage of the bomber, while the former issued a poster of her after her death. Hamas spokesman Abdel Aziz Rantisi said that the attack showed that "our [Palestinian] fighters are capable of reaching them (Israelis) in every corner of our occupied land." He added, "As long as the occupation remains on our land and as long as the occupation soldiers are breathing our air, we will continue our resistance." The Palestinian Authority (PA) condemned the attack, with Labor Minister Ghassan Khatib asserting, "We reject [the attacks] because they harm us politically and morally and don't represent the Palestinian position."

The 19-year-old suicide bomber, Hiba Azem Daraghmeh (Heba Daraghmeh, Hiba Azam Dragma), had been a freshman at an Al-Quds Open University campus in Jenin. The brilliant but deeply troubled young woman was from the West Bank village of Tubas. She was a student of English literature who some described as being deeply religious and modest to the point of obsession, possibly on account of being raped by a relative when she was just 14 years old. Despite this, Hiba put aside her traditional garments (that hid almost her entire body) clothing on the day of the attack in favor of Western-style jeans and a T-shirt. Although this mode of dress was interpreted as part of a disguise to avoid arousing suspicion, her mother, Fatmah Daragmeh, later noted that prior to the rape her daughter had worn clothing of this type on a regular basis. She went on to say that the sexual attack had fundamentally changed her daughter: "More and more, she became religious. More and more, she read the Koran, and more and more, she became distant from me. I believed it was my punishment for keeping our secret [the rape]. And now I believe her death is my punishment as well."

Immediately after Hiba's death, Yusef al-Qaradawi from Qatar repeated a claim made by other militant religious leaders: that a woman could reach Paradise by committing a suicide bombing. It was a view that had also been echoed in the more secular rhetoric of Yasser Arafat on January 27, 2002, in a speech where he outlined the importance of women to the success of the Intifada. In it, he said, "Women and men are equal. You are my army of roses that will crush Israeli tanks." To emphasize the nature of the equality, he used the term *Shahida,* a feminized version of the Arab word for martyr, *shahide.* Arafat's speech was followed by a suicide attack carried out by 26-year-old Wafa Idris that killed 1 and wounded 131 at a mall in downtown Jerusalem. That strike, like the Amaqim bombing, was claimed by al-Aqsa Martyrs' Brigades.

The Amaqim bombing was the last in a series of terrorist acts that had begun on Saturday, May 17. The first involved a student from Hebron's Polytechnic

University, who blew himself up in Gross Square. The attack, which Hamas claimed, killed a husband and his pregnant wife. The second and third attacks occurred on Sunday, May 18, targeting a bus near French Hill in Jerusalem (7 dead and 20 injured) and a police checkpoint in the northern part of the city (1 dead, the bomber). Once again Hamas took responsibility for the attacks, and in common with strike on Gross Square, both perpetrators were students from the Polytechnic University in Hebron. Then, on Monday, May 19, a Palestinian militant on a bicycle detonated a device next to a military jeep near Kfar Darom in the southern Gaza Strip. Three members of the Israeli Defense Forces (IDF) were injured in the ensuing explosion. For the third time, Hamas assumed credit for the incident.

See also: al-Aqsa Martyrs' Brigades; Hamas (Islamic Resistance Movement); Palestinian Islamic Jihad (PIJ)

Further Reading

Bloom, Mia. *Dying to Kill: The Allure of Suicide Terror.* New York: Columbia University Press, 2005.
"Islamic Jihad Claims Responsibility for Bomb in Northern Israel—Radio." *Asia Africa Intelligence Wire,* May 19, 2003. http://www.accessmylibrary.com/coms2/summary_0286-23313479_ITM, accessed December 20, 2011.
Victor, Barbara. *Army of Roses: Inside the World of Palestinian Women Suicide Bombers.* New York: St. Martin's, 2003.

Donna Bassett

AMIR, YIGAL

On the evening of November 4, 1995, while leaving a peace rally he had just addressed in the Kings of Israel Square, Tel Aviv, Israeli prime minister and elder statesman Yitzhak Rabin was shot twice and mortally wounded. The assassin was Yigal Amir, a young Jewish extremist who later claimed he had no regrets over his actions and had been acting "on orders from God." He justified his actions as revenge for Rabin's signing of the Oslo Accords with Yasser Arafat in September 1993 and his willingness to bargain away biblical lands captured in the 1967 Six-Day War in return for peace with the Palestinians.

Amir was born in 1970 into a large, poor family in Herzliya, north of Tel Aviv. His parents were Orthodox Sephardic Jews who had immigrated to Israel from Yemen, and his father earned a living writing Holy Scripture. As a teenager Amir was ultra-Orthodox and, as well as being a hard worker, was noted for his extreme religious and political views. When he reached the age of 18, unlike many of his contemporaries, who sought to avoid military service, Amir volunteered for a five-year Hesder program, which combined combat training with the 1st Golani Infantry Brigade with periods of religious scholarship. He subsequently developed a reputation as an excellent soldier who would always volunteer for extra duties.

In 1992 Amir worked as an emissary in the Liaison Bureau in Riga, Latvia, where he taught Hebrew. As part of his preparation, he was trained in the use of handguns by the domestic intelligence and security service, the Shin Bet. After three months abroad, he returned to Israel, where he enrolled as a law student in the religious Bar-Ilan University near Tel Aviv. By this stage he had become an active member of Eyal, a right-wing Jewish extremist group that was an offshoot of the outlawed Kach movement. The extremist Rabbi Meir Kahane had founded the latter organization before his assassination at the hands of an Islamist cell in New York in 1990.

The Israeli authorities, and in particular the Shin Bet, were fully aware of Amir's affiliation with Eyal, which was in fact a front organization established by the intelligence service as a means of drawing in and identifying Jewish right-wing extremists who might pose a realistic threat to the Israeli state. Indeed, the leader of Eyal and Amir's mentor was Avishai Raviv, a Shin Bet agent provocateur. In addition, the Shin Bet had been previously tipped off that plans to kill Prime Minister Rabin had been overheard and that the assassin's profile fit Amir's description: a member of Eyal who was short and in his mid-20s, with dark features and black hair.

Amir had been following the prime minister's movements and planning an attack for at least a year. Initially, he held discussions with his brother Hagai as to proposed tactics, including the possibility of a bomb or use of a sniper's rifle. However, ultimately Amir believed that the only way to ensure a successful assassination was for a lone gunman to shoot the prime minister at close range. It has been suggested that Amir may have made up to a dozen attempts to kill Rabin, including one in January 1995 when the Israeli leader traveled to the Yad Vashem Holocaust Memorial to mark the 50th anniversary of the liberation of the Nazi Auschwitz concentration camp. Rabin never made the appointment, however, going instead to Beit Leid junction, where two suicide bombers from Palestinian Islamic Jihad disguised in Israeli uniforms had killed 21 soldiers and wounded dozens more.

Despite these setbacks Amir remained committed to assassinating Rabin. On the evening of November 4, 1995, Amir boarded a bus to the Kings of Israel Square, where the prime minister was to address a peace rally. He was armed with a nine-millimeter Beretta semiautomatic pistol loaded with dumdum bullets designed by his brother to enhance gunshot wounds. Upon arrival the 25-year-old Amir made his way to a supposedly secure parking area next to Rabin's vehicle, around 30 meters (98 feet) from the stage. With his Jewish features and casual dress, he was able to chat with police, convincing one Shin Bet officer that he was a driver for one of the performing pop stars. At no stage was he either detained or searched.

At 9:40 P.M., having delivered speeches, Rabin and Deputy Prime Minister Shimon Peres made their way from the stage down steps to their awaiting cars. While Amir stood in the shadows at the bottom of the stairwell, Rabin stopped to talk to event organizers, while Peres and his protective detail walked past safely. Amir waited for the prime minister to reach the bottom of the stairs, where he fired three shots at point-blank range. Two rounds struck Rabin in the back, while the third wounded a Shin Bet officer, Yoram Rubin, in the shoulder. The police immediately detained Amir, and despite his injuries, Rubin rushed Rabin to the Ichilov Hospital. However, the prime minister was already unconscious upon arrival and was pronounced dead 90 minutes later.

At his trial Amir showed no remorse. He claimed his decision to kill Rabin was based on the judgments of two militant rabbis who had sanctioned the prime minister's death on the grounds that he had betrayed the Israeli people and deliberately risked Jewish lives. These justifications were respectively based on the ancient Talmudic laws of *din moser* and *din rodef.* At sentencing in 1996, Amir was imprisoned for life, while his brother was given a 12-year jail term for conspiracy.

See also: Kahane Khai; Oslo Accords

Further Reading

Fetherling, George. *A Biographical Dictionary of the World's Assassins.* London: Robert Hale, 2002.
Juergensmeyer, Mark. *Terror in the Mind of God: The Global Rise of Religious Violence.* Berkeley: University of California Press, 2001.
Katz, Samuel. *The Hunt for the Engineer: The Inside Story of How Israel's Counterterrorist Forces Tracked and Killed the HAMAS Master Bomber.* Guilford, CT: Lyons, 2002. Chapter 6, "The Autumn of the Assasin."
McTernan, Oliver. *Violence in God's Name: Religion in an Age of Conflict.* London: Darton, Longman and Todd, 2003.
Stern, Jessica. *Terror in the Name of God: Why Religious Militants Kill.* New York: Harper Collins, 2003.

Richard Warnes

AMMAN HOTEL BOMBINGS

On November 9, 2005, a trio of Iraqi suicide bombers detonated devices at three separate hotels in Amman, Jordan. The attacks, organized by Abu Musab's al-Zarqawi's Tanzom Qa'idat al-Jihadi Bilad al-Rafidyan (QJBR, or Al Qaeda in Iraq [AQI]), resulted in the deaths of 62 people and the reported wounding of 115 others. The most deadly explosion occurred at the Radisson SAS, where one of the terrorists detonated himself in the middle of a wedding celebration attended by Jordanians and Palestinians. The bombings produced a major backlash against AQI within Jordan, and to some extent the larger Middle East, depriving the group of much of its earlier popularity.

Prior to the November 2005 bombings, al-Zarqawi had been linked to several unsuccessful plots in Jordan. In 1999 he was implicated in the failed "millennium plot" that was to have targeted the Radisson SAS and various other tourist sites in the country. In August 2005 he was tied to another unsuccessful strike, this time a rocket attack in 'Aqaba. Overall Jordan's General Intelligence Department (GID) believed al-Zarqawi had been behind at least a dozen attempted acts of terrorism, although some security officials gave numbers as high as 150. The Amman bombings dramatically broke this pattern and were generally seen as indicative of a change in targeting preferences away from fortified strategic buildings toward "soft" civilian-centric venues. AQI itself claimed the hotels had been selected because they were frequented by the intelligence services who were coordinating activities against the mujahideen in Iraq, by North Atlantic Treaty Organization (NATO) commanders, by Shi'a militias, and by Jewish and Christian tourists. The group also asserted that the properties were centers of vice and prostitution.

There is no indication that Al Qaeda's central command had any role in planning the attacks. Indeed, in July 2005, Ayman al-Zawahiri, then Osama bin Laden's

A Jordanian policeman stands guard in the damaged lobby of the Grand Hyatt hotel in Amman, Jordan, November 10, 2005. Al Qaeda in Iraq issued an Internet claim of responsibility for this attack and two other suicide bombings on Western hotels that killed 62 people. (AP Photo/ Hussein Malla)

second in command, had advised al-Zarqawi to focus on expelling American forces from Iraq and consolidating the establishment of an Islamic state before attempting to export the jihad to neighboring countries.

Perhaps indicative of Al Qaeda's noninvolvement, actual preattack preparations appeared to be minimal. On November 5, 2005, four members of AQI—Ali Hussein al-Shumari, 35; his wife, Sajida Mubarak al-Rishawi, 35; Rawad Jassem Muhammad Abed, 23; and Safaa Muhammad Ali, 23—crossed the border from Iraq to Jordan with fraudulent passports. The terrorists then rented an apartment in a neighborhood of Amman and hired a car. According to the GID, once the team had crossed the border into the country all communications with the AQI leadership were cut.

It is unclear whether the bombers assembled their suicide belts once in Amman or whether the devices were smuggled in separately. An AQI statement issued on the Internet two days after the bombings asserted that that the attackers conducted "one month" of surveillance before carrying out their mission. However, this is clearly contradicted by the date the bombers entered the country, only three days prior to the explosions. In fact, several witnesses claimed to have seen two men canvassing one of the targeted properties, the Days Inn, just one day before it was hit.

On the evening of September 9, the suicide bombers traveled to their respective hotels: al-Rishawi and al-Shumari to the SAS Radisson; Muhammed Abed to the Grand Hyatt; and Muhammad Ali to the Days Inn. At approximately 8:50 P.M. the attacks were launched.

At the Raddison SAS, al-Rishawi failed to detonate her suicide belt due to technical difficulties and fled the scene. Her husband then reportedly jumped on a table in the center of the room and triggered his device. The ensuing blast was the most lethal of the three, as it took place in the middle of a wedding reception.

The attack at the Grand Hyatt took place in the lobby, resulting in the death of several Palestinian officials, including the head of military intelligence for the West Bank, Major General Bashir Nayef. American-Syrian filmmaker Mustafa Akkad and his daughter were also among those killed. The explosion at the Days Inn occurred immediately outside the hotel and was initially thought to have been the result of a car bomb. However, it was later determined that the perpetrator had merely detonated his suicide belt inside the vehicle. Three members of a Chinese military delegation were among the fatalities.

The day after the bombings a statement claiming responsibility in the name of "Al-Baraa bin Balik Brigade" was posted on a website often used by AQI. A second communiqué clarifying the reasons behind the attacks was issued shortly thereafter, apparently in an attempt to ameliorate the condemnation already building within the Arab media and on the streets of Jordan. A third message appeared on Friday, November 11, which provided more details about the operation and confirmed that the bombers were all Iraqis and included three males and one female. It is not clear whether the GID was aware at this time that al-Rishawi had been involved or whether the statement alerted them that she was still at large.

Following the attacks, the border with Iraq was immediately closed, and a heavy security dragnet was instituted across the capital. Over the next couple of days 120 suspects were rounded up in what was described as the country's largest manhunt in history. Al-Rishawi was eventually traced to Salt, a town northwest of Amman, where she had taken refuge in a house owned by a local family.

There is well-documented evidence that before the bombings the majority of the population of Jordan was sympathetic to AQI and believed that suicide bombings could be legitimate if carried out to defend Muslim lives. These attitudes changed dramatically following the attacks. According to surveys conducted by the Pew Research Center, whereas 57 percent of respondents had declared militant martyrdom as sometimes or often justified in early 2005, only 29 percent did so in 2006. Confidence in bin Laden and Al Qaeda affiliates similarly plummeted, from 61 percent in 2005 to 24 percent in 2006. Even Internet polling of jihadis showed a high level of discomfort with the Amman bombings.

Condemnation of the attacks was visibly reflected in mass public protests that sprang up in Amman, with some gatherings numbering as many as 200,000 people. Demonstrators berated AQI and vocally reaffirmed their support for and loyalty to the Jordanian government, then a key U.S. ally in the so-called global war on terror. Arguably more significantly, al-Zarqawi's own clan, the al-Khalaliyah, published advertisements in local newspapers denouncing the attacks, disowning the AQI leader and pledging allegiance to the king.

The overwhelming public narrative surrounding the bombings was that they mindlessly targeted civilians. The images and stories from the attack on the wedding at the Radisson SAS triggered a particularly dramatic backlash, not least because it had resulted in the indiscriminate slaughter of innocent Jordanian and Palestinian Muslims. Ashraf al-Khalid, the groom at the celebration, later became a public activist against terrorism and cofounded the global survivors' network.

Despite the overwhelming revulsion the bombings caused, conspiracy theories fueled stories among a small minority that the attacks were legitimately aimed at foreign intelligence agencies and that intended Jewish targets had received advanced notice of the impending strikes. The activities of the head of West Bank intelligence, Major General Bashir Nayef, and the Chinese military delegation that died in the explosion at the Days Inn attacks remain largely unexplained. Furthermore, *Haaretz* reported that Israeli citizens were escorted out of the Raddison SAS shortly before the attacks and alleged an advisory warning against travel to Jordan had been posted before the bombings actually occurred.

See also: Millennium Plots; Tanzom Qa'idat al-Jihadi Bilad al-Rafidyan (QJBR); Zarqawi, Abu Musab al-; Zawahiri, Ayman al-

Further Reading

Blumenkrantz, Zhoar, and Yoav Stern. "Scores Dead in Three Amman Hotel Bombings; Israelis Evacuated before Attack." *Haaretz,* November 10, 2005. http://www.haaretz.com/print-edition/news/scores-dead-in-three-amman-hotel-bombings-israelis-evacuated-before-attack-1.173770, accessed January 31, 2012.

"English Translation of Ayman al-Zawahiri's Letter to Abu Musa'ab al-Zarqawi." *Weekly Standard,* October 12, 2005.

"The Fallout from the Amman Bombings." Jane's Terrorism and Insurgency Center, December 15, 2005. http://jtic.janes.com, accessed January 31, 2012.

Fattah, Hassan M. "Jordan Arrests Iraqi Women in Hotel Blasts." *New York Times,* November 14, 2005.

Garwood, Paul. "Al-Qaida in Iraq Claims Four Iraqis Were Bombers; Scores Detained." *Seattle Times,* November 11, 2005.

"JTIC Exclusive Interview: Major-General Samih Asfoura, Director, Jordanian General Intelligence Department." Jane's Terrorism and Insurgency Center, December 22, 2005. http://jtic.janes.com, accessed January 31, 2012.

Phillips, James. "Zarqawi's Amman Bombings: Jordan's 9/11." Heritage Foundation, Washington D.C., November 18, 2005. http://www.heritage.org/research/reports/2005/11/zarqawis-amman-bombings-jordans-9–11, accessed January 31, 2012.

"Suicide Bombers Hit Amman Hotels." Jane's Terrorism and Insurgency Center, November 10, 2005. http://jtic.janes.com, accessed January 31, 2012.

"Unfavorable Views of Jews and Muslims on the Increase in Europe." Pew Research Center, Washington D.C., September 17, 2008. http://www.pewglobal.org/2008/09/17/chapter-3-muslim-views-on-extremism-and-conflict/, accessed January 31, 2012.

Gregory Wyatt

AMMAN TOXIC CHEMICAL BOMB PLOT

The Amman toxic chemical plot was discovered and broken up by Jordanian authorities in 2004 days before it was about to be launched. The operation was to have involved simultaneous strikes against the American embassy in Jordan, the Jordanian prime minister's office, and the headquarters of the Jordanian General Intelligence Department (GID). Had it been successful, security officials believe a toxic cloud with a two-kilometer (1.2-mile) radius would have been unleashed across Amman, killing 80,000 people and injuring 160,000 more. If these approximations are correct, the attacks would have dwarfed the 9/11 bombings of the Pentagon and World Trade Center in the United States.

Jordanian authorities maintain that the attack was being planned by a cell of the Kataeb Al Tawhid (Battalions of Monotheism), an organization that has ties to Al Qaeda. The ringleader of the group was a Jordanian named Azmi al-Jayyousi, who reported directly to Abu Musab al-Zarqawi, the emir of Al Qaeda in Iraq (AQI). Al-Jayyousi allegedly received training and planned the attack in Iraq before moving to Jordan to oversee logistical planning. The plot was broken up on April 20, 2004, after the GID received intelligence that a major terrorist operation was in the final stages of being organized. A subsequent raid by the kingdom's special forces on al-Jayyousi's hideout led to the discovery of explosives and 20 tons of toxic chemicals including hydrogen peroxide, cyanide salts, pesticides, and sulfuric acid (which apart from acting as a blistering agent can also be used to increase the yield of conventional bombs).

The men accused of planning the attack were Jordanian, Syrian, and Palestinian. Four males—Muwaffaq Adwan, Hassan Simsmiyyeh, Salah Marjehm, and Ibrahim Abu al Kheir—were killed during the raid. Al-Jayyousi, Ahmad Samir, Hussein Sharif Hussein, Anas Sheikh Amin, Mohammad Salameh Shaaban, and Husni Sharif Hussein were all arrested. Sulayman Khalid Darwish, Haytham Omar Ibrihim, and Abu Musab al-Zarqawi escaped. After his arrest, al-Jayyousi admitted to having planned the attack, asserting that he reported directly to al-Zarqawi and had received chemical weapons training from AQI. Al-Jayyousi later retracted the confession, which had been aired on Jordanian television before his trial, claiming it had been obtained under duress.

Al-Zarqawi responded to al-Jayyousi's statements in an audiotape, of unconfirmed authenticity, acknowledging there had been a plan to launch an attack on the GID's headquarters. However, he denied that the intended strike was to have involved chemical weapons, stating, "The chemical and poisonous bomb is a fabrication by the evil Jordanian mechanism. God knows that if we possessed such a bomb that we would not have hesitated for a second to avidly seek to strike Israeli cities such as Eilat, Tel Aviv and others."

The trial of al-Jayyousi, his comrades, and another seven suspected accomplices commenced on September 15, 2004. All of the men pleaded not guilty, setting the scene for a lengthy judicial hearing that eventually concluded on February 16, 2006. Two of those on trial were acquitted, and two received short prison terms. Al-Jayyousi and seven others were sentenced to death. Three others were charged in absentia, including al-Zarqawi. The verdict was appealed, and on May 21, 2008, the various capital punishments were overturned in favor of life imprisonment—although for al-Zarqawi this was moot as he had already been killed in a targeted U.S. air strike on June 7, 2006.

The foiled attacks did not receive significant media attention when the story first broke in 2004, and most reports that did emerge adopted the government's perspective and estimate of casualties. Debate has since emerged over the nature and seriousness of the plot. Many suspected that Jordanian authorities had deliberately exaggerated the seriousness of the incident to justify the kingdom's highly draconian antiterrorism policies. U.S. officials were also skeptical that the chemicals discovered at al-Jayyousi's house were intended to create a chemical weapon or increase the yield of a conventional bomb. While investigators did apparently carry out simulations during the trial to verify the magnitude of the supposed toxic cloud, no details of these experiments were ever made public. Moreover, independent experts who surveyed the list of recovered chemicals argued that the terrorist cell clearly had no idea how to construct a chemical weapon— al-Jayyousi, with only a sixth-grade education, certainly had no relevant expertise—and that with only 20 tons of material available it would have extremely difficult, if not impossible, to have caused mass casualties.

Most expert observers now agree that the Amman plot was really an amateur attempt to incorporate minimally effective crude toxic materials in a conventional attack. The Jordanian government either honestly misunderstood the seriousness of the threat or exaggerated it for political reasons.

See also: Tanzom Qa'idat al-Jihadi Bilad al-Rafidyan (QJBR); Zarqawi, Abu Musab al-

Further Reading

Central Intelligence Agency. "Terrorist CBRN: Materials and Effects." May 2003. https://www.cia.gov/library/reports/general-reports-1/CBRN_threat.pdf, accessed February 1, 2012.

Parachini, John. "Putting WMD Terrorism into Perspective." *Washington Quarterly* 26, no. 4 (2003).

Pita, Rene. "Assessing al-Qaeda's Chemical Threat." *International Journal of Intelligence and Counterintelligence* 20 (2007).

Smith, Paul J. *The Terrorism Ahead: Confronting Transnational Violence in the Twenty-First Century.* Armonk, NY: M.E. Sharpe, 2008.

Spyer, Jonathan. "The Al-Qai'ida Network and Weapons of Mass Destruction." *Middle East Review of International Affairs* 8, no. 3 (2004).

Megan Gregory

ANGRY BRIGADE

The Angry Brigade was an anarchist group that was active in the United Kingdom during the early 1970s. The organization espoused violent popular revolution and usually targeted property connected to individuals in industries that were perceived as exploitative—politicians, government departments, and members of the security forces and police (which were castigated as tools of a coercive state).

The Angry Brigade's first action was the planting of an improvised explosive device (IED) at a police station in Paddington, London, on May 22, 1970. By the end of 1971, the group had claimed responsibility for a further eight bombings, most of which were also accompanied by rambling communiqués justifying the attacks on the basis of vague anarchist ideological tenets. While mostly innocuous, some of the Angry Brigade's intended targets were high profile and included a cabinet minister, leading industrialists, and senior police officers.

In August 1971 eight people were arrested and charged with a number of offenses relating to Angry Brigade and other attacks dating back to 1968. The defendants became known as the Stoke Newington Eight, and four of them were eventually found guilty. During the trial, which ended in December 1972, the prosecution directly attributed 25 bombing to the Angry Brigade. In all, a total of 12 people were arrested for offenses relating to the group's activities. Five were convicted, five were acquitted, and two had the charges withdrawn.

Further Reading

The Angry Brigade 1967–1984: Documents and Chronology. Introduction by Jean Weir. London: Elephant Editions, 2005.

Carr, Gordon. *The Angry Brigade: A History of Britain's First Urban Guerilla Group.* London: PM, 2010.

Vague, Tom. *Anarchy in the UK: The Angry Brigade.* London: AK, 1997.

Lindsay Clutterbuck

ANSAR AL-ISLAM (AAI)

Ansar al-Islam (AaI) is an Islamic militant organization currently active in Iraq. It was founded in 2001 as an organization dedicated to promoting strict Islamist ideology within Iraqi Kurdistan. However, the group quickly transformed into a key insurgent movement in the wake of the U.S.-led invasion of Iraq in 2003. That same year AaI birthed the terrorist group Ansar al-Sunnah, which rejoined its parent organization in 2007. Alongside Al Qaeda in Iraq (AQI), AaI is responsible for a great deal of the violence that took place in Iraq following the 2003 invasion.

Although officially founded in 2001, AaI traces its origins to the mid- to late 1990s and the Islamic Movement of Kurdistan (IMK), a political movement operating in Iraqi Kurdistan. The IMK had been jockeying for political power by competing in local elections against secular Kurdish political parties like the Kurdistan Democratic Party and the Patriotic Union of Kurdistan (PUK). Beginning in the late 1990s, the IMK splintered into a number of factions. Two of these ultimately merged on September 1, 2001 to form Jund al-Islam. After some early battlefield successes—most notably, the killing of 42 PUK fighters in an ambush that same month—Jund al-Islam managed to draw a few more former IMK leaders into its ranks and renamed itself AaI on December 10, 2001.

Upon its founding, AaI declared war on all secular political parties in Iraqi Kurdistan. In a series of attacks throughout 2002, the group took part in targeted killings of members of rival secular Kurdish groups, including the attempted assassination of Barham Salih, a high-level PUK member. It also engaged in skirmishes and pitched battles with PUK forces. These attacks allowed AaI to carve out enough space to implement its form of strict Islamic government in northeastern Iraq. Under the guidance of its spiritual leader and its founder, Mullah Krekar, the group began implementing sharia law, enforcing it through bombings of businesses it deemed un-Islamic, acid attacks on women it deemed immodest, and beheadings of those it deemed to be apostates.

During late 2001 and early 2002, AaI also experienced an inflow of veteran jihadists who were fleeing Afghanistan in the wake of the U.S.-led invasion. Many of these fighters were foreigners- the vast majority Arabs. Most prominent among them was Abu Musab al-Zarqawi, a Jordanian salafist and the future founder of Tanzom Qa'idat al-Jihadi Bilad al-Rafidyan (QJBR), otherwise known as AQI. The connection to Al Qaeda and al-Zarqawi's network propelled the AaI to international notoriety when Colin Powell highlighted the group during his speech before the United Nations Security Council in the run-up to U.S.-led invasion of Iraq. Powell claimed that al-Zarqawi had linked up with AaI and was helping it manufacture poisons, such as ricin, in its camps in northern Iraq. Although the extent of the connection between al-Zarqawi and AaI remains a matter of debate, consensus exists that the AaI at one point hosted al-Zarqawi, who then derived parts of his network from the group.

Following the U.S.-led invasion of Iraq, AaI was dealt a serious blow. The PUK, backed by U.S. special forces, targeted a major base of AaI in March 2003, killing hundreds of AaI militants and forcing the group to scatter throughout mountainous Iraqi Kurdistan. While this attack proved to be a serious setback, it did not eliminate the group altogether. Some of the AaI remnants that survived the onslaught were believed to have taken refuge in Iran and quickly reconstituted themselves. In November 2003 these elements reemerged as Ansar al-Sunnah. Ansar al-Sunnah would ultimately acknowledge its roots in AaI and revert to its original name in November 2007.

See also: Ansar al-Sunnah (Sunni Army)

Further Reading

International Crisis Group. *Radical Islam in Iraqi Kurdistan: The Mouse That Roared?* Iraq Briefing, February 7, 2003.

Rubin, Michael. "The Islamist Threat in Iraqi Kurdistan." *Middle East Intelligence Bulletin* 3, no. 12 (December 2001).

Schanzer, Jonathan. "Ansar al-Islam: Back in Iraq." *Middle East Quarterly* 11, no. 1 (Winter 2004).

Schanzer, Jonathan. "Ansar al-Islam: Postmortem or Prelude to More Attacks?" Washington Institute for Near East Policy, Washington D.C., April 3, 2003.

Nate Shestak

ANSAR AL-SUNNAH (SUNNI ARMY)

Formed in 2003, Ansar al-Sunnah was a salafist-jihadist organization that fought in Iraq. The group emerged out of the ashes of Ansar al-Islam, a Kurdish Islamic militant group that was decimated by Kurdish and U.S. military forces during the U.S.-led invasion of Iraq. Alongside the Islamic Army of Iraq (IAI) and Tanzom Qa'idat al-Jihadi Bilad al-Rafidyan (QJBR), more commonly known as Al Qaeda in Iraq (AQI), Ansar al-Sunnah represented one of the deadliest Sunni Iraqi insurgent movements and was responsible for much of the violence that plagued Iraq following the U.S. invasion. In November 2007 the group reverted to its original name of Ansar al-Islam. Under this banner, it remains active in the insurgency in Iraq.

Ansar al-Sunnah traces its origins to its predecessor, Ansar al-Islam. During the political turmoil that beset semiautonomous Iraqi Kurdistan in the mid- to late 1990s, the Islamic Movement of Kurdistan (IMK) competed for political power with secular political parties like the Patriotic Union of Kurdistan (PUK) and the Kurdish Democratic Party (KDP). The IMK splintered into a number of factions, two of which would ultimately join together to form Jund al-Islam in September 2001. Upon its founding, Jund al-Islam declared war against the secular political parties in Iraqi Kurdistan and killed 42 PUK fighters in an ambush later that same month. After this early battlefield success, Jund al-Islam drew two former IMK commanders into its ranks. In December 2001, under the guidance of its spiritual leader, Mullah Krekar, the group ultimately renamed itself Ansar al-Islam. Ansar al-Islam's principal objective was to oppose the secular political vision of other Kurdish political parties and to establish a strict Islamic form of government in Iraqi Kurdistan.

In March 2003 Ansar al-Islam was dealt a serious blow when PUK fighters, in conjunction with U.S. special forces, attacked the group's base in Iraqi Kurdistan and killed hundreds of fighters. The attack destroyed much of the group, forcing it to scatter throughout northern Iraq. Many analysts questioned whether the group had been defeated altogether. However, pronouncements of Ansar al-Islam's death proved premature as it quickly reconstituted itself and reemerged in September of that year under the banner of Ansar al-Sunnah.

The group's rebirth as Ansar al-Sunnah marked a turning point in terms of the group's ideology and its goals. Like Ansar al-Islam, Ansar al-Sunnah maintained a slightly nationalistic bent. However, it married these nationalistic tendencies with the radical salafi-jihadist ideology of groups like AQI. In other words, while Ansar al-Sunnah still focused on stymieing the expansion of secular political voices in Kurdistan, its stated goals broadened to encompass the expulsion of foreign elements from Iraq, the establishment of a Sunni Islamic form of government for all of Iraq, and the marginalization of Iraq's Shi'a.

Led by Abu Abdullah al-Shafi until his capture in May 2010, Ansar al-Sunnah was one of the largest and most lethal insurgent movements in Iraq. At one time, the group boasted of having 16 brigades, although, like many Iraqi insurgent groups, its exact fighting strength is difficult to gauge. Given its ties to AQI, Ansar al-Sunnah's ranks included some foreign fighters. Some sources allege that Iran assisted Ansar al-Sunnah in facilitating the inflow of these external combatants. However, given its origins as a Kurdish separatist movement, the vast majority of its fighters were Iraqis and Kurds. Ansar al-Sunnah's group structure was only loosely hierarchical, and like other Iraqi insurgent movements, its leadership consisted of separate "emirs" for individual Iraqi provinces.

At one point Ansar al-Sunnah was purported to have European connections. Mullah Krekar, the founder of Ansar al-Islam, lives under de facto house arrest in Norway and has allegedly supplied funding to the group from Europe. In addition, the group's website was run out of a server in Germany, and authorities have claimed an Ansar al-Sunah presence in that country. However, no specific plots emanating from the group have surfaced to date.

Ansar al-Sunnah's home base and sphere of operation always remained in Iraq, though. Based out of Mosul, the group conducted its operations throughout much of northern, western, and central Iraq, often alongside IAI and AQI. These operations wreaked a sanguinary havoc on Iraq from 2003 through 2007 on a scale exceeded only by AQI. Keeping with its aims of countering secular Kurdish political forces, the group's first major operation took place on February 1, 2004, when two of its suicide bombers targeted KDP and PUK political offices in Irbil. The blasts left 109 dead and at least 200 wounded. This operation was followed by another mass-casualty attack in Irbil on May 3, 2005, when a suicide bomber targeted a crowd outside of a police recruiting station and a KDP political office, killing at least 60 and wounding at least 150. Throughout its existence, the group would continue to pummel the PUK and KDP. As the May 3, 2005, attack on the police center exemplifies, the group also actively targeted the Iraqi state. Indeed, it staged a number of attacks in the lead-up to Iraq's first elections in January 2005.

While the group did not demonstrate the same zeal for sectarian killing as AQI, it nonetheless participated in the sectarian violence that tore through Iraq from 2005 through 2007. This participation was motivated by the group's overarching vision of a strictly Sunni Islamic state. The group made the conscious decision to rename itself Ansar al-Sunnah, signifying an effort to appeal to Sunni Islamic sensibilities. On January 12, 2005, the group assassinated Sheik Mahmoud Finjan, an assistant to the powerful Shi'ite clerice Ayatollah al-Sistani. It would undertake other sectarian attacks but generally refrained from mass-casualty attacks explicitly targeting the country's Shi'a.

In keeping with Ansar al-Sunnah's goal of expelling foreign elements from Iraq, the group also widely targeted Western and international elements operating within Iraq. In many of these attacks, the group engaged in kidnapping, torture, and beheading. Heavily targeting contractors working for Western forces in Iraq, the group displayed incredible ruthlessness in its kidnapping operations. It rarely issued any demands, instead using its captives primarily for propaganda purposes, and it ultimately executed the vast majority of its abductees. Perhaps the most notorious example of this tactic was the August 2004 execution of 12 Nepalese contractors. Eleven of the 12 were beheaded in a widely distributed propaganda video, while the 12th was shot.

Ansar al-Sunnah also focused much of its efforts on U.S. forces and other military targets. As such, it represented one of the largest and most lethal insurgent challenges to American interests in Iraq. The group carried out the deadliest attack on U.S. forces in postinvasion Iraq when, on December 21, 2004, an Ansar al-Sunnah suicide bomber infiltrated a U.S. military dining hall on a base in Mosul and detonated his explosives. The ensuing blast killed 22 people, including 18 U.S. soldiers, and wounded nearly 70 others. In addition to this attack, the group constantly targeted U.S. and Iraqi military forces with guerrilla-warfare tactics, including widespread use of improvised explosive devices, mortar attacks, and ambushes. These attacks were invariably accompanied by online propaganda videos and written releases or attack claims, all of which recounted the group's purported battlefield successes. Of note is the fact that such propaganda would be released in both Arabic and Kurdish, further signifying the group's Kurdish and Iraqi nationalist tinge.

Although Ansar al-Sunnah collaborated with AQI and was arguably its strongest ally, Ansar al-Sunnah deliberately maintained a certain degree of distance between itself and the broader Al Qaeda network. The two groups espouse similar ideologies, but AQI's foreign leadership did not mesh with Ansar al-Sunnah's Iraqi nationalist undertones. In addition, tensions between the groups flared over the killing of Ansar al-Sunnah militants by AQI. In 2006 Ansar al-Sunnah rejected calls from Al Qaeda to join the Islamic State of Iraq—an umbrella organization of Sunni extremist groups that AQI formed in an attempt to reaffirm its ties with Iraq's Sunnis and put an Iraqi face on its movement—and instead simply chose to appoint a liaison. Nevertheless, the two groups maintain cordial relations. Ansar al-Sunnah still eulogized Abu Omar al-Baghdadi and Abu Ayyub al-Masri, the leaders of the Mujahideen Shura Council (MSC) and AQI, respectively, upon their deaths.

In December 2007, Ansar al-Sunnah released a communiqué that offered an overview of the group's origins as remnants of Ansar al-Islam and stated that the group was reverting to its old name. Under the name Ansar al-Islam, the group remains active in the Iraqi insurgency, but it has continued to resist entreaties from AQI to join the Islamic State of Iraq. Like all other Sunni insurgent movements, the group has seen its fortunes decline since mid-2007. The surge in coalition forces, paired with AQI's overreach and its rejection by most of Iraq's Sunnis, has led to a significantly less favorable operating environment for the group. Nonetheless, it remains operationally active and still possesses the capability to significantly threaten the Iraqi state.

See also: Ansar al-Islam; Jamaa al-Tawhid wa'a Jihad; Tanzom Qa'idat al-Jihadi Bilad al-Rafidyan; Zarkawi, Abu Musab al-

Further Reading

Gregory, Kathryn. "Ansar al-Islam (Iraq Islamists/Kurdish Separatists), Ansar al-Sunnah." Council on Foreign Relations, Washington D.C., November 5, 2008.
Khalil, Lydia. "The Transformation of Ansar al-Islam." *Terrorism Monitor* 3, no. 24 (December 21, 2005).
Lia, Brynjar. "The Ansar al-Islam Group Revisited." Norwegian Defence Research Establishment, Kjeller, June 15, 2006.

Nate Shestak

ANTHRAX ATTACKS (UNITED STATES)

On September 18, 2001, one week after the terrorist attacks of September 11, five letters contaminated with anthrax bacteria were mailed in the United States to five media outlets. Over the next month, two more letters were sent. Altogether, the anthrax letters (which were mailed from a postal box in New Jersey) resulted in the deaths of 5 people and the infections of 17 more.

The anthrax-laced letters originally sent on September 18 were sent to the offices of ABC News, CBS News, NBC News, the *New York Post,* and the *National Enquirer.* Nearly a month later, two more letters were sent to Democratic senators Tom Daschle and Patrick Leahy at the Senate building in Washington, D.C. The postal service misdirected Leahy's letter, but the letter addressed to Daschle was opened by an aide, who became infected. Unlike the earlier letters, the second set of letters contained higher-quality weapons-grade anthrax capable of infecting victims with greater lethality.

In response to the attacks, thousands of people who came in contact with or near the envelopes began taking strong doses of ciprofloxacin ("cipro"), an antibiotic capable of preventing anthrax infections. In addition, the federal government began radiation treatment of all incoming mail to defuse any possible anthrax inside. Post office employees began wearing gloves and masks and warned all Americans to carefully examine their mail and report any suspicious letters or packages.

Five people died from the anthrax infection: one employee at the *National Enquirer,* two post office employees, and two other unconnected people whose mail was likely cross-contaminated by the anthrax letters. Government officials began

A hazardous materials worker tasked with inspecting buildings and offices on Capitol Hill in Washington, D.C., for evidence of anthrax is hosed down to prevent possible contamination, October 23, 2001. Many Americans believed that Al Qaeda was behind the series of anthrax-laced letters that emerged shortly after 9/11, although subsequent investigations suggested that the letters were the work of Bruce Edwards Ivins, a scientist working at a government biodefense lab in Maryland. (AP/Wide World Photos)

an investigation immediately after discovering the anthrax letters. Following a variety of leads, the investigators profiled the suspect as a chemical or biological engineer in the United States who had likely worked at government facilities in the past. Some microbiologist experts who examined the anthrax stated that its quality was likely greater than that of the anthrax found in either U.S. or Russian stockpiles and thus was likely created in recent government anthrax programs.

The Federal Bureau of Investigation eventually concluded that Dr. Bruce Ivins, a microbiologist working at the U.S. Army's Bio-Defense Laboratory in Maryland, was responsible for the attacks. To this day, however, questions remain about his guilt, and there continues to be speculation that the true perpetrator is still on the loose. Ivins committed suicide in 2008.

Further Reading

"American Anthrax Outbreak of 2001." University of California at Los Angeles (UCLA) Department of Epidemiology, August 24, 2008. http://www.ph.ucla.edu/epi/bioter/ detect/antdect_intro.html.

Croddy, Eric A., and James Wirtz. *Weapons of Mass Destruction.* Santa Barbara, CA: ABC-CLIO, 2005.

Shane, Scott. "Colleague Rebuts Idea That Suspect's Lab Made Anthrax in Attacks." *New York Times,* April 23, 2010.

"Troubled Scientist's Anthrax Attack May Have Been Misguided Attempt to Test Cure." Associated Press, August 1, 2008.

"2001 Anthrax Attacks." *History Commons.* http://www.historycommons.org/project. jsp?project=2001anthraxattacks (accessed July 9, 2012).

Peter Chalk

ARAFAT, YASSER

Yasser Arafat, officially named Mohammed Abdel Raouf Arafat al-Qudwa al-Husseini, was born on August 24, 1929. Arafat always stated that he was born in Jerusalem, but to discredit him, Israeli officials began to claim in the 1970s that he was born in Cairo. There is also some dispute about his date of birth, which is occasionally given as August 4, 1929. He went by the name Yasser as a child.

Arafat's father was a Palestinian textile merchant. Neither Arafat nor his siblings were close to their father. His mother, Zahwa, also a Palestinian, was a member of a family that had lived in Jerusalem for generations. She died when Arafat was five years old, and he then lived with his mother's brother in Jerusalem. Arafat vividly remembered British soldiers invading his uncle's house one night, destroying possessions and beating the residents. When Arafat was nine years old his father brought him back to Cairo, where his older sister raised him.

As a teenager in Cairo, Arafat became involved in smuggling arms to Palestine to aid those struggling against both the British authorities and the Jews living there. He attended the University of Fuad I (later Cairo University) in Cairo but left to fight in Gaza against Israel in the Israeli War of Independence of 1948–1949. When the Arabs lost the war and Israel was firmly established, Arafat was inconsolable. He briefly attended the University of Texas but then returned to Cairo University to study engineering. He spent most of his time with fellow Palestinian students spreading his hopes for a free Palestinian state.

Arafat became president of the Union of Palestinian Students, holding that position from 1952 to 1956. He joined the Muslim Brotherhood in 1952. He finally graduated from college in 1956 and spent a short time working in Egypt. During the 1956 Suez Crisis he served as a second lieutenant in the Egyptian Army. In 1957 he moved to Kuwait, where he worked as an engineer and formed his own contracting company.

In 1958 Arafat founded the al-Fatah organization, an underground guerrilla group dedicated to the liberation of Palestine. In 1964 he quit his job and moved to Jordan to devote all his energies to the promotion of Palestinian nationhood and to organize raids into Israel. The Palestine Liberation Organization (PLO) was founded that same year.

In 1968 the Israel Defense Forces attacked al-Fatah at the small Jordanian village of Al Karameh. The Palestinians eventually forced the Israelis back, and Arafat's face appeared on the cover of *Time* magazine as the leader of the Palestinian movement. In consequence, Palestinians embraced al-Fatah, and Arafat became a national hero. He was appointed chairman of the PLO the next year and within four years controlled both the military (the Palestine Liberation Army) and political branches of the organization.

By 1970 the Palestinians had assembled a well-organized unofficial state within Jordan. However, King Hussein of Jordan deemed them a threat to security and sent his army to evict them. Arafat enlisted the aid of Syria, while Jordan called on the United States for assistance. On September 24, 1970, the PLO agreed to a cease-fire and agreed to leave Jordan. Arafat moved the organization to Lebanon, which had a weak government that was not likely to restrict the PLO's operations. The PLO soon began launching occasional attacks across the Israeli border.

Arafat did not approve of overseas attacks because they gave the PLO a bad image abroad. He publicly dissociated the group from Black September, the organization that killed 11 Israeli athletes at the 1972 Munich Olympics, although there is now evidence of his involvement. In 1974 he limited the PLO's attacks to Israel, the Gaza Strip, and the West Bank. Although Israel claimed that Arafat was responsible for the numerous terrorist attacks within the country during the 1970s, he denied responsibility. In 1974 he spoke before the United Nations General Assembly as the representative of the Palestinian people and condemned Zionism but offered peace, which won him praise from the international community.

During the Lebanese Civil War, the PLO initially sided with the Lebanese National Front against the Lebanese forces, which were supported by Israel and backed by Defense Minister Ariel Sharon. As such, when Israeli forces invaded southern Lebanon, the PLO ended up fighting against the Israelis and then the Syrian militia group Amal. Thousands of Palestinians, many of them civilians, were killed during the struggle, and the PLO was forced to leave Lebanon in 1982 and relocate to Tunisia, where it remained until 1993.

During the 1980s Iraq and Saudi Arabia donated millions of dollars to Arafat to help him rebuild the PLO. Arafat approved the First Intifada (1987) against Israel.

In 1988 the Palestinians declared Palestinian statehood at a meeting in Algiers. Arafat then announced that the Palestinians would renounce terrorism and recognize the state of Israel. The Palestinian National Council elected Arafat president of this new, unrecognized state in 1989.

Arafat and the Israelis conducted peace negotiations at the Madrid Conference in 1991. Although negotiations were temporarily set back when the PLO supported Iraq in the 1991 Persian Gulf War, over the next two years the two parties held a number of secret discussions. These negotiations led to the 1993 Oslo Accords in which Israel agreed to Palestinian self-rule in the Gaza Strip and the West Bank. Arafat also officially recognized the existence of the state of Israel. Despite the condemnation of many Palestinian nationalists who viewed Arafat's moves as a sellout, the peace process appeared to be moving in a positive direction in the mid-1990s. Israeli troops withdrew from the Gaza Strip and Jericho in May 1994. Arafat was elected leader of the new Palestinian Authority (PA) in January 1996 with 88 percent of the vote in elections that were by all accounts free and fair (but with severely limited competition because Hamas and other opposition groups refused to participate).

Later that same year, Benjamin Netanyahu of the Likud Party became prime minister of Israel, and the peace process began to unravel. Netanyahu, a hard-line conservative, condemned terrorism and blamed Palestinians for numerous suicide bombings against Israeli citizens. He also did not trust Arafat, who he charged was supporting terrorists. Arafat continued negotiations with the Israelis into 2000. That July, with Ehud Barak having replaced Netanyahu as Israeli prime minister, Arafat traveled to the United States to meet with Barak and President Bill Clinton at the Camp David Summit. Despite generous concessions by Barak, Arafat refused to compromise, and a major chance at peace was lost.

After the collapse of the peace process, the Second (al-Aqsa) Intifada began. From the outset of hostilities in 2000, Arafat was a besieged man who appeared to be losing influence and control within the Palestinian and larger Arab communities. His inability or unwillingness to stop suicide attacks against Israel resulted in his virtual captivity at his Ramallah headquarters from 2002. In declining health by 2004, the PLO leader was beginning to look increasingly like a man past his time.

Flown to France for medical treatment, Arafat died on November 11, 2004, at Percy Military Hospital outside Paris, France. For a time, there was much intrigue and conspiratorial conjecture concerning his mysterious illness and death. Rumors persist that he was assassinated by poisoning, although it is equally likely that he succumbed to unintentional food poisoning. He is buried at his former headquarters in the city of Ramallah.

See also: al-Fatah; Palestine Liberation Organization (PLO)

Further Reading

Aburish, Said K. *Arafat: From Defender to Dictator.* New York: Bloomsbury, 1998.
Gowers, Andrew. *Arafat: The Biography.* Rev ed. London: Virgin Books, 1990.
Hart, Alan. *Arafat: A Political Biography.* Rev. ed. London: Sidgwick and Jackson, 1994.
Laqueur, Walter, and Barry Rubin, eds. *The Israel-Arab Reader: A Documentary History of the Middle East Conflict.* London: Penguin, 2001.

Said, Edward W. *Peace and Its Discontents: Essays on Palestine in the Middle East Process.* New York: Vintage Books, 1995.

Tessler, Mark. *A History of the Israeli-Palestinian Conflict.* Bloomington: Indiana University Press, 1994.

Wallach, Janet, and John Wallach. *Arafat: In the Eyes of the Beholder.* Secaucus, NJ: Carol, 1997.

Amy Hackney Blackwell

ARMENIAN SECRET ARMY FOR THE LIBERATION OF ARMENIA (ASALA)

The Armenian Secret Army for the Liberation of Armenia (ASALA), sometimes referred to as the 3rd October Organization and the Orly Group, was founded by Hagop Hagopian during the Lebanese Civil War. It was established in 1975 from among the Armenian community with the assistance of the wider diaspora. ASALA cadres initially trained in Palestinian militant camps in Beirut. While the group had close links to the Palestine Liberation Organization (PLO) and the more hard-line Popular Front for the Liberation of Palestine (PFLP)—a Marxist-Leninist ideology and subsequent links to the Soviet Union—its primary objective was to "compel the Turkish Government to acknowledge publicly its responsibility for the Armenian Genocide in 1915, pay reparations and cede territory for an Armenian homeland."

During World War I, the Armenian community had been seen by elements of the Ottoman Empire as potential fifth columnists, loyal to their Russian coreligionists who were at that time in conflict with Turkish forces in Anatolia. In 1915 the Young Turk movement used the justification of security to order the mass deportation of the Armenian community, who were force-marched to camps located in the Syrian Desert. In the course of these actions it is estimated that up to one and a half million Armenians died, while many others emigrated to the United States, the Middle East, and Europe.

In 1965, on the 50th anniversary of these events, there was an international campaign among Armenian expatriates to pressure the Turkish authorities to acknowledge the deaths and make reparations, with little response. In 1973 an elderly survivor of the expulsions, Gourgen Yanikian, acted as a catalyst for later attacks when he invited two Turkish diplomats from the Los Angeles consulate out for a meal before shooting them dead. Following an initial bomb attack against the World Council of Churches' Beirut office in January 1975, ASALA used similar tactics, targeting Turkish diplomats and politicians in Europe, the United States, and Middle East. Later, they returned to bombings and hostage taking, ultimately killing 46 people and wounding around 300 between 1975 and 1986.

Of the fatalities, around 36 were Turkish diplomats or members of their families. Prominent cases included

- The Turkish ambassador to Paris and his bodyguard (October 1975)
- Oktar Cirit at the Turkish embassy in Beirut (February 1976)
- The Turkish ambassador to the Vatican (June 1977)
- The wife of the Turkish ambassador to Madrid (June 1978)
- Ahmet Benler, son of the Turkish ambassador to the Hague (October 1979)

- Galip Ozmen and his daughter Neslihan at the Turkish embassy in Athens (July 1980)
- Resat Morali at the Turkish embassy in Paris (March 1981)
- Mehmet Savas Yergus at the Turkish consulate in Geneva (June 1981)
- The Turkish honorary consul in Boston (May 1982)
- The Turkish military attaché in Ottawa (August 1982)
- Dursun Aksoy, the Turkish ambassador to Brussels (July 1983)
- Isik Yonder at the Turkish embassy in Tehran (April 1984)

During 1980 and 1981 a series of bombs in Switzerland and France were also associated with ASALA demands for the release of imprisoned colleagues. In one notable attack on September 24, 1981, four members of the group launched Operation Van, named after the former Armenian-populated town in eastern Turkey. The team seized the Turkish consulate in Paris; killed Cemal Ozen, a security guard; and took 56 members of the staff hostage. The captives were held for some 16 hours before the terrorists surrendered to the French authorities.

By 1982 ASALA had reached the height of its powers, issuing an eight-point political program to the Turkish government. However, in June 1982 the Israeli invasion of Lebanon forced ASALA (and many Palestinian groups) out of Beirut. The organization subsequently relocated to the Bekaa Valley, where it fell increasingly under the influence of Syria. ASALA also formed a close relationship with the Abu Nidal Organization (ANO), which served to escalate the militancy and violence of its agenda.

On August 7, 1982, ASALA carried out an attack at Esenboga Airport, Ankara, where two terrorists opened fire on passengers in a waiting room, killing 9 and wounding over 80. The following year members of the group bombed the Turkish Airlines desk at Orly Airport near Paris. The strike left eight people dead, predominantly French nationals.

Disagreements over such indiscriminate attacks led to a split in the organization between the hard-line ASALA-Militant, led by Hagopian, and ASALA-Mouvement Revolutionnaire, led by Monte Melkonian. A bitter feud developed between the two factions, and most of their energies focused on killing rival members (Hagopian was assassinated on an Athens street in April 1988), with the remnants of the original ASALA becoming increasingly moribund. Despite a token attack in 1991 against the armored limousine of the Turkish ambassador to Budapest, the organization continued to fragment and by the mid-1990s had essentially ceased to exist.

See also: Abu Nidal Organization (ANO); Justice Commandos of the Armenian Genocide (JCAG); Palestine Liberation Organization (PLO); Popular Front for the Liberation of Palestine (PFLP)

Further Reading

Dobson, Christopher, and Ronald Payne. *War without End: The Terrorists: An Intelligence Dossier.* London: Harrap, 1986.

Gunter, Michael. *Transnational Armenian Activism.* Conflict Studies 229. Research Institute for the Study of Conflict and Terrorism, London, 1990.

Iacovou, Christos. "ASALA: Terrorism as a Political Issue." International Institute for Counter-Terrorism, Herzliya, 1999. http://www.ict.org.il/articles/articledet.cfm?articleid=80.

Richard Warnes

ARYAN NATIONS (AN)

The Aryan Nations (AN), founded by Richard Butler in the 1970s as an extension of the Christian Identity group, is a far-right white supremacist organization that the Federal Bureau of Investigation (FBI) deems a domestic terrorist threat. Up until 2001 the group was based near Hayden Lake, Idaho, with loosely affiliated state chapters across several states.

In August 2001 Ray Redfeairn, a leading AN adherent, recruited Dave Hall. The new member turned out to be an FBI informant and exposed many of the group's illegal activities. Following this embarrasing relevation, Redfeairn was removed from the organization, and together with AN's propaganda minister, August Kreis, formed a splinter movement. The new faction was short-lived as a result of Redfeairn's death in October 2003.

Subsequently AN split into three main entities. Kreis and Charles Juba led one group based in Ulysses, Pennsylvania. Juba quit in March 2005, and Kreis moved his headquarters to Lexington, South Carolina. In 2007 the Holy Order of the Phinehas Priesthood broke away from Kreis and based itself in New York. It was viewed, as of 2011, as the enforcement and terrorism wing of AN. In 2009 a third arm emerged as a result of the merger between Aryan Nations Revival—based in Texas and led by Jay Faber—and the original AN from Idaho, now led by Pastor Jerald O'Brien.

AN adherents generally subscribe to Dominion theology, a reinterpretation of Christian Identity doctrine. In addition to anti-Semitism and racism, Dominionists articulate postmillennial Bible-based beliefs that call on each individual member to actively hasten the inevitable apocalypse in order to end the tribulations that afflict the American Christian white man. Proslyetizers contend that this period of reckoning will be followed by a 1,000-year period of Christian rule, after which the Messiah (Christ) will return to earth.

As with other far-right racist movements, AN subscribes to the concept of "leaderless resistance." Articulated by Louis Beam as an organizing principle designed to defeat the state tyrant, its genesis comes from the adventure novel *Hunter,* William Pierce's sequel to the *Turner Diaries* (which he wrote under the pseudonym Andrew McDonald). Under this construct, autonomous phantom cells are established in several regions. Although they act completely independently of one another, it is assumed their individual terrorist attacks will eventually combine to create the necessary conditions for sparking a nationwide white supremacist revolution.

Timothy McVeigh represented the culmination of the growth and potential reach of AN and various offshoots such as the Order and New Order (generically lumped under the banner of the "Militia Movement"). Born and raised in Pendleton, New York, and a veteran of the First Gulf War, McVeigh was directly inspired by the ideas of Pierce and was an ardent promoter of postmillennial theory. In 1995 he translated his supremacist "passion" into concrete action with the bombing of the Alfred P. Murrah Federal Building in Oklahoma City. Prior to 9/11 this was the most destructive act of terrorism to have ever been carried out on the U.S. mainland, leaving 168 people dead (including 19 children) and nearly 800 injured.

See also: Ku Klux Klan (KKK); McVeigh, Timothy; Oklahoma City Bombing

Further Reading

Aho, James A. *The Politics of Righteousness: Idaho Christian Patriotism.* Seattle: University of Washington Press, 1990.

Barkun, Michael. *Religion and the Racist Right: The Origins of the Christian Identity Movement.* Chapel Hill: University of North Carolina Press, 1997.

De Armond, Paul. "Christian Patriots at War with the State." Public Good Project, San Francisco, 1996. http://www.publicgood.org/reports/belief/, accessed September 14, 2011.

Flynn, Kevin, and Gary Gerhardt. *The Silent Brotherhood: Inside America's Racist Underground.* New York: Free Press, 1989.

Hoffman, Bruce. *Inside Terrorism.* London: Victor Gollancz, 1998. Pp. 105–20.

"Timothy McVeigh." History Guy Website. Last modified May 14, 2011. http://www. historyguy.com/biofiles/mcveigh_timothy.html, accessed September 14, 2011.

Donna Bassett

ASAHARA, SHOKO

Shoko Asahara is the founder and former leader of Aum Shinrikyo, the group responsible for the sarin gas attack on the Tokyo subway system in 1995. His birth name was Chizuo Matsumoto. The son of a family of poor tatami mat makers in Kumamoto Prefecture, he was afflicted at birth with infantile glaucoma. Blind in his left eye and almost blind in his right eye, he attended a special school and graduated in 1977. Failing to get accepted to a university, Matsumoto pursued a career as an acupuncturist, a career traditionally taken up by Japanese with visual disabilities. He also moved to Tokyo in 1977 and married Ishii Tomoko the next year. They eventually had six children together.

Matsumoto began to intensively pursue enlightenment in the early 1980s. From 1981 to 1984, he was an ardent member of Agonshu, one of Japan's "new" Buddhist groups, where he became acquainted with yoga and the Buddhist Agama literature. He eventually left and began to gather disciples as a yoga teacher before embarking on a pilgrimage to the Himalayas in 1987. It was here that Matsumoto believed he had attained enlightenment and a commissioned right from the Dalai Lama to revive true Buddhism in the land of his birth.

Upon his return from India, Matsumoto altered his name to Shoko Asahara (referring to himself as the "Venerable Master") and changed the title of his then-small group from Aum shinsen-no-kai ("group of mountain ascetics") to Aum Shinrikyo ("AUM Supreme Truth"). A form of Tantric Buddhism, Aum Shinrikyo's teachings emphasized yoga practices and spiritual experiences. By the time of the subway incident, Asahara had acquired a large communal facility near Mount Fuji and a following of approximately 10,000 members in Japan, with an estimated 30,000 followers in Russia.

Shoko Asahara, founder and leader of the Japanese cult Aum Shinrikyo, was accused of masterminding the 1995 sarin gas attack on Tokyo's subway in which 12 people died and 5,000 were poisoned. (Getty Images)

In addition to the usual teachings that go hand in hand with mainline Buddhism, Asahara was also fascinated with forecasting the future. His preoccupation with divination may have grown out of the weakness of his physical senses. Before undertaking yoga and meditation practices, he pursued the study of such divinatory practices as astrology. Like many other Japanese spiritualists, he was fascinated by Western biblical prophecies as well as by the premonitions of Nostradamus. No doubt influenced by the apocalyptic flavor of these predictions, Asahara himself began preaching a doomsday message to his followers: An ultimate confrontation would take place between Japan and the United States before the end of the century that would in all likelihood decimate his home country.

Asahara was, in fact, so certain about his future vision that he actually began to prepare for war. Unable to match the conventional military might of the United States, Aum scientists investigated how to produce and disseminate a whole range of unconventional weapons, from biological agents to poison gas. Then on March 20, 1995, Asahara ordered the sarin attack on the Tokyo subway in an attempt to cripple the Japanese government. Twelve people died, and thousands were injured in the incident, the blame for which was quickly directed at Aum. Although Asahara managed to escape capture for nearly two months, he was eventually arrested on May 16, 1995. His group was subsequently disbanded (though it later reformed under the name Aleph), and Asahara himself convicted of murder and sentenced to death.

See also: Aum Shinrikyo; Tokyo Subway Sarin Attack

Further Reading

Kaplan, David, and Andrew Marshall. *The Cult at the End of the World: The Incredible Story of Aum.* London: Hutchinson, 1996.

Kisala, Robert J., and Mark R. Mullins, eds. *Religion and Social Crisis in Japan.* London: Palgrave MacMillan, 2001.

Lifton, Robert. *Destroying the World to Save It: Aum Shinrikyo, Apocalyptic Violence and the New Global Terrorism.* New York: Henry Holt, 1999.

Reader, Ian. *Religious Violence in Contemporary Japan: The Case of AUM Shinrikyo.* Honolulu: University of Hawaii Press, 2000.

James R. Lewis

ASBAT AL-ANSAR

Asbat al-Ansar ("the Partisan's League") is a Salafist Sunni extremist organization based in Lebanon. The group was established by Hisham al-Shuraydi with the ostensible goals of overthrowing the central government in Beirut and preventing the spread of anti-Islamic influences across the country. It is also bitterly opposed to any peace agreement with Israel.

The current leader of Asbat is Abd al-Karim al-Sa'di (aka Abu Mihjin), who took over command in 1991 after al-Shuraydi was assassinated. His present whereabouts are unknown, although most of the group's cadres are based in the Ayn al-Hilwah Palestinian refugee camp near Sidon.

Asbat al-Ansar has carried out numerous attacks in Lebanon, including assassinations of rival religious leaders and bombings of nightclubs, theaters, fast-food restaurants, and liquor stores. In 2000 the group fired a rocket-propelled grenade at the Russian embassy in protest of Moscow's military campaign in Chechnya, and it is also thought to have been responsible for the 2002 murder of U.S. missionary Bonnie Witherall in Sidon.

Asbat al-Ansar has publicly proclaimed its support for Al Qaeda in Iraq (AQI) and was thought to have sent at least some of its members to fight coalition forces when they were stationed in the country. Despite this, the group is not thought to have any formal ties with Al Qaeda or its various affiliates.

Asbat al-Ansar has been involved in fighting and clashes with other militant groups operating in Lebanon, including al-Fatah. The organization was also heavily criticized for its failure to back Fatah al-Islam during the latter's confrontation with the Lebanese Armed Forces in 2007.

Asbat al-Ansar is thought to have no more than 300 active members. However, it retains significant influence in Palestinian refugee camps inside and outside of Lebanon and can count on these radicalized disenfranchised elements for both logistical and operational support. This, combined with Beirut's general inability to project power across the country, will ensure its survival for the foreseeable future.

The United States, European Union, United Kingdom, and Canada have all designated Asbat al-Ansar as a proscribed terrorist organization. Lebanon outlawed the group in 2002, and the government has sentenced Mihjin to death in absentia for the murders of four judges as well as the former head of the Association of Islamic Charitable Projects.

See also: Tanzom Qa'idat al-Jihadi Bilad al-Rafidyan (QJBR)

Further Reading

Fisk, Robert. "Lebanon Moves to Enforce Its Will: A Standoff with a Palestinian Group's Leader Threatens War." *The Independent* (UK), January 12, 1996.
Gelfand, Robert. "Portaits of Groups U.S. Links to Terror." Agence Presse-France, September 25, 2001.
"In the Spotlight: Asbat al-Ansar (Band of Partisans)." CDI Terrorism Project, November 25, 2001. http://www.cdi.org/terrorism/asbat.cfm, accessed January 7, 2012.
National Counterterrorism Center. "Asbat al-Ansar—Terrorist Groups." http://www.nctc.gov/site/groups/asbat_al_ansar.html, accessed January 6, 2012.
"Palestinian Group Asbat al-Ansar Denies Links with Bin Laden." Deutsche Presse-Agentur, September 25, 2001.

Edward F. Mickolus

ASHDOD PORT ATTACK

On Sunday March 14, 2004, a double suicide attack by two 18-year-old terrorists, one each from Harakat al-Muqawama al-Islamiya (Hamas) and the al-Aqsa Martyrs' Brigades of al-Fatah, killed 10 people and wounded 16 at the Port of Ashdod. The terminal, around 40 kilometers (25 miles) south of Tel Aviv, is one of Israel's largest ports, along with Haifa and Eilat. The two bombers managed to circumvent vigorous security checks at the facility by hiding in an ocean shipping cargo container that had been trucked from Gaza; the crate held a secret compartment that was complete with food, water, sleeping accommodations, and weapons.

The attack is believed to have been financed and directed by Nizar Rayan, a senior leader in Hamas, who acted as a liaison between the political leadership of the organization and its armed wing, the Izzedine al-Qassam Brigade. As a doctor of Islamic law, he was considered a leading clerical authority within Hamas, particularly after an Israeli strike killed its leader, Sheikh Yassin, in 2004. Rayan strongly advocated and supported suicide attacks against Israel before he himself was killed when his home in Gaza was bombed during an Israeli air strike in January 2009.

The suicide bombers in the Ashdod Port attack were Nabil Massoud and Mahmoud Salem, both schoolboys from the Jabalya refugee camp in Gaza. The container they were hiding in had been trucked to the Karni checkpoint, a major crossing between Gaza and Israel. Despite detailed inspections, the false compartment was missed. A few hours later the "trojan horse" container was unloaded within the security perimeter of the port, and two men emerged.

The first terrorist managed to gain entry to an engineering machine workshop, where he detonated his bomb among workers, killing five. The second terrorist triggered his explosives in a nearby storage and refrigeration area adjacent to the port, killing five more people. In addition to the 10 fatalities, another 16 were injured, some seriously.

Despite the number of casualties, many believe that the suicide attack could have been far worse. The port complex contained large stores of fuel, bromine, ammonia, and other hazardous chemicals, which a Hamas communiqué later confirmed had been the ultimate target of the terrorists. For whatever reason neither bomber managed to reach the storage tanks, and both detonated their suicide explosive packs several feet away. That said, the operation generated considerable publicity, and even though it did not result in mass casualties, it still graphically highlighted Hamas's ability to breach tight security by employing new and sophisticated tactics.

See also: al-Aqsa Martyrs' Brigades; Hamas (Islamic Resistance Movement)

Further Reading

"Fatah: Ashdod Bombers Used Tunnels to Cross Gaza." UJA Federation, New York. http://www.jewishtoronto.com/page.aspx?id=59415.

Israeli Ministry of Foreign Affairs. *Suicide Bombing at Ashdod Port.* March 14, 2004. http://www.mfa.gov.il/MFA/MFAArchive/2000_2009/2004/3/suicide%20bombing%20at%20Ashdod%20Port%2014-Mar-2004.

"Port Blast." Maritime Union of Australia, Sydney, August 6, 2004. http://www.mua.org.au/news/port-blast/.

Richard Warnes

ATEF, MOHAMMED

Mohammed Atef was born in 1944 in Menoufya, Egypt, in the Nile Delta, about 35 miles north of Cairo. His birth name was named Sobhi Abu Sitta. After graduating from high school, he served his required two years of military service in the Egyptian Army. Reports that Atef was a policeman in Egypt have been denied by the Egyptian government, but nearly all sources assert that he was.

Atef became an Islamist extremist early in his career, and in the late 1970s, he joined an Egyptian terrorist organization, the Egyptian Islamic Jihad (EIJ). Evidently a low-ranking member, he did not meet with its leader, Ayman al-Zawahiri, while both were in Egypt. Despite his involvement in this group, he escaped arrest after the crackdown on extremists that followed the assassination of Egyptian president Anwar Sadat in 1981.

In 1983 Atef left Egypt for Afghanistan to fight with the mujahideen ("holy warriors" or freedom fighters) against the Soviet forces. There he first met al-Zawahiri, who then introduced him to Osama bin Laden. Atef and bin Laden became close friends. Atef also became acquainted with Abdullah Azzam and admired him greatly, but in the subsequent battle between Azzam and al-Zawahiri for bin Laden's support, Atef supported al-Zawahiri. In 1999 Egyptian authorities sentenced Atef to a seven-year prison term in absentia for his membership in the EIJ, but he never returned to Egypt.

Atef's close personal relationship with bin Laden made him an important member of Al Qaeda; indeed, when the movement was founded, he was a charter member. Ubaidah al-Banshiri was Al Qaeda's head of military operations, and Atef assisted him. He was active in organizing Somali resistance to the American military presence in 1992, but some evidence suggests that his stay there was not entirely successful. Atef also served as bin Laden's chief of personal security. Al-Banshiri's death in a boating accident in Africa allowed Atef to replace him in 1996. From then until his death in 2001, Atef was in charge of all military operations for Al Qaeda, although he always remained subordinate to bin Laden, even after bin Laden's eldest son married one of Atef's daughters in January 2001.

Atef was aware of the September 11 plot from its beginning. Khalid Sheikh Mohammed had apparently outlined the plan to bin Laden and Atef as early as 1996. Bin Laden finally agreed on the basics of the plot in 1998, and it was Atef's job to search Al Qaeda's training camps for suitable candidates for a martyrdom mission that required operatives to live unnoticed in America. Once the members of the Hamburg Cell were picked and recruited by bin Laden, Atef explained the outlines of the plot to Mohamed Atta, Ramzi bin al-Shibh, Ziad Jarrah, and Marwan al-Shehhi.

Atef was killed on November 18, 2001, during the early stages of the U.S.-led military campaign to oust the Taliban in Afghanistan. While his death was a major blow to Al Qaeda (bin Laden had announced that in the case of his death Atef would assume the mantle of leadership), he was quickly replaced as military commander by Abu Zubaydah.

See also: Al Qaeda; Atta, Mohamed; bin Laden, Osama; September 11 (2001)

Further Reading

Bergen, Peter L. *The Osama bin Laden I Know: An Oral History of al-Qaeda's Leader.* New York: Free Press, 2006.
Dawoud, Khaled. "Mohammed Atef: Egyptian Militant Who Rose to the Top of the al-Qaida Hierarchy." *The Guardian* (London), November 19, 2001.
Scheuer, Michael. *Through Our Enemies' Eyes: Osama bin Laden, Radical Islam and the Future of America.* Rev. ed. Washington, DC: Potomac Books, 2006.

Stephen E. Atkins

ATLANTA ABORTION CLINIC BOMBINGS

On January 16, 1997, two bombs detonated 45 minutes apart at an abortion clinic in Atlanta, Georgia. The attack injured six people. The first explosion occurred around 9:30 A.M. and shattered the southwestern corner of the building. Four people were inside at the time, but nobody was injured. The second bomb, which caused all of the injuries and targeted authorities and rescue workers who had rushed to the scene, blew up in a trash container outside the northwestern corner of the building.

A bystander saw a man near the clinic take off a blond wig and then hurriedly drive away in a 1989 Nissan pickup. The witness wrote down the license plate of the fleeing truck and gave it to the authorities, who then traced the vehicle to a man named Eric Robert Rudolph. The clinic explosions bore similarities to the July 27, 1996, Centennial Olympic Park series of bombs that killed 1 person and injured more than 100 others. That event, like the one at the Atlanta clinic, also targeted the crowd that gathered after the first device exploded.

On January 29, 1998, another abortion clinic was targeted, this time in Birmingham, Alabama. The attack killed an off-duty police officer who was moonlighting at the building as a private security guard and badly injured a counselor and nurse. The second incident was also tied to Rudolph. The day after the Birmingham bombing, Rudolph returned to his rural home near Murphy, North Carolina, and with the alleged assistance of sympathizers ventured into the nearby hills, where he hid in a makeshift camp.

On November 15, 2000, federal grand juries in Atlanta and Birmingham indicted Rudolph on 23 counts for the Centennial Olympic, Atlanta clinic, and Birmingham bombings, as well as a February 1997 attack on the Otherside Lounge—a gay bar in Atlanta—that injured five people. The Federal Bureau of Investigation (FBI) offered a $1 million reward for information leading to Rudolph's arrest.

On May 31, 2003, the authorities captured Rudolph. As part of a plea bargain to avoid the death penalty, Rudolph provided the location of more than 250 pounds of dynamite buried in the mountains of North Carolina. FBI agents and members of the Alcohol, Tobacco, and Firearms Bureau subsequently found the massive stash in three different locations. On August 21, 2005, after years on the run, a federal judge sentenced Rudolph, then 39, to life in prison without parole plus $2.3 million in damages. Before he was convicted, Rudolph apologized to his victims in the Olympics bombing.

The Atlanta and Birmingham bombings were part of a general trend of attacks against American abortion clinics. In 1996 the federal government said that violence aimed at these facilities and people who work in them—including shootings, bombings, arson, death threats, chemical attacks, and clinic blockades—had occurred in at least 28 states as well as the District of Columbia. Statistics from the Justice Department show that there were at least 15 bombings or arsons at abortion clinics every year from 1993 to 1995.

See also: Centennial Olympic Park Bombing; Rudolph, Eric

Further Reading

Baird-Windle, Patricia, and Eleanor J. Bader. *Targets of Hatred: Anti-Abortion Terrorism.* New York: Palgrave, St. Martin's, 2001.

"Blast Probed at Atlanta Family Planning Clinic." *CNN,* January 16, 1997. http://cgi.cnn.com/US/9701/16/atlanta.blast.update/, accessed May 2, 2011.

Hillard, Robert L., and Michael C. Keith. *Waves of Rancor: Tuning In the Radical Right.* New York: M. E. Sharpe, 1999.

Schuster, Henry (with Charles Stone). *Hunting Eric Rudolph.* New York: Penguin, 2005.

Donna Bassett

ATTA, MOHAMED

Mohamed al-Amir Awad al-Sayyid Atta was born on September 1, 1968, in the village of Kafr el-Shaykh in the Egyptian delta and had a strict family upbringing. His father was a middle-class lawyer with ties to the fundamentalist Muslim Brotherhood. Atta's family moved to the Abdin District of Cairo in 1978, when he was 10. His father, who had a dominating personality, insisted that his children study, not play; thus Atta's early family life allowed him few friends.

After attending high school, Atta enrolled at Cairo University in 1986. He successfully graduated in 1990 but failed to earn the grades necessary to embark on a master's course. On the recommendation of his father, he subsequently applied to study urban planning in Germany, commencing his coursework in Hamburg in July 1992. Up to this point in his life, Atta appeared to be an academic preparing for a career as a teacher at a university.

In 1995, however, Atta became active in Muslim extremist politics. After a pilgrimage to Mecca, he initiated

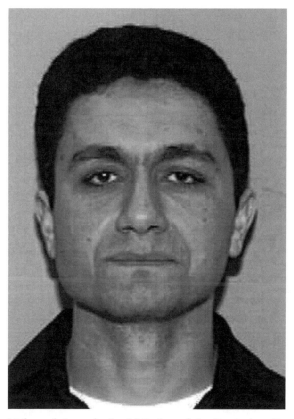

Mohamed Atta, the lead hijacker of the September 11, 2001, American Airlines flight 11 that crashed into the North Tower of the World Trade Center. (AP/Wide World Photos)

contact with Al Qaeda recruiters, who viewed him as an ideal candidate for the movement: intelligent, patient, dedicated, and disturbed by the "Americanization" of Egyptian society.

After returning to Hamburg to continue his studies, Atta attended the al-Quds Mosque, where his final conversion to militant extremism took place. There, Atta met an Islamist recruiter, Muhammad Heydar Zammar, who steered him into the Al Qaeda organization. Several of his friends, Ramzi bin al-Shibh, Marwan al-Shehhi, and Ziad Jarrah, also joined the movement at this time, and Atta subsequently became the leader of the so-called Hamburg Cell.

In 1998 Atta left for Kandahar, Afghanistan, to receive military and terrorist training at the Al Qaeda camp at Khaldan. He so distinguished himself there that Al Qaeda leaders decided to recruit him for a future suicide attack. Atta, Jarrah, and al-Shehhi subsequently met and talked with Osama bin Laden, who asked them to pledge loyalty to him and accept a martyrdom mission. They all agreed, and Mohammed Atef, Al Qaeda's military chief at the time, briefed them on the general outlines of the September 11 (9/11) operation. Atta and the others then returned to Germany to finish their academic training.

After Atta completed his degree in 1999, Al Qaeda's leaders assigned him responsibility for 9/11, a plan originally hatched by Khalid Sheikh Mohammed. Atta arrived in the United States on June 2, 2000, and although his orders placed him in charge of a large cell, only he, Jarrah, and al-Shehhi knew the full details of his mission. Several times Atta flew back to Germany and Spain to coordinate with Al Qaeda planners and facilitate the entry of additional cell members into the United States. Most of Atta's time in the United States was spent in pilot lessons in Florida, the bulk of which took place at Huffman Aviation in Sarasota, Florida. He also used simulators and manuals to train himself on how to fly large commercial aircraft in preparation for the September 11 mission.

Atta commanded the first team of hijackers that were used in the 9/11 attacks. Approximately 15 minutes after American Airlines Flight 11 took off from Boston's Logan International Airport, his team seized control of the aircraft using box cutters as weapons. Atta then redirected the aircraft toward New York City and the World Trade Center complex, where it crashed into the north tower of the World Trade Center at about 8:45 A.M.

See also: Al Qaeda; bin al-Shibh, Ramzi; bin Laden, Osama; Hamburg Cell; Mohammed, Khalid Sheikh; September 11 (2001)

Further Reading

Fouda, Yosri, and Nick Fielding. *Masterminds of Terror: The Truth behind the Most Devastating Terrorist Attack the World Has Ever Seen.* New York: Arcade, 2003.
McDermott, Terry. *Perfect Soldiers: The Hijackers: Who They Were, Why They Did It.* New York: HarperCollins, 2005.
Miller, John, Michael Stone, and Chris Mitchell. *The Cell: Inside the 9/11 Plot, and Why the FBI and CIA Failed to Stop It.* New York: Hyperion, 2002.

Stephen A. Atkins

AUM SHINRIKYO

Aum Shinrikyo, known in the West as Aum Supreme Truth, is a Japanese religious group that mixed Buddhist and Hindu beliefs. The group made headlines around the world in 1995 when several of its followers carried out a deadly sarin nerve gas attack on the Tokyo subway. The group's name is made up of the Hindu syllable "Omm," representing the creative and destructive forces of the universe, and three kanji characters: "shin" (truth, reality, Buddhist sect), "ri" (reason, truth), and "kyo" (teaching faith, doctrine). The name translates loosely as the "Teaching of Supreme Truth."

The group was founded by Chizuo Matsumoto, a half-blind yoga instructor who began to gather followers through his yoga classes in Tokyo in 1984. During a trip to India in 1986, Matsumoto claimed to have received enlightenment while on a hike in the Himalayas. Upon his return to Japan the following year, Matsumoto changed his name to the "holy" Shoko Asahara. He altered the title of his group to Aum Shinrikyo, and it started to take on an explicit apocalyptic character based on predictions concerning the impending destruction of the universe.

Aum's application for religious tax exempt status under Japanese law—was denied in 1989 but granted several months later after the group mounted a legal campaign against the government. In fact, the group would use legal recourse on several occasions, both to defend its views and rights and to gather public attention.

In the same year, the group came under fire through a growing public outcry against brainwashing carried out on young people who joined the group. A group of families hired Sakamoto Tsutsumi, a lawyer from Yokohama with experience in cult brainwashing. At the same time the *Sunday Mainichi*, a prominent Japanese newspaper, began to run an expose of the group's activities based on reports from former members and families of members. Already under attack from the press, the group could hardly accept Sakamoto's discovery of a series of fake tests concerning Asahara (the group's founder had claimed to have a unique type of blood that made him different from all other people; Sakamoto's investigation found out that the alleged tests done at Kyoto University never took place). Soon after, Sakamoto and his wife and infant son disappeared. The bodies were found six years later in remote mountain locations, but despite suspicions that the group had been responsible, no direct evidence implicating Aum Shinrikyo was ever found.

In 1989 the group established a political party with the hopes of broadcasting their views within the Japanese society at large, but all 25 candidates failed to gain enough votes to be elected. Their complete defeat made the group the subject of numerous jokes, further distancing them from mainstream public opinion. This also enhanced the feeling of persecution among the group's followers and their sense that they needed to prepare for the coming Armageddon.

In 1995, following the Tokyo subway sarin gas attack that left 12 commuters dead and thousands injured, Asahara and several other senior members of the group were arrested and accused of masterminding the attack. Asahara himself was found guilty and sentenced to death. While it is unclear why Aum committed these atrocities, some believe it was an effort to divert police attention away from the group, which was coming under increased scrutiny from the authorities.

Despite the trials of Asahara and other top members, the group continues to operate and is currently led by Fumihiro Joyo, a charismatic leader and one of Asahara's main executives. The group is now called Aleph, the first of the Hebrew letters, a name that stands for a new beginning. As of January 2010, the group is still under police surveillance. Small branches of the group exist in New York, Sri Lanka, and Russia.

See also: Asahara, Shoko; Tokyo Subway Sarin Attack

Further Reading

Hall, John R., Philip D. Schuyler, and Sylvaine Trinh. *Apocalypse Observed: Religious Movements and Violence in North America, Europe, and Japan.* London: Routledge, 2000.

Stalker, Nancy. "Religious Violence in Contemporary Japan: The Case of Aum Shinrikyo." *Pacific Affairs* 75 (2002).

Wessinger, Catherine. *How the Millennium Comes Violently: From Jonestown to Heaven's Gate.* New York: Seven Bridges, 2000.

Jose M. Valente

AUSTRALIAN EMBASSY (JAKARTA) BOMBING

On September 9, 2004, a bomb hidden in a white Daihatsu minivan detonated in front of the Australian embassy in Jakarta, Indonesia. The attack took place at approximately 10:30 A.M. and killed 9, wounding another 161. The diplomatic mission was badly damaged, as were surrounding buildings in the Kunigan business district. Although serious, the incident could have been far worse had the vehicle transporting the explosives exploded inside the embassy's perimeter walls; as it was, no one inside the building was killed, and the majority of those wounded sustained only minor injuries. Virtually all of the casualties were Indonesian nationals, many of them Muslim.

Jemaah Islamiyah (JI), an Islamic militant organization with alleged ties to Al Qaeda, claimed responsibility for the bombing. The group had carried out several previous attacks in Indonesia, including strikes against tourist venues in Bali in 2002 (which left 191 people dead) and the J.W. Marriott in Jakarta the following year. Authorities believed the 2004 incident was the work of a highly militant JI faction that apparently believed the group's goal of a Southeast Asian caliphate could be "fast-tracked" through an indiscriminate campaign of mass-casualty terrorism.

The device used in the attack was based on potassium chlorate and contained between 200 kilograms (400 pounds) and one ton (2,204 pounds) of explosives. Its composition suggested that the bomb-manufacturing techniques of JI had evolved only marginally since the 2002 Bali atrocity. Experts believed this was partly due to more effective counterterrorism strategies in Indonesia, which had denied the group a secure safe haven in which to test, refine, and improve explosives and their delivery systems.

In line with many of JI's attacks, the bombing took the form of a suicide operation. Subsequent investigations identified two people as the chief bomb makers: a former university lecturer, Dr. Azahari bin Husin (Azhari Husin); and an electronics expert, Dulmatin (also known as Joko Pitono and Genius). Both were also believed to have been involved in the manufacture of the explosives used in the 2002 Bali attack and to be key players in JI's militant faction. Husin, who had earned a doctorate from the University of Reading in Great Britain, was later killed in a police raid in November 2005; five years later authorities also fatally shot Dulmatin after tracing him to a hideout in Jakarta.

The actual perpetrator was an Islamist militant by the name of Heri Golun. Oddly enough, even though the weapon of choice was a truck bomb, he did not know how to drive. It has since been alleged that the inexperienced Golun was given some basic training on how to operate a van and was assisted in guiding the attack vehicle through the midmorning rush hour by an accomplice before he was allowed to take over. If true, this could explain why the van did not crash through the gates of the embassy in the more dramatic fashion of previous suicide vehicle bombers but detonated in the street in front of the embassy after having emerged from a side street.

Following the bombing, Indonesian police arrested six suspected JI members. Among them was Iwan Darmawan (also known as Rios), who was alleged to have been the chief planner for the attack. He was detained with two other militants on the main island of Java. According to authorities the trio were all wearing explosive belts but did not have time to detonate them before they were seized.

Rios later confessed his involvement in the bombing. He claimed that Al Qaeda had financed the operation through an intermediary based in Malaysia. There is also evidence to suggest that additional monies were needed to cover the cost of the attack and that these were raised through donations, illegal gold trafficking, and criminal activities that targeted non-Muslims.

On September 13, 2005, Rios was sentenced to death for his participation in the event, after which he recanted his previous confession, saying, "I'm innocent and I wasn't involved in this." Although the sentence was appealed, it was upheld by the Indonesian High Court the following December. At the time of writing, Rios had still to be executed and remained in prison. Another accomplice, Irun Hidayat, was charged with providing housing and money to the perpetrators. He was convicted on July 21, 2005, and sentenced to three years for his role in the attack. Hidayat had been inducted into Darul Islam by Kang Jaja in 1987 at age 15. He was a close friend of Rois and was the local head of the religious council of the Indonesian Muslim Workers Union (Perserikatan Pekerja Muslim Indonesia [PPIM]).

There was some speculation that the attack was designed to influence the upcoming September 20 elections in Indonesia. Others believed it was in commemoration for 9/11 given that it occurred just two days before the bombings in New York and Washington. It was also suggested that the attack could have been prompted by Canberra's support for the U.S.-led global war on terror and participation in the invasion of Iraq.

Following the bombing, Australian prime minister John Howard announced that he would be setting up a fund to assist the victims of the attack and that his government would make an initial kick-off contribution. He also encouraged the public to donate, saying that "it is the least that this country can do as a measure, not only of our respect for them, our compassion for their families, but also as a practical help to people who will need help in this very tragic situation."

See also: Al Qaeda; Bali Bombings (2002); bin Husin, Azahari; Jemaah Islamiyah (JI); Marriott Hotel (Jakarta) Bombing (2003 and 2009)

Further Reading

Chalk, Peter, Angel Rabasa, William Rosenau, and Leanne Piggott. *The Evolving Terrorist Threat to Southeast Asia: A Net Assessment.* Santa Monica, CA: RAND, 2009.

International Crisis Group. *Terrorism in Indonesia: Noordin's Networks.* Asia Report no. 114, May 5, 2006.

Jackson, Brian, John Baker, Kim Cragin, John Parachini, Horacio Trujillo, and Peter Chalk. *Aptitude for Destruction.* Vol. 2, *Case Studies of Organizational Learning in Five Terrorist Groups.* Santa Monica, CA: RAND, 2005.

Sidel, John. *Riots, Pogroms, Jihad: Religious Violence in Indonesia.* Ithaca, NY: Cornell University Press, 2006.

Donna Bassett

AUTODEFENSAS UNIDAS DE COLOMBIA (AUC)

The Autodefensas Unidas de Colombia (AUC, or United Self-Defense Forces of Colombia) was a loose umbrella movement of self-defense militias and paramilitary groups that battled left-wing guerrillas in Colombia for over a decade. The organization was formed in April 1997 as a successor to the Autodefensas Campesinas de Córdoba y Urabá under the leadership of Carlos Castaño. Although many Colombians initially considered the AUC as a necessary evil to contain the violence and insurgency of the Fuerzas Armadas Revolucionárias de Colombia (FARC, or Revolutionary Armed Forces of Colombia) and Ejército de Liberación Nacional (ELN, or National Liberation Army), they increasingly came to be viewed as a significant threat in their own right. The United States, European Union, and several other countries all shared this view and proscribed the AUC as a terrorist organization.

At its height the AUC could count on a membership of around 31,000 cadres that effectively controlled large tracts of territory in Colombia's northern Antioquia province and eastern plains. The movement's strategy and tactics closely mirrored those of FARC and the ELN, with the basic aim to extend control at the local level through intimidation and bribery. The movement was responsible for most of the mass killings attributed to organized armed groups in Colombia during the late 1990s and 2000s. It is estimated that in its first two years alone, the AUC (and related paramilitary affiliates) killed over 19,000 people. According to the Colombia National Police, during the first 10 months of 2000, the AUC carried out 804 assassinations, 203 kidnappings, and 507 murders. Most violence was directed against FARC and the ELN, their sympathizers, and villages suspected of providing the two guerrilla groups with sanctuary. The movement also routinely terrorized local populations to instill fear and compel support.

The AUC funded itself almost exclusively on the drug trade, working in collaboration with Mexican cartels to ship cocaine to the United States. In a televised interview in March 2000, Castaño himself admitted that narcotics trafficking and taxation of coca production in Antioquia and Córdoba provided up to 70 percent of the financing for his forces (with rest largely coming from extortion). A 2003 Colombian peace commission report claimed that the AUC derived possibly as much as 80 percent of its revenue from drugs and that self-defense militias in general monopolized up to 40 percent of the country's entire narcotics industry.

There have been repeated allegations that the AUC cooperated both tacitly and openly with the Colombian military. In one paramilitary massacre at the town of El Tigre in January 1999, eyewitnesses said the gunmen arrived in trucks belonging to the army's 24th Brigade. Left-wing guerrillas and human rights activists both claimed this incident was consistent with an established relationship aimed at eliminating the civilian supporters of FARC and the ELN. Press reports have also alleged that a number of senior militia leaders in the province of Putumayo previously served as noncommissioned officers in the army.

On April 16, 2004, there was an attack on AUC supreme leader and cofounder Carlos Castaño. He was never seen again. Press reports speculated that his disappearance could hurt the peace process with the Uribe government. In 2006 a Venezuelan newspaper, *Nuevo Diario Occidente,* reported that Vincent Castaño had hired an assassin, who had confessed to police that he killed Carlos Castaño in 2004. The confession led police to a body in August 2006. DNA tests a month later confirmed it was Carlos.

In 2003 Carlos Castaño had affirmed that he was ready to discuss a possible cease-fire with the Colombian government. His announcement generated widespread opposition among certain elements of the AUC that rejected any notion of laying down arms. As noted, Castaño later disappeared following an attack on his headquarters in April 2004.

Although there was speculation that Castaño's murder could hurt the slowly unfolding peace process, talks proceeded and culminated in 2005 when the AUC declared a cease-fire and agreed to disarm in accordance with a so-called Justice and Peace Law (Law 975) passed that same year. The legislation, which originated from the 2003 Santa Fé de Ralito Accord, limited jail terms for the highest-ranking members of the AUC to eight years if they confessed the entirety of their crimes and returned all stolen property. More junior paramilitaries who demobilized were enrolled in a 18-month program that provided them with a stipend, living accommodations, counseling, and help with reincorporating into mainstream society.

Not surprisngly, the law was the subject of considerable controvery, with critics in both Colombia and the United States charging it effectively shielded paramilitary leaders from prosecution or extradition for serious crimes. Despite these objections, the demobilization, disarmament, and reintegration (DDR) process continued and had largely been completed by 2006, by which time up to 30,000 paramilitaries had surrendered and laid down their arms.

Problematically the DDR program was quickly overwhelmed (the government estimated that there were no more than 20,000 paramilitaries who needed to be processed), and many of those who entered it never received a job and complained that Bogotá had not lived up to its side of the bargain. Initial dissatisfaction with the peace dividend translated into widespread disillusionment, driving many to join preexisting criminal gangs. These reconfigured entities, euphemstically referred to as *bandas criminales* (criminal groups), are thought to number around 5,000 members, organized into 11 main syndicates. Four of these have since become central players in the Colombian cocaine trade and make no pretence of seeking political or ideological objectives: the Don Mario Gang, the Ejército Revolucionario Popular Anticomunista (Erpac), the Rastrojos, and Los Paisas.

See also: Ejército de Liberación Nacional (ELN); Fuerzas Armadas Revolucionarias de Colombia (FARC)

Further Reading

Bergquist, Charles, Ricardo Peñaranda, and Gonzalo Sánchez, eds. *Violence in Colombia 1990–2000: Waging War and Negotiating Peace.* Wilmington, DE: SR Books, 2001.

Chalk, Peter. *The Latin American Drug Trade: Scope, Dimensions, Impact and Response.* Santa Monica, CA: RAND, 2011.

Cragin, Kim, and Bruce Hoffman. *Arms Trafficking and Colombia.* Santa Monica, CA: RAND, 2003.

Kirk, Robin. *More Terrible than Death: Violence, Drugs, and America's War in Colombia.* New York: Public Affairs, 2004.

Porch, Douglas, and María Rasmussen. "Demobilization of Paramilitaries in Colombia: Transformation or Transition?" *Studies in Conflict and Terrorism* 31, no. 6 (2008).

Romero, Mauricio. "Changing Identities and Contested Settings: Regional Elites and the Paramilitaries in Colombia." *International Journal of Politics, Culture and Society* 14, no. 1 (2000).

Saab, Bilal, and Alexandra Taylor. "Criminality and Armed Groups: A Comparative Study of FARC and Paramilitary Groups in Colombia." *Studies in Conflict and Terrorism* 32, no. 6 (2009).

Peter Chalk

AYYASH, YAHYA

Yahya Ayyash, known as "the Engineer," was the chief bomb maker for Hamas. On April 6, 1994, he began a 24-month terror campaign that for a while made him the most wanted man in Israel. He also trained other militants—teaching them how to manufacture Qassam rockets developed by Nidal Fat'hi Rabah Farahat and Adnan al-Ghoul—and introduced the whole concept of martyrdom to the Palestinian conflict. Ayyash was assassinated on January 5, 1996, when Shin Bet, the Israeli domestic intelligence service, detonated a booby-trapped cell phone while he was taking a call. He was revered by Palestinians and would later have buildings and streets named after him.

Born in Rafat near Nablus in the Gaza Strip in March 1966, Ayyash obtained good grades at secondary school and in 1991 earned a bachelor's degree in electrical engineering from Beir Zeit University in the West Bank. He was reportedly a devout scholar of the Koran and intended to go to Jordan to study for his master's degree but was prevented from doing so by Israeli authorities. Instead, he joined the Ezzul Deen Al Qassam Brigade, the military wing of Hamas in early 1992, the same year he got married.

Because TNT and other high explosives were not available in the Palestinian Occupied Territories, Ayyash specialized in making bombs out of raw materials that were locally available. Most of his devices were therefore primitive in both design and construction. Even so, during his career, Ayyash was held personally responsible for the deaths of 130 Israelis and the injury of another 500.

The principal trigger for Ayyash's string of bombings appears to have been the Hebron massacre of February 25, 1994, when an American Zionist extremist, Baruch Goldstein, indiscriminately killed 29 Muslims and wounded more than 125. The attack, carried out with an assault rifle and hand grenades, caused outrage among Palestinians and Muslims—not least because the victims were all praying at the Al-Ibrahimi mosque when they were executed.

Although popular with Hamas, Ayyash's terrorist activities caused some concern within the Palestinian Authority (PA), which at the time was entertaining negotiations with Israel. Following the assassination of Prime Minister Yitzhak Rabin on

November 4, 1995, the PA's security division began to cooperate with Shin Bet in the hunt for Ayyash. During subsequent surveillance it was discovered that Ayyash sometimes spent the night at the Gaza City home of Osama Hamad—an old friend whose uncle, Kamil, had worked with Shin Bet in the past. The PA urged him to cooperate again, which after sustained prodding he eventually agreed to do. The Israeli agents supplied Kamil with a phone, which they said was bugged so they could listen to Ayyash's conversations; what they did not tell him was that it was also loaded with 15 grams (0.5 ounces) of RDX high explosive.

Kamil gave the cell to Osama, knowing that Ayyash frequently used his nephew's devices. At 8 A.M. on January 5, 1996, the Engineer received a call from his father. An Israeli plane picked up the conversation and relayed it to a Shin Bet command post. The intelligence service then detonated the explosive remotely.

Roughly 100,000 mourners attended Ayyash's funeral. After 40 days of mourning, the military wing of Hamas launched four revenge suicide bombings that killed 60 Israelis and wounded many others. Ali Hassan Salameh, a professionally trained terrorist, orchestrated the campaign. He was captured by pure luck in Hebron, and at the time it was thought that apart from avenging Ayyash's death, he was also trying to affect the May 29, 1996, elections that ended up replacing incumbent Israeli prime minister Shimon Peres with Benjamin Netanyahu. Salameh flatly denied this and declared that he simply wanted to kill Israelis.

See also: Dizengoff Shopping Center Bombing; Goldstein, Baruch; Hamas (Islamic Resistance Movement); Hebron Mosque Massacre; Jerusalem Bus Attacks (1996)

Further Reading

Forest, James J. F., ed. *Teaching Terror: Strategic and Tactical Learning in the Terrorist World.* Lanham, MD: Rowman & Littlefield, 2006.

Katz, Samuel M. *The Hunt for the Engineer: The Inside Story of How Israel's Counterterrorist Forces Tracked and Killed the Hamas Master Bomber.* Guilford, CT: Lyons Press, 1999.

Levitt, Matthew. *Hamas: Politics, Charity, and Terrorism in the Service of Jihad.* New Haven, CT: Yale University Press, 2006.

Milton-Edwards, Beverley, and Stephen Farrell. *Hamas: The Islamic Resistance Movement.* Malden, MA: Polity, 2010.

Pedahzur, Ami. *Suicide Terrorism.* Cambridge, UK: Polity, 2005.

Donna Bassett

AZHAR, MASOOD

Maulana Masood Azhar is the current emir of the Pakistani terrorist group Jaish-e-Mohammed (JeM). Born in Bahawalpur on August 7, 1968, to a retired school-teacher, Azhar has a younger brother named Mufti Abdul Rauf and another named Ibrahim Akhtar Alvi—both of whom are also active JeM members. Azhar was educated at Jamia Uloom-e-Islami in Binori Town and after graduating in 1989 reportedly attempted a 40-day militant training course in Afghanistan but failed to complete it. That same year he met Fazlur-Rahman Khalil, the leader of

Harakat-ul-Mujahideen (HuM), who urged him to start an Urdu magazine called *Sada-i-Mujahid* and an Arabic periodical named *Sawt ul-Kashmir*. According to Indian interrogators, Azhar admitted to meeting with members of the Somali Islamist group al-Ittihad al-Islami (AIAI) in Nairobi, Kenya, and may have acted as a link between Somali militants and Al Qaeda. In the early 1990s Azhar was appointed the general secretary of HuM and as part of this role traveled abroad, particularly to the United Kingdom, to raise funds and conduct *dawa* (outreach). When HuM merged with the militant group Harakat ul-Jihad al-Islami (HuJI) to form Harakat-ul-Ansar (HuA) in 1993, Azhar was reportedly put in charge of dawa for the new organization.

In February 1994 Azhar was arrested in India while assisting with the HuM-HuJI merger. During his time in prison he welcomed Pervez Musharraf's rise to power in Pakistan and wrote several articles for publication in jihadi magazines run by the al-Rashid Trust. Following several failed attempts to secure his release from incarceration via kidnappings, Azhar was eventually freed in exchange for the safe return of hostages seized during the hijacking of Indian Airlines Flight 814 in 1999. Although HuM effected his release, Azhar did not return to the movement and, instead, formed JeM as a breakaway faction on his return to Pakistan in 2000; he was supported in this endeavor by Mufti Nizamuddin Shamzai and Maulana Yusuf Ludhianvi—both of whom were close to Fazlur Rehman, the fiery emir of the Deobandi Jamiat Ulema-e-Islam-Fazlur—in addition to fellow Punjabis. Azhar was also thought to have the backing of Pakistan's InterServices Intelligence (ISI) Directorate, the Sipah-e-Sahaba, and its militant arm, Lashkar-e-Jhangvi (LeJ), which he greatly admired and was very close to. However, his group repeatedly clashed with HuM as a result of disputes related to property, and he had poor relations with Hafiz Saeed, the leader of Lashkar-e-Taiba (LeT), due to conflicting theological viewpoints.

In 2000 JeM founded the al-Akhtar Trust, which was involved in providing donations and medical treatment to Al Qaeda and providing financial and logistical aid to the Taliban. The ostensible charity provided an important link to Afghanistan and Osama bin Laden's transnational militant network, illustrating the extent and depth of Azhar's connections with both.

In 2003 Azhar expelled a dozen ranking members of JeM, including Maulana Abdul Jabbar, after revelations that they had organized attacks against Western and Christian targets in Pakistan without his authorization. In July of the same year, he informed the Punjab governor that he had removed these cadres, that he should not be held responsible for their actions, and that all should be arrested. The move caused a major schism within JeM, with hardline members deserting Azhar and joining the expelled members to form Jamaat ul-Furqaan. Jabbar further accused the JeM emir of personally profiting from jihad (pointing out that he lived in one of Bahawalpur's best neighborhoods and drove Land Cruisers), being a lackey of the Pakistani intelligence agencies, and appointing friends and family members to plum positions in seminaries and publications. Both JeM and Jamaat ul-Furqaan suffered from crackdowns following failed assassination attempts against Musharraf, and although Azhar was considered to be relatively close to (and obedient to) the ISI, this episode and his group's past ties to Al Qaeda served to significantly undercut his position in the eyes of the military.

There is some indication that Azhar has taken a harder rhetorical stance against the Pakistani state in recent years. In November 2007 he made statements supportive of Maulana Fazlullah, the leader of the highly extremist Tehrik-e-Nefaz-e-Shariat-e-Mohammadi, and referrred to the military as an infidel entity beholden to the United States. Such comments appear to have been designed to rehabilitate Azhar's image and standing among militants fiercely opposed to Islamabad and its actions against jihadists in the Federally Administered Tribal Areas (FATA). That said, JeM continues to operate openly in Pakistan, reportedly rents out gunmen to Punjabi politicians during elections, and receives assistance from the ISI—all of which would indicate that Azhar has not completely broken with the military. Azhar has also assisted the Pakistani government in negotiations with Deobandi clerics and militants who have rebelled against the state and in 2009 reportedly dispatched his brother Abdul Rauf to negotiate with members of the Amjad Farooqi Group during their assault on the army's general headquarters. These actions have ensured that Azhar remains a figure of scorn among members of the so-called Punjabi Taliban, who advocate a highly antiestablishment line and have emerged as arguably one of the main internal threats to the present Pakistani administration. This was graphically illustrated in April 2010 when Punjabi militants operating in FATA areas forced a known JeM cadre, Khalid Khwaja, to denounce Azhar as a proxy of the ISI prior to executing him.

Azhar currently resides in Model Town, Bahawalpur, where he was placed under temporary house arrest in December 2008 following LeT's Mumbai attacks; he had been previously arrested in December 2001 after a joint JeM-LeT attack on the Indian Parliament. Azhar remains a prolific writer and speaker and helps oversee JeM's training camp in Balakot in Pakistan's Khyber-Pakhtunkhwa province.

See also: Harakat-ul-Mujahideen (HuM); Harakat-ul-Ansar (HuA); Harakat-ul-Jihad-al-Islami (HuJI); Lashkar-e-Taiba (LeT); Highjacking of Air India 814; Jamaat-ul-Furqaan (JuF)

Further Reading

Mir, Amir. *The True Face of Jehadis.* Lahore, Pakistan: Mashal Books, 2004.

Raman, B. "Jaish-e-Mohammad Rebaptised?" South Asia Analysis Group, Paper 337, October 2001. http://www.southasiaanalysisgroup/papers4/paper337.html.

Rana, Muhammad Amir. *A to Z of Jehadi Organizations in Pakistan.* Lahore, Pakistan: Mashal Books, 2005

Swami, Praveen. "Masood Azhar: In His Own Words." *Frontline* 18, no. 21 (October 2001). http://www.thehindu.com/fdline/fl1821/1821/0190.htm.

Zahab, Mariam Abou, and Oliver Roy. *Islamist Networks: The Afghan-Pakistan Connection.* New York: Columbia University Press, 2004.

Ben Brandt

AZZAM, SHEIKH ABDULLAH YUSSUF

Sheikh Abdullah Yussuf Azzam was one of the spiritual leaders of the international radical Islamist movement. His ideas of jihad inspired the September 11, 2001, terrorists. Before his death, he traveled around Europe, the Middle East, and the United States advocating religious warfare against the West.

A Palestinian by birth, Azzam devoted his life to building the Islamist movement. He was born in 1941 in the small village of Selat al-Harithis, near Jenin, Palestine. Most of his early schooling took place in Jordanian religious schools. After graduating from Khadorri College, he taught in the village of Adder in South Jordan. In the early 1960s, he attended the Sharia College of Damascus. Azzam fought with the Palestinians in the Six-Day War in 1967 but left the Palestinian resistance movement because he considered it "a political cause insufficiently rooted in Islam." In 1967 he moved to Egypt, where he worked toward a master's degree in Islamic law at Cairo's famous al-Azhar University. Among his acquaintances was Omar Abdel Rahman, with whom he often talked about the creation of an Islamist state. After graduation, Azzam taught for a couple years before returning to al-Azhar University to study for a PhD in Islamic jurisprudence. Azzam received his doctorate in 1971, after which he took a teaching job at the University of Jordan. In 1980 he was dismissed from the university because of his activity with the Palestinian movement. He found a job leading prayers at the school mosque at King Abdul Aziz University in Jeddah, Saudi Arabia. Among his students there was Osama bin Laden. Azzam refused to return to Palestine because of his continued unhappiness with the secularism of the Palestine Liberation Organization (PLO). Later, when his views crystallized, he helped start Hamas in December 1987 to serve as a counterweight to the PLO.

Azzam was a proponent of the use of holy war, or jihad, to liberate the Muslim world from what he considered the tyranny of the secular West. He wanted to reestablish the caliphate by any means possible. J. Boyer Bell described Azzam's tactics as use of "jihad and the rifle alone; no negotiations, no conferences, no dialogues." Azzam taught this doctrine of jihad at every turn at King Abdul Aziz University. Although his teachings made the Saudi government nervous, authorities left him alone. After the invasion of Afghanistan by the Soviet Army in 1979, Azzam decided to place his Islamist doctrine and himself at the service of the Afghan fighters. At the same time, Saudi authorities expelled him from his teaching post. In November 1981 he found a position teaching Arabic and the Koran at the International Islamic University in Islamabad, Pakistan, but he soon found the war in Afghanistan more important than his teaching.

Azzam moved to Peshawar, Pakistan, to organize the mujahideen fighters in their operations against the Soviets. He traveled throughout the Arab world—and even Europe and the United States—recruiting fighters and raising money. His former student, bin Laden, who was also in Pakistan, began working with him. They founded the Mujahideen Services Bureau (MSB) in 1984, with Azzam providing the inspiration and theology and bin Laden the funding (from his personal fortune). It was also in 1984 that Azzam issued a fatwa making it obligatory for every able-bodied Muslim to fight against the Soviets in Afghanistan. Azzam made frequent trips into Afghanistan to preach global jihad, but he avoided the fighting. His sermons and other discourses reached most of the 16,000 to 20,000 Afghan War veterans. He also made several trips to the United State looking for money and recruits for the war. While in the United States, he established branches of the MSB. Both abroad and in Pakistan he constantly preached the necessity of jihad, expressing himself best in his own works explaining his doctrine of jihad.

Azzam's ideas became more radical as the war in Afghanistan progressed. He became convinced of a conspiracy on the part of Pakistan and the United States to weaken the Islamist cause. In 1987 he conceptualized an Islamist vanguard, or al-Qaeda al-Sulbah (the Solid Base), to carry the creation of a purified Islamist society. It was this concept of an Islamist base organization that bin Laden later developed into Al Qaeda.

Azzam and bin Laden's relationship deteriorated because they disagreed over the strategy of exporting terror. Azzam first wanted to concentrate on building an Islamist society in Afghanistan. He opposed launching a terrorist campaign against Arab regimes before consolidating affairs in Afghanistan and Pakistan. Azzam was not adverse to the idea of rolling back Christian encroachment on formerly Muslim lands, but he opposed internal Muslim infighting. In contrast, bin Laden aimed to liberate the Muslim community everywhere—including in Muslim countries. Ayman al-Zawahiri, who was even more radical in his views than bin Laden, used his close contacts with bin Laden to undermine Azzam. This open disagreement between Azzam and bin Laden led the latter to break with Azzam in 1987, something partly caused by Azzam's increasing closeness with Ahmad Shah Massoud. Azzam believed that Massoud was a possible future leader of an Islamic Afghanistan. Bin Laden and al-Zawahiri violently disagreed with Azzam over this. Azzam's career ended abruptly on November 24, 1989, when a bomb exploded under his car in Peshawar, killing him, two of his sons, and a companion. He was killed shortly after a meeting where he had been forced to justify his spending on Islamist operations. At first, suspicion centered on Pakistani security forces as the killers, but there is no satisfactory evidence of who planted the bomb—although the person who benefited most was al-Zawahiri. Regardless of the intent of the assassins, Azzam's stature in the Islamist movement remains strong because his backers have continued to advance his cause.

See also: Abdel-Rahman, Omar; Al Qaeda; bin Laden, Osama; Masri, Abu Hamza al- (Mustafa Kamel Mustafa); U.S. Embassy (East Africa) Bombings; Zawahiri, Ayman al-

Further Reading

Boyer Bell, J. *Murders on the Nile: The World Trade Center and Global Terror.* San Francisco: Encounter Books, 2003.

Gunaratna, Rohan. *Inside Al Qaeda.* New York: Columbia University Press, 2002.

Sageman, Marc. *Understanding Terror Networks.* Philadelphia: University of Pennsylvania Press, 2004.

Wright, Lawrence. *The Looming Tower: Al-Qaeda and the Road to 9/11.* New York: Knopf, 2006.

Stephen E. Atkins

B

BAADER, ANDREAS

Andreas Baader, a founder and leading member of the Baader-Meinhof Gang and Rote Armee Fraktion (RAF), or Red Army Faction, was born in Munich on May 6, 1943. His father, Dr. Berndt Phillipp Baader, was then serving in the German Army on the Eastern Front and in 1945 was reported missing, believed killed. Baader, nicknamed Andi, was thus raised by his mother, Anneliese, an aunt, and his grandmother—all of whom spoiled him. Though considered intelligent and strong-willed, he was lazy at school, rejecting any form of authority. This rebellion manifested itself at home, where he refused to conform to normal behavior, failing to wash and eat meals. He also rejected religion and tried to stop his mother from celebrating Christmas. As a teenager, he became obsessed with fast cars and was arrested on a number of occasions for driving without a license.

In 1963, at the age of 20, Baader went to West Berlin and became involved in the student subculture of the city, mixing in bars and cafés, where his dark features endeared him to many women. One of the females he met was Gudrun Ensslin, a teacher in training and the daughter of a Lutheran vicar; she was already actively involved in the left-wing student movement. Baader not only became her lover but also fully adopted her political activism.

Baader's meeting with Ensslin coincided with a wave of student demonstrations and the growth of left-wing extremism in Europe, fueled by protests against the Vietnam War and perceived U.S. imperialism. These factors were exacerbated in Germany by opposition to the older generation and their values, which were seen as tainted by the country's Nazi past. When the shah of Iran visited West Berlin in 1967, violent protests erupted, leading to clashes with the police. During one of these clashes, a student demonstrator, Benno Ohnesorg, was shot dead. This led to further violent protests across the country and an escalation of tensions between radical students and the German authorities. These were heightened at Easter 1968 with the attempted assassination of student leader Rudi Dutschke and the introduction of emergency legislation granting the security forces increased powers to quell unrest.

Collectively these events convinced a small number of radical activists, including Baader and Ensslin, that they needed to go beyond traditional street demonstrations and adopt a more direct campaign of violence. Consequently Baader, Ensslin, and two colleagues, Thorwald Proll and Horst Sohnlein, drove from Munich to Frankfurt armed with incendiary bombs. On the evening of April 2, 1968, these were used to start fires in the Kaufhaus and Kaufhof department stores, causing severe damage. That same evening, Baader and his colleagues were arrested; they were convicted in October and sentenced to three years imprisonment. One of those who covered the trial was a journalist from the left-wing paper *Konkret,* Ulrike Meinhof.

The quartet was later released on bail pending an appeal. However, when the Federal High Court rejected this, Baader, Ensslin, and Proll went underground, escaping to France and later Italy. Early in 1970, Baader and Ensslin returned to Germany under assumed names, but in April Baader was recaptured. While held in Tegel prison, Baader was visited by his lawyer friend Horst Mahler and journalist Ulrike Meinhof, and on May 14, while he was attending the Central Institute for Social Issues, under the excuse of working on a book with Meinhof, Baader was rescued from his guards by armed colleagues. In the course of the rescue Georg Linke, a member of the institute's staff, was shot and severely wounded. On June 5, 1970, Baader and the other key members of what was now being popularly called the Baader-Meinhof Gang, formally founded the RAF, officially appointing Ensslin as the group's leader. Later that month, Baader traveled with other members of the group via Damascus to a Palestinian al-Fatah camp outside of Amman in Jordan, where the group received training in basic firearms and explosives handling.

Returning to Germany in August 1970, Baader, Ensslin, Meinhof, and around 20 other members of the Baader-Meinhof Gang, or RAF, reestablished contacts across the country, recruited new members, and prepared for the first phase of terrorist violence. Initially the group organized a series of armed bank robberies to raise funds. Inevitably there were a number of shooting exchanges with the police, during which several officers and a couple of RAF members were killed. Despite being the subject of national police and security manhunts, Baader and his colleagues evaded arrest and in May 1972 launched a series of bomb attacks against "imperialist" German and U.S. military targets, killing 4 and injuring around 40.

At the end of that same month, the police, acting on a tip-off, started watching a garage in Frankfurt that was suspected of serving as an RAF bomb-making factory. A day later, a Porsche pulled up at the site. Baader and Holger Meins (a German cinematography student who also became a leading member in RAF) exited the car and entered the garage, leaving fellow colleague Jan-Caral Raspe outside to keep watch. The police immediately closed in and, after a foot chase, arrested the latter. Meanwhile, another squad surrounded the garage, and a siege developed. After a brief exchange of fire, a sniper shot Baader in the leg, and he and Meins surrendered. Within weeks an informer led the police to an RAF safe house, where Meinhof was apprehended; Ensslin was also identified and arrested while out shopping in Hamburg.

Baader and the others were held in Stammheim prison. However, their trial was delayed for several years while a secure courthouse and holding facilities were built. In protest at the delay and their solitary confinement, Baader and the group went on hunger strike for 140 days, during which time Meins died (in 1974). Various attempts were made by RAF extremists to force the German authorities to release the remaining leaders, but without success, and in May 1976, just prior to the trial, Meinhof hanged herself.

By July 1977 the trial of Baader, Ensslin, and Raspe was completed, and all three were sentenced to life imprisonment. In reaction, the RAF stepped up their campaign of violence in an attempt to coerce the West German authorities into acceding to their release. Events finally came to a head on September 5, 1977, when an RAF commando killed four bodyguards and kidnapped the president of the employer's association, Hanns-Martin Schleyer. Despite demands for the release of Baader and his colleagues, the German government refused to compromise.

To increase the pressure, four members of the Popular Front for the Liberation of Palestine (PFLP) working on behalf of the RAF seized Lufthansa Flight LH 181 on October 13. The terrorists immediately issued a communiqué threatening to kill the passengers if Baader and his colleagues were not set free. After five days of fruitless negotiation, members of the German elite antiterrorist Grenzschutzgruppe-9 (GSG-9) successfully stormed the plane, freeing all the passengers, killing three hijackers, and wounding a fourth.

Although no one knows the exact details of what then transpired in Stammheim prison, it is believed that in the early morning of October 18, Raspe heard of the rescue on a radio in his cell, communicating the news to Baader and the others. It appears that while Raspe shot himself with a concealed pistol and Ensslin hung herself with a loudspeaker cable, Baader removed a hidden pistol from his record player and fired a round through his neck and skull.

Despite the deaths of Baader and other RAF leaders under contentious circumstances, future generations of the group continued their terrorist campaign throughout the 1980s and into the 1990s. Suffering from a loss of ideological purpose following the collapse of the Soviet Union, the RAF eventually issued an eight-page letter in April 1998 that officially announced the group's disbanding and termination of all violent actions.

See also: Baader-Meinhof Gang; Lufthansa Hijacking (1977); Meinhof, Ulrike; Raspe, Jan-Carl; Rote Armee Fraktion (RAF)

Further Reading

Aust, Stefan. *The Baader-Meinhof Complex.* London: Bodley Head, 2008.

Kushner, Harvey. *Encyclopedia of Terrorism.* Thousand Oaks, CA: Sage, 2003.

Otte, Thomas. "Red Army Faction: The Baader-Meinhof Gang." In Martha Crenshaw and John Pimlott, ed., *International Encyclopedia of Terrorism.* Chicago: Fitzroy Dearborn, 1977.

Rojahn, Christoph. *Left-Wing Terrorism in Germany: The Aftermath of Ideological Violence.* Conflict Studies 313. Research Institute for the Study of Conflict and Terrorism, London, 1998.

Richard Warnes

BAADER-MEINHOF GANG

The Baader-Meinhof Gang, named after two of its key members and later to become known as the Rote Armee Fraktion (RAF, or Red Army Faction), had its roots in the radical student movement of the late 1960s and a resurgence of Marxist-Leninist theories in Europe. This coincided with protests against the Vietnam War and what was perceived as U.S. imperialism. Opposition to the political "Grand Coalition" between the Christian Democrats and Social Democrats heightened tensions, as did the younger generation's criticism of their parents for the Nazi period and the unwillingness of German society to confront its past.

In 1967 during a visit to West Berlin by the shah of Iran, protests erupted; during increasingly violent scenes with the police, a young student protester, Benno Ohnesorg, was shot dead on June 2. This in turn led to violent student protests across the country. The West German authorities responded by amending the Constitution with a "Basic Law" extending their ability to introduce emergency measures. A small core element of the extreme left took these events to signal that demonstrations and protests were ineffectual and that the only way forward was the use of terrorism.

Consequently, during March 1968, left-wing activist Andreas Baader, his partner Gudrun Ensslin, and their colleagues Horst Sohnlein and Thorwald Proll firebombed two Frankfurt department stores in emulation of a similar attack the

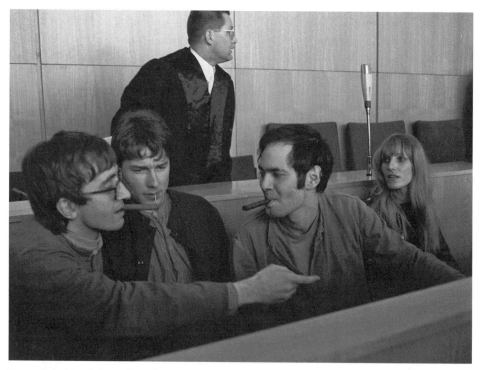

Horst Sohnlein, left, and Andreas Baader joke around with their extinguished cigars, which they lit earlier as Thorwald Proll and Gudrun Ensslin look on, during the opening of the department store arson trial in Frankfurt am Main, West Germany, October 14, 1968. (AP Photo/ Peter Hillebrecht)

previous year in Brussels. Although no one was actually injured, the group was quickly arrested and convicted in October 1968. However, they were granted bail pending an appeal, and when this was rejected in November, they fled abroad.

In early 1970 Baader and Ensslin returned to Germany under false identities, but in April Baader was recaptured and imprisoned. However, on May 15, with the assistance of left-wing *Konkret* journalist Ulrike Meinhof, other members of the group, including Horst Mahler, Ingrid Schubert, and Irene Goergens, freed Baader during an escorted visit to the German Central Institute for Social Issues. On June 5, 1970, the organization formally established itself as the RAF, appointing Ensslin as the group's leader; however, it was still popularly known as the Baader-Meinhof Gang.

That summer, in the first phase of Baader-Meinhof terrorism, a group of over 20 male and female members traveled to a Palestinian al-Fatah training camp near Amman in Jordan. There they practiced the use of firearms with Kalashnikov rifles, the use of grenades, and "urban guerrilla tactics." Although they met Ali Hassan Salameh, a leading figure in the Black September movement, their liberated attitude upset their Palestinian hosts, and they were asked to leave.

Upon returning to Germany, the Baader-Meinhof Gang launched a series of attacks on property and carried out a number of fund-raising bank robberies, becoming the focus of a massive manhunt by the authorities. Inevitably, confrontations with the police occurred, and during 1971, while the group shot and killed three officers, several of its members were arrested.

In May 1972 an expanded Baader-Meinhof Gang that by this time had established a number of regional cells commenced a systematic terrorist campaign against more high-profile "imperialist" German and U.S. targets. Prominent incidents included an attack on the U.S. Army's V Corps headquarters in Frankfurt on May 5, 1972; the bombing of the U.S. Army European headquarters on May 24, 1972; and an assault on the Axel Springer press building in Hamburg.

Police eventually traced Baader to a bomb-making garage at the end of May 1972, where he was captured along with several of his colleagues. Within weeks Meinhof and Ensslin were also arrested, dealing a crippling blow to the organization. However, a new generation of RAF activists would soon arise and conduct a wave of terrorism throughout the 1980s and 1990s that would pose a far more serious threat to German democracy.

See also: al-Fatah; Baader, Andreas; Meinhof, Ulrike; Raspe, Jan-Carl; Rote Armee Fraktion (RAF)

Further Reading

Alexander, Yonah, and Dennis Pluchinsky. *Europe's Red Terrorists: The Fighting Communist Organizations.* London: Frank Cass, 1992.

Aust, Stefan. *The Baader-Meinhof Complex.* London: Bodley Head, 2008.

Otte, Thomas. "Red Army Faction: The Baader-Meinhof Gang." In Martha Crenshaw and John Pimlott, eds., *International Encyclopedia of Terrorism*. Chicago: Fitzroy Dearborn, 1997.

Peters, Butz. *Tödlicher Irrtum: Die Geschichte der RAF.* Frankfurt: Fischer Taschenbuch, 2007.

Richard Warnes

BABBAR KHALSA (BK)

Babbar Khalsa (BK) is an Indian terrorist organization that seeks the creation of an independent Sikh state to be known as Khalistan. Sukhdev Singh Babbar and Talwinder Singh Parmar formed the group in 1978, and it was most active throughout the 1980s during the so-called Punjab insurgency. BK's influence waned in the 1990s after several senior members were killed in battles with the police, although it continues to exist and is thought to enjoy significant financial and political support in the United States, Canada, the United Kingdom, Germany, France, Belgium, Norway, Switzerland, and Pakistan. BK has also spawned several splinter factions. One of the most recent to emerge is the Khalistan Tiger Force, which Jagtar Singh Tara set up on March 13, 2011.

BK is best known for the bombing of Air India Flight 182 in Irish airspace on June 23, 1985. The attack killed 329 people and prior to 9/11 was the deadliest act of aviation terrorism in history. The incident occurred within an hour of an explosion at Japan's Narita Airport, which apparently involved a second BK device that detonated prematurely and was intended for another Air India flight with 177 people aboard. Although several BK members were arrested and tried for complicity in the 1985 attack, only one, Inderjit Singh Reyat, was convicted. In 2003 he pleaded guilty and was given a 15-year sentence for building both the Narita and Flight 182 bombs.

In early 1986 Parmar and others were arrested after being wiretapped discussing plans to blow up the Indian Parliament building in New Delhi. The group's current leader, Wadhwa Singh, and deputy chief, Mehal Singh, are both allegedly hiding in Pakistan. India is seeking their extradition along with 18 other terrorists.

BK is part of an alleged militant movement cosponsored by German-based extremist groups and Islamabad's Inter Services Intelligence (ISI) Directorate. The purported goal of this network, which is jointly led by Gurdial Singh Lalli of the International Sikh Youth Federation (ISYF), Resham Singh of BK, and Harmeet Singh of Kamagata Maru Dal of Khalistan, is to revive terrorism in the Indian Punjab. Indian authorities additionally claim that a former ISI chief, Javed Nasir, is currently coordinating the activities of Khalistani and Kashmiri militants and in 2002 tasked Lashkar-e-Taiba (LeT) with the training of Sikh extremists at various camps in Pakistan.

There have also been reports that BK is working with D-Company, a major organized crime syndicate operating in both India and Pakistan. The reputed don of the organization, Dawood Ibrahim, is charged with orchestrating a series of bombings in 1993 that killed 257 people and wounded another 700 in Mumbai. He is believed to be helping fund BK by channeling a percentage of the proceeds from a stolen-car racket to Wadhwa Singh.

The United States, which put Dawood on its list of global terrorists in 2003, says that D-Company is involved in large-scale narcotics shipments throughout Western Europe and is also complicit in laundering money for Al Qaeda through the *hawala* system. Dawood himself is one of India's most wanted men and is also subject to an Interpol international arrest warrant for organized crime and counterfeiting.

See also: Air India Flight 182 Bombing; Bombay Bombings (1993); Tokyo Airport Attack

Further Reading

"Babbar Khalsa International." South Asia Terrorism Portal, Institute for Conflict Management. http://www.satp.org/satporgtp/countries/india/states/punjab/terrorist_outfits/BKI.htm, accessed September 1, 2011.

Clarke, Ryan. *Lashkar-I-Taiba: The Fallacy of Subservient Proxies and the Future of Islamist Terrorism in India.* Carlisle, PA: U.S. Army War College, Strategic Studies Institute, March 2010. http://www.strategicstudiesinstitute.army.mil/pdffiles/pub1973.pdf, accessed September 1, 2011.

Jiwa, Salim. *The Death of Air India Flight 182.* London: W.H Allen, 1986.

King, Gilbert. *The Most Dangerous Man in the World: Dawood Ibrahim.* New York: Penguin Books, 2004.

Donna Bassett

BAGHDAD MINISTRY OF JUSTICE AND PROVINCIAL COUNCIL BUILDING BOMBINGS

On October 25, 2009, two suicide bombings near the center of Baghdad, Iraq, killed some 160 people and wounded more than 720 others. The attacks occurred within 15 minutes of each other (at 10:15 and 10:30 A.M.) and targeted the Justice Ministry, the Ministry of Municipalities and Public Works, and the Provincial Council; the blasts also destroyed the medical clinic that was part of the only Anglican Church in Iraq. They occurred at the height of a Sunni Muslim terrorist campaign that was primarily designed to show the Iraqi population two things: first, that the Shiite Muslim-led government of Prime Minister Nouri al-Maliki could not provide public safety as American military forces withdrew from the country; and, second, that his administration did not have the required sense of direction in the face of the January 2010 national elections.

The strikes cost roughly $120,000 and took the form of vehicle-borne improvised explosive devices (VBIEDs) that consisted of a minivan and a 26-seat day care bus. The operation itself was both strategically and tactically significant. Not only were the devices constructed and deployed in the most secure part of Iraq—the heavily fortified Green Zone—but the bombings were also executed at a time when it had become increasingly difficult to conduct any type of attack. Overall, it was the deadliest act of terrorism in the country since a series of VBIEDs had killed 500 people in northern Iraq in August 2007.

The mastermind behind the operation was Manuf al-Rawl. He had already been implicated in a series of explosions on August 19, 2009, that struck Iraq's finance and foreign ministries and left 122 people dead. He was captured in a raid on March 11, 2010, and later confessed that the October bombings were designed to compound the destabilizing effects of the earlier ones. In the end, however, the withdrawal of U.S. troops continued unabated, and al-Maliki, who had staked his political future on a pledge to bring peace to Iraq, was elected to a second term in January 2010.

Indeed, the attacks probably did more to hurt the Sunni cause than to advance it. One of the government buildings hit was the Justice Ministry. At the time it was attempting to reduce the number of inmates in Iraq's chronically overcrowded prisons. The attacks halted this process and served to further backlog outstanding criminal cases. Both aspects generated considerable dissatisfaction among the Sunnis, who make up only 20 percent of the population but 80 percent of those in jail.

The day after the explosions, Al Qaeda in Iraq (AQI) posted a message on the Internet taking credit for the attacks. The group is a Sunni umbrella association of semiautonomous terrorist organizations made up mostly of Iraqis. It was forged in the aftermath of the 2003 American invasion to overthrow Saddam Hussein and according to U.S. intelligence sources has a largely foreign leadership. At the zenith of the Iraqi insurgency, AQI effectively governed large parts of the country and in common with the Taliban in Afghanistan was able to operate, recruit members, and raise funds openly. By 2010, however, nearly three-quarters of the group's top commanders had been eliminated, and as a result of brutality and indiscriminate violence it had lost much of its original internal backing.

See also: Al Qaeda; Tanzom Qa'idat al-Jihadi Bilad al-Rafidyan (QJBR)

Further Reading

Atwan, Abdel Bari. *The Secret History of al Qaeda.* Berkeley: University of California Press, 2008.

Forest, James, ed. *Teaching Terror: Strategic and Tactical Learning in the Terrorist World.* Lanham, MD: Rowman & Littlefield, 2006.

Hafez, Mohammed. *Suicide Bombers in Iraq: The Strategy and Ideology of Martyrdom.* Washington DC: U.S. Institute of Peace Press, 2007.

Pirnie, Bruce, and Edward O'Connell. *Counterinsurgency in Iraq (2003–2006) RAND Counterinsurgency Study.* Vol. 2. Santa Monica, CA: RAND, 2008.

Donna Bassett

BAHAJI, SAID

Said Bahaji was an active member of the Hamburg Cell and served as its administrative secretary. This role gave him access to all the planning for the September 11 conspiracy. He also served as a conduit between the Hamburg Cell and Al Qaeda.

Bahaji was a product of mixed cultures. He was born on July 15, 1975, at Haselünne, Lower Saxony, Germany. His father was Moroccan and his mother

German. His father ran discotheques in Germany but was never successful. Bahaji lived in Germany until age nine, when the family moved to Meknès, Morocco, where his father became a farmer. In Meknès Bahaji attended the local school. After graduation he returned to Hamburg, Germany, to continue his education. With a desire to study electronics, Bahaji enrolled in an electrical engineering program at the Technical University of Hamburg-Harburg in 1996. He became an excellent computer programmer. Because Bahaji was a German citizen, he had a military obligation to fulfill. He served with the 72nd Tank and Rifle Battalion in Hamburg's Fischbek district, although his tour of duty ended with a military discharge after five months because of asthma and allergies. Bahaji married a Turkish woman in 1999, and they had a son.

Bahaji held pro-Western views until he began attending the al-Quds Mosque. Mounir el-Motassadeq introduced him to Mohamed Atta and Ramzi bin al-Shibh. Within weeks of this introduction, Bahaji began making militant Islamist remarks. Shortly after meeting Atta and bin al-Shibh, Bahaji decided to share an apartment with them at 54 Marienstrasse. They soon formed what came to be known as the Hamburg Cell. Each member of the cell had a job. Bahaji's job was that of administrative secretary, paying bills and handling the cell's administrative duties. His computer skills were invaluable. He made certain that the cell's bills were paid on time to attract as little attention as possible. Bahaji was never considered a candidate for the September 11 plot team, but he continued to conduct support activities from Hamburg. He was in frequent contact with the leaders of the September 11 conspiracy, providing them with money and with instructions from their Al Qaeda contacts.

Preparing for the backlash from the September 11 attacks, Osama bin Laden ordered Al Qaeda personnel to destroy records and return to his protection in Afghanistan. Responding to these orders, Bahaji left Germany on September 4, 2001, for Afghanistan. His whereabouts since then are unknown, although his German passport was found by Pakistani troops during military operations in South Waziristan in October 2009. His mission to supply logistic support for the Hamburg Cell had been successful.

See also: al-Quds Mosque; Atta, Mohamed; Hamburg Cell

Further Reading

McDermott, Terry. *Perfect Soldiers: The 9/11 Hijackers: Who They Were, Why They Did It.* New York: HarperCollins, 2005.

Stephen E. Atkins

BALI BOMBINGS (2002)

On October 12, 2002, devastating suicide bombings rocked the Indonesian island of Bali. The attacks, carried out by an Indonesian-based Islamist group known as Jemaah Islamiyah (JI), were the deadliest in Southeast Asian history and remain the most serious act of international terrorism since the 9/11 strikes in the United States.

About an hour before midnight on October 12, a suicide terrorist later identified as Iqbal walked into Paddy's Bar in the resort town of Kuta and detonated
an explosive device hidden in his backpack. As panicked civilians ran into the
street to flee the scene, another, 400-pound vehicle-borne improvised explosive
device (VBIED) concealed in a Mitsubishi L300 van, detonated across the street
outside the Sari nightclub. It was this blast that caused the majority of fatalities. A third, significantly smaller bomb also exploded at the U.S. consulate in
the nearby city of Denpasar, although it caused only minor injuries and minimal
property damage.

The attacks killed 202 individuals, including 88 Australians, 38 Indonesians,
24 Britons, and 7 Americans. Another 240 people were injured, many with severe
burns. The local hospital was soon overwhelmed, and many of the wounded had
to be flown to the Australian city of Darwin for extensive burn treatment. Two days
later, the United Nations Security Council (UNSC) unanimously passed Resolution 1438 condemning the attacks.

Although JI, a Southeast Asian Islamist organization with suspected links to Al
Qaeda, was immediately suspected, its leader, Abu Bakar Bashir, quickly denied
the group's involvement, instead blaming the United States for the attacks. Several

A police officer stands guard outside the ruins of the Sari Nightclub in Bali, which was destroyed
by a suicide bomber on October 12, 2002. The attack occurred minutes after another explosion at Paddy's Bar. The twin strikes left 202 people dead and remain the worst act of terrorism in Southeast Asia. (AP/Wide World Photos)

days after the bombings, the Arab news network Al Jazeera released an audio recording from Al Qaeda leader Osama bin Laden, who claimed that the attacks were conducted in retaliation for the U.S. War on Terror and Australia's involvement in securing East Timor's independence from Indonesia in 1999.

Because of the limited and at times contradictory information released by the Indonesian government in the immediate days after the attack, there are conflicting reports about the composition of the VBIED. Some sources claim the device was made out of ammonium nitrate, others believe it consisted of 1.2 tons of black powder connected to a cable detonator with PETN, while still others say it was constructed of TNT, chlorate, and RDX detonators. Whatever the exact nature of the compound, it is now known that the explosives were mixed in Denpasar (about 15 minutes from Kuta) and packed in at least a dozen filing cabinets that were then stored in the back of the minivan in place of the vehicle's rear seats. This device as well as the other two bombs was detonated by cell phone.

Police quickly traced the purchase of the Mitsubishi L300 van to Amrozi bin Haji Nurhasyim, largely because he had used his own name to purchase the vehicle. Other key individuals who were rounded up within months of the attack included Amrozi's two brothers, Mukhlas (also known as Ali Ghufron) and Ali Imron, Imam Samudra, and Wan Min Wan Mat (arrested in Malaysia). The chief architect of the operation, Riduan Isamuddin (also known as Hambali), was captured in Thailand in 2003. Two other main individuals who played a direct supervisory role, Azahari bin Husin and Noordin Mohamed Top (who acted as JI's principal explosives and financial experts, respectively) escaped arrest. However, both were later killed in police raids—the first in 2005, the second in 2009.

Subsequent testimony from the captured terrorists revealed that the funding for the bombings amounted to around $35,000, the bulk of which came from the theft of a gold store in Central Java. The targets were selected just two days prior to the attack and largely chosen on account of their patrons—Western tourists. Following his arrest, Samudra asserted, "I saw lots of whitey's dancing and lots of whitey's drinking there. That place—Kuta and especially Paddy's Bar and the Sari nightclub—was a meeting place for US terrorists and their allies, who the whole world knows to be the monsters" (cited by the Australian Broadcasting Corporation/ABC).

It also became apparent that the sites had advantages owing to the nature of their construction. Paddy's had an open front, which both allowed easy access for Iqbal and ensured that its occupants would be quickly funneled to the site of the main VBIED. The Sari Club consisted of bars with highly flammable thatched roofs and high walls that would act to force the direction of the minivan blast back toward the street where most people were congregated. The operatives apparently developed four backup plans for detonating the explosives in the event that the initial attempt failed: the first by cell phone; the second by a trigger that would be manually armed; the third by a timer; the fourth by a secondary switch set to go off if one of the drawers of the filing cabinet was opened.

Legal proceedings against those arrested began on April 30, 2003. Three were sentenced to death: Amrozi, Samudra, and Mukhlas. After several appeals and stays, the executions were eventually carried out by firing squad on November 9, 2008. Ali Imron, who reportedly showed remorse for his role in orchestrating the attacks, received a sentence of life imprisonment on September 18, 2003. Wan Min Wan Mat, the financial conduit for the attacks, agreed to testify in the trial against Mukhlas in return for a reduced jail term. He was subsequently released in 2005 after Malaysian authorities concluded that he no longer posed a threat to national security.

On October 15, 2004, Bashir was charged with complicity in the Bali attacks as part of a larger indictment for a 2003 bombing in Jakarta. Although acquitted of the latter, he was convicted of conspiracy in connection with the former. He was not indicted on any specific charge of terrorism and received a sentence of only two and a half years in prison (which was later commuted to time served). Bashir was again arrested in 2011, this time for running a militant training camp in Aceh, northern Sumatra. After a highly charged trial he was incarcerated for 15 years.

One of the more important implications of the Bali bombings was that it forced the Indonesian government to admit it had a serious domestic terrorist threat in its midst; prior to the attack Jakarta had insisted that if there were any extremists in the country, they were foreign and it was the responsibility of these states to deal with them. A slew of initiatives were quickly passed, including two antiterrorism regulations, an overhaul of the law enforcement and intelligence infrastructures, the formation of a new elite counterterrorist unit (Detasemen Khusus—88/Special Detachment—88), and the establishment of a coordinating body to better stream-line and integrate counterterrorism responses within the security forces (the Ter-rorism Eradication Coordinating Desk).

These various measures have paid dividends, substantially eroding JI's opera-tional and organizational presence in the country. Many of the group's top leaders have been either arrested or killed, and at least 450 additional militants have been detained. Although Bali was hit by another suicide attack in 2005 (which resulted in 26 deaths and 100 injuries), there have been no major incidents since then. Re-flecting the improved situation, the United States lifted its travel warning for In-donesia in 2008, with Washington's embassy in Jakarta affirming that the decision stemmed from the objective improvements that have been made in internal secu-rity and progress against JI.

On October 12, 2004, the second anniversary of the Bali bombings, a memorial to the victims of the attacks was unveiled in Kuta. Similar monuments have been erected in Melbourne, Sydney, Perth, and London. The atrocity was also immortal-ized in a 2007 Indonesian film called *The Long Road to Heaven*. Directed by Enison Sinaro, this cinematic production chronicles the planning and execution of the at-tacks, as well as the sentencing of the suspects.

See also: Al Qaeda; Bali Bombings (2005); Bashir, Abu Bakar; Jemaah Islamiyah (JI)

Further Reading

"Bali Death Toll Set at 202." *BBC News*, February 19, 2003. http://news.bbc.co.uk/2/hi/asia-pacific/2778923.stm, accessed October 21, 2011.

Chalk, Peter, Angel Rabasa, William Rosenau, and Leanne Piggott. *The Evolving Terrorist Threat to Southeast Asia: A New Assessment.* Santa Monica, CA: RAND, 2009.

Firdas, Irwan. "Indonesia Executes Bali Bombers." *Jakarta Post* (Indonesia), November 9, 2008. http://www.thejakartapost.com/news/2008/11/09/indonesia-executes-bali-bombers.html, accessed October 21, 2011.

Onishi, Norimitsu. "Indonesia Sentences a Radical Cleric to 15 Years." *New York Times*, June 17, 2011.

Parkinson, Tony. "Bin Laden Voices New Threat to Australia." *The Age* (Australia), November 14, 2002. http://www.theage.com.au/articles/2002/11/13/1037080786315.html, accessed October 12, 2011.

Ramakrishna, Kumar, and See Seng Tan, eds. *After Bali: The Threat of Terrorism in Southeast Asia.* Singapore: Institute of Defense and Strategic Studies, 2003.

Spencer C. Tucker

BALI BOMBINGS (2005)

On the evening of October 1, 2005, three suicide bombers detonated improvised explosive devices (IEDs) in near-simultaneous attacks on various locations on the Indonesian island of Bali. The targeted venues included the Raja Restaurant in Kuta Square and the Nyoman Cafe and Mandega Cafe in Jimbaran Beach. The attack left 26 people dead (including 21 Bali Hindus, 4 Australians, and 1 Japanese citizen) and at least another 129 injured. The incident was the most devastating act of terrorism in Indonesia since the 2002 Bali bombings.

Indonesian authorities identified the three perpetrators as Salik Firdaus (responsible for the bombing at the Nyoman Cafe), Aip Hidayat (responsible for the bombing at the Raja Restaurant), and an individual known as Misno (responsible for the bombing at the Mandega Cafe). Further investigations revealed that the masterminds behind the attacks were two leading Malaysian members of Jemaah Islamiyah's (JI) so-called pro-bombing faction: Noordin Mohamed Top and Azahari bin Husin. Both men had been directly tied to several prior incidents, including the Bali bombings of 2002 (which remain the most devastating terrorist attack since 9/11), the 2003 strike on the J.W. Marriott in Jakarta, and the 2004 bombing of the Australian embassy, again in the Indonesian capital.

Subsequent law enforcement operations identified a series of investigative leads, one of which led to the location of Azahari bin Husin's hideout in the Javanese town of Malang. Members of Indonesia's elite antiterrorist unit Densus-88 (D88) were subsequently deployed to the area and in an ensuing raid fatally shot him on November 9, 2005. Although Top escaped the authorities, he was eventually killed on September 17, 2009, again in an operation spearheaded by Densus-88.

The October 1, 2005, suicide bombings three years after the previous attacks underscored the severe economic impact that can result from terrorism targeting tourist destinations. The United States and several other governments immediately issued travel warnings for Indonesia, and many hotels in Bali suffered enormous losses as a result of cancellations. Despite the tragic loss of life, destruction, and impacts on the region, the attacks ultimately proved to be a disaster for JI, which suffered from a huge loss of grassroots support given that many of the casualties had been Muslims.

See also: Australian Embassy (Jakarta) Bombing; Bali Bombings (2002); Jemaah Islamiyah (JI); Marriott Hotel (Jakarta) Bombing (2003 and 2009)

Further Reading

"Azahari Killed in Raid." *Jakarta Post* (Indonesia), November 10, 2005. http://www.theja kartapost.com/news/2005/11/10/azahari-killed-raid.html, accessed February 16, 2012.
Federal Bureau of Investigation. *Terrorism 2002–2005.* Washington, DC: U.S. Department of Justice, 2006. Available online at http://www.fbi.gov, accessed February 16, 2012.
Ismail, Noor Huda. "The July 17 Jakarta Suicide Attacks and the Death of Noordin Top." *CTC Sentinel* 2, no. 9 (September 2009).
Komandjaja, Eva. "Police Identify Third Bali Suicide Bomber." *Jakarta Post* (Indonesia), November 20, 2005. http://www.thejakartapost.com/news/2005/11/20/police-identify-third-bali-suicide-bomber.html, accessed February 16, 2012.
Office of the Coordinator for Counterterrorism. *Country Reports on Terrorism 2006.* Washington, DC: U.S. Department of State, 2007. Available online at http://www.hsdl.org, accessed February 16, 2012.

Paul Kemppainen

BALTIC EXCHANGE BOMBING

On Friday April 10, 1992, the Provisional Irish Republican Army (PIRA, or the "Provos") detonated a huge vehicle-borne improvised explosive device (VBIED) outside the offices of the historic Baltic Exchange at 30 St. Mary Axe, London, United Kingdom. The bombing took place one day after British elections that saw Gerry Adams of Sinn Féin (the political wing of the Provos) lose his seat and John Major return as the prime minister of a conservative-led government. The attack was conducted as part of the group's so-called English Campaign and was primarily designed to inflict large-scale economic damage on the English mainland in an effort to force the United Kingdom out of Northern Ireland. It was the first of several large-scale bombings to occur over the next four years, including incidents in both London and Manchester.

The VBIED, which detonated at 9:20 P.M., was packed in a large white truck parked across the street from the Hong Kong and Shanghai Bank (HKSB). It was composed of 300 pounds of ammonium nitrate wrapped around military-grade Semtex; a similar device was used the following year in Bishopsgate, an attack that again targeted the heart of London's financial district. A man using a known PIRA code word phoned in a warning to British Rail's Waterloo station that a bomb was going to go off near the Baltic Exchange but gave only 20 minutes notice.

In addition to damaging the Exchange's facade, the blast caused extensive damage to several neighboring buildings in the vicinity of St. Mary Axe, with the overall cost estimated at £800 million (approximately $1.2 billion). This was four times the amount caused by more than 10,000 explosions that had occurred during the so-called Troubles in Northern Ireland up to that point.

Apart from structural damage, the truck bomb left 3 people dead (Paul Butt, Thomas Carey, and Danielle Carter) and 91 injured—14 of whom required urgent medical treatment. The low number of fatalities and serious casualties was largely due to the fact that VBIED detonated after hours on a Friday evening—a time when the City of London is largely devoid of human traffic.

Although a trading floor had reopened by the following Wednesday, authorities were unable to fully restore the building's operations in a manner that was consistent with the requirements of the English Heritage Board. The site was sold to Trafalgar House in 1995. The hope was that the interior of the Exchange Hall, which was regarded as stable, could be preserved and incorporated in any new development at the site. However, authorities later determined that the damage to the building was far more severe than originally thought, and plans for restoration were halted over the objections of architectural preservationists, who sought a judicial review of the decision. This was rejected, and 30 St. Mary Axe is now home to the offices of the reinsurance firm Swiss Re, which given its configuration is commonly referred to as the Gherkin.

See also: Bishopsgate Bombing; City of London Bombings (1996); Manchester City Bombing; Provisional Irish Republican Army (PIRA)

Further Reading

De Baróid, Ciarán. *Ballymurphy and the Irish War.* London: Pluto, 2000.

"Historic London Building to Be Reassembled in Central Tallin." *Baltic Times,* June 13, 2007. http://www.baltictimes.com/news/articles/18054, accessed November 09, 2011.

"Pavilions of Splendour." English Heritage. http://www.heritage.co.uk/apavilions/baltic.html, accessed November 9, 2011.

Edward F. Mickolus

BANBRIDGE BOMBING

On August 1, 1998, a 500-pound vehicle-borne improvised explosive device (VBIED) detonated outside of a shoe store in Banbridge, County Down, Northern Ireland. The attack wounded 35 people—including two members of the Royal Ulster Constabulary (RUC)—and damaged 200 homes. Repair costs ran into the millions of pounds.

The police, who had received three coded telephone warning messages, were in the process of evacuating the area when the device went off. The RUC later said the calls had given them only 20 minutes to clear the busy street. The Real Irish Republican Army (RIRA), the Republic of Ireland–based military wing of the 32 County Sovereignty Council, claimed credit for the attack.

The VBIED was packed in a Vauxhall Cavalier that had been abandoned in Newry Street close to where another device had been discovered and made safe the previous January. According to Irish authorities, that bomb, also estimated at 500 pounds, had been planted and left by the Continuity Irish Republican Army (CIRA).

The Banbridge strike was followed by an even more devastating attack two weeks later—the Omagh bombing (likewise carried out by RIRA), which killed 29 people. These incidents sparked fear of a major surge in dissident Republican violence, which was further exacerbated by the discovery of a massive explosive device at a RIRA checkpoint in South Armagh in September.

The intensification of dissident activity at this time strongly suggested that arms and explosives were making their way to CIRA and RIRA from external sources. Indeed, in August 1998 Michael Campbell, brother of the jailed RIRA leader and former "chief of staff" Liam Campbell, had appeared in court in Lithuania on charges of attempting to procure weapons and bomb-making equipment for use in Ireland. His case was one of several involving dissident Irish militants at this time who had been detained on suspicion of gunrunning in Eastern Europe.

Lacking the expertise and manpower required for more sophisticated ambushes and sniper attacks against police and security personnel, groups such as CIRA and RIRA have long relied on indiscriminate civilian-oriented attacks. These have mostly come in the form of booby-trap bombs, "barrack-buster" mortar strikes, and—most worrying—VBIEDS. Although basic, these assaults have the potential to inflict major damage as was vividly demonstrated by the Banbridge and Omagh bombings. However, they also galvanized public disgust and revulsion and, ironically, served as a force to unite the Catholic and Protestant populations behind a concerted drive for long-term peace in Northern Ireland.

See also: Continuity Irish Republican Army (CIRA); Good Friday Agreement; Provisional Irish Republican Army (PIRA); Real Irish Republican Army (RIRA)

Further Reading

"Arson Attacks Follow Bombing." *BBC,* August 2, 1998. http://news.bbc.co.uk/2/hi/events/northern_ireland/latest_news/143814.stm, accessed May 2, 2011.

McKittrick, David, and David McVea. *Making Sense of the Troubles.* London: Penguin Books, 2000.

Oppenheimer, A. R. *IRA: The Bombs and the Bullets: A History of Deadly Ingenuity.* Foreword by Richard English. Dublin: Irish Academic Press, 2009.

Donna Bassett

BANCA DE AGRICULTURA BOMBING

On December 12, 1969, an improvised explosive device (IED) was detonated in the National Bank of Agriculture (Banca de Agricultura) in the Piazza Fontana, Milan, Italy. The attack killed 17 people and wounded another 90, most of whom were conducting business after the end of the workday at a nearby fruit and vegetable market. The bombing occurred the same day that three smaller IEDs were detonated in Rome—one at the National Bank of Labor, one at a monument to

King Vittorio Emmanuele II, and one at the Tomb of the Unknown Soldier (which collectively injured 17)—and was part of a series of 149 incidents that took place in 1969.

Following the explosion, the Italian military secret service, the Servisio Informazioni Difesa (SID, or Defense Information Service), rounded up and questioned 150 left-wing activists. Four days later, nine individuals were arrested, including railway worker Giuseppe Pinelli and a ballet dancer named Pietro Valpreda. Another five people were detained on December 19. All were alleged to be members of the Anarchist Black Cross movement or otherwise tied to radical left-wing organizations.

One day after being apprehended, Pinelli allegedly committed suicide by throwing himself out of a window while being questioned at the central police headquarters. However, eyewitnesses said he was either dead or unconscious at the time of the incident, an account that was subsequently vindicated in an autopsy. Approximately 20,000 attended Pinelli's funeral (on December 20), by which time rumors had begun to circulate that he had been deliberately killed by the far right, elements of which were now also believed to be behind the Piazza bombing.

These rumors started to take on a more concrete form in 1970 when a warrant was issued for the arrest of Stefano Delle Chiaie, a member of Ordine Nuovo (ON, or New Order) and the founder of Avangaurdia Naszionale (National Vanguard). This was followed two years later by the apprehension of Pino Rauti, the leader of ON, along with Franco Freda, both of whom were charged with the Milan bombing. To the outrage of many, however, a judge decided to release Rauti on April 24, ruling that there were insufficient grounds to hold him. Although Freda was sentenced to 15 years for subversive association, he was released in 1985.

Over the course of the next 14 years, ongoing investigations increasingly pointed to the right as the perpetrators of the Piazza bombing. Eventually, in 1986 the SID agent Guido Giannettini and several other extremists were convicted for the attack and sentenced to life imprisonment. In January 1987, however, all were released due to a lack of evidence. That same year, the left-wing radicals who had originally been detained were also freed.

In 1989 Delle Chiaie was captured in Venezuela and extradited back to Italy to stand trial for the Rome bombing. He was acquitted. On June 20, 2001, former ON members Delfo Zorzi, Carlo Maria Maggi, and Giancarlo Rognoni were convicted. They were all acquitted in 2004, although speculation remained that they had played a direct role in the incident as well as the 1974 explosion in the Piazza della Loggia, which killed 8 and wounded over 90.

While the authorities were ultimately unable to resolve the case, evidence had come to light indicating a robust relationship between the neo-fascist community and some elements of the secret services. Indeed, one of the only convictions was of a SID general and captain who were found guilty of furnishing a false passport to a suspect in the bombing and generally trying to impede the course of the investigation.

Further Reading

Beck, Chris, Reggie Emilia, Lee Morris, and Ollie Patterson. *Strike One to Educate One Hundred: The Rise of the Red Brigades in Italy in the 1960s–1970s.* Chicago: Seeds beneath the Snow, 1986.

Christie, Stuart. "Stefano Delle Chiaie: Portrait of a Black Terrorist." *Black Papers* no. 1 (London: Anarchy Magazine/Refract Publications, 1984).

"Italy: The Injustice of Justice." *Time,* November 27, 1972. http://www.time.com/time/magazine/article/0,9171,944528,00.html, accessed August 11, 2011.

Meade, Robert. *Red Brigades: The Story of Italian Terrorism.* New York: St. Martin's, 1990.

Donna Bassett

BANDARANAIKE INTERNATIONAL AIRPORT ATTACK

On July 24, 2001, a 14-man suicide squad from the Liberation Tigers of Tamil Eelam (LTTE, or Tamil Tigers) staged an audacious assault on the Katunayake Air Force Base (KAB) and Sri Lanka's Bandaranaike International Airport (BIA), 18 miles north of Colombo. The well-armed attackers penetrated the 800-acre high-security complex in three waves and over the course of six hours successfully destroyed 26 military and commercial aircraft. The incident left 20 people dead (including all the perpetrators), led to the closure of the country's only international airport, and caused millions of dollars of damage.

The attack took place on the anniversary of the so-called Black July Riots, which over the course of two days in July 1983 are alleged to have killed between 2,000 and 3,000 Tamils. This particular event, triggered in part by a rebel land mine that killed 13 Sri Lankan soldiers, is often viewed as one of the main defining moments for the LTTE's war, and it remains a day of remembrance for thousands in the international Tamil diaspora (many of whom were forced to flee overseas as a result of the violence).

Planning for the operation is believed to have taken several months. The suicide team arrived on the eve of the attack and, pretending to be a group of young Sinhalese males enjoying an evening picnic, set up position in a playground near the target location. At around 10 P.M. the attackers changed into military clothes and under cover of darkness cut a hole in the chain-link fence controlling access to the KAB. Their movements were assisted by a routine nationwide blackout that began at 9:45 P.M. to reduce power consumption. After gaining entrance, the squad split into two teams and made their way to the apron and hangars where both fixed-wing military planes and helicopters were parked.

At around 3:50 A.M. the terrorists commenced their attack, opening fire with six light antitank weapons, three rocket-propelled grenades, one 40-millimeter grenade launcher, nine T-56 assault rifles, and three general-purpose machine guns. Over the course of the next hour they destroyed eight aircraft on the apron (two Israeli Kfirs, one Ukrainian MIG-27, two Mi-7 helicopter gunships, and three Chinese K-8 advanced trainers) and damaged two in the hangars; three airmen were also killed, as were eight LTTE cadres.

As resistance from the KAB mounted, the surviving members of the Tiger squad ran across the runway to BIA. After killing security guards, they ruptured an oil tanker with machine-gun rounds and then ignited the leaking fuel with the grenade launcher. The resulting blaze spread to a nearby A-330 Airbus and destroyed it. A lone attacker then detonated a charge on another A-330, which ripped its two wings from the fuselage. The remaining attackers had by now approached the main terminal. One suicide bomber set off his explosives in the departure cargo-holding area while three others entered the duty-free complex through an air-conditioning duct. Although two were killed, the final cadre managed to climb onto the building's roof. Benefiting from a clear line of sight, he critically damaged a third plane, an A-340.

After a total of six hours of intense fighting, 26 aircraft had been destroyed or badly damaged, including two civilian jets that were hit by friendly fire. Sri Lankan Airways reported that half of its fleet had been effectively taken out of service, at a cost of at least $350 million. The economic impact on the air force was less but still significant at $19.3 million.

Despite the amount of damage suffered in the course of the attack, the civilian airport was able to renew its operations within 24 hours. However, many governments and tour operators advised people to postpone or cancel planned trips to Sri Lanka, which led to a 15.5 percent drop in tourist revenue and contributed to a significant slowdown in economic growth (from an expected 4.5 percent to 2.5 percent). Sri Lanka's tourist board attempted to minimize the fallout by offering discounts to travelers, but expectations were low. Indeed, officials worked with a worst-case scenario, estimating that over the next six months there would be a 50–60 percent reduction in arrivals.

An additional consequence of the attack involved insurance costs and "risk premiums." A $40 per ticket security fee was added to air tickets, an addition that was so prohibitively expensive to some visitors that a group of Buddhist pilgrims were stranded in India as a direct result. Lloyd's of London also extended its "war risk" rating to the Port of Colombo. The resulting surcharge increase, which ran to around $450,000 per vessel, forced some shipping companies to avoid the terminal altogether.

To make matters worse, the widely reported behavior of the airport staff did little to increase tourist confidence. Several travelers complained that no one from the airport or the airlines had been willing to help guide them to safety. Others claimed that they were forced to flag down private buses in order to make the return trip to Colombo and that it was at least two hours before anyone in authority offered to assist them in finding a hotel or to provide transportation.

In an attempt to reassert its authority and establish a sense of renewed confidence in the country, the government carried out retaliatory air strikes against LTTE ground bases in Vishwamadhu (17 kilometers [10 miles] southeast of Kilinochi) and Trincomalee. The strikes were launched from the KAB in an attempt to demonstrate to the world (and the people of Sri Lanka) that the Tigers had failed to inflict meaningful harm on the base.

Three committees of inquiry were also established. The first, under Air-Vice Marshal Vijitha Thennekoon, was given the responsibility of investigating the security and intelligence failures that had allowed the Tigers to attack the KAB and BIA; the second, under Justice D. Jayawickrama, was mandated with assessing the mechanics of the LTTE assault. The third, under Defense Secretary Chandana de Silva, was charged with suggesting how to improve security at the international airport and other civil airports in the country. Critics dismissed these commissions as a waste of time, asserting they were merely formed as a means of pacifying public opinion. The punitive recommendations of the commissions—the arrest of several air force personnel, the permanent suspension of 11 others, and the replacement of the base commander and ground defense officer—were also seen as having little consequence for preventing similar events from occurring again.

Many experts concluded the LTTE attack revealed critical weaknesses in Sri Lanka's national security apparatus, especially its ability to collect and analyze tactical actionable information in order to develop appropriate threat forecasts to protect critical infrastructure. Others also lambasted the government's ineptitude in understanding the basics of counterintelligence, pointing out that throughout the assault the perpetrators had demonstrated an intimate understanding of the layout of both the KAB and BIA—knowledge that could have been procured only with the assistance of insiders. Finally, glaring deficiencies in base security were highlighted, including insufficient policing of the perimeter fence, no electrification of barriers, a lack of adequate lighting, the absence of patrol dogs, and routine (hence easily predicted) guard schedules. These assessments came despite reports that the government had invested 40 percent of its total war budget in professionalizing and increasing the capacity of both civilian and military intelligence agencies.

See also: Liberation Tigers of Tamil Eelam (LTTE)

Further Reading

Byman, Daniel, Peter Chalk, Bruce Hoffman, William Rosenau, and David Brannan. *Trends in Outside Support for Insurgent Movements.* Santa Monica, CA: RAND, 2001.
Davis, Mike. *Buda's Wagon: A Brief History of the Car Bomb.* New York: Verso Books, 2007.
Gunaratna, Rohan. "Intelligence Failures Exposed by Tamil Tiger Airport Attack." *Jane's Intelligence Review,* September 2001.
Tampoe, Mahen. *From Spices to Suicide Bombers and Beyond: A Study of Power, Politics, and Terrorism in Sri Lanka.* London: Athena, 2006.

Donna Bassett

BANGLADESH BOMBINGS

On August 17, 2005, Bangladesh was struck by a series of 500 nearly simultaneous explosions from 11:00 to 11:30 A.M. The well-organized bombings hit 63 of the country's 64 districts. In the capital city of Dhaka alone there were 28 attacks. Targets included the Supreme Court complex, the Bangladesh Secretariat, the prime minister's office, the Dhaka Judges Court, Dhaka University, Dhaka Sheraton Hotel, Zia International Airport, Ramna police headquarters, Hotel Sonargaon, the National Press Club, the New Market, the Bangladesh Bank, and the airport rail station.

Jama'at ul-Mujahideen Bangladesh (JMB) claimed responsibility for the explosions. Leaflets from the group were found at some of the bombing sites, asserting that it was time to implement full Islamic law in Bangladesh and warning the United States and the United Kingdom to leave all Muslim countries. Another group called Harakat ul-Jihad al-Islami (HuJI) was also alleged to have assisted JMB in carrying out the attacks. In total, 2 people were killed and more than 100 injured. Although most of the casualties were relatively minor, the attacks caused widespread panic across the country, leading to massive traffic jams as worried parents rushed to local schools to retrieve their children.

Investigators subsequently found that a huge sum of money had been used to buy the materials for the bombings. The monetary paper trail showed that the funds had originated from JMB's Dhaka chapter and had been wired to an account at the Chittagong branch of Islami Bank. Once the explosives had been purchased, they were sent to the capital in small lots beginning in May 2005.

The August bombings were not the only terrorist incidents to take place in Bangladesh that year. On January 27 a former finance minister, Shah AMS Kibria, was assassinated, and the following month the offices of two local aid agencies, Grameen and Brac, were bombed. The latter attack was linked to JMB and Jagrata Muslim Janata Bangladesh (JMJB). The August explosions came just a few days after the government of Bangladesh had told reporters that Islamic militants were a figment of their imaginations. This statement seemed absurd. There had been numerous terrorist incidents in the country during the previous five years, including attacks on the British High Commissioner, shrines, journalists, and movie theaters.

Several of those arrested in the aftermath of the bombings claimed that the operation had been carried out under the leadership of JMB's Abdur Rahman. Furthermore, it appeared that several groups thought to be otherwise independent were somehow connected to the incidents, collectively working under the banner of a shadowy entity called al-Mujahideen (AM). Two years earlier, authorities had found and decoded militant documents that revealed the existence of multiple AM training centers in more than 50 districts. Many of these were allegedly based in mosques and madrassas in the north.

On September 16, police detained Maulana Shahidullah Faruk, JMB's section commander in Chapainawabganj. They also arrested Mohammad Tufan, an explosives expert from Shibganj. In addition, the authorities found large quantities of bomb-making materials and firearms in residences belonging to other militants in Tanore and Rajshahi.

In February 2006, 21 men who had been found guilty of having carried out the August bombings were condemned to death by hanging. Three of the defendants were sentenced in absentia. All of the men, who were aged between 20 and 25, were JMB members. In January 2007, three more JMB cadres, Abdul Qaiyum (alias Bhodu), Minhajul Islam (alias Sohel Rana), and Abu Sayeed (alias Hussain), were executed. An additional five members were imprisoned for life in August 2010.

Despite these arrests, conspiracy theories continue to surround the August bombings. Some have suggested that the Awami League (AL), the former opposition party, was behind the attacks in an attempt to discredit the then ruling Bangladesh Nationalist Party (BNP). The AL has, in turn, alleged that the escalation of terrorism in 2005, combined with the slow pace of convictions, was due to the fact that powerful sympathizers within the ranks of two mainstream political parties, the Jamaat-e-Islami and Islami Oikya Jote (IOJ), were protecting militants in the country. Both groups as well as the BNP have dismissed these charges as baseless and irresponsible.

See also: Harakat-ul-Jihad-Islami Bangladesh (HuJI B); Jama'at ul-Mujahideen Bangladesh (JMB)

Further Reading

"Bombs Explode across Bangladesh." *BBC News,* August 17, 2005. http://news.bbc.co.uk/2/hi/south_asia/4158478.stm, accessed July 1, 2011.

Karlekar, Hiranmay. *Bangladesh: The Next Afghanistan?* New Delhi: Sage, 2005.

"Three Death Sentences for August 2005 Bombings." *Asia News,* January 25, 2007. http://www.asianews.it/news-en/Three-death-sentences-for-August-2005-bombings-8320.html#, accessed July 1, 2011.

Donna Bassett

BASAYEV, SHAMIL

During his life, Shamil Basayev held roles in various unrecognized governments of the Chechen separatist movement. These included the positions of divisional general of the military and vice president of the Republic of Ichkeria, deputy defense minister of Abkhazia, and the leader of the Islamic Republic of Dagestan. He was also an emir of the Majlis al-Shura (Council of Muslims) of Chechnya and Dagestan, an umbrella organization of North Caucasus insurgent groups, as well as the self-declared military commander of the Islamist International Peace Brigade and the leader of Riyad us-Saliheyn Martyrs' Brigade.

Basayev's prominence as a rebel leader can be traced back to Yeltsin's decision to send troops to quash Chechnya's bid for independence in 1994. That year he buried a radioactive dispersal device (or "dirty bomb") in a Moscow park, threatening to detonate it if Chechyna was not granted independence. A year later Basayev assaulted the town of Budennovsk, Russia, with 100 fighters. His forces attacked various government offices, killing at least 20 police and soldiers and wounding 21 others, and then seized a hospital, taking between 1,500 and 1,800 hostages, most of them civilians. After Russian troops failed to retake the building, Prime Minister Viktor Chernomyrdin opened negotiations and eventually agreed to halt military actions and grant a degree of self-rule to Chechnya if the captives were freed. This brought a temporary end to the ongoing conflict, which would later be referred to as the First Chechen War.

Basayev's popularity reached a peak following the raid in Budennovsk. In 1997 he unsuccessfully ran for the presidency of Chechnya, a post that another rebel commander, Aslan Maskhadov, won. However, he was included in the provincial government as prime minister. During his tenure, Basayev signed an agreement

Shamil Basayev speaks at rebel's positions in the mountains in the Botlikh region, near the village of Ansalta, during a raid in Dagestan. He was Chechnya's most feared warlord, who terrified Russia and outraged the world with cunning and savage attacks that observed no limits, targeting hospitals, a theater, and even schoolchildren. Basayev was killed in Ingushetia on July 10, 2006. (AP Photo)

with Yeltsin that further extended the scope of autonomy in Chechyna. However, the Russian president refused to consider the question of independence, which prompted Basayev to resign as prime minister and turn once again to armed resistance.

In 1999 Basayev led a group of Chechen rebels into Dagestan to establish an Islamic state. The move was denounced by Maskhadov, who Basayev publicly acknowledged had not known of the plan. Nevertheless, the incursion, along with a wave of bomb attacks across Russia, was used by Russian president Vladimir Putin as justification for a renewed offensive against Chechnya. Maskhadov's government was declared invalid, and Russian troops took control of Grozny, installing a pro-Moscow administration in 2000. Although Basayev managed to escape to the mountains in the south, he stepped on a land mine while fleeing and lost a foot.

Events in 2000 marked the onset of the Second Chechen War. Basayev immediately declared an intention to attack Russian targets as well as any international organizations perceived as supporting the government in Moscow. He soon made good on these threats, orchestrating a series of deadly terrorist attacks both within and outside Chechnya. In December 2002 suicide bombers destroyed an administration complex in Grozny, killing 78 and wounding 150. In May 2003 a car bombing at a government compound in Znamenskoye killed 60 and wounded 200.

That same month a female suicide bomber attempted to assassinate pro-Moscow Chechen president Akhmad Kadyrov at a religious festival in Iliskhan-Yurt. Although the attack failed, 18 people were killed and 43 wounded. Finally, in October 2005, Chechen rebels staged multiple attacks on the police, army, and Federal Security Service facilities in the city of Nalchik in the republic of Kabardino-Balkaria, killing 139.

Outside Chechnya, Basayev took responsibility for two of the most serious terrorist attacks to have ever been perpetrated on Russian soil. The first involved the seizure of the Moscow Dubrovka Theater in October 2002, which resulted in the deaths of 120 hostages (although many of these fatalities were reputedly the fault of the special forces, who reportedly piped an overly concentrated mix of poisonous gas through the ventilation system in an effort to incapacitate the attackers). The second took place in September 2004 when Chechen rebels seized a school in the town of Beslan. After a standoff of several days, Russian forces stormed the building, precipitating a major firefight that left 331 people in the school dead.

Although Basayev is now known to have been a committed Islamist terrorist with a $10 million bounty on his head, sources close to Basayev describe him as a man who adopted fundamentalist Islam simply as a reason to exercise his longtime love of fighting. Some analysts also contend that his adherence to an extremist Muslim ideology was merely an attempt to extract money and other forms of material support from the Middle East. Despite these allegations, Basayev himself consistently denied that he received any money or backing from either Al Qaeda or Osama bin Laden.

Basayev was killed by an explosion in Ingushetia on July 10, 2006. Russian officials claimed that his death was the result of an effective operation by the country's Federal Security Service. However, Chechen rebels denied this, asserting that the explosion was due to the spontaneous detonation of homemade bombs that Basayev and others were transporting for a series of attacks on unspecified locations.

See also: Moscow Theater Attack; Beslan School Hostage Crisis

Further Reading

"Basayev: Russia's Most Wanted Man." *CNN,* September 8, 2004. http://www.cnn.com/2004/WORLD/europe/09/08/russia.basayev/.

"Chechen Terror Leader Shamil Basayev Killed in Russia." *FoxNews,* July 10, 2006. http://www.foxnews.com/story/0,2933,202753,00.html.

"Mastermind of Russian School Siege Killed." *CNN,* July 10, 2006. http://www.cnn.com/2006/WORLD/europe/07/10/russia.basayev/.

Reeker, Philip. "Designation of Shamil Basayev under Executive Order 13224." United States Department of State Press Statement, August 8, 2003.

Steele, Jonathan. "Shamil Basayev." *The Guardian* (UK), July 11, 2006.

Horacio Trujillo

BASHIR, ABU BAKAR

Abu Bakar Bashir is a radical Muslim cleric who was sentenced to prison in 2005 for his role in a series of Indonesian bombings and who is suspected of being the spiritual leader of the Jemaah Islamiyah (JI) terrorist group. Bashir was born in the Indonesian region of East Java in 1938. As a young man, he became a cleric and a teacher of Islam. At the same time, he began to advocate for the formation of an Islamic state under sharia law, first in Java and then in the nation as a whole. During his years teaching Islam in the Java region, Bashir gained a following among radical Muslims, who supported his demands that Indonesia become an Islamic state under sharia. He joined the group Darul Islam, dedicated since the 1940s to leading Indonesia to Islam, sometimes by violent means. These demands were not endorsed by the country's secular government, and the Indonesian leader Suharto had Bashir jailed for subversive speech in the late 1970s.

After Bashir was released from prison, he continued his calls for Indonesia to become a Muslim theocracy, moving to Malaysia in 1985 to avoid further prison time. In 1998, shortly after Suharto's authoritarian regime collapsed, Bashir returned to Indonesia, where in 2000 he joined the executive council of the newly formed Mujahideen Council, devoted to the Islamization of Indonesia.

In October 2002 two massive bombs were detonated outside nightclubs on the Indonesian island of Bali, an attack that killed more than 200 people and was blamed on the Islamic terrorist group JI, believed to have links to Al Qaeda. Bashir, viewed by Indonesian police officials as the religious head of the secretive group, was arrested and charged with spiritually guiding the group and masterminding the Bali bombings, in addition to being implicated in a series of church bombings in 2000 and a failed assassination attempt on then Indonesian president Megawati Sukarnoputri. In 2003 Bashir was charged in the bombing of a Marriott hotel in the capital, Jakarta, for which JI was also blamed.

Bashir, who despite his vocal support of Osama bin Laden and Al Qaeda had publicly denied any connection with JI and claimed that the charges against him were part of a U.S. conspiracy, was found not guilty of treason for serving as JI's spiritual leader in his first trial in 2003. In a second trial for complicity in the 2002 and 2003 bombings that began in late 2004, Bashir was ultimately convicted of conspiracy to commit the Bali bombings. However, he was acquitted on similar charges pertaining to the Jakarta hotel bombing due to a lack of evidence.

In February 2005 Bashir was sentenced to 30 months in prison for his role in the Bali attacks. Despite his conviction, many governments around the world, including those of the United States and Australia, expressed their dismay at the short sentence, believing it was inadequate punishment for participating in the Bali attacks, in which more than 200 people, mostly Australian tourists, had been killed. Bashir's sentence was questioned again on October 1, 2005, when—almost three years to the day after the 2002 Bali attacks—three suicide bombers allegedly linked to JI caused more mayhem in Bali tourist areas, killing more than 25 people.

See also: Bali Bombings (2002); Bali Bombings (2005); Jemaah Islamiyah (JI)

Further Reading

Ahtisaari, Martti. *How the Jemaah Islamiyah Terrorist Network Operates*. Darby, PA: Diane, 2003.
Bertrand, Jacques, ed. *Nationalism and Ethnic Conflict in Indonesia*. Cambridge: Cambridge University Press, 2003.
Kingsbury, Damien. *The Politics of Indonesia*. Melbourne: Oxford University Press, 2002.

Peter Chalk

BEAM, LOUIS

Louis Beam was a key theorist and strategist for the U.S. white supremacist movement. He is best known for his Ku Klux Klan (KKK) affiliation and ties to Aryan Nations (AN) and his violence against Vietnamese shrimp fishermen in Louisiana in the 1980s; he was one of the first proponents of leaderless resistance.

There is some mystery about Beam's early life. Most biographical materials only provide his birth date as 1946 in Braunfels, Texas, northeast of San Antonio. During the Vietnam War, he enlisted in the army and served as a helicopter gunner. While deployed he allegedly said his main goal was to rack up at least 50 kills, and he reportedly reveled in any chance to fatally engage the enemy.

Beam returned home in 1968 and immediately joined the Texas chapter of the United Klans of America. He was arrested in the early 1970s for the bombing of a left-wing radio station in Houston, Texas, and a machine-gun attack on a local Communist Party group. However, the charges were subsequently dropped in both cases. He was later apprehended for an attempted assault on Deng Xiaoping during the Chinese Communist leader's visit to Texas, although he again never faced court.

Beam joined David Duke's Knights of the KKK in 1976 and rose rapidly through the ranks to become a state leader. He led guerrilla-warfare workshops and pushed for the recruitment of Klansmen from among the soldiers at Fort Hood in Texas. In 1981 he led a campaign of violent harassment of Vietnamese fishermen, adopting the catchphrase "Where ballots fail, bullets will prevail." As part of this effort he encouraged Texan shrimpers to burn immigrant trawlers—at least two of which were destroyed—and set fire to crosses outside their homes. In justifying his actions, Beam declared that only direct (violent) action could rescue the country from the enemy. In response, the Southern Poverty Law Center filed injunctions against the KKK and successfully won court orders for Beam to close five paramilitary training camps.

Beam was obsessed with the fear that nonwhites were overrunning the United States. He looked at the fight with the Vietnamese fishermen as the first round of the battle to reclaim America for the Caucasian majority. In this endeavor Beam received overt support from Richard Butler, the head of the neo-Nazi AN, cementing a relationship that later saw him move to an AN compound, where he formed a secret domestic terrorist group known as the Order. The organization achieved notoriety for several brazen robberies and assassinations in 1983 and 1984.

Authorities arrested Beam in 1982 for kidnapping his toddler daughter from his estranged wife, Kara Mikels. However, she dropped the case, allegedly as a result of KKK threats. After his release from detention, Beam along with two other colleagues set up the first white supremacist online bulletin board, marking the beginning of his leaderless resistance "innovation" that used cyberspace, rather than physical territory, as a medium in which to organize. Beam argued that this principle was the best way to insulate a covert movement from the attention of law enforcement and reflected his own fear that federal authorities were closing in on him. In the latter regard he was right. In April 1987, Beam, along with 12 other prominent leaders of the neo-Nazi movement, such as Butler, was indicted for conspiracy to overthrow the U.S. government. The Federal Bureau of Investigation (FBI) put him on its ten-most-wanted list.

Beam immediately fled to Mexico with his fourth wife, Sheila Toohey. However, he was quickly discovered, and federal authorities surrounded the building in Chapala where the pair was hiding. After a brief shoot-out that left one police officer dead, Beam was extradited back to the United States. In April 1988 an all-white jury in Arkansas acquitted Beam and his accomplices of the federal conspiracy charges—a significant victory for the far right. The following year, Beam refused Butler's offer to become head of the AN and continued to work alone. He gradually disappeared from public view and confined himself to writing articles for his web page.

Toohey later accused Beam of sexually molesting his two young daughters during a 2002 custody dispute. She also alleged that Beam refused to let the girls swim in a hotel pool with African Americans. Again, the charges against him were dropped. Beam now lives with his fifth wife near New Braunfels.

See also: Aryan Nations (AN); Ku Klux Klan (KKK); McVeigh, Timothy; Oklahoma City Bombing; Rudolph, Eric

Further Reading

Dees, Morris. *Gathering Storm: America's Militia Threat.* New York: Harper Collins, 1996.
Dees, Morris. *A Season for Justice: A Lawyer's Own Story of Victory over America's Hate Groups.* New York: Touchstone Book, 1991
Flynn, Kevin, and Gary Gerhardt. *The Silent Brotherhood: Inside America's Racist Underground.* New York: Free Press, 1989.
Stanton, Bill. *Klanwatch: Bringing the Ku Klux Klan to Justice.* New York: Grove Weidenfeld, 1991.

Donna Bassett

BEERSHEBA BUS BOMBINGS

On August 31, 2004, at approximately 2:55 P.M., two Hamas suicide bombers blew up Metro Dan buses no. 6 and no. 12. The vehicles were 100 yards apart near the city hall in Beersheba (Be'er Sheva). The attacks killed 16, including several students returning from school, and hospitalized 97. The terrorists were later identified as Ahmed Kawasma (Ahmad Qawasme, Ahmed Qawasmeh) and Nassim Jabri (Nassem Jabari).

Following the incident Hamas sent a so-called military communiqué to Israeli prime minister Ariel Sharon and defense minister Shaul Mofaz taking credit for the bombings and affirming that the attack was a response to the assassinations of Hamas founder and spiritual leader Sheikh Ahmad Yasin. It further asserted solidarity with the Palestinian political prisoners on hunger strike and announced a determination to continue with jihad. A videotape was eventually released that showed the two suicide bombers posing with rifles next to posters of Sheikh Ahmad Yasin and Abdel-Aziz al-Rantissi. The 22-year-old Jabri and 26-year-old Kawasma were neighbors from the West Bank community of Hebron.

Yasin, three bodyguards, and four passersby had been killed on March 22, 2004, when Israeli helicopter gunships fired on his motorcade as he was leaving Gaza City's Islamic Group Mosque. An additional 15 others were wounded, including two of Yasin's sons. The targeted assassination was carried out in response to twin suicide bombings earlier that month at the Port of Ashdod, which had killed 11. Yasin's assassination triggered a wave of protests, and the Abu hafs al-Masri Brigades website vowed vengeance against Israel and the United States.

Following the attacks in Beersheba, Hamas members drove through the city streets in a vehicle equipped with loudspeakers announcing that a cell from Hebron was responsible for the twin suicide bombings and that Yasin could now rest in peace. Members of the public threw sweets into the air and sang to celebrate. "Revenge is sweet," said one activist.

Meanwhile, Palestinian prime minister Ahmed Qorei issued a statement condemning the attack and calling for an immediate cessation of any future actions of this kind. He went on to say that these types of bombings harmed Palestinian national interests as they provided Israel with the "perfect" pretext to continue with assassinations, incursions, and the expansion of settlements.

The bombings took place on the same day that Sharon announced a timetable for the full withdrawal of all of its estimated 7,000 settlers from Gaza along with the troops assigned to protect them. The Israeli government was also apparently intending to redeploy soldiers from portions of the West Bank as well. The attacks immediately halted these plans and were used as justification for the construction of a protective barrier to keep suicide bombers from entering Israel. Ranaan Gissin, Sharon's chief spokesman, was quoted as saying that the work on the southern portion of the West Bank barrier would be speeded up, adding that had a fence been in place it would have been much harder to get into Beersheba from Hebron. Israel later accused Syria of having been involved in the attack, claiming that the operation had been planned in Damascus. A spokesman for Sharon said, "The fact that Hamas is operating from Syria will not grant it immunity."

The Beersheba bombings triggered a wave of actions and counteractions. On September 1, bulldozers were used to destroy the homes of the two suicide bombers. In an allegedly unrelated strike in Gaza, Israeli forces surrounded 10 apartment blocks and ordered the residents to leave. Two buildings were then demolished. Authorities claimed that Palestinian militants were using the area as a staging platform to fire mortars, rockets, and antitank missiles at Israeli soldiers and settlers. Although officials claimed no one was injured in the forced Gaza eviction, others reported the demolition wounded six Palestinians and left dozens of families homeless.

On September 7 an Israeli air strike on a sports field dedicated to Yasin killed 14 people and injured at least 20 others. The attack, which occurred in the eastern Shajaiyeh district of Gaza City, was justified as a legitimate and "clean" operation aimed at destroying a terrorist training facility. Hamas denied the accusation, claiming that the site was being used as a summer camp for Palestinian youth. The group swore vengeance and quickly responded by firing mortars and rockets at Jewish settlements in Gaza.

Later that same month an improvised explosive device destroyed a car belonging to Izz el-Deen Sheikh Khalil. According to witnesses, the 39-year-old Hamas leader answered a call to his mobile phone moments before the explosion. The blast killed Khalil and wounded three passersby. Although Israel did not take responsibility for the assassination, unnamed sources claimed the attack was in response to the Beersheba bombings. Public Security Minister Gideon Ezra neither confirmed nor denied that his government had had a hand in Khalil's death, ominously adding, "I'm not sorry this happened." Hamas not surprisingly blamed Israel for the murder and threatened further retaliation. Syria made similar allegations, affirming that the incident was evidence of the Jewish state's active intention to shake regional security and stability.

See also: al-Aqsa Martyrs' Brigades; Ashdod Port Attack; Hamas (Islamic Resistance Movement)

Further Reading

Levitt, Matthew. *Hamas: Politics, Charity, and Terrorism in the Service of Jihad.* New Haven, CT: Yale University Press, 2006.

Milton-Edwards, Beverley, and Stephen Farrell. *Hamas: The Islamic Resistance Movement.* Malden, MA: Polity, 2010.

Mishal, Shaul, and Avraham Sela. *The Palestinian HAMAS: Vision, Violence, and Coexistence.* New York: Columbia University Press, 2000.

Rabasa, Angel, Peter Chalk, Kim Cragin, Sara Daly, Heather Gregg, Theodore Karasik, Kevin O'Brien, and William Rosenau. *Beyond al-Qaeda: The Outer Rings of the Terrorist Universe, Part 2.* Santa Monica, CA: RAND, 2006.

Donna Bassett

BEILEN TRAIN SIEGE

The South Moluccans originating from the Molucca, or the Spice Islands, between Celebes and New Guinea had been some of the Netherlands' most ardent supporters in the former Dutch East Indies (Indonesia). Many served in the Dutch military and remained loyal during the fighting against Sukarno and his supporters, who sought Indonesian independence in the aftermath of World War II. Consequently, when the Dutch withdrew from Indonesia on December 27, 1949, around 12,000 Moluccans left with them and settled in the Netherlands. Their descendants tended to form inner-city ghettoes in the poorer parts of the country, with most taking menial or labor jobs.

Certain elements within the next generation of Moluccans living in the Nether-lands soon felt betrayed, however. Three main factors animated their resentment: first, that the Dutch had handed over their home islands to Indonesia; second, that the government failed to condemn the ensuing repression of the remaining Moluccans when the Indonesian military took control; and, third, that they per-ceived themselves as discriminated against in Dutch society. A number of youths from this more radical section of the Moluccan diaspora subsequently formed the Vrije Zuidmolukse Jongeren (VZJ), or Moluccan Youth Organization, with the intention of taking direct action to ensure their grievances were heard and recognized.

On December 2, 1975, seven armed members of the VZJ hijacked a train near Beilen and Wijster. When the driver tried to resist, he was shot and wounded before being taken to the luggage car and killed. The terrorists then forced the hostages to tape newspapers over the windows to obscure outside vision and placed chains, padlocks, and what were believed to be explosives on the doors. The VZJ terrorists demanded the release of Moluccan prisoners in Indonesia, a more forceful stance toward Moluccan independence on the part of the Nether-lands' government, publicity for their cause, and safe passage out of the country. The Dutch authorities for their part played out the siege, relying on psycholo-gists and interventions from leaders in the Moluccan community to deliberately extend negotiations for minor concessions in order to wear down the hostage takers.

On the second day of the siege as the VZJ negotiated with the police, who had set up a command post at a nearby farm, tensions rose. Subsequently, Robert de Groot, one of the hostages who had initially been argumentative with the terror-ists, was shot and thrown off the train but survived his wounds. The following day, after further demands were ignored, the terrorists shot and killed another hostage, E. J. Bierling. Nevertheless, over the remaining days no further killings occurred, and the tactics of prolonged negotiation and interventions from Moluccan com-munity leaders appeared to be working. This was confirmed on December 14, when the terrorists, surrounded by Dutch police and members of the Royal Neth-erlands Marine Corps (RNLMC), surrendered to the Moluccan president in exile, Manusama, before handing themselves over to the authorities.

Although the siege ended peacefully, 2 of the original 52 hostages had been killed. Five days later, a parallel siege of the Indonesian consulate in Amster-dam also ended peacefully, though one hostage died jumping from a high window.

See also: De Punt Train Siege

Further Reading

Brogan, Patrick. *World Conflicts: Why and Where They Are Happening.* London: Bloomsbury, 1989.

Griffiths, John. *Hostage: The History, Facts and Reasoning behind Hostage Taking.* London: Andre Deutsch, 2003.

Newton, Michael. *The Encyclopedia of Kidnappings.* New York: Checkmark Books, 2002.

Rasser, Martijn. "The Dutch Response to Moluccan Terrorism 1970–1978." *Studies in Conflict and Terrorism* 28 (2005).

Schmid, Alex. "Countering Terrorism in the Netherlands." *Terrorism and Political Violence* 4 (1992).

Richard Warnes

BEN YEHUDA SHOPPING MALL BOMBING

At 3 P.M. on September 4, 1997, three Palestinians set off bombs full of nails in Ben Yehuda Street in the center of Jerusalem, killing themselves and five others and wounding 190 shoppers. Hamas took credit, warning that it would carry out more attacks until Israel agreed to release imprisoned members of the group.

Just over two weeks later Israel announced that four Palestinians were responsible for the Ben Yehuda Street bombing. The government said all had lived in the West Bank village of Asirah Shamaliya, north of Nablus, and identified them as Mouaia Jarara, 23; Bashar Zoualha, 24; Touwafik Yassin, 25; and Yosef Shouli, 23.

On January 14, 1998, two Hamas members were arrested in Nablus after Palestinian intelligence uncovered a safe house that was being used to store 1,500 pounds of explosive materials. The pair were subsequently tried and sentenced to 15 years of hard labor for building the bombs and recruiting the suicide terrorists who carried out the attack in Jerusalem.

Palestinian leaders were quick to condemn the Ben Yehuda Street violence. The cabinet secretary for the Palestinian Authority (PA), Amin Abdul Rahman, called the bombings a crime against civilized people. However, the Israeli government discounted the statement as largely meaningless, accusing the PA of not doing enough to curtail the activities of groups like Hamas.

The Palestinian-Israeli peace process had already been put in jeopardy as a result of an earlier bombing at the Ben Yehuda Market on July 30, 1997. The second attack was apparently intended to sabotage the diplomatic mission of U.S. secretary of state Madeleine Albright, who was scheduled to arrive the following week. She did not cancel her visit to the region but had little success in forwarding the peace process. Following the second bombing, Prime Minister Binyamin Netanyahu announced that he was no longer bound by the 1993 Oslo Peace Accords and would suspend Israeli withdrawal from the West Bank. It would take several years before the two sides resumed talks.

The Ben Yehuda bombing was just the latest in a series of attacks on or in the vicinity of the street going back decades. Some earlier incidents included the bombing of four British Army trucks on February 22, 1948 (58 Jewish civilians killed and 140 injured); the detonation of a refrigerator packed with five kilograms (11 pounds) of explosives at nearby Zion Square on July 4, 1975 (15 killed, 77 injured); a bombing near the pedestrian mall on November 13, 1975 (7 killed, 45 wounded); an improvised explosive device attack at the corner of Ben Yehuda and Ben Hillel Streets (33 wounded); and a blast on March 24, 1979, in Zion Square (1 killed, 13 injured).

See also: Oslo Accords; Hamas (Islamic Resistance Movement)

Further Reading

Levitt, Matthew. *Hamas: Politics, Charity, and Terrorism in the Service of Jihad.* Foreword by Dennis Ross. New Haven, CT: Washington Institute for Near East Policy, Yale University Press, 2006.

Milton-Edwards, Beverley, and Stephen Farrell. *Hamas: The Islamic Resistance Movement.* Malden, MA: Polity, 2010.

Mishal, Shaul, and Avraham Sela. *The Palestinian HAMAS: Vision, Violence, and Coexistence.* New York: Columbia University Press, 2000.

Donna Bassett

BESLAN SCHOOL HOSTAGE CRISIS

The Beslan school operation was the latest in a series of attacks carried out by Chechen rebels in an effort to gain independence for Chechnya, which first broke away from Russia in November 1991 after the fall of the Soviet Union. In 1994 President Boris Yeltsin sent troops to regain control of the province, triggering a bloody insurgency that has resulted in the fatalities of countless troops and civilians. Less than a month before the Beslan attack, Chechen suicide bombers blew up two civilian airliners; earlier that year, they assassinated Akhmad Kadyrov, the pro-Russian Chechen president installed by Moscow authorities and, in a separate incident, invaded the Interior Ministry in the neighboring republic of Ingushetia.

The Beslan hostage crisis commenced on the morning of September 1, 2004, when 32 heavily armed Chechen, Ingush, Russian, and Arab terrorists stormed and seized School Number One, where an estimated 1,200 students, teachers, and parents were attending opening ceremonies for the first day of classes. Twelve people were killed within the first few minutes after the attackers opened fire, and a few others managed to escape. The remainder, which numbered more than 1,000, were shepherded into the gymnasium, where they were surrounded by a ring of guns, bombs, and detonators. Temperatures soon rose in the building, and as the days wore on many hostages fainted and faced dehydration.

Soon after the takeover, Russian and North Ossetian police blockaded the school and managed to make contact with the hostage takers. The terrorists immediately demanded full recognition of Chechnya's independence and the withdrawal of all Russian troops from the province. Although the attackers agreed to release 26 hostages on September 2, they refused to allow any food or water into the school, and negotiations soon broke down. However, talks commenced the next day, and the attackers agreed to allow medical personnel to access the building and retrieve the bodies of those who had been killed when the school was seized two days earlier.

It remains unclear exactly what happened next, but when emergency workers entered the school, a series of explosions went off and the gymnasium roof collapsed. At that point, police stormed the building. Adding to the confusion, hundreds of civilians—mainly hostages' families who had been watching the crisis from the other side of police blockades just over 300 feet away—also ran into the school. In the ensuing gunfight, hundreds were killed, and more than 700 were injured. According to Russian police, all but one of the hostage takers were killed either within the school or after being tracked down nearby. The sole survivor, Nur-Pashi Kulayev, was convicted and sentenced to life in prison in May 2006. Shamil Basayev, commander of the Chechen separatist movement since the mid-1990s, later claimed responsibility for the siege.

Much about the siege, particularly what specifically sparked the September 3 explosions that brought about

An elderly woman carries a small child past the ruins of Beslan School Number 1 just days after a deadly hostage crisis that took the lives of several hundred people, mostly young children, in North Ossetia, Russia in 2004. (AP/Wide World Photos)

its violent end, remains unknown, and many victims' families accused then Russian president Vladimir Putin and other top officials of a cover-up. A subsequent report compiled by North Ossetian officials concluded that Russian troops fired rocket-propelled grenades and flamethrowers into the school gym, and this caused the roofs collapse and further explosions. The Kremlin denied the charges, claiming that it was the hostage takers who first detonated the charges and that they were responsible for the high death toll. A Russian legislative commission repeatedly delayed the release of its own findings, saying the final report still had "many holes."

Other investigations have raised the possibility that a bomb hung from the gym's ceiling may have fallen and exploded accidentally. Many have also blamed North Ossetian police for failing to prevent the crisis in the first place, especially given that Moscow officials had previously warned of an imminent attack in the region. Numerous people, including families of the victims, are doubtful that the facts behind the siege will ever be fully known.

Further Reading

Abdullaev, Nabi. "Beslan Tragedy Reveals Flaws in Russian Security Operations." *Eurasia Daily Monitor,* 1, no. 79 (September 7, 2004).

Baker, Peter, and Susan Glasser. "Hostage Takers in Russia Argued before Explosion." *Washington Post,* September 7, 2004.

Chamberlain, Gethin. "Blood of Beslan's Innocents." *The Scotsman* (Glasgow), September 4, 2004.

Mulvey, Stephen. "The Hostage Takers." *BBC News,* September 9, 2004.

Ostrovsky, Simon. "Over 300 Killed in School Carnage." *Moscow Times,* September 6, 2004.

Walsh, Nick. "When Hell Came Calling at Beslan's School No. 1." *The Observer* (London), September 5, 2004.

Edward F. Mickolus

BHAGWAN SHREE RAJNEESH CULT

The Bhagwan Shree Rajneesh cult was a social movement based around the beliefs of its spiritual leader and guru, Bhagwan Shree Rajneesh. Despite his public admonishments for institutionalized religion, Rajneesh's teachings were a blend of Buddhism, Hinduism, and Western social and psychological schools of thought. While there are many contradictions in what he preached, some of the consistent tenets are the quest for enlightenment, individualism, sexual openness, and meditation. Rajneesh, who changed his name several times, anointed his followers as *sannyas,* who thereafter took on new identities and were given a necklace with his picture to wear (a *mala*) and dressed in orange robes.

While working as a professor at Jabalpur University in the 1950s and 1960s, Rajneesh spread his ideas through lectures and meditation instruction. He developed a significant following and formed the Life Awakening Movement (LAM), which provided significant financial support for his lectures and classes. LAM subsequently evolved into the Neo-Sannyas International Movement, which funded the creation of an ashram in Poona, India, that drew thousands of visitors a year. However, amid tension with Delhi over allegations of the involvement of some sannyas in prostitution, drug use, and trafficking, Rajneesh moved to establish a commune in Antelope, Oregon, in 1981.

In the United States, Rajneesh's secretary, Sheela Silverman, known as Ma Anand Sheela, purchased a 64,000-acre plot, where the "Rancho Rajneesh" was established to run the group's day-to-day operations. The new commune violated zoning laws, which triggered a series of legal battles with county and state officials. At first, the Rajneeshees attempted to use existing legislative statutes to gain recognition of their city, which included a police station, airfield, and public transportation system (the Rajneeshpuram), and then started to bus in homeless men to vote for one of their own as county commissioner.

Unsuccessful, the Rajneeshees turned to intimidation tactics and, finally, to violence. The group attempted to poison county officials, set fire to Wasco County Planning Department buildings, and conspired to assassinate the U.S. attorney for the District of Oregon, Charles Turner. However, the cult is most well known for conducting the first and largest act of bioterrorism on American soil. Undertaken in 1984, this attack involved the contamination of several restaurant salad bars located in the Dalles with salmonella. Although no one was killed, over 700 people fell ill. Federal authorities subsequently issued warrants for the group's leaders, including Sheela and Rajneesh. The latter was arrested while attempting to flee the country in his private jet, fined $400,000, and deported; the former was sentenced to two years in prison. In the wake of their detentions, the commune quickly dissolved. Rajneesh returned to Poona where he set up the Osho International Meditation Resort and continued instructing and lecturing until his death in 1990.

Further Reading

Carter, Lewis F. *Charisma and Control in Rajneeshpuram: A Community without Shared Values.* New York: Cambridge University Press, 1990.
Gordon, James S. *The Golden Guru: Bhagwan Shree Rajneesh.* New York: Penguin, 1988.
McCormick, Win, ed. *The Rajneesh Chronicles: The True Story of the Cult That Unleashed the First Act of Bioterrorism on U.S. Soil.* Portland, OR: Tin House Books, 2010.
Zaitz, Les. "Rajneeshees in Oregon: The Untold Story." *The Oregonian,* April 14, 2011.

Michael McBride

BIN AL-SHIBH, RAMZI

Ramzi bin al-Shibh was one of the chief planners of the September 11 attacks in the United States. He was an active member of the Hamburg Cell. Frustrated by his inability to obtain a visa to participate in the September 11 attacks, bin al-Shibh stayed in Hamburg, Germany, where he continued to provide logistical support for the conspirators until the eve of the attack.

Bin al-Shibh was a Yemeni. He was born on May 1, 1972, in Ghayl Bawazir in the province of Hadramaut, Yemen. His father was a merchant. The family moved to the city of Sana'a in northern Yemen when bin al-Shibh was a small boy. His father died in 1987 when his son was 16. Bin al-Shibh was an enthusiastic child, and from the beginning he was more religious than the rest of his family. After finishing his schooling, he began working as a messenger boy at the International Bank of Yemen. For a time he studied at a business school before deciding to leave Yemen. In 1995 he applied for a U.S. visa, but his application was turned down. Determined to leave Yemen, bin al-Shibh then traveled to Germany, where he claimed to be a Sudanese citizen seeking political asylum, using the name Ramzi Omar. German authorities were suspicious of his claim for political asylum, and it was initially turned down. Germany received more than 100,000 political asylum seekers annually, most wanting access to Germany's generous welfare system that would guarantee free health care and money for food and lodging almost indefinitely. Bin al-Shibh spent two years at a special camp, the so-called Container Camp, awaiting his appeal. During the period pending the appeal of his asylum claim, he joined the al-Quds Mosque in Hamburg, where he met Mohamed Atta and other Islamist militants. After his appeal was denied by the German government, bin al-Shibh returned to Yemen in 1997. Shortly thereafter, he returned to Germany, this time using his true name. This time, bin al-Shibh enrolled in a school in Hamburg, although academic problems led to his expulsion in September 1998.

Bin al-Shibh was an active member of the Hamburg Cell. There he was known by associates as Omar. He roomed with Atta and Marwan al-Shehhi beginning in 1998. In the summer of 1998, bin al-Shibh traveled to Afghanistan for special training at one of Al Qaeda's camps. He was obviously a top student because leaders of Al Qaeda selected him for a special mission. A fellow recruit testified that bin al-Shibh had extensive contact with Osama bin Laden while in Afghanistan. Along with Atta, Ziad Jarrah, and al-Shehhi, he was recruited by bin Laden for a special martyrdom mission. Mohammed Atef, the military commander of Al Qaeda, gave them a briefing on the outlines of the September 11 plot. After returning to Germany, bin al-Shibh joined with Atta and al-Shehhi in working at a warehouse packing computers for shipping.

Bin al-Shibh's personality and abilities made him one of the leaders of the Hamburg Cell. He became one of the chief recruiters for the Hamburg Cell because he was better liked and more influential in the Muslim community than Atta. Bin al-Shibh also traveled extensively throughout Germany and was able to recruit others for the Hamburg Cell.

Bin al-Shibh also served as the cheerleader for the Hamburg Cell. He gathered cassette tapes of jihad activities in Chechnya, Bosnia, and Kosovo and played them to Muslim audiences all over Hamburg. The longer he was active in the cell, the more militant his beliefs became. He believed that the highest attainment in life was to die for the jihad. Only bin al-Shibh's inability to obtain a visa prevented him from joining Atta's suicide team on September 11. Four times he sought a visa—three times in Berlin and once in Yemen. Bin al-Shibh was turned down each time because consular officers believed that, being Yemeni, he might be an unlawful immigrant. He even tried using other people's names but with no luck. Instead, bin al-Shibh provided logistical support and money from Germany. He kept in close contact with Atta and served as his banker. He also protected the men of the Hamburg Cell by keeping them registered as students. Bin al-Shibh was the only member of the Hamburg Cell to attend the January 2000 Kuala Lumpur meeting where midlevel Al Qaeda operatives discussed future operations.

Another of bin al-Shibh's responsibilities was recruitment. He recruited Zacarias Moussaoui into Al Qaeda. Bin al-Shibh gave Moussaoui funds for pilot training in the United States. Although Moussaoui was not a part of the Hamburg Cell and the September 11 plot, he was being considered for a future martyrdom mission.

When bin al-Shibh finally learned the date of the attack on the World Trade Center complex, the Pentagon, and the U.S. Capitol or White House in late August 2001, he began to shut down operations in Germany. He was aware that all members and anyone affiliated with the Hamburg Cell would be subject to arrest. In early September bin al-Shibh fled to Pakistan, where he thought he would be safe from American reprisal.

Bin al-Shibh was captured in an apartment complex in Karachi, Pakistan, on September 11, 2002, after a gunfight with Pakistani security forces. On September 16,

2002, the Pakistani government turned bin al-Shibh over to American security officials, who moved him out of Pakistan to a secure interrogation site. Since his arrest, bin al-Shibh has been cooperative in providing intelligence on the nuclear, biological, and chemical capabilities of Al Qaeda, as well as on how the Al Qaeda organization functions. Despite this cooperation, bin al-Shibh has expressed no regrets about his involvement with Al Qaeda; had he not been captured, he would likely still be an active participant. In August 2006 bin al-Shibh was transferred to the Guantánamo Bay Detainment Camp with 13 other high-profile terrorist suspects. One of five "enemy combatants" originally slated for trial in New York City in 2010 before the controversial plan was dropped, he remains in custody at Guantánamo Bay.

See also: Al Qaeda; Atta, Mohamed; Hamburg Cell; Jarrah, Ziad Samir; Mohammed, Khalid Sheikh; Moussaoui, Zacarias; Shehhi, Marwan Yousef Muhammed Rashid Lekrab al-

Further Reading

Fouda, Yosri, and Nick Fielding. *Masterminds of Terror: The Truth behind the Most Devastating Terrorist Attack the World Has Ever Seen.* New York: Arcade, 2003.
McDermott, Terry. *Perfect Soldiers: The Hijackers: Who They Were, Why They Did It.* New York: HarperCollins, 2005.
Posner, Gerald. *Why America Slept: The Failure to Prevent 9/11.* New York: Ballantine Books, 2003.

Stephen E. Atkins

BIN HUSIN, AZAHARI

Azahari bin Husin was one of Jemaah Islamiyah's (JI) top explosives experts. He was behind some of the bloodiest acts of terrorism in Southeast Asia in recent years—for which he was given the title "Demolition Man"—and worked closely with Noordin Mohamed Top, the self-defined head of JI's pro-bombing faction. He was killed in 2005.

Bin Husin was born to a middle-class family in Malaysia on September 14, 1957. He attended high school in Australia before returning to his home country, where he earned a university degree in engineering. In the late 1980s, bin Husin traveled to Great Britain and enrolled in a doctoral program at the University of Reading. He successfully graduated in 1990, writing his dissertation on property prices in Malaysia. According to a statement released by the university in October 2005, "when Azahari Husin was at Reading, he appeared to be a completely normal student."

Having secured his doctorate, bin Husin returned once again to Malaysia to teach at Universiti Teknologi Malaysia (UTM). During this time he became more closely involved with radical Islamist elements in the country, including Top, a student at UTM and a future key financier and recruiter for JI. In 1999 bin Husin traveled to Kandahar, Afghanistan, to receive terrorist training at an Al Qaeda camp. The trip was arranged by Riduan Isamuddin, otherwise known as

Hambali, who was Osama bin Laden's principal liaison between South and Southeast Asia.

In 2000 bin Husin flew back to Malaysia and reconnected with Top. The two fled to Indonesia in early 2000 after the government began to crack down on radical Islamist elements in the country as a response to the 9/11 terrorist attacks in the United States. In exile, Top and bin Husin were instrumental in developing an operational cell that would be tied to several high-profile acts of terrorism over the next several years. These included the 2002 bombings of nightclubs in Bali (over 200 killed), the 2003 bombing of the JW Marriott Hotel in Jakarta (12 killed), and the 2004 bombing of the Australian embassy (24 killed).

Bin Husin and Top are also credited with expanding the use of suicide terrorism in Southeast Asia through their dissemination of handbooks extolling the virtues of martyrdom in furthering the jihadist cause across the region. They also disseminated instructional videos on how to prepare explosives and perform tasks associated with self-sacrifice, such as ritual prayers and the narration of a final will and testament.

Following the Australian embassy bombing, bin Husin and Top became progressively sidelined within JI, largely because this attack had mostly killed Muslims and triggered a major popular backlash against the movement. The two increasingly started to operate on their own, portraying themselves as the true leaders of the Islamist cause in Southeast Asia.

On November 9, 2005, Indonesia's elite counterterrorism unit, Densus-88, traced bin Husin to a safe house in Malang, East Java. The police surrounded the building and ordered its occupants to surrender. Rather than give themselves up, however, bin Husin and two others blew themselves up. Following his death, Top assumed the mantle as the head of JI's so-called pro-bombing faction, orchestrating the 2005 bombings in Bali before he himself was killed in 2009.

See also: Australian Embassy (Jakarta) Bombing; Bali Bombings (2002); Jemaah Islamiyah (JI); Marriott Hotel (Jakarta) Bombing (2003); Marriott Hotel (Jakarta) Bombing (2009); Top, Noordin Mohamed

Further Reading

Collins, Nancy-Amelia. "Top Asian Terrorist Leader Dead in Indonesia." Voice of America, November 10, 2005. Online at VOAnews.com, accessed December 2006

International Crisis Group. *Terrorism in Indonesia: Noordin's Networks.* Asia Report no. 114, May 5, 2006.

Kirkup, James. "Demolition Man and Money Man Hunted." *The Scotsman,* October 3, 2005.

"Leading Bali Bomb Suspect Reported Shot Dead." ABC National Radio (Sydney), November 9, 2005.

Retnowati, Heri. "4-Key Asian Militant Dead, but Threat Remains." *Reuters,* November 9, 2005. http://today.reuters.com/news/articlebusiness.aspx?type=tnBusinessNews&storyID=nJAK121200&imageid=&cap&from=business, accessed December 2006.

Horacio Trujillo

BIN LADEN, OSAMA

Osama bin Laden was an Islamist extremist and, as head of Al Qaeda, the world's most notorious terrorist leader. He was directly linked to the notorious September 11, 2001, suicide attacks on the United States as well as numerous other acts of terrorism across the globe.

Born on March 10, 1957, in Riyadh, Saudi Arabia, Usamah bin Muhammad bin 'Awa bin Ladin was most usually known as Osama bin Laden. His father, Muhammad bin Awdah bin Laden, was a highly successful and immensely wealthy construction manager from Yemen who was closely linked to the Saudi royal family and whose business ventures included the development of major highways and the reconstruction of the Muslim holy cities of Medina and Mecca. Bin Laden Sr., who was strongly opposed to Israel, reportedly had 21 wives and fathered 54 children. Osama was the 17th son and only child of his father's 10th wife, Hamida al-Attas. Bin Laden Sr. died in a plane crash in 1967, leaving behind an estate reported at $11 billion. Of this, an estimated $40 to $50 million went to Osama.

The family moved a number of times but settled in Jeddah, Saudi Arabia. There, bin Laden attended al-Thagr, the city's top school. He had some exposure to the West through vacations in Sweden and a summer program in English at Oxford University. At age 17, bin Laden married a 14-year-old cousin of his mother and in 1977 enrolled at King Abdulaziz University (now King Abdul Aziz University) in Jeddah, where he majored in economics and business management. Bin Laden was an indifferent student, but this was at least in part because of time spent in the family construction business. He left school altogether in 1979, evidently planning to work in the family's Saudi Binladen Group that then employed 37,000 people and was valued at some $5 billion. This plan was apparently blocked by his older brothers.

As a boy, bin Laden had received religious training in Sunni Islam, but around 1973 he began developing a more fundamentalist bent and interest in the Muslim Brotherhood (MB). This orientation, which was apparently strong enough to alarm other family members, was strongly reinforced by the influence of two key individuals: Muhammad Qutb, brother of the MB's martyred leader Sayyid Qutb and his mentor in religious study at the university; and Sheikh Abdullah Yussuf Azzam, a proponent of jihad (holy war).

Two events were also to have a profound impact on bin Laden. The first was the seizure of the Grand Mosque in Mecca by Islamists led by Juhayman ibn-Muhammad-ibn Sayf al-Otaibi and the subsequent martyrdom of the group. The incident impressed on bin Laden that those who truly believed in their religious convictions were not only imbued with qualities of absolute loyalty but, more tellingly, willing to contemplate self-sacrifice if circumstances required it. The second, and arguably more significant, event was the Soviet Union's invasion and subsequent occupation of Afghanistan between 1979 and 1989. It is safe to say that this episode marked probably the most important turning point in bin Laden's life.

Following Moscow's incursion into Afghanistan in 1979, bin Laden traveled to Pakistan, where he met with Afghan leaders Burhanuddin Rabbani and Abdul Rasul Sayyaf. He then returned to Saudi Arabia, where he recruited some 10,000 volunteers to form the bedrock of a resistance movement—the mujahideen (freedom fighters, holy warriors)—dedicated to driving the Soviets out of Afghanistan. Bin Laden also procured a wide array of construction equipment to build roads, tunnels, shelters, hospitals, and other infrastructure for assisting the rebel campaign.

Bin Laden's organizational skills and financial assets were probably his most important contribution to the Afghan resistance, however. He worked actively with Sheikh Abdullah Yussuf Azzam to train mujahideen recruits, providing much of the funding for this from his personal fortune as well as supplemental financial contacts he tapped in Saudi Arabia. A centerpiece of this mobilization effort was the Mujahideen Services Bureau, which he and Azzam established in conjunction with Pakistan's Inter-Services Intelligence (ISI) Directorate. Between 1985 and 1989, approximately 150,000 soldiers entered Afghanistan after "graduating" from camps run by the bureau.

In 1986 bin Laden, now having relocated to Peshawar, Pakistan, joined a mujahideen field unit and took part in actual combat. Notably, this included the 1987 Battle of the Lion's Den near Jaji. This experience helped to greatly enhance bin Laden's prestige and standing among jihadis fighting in Afghanistan.

The mysterious assassination of Azzam on November 14, 1989, opened the way for bin Laden to assume a greater role in extremist Islamic politics. While he agreed with Azzam about the need for jihad against the enemies of Islam, bin Laden carried this philosophy a step further in insisting that it should be extended to a holy war on behalf of Muslims around the world. It was this objective that was to define the ideology and subsequent direction of the Al Qaeda ("the Base") movement that he had founded with Azzam in the fall of 1989 (and that he now exclusively led after the death of the latter).

With the end of the Soviet-Afghan War, bin Laden returned to Saudi Arabia, where he was universally acclaimed as a hero by both the people and the government. Bin Laden subsequently approached Prince Turki al-Faisal, head of the Saudi intelligence services, offering to lead a guerrilla war to overthrow the Marxist government of South Yemen. Turki, however, rejected the suggestion, after which bin Laden settled in Jeddah and worked in the family construction business. All this changed after Saddam Hussein sent his army into Kuwait in August 1990.

The Iraqi military takeover of Kuwait directly threatened Saudi Arabia, and bin Laden once again offered his services to the government—this time with an entreaty to recruit as many as 12,000 men to defend the kingdom. As before, Riyadh rebuffed his overture and instead turned to the United States and other allied powers to liberate Kuwait using Saudi Arabia as a base from which to launch a counteroffensive. Incensed at both the rejection of his services and the injection of hundreds of thousands of infidels into his homeland, bin Laden bitterly denounced the Saudi regime and demanded that all foreign troops leave at once. His vocal opposition to Riyadh brought him a brief period of house arrest.

Following the end of the Gulf War, bin Laden left Saudi Arabia and together with his family moved first to Pakistan and then to Sudan, where he owned property around Khartoum. He also transferred a considerable degree of money to the East African country, investing in a series of successful business ventures, including a road-building company, which added considerably to his personal fortune.

From Sudan, bin Laden mounted increasingly acerbic attacks on the Saudi royal family and the kingdom's religious leadership, accusing them of being false Muslims. These verbal assaults eventually led Riyadh to strip him of his citizenship (April 1994) in addition to freezing those financial assets he still retained in the kingdom (by now his share of the family business was estimated to be about $7 million).

It was at this time that bin Laden started to concertedly organize the terrorist activities of Al Qaeda and exhort Muslims from around the world to join in a defensive jihad directed against the West and tyrannical secular Islamic governments. Bin Laden established a jihadist training camp at Soba, north of Khartoum; sent advisors and equipment to assist rebels fighting Western peacekeeping troops that had been dispatched to Somalia following the fall of the Siad Barre dictatorship in 1991; and commenced terrorist activities against American interests in Saudi Arabia. As part of the latter endeavor, he orchestrated a car bombing in Riyadh on November 13, 1995, that killed 5 Americans and 1 Saudi and wounded 60 others. Other similar actions followed.

Largely as a result of mounting Saudi and U.S. pressure, the Sudanese government asked bin Laden to leave the country in 1996, after which he relocated to Afghanistan. The South Asian state was a natural choice from which to base his future activities. The Islamic fundamentalist Taliban had come to power, and bin Laden had forged a close relationship with its head, Mullah Mohammad Omar. Although there was some unease among certain elements within the Taliban leadership over the possible consequences of hosting a by now internationally acknowledged terrorist, scruples were quickly overcome by bin Laden's promises of financial assistance and contacts in the Arab world. The Taliban subsequently permitted him to establish a network of training camps across the country. The alliance was sealed when bin Laden ordered Al Qaeda to assist Omar's regime in repelling the Northern Alliance (NA) forces of General Ahmed Shah Massoud.

Now firmly ensconced in Afghanistan, bin Laden began planning a series of attacks against the perceived worldwide enemies of Islam. His principal target was the United States, and on August 23, 1996, he issued a call for jihad against the Americans for their presence in Saudi Arabia. Two years later he broadened this message in the now-infamous "Khost fatwa" that urged Muslims worldwide to kill Americans and Jews whenever and wherever they were able. The double suicide bombings of Washington's embassies in Kenya and Tanzania, which collectively killed over 200 and injured 4,000, followed in August of that year.

It is thought that arrangements for the September 11, 2001 (9/11), strikes on the United States also started around this time. The plan, which was to involve the simultaneous hijacking of several commercial airliners that would then be flown into prominent buildings in New York City, northern Virginia, and

Washington, D.C., was hatched by Khalid Sheikh Mohammed and marked the zenith of Al Qaeda aggression against America.

Bin Laden approved the 9/11 operation in the expectation that, if successful, it would trigger a vigorous and unconstrained U.S. response that would, in turn, produce an outpouring of support for his cause from within the Arab world. The first assumption proved correct. Following the attacks on the World Trade Center and Pentagon, Washington demanded that the Taliban turn over bin Laden and take action against Al Qaeda. When Omar and his coleaders refused, U.S. forces, assisted by an international coalition made up largely (but not exclusively) of other Western nations, invaded Afghanistan, joined with the Northern Alliance, and drove the Taliban from power. The second assumption, however—that a forceful American response would bring a Muslim backlash—proved false, and indeed, for a certain period of time, the United States enjoyed an unprecedented degree of support and sympathy from Islamic and non-Islamic states alike.

After the fall of the Taliban, bin Laden retreated into his stronghold in Tora Bora, a cave complex in the White Mountains of eastern Afghanistan, where he remained until December 2001. Efforts to capture him and his followers were botched, and he fled the country along with his second in command, Ayman al-Zawahiri. Despite a reward of $50 million for his arrest—dead or alive—bin Laden continued to thwart efforts to bring him to justice for a decade. He was eventually tracked to a compound at Abbottabad, just outside the Pakistani capital. On May 2, 2011, American commandos from the elite Sea, Air, and Land (SEAL) Team Six stormed the complex and shot bin Laden in the head; his body was seized and later buried at sea. It remains unclear whether the Al Qaeda chief was deliberately executed or killed in an exchange of fire.

Although bin Laden's death was welcomed around the world, it severely strained Washington's relations with the Pakistani government, which, because it had been given no advance notice of the operation, saw the raid as an unacceptable violation of national sovereignty. Further fueling tensions has been widespread speculation that bin Laden had been living in Abbottabad with the knowledge, if not the direct protection, of Islamabad's ISI. Al-Zawahiri was appointed the new leader of Al Qaeda in June 2011.

See also: Al Qaeda; September 11 (2001); Taliban; U.S. Embassy (East Africa) Bombings; Zawahiri, Ayman al-

Further Reading

Atkins, Stephen E. *The 9/11 Encyclopedia.* Westport, CT: Praeger Security International, 2008.

Bergen, Peter L. *Holy War, Inc.: Inside the Secret World of Osama bin Laden.* New York: Touchstone, 2002.

Bergen, Peter L. *Manhunt: The Ten-Year Search for Bin Laden: From 9/11 to Abbottabad.* New York: Random House, 2012.

Bergen, Peter L. *The Osama bin Laden I Know: An Oral History of al Qaeda's Leader.* New York: Free Press, 2006.

Callianan, Rory. "New Faces Mask Same Terrorist Threat." *Weekend Australian,* May 7–8, 2011.

Esposito, John L. *Unholy War.* New York: Oxford University Press, 2002.

Hon, Chua Chin. "Osama Killed." *Straits Times,* May 3, 2011.

"How Courier Led CIA to Osama." *Straits Times,* May 4, 2011.

Randal, Jonathan. *Osama: The Making of a Terrorist.* New York: Knopf, 2004.

Scheuer, Michael. *Through Our Enemies' Eyes: Osama bin Laden, Radical Islam and the Future of America.* Dulles, VA: Brassey's, 2006.

Shane, Scott. "Qaeda Chooses Chief and U.S. Cites His Flaws." *New York Times,* June 17, 2011.

Zuhur, Sherifa. *A Hundred Osamas: Islamist Threats and the Future of Counterinsurgency.* Carlisle Barracks, PA: Strategic Studies Institute, U.S. Army War College, 2006.

Harry Raymond Hueston and Spencer C. Tucker

BIRMINGHAM PUB BOMBINGS

Prior to the suicide attacks on the Underground and a local bus in London on July 7, 2005, which killed 52 people, the greatest previous loss of life in a terrorist attack on the British mainland occurred in Birmingham on November 21, 1974. During the evening of that day a total of seven improvised explosive devices (IEDs) planted by the Provisional Irish Republican Army (PIRA) went off in public buildings in the Birmingham city center.

The two most powerful IEDs were left in public houses (pubs) and exploded without warning within minutes of each other. The first was at the Mulberry Bush, the second at the Tavern in the Town, located only a short distance away. Twenty-one people were killed, and over 180 were injured in the twin bombings. A warning of the impending attacks had been phoned to a local newspaper, stating the IEDs had been placed in the Rotunda, an office block that was the highest building in the city. Six minutes later, as police were clearing the building, the bombs went off in the two pubs. Public outrage caused PIRA to try to distance itself from the explosions, with the group's leadership denying that it sanctioned indiscriminate attacks, claiming instead that the IEDs had been detonated by a hitherto-unknown organization, Red Flag 74 (which had called in the Rotunda warning). It took a full 11 years before PIRA eventually acknowledged responsibility for the bombings.

In the immediate aftermath of the attacks a groundswell of anger swept across Britain, and many innocent members of the Irish community were verbally threatened and physically assaulted. In Birmingham itself some factories were forced to close as a result of violence between English and Irish workers.

Another consequence of the bombings was the introduction of emergency legislation in the guise of the Prevention of Terrorism Act of 1974, which was replaced by the Prevention of Terrorism (Temporary Provisions) Act two years later. These statutes, which Parliament had to renew on an annual basis, gave the police the right to arrest, detain, and question individuals over a period of days if they were suspected of being involved in the commission, preparation, or instigation of an act of terrorism on the British mainland. They remained in force until the passage of permanent legislation—the Terrorism Act—in 2000.

Six people were eventually convicted for carrying out the Birmingham bombings and in August 1975 were sentenced to life imprisonment. Throughout their

Firemen search the debris of one of two pubs in the center of Birmingham, England, that was destroyed by bombs in November 1974. The blasts, which killed 21 and injured over 180, were the work of the Provisional Irish Republican Army (PIRA). (AP/Wide World Photos)

trial and for many years afterward, the prosecution's evidence was strongly challenged, and doubts were raised as to whether the right people had been jailed. Eventually, after two appeals, the convictions were quashed as a miscarriage of justice, and all six were released from prison in March 1991 after serving 16 years.

See also: Provisional Irish Republican Army (PIRA)

Further Reading

Gibson, Brian. *The Birmingham Bombs.* London: Barry Rose, 1976.
McGladdery, Gary. *The Provisional IRA in England: The Bombing Campaign 1973–1997.* Dublin: Irish Academic Press, 2006.
Mullin, Chris. *An Error of Judgment: The Truth about the Birmingham Bombings.* London: Chatto and Windus, 1986.

Lindsay Clutterbuck

BISHOPSGATE BOMBING

On April 24, 1993, the Provisional Irish Republican Army (PIRA, or the "Provos") detonated a large vehicle-borne improvised explosive device (VBIED) in Bishopsgate—the heart of the City of London's financial district. The attack was integral to the group's so-called English Campaign and was meant to inflict large-scale economic harm in an effort to drive the British government to the negotiating table. The explosion killed 1, injured 44, and caused an estimated £350 million in damage. Buildings up to 500 meters (546 yards) away were caught in the blast, with 1.5 million square feet of office space being affected and over 500 tons of glass broken.

The device, composed of around 1,000 tons of fertilizer and similar to the one that devastated the Baltic Exchange the previous year, was packed into the back of a Ford Iveco tipper truck that had been stolen from Trafford Park in Manchester and parked outside the Hong Kong and Shanghai Bank (HKSB). A series of coded warnings were phoned in to the police that a massive bomb had been primed and that the area should be immediately cleared. The VBIED detonated at 10:25 A.M. while the police were still in the process of evacuating people. Luckily, however, it was a Saturday morning, when Bishopsgate is largely devoid of people. Most of those wounded were security guards, builders, maintenance staff, and office personnel working over the weekend. There was only one fatality—Ed Henty, a 34-year-old freelance photographer with the *News of the World*; he was killed after ignoring warnings and rushing to the scene.

PIRA claimed responsibility for the attack and in an April 29 edition of *An Phoblacht* described how the bombers had spotted and managed to exploit a breach "in the usually tight security around the City." The group leadership further called on the British government to end its futile and costly war in Ireland and "pursue the path of peace."

A month after the bombing, the British government introduced the so-called Ring of Steel initiative to enhance security in the city. Most routes into the one-square-mile area were closed or made exit-only, and armed police were stationed at the eight routes that were left open. Closed-circuit television cameras were also introduced to monitor all vehicles entering and leaving the city, including two at each entry/departure point—one to read the vehicle's license plate and one to monitor the driver and passenger.

The economic cost of the attack was initially set at £1 billion. Even though this figure was later revised to £350 million, the ensuing payouts by insurance companies triggered a crisis in the industry and nearly resulted in the collapse of the Lloyd's of London group. A scheme known as Pool Re was subsequently introduced whereby the government would act as the reinsurer of last resort for losses over £75 million. Pool Re was later to inform the development of the Terrorism Risk Insurance Act (TRIA) in the United States, instituted following the September 11, 2001, attacks in Washington and New York.

PIRA carried out a number of additional attacks that same year before declaring a unilateral cease-fire in August 1994. However this was called off in 1996 after the British government announced that it would allow Sinn Féin (the Provos' political wing) to participate in political negotiations only if the Provos committed to full disarmament. That year saw a series of bombings in mainland England, including two major attacks in London (Canary Wharf) and Manchester that almost jettisoned the entire peace process. PIRA eventually reinstated their cease-fire in

1997, paving the way for an eventual settlement in the guise of the 1998 Good Friday Agreement.

See also: Baltic Exchange Bombing; City of London Bombings (1996); Good Friday Agreement; Manchester City Bombing; Provisional Irish Republican Army (PIRA)

Further Reading

"The Bishopsgate Bomb: Police Reveal How IRA Attack Was Planned: Registration Plates Traced." *The Independent,* April 28, 1993.

Chalk, Peter, Bruce Hoffman, Robert Reville, and Anna-Britt Kasupski. *Trends in Terrorism: Threats to the United States and the Future of the Terrorism Risk Insurance Act.* Santa Monica, CA: RAND, 2005.

Coaffee, Jon. *Terrorism, Risk and the City: The Making of a Contemporary Urban Landscape.* Aldershot, UK: Ashgate, 2003.

Kelly, Owan. "The IRA Threat to the City of London." *Internet Law Book Reviews* (1986–1993). http://www.rjerrad.co.uk/law/city/irathreat.htm, accessed November 8, 2012.

"1993: IRA Bomb Devastates City of London." *BBC,* April 24 1993. *BBC on This Day.* http://news.bbc.co.uk/onthisday/hi/dates/stories/april24/newsid_25230000/2523345.stm, accessed November 8, 2012.

"1994: IRA Declares 'Complete' Ceasefire." *BBC,* August 31, 1994. *BBC on This Day.* http://news.bbc.co.uk/onthisday/hi/dates/stories/august/31/newsid_3605000/3605348.stm, accessed November 8, 2012.

Schmidt, William. "1 Dead, 40 Hurt as a Blast Rips Central London." *New York Times,* April 25, 1993.

Edward F. Mickolus

BLACK SEPTEMBER ORGANIZATION (BSO)

The Black September Organization (BSO) was a Palestinian terrorist group that was established in the autumn of 1971. It was named after the forced expulsion of the Palestine Liberation Organization (PLO) from Jordan in September 1970 (Black September). Although the BSO was alleged to be an offshoot of al-Fatah, the dominant wing of the PLO controlled by Yasser Arafat, the extent to which it was tied to the latter remains somewhat unclear. While its main founders, Salah Khalaf and Sabri al-Banna (also known as Abu Nidal), were close associates of Arafat, and despite indications that PLO funds were used to underwrite its operations, the precise extent of control or influence that Arafat or the PLO had over BSO actions has never been established. Far more apparent was the direct involvement of other militant groups in BSO's ranks, including, notably, the Popular Front for the Liberation of Palestine (PFLP).

BSO's first act took place in November 1971, when several members attacked and killed Jordanian prime minister Wasfi Tal in Cairo, Egypt. The assassination was said to be retribution for Tal's hard-line policies toward the Palestinians and the PLO's subsequent eviction from Jordan. A month later the group struck again when it unsuccessfully tried to assassinate a Jordanian ambassador. BSO was also likely responsible for two acts of sabotage—one in West Germany and the other in the Netherlands. Three months later, members of the organization hijacked

Sabena Airlines Flight 572, a Belgian jetliner that had just left Vienna en route to Tel Aviv. A daring commando raid by Israel's Sayeret Maktal resolved the crisis, leaving just one passenger dead; the Israelis killed two hijackers and took another two prisoners.

Without a doubt, BSO's most spectacular terrorist scheme unfolded during the 1972 Olympic Games in Munich. There, in front of major media networks assembled to cover the sporting event, members of the group murdered 11 Israeli athletes, 9 of whom they had previously kidnapped; one police officer was also fatally shot during an abortive hostage-rescue attempt. The killings shocked the global community and were directly responsible for a major overhaul of West Germany's counterterrorist capabilities, leading to the eventual creation of the elite Grenzschutzgruppe-9 (GSG-9), which was to play a major role in rapid-reaction operations during the 1970s.

The Munich Olympics massacre was a major coup for the BSO, projecting the PLO and the Palestinian cause for which it was fighting into the limelight of world attention. It also encouraged a wave of subsequent high-profile attacks and hijackings that were to dominate much of the European and international terrorist landscape for the next two decades.

The exposure and notoriety of the 1972 assault saw the Israelis take immediate and bold steps to crush the BSO and hunt down those responsible for the killings. Despite this pressure, the BSO managed to stage another significant attack, this time on the Saudi embassy in Khartoum, Sudan, in March 1973, which left two American diplomats and the Belgian *chargé d'affaires* dead. This was to prove the group's last main operation, however, as in the autumn of that year (around the time of the Yom Kippur War) Arafat started to strongly advocate for it to be disbanded. The following year, the PLO chairman declared a moratorium on all terrorist strikes outside Israel and the Occupied Territories (Gaza and the West Bank), which effectively marked BSO's final demise and replacement by the even more fanatical Abu Nidal Organization (ANO).

See also: al-Fatah; Arafat, Yasser; Khalaf, Salah; Munich Olympic Games Massacre; Sabena Airlines Hijacking

Further Reading

Dobson, Christopher. *Black September: Its Short, Violent History.* New York: Macmillan, 1974.
Livingstone, Neil C., and David Haley. *Inside the PLO.* New York: William Morrow, 1990.
Yodfat, Aryeh Y., and Yuval Arnon-OHannah. *PLO Strategy and Tactics.* New York: St. Martin's, 1981.

Paul G. Pierpaoli Jr.

BLOODY FRIDAY

Friday July 21, 1972, has become infamous as Bloody Friday—the day the Provisional Irish Republican Army (PIRA) planted and detonated 22 bombs in the city center of Belfast. The devices exploded in quick succession, overwhelming the ability of the police and army to respond to both false and genuine warning calls that PIRA phoned in before the attacks and to the chaos caused by the bombs themselves. Nine people were killed (four employees of Ulsterbus, two soldiers, two women, and a young boy) and 130 were injured, 77 of whom were women and children.

Thirty years later, on the anniversary of the day and as part of the wider peace process then under way, PIRA issued an acknowledgment of its responsibility for the attacks. The group stated that while "it was not our intention to kill or injure non-combatants, the reality is that on this and a number of other occasions, that was the consequence of our actions." PIRA went on to offer its "sincere apologies and condolences" for all the deaths and injuries caused by its actions.

The attacks on Bloody Friday took place following the breakdown of secret peace talks between PIRA and the secretary of state for Northern Ireland, William (Willy) Whitelaw. Declaring that the British had no genuine interest in resolving the situation in Northern Ireland, PIRA commander Sean MacStiofain declared the immediate beginning of a military offensive of the "utmost ferocity and ruthlessness." He made good on his word, with the bombings constituting the zenith of what was already a period of intense violence in the province. The yearly number of fatalities at the time—258 civilians, 108 army/paramilitary personnel (77 Republicans, 11 loyalists, 16 members of the Royal Ulster Constabulary, and 24 troops belonging to the Ulster Defence Regiment and Royal Irish Regiment)—would never be exceeded.

As a direct result of the attacks, on July 31 the British Army received the political go-ahead to implement a plan to remove the barricaded "no-go" areas set up by PIRA in the Creggan and Bogside areas of Londonderry (known collectively as Free Derry) as well as parts of Belfast itself. Code-named Motorman and involving thousands of troops, the operation proved to be a resounding success. Not only was there little resistance to the dismantling of the barricades, but the rate of PIRA bombing and shooting attacks immediately dropped and continued to decline over the next several years.

From the perspective of PIRA, the success of Motorman meant the loss of safe areas in which to plan and prepare for attacks and disseminate propaganda. Over the longer term it also deprived the group of the operational ability to maintain the type of constant, high-level military activity needed to pressure the British government and force concessions. In addition, the carnage caused by Bloody Friday made it impossible for London to meet with PIRA again. Taking all these factors into account, the events of July 21, 1972, marked a significant watershed in the fortunes of PIRA that it would take the group some years to recover from.

See also: MacStiofain, Sean; Provisional Irish Republican Army (PIRA)

Further Reading

"Bloody Friday: What Happened?" *BBC News,* July 16, 2002. http://news.bbc.co.uk/2/hi/uk_news/northern_ireland/2132219.stm.

Coogan, Tim. *The Troubles: Ireland's Ordeal 1966–1995 and the Search for Peace.* London: Hutchinson, 1995. Pp. 158–60.

Smith, M. *Fighting for Ireland? The Military Strategy of the Irish Republican Movement.* New York: Routledge, 2007.

Lindsay Clutterbuck

BLOODY SUNDAY

Bloody Sunday usually refers to January 30, 1972, the day British paratroopers fired on a peaceful, illegal civil rights march in Londonderry ("Derry"), Northern Ireland. The incident resulted in the killing of 14 civilians and the wounding of 17 others. It was the opening of a fierce new chapter in the Northern Ireland "Troubles" and is often viewed as the main trigger for the subsequent terrorist campaign of the Provisional Irish Republican Army (PIRA), which claimed the lives of 3,600 people.

A previous Bloody Sunday had occurred on November 21, 1920, an event that was part of the wider political struggle for an independent Irish republic that had begun earlier in the century. The day of violence left 31 people dead and was responsible for the United Kingdom's Government of Ireland Act. This piece of legislation set up two parliaments in Ireland: one for 6 counties, another for 26 counties. The 6 counties of Northern Ireland remained under direct British rule, and discrimination against their Catholic population was routine.

In response to ongoing persecution, a broad-based, peaceful civil rights movement formed in 1967 and called for reforms such as one vote for each citizen, equal opportunity for housing and employment, and the abolition of the Special Powers Act (which essentially enabled British police forces to act with impunity). Most of those who supported these changes were not interested in a free and united Ireland but merely wanted justice within the six northern counties. The British government and Protestant majority were reluctant to accede to these and other demands, resulting in the escalation of tension on both sides. Matters came to a head on January 30, 1972, when an estimated 30,000 people congregated in Derry to protest internment—the practice of holding political prisoners without trial.

The British government had not approved the march, and members of 1 Battalion, the Parachute Regiment (1 PARA), were dispatched to make arrests. Scuffles quickly broke out and were contained using tear gas, water cannons, and rubber bullets. At roughly 4 P.M., however, the troops began to fire on the demonstrators with live ammunition. The army claimed that the soldiers were responding to a sniper hidden in the crowd; other witnesses said the protesters were unarmed and were murdered in cold blood.

Two days after the confrontation, the British government adopted a resolution calling for a tribunal to investigate the events of the day. Lord Chief Justice Widgery was commissioned to undertake the inquiry. His report, which was produced 10 weeks later, supported the army's account. Most Irish people rejected these findings as a whitewash, claiming that Widgery was not impartial and had blithely overlooked vital pieces of forensic evidence.

An armed soldier attacks a protestor in Northern Ireland on January 30, 1972. In a horrific display of the violence that characterized the troubles in Northern Ireland, British paratroopers killed 14 civilians on a civil rights march in Derry City on what came to be known as Bloody Sunday. (Hulton Archive/Getty Images)

In the run-up to the negotiation of the Good Friday peace accord, then prime minister Tony Blair decided to open a second inquiry to reexamine Bloody Sunday. A new commission under Lord Saville was established in January 1998, which during the course of the next six years heard statements from 921 witnesses and considered over 60 volumes of written evidence. A 5,000-page report was eventually released on June 15, 2010. The probe, which cost nearly £200 million (making it one of the most expensive in British legal history), concluded that "the firing by soldiers of 1 PARA on Bloody Sunday caused the death of thirteen people and injury to a similar number, none of whom was posing a threat of causing death or injury." Lord Saville also stated that the soldiers had lost control and had concocted lies in an attempt to hide their acts.

Although there were no prosecutions—the soldiers had been granted broad protection against criminal charges and anonymity at the outset of the hearings—the Saville Inquiry was widely welcomed in Northern Ireland as a final vindication of the victims of Bloody Sunday. Prime Minister David Cameron formally apologized for the incident in June 2010, saying it was both "unjustified and unjustifiable."

See also: Good Friday Agreement; Provisional Irish Republican Army (PIRA)

Further Reading

Burns, John, and Eamon Quinn. "Cameron Says 1972 N. Ireland Killings Were 'Unjustified.'" *New York Times,* June 15, 2010.
Dermot, P. *Bloody Sunday and the Rule of Law in Northern Ireland.* London: Gill and Macmillan, 2000.
Geraghty, Tony. *The Irish War.* Washington, DC: Johns Hopkins University Press, 2000.
McCann, Eamonn. *Bloody Sunday in Derry.* Brandon, Ireland: Printing Press, 1998.
Purdie, Bob. *Politics in the Streets: The Origins of the Civil Rights Movement in Northern Ireland.* Belfast: Blackstaff, 1990.

Edward F. Mickolus

BOJINKA OPERATION

The Bojinka plot (also known as the Manila air plot) was a conspiracy engineered by Khalid Sheikh Mohammed and his nephew Ramzi Yousef. The plan was primarily aimed at bombing 12 U.S. airliners as they crossed the Pacific Ocean but also included other goals, such as assassinating President Bill Clinton and Pope John Paul II during their respective visits to Manila in November 1994 and January 1995.

Mohammed and Yousef began planning Bojinka in 1994 when both men rented an apartment in the capital and started gathering the necessary chemicals and equipment for the plane bombs. They were later joined by a third man, Abdul Hakim Murad, who had undergone terrorist training in Pakistan; Murad's role was to help purchase explosives and timing devices in the Philippines.

The aviation part of the plan called for the targeting of U.S.-flagged airlines that served routes in East or Southeast Asia. Five individuals were envisaged to carry out the attacks. Each would board one leg of the flight, assemble and place the bomb, and then exit the aircraft during the first layover. The bombs were timed to detonate as the airplane proceeded across the Pacific Ocean toward the United States. Most of the targeted flights were bound for Honolulu, Los Angeles, San Francisco, or New York. Four of the five bombers were to return to Karachi, Pakistan, while the fifth would return to Doha, Qatar. Mohammed left the Philippines for Pakistan in September 1994, and later Yousef met him in Karachi, where both men enlisted a fourth man, Wali Khan Amin Shah (also known as Usama Asmurai). Yousef and Shah returned to the Philippines to continue preparations for the operation. Yousef decided to conduct at least two trial runs for their improvised explosive device, by detonating one in a Manila movie theater on December 1, 1994, and a second one 10 days later on an actual airline flight. For the airline test, Yousef chose a Philippine Airlines 747 aircraft that was scheduled to fly from Manila to Tokyo, via Cebu. Yousef boarded the aircraft in Manila, during which time he positioned the explosive device under a passenger seat. Upon landing in Cebu, Yousef disembarked from the jet, which flew back to Manila before heading to Japan. While the Philippine Airlines aircraft was roughly 190 miles east of Okinawa, the bomb exploded, killing a 24-year-old Japanese national and injuring eight others. The pilot was able to maintain control of the aircraft and land it in nearby Naha, Okinawa. Soon after, the Philippines-based Abu Sayyaf Group (ASG) called an Associated Press office in Manila and claimed it had conducted the attack. Authorities learned about (and hence disrupted) the Bojinka/Manila air plot on January 7, 1995, when volatile explosive compounds ignited a fire in the apartment that Yousef and Murad were renting. Neighbors who witnessed smoke coming out of the unit quickly alerted security personnel, who after being denied entry called the police and fire department. Investigators subsequently discovered an assortment of items suggesting criminal behavior, including cartons of chemicals, Casio timers, and juice bottles with unknown substances inside. In addition, they found photographs of Pope John Paul II, Bibles, and confessional materials, which would later be linked to the assassination plot. Realizing their plan had been disrupted, Yousef and Murad attempted to flee the area. Although the police quickly detained the latter (who was apprehended while attempting to retrieve a laptop computer that had been left in the apartment), the former managed to escape to Pakistan. However, soon after he arrived in that country U.S. embassy officials in Islamabad received a tip that Yousef was hiding somewhere in the city; he was subsequently discovered at a guest house, where he was arrested on February 7, 1995. In 1995 Yousef, Murad, and Shah (who had fled to Malaysia) were extradited to the United States. They were charged with various terrorism-related offenses related to the Bojinka plot and prosecuted in a federal court in Manhattan. The men's trial lasted more than three months, and the jury heard from more than 50 witnesses and viewed over 1,000 exhibits. A critical part of the U.S. government's case involved the contents of the laptop that was seized in the Manila apartment in 1994; it contained airline schedules, photographs, evidence of money transfers, and a threat letter that warned of future attacks on American interests by the "Fifth Division of the Liberation Army." Ultimately, a federal jury in New York convicted the three men for their role in the Bojinka plot. Yousef was also convicted on a separate count for his role in bombing the Philippine Airlines 747 jet. The significance of the Manila/Bojinka air plot is that it would provide a conceptual blueprint for subsequent aviation plots, including the 9/11 attack in the United States and the liquid-explosives airline plot that was disrupted in the United Kingdom (August 2006). It has also been speculated that Bojinka may have provided the inspiration for other major attempted airline attacks, including those carried out by Richard Reid (the "shoe bomber") and Umar Farouk Abdulmutallab (who attempted to detonate explosives hidden in his underwear on Christmas Day, 2009).

See also: Abu Sayyaf Group (ASG); Yousef, Ramzi Ahmed

Further Reading

Bonner, Raymond. "Echoes of Early Design to Use Chemicals to Blow Up Airlines." *New York Times,* August 11, 2006.
"Disparate Pieces of Puzzle Fit Together." *Washington Post,* September 23, 2001.

Elegant, Simon. "Asia's Own Osama." *Time,* April 1, 2002.

"The Man Who Wasn't There." *Time,* February 20, 1995.

McDermott, Terry. "The Plot." *Los Angeles Times*, September 1, 2002.

McKinley, James. "Suspected Bombing Leader Indicted on Broader Charges." *New York Times,* April 1, 1995. http://www.nytimes.com/1995/04/14/nyregion/suspected-bombing-leader-indicted-on-broader-charges.html.

"Muslim Militants Threaten Ramos Vision of Summit Glory." *The Australian,* January 13, 1996.

"Plane Terror Suspects Convicted on All Counts." *CNN.com,* September 5, 1996. http://www.cnn.com/us/9609/05/terror.plot/index.html.

Ressa, Maria. "Philippines: U.S. Missed 9/11 Clues Years Ago." *CNN.com*, July 26, 2003. http://www.cnn.com/2003/WORLD/asiapcf/southeast/07/26/khalid.confession/index.html.

Spaeth, Anthony. "Rumbles in the Jungle." *Time,* March 4, 2002.

Paul Smith

BOLOGNA BASILICA BOMB PLOT

Four Moroccans and an Italian were arrested in Bologna, Italy, on August 19, 2002, on suspicion of plotting to attack the Basilica of San Petronio. The group was apprehended while videotaping the central altar and a 15th-century fresco (by Giovanni da Modena) depicting the prophet Muhammad being devoured by demons in hell. In 2001 a number of Italian Muslims had asked the Vatican to have the wall painting removed or to have the offending parts covered.

The five told police they were tourists, but Italian authorities claimed they were Moroccans who were affiliated with Al Qaeda. Prosecutor Paolo Giovagnoli further claimed that the men, all of whom were from Padua, were overheard saying, "If they don't take (the fresco) away, everything will come tumbling down." They were further accused of saying, "That which [Osama] bin Laden does is just what's needed." The conversation was allegedly spoken in Berber. Judge Diego Di Marco rejected the prosecution's case and released the five men on August 21 for lack of evidence.

The Milan daily *Corriere della Sera* had earlier reported that Islamic militants linked to the Al Qaeda network were plotting to bomb the basilica in June because of the offensive fresco. The allegations seemed to be supported by the fact that plainclothes police officers had been assigned to the church in June. The newspaper also said that the paramilitary police had been involved in a more general surveillance operation against jihadi extremists thought to be operating in Italy. These investigations had led to the arrest of nine people, seven of whom were Tunisians who were later convicted in Milan. The men were sentenced for providing logistic support to Al Qaeda recruits transiting in and out of Europe.

A confusing statement issued by interior minister, Guiseppe Pisanu, at a political rally in Sardina on the day of the Bologna arrests seemed to merge this plot with the Milan incident. He claimed that that a major terrorist attack on Italian soil had been thwarted by the preventive actions of law enforcement and intelligence officials, going on to assert that those suspected of targeting the San Petronio basilica were also intending to strike the subway in Milan. According to Pisanu, two individuals had been arrested in connection with the alleged plot, and three others had been expelled from Italy. One individual was said to still be at large, while another remained under surveillance. The Interior Ministry did not immediately confirm these details.

The Bologna incident was the latest in a string of alleged terrorist acts that had been preempted by the authorities. Prosecutor Giovagnoli later announced that nothing had turned up to indicate any link between the planned attack on the San Petronio basilica and other alleged jihadist cells based in Italy.

See also: Al Qaeda

Further Reading

Buruma, Ian. *Murder in Amsterdam: The Death of Theo van Gogh and the Limits of Tolerance.* New York: Penguin, 2006.
Vidino, Lorenzo. *Al Qaeda in Europe: The New Battleground of International Jihad.* Amherst, NY: Prometheus Books, 2006.

Donna Bassett

BOLOGNA TRAIN STATION BOMBING

On August 2, 1980, a bomb containing approximately 20 kilograms (44 pounds) of TNT exploded at Bologna Central Station, one of the principal railway hubs in Italy. The device had been hidden in a suitcase and placed in an air-conditioned waiting room crowded with passengers trying to escape the summer heat. The ensuing blast killed 85 and wounded approximately 200.

Three hours later a member of the neo-fascist Nuclei Armati Rivoluzionari (NAR, or Armed Revolutionary Nuclei) phoned a Rome newspaper and claimed responsibility for the attack. The caller said the action had been taken in retaliation for a Bologna judge's decision to try eight men in connection with the bombing of the Italicus Express from Rome to Brenner in 1974. That incident, which had been attributed to another far-right group, Ordine Nero (Black Order), had killed 12 people. The NAR spokesman also said his organization was behind the midair destruction of an Italian DC-9 on June 27, 1980; the plane crashed into the Tyrrhenian Sea, killing all 81 passengers and crew.

However, NAR was not alone in its claim of responsibility. Another caller, supposedly from the Brigate Rosse (Red Brigades), took credit for the attack, as did a third person who said he was with the Organized Communist Movements. Representatives of both groups later denied they had anything to do with the bombing.

On August 4, Italian neo-fascist Marco Affatigato was arrested in France and, after being held for questioning, was extradited to Italy. He had been on the run since 1978 and was wanted for helping Mario Tutti, a member of Ordine Nero, escape from prison. Police also sought to question Paolo Signorelli, Franco Freda, Claudio Mutti, and Stefano Delle Chiaie.

On August 5, 1980, a mass nationwide strike brought Italy to a standstill for two hours. Those participating openly expressed their outrage at the bombing and demanded that those responsible for the atrocity be rapidly brought to justice.

Sadly, this was not to be. On August 16, authorities issued an arrest warrant for Luca de Orazi. The 17-year-old neo-Nazi was charged with subversion. Raids carried out on August 29 in three Italian cities, including Rome, led to the detention of a dozen more suspects and the identification of 16 others who might have played a role in the bombing.

And yet it was a bank fraud investigation in March 1981 that ultimately led authorities to their first real break in the case. During the course of the probe, police discovered a membership list for a far-right organization called Propaganda Due. The document was found in the office of Licio Gelli, a highly successful Italian financier, alleged to have brokered arms and oil deals involving Libya, Italy, and Argentina during the 1970s.

The list contained the names of 953 people. Most were Italian, and they included military intelligence officials, 195 military officers, five ministers or ex-ministers, a party secretary, magistrates, Members of Parliament, industrialists, publishers, journalists, members of the media, bankers (including Michele Sindona and Roberto Calvi), criminals, and a host of other prominent Italian leaders. Several foreign nationals from Uruguay, Brazil, and Argentina were also mentioned. One, José López Rega, was the founder of the Argentine Anticommunist Alliance (Triple A).

In addition, authorities found a detailed paper titled "Plan for Democratic Rebirth," which outlined a strategy to install an authoritarian government in Italy. As part of this plan, it called for the suppression of trade unions, consolidation of the media for maximum control, and the rewriting of the constitution.

The scandal ultimately led to the resignation of Italian prime minister Arnaldo Forlani and his entire coalition cabinet on May 26, 1981. A police chief also shot himself, and a former minister tried to commit suicide by taking an overdose of barbiturates. The magistrates investigating the Bologna bombing concluded that members of a subversive organization, probably Propaganda Due, were responsible for the attack. They suspected that Gelli was involved and that members of the secret services who were part of his group had participated in a cover-up designed to make it impossible to discover the truth or to obtain convictions.

By this time the investigation had indeed become unduly complicated. Some of the supposed "evidence" appeared specifically designed to falsely implicate French and German neo-fascists in the attack. While a number of militants confirmed they had worked with NAR and other Italian right-wing extremists in the past, they denied having anything to do with the August bombing. Although unrelated to the Bologna attack, this line of inquiry did uncover an intricate network of connections tying European neo-fascists with narco-traffickers in South America, especially Bolivia.

Two years later Spanish police rounded up seven people suspected of involvement in the Bologna bombing. Far from clarifying matters, however, the detentions further muddied the picture. The group was widely believed to be behind an attack on a Paris synagogue on October 3, 1980, which itself was linked to a hard-line branch of the Palestinian movement, possibly related to the Abu Nidal Organization (ANO).

Meanwhile, Gelli had fled to Switzerland, where he narrowly managed to avoid capture while attempting to withdraw tens of millions of dollars from a special bank account in Geneva. He traveled to South America and was eventually arrested and extradited back to Italy in 1987. Gelli was imprisoned but in 1998 escaped while out on parole. He was tracked down to Cannes on the French Riviera and recaptured. In a new trial, the former financier was acquitted of masterminding the Bologna attack due to lack of evidence but was found guilty of deliberately hindering the investigation into the attack. Gelli received a sentence of 10 years (later reduced to 7) and was jailed along with Francesco Pazienza and two ex–Servizio per le Informazione e la Sicurrez Militarire (Military Intelligence and Security Service) officers (General Pietro Musumeci and Colonel Giuseppe Belmonte).

Many have referred to the Bologna (and Italicus Express) bombing as a subset of a much larger "strategy of tension." The aim of this supposed campaign was to destabilize society by creating adverse economic conditions, subverting law and order, and promoting social divisions. The long-term goal was to exploit the threat of violent extremism to stampede the public into demanding the abrogation of a democratically elected government and its replacement by a military or authoritarian dictatorship. This objective was allegedly to be achieved by protecting extremist right-wing organizations and, in some instances, directly participating in their attacks.

The idea of a strategy of tension has been used to explain the wave of violent attacks that engulfed Italy during the 1970s and 1980s. Authorities attributed these acts of so-called political terrorism to various radical right-wing and far-left organizations. Many of these groups, while notionally ideologically distinct, often overlapped in complex and unexpected ways, and several moved to establish mutually beneficial relationships with international arms and narcotics trafficking networks based outside Italy. This veritable witches brew of extremism and criminality led many police and security officials of the day to review materials and report in a manner that was problematic at best. Fantasy often discredited fact, disrupting investigations and creating a sort of "Great Game Preserve" where illegal entities operated with near impunity. Given this background, it is not surprising that certain aspects of the Bologna train station attack remain unclear to this day.

See also: Banca de Agricultura Bombing; Rome-Messina Train Bombing

Further Reading

Christie, Stuart. "Stefano Delle Chiaie: Portrait of a Black Terrorist." *Black Papers no. 1.* London:Anarchy Magazine/Refract Publications, 1984.

Della Porta, Donna. "Institutional Responses to Terrorism: The Italian Case." *Terrorism and Political Violence* 4, no. 4 (Winter 1992).

Furlong, Paul. "Political Terrorism in Italy: Responses, Reactions and Immobilism." In Juleit Lodge, ed., *Terrorism: A Challenge to the State.* Oxford: Martin Robertson, 1981.

Meade, Robert C., Jr. *Red Brigades: The Story of Italian Terrorism.* New York: St. Martin's, 1990.

Rodota, S. "La Risposta Dello Stato al Terrorismo: Gli Apparati." In G. Pasquino, ed., *La Prova Delle Armi.* Bologna: Il Muno, 1984.

Donna Bassett

BOMBAY BOMBINGS (1993)

On March 12, 1993, there were 13 bomb attacks across the Indian city of Bombay (Mumbai) over a period of approximately two hours. The explosives had been planted in a range of objects, including cars, motor scooters, and briefcases. At least 257 people were killed, and between 700 and 1,400 were wounded.

The first bomb, which was packed in a car, detonated at 1:28 P.M. outside the Bombay Stock Exchange. The massive blast, which rained glass and concrete onto street vendors, vehicles, and traders both inside and outside the building, resulted in 84 fatalities and at least 217 injuries, many of them serious. Almost an hour later, a second device exploded at the main branch of Air India, completely destroying the Bank of Oman, which rented space at the street level of the office tower. This attack killed 20 and wounded 87. It was rapidly followed by several other smaller bombings that targeted luxury hotels, movie theaters, hospitals, Bombay University, assorted bazaars and markets, a passport office, and a gas station next to the headquarters of a radical Hindu group. At 2:55 P.M. the most serious incident occurred when an explosion ripped through Bombay's Century Bazaar, leaving 113 dead and 227 injured.

Three additional unexploded bombs were found on March 14 and March 15 and successfully defused. The devices were hidden on three scooters and consisted of 40 pounds of Semtex linked to a chemical pencil timer delay detonation mechanism. Police later detained the owner of the motorcycles and his mechanic, both of whom were Muslims. The two men claimed they had sold the scooters for cash and were not involved in the bombings.

A brown van was subsequently found near the site of the Century Bazaar attack. The vehicle, which contained seven AK-56 rifles and four grenades, was traced to Yaqub Memon (Momen), a Muslim whom police described as a notorious drug smuggler. His brother, Ismail Memon ("Tiger" Memon), was a known member of D-Company—a major crime syndicate headed by Dawood Ibrahim, one of India's leading underworld mafia bosses.

Witnesses reported seeing a great deal of activity outside a residence linked to the Memon brothers the night before the attack. A number of people also said they had seen individuals resembling the Memon brothers enter one of the hotels that was subsequently bombed. Based on these testimonies and the discovery of the brown van, police opened an investigation into the two Memon brothers as well as Dawood—all of whom were described as subjects of particular interest.

The working theory at this stage was that the attackers were local criminals, Kashmiri jihadists, or Sikh separatists who had had received logistical help from D-Company. Although various other perpetrating parties had been postulated, including Iranian militants, members of the Liberation Tigers of Tamil Eelam, and guerrillas with the Marxist People's War Group, these were dismissed for two main reasons: Either they had largely not operated in India, or they lacked the technical experience to execute large-scale, coordinated bombings of the magnitude that occurred in Bombay.

The rationale for the attack was open to debate. Some experts believed that the bombings were carried out in response to the December 6, 1992, destruction of the Babri Mosque in Ayodhya by Hindu extremists. The series of riots that followed killed approximately 900 and wounded over 2,000, most of whom were Muslims. Others suggested that the motivation was financial, not ideological. Dawood is known to do business with Hindu crime networks, including the son of a Hindu nationalist leader. More important, perhaps, criminal syndicates like D-Company have been known to generate destabilization in the form of terrorism and riots to seek economic gains or to manipulate elections to suit their own interests.

Meanwhile, Indian authorities had made their first arrests in the case, formally charging 26-year-old Mangeshkar Gajanand Pawar and 30-year-old Piloo Khan (Tilu Khan) for planting several of the bombs that detonated on March 15. The two men had been previously arrested and convicted at least 18 times on charges including murder, attempted murder, kidnapping, extortion, and narcotics trafficking. However, before the pair could be questioned, they managed to escape after engaging the police in a shoot-out in northern Bombay.

Despite this setback, the investigation into the Memons had begun to bear fruit. On March 17, the police arrested two people who allegedly had been hired by the brothers to place and trigger the explosives. One had driven a scooter bomb and had parked it at Zaveri Bazaar. Another had positioned a car bomb at Century Bazaar. The following month India's home minister, S. B. Chaven, announced that the police had identified at least 20 underworld figures who had trained in a camp near Islamabad Airport in Pakistan and that Ibrahim Abdul Razak Memon and other family members were pivotal figures in planning the attack. According to Chaven, Ibrahim Memon had traveled to Dubai on no fewer than three occasions to meet with Dawood Ibrahim about matters specific to the bombings. Another individual tied to the operation, Dawood Mohammad Fanse, had also gone to Dubai on related matters. Following these various exchanges, a large consignment of arms and explosives had apparently been arranged and smuggled into the Raigarh District of Maharashtra on February 2–3.

It was later revealed that the men who participated in planting the bombs included a mix of criminals and terrorists. At least one was a member of the Jammu and Kashmir National Liberation Front (JKNLF). Others had ties to Jama'at-i-Islami (Jamat-e-Islami), Seva Sangh, the Students Islamic Movement of India (SIMI), or Sikh militants. It was alleged that at least one of the men, Abdul Khadar, had been in touch with a senior Pakistan High Commission official working in the consulate wing. He had allegedly connected Khadar with an Inter-Services Intelligence (ISI) official in Islamabad, Pakistan, who had in turn put him in touch with Abdur Rashid Trabi and Amir in Pakistan.

By the end of April a total of 88 suspects were being held under the Terrorism and Disruptive Activities Act. In addition, police had begun questioning film star Sanjay Dutt about his alleged ties to Dawood Ibrahim; he was also arrested that month. Over the course of the next two to three months, ongoing investigations led to the detention of 189 individuals, all of whom were charged with conspiracy. Hundreds of witnesses and 10,000 pages of statements had additionally been collected and were being examined by at least 40 lawyers.

A major break occurred in July 1994 when Yaqub was arrested in Kathmandu while consulting with his lawyer. He was extradited back to India on August 4. Following his capture, the rest of the family fled Karachi for the United Arab Emirates. Agents with Delhi's Bureau of Criminal Investigation were aware of their departure, and in a remarkable operation that lasted more than three weeks, they cornered them in Dubai. The Memons were returned to India in two groups—first, Yakub's father (Razzak), mother (Rubina), and three brothers (Essa, Yusuf, and Suleiman) and, second, his wife (Rahin) and newborn daughter. Only Tiger and Ayub Memon remained at large, both of whom have yet to be captured and remain on India's most wanted list.

On October 16, 2003, the U.S. Treasury Department designated Dawood Ibrahim as a global terrorist with links to Al Qaeda. This decision was made after evidence came to light that suggested Dawood had reached a financial agreement with Osama bin Laden allowing Al Qaeda to use the group's smuggling routes. The designation and subsequent arrest of 10 members of D-Company forced Dawood to relocate to Karachi, where he proceeded to invest in real estate, expand his global smuggling network, and venture into new business opportunities such as gambling and match fixing.

Dawood was later tied to the Bombay attacks. One of the gunmen arrested in the aftermath of the assault, Ajmal Amir Kasab, testified that D-Company had provided Lashkar-e-Taiba (LeT) with the arms and explosives used in the operation. He is currently India's most wanted man and is also the subject of an Interpol international arrest warrant. He is widely believed to still be in Karachi, although Pakistani intelligence denies any knowledge of his whereabouts.

In October 2006 Essa and Rubina Memon were convicted for complicity in the bombings and sentenced to life imprisonment. Charges against Yusuf Memon were dismissed on medical grounds, and he was sent to a hospital for treatment of chronic schizophrenia. On July 27, 2007, Yaqub Memon was sentenced to death by hanging. His execution was stayed in 2008. Three other members of the family were acquitted.

Others found guilty included Shoaib Ghansar, Asghar Mukadam, Shahnawaz Qureshi, Abdul Ghani Turk, Parvez Shaikh, Mohammed Iqbal Mohammed Yusuf Shaikh, Mohammed Farooq Pawale, Mushtaq Tarani, Zakir Hussain, Abdul Akhtar Khan, and Firoz Amani Malik. All were given life sentences. Another 18 individuals were indicted on lesser charges, receiving punishments that ranged from prison time to a variety of fines.

See also: Al Qaeda; Bombay Bombings (2003); Lashkar-e-Taiba (LeT); Mumbai Attacks (2008); Students Islamic Movement of India (SIMI)

Further Reading

Farah, Douglas. *Blood from Stones: The Secret Financial Network of Terror.* New York: Random House, 2004.

King, Gilbert. *The Most Dangerous Man in the World: Dawood Ibrahim.* New York: Penguin Books, 2004.

"1993: Bombay Hit by Devastating Bombs." *BBC,* May 12, 1993. *BBC On This Day.* http:// news.bbc.co.uk/onthisday/hi/dates/stories/march/12/newsid_4272000/4272943.stm, accessed July 24, 2011.

"A Tear for Yakub Memon." *Bist Reads Best Reads* #42, June 15, 2009. http://bistreads. blogspot.com/2009/06/tear-for-yakub-memon.html, accessed July 24, 2011.

Zaidi, Hussain S. *Black Friday: The True Story of the Bombay Bomb Blasts.* New York: Penguin Books, 2003.

Donna Bassett

BOMBAY BOMBINGS (2003)

During 2003 several high-profile bombings took place in the Indian port city of Bombay (Mumbai). The attacks collectively killed 71 and injured scores of others. The first explosion took place on January 27 in a crowded street market, injuring at least 27 people. Authorities said that the device, which contained nails, was homemade and had been planted on a bicycle that was left outside the Vile Parle railway station.

On March 13, a second, larger bomb detonated on an evening commuter train after it left the Victoria Terminus in Mulund Station. The blast killed 11, wounded at least 60, and blew the roof off of the coach near the women's compartment where the device had been hidden. Police suspected that militants with ties to the banned Students Islamic Movement of India (SIMI) were responsible, noting that the explosion took place just one day after the 10th anniversary of the deadly 1993 Bombay bombings (which killed more than 250). However, no evidence to link SIMI to the incident ever emerged. Seven years later the Anti-Terrorist Squad arrested 44-year-old W. Murtuza (Babu) for carrying out the March attack as well as the earlier one in January. He is believed to be a friend of Indian Mujahideen (IM) leader Iqbal Shahbhandari (Bhatkal).

On July 27, a third improvised explosive device (IED) was triggered on a bus near a telephone exchange in the suburb of Ghatkopar, killing 3 and wounding 40. The blast tore the roof off the vehicle, shattered windows, and damaged nearby cars. Police initially believed that militants with ties to the Pakistan-based Lashkar-e-Taiba (LeT) were behind the attack, which became the justification for a strike called by the extreme militant Shiv Sena and Bharatiya Janata parties that disrupted transportation and trading throughout the city. The authorities eventually concluded that underworld gangs linked to Dawood Ibrahim—a Muslim gangster based in Pakistan who was alleged to have financed the 1993 Bombay bombings— were behind the attacks.

Three days after the July 27 attack, Bollywood special effects artist Dilnawaz Khan, his wife and three children, and two others were killed when their house blew up. An additional 24 others were wounded. Forensic evidence showed that sticks of gelignite caused the explosion, which caused some to question whether the incident was just a horrific accident as Khan was reported to have occasionally left incendiary devices used to generate special effects at his residence. Police officials did point out, however, that it is highly irregular, and indeed improper, for explosives to be stored in a family residence. They also noted that

A car damaged in a bomb blast lies next to the Gateway of India, background, in Mumbai (formerly Bombay), India, on August 25, 2003. A series of bombings hit the city that year, collectively killing 71. (AP/Wide World Photos)

the movie industry was riddled with connections to underworld figures such as Dawood.

On August 25, at least 52 people were killed and more than 150 wounded when a pair of IEDs detonated within 15 minutes of each other during lunchtime. The bombs had been hidden in the trunks of taxis prepositioned at two locations in Bombay. The first was deposited in a car parked in front of the Taj Mahal Hotel near the Gateway of India, a popular tourist area. The site is close to the sea, and the blast was so powerful that it actually threw people into the water. The second was placed in a taxi left near the jewelry market in the Zaveri Bazaar near the Hindu Mumba Devi temple. The vehicle had been parked in front of a multistory building that contained shops on the ground floor and apartments on the upper floors. No immediate claims of responsibility were made, but some suspected militants with ties to SIMI or members of LeT were responsible for the attacks. Meanwhile, police found nine detonators on train tracks in a railway tunnel 75 miles north of Bombay. Authorities believed the target was a train taking Hindus to a religious festival. It was not clear whether the two incidents were related.

The twin bombings had an immediate and powerful impact on the Indian stock market. National shares fell by 119 points, or nearly 3 percentage points, and the rupee lost 0.15 percent against the dollar. The value of gold was also impacted, bringing to an abrupt end a five-day rally that had driven prices to their highest level in 29 months. Commenting on the situation, Chief Minister Sushil Kumar

Shinde said, "The explosions were aimed at targeting the economic activity of the city as well as Bombay as a tourist destination."

Soon after the bombings, police arrested six people in connection with the attacks: Ashrat Shafiq Mohammed Ansari, Syed Mohammed Haneef (Haneef Sayyed), his wife Fahmeeda Syed Mohammed Haneef, Zahid Patni, Mohammed Ansari Ladoowala, and Mohammed Hasan Batterywala. All were held under the Prevention of Terrorism Act and charged with carrying out the July 27 and August bombings, belonging to a proscribed organization (LeT), and conspiring to kill and damage public property.

On September 12, two men opened fire on police when the car the men were traveling in was ordered to stop near Shivaji Park. Both were shot and killed. In a subsequent search of their vehicle, police discovered detonators, explosives, and various firearms. One of the men, Abdul Rehman Aydeet (alias Naseer), was thought to be have been involved in the August 25 attacks. This suspicion was confirmed a month later during the questioning of Patni, a Dubai storekeeper and childhood friend of Ansari. During his interrogation, Patni confessed to being part of the team that carried out the two explosions. He claimed that Naseer was a principal member of the group, which called itself the Gujarat Muslim Revenge Force, and that they had all plotted with the assistance of and supervision from LeT. He agreed to turn approver in the case and provide star witness testimony.

The trial—which was to last several years—began in September 2004. In 2008 Laddoowala and Batterywala were freed for lack of evidence. Although Special Prosecutor Ujjwal Kikam challenged the decision, the Supreme Court overruled the appeal and ordered their full discharge. On July 27, 2009, Ashrat Ansari, Haneef Sayed, and Fehmeeda Sayed were convicted. On August 6, the trio was sentenced to death.

See also: Bombay Bombings (1993); Lashkar-e-Taiba (LeT); Mumbai Attacks (2008); Students Islamic Movement of India (SIMI)

Further Reading

"At Least 48 Die in Mumbai Blasts." *Rediff.com,* August 25, 2003. http://www.rediff.com/news/2003/aug/25blast.htm, accessed July 26, 2011.

"Indians Sentenced to Death over 2003 Mumbai Blasts." *Reuters,* August 6, 2009. http://www.reuters.com/article/2009/08/06/us-india-mumbai-idUSTRE5751CS20090806, accessed July 26, 2011.

"IN PICS—2003 Twin Mumbai Blasts Convicts Sentenced to Death." *WordPress.com,* August 7, 2009. http://yousob.wordpress.com/2009/08/, accessed July 26, 2011.

"2003 Mumbai Blasts Accused Get Death Sentence." *Defense India Forum,* August 6, 2009. http://defenceforumindia.com/international-politics/4100-2003-mumbai-blasts-accused-get-death-sentence.html, accessed July 26, 2011.

"2003 Mumbai Blasts: All Accused Convicted under POTA." *Indian Express,* July 27, 2009. http://www.indianexpress.com/news/2003-mumbai-blasts-all-accused-convicted-un/494619/, accessed July 26, 2011.

Donna Bassett

BRIGATE ROSSE (BR)

Brigate Rosse (BR, or the Red Brigades) was an extreme left-wing terrorist organization that was active in Italy during the 1970s and 1980s. The group was formed in 1969 and claimed responsibility for numerous bombings, assassinations, kidnappings, and robberies that were carried out to force the country's removal from NATO and to destroy the power of industrialists, who were denigrated as the "enemy of the people."

Like many other so-called fighting communist organizations of the time, BR grew out of the social turbulence of the 1960s, opposition to the Vietnam War, and the apparent failure of the New Left to hail in a new era of peace, equality, and justice. The group emerged along with a number of like-minded entities in Europe, including the German Rote Armee Fraktion (RAF), the French Action Directe (AD), and the Belgian Cellules Communistes Combattantes (CCC), all of which shared a hatred of the United States and its allies, a commitment to the violent overthrow of the bourgeois technological-military complex, and a stated allegiance to a revolutionary brotherhood committed to solidarity with liberation movements around the world.

Initially, BR confined most of its activities to the distribution of leaflets and the release of statements that attacked and criticized government policies and Italian industrialists. Although the group conducted a number of bank robberies, it did not manifest as a serious threat until 1974 when members abducted prosecutor Mario Sossi. He was subsequently freed in exchange for the release of eight BR prisoners. The success of this operation encouraged the group to adopt kidnappings as its main tactic, directed against prominent business executives, government officials, and politicians. If the BR's demands were met, the hostages were typically freed; if not, they were executed.

In 1976 BR suffered from the arrest of its two main ideologues, Renato Curcio and Alberto Franceschini. Although the former was sprung from jail, he was quickly rearrested and returned to prison. BR vowed further acts of violence if he was not immediately released and made good on this threat two years later with their most famous operation, the March 1978 seizure of Aldo Moro—a former prime minister and the reformist leader of the Christian Democratic Party. The group attempted to use him as a bargaining chip to overturn the sentences of other convicted members, but the government refused to negotiate. Eventually, after 54 days in captivity, a people's court found Moro guilty of crimes against the people and passed a verdict of death. He was subsequently shot in the back of the head, and his body was left in the trunk of the car in the center of Rome.

Moro's murder, which was widely condemned, generated a strong response from the Italian authorities. Concerted police operations led to dozens of arrests of suspected BR supporters and sympathizers, many of whom received lengthy jail terms. Curcio was also dealt with extremely harshly and after several hearings was sent to prison for over 40 years. Many other left-wing activists fled to either France or South America, with an estimated 600 leaving Italy by the end of 1980.

Despite these setbacks BR remained active, and in 1981 the group's executive committee voted to strike back with a series of audacious attacks code-named Winter of Fire. The first of these took place on December 17, when four members of the group posing as plumbers kidnapped General James Dozier, a U.S. Army staff officer and deputy commander of NATO land forces in southern Europe. Like Moro he was tried in a people's court and sentenced to death. However, before the execution could be carried out, Italian police traced his location to an apartment in Padua. A 12-man commando team from the elite Nucleo Operativo Centrale di Sicurezza (Central Security Operations Service) mounted a rescue operation and successfully freed Dozier without firing a single shot. Captured in the raid was Antonio Savasta, the top BR commander in northern Italy. While in custody he called on the group to lay down their weapons and provided more than 200 names to the authorities. His information decimated the BR, precipitating a downward spiral that, as with other left-wing terrorist movements in Europe, was compounded by the collapse of the Soviet Union and the subsequent end of the Cold War.

Although BR had effectively ceased to exist as a viable entity by 1989, smaller splinter elements have continued to carry out sporadic attacks in Italy, notably the New Red Brigades for the Construction of Combative Communists (NBR-CCC) and the Nucleus of Revolutionary Proletarian Initiative. Incidents attributed to these entities have included the May 1999 murder of Massimo D'Antona, advisor to the cabinet of Massimo D'Alema; the March 2002 killing of Marco Bingi, chief counsel to Prime Minister Silvio Berlusconi; and an April 2002 car bombing in Rome. These strikes have raised fears that the BR may be attempting to revive their organization, riding on the back of widespread popular anger over political corruption and government mismanagement of the economy.

See also: Action Directe (AD); Cellules Communistes Combattantes (CCC); Curcio, Renato; Dozier (James) Kidnapping; Moro (Aldo) Kidnapping and Murder; Rote Armee Fraktion (RAF)

Further Reading

Alexander, Yonah, and Dennis Pluchinsky. *Europe's Red Terrorists: The Fighting Communist Organizations.* London: Frank Cass, 1992.

Bartali, Roberto. "Brigata Rosse and Moro Kidnapping: Secrets and Lies." http://www.robertobartali.it/english.htm, accessed October 20, 2011.

Drake, R. "Contemporary Terrorism and the Intellectuals: Italy." In Paul Wilkinson and Alasdair Stewart, eds., *Contemporary Research on Terrorism.* Aberdeen: Aberdeen University Press, 1987.

Jamieson, Alison. "Identity and Morality in the Italian Red Brigades." *Terrorism and Political Violence* 4 (1990).

Peter Chalk

BRIGHTON BOMBING

At 2:54 A.M. on October 12, 1984, a bomb planted under the bathroom floor of Room 629 in the Grand Hotel in Brighton blew a massive hole through the top three floors of the seven-story building. The explosion left 5 people dead, injured

34, and narrowly missed killing Prime Minister Margaret Thatcher, her husband (Denis), and many of her cabinet who were at the hotel for the annual Conservative Party conference.

The bomb was placed to cause five of the hotel's eight stories to collapse. However, the building remained standing even though the central section collapsed into the basement. Eyewitnesses saw a piercing flash that lit up the entire seafront. Flying masonry ripped the heads off nearby parking meters, and one of the hotel's chimneys crashed through ceilings and floors, plunging sleeping guests into the foyer and basement.

Those killed were Anthony Berry, 58, a Member of Parliament (MP); Roberta Wakeman (who was married to the chief whip); Muriel Maclean; Jeanne Shattock; and Eric Taylor. The injured included John Wakeham, Trade Minister Norman Tebbit, and his wife (who remains paralyzed).

Thatcher had just left the bathroom to do some paperwork when the blast occurred. If it had gone off moments earlier, she would have been killed in the bathroom, which sustained massive damage. Sir Geoffrey Howe, the foreign secretary, also narrowly escaped death after leaving his sitting room, which was also decimated in the explosion.

Immediately after the bombing, Thatcher and her husband quickly changed their clothes and were escorted by security guards to a Brighton police station. They were then transferred to Sussex Police Headquarters at Lewes, where they stayed for the rest of the night. At Mrs. Thatcher's insistence the conference opened on schedule at 9:30 A.M. In the keynote speech, the prime minister omitted most of her planned attacks on the opposition Labour Party and instead focused on the bombing, which she called an inhuman, undiscriminating attempt to massacre innocent, unsuspecting men and women as well as cripple a democratically elected government. After her opening remarks, Thatcher went immediately to the Royal Sussex County Hospital to visit the injured. Four people had already died, and Maclean, who was on a drip, passed away later. Wakeham was still unconscious and remained so for several days. He had to be operated on daily for some time to save his legs, which had been badly crushed.

A Provisional Irish Republican Army (PIRA, or the "Provos") statement sent to the Press Association by the group's publicity bureau in Dublin claimed credit for bombing, castigating the "British cabinet and the Tory warmongers" and ominously declaring, "Today, we were unlucky. But remember we have only to be lucky once. You will have to be lucky always." The communiqué, which was signed by P. O'Neill, claimed that a 100-pound gelignite bomb had been used in the attack, although investigators later determined that the device was probably no more than 20 pounds in weight.

PIRA had set out to kill Thatcher because the group blamed her intransigence for the death of the Long Kesh hunger strikers in 1981. The Provos vowed never to forget this incident and repeatedly expressed their hatred for the prime minister and her Tory administration. The bombing was also a direct attempt to destroy the British government, and it remains one of PIRA's most politically significant attacks, on a par with the February 7, 1991, mortar attack on 10 Downing Street.

The Brighton attack was also highly sophisticated in terms of weapons expertise. The bomb employed a delay-timer mechanism based on technology used in home video recorders, which had become extremely popular during the 1980s. This enabled the operatives to avoid undue suspicion by planting the device months in advance, with actual detonation occurring 24 days, 6 hours, and 36 minutes later.

The technical ingenuity involved in the bomb's placement at the conference site weeks before the event, and the use of a detonation timing device powered by a computer microchip, told the British security forces and the world how sophisticated PIRA weapon construction had become. Nor was it a one-off event. The subsequent attack on the Baltic Exchange (April 10, 1992)—London's leading shipping market—was similarly planned months in advance, further underscoring the depth of PIRA's logistic planning and bomb-making capabilities.

After the bombing, Security Service (MI5) agents and Metropolitan Police Special Branch officers began to tail Patrick Joseph Magee, a resident of Belfast whose expertise in timers had been known to British authorities for many years. He had also been linked to the construction of an improvised explosive device that had been hidden in a flowerpot at the New University of Ulster at Coleraine in August 1977, a week before the planned visit of the Queen of England.

Despite this surveillance, it was not until June 1985 that police had gathered sufficient evidence to arrest Magee. He was apprehended in an apartment in Glasgow, Scotland. The raid uncovered details of a planned multipronged bombing campaign that was to have targeted British resorts during the summer of 1985. Magee and four others—Ella O'Dwyer, Martina Anderson, Gerald McDonnell, and Peter Sherry—were arrested.

It is now known that Magee checked into the Grand Hotel a month before the conference under the name of Roy Walsh, a volunteer who had been involved in the 1973 bombing of the Old Bailey court in London. He unscrewed the hardboard in the small space under the bathtub of the shower in room 629, which was within range of the prime minister's anticipated suite; inserted the bomb, wrapped in cellophane to disguise the tell-tale marzipan aroma of gelignite; and set the long-delay timer. He checked out three days later.

Sussex police pinpointed the date the package was primed and placed behind the bath panel of room 629 by matching a palm and fingerprint on the cellophane with those of the man who had checked into the hotel as Roy Walsh. The same prints were later found at the London Rubens hotel in Victoria, where a bomb was discovered and successfully defused. Incredibly, these prints matched those taken from Magee when he had been arrested for a teenage driving offence many years earlier.

On June 29, 1985, Magee was charged in a London court with the murder of those killed in the Brighton bombing. Fingerprints on a hotel registration card linked him to the hotel. Investigators disclosed that Magee had planted the bomb and had set it to explode at a time when conference delegates would be asleep.

On June 11, 1986, Magee was found guilty of murder stemming from the Brighton bombing as well as of conspiring to cause explosions. He received eight life sentences. The following day the same London court convicted O'Dwyer, Anderson,

McDonnell, and Sherry for participating in the planned attacks on British resorts. After being sentenced, Magee was transferred to Maghaberry prison in 1994. He was subsequently transferred to Long Kesh and eventually released under the terms of the 1998 Good Friday Agreement.

The Brighton bombing was part of a larger PIRA campaign that focused on hitting high-prestige targets in mainland Britain. Some of the most infamous strikes associated with the strategy, which commenced at the end of the 1970s and continued into the 1990s, included bombings of the Chelsea barracks (October 1981), Hyde and Regent's Parks (both in July 1982), Harrods department store (December 1983), the Baltic Exchange (April 1992), the City of London (April 1993), and Canary Wharf (February 1996); the assassination of Lord Mountbatten (August 1979); the Enniskillen massacre (November 1987); and the 10 Downing Street mortar attack (February 1991).

Small five- to eight-member cells conducted most of these attacks, using arms and explosives obtained from Libya. While the strategy appeared somewhat incoherent, involving a mixture of attacks on troops and civilians, the effect was deadly, far-reaching, and entirely fitting for one of the world's most experienced terrorist groups. The Provos' ability to carry out "spectaculars"—the term used to describe large-scale attacks with maximum impact and publicity exposure—not only enhanced PIRA's reputation as a real terrorist force but also, most important, provided the group with the means to target the political and economic heart of the British government.

See also: Downing Street Mortar Attack; Harrods Bombing; Mountbatten (Lord) Assassination; Provisional Irish Republican Army (PIRA); Regent's Park and Hyde Park Bombings

Further Reading

McKittrick, David, and David McVea. *Making Sense of the Troubles.* London: Penguin Books, 2000.

"1984: Tory Cabinet in Brighton Bomb Blast." *BBC,* October 12, 1984. http://news.bbc.co.uk/onthisday/hi/dates/stories/october/12/newsid_2531000/2531583.stm, accessed May 2, 2011.

Oppenheimer, A. R. *IRA: The Bombs and the Bullets: A History of Deadly Ingenuity.* Foreword by Richard English. Dublin: Irish Academic Press, 2009.

Thatcher, Margaret. *The Downing Street Years.* BBC Television Mini-Series, 1993. http://www.margaretthatcher.org/document/109119, accessed May 2, 2011.

Donna Bassett

BROOKLYN BRIDGE BOMB PLOT

On May 1, 2003, a Columbus, Ohio, trucker named Iyman Faris (alias Mohammad Rauf) pleaded guilty to plotting to destroy the Brooklyn Bridge and launch a simultaneous attack designed to derail trains near Washington, D.C. The plot was allegedly to have been carried out with direct Al Qaeda sanction and support.

Faris, born on June 4, 1969, in Pakistan-occupied Kashmir, entered the United States in 1994 on a student visa. He married Geneva Bowling in 1995 while he was working at H&M Auto in Columbus, Ohio, and obtained U.S. citizenship in 1999. He allegedly returned to Pakistan the following year. The couple later divorced amicably in April 2000.

According to court documents, Faris's first contact with Al Qaeda occurred in late 2000 when he traveled from Pakistan to Afghanistan with a longtime friend who was already an operative in the terror group. During a series of subsequent visits, Faris was apparently introduced to Osama bin Laden and at least one senior operational leader (identified only as C-2 but thought to be number 3 in Al Qaeda), who allegedly instructed Faris to assess the feasibility of conducting attacks in New York and Washington, D.C., when he returned to the United States.

While continuing his job as an independent trucker, Faris conducted surveillance in New York City to ascertain the feasibility of destroying a major bridge by cutting the suspension cables with gas cutters. He also procured equipment to conduct a second, simultaneous attack aimed at derailing a train in the Washington, D.C., area. In communications with Al Qaeda, Faris referred to the gas cutters as "gas stations" and tools for the strike on the train as "mechanics shops."

In coded messages sent to his handlers in Afghanistan via an unnamed third party in the United States, Faris said he was still trying to obtain "gas stations" and rent "mechanics shops" and was continuing to work on the project. After scouting the Brooklyn Bridge and deciding its security and structure meant the plot was unlikely to succeed, he passed along a message to Al Qaeda in early 2003 that simply said, "The weather is too hot."

In addition to scouting for the New York and Washington, D.C., attacks, Faris also carried out several other tasks for Al Qaeda. These included acting as a cash courier, providing information about ultralight aircraft as potential getaway vehicles, ordering 2,000 sleeping bags for militants based along the Afghan-Pakistani border, obtaining extensions for six airline tickets for jihadists traveling to Yemen, and delivering cell phones to Khalid Sheikh Mohammed. It was the latter who, after he was captured in early 2003, provided information on Faris and his various activities.

On March 19, 2003, two agents from the Federal Bureau of Investigation (FBI) and one antiterror officer visited Faris and confronted him with Mohammed's testimony and voice recordings intercepted from telephone calls as part of the National Security Agency's secret eavesdropping program. Faced with overwhelming evidence, Faris agreed to work as a double agent, reporting to the FBI and cooperating with ongoing federal investigations into Al Qaeda. He was ordered to leave his home in Columbus and stay at a safe house in Virginia, from where he would continue to engage in discussions with his contacts and handlers. This cooperation continued until May 1, 2003, when Faris pleaded guilty to the New York and Washington, D.C., plots. He was eventually convicted on October 28, 2003, and sentenced to 20 years in prison for conspiracy to provide material support to terrorism.

See also: Al Qaeda; Mohammed, Khalid Sheikh

Further Reading

Emerson, Steven. *Jihad Incorporated: A Guide to Militant Islam in the US*. Foreword by Peter Hoekstra. Amherst, NY: Prometheus Books, 2006.

Donna Bassett

BURGOS CAR BOMBING

Early on the morning of July 29, 2009, at around 4 A.M., a large car bomb exploded outside the Guardia Civil (Civil Guards) married quarters at their base in the northern town of Burgos. Believed to be the work of the Basque separatist terrorist organization Euskadi Ta Askatasuna (ETA), the blast tore off the front facade of the 14-story block, damaging nearby local buildings and shattering windows. The explosion left a crater 7 meters (22 feet) deep and spread wreckage hundreds of feet, including the remains of the car, which was later recovered some 230 feet from the site of the blast.

The bomb involved between 200 and 300 kilograms (440–661 pounds) of explosives and was packed in a car that authorities believed had been stolen in France. The vehicle was apparently driven across the border to the Guardia Civil barracks in Burgos, one of Spain's historic cities. The car bomb—or vehicle-borne improvised explosive device (VBIED)—was parked on wasteland at the back of the barracks. Given that this was the side of the building where the Guardia Civil and their families were asleep, and taking into account the amount of explosives and the timing of the attack, it can only be assumed that the intention was to kill en masse.

Miraculously, out of approximately 120 people asleep in the barracks block, no one was actually killed in the attack. However, the explosion wounded 48 people, 38 of whom had to be taken to the hospital, mostly with serious cuts and abrasions caused by flying shards of glass. Many of those injured were the wives and children of the Guardia Civil.

The Burgos car bomb graphically highlighted that the ETA maintained a viable and lethal capability, despite a lull in their activities since the mid-2000s. More ominously, it demonstrated a continuing intent to attack "soft" targets of opportunity where there was a realistic prospect of a high death toll.

See also: Carrero-Blanco (Luis) Assassination; Euskadi Ta Askatasuna (ETA)

Further Reading

"Dozens Injured in Spain Car Bomb Blast." *The Guardian Online*, July 29, 2009. http://www.guardian.co.uk/world/2009/jul/29/suspectedcar-bomb-explodes-spain.

"ETA Blamed for Massive Car Bomb in Burgos." *The Times Online*, July 30, 2009. http://www.timesonline.co.uk/tol/news/world/europe/article6731355.

"Spanish Barracks Hit by Car Bomb." BBC News, July 29, 2009. http://news.bbc.co.uk/1/hi/8173727.

Richard Warnes

C

CAHILL, JOE

Joe Cahill was born in May 1920 on Divis Street, West Belfast. He was a key figure in the founding of the Provisional Irish Republican Army (PIRA, or the Provos) and was once a commander of the group's Belfast Brigade. At the age of 17 he joined Na Fianna Éireann, a Republican-oriented scouting movement. In 1938 he became a volunteer in the local Clonard "C" Company of the Belfast Brigade of the Irish Republican Army (IRA) and narrowly escaped the death penalty in 1942 for the murder of Constable Patrick Murphy (largely as a result of pressure on the British government by Éire and the Vatican). Released from prison in 1949, Cahill resumed militant activities in Belfast and played a leading role in the IRA's border campaign during the 1950s.

Angered by the IRA's failure to defend Catholic areas during sectarian riots in 1969, Cahill and Billy McKee declared they would no longer take orders from their parent movement and instead pledged allegiance to a new organization, PIRA. In 1971 Cahill became the commander of the PIRA's Belfast Brigade and authorized the beginning of bombing operations against British troops deployed in Northern Ireland as well as members of the Royal Ulster Constabulary.

The following year Cahill was appointed PIRA's chief of staff and put in charge of organizing arms shipments to Northern Ireland from the United States—working in collaboration with the Northern Irish Aid Committee (NORAID)—and Colonel Muammar Qaddafi's regime in Libya. The position proved to be short-lived as in 1973 he was imprisoned for allegedly masterminding a major gunrunning operation to smuggle weapons from Libya onboard a commercial vessel known as the *Claudia*. The Cypriot-registered ship was seized in Waterford Bay with a cargo consisting of five tons of munitions, including 250 assault AK-47s, 247 Webley revolvers, 20,000 rounds of ammunition, 100 antitank mines, 600 pounds of TNT, 500 pounds of gelignite, 300 hand grenades, and 100 cases of antipersonnel mines.

After his release, Cahill devoted most of his time to political work and the organization of aid for Republican prisoners and their families. Although he served on PIRA's Army Council until as late as the 1990s, he became a strong supporter of Gerry Adams and fully endorsed the 1998 Good Friday Agreement that laid the framework for PIRA's eventual disarmament and demobilization. He died in July 2003 as a result of being exposed to asbestos while working at the Harland and Wolff shipyards in his 20s. He was 84.

See also: Adams, Gerry; Good Friday Agreement; Irish Republican Army (IRA); Provisional Irish Republican Army (PIRA)

Further Reading

Anderson, Brendan. *Joe Cahill: A Life in the IRA.* Dublin: O'Brien, 2002.
Coogan, Tim. *The Troubles. Ireland's Ordeal 1966–1995 and the Search for Peace.* London: Hutchinson, 1995.
O'Brien, Brendan. *The Long War—the IRA and Sinn Féin.* Dublin: O'Brien, 1995.

Edward F. Mickolus

CARRERO-BLANCO (LUIS) ASSASSINATION

On December 20, 1973, the Basque separatist terrorist group Euskadi Ta Askatasuna (ETA), or Basque Fatherland and Freedom, successfully assassinated the Spanish prime minister, Admiral Carrero-Blanco, with a massive bomb that detonated as his car passed. Due to his advanced age and declining health, Spanish dictator Francisco Franco had nominated Carrero-Blanco as his heir apparent, so that the ETA's assassination of the admiral had significant long-term implications.

During the 1970s, the ETA stepped up their campaign of violence in Spain, conducting a series of audacious kidnappings and bombings. These actions triggered a draconian response from the state that resulted in the death of the leading ETA member, Eustaquio Mendizabal (also known as Txikia). Partly in response to his death, the group decided to kidnap Carrero-Blanco. As planning for the operation (code-named Ogre) proceeded, however, it became apparent that due to the level of Carrero-Blanco's security, kidnapping was not a feasible option. As a result, and given his appointment as prime minister in June 1973, the ETA's higher command determined that the best course of action was an assassination.

In November 1973 an ETA commando (named Txikia in honor of the group's former leader) was dispatched to Madrid. Led by Jose Miguel Ordenana (also known as Argala), the cell rented a basement apartment at 104 Claudio Coello Street. The team quickly established that every morning at around 9:00 A.M. Carrero-Blanco attended Mass at the Catholic Church of San Francisco de Borja, leaving afterward for his office by a set route in his chauffeur-driven limousine. Consequently, from the basement they began digging a tunnel out under the road, with the intention of filling it with explosives and detonating them at the exact moment that Carrero-Blanco's car passed.

Despite numerous problems and the danger of collapse, the ETA team managed to complete the construction of a crude tunnel, which opened into a T shape, by December 17. This was filled with around 80 kilograms (176 pounds) of commercial Goma 2 Eco quarrying explosive, which was wired to a detonator on the street above. To ensure Carrero-Blanco's vehicle slowed at exactly the right location, a blocking car was double-parked at the attack site.

On December 20 at around 9:36 A.M., Carrero-Blanco's limousine slowed down at the blocking car, and Argala, disguised along with his colleagues as electricians, initiated the massive charge. The blast threw the vehicle five stories onto the church roof, killing Carrero-Blanco, his police bodyguard, Inspector Juan Antonio Bueno Fernandez, and his driver, Jose Luis Perez Mojeda. The ETA members then shouted there had been a gas explosion before using the ensuing confusion to make their escape.

The death of the hard-liner prime minister Carrero-Blanco was undoubtedly a factor in Spain's relatively peaceful transition to democracy. Nevertheless, in December 1978, as a somewhat ironic postscript to the assassination, Argala was himself killed by a booby-trapped car bomb in France.

See also: Burgos Car Bombing; Euskadi Ta Askatasuna (ETA)

Further Reading

Clark, Robert. *The Basque Insurgents: ETA 1952–1980.* Madison: University of Wisconsin Press, 1984.
Hollington, Kris. *How to Kill: The Definitive History of the Assassin.* London: Century, 2007.
Woodworth, Paddy. *Dirty War Clean Hands: ETA, the GAL and Spanish Democracy.* New Haven, CT: Yale Nota Bene, 2002.

Richard Warnes

CASABLANCA BOMBINGS

At 9:30 P.M. on May 16, 2003, five simultaneous explosions struck the city center of Casablanca in Morocco. The attacks, carried out by 14 suicide bombers, instantly killed 29 bystanders and 12 of the perpetrators (2 were arrested before they could detonate their devices); another 4 people later succumbed to their injuries. Eight of the dead were Europeans, including three Spaniards, and the rest Moroccan. Total casualties exceeded 100. The incident remains the most serious act of terrorism in the country's history.

The first, and most deadly, explosion took place at the Casa de España restaurant while people were eating dinner and playing bingo. The terrorists knifed a guard at the front door, stormed into the building, and blew themselves up. The assault resulted in 29 fatalities.

The five-star Saudi-owned Hotel Farah was hit next, leaving a guard and a porter dead. Another terrorist, who apparently became lost while trying to make his way to a Jewish cemetery, blew himself up at a fountain 150 yards from the venue, killing three Muslim civilians. Two additional bombers attacked a Jewish social center but failed to cause any casualties as the building was closed and empty (although it would have been packed the next day).

The final explosion occurred at a Jewish-owned Italian restaurant located near the Belgian consulate, killing two police officers. Speculation remains as to which of the two buildings was the intended target.

Members of Salafia Jihadia, an offshoot of the Moroccan Islamic Combatant Group (MICG), carried out the attack with the logistical and financial support of Al Qaeda. The suicide bombers were all recruited from the shanty town of Sidi Moumen, a poor suburb of Casablanca. The local leader was Mohamed Omari. He picked the targets and planned the bombings in cooperation with Abdelhaq Bentassir, the national coordinator for MICG. It appears that Abu Musab al-Zarqawi, the deceased head of Al Qaeda in Iraq (AQI), approved the operation on behalf of Al Qaeda. Working through Bentassir, he sent $50,000 to $70,000 to finance the attacks and obtained Osama bin Laden's "blessing" for the mission in a taped message.

Despite receiving two warnings that a major incident was imminent, Moroccan authorities failed to prevent the bombings. However, police moved quickly to identify and detain suspects thought to have played either a central or a peripheral role in the explosions, no doubt benefiting from information provided by the two surviving terrorists. Within 12 months more than 2,000 people had been arrested and put on trial.

In April 2008 nine of those convicted tunneled their way out of the Kenitra jail complex, north of Rabat. According to Abderrahim Mahtade, who represents a prisoner's advocacy group, one of the escapees had been sentenced to death, six had been given life sentences, and two had received 20-year terms.

Following the Casablanca attacks, which came on the heels of the Riyadh compound bombings, the U.S. Department of Homeland Security raised the American threat level to orange (high), one step below the critical threshold of red (severe).

See also: Al Qaeda; Zarqawi, Abu Musab al-

Further Reading

Finn, Peter, and Keith Richburg. "Madrid Probe Turns to Islamic Cell in Morocco." *Washington Post,* March 20, 2004. http://www.washingtonpost.com/ac2/wp-dyn/A9282-2004Mar19?language=printer, accessed August 5, 2011.
"9 Jihadis Convicted of 2003 Casablanca Bombings Escape from Jail." *Reuters,* April 7, 2008. Available online at http://patdollard.com/2008/04/9-jihadis-convicted-for-2003-casablanca-bombings-escape-prison/, accessed August 5, 2011.
"Terror Blasts Rock Casablanca." *BBC News,* May 17, 2003. http://news.bbc.co.uk/2/hi/africa/3035803.stm, accessed August 5, 2011.

Peter Chalk

CELLULES COMMUNISTES COMBATTANTES (CCC)

During the 1970s, Belgium escaped the worst excesses of terrorist violence seen in many other European countries. Most of the acts that did occur were linked to foreign organizations operating on its territory rather than domestic terrorist groups per se. For these reasons (and despite its small size), the short-lived actions of the Belgian Cellules Communistes Combattantes (CCC, or Communist Combatant Cells) had a disproportionate impact. Indeed, it was widely suggested at the time that the organization was comprised of agents provocateurs from the extreme right, but no evidence has emerged to support this allegation.

Pierre Carette, a left-wing activist and printer who had previously interacted with Action Directe (AD), the Rote Armee Fraktion, and other European "fighting communist organizations," established the CCC as a Belgian parallel. Although it did not have the roots or numbers of these more traditional groups, its first attack on Litton Data System's office, Brussels, in October 1984 came as a surprise to the Belgian authorities. There then followed a rapid series of nearly 26 bombings over the next 14 months. Attacks were directed against NATO, U.S., Belgian, and German targets and included oil pipelines, multinational headquarters, and military bases.

During this spate of violence, the CCC always gave warnings and avoided casualties. However on May 1, 1985, a van full of explosives left outside the Belgium Employers Federation exploded as two firemen approached it, killing both. The event triggered a forceful response by the Belgian authorities and led to the arrest of Carette and three leading commanders at the end of the year. Documents seized at the time of their apprehension revealed the group had been planning the assassination of various financial and political figures.

The arrest of Carette and his colleagues dealt a decisive blow to the CCC, largely because it lacked a popular support base in Belgium and was not closely tied to the wider European extreme left movement. However, its actions still resonate in a country that has historically had little direct experience of terrorism.

See also: Action Directe (AD); Rote Armee Fraktion (RAF)

Further Reading

Alexander, Yonah, and Dennis Pluchinsky. *Europe's Red Terrorists: The Fighting Communist Organisations.* London: Frank Cass, 1992.
Jenkins, Philip. "Strategy of Tension: The Belgian Terrorist Crisis 1982–1986." In E. Moxon-Browne, ed., *European Terrorism.* Aldershot, UK: Dartmouth, 1993.
Petermann, Simon. "The CCC Phenomenon in Belgium: Unbacked Terrorism." In Naomi Gal Or, ed., *Tolerating Terrorism in the West.* London: Routledge, 1991.

Richard Warnes

CENTENNIAL OLYMPIC PARK BOMBING

On July 27, 1996, an improvised explosive device (IED) bomb hidden in a knapsack detonated at the Centennial Olympic Park in Atlanta, Georgia, killing 2 people and wounding 111 others. The fatalities were Alice Hawthorne, who died in the cross-blast, and a Turkish cameraman, Melih Uzunyol, who had a heart attack while running to film the devastation. Among those injured were six state troopers and one Georgia Bureau of Investigation agent.

Bomb experts said the crudely made device, filled with masonry nails that served as shrapnel, was designed to kill. The pack used a steel plate to direct the blast and could have done more damage, but it had tipped over at some point. It was the largest pipe bomb in U.S. history, weighing in excess of 40 pounds.

Initial suspicions centered around Richard Jewell, a contract guard with AT&T, who brought the bomb to the attention of the authorities. The Justice Department formally declared on October 26 that he was not a target of investigation. On December 9, the Federal Bureau of Investigation (FBI) asked for any photographs or videotapes taken in the park on the night of the bombing and offered a $500,000 reward. The bureau also released a tape of a 911 call warning of the impending attack.

On February 21, 1997, a dynamite bomb exploded at the Otherside Lounge, a gay/lesbian bar in Atlanta's Piedmont Road neighborhood, injuring five people. A second device was found in the parking lot the next morning, where it was defused. Both were similar to an IED used to attack abortion clinics in Atlanta and Birmingham the month before, and all four bore a strong resemblance to the Centennial Park bomb.

On May 5, 1998, the FBI charged Eric Rudolph with the Birmingham clinic bombing and linked it to the Centennial Park incident, saying that the two IEDs employed in the attacks were very similar in design. The bureau offered a $1 million reward for information leading to Rudolph's arrest and placed him on the 10 Most Wanted Fugitives list. Five months later, Attorney General Janet Reno and FBI Director Louis Freeh jointly announced that Rudolph was the chief suspect in four unsolved acts of terror—the Centennial Park attack and the 1997 bombings of the Otherside Lounge and the Atlanta and Birmingham abortion clinics.

Rudolph was eventually captured on May 31, 2003. As part of a deal, Rudolph provided authorities with the location of more than 250 pounds of dynamite buried in the mountains of North Carolina. FBI agents and officers with the Alcohol, Tobacco and Firearms Bureau subsequently found the massive stash in three different locations near populated areas.

Rudolph's justification for the Centennial Park bombing was political. In a statement made on April 13, 2005, he asserted, "In the summer of 1996, the world converged upon Atlanta for the Olympic Games. Under the protection and auspices of the regime in Washington millions of people came to celebrate the ideals of global socialism. . . . The purpose of the attack on July 27 was to confound, anger, and embarrass the Washington government in the eyes of the world for its abominable sanctioning of abortion on demand."

Rudolph later claimed that he had intended to carry out a much larger bombing campaign at the Atlanta Games site, involving five IEDs detonated over several days. He maintained that he intended to make phone calls well in advance of each explosion, leaving only armed uniformed government personnel exposed to potential injury. When asked why he had not proceeded with the more elaborate attack, Rudolph responded that poor planning on his part made it impossible.

On August 21, 2005, after years on the run, Rudolph was sentenced by a federal judge to four consecutive life sentences plus $2.3 million in damages for the Centennial Park, Otherside Lounge, and Atlanta and Birmingham abortion clinic bombings. Before he was sentenced, he apologized to the victims of the Olympic Games attack. Rudolph was sent to the ADX Florence Supermax federal prison, where he spends 22-1/2 hours per day alone in his 80-square-foot cell.

See also: Atlanta Abortion Clinic Bombings; Rudolph, Eric

Further Reading

Hillard, Robert L., and Michael C. Keith. *Waves of Rancor: Tuning In the Radical Right.* Armonk, NY: M. E. Sharpe, 1999.
Schuster, Henry (with Charles Stone). *Hunting Eric Rudolph.* New York: Penguin, 2005.

Donna Bassett

CENTRAL BANK (COLOMBO) BOMBING

On January 31, 1996, a 400-kilogram (881-pound) truck bomb was detonated at the 11-story Central Bank complex in Colombo, Sri Lanka. At least 90 individuals (some sources say 91, others 96) were killed, and more than 1,400 wounded, and huge reserves of Sri Lankan currency and gold were buried by the blast. At least 400 cars were also damaged, as were several nearby buildings, including the twin towers of the Colombo's World Trade Centre, the Mercantile Building, the Lighthouse Clock Tower, the Hotel Ceylon Intercontinental, the Galadari Hotel, the Reuters office building, the Ceylon Hotels Corporation, ABN AMRO, Cargo Boat, George Steuarts, and the offices of Air Lanka and American Express. It was and continues to remain the most deadly act of terrorism in Sri Lankan history.

Authorities suspected the Liberation Tigers of Tamil Eelam (LTTE, or Tamil Tigers) of having carried out the attack. Although the group did not officially claim responsibility, an alleged Tiger spokesman did openly admit the organization's complicity, and the incident is generally regarded as an LTTE operation.

It was later reported that the blue-and-brown Isuzu truck carrying the bomb, which was hidden beneath sacks of rice, stopped near the bank at approximately 10:45 A.M. Security staff confronted the driver, whereupon he crashed the vehicle into the barricade erected in front of the building. Two men then climbed out of a three-wheel motorized rickshaw that accompanied the truck and, after killing two guards with automatic gunfire, fired a rocket-propelled grenade at the bank's metal gates in an attempt to weaken them. The truck attempted to smash through the barrier but failed to fully penetrate it. According to witnesses the driver backed up and tried again. Either through intent or due to the force of the repeated crashing, the bomb suddenly detonated. The force of the blast killed the driver, collapsed part of the first two floors, and left a crater eight feet deep, hurling debris up to a kilometer (half a mile) away. Many small stalls selling newspapers, cigarettes, and food items were also destroyed in the blast.

One victim, who lost both eyes and his left leg in the attack, later said, "I heard some noises, and so I rushed to the window to see what was happening. Barely a moment later, the whole building shook. . . . Concrete blocks had been loosened and were falling, the glass had shattered." After that, all he remembered was his friend helping him out of the building, after which he was rushed to a hospital, where he slipped into a coma that lasted two weeks. He was 1 of 26 people who were permanently incapacitated by the attack and of at least 100 individuals who lost their eyesight.

View of the bombed Central Bank in Colombo, Sri Lanka. Suspected Tamil rebels destroyed the bank with a truck laden with explosives. At least 90 people were killed and 1,400 injured in the attack, which gutted several buildings in the city center on January 31, 1996. (AP Photo/ Dexter Cruez)

Fires hampered initial rescue operations, and there were concerns about additional detonations occurring. Others feared the entire bank might collapse as a result of the blast. That said, helicopters were able to save several office workers trapped on the rooftops of burning buildings, and first responders managed to evacuate the Hotel Ceylon Intercontinental.

Although the driver of the truck died in the attack, the gunmen did not. According to witness statements, the two men managed to climb back into the three-wheeled taxi (scooter-rickshaw) just prior to the blast and flee the scene. The escape was short-lived, however, as local citizens captured the pair at the nearby Fort railway station. They were carrying four grenades, a suicide kit, two bombs, and a couple of walkie-talkies.

A police investigation later revealed that the two men, 24-year-old Rasu (Raghu, Ragunathan, Raju, also known as Sivasamy Dharmendra) and 26-year-old Kittu (Kutti, also known as Subramanium Vigneswaram), admitted to being members of the LTTE. They claimed to have entered Colombo from Jaffna in the north of the country on January 8. The gunmen along with the driver (whose identity was confirmed as Raju/Raj) apparently drove the truck from Vavuniya, some 155 miles away, the day before the attack. It was later alleged that two other three-wheeled vehicles had been part of the convoy but had escaped unnoticed.

The capture of the gunmen led to the eventual arrest of 34 other alleged plotters. Of those, 11 were charged with membership in the LTTE. Ten of these individuals were indicted on a total of 712 counts, including intention to cause death and murder.

The day after the bombing, the governor of the Central Bank of Sri Lanka contacted the heads of the country's commercial banks and transferred all international financial transactions normally handled by his institution. He also temporarily suspended Treasury Bill auctions. These actions only marginally ameliorated the economic impact of the attack, however, largely because of a lack of modern technology that was able to read records of old banking transactions. In addition to direct losses, the incident had serious repercussions on tourism and foreign investment. The numbers of foreigners visiting the country plummeted by 40 percent, and hundreds of workers had to be laid off.

In the aftermath of the bombing, a group calling itself the Ellalan Force contacted several travel agencies, both regional and international, instructing them to boycott Sri Lanka. The group also warned that it would attack the staff of the embassy of Malaysia in reprisal for Kuala Lumpur's decision to revoke the permanent resident status of all foreign nationals supporting LTTE activities. Similar threats were made against Tokyo's mission after it refused to issue a visa to Neelam Thiruchelvam, a Tamil United Liberation Front Member of Parliament who was scheduled to visit Japan for a seminar.

Although the LTTE denied any association with the Ellalan Force in statements posted on their main Internet website, Tamil News, most Sri Lankans completely rejected these disavowals. Many noted that the Central Bank bombing came on the heels of the capture of Jaffna City in December 1995. This was deemed to have been a major government success, not least because the small metropolis represented the symbolic heart of a future Tamil state. The presumed wisdom was that the attack had been conducted in direct response to this victory and was aimed at cowing Colombo into submission. Deputy Defense Minister Anuruddha Ratwatte firmly rebutted any question that this would occur and in an official release affirmed, "If [Tamil Tiger chief] Velupillai Prabhakaran thinks that by these acts he can stop our military offensive, he is dreaming. . . . We say quite clearly that these acts will make us even more determined to destroy terrorism."

On October 15, 1997, the Central Bank was again damaged after a truck bomb detonated outside Sri Lanka's World Trade Center. This attack killed 10 civilians and was again blamed on the LTTE.

Following the Central Bank bombing, the LTTE's supreme leader Velupillai Prabhakaran was tried in absentia. He was found guilty on 51 criminal counts and sentenced to 200 years in prison. He was one of 11 individuals indicted for the bombing. Others included Chellathamby Navaratnam (Chettikulam Navaratnam, Sellathamby Navaratnam), who was accused of transporting the explosives used in the bombing, and Pottu Amman, the Tigers' chief of intelligence.

Prabhakaran and Amman were both killed in 2009 during a major army onslaught that finally decimated the LTTE. Navaratnam was taken into custody that same year after trying to escape from one of the Tamil refugee camps that were erected after the final defeat of the Tigers. He had been hiding in LTTE-controlled areas for over 13 years.

See also: Colombo World Trade Centre Bombing; Liberation Tigers of Tamil Eelam (LTTE)

Further Reading

Bandarage, Asoka. *The Separatist Conflict in Sri Lanka: Terrorism, Ethnicity, Political Economy.* Bloomington, IN: iUniverse, 2009.

Cragin, Kim, Peter Chalk, Sara Daly, and Brian Jackson. *Sharing the Dragon's Teeth: Terrorist Groups and the Exchange of New Technologies.* Santa Monica, CA: RAND, 2007.

Gunaratna, Rohan. *Sri Lanka's Ethnic Crisis and National Security.* Colombo, Sri Lanka: South Asian Network on Conflict Research, 1998.

Jackson, Brian, John Baker, Kim Cragin, John Parachini, Horacio Trujillo, and Peter Chalk. *Aptitude for Destruction.* Vol. 1, *Organizational Learning in Terrorist Groups and Its Implications for Combating Terrorism.* Santa Monica, CA: RAND, 2005.

Donna Bassett

CHRISTMAS DAY (2009) AIRLINE TERROR PLOT

On December 25, 2009, Nigerian citizen Umar Farouk Abdulmutallab unsuccessfully attempted to bomb Northwest Airlines Flight 253 from Amsterdam to Detroit as it approached its final destination. The device, which consisted of a six-inch packet of powdered PETN (which becomes a plastic explosive when mixed with triacetone triperoxide/TAPN) sewn into his underwear and a syringe of liquid acid, ignited a small fire that was promptly put out by a passenger and flight crewmembers. After the incident, officials discovered that Abdulmutallab had been in regular communication with Anwar al-Awlaki, an American-born Islamist widely believed to be the chief ideologue of Al Qaeda in the Arabian Peninsula (AQAP) in Yemen.

Public responses included a barrage of criticisms of U.S. national security and intelligence organizations for not preventing the attempted bombing, especially given the millions that had been invested to improve aviation security since 9/11. Of particular concern was the fact that U.S. officials had received a warning from Abdulmutallab's father in November 2009, who was concerned over his son's increasingly extremist views. Although the 23-year-old Nigerian had been put on watch lists and even denied a visa renewal by Britain in May 2009, his name was apparently lost among thousands of others and not flagged. Critics also asked why X-rays checks had failed to detect the explosive materials he carried.

Three days after the attempted attack, President Barack Obama publicly addressed the incident while on vacation in Hawaii, receiving some criticism that he showed a lack of concern for Americans' fear for their safety. He mandated a thorough investigation of the event, which he officially blamed on AQAP a week later. A declassified report subsequently released to the public in January 2010 detailed the intelligence and defense agencies' failures to streamline their information and "connect the dots." The president ordered further reforms to fix these weak links and also instigated heightened security measures at airports, including the installation of whole-body scanners in airports and delaying the release of Yemeni prisoners at Guantánamo Bay. He also announced that he would more than double the $70 million in security aid that Washington had sent to Yemen in 2009 and, along with the United Kingdom, would jointly finance a new counterterrorism unit in the country.

Abdulmutallab was taken into custody on December 26, 2009, and charged with eight felonies, including the attempted use of a weapon of mass destruction and the attempted murder of 289 civilians. At the time of writing he was in U.S. custody awaiting sentencing after pleading guilty on all counts.

See also: Al Qaeda; Al Qaeda in the Arabian Peninsula (AQAP)

Further Reading

Baker, Peter. "Obama Says Al Qaeda in Yemen Planned Bombing Plot, and He Vows Retribution." *New York Times,* January 3, 2010.

Borzou, Daragahi. "Bin Laden Takes Responsibility for Christmas Day Bombing Attempt." *New York Times,* January 24, 2010.

Margasak, Larry, Lara Jakes, and Jim Irwin. "Man Cites Orders from al-Qaeda in Failed Bid to Blow Up Plane." *Globe and Mail* (Canada), December 26, 2011.

Savage, Charlie. "Nigerian Indicted in Terrorist Plot." *New York Times,* January 6, 2010.

"'Underwear Bomber' Abdulmutallab Pleads Guilty." *BBC News,* October 12, 2011. http://www.bbc.co.uk/news/world-us-canada-15278483, accessed October 27, 2011.

Peter Chalk

CHRISTMAS EVE BOMBINGS

On December 24, 2000, Islamic militants carried out a series of coordinated bombings attacks in Indonesia, targeting Christians and Christian-owned properties. They deployed 34 improvised explosive devices (IEDs), most left in cars parked outside selected venues, of which an estimated 19 detonated as planned. An additional 15 bombs were found before they detonated. Most, but not all, were successfully defused. In total, 10 cities in three provinces were hit: 6 in Java (Jakarta, Bekasi, Bandung, Sukabumi, Ciamis, and Mojokerto), 3 in Sumatra (Medan, Pematang and Sinatar), and 1 in Lombuk (Mataram). The combined attacks left 19 people dead, another 120 wounded, and are thought to have cost around $47,000.

Because the bombings took place over such a large area and were highly coordinated, the press speculated that rogue elements of the Indonesian military might have been involved, accusing them of trying to manipulate religious conflict in an effort to shore up the army's influence, which had been abruptly curtailed following the fall of the Suharto regime in 1998. President Abdurrahman Wahid, who was under pressure to resign because of worsening political and economic conditions at the time of the explosions, accused his opponents of complicity, claiming they were trying to discredit him by creating fear and panic.

Several Islamist entities denied any responsibility for the attacks. The paramilitary organization Laskar Jihad issued a statement denouncing the bombings as "immoral and politically motivated." Gerakan Aceh Merdeka (GAM, or the Free Aceh Movement) similarly distanced itself from the incidents, with the group's spokesman, Teungku Amni bi Marzuki, affirming, "We have no connection with the bombings in several places in Indonesia because the conflict in Aceh is not a religious conflict."

On December 26 it was announced that two people had been arrested in connection with the attacks—one of whom (Dedi Mulyadi) later claimed to have received training in Afghanistan during the early 1990s. They were detained at a house in the Antapani area of Bandung after an IED exploded prematurely during the construction process. Both men were seriously injured in the blast, which killed three additional suspects and 10 civilians and injured at least 95 others. Authorities also announced that documents had been found in the course of the detentions implicating Jemaah Islamiyah (JI) field commander Nurjaman Riduan Isamuddin (Hambali) in the bombings. Abu Bakar Bashir (Abu Bakar Ba'asyir, also known as Abdus Samad), the spiritual leader of the group, was later tried for his alleged involvement but found not guilty. During the course of his trial, it was alleged that the attacks were part of a campaign of terror aimed at tilting the religious balance in Southeast Asia in order to create a pan-regional caliphate that was to include Indonesia, the southern Philippines, the Malay Muslim provinces of Thailand, and Brunei.

It is now known that the first planning meeting for the operation took place in Kuala Lumpur in October 2000. It was here that cities were selected for attack and arrangements made for the procurement of explosives; the latter material was sourced out of Manila with the help of JI's representative in Singapore, Faiz bin Abubakatheafana. At a subsequent gathering held on or around December 15, principal team members were identified, provided with money, and given basic instruction in bomb-making techniques. They were also told to place the IEDs in different churches and that, if a suitable venue was not available, other "infidel" or Chinese-owned properties should be targeted.

On January 25, 2011, JI leader and explosives expert Umar Patek, also known as Pak Taek, Abu Syekh, and Zachy, was arrested in Pakistan. Like Al Qaeda leader Osama bin Laden, he had been hiding in Abbottabad. He was extradited to Indonesia the following August and under interrogation admitted his complicity in the Christmas Eve explosions as well as the 2002 attacks in Bali. Patek's capture was a major blow to JI's so-called pro-bombing faction and removed arguably the most dangerous terrorist in Southeast Asia from circulation.

See also: Bashir, Abu Bakar; Jemaah Islamiyah (JI)

Further Reading

Abuza, Zachary. *Militant Islam in Southeast Asia: Crucible of Terror.* Boulder, CO: Lynne Rienner, 2003.

Chalk, Peter, Angel Rabasa, William Rosenau, and Leanne Piggott. *The Evolving Terrorist Threat to Southeast Asia: A Net Assessment.* Santa Monica, CA: RAND, 2009.

Sidel, John T. *Riots, Pogroms, Jihad: Religious Violence in Indonesia.* Ithaca, NY: Cornell University Press, 2006.

Turnbull, Wayne. "A Tangled Web of Southeast Asian Islamic Terrorism: The Jemaah Islamiya Terrorist Network." Monterey, CA: Monterey Institute of International Studies, July 31, 2003. Available online at http://www.terrorismcentral.com/Library/terrorist groups/JemaahIslamiyah/JITerror/WJ2000.html.

Donna Bassett

CITY OF LONDON BOMBINGS

Between February and September 1996, the Provisional Irish Revolutionary Army (PIRA, or the "Provos") carried out a series of bombings and attempted bombings in London. Although the attacks did not result in a large-scale loss of life, they caused considerable economic damage and dangerously threatened the nascent peace process with the UK government that was then under way.

The first, and most serious, incident occurred on February 9, when PIRA set off a 500-pound vehicle-borne improvised explosive device (VBIED) composed of a mixture of ammonium nitrate and fuel oil 80 yards from South Quay Station on the London Dockland's Light Railway. The target was Canary Wharf, one of the city's largest office and apartment complexes. The blast killed two men working at a nearby news agency and injured 106 other people, at least 36 of whom were hospitalized. Insurance assessors later calculated the property damage at $127.5 million. The attack brought to an end PIRA's 17-month cease-fire, which was called off in reaction to the British government's insistence that it disarm before Sinn Féin—the Provos' political wing—could be included in peace talks.

The Docklands bombing (also known as the Canary Wharf bombing) was quickly followed up on February 18 when an improvised explosive device (IED) was detonated on a double-decker bus near Trafalgar Square, killing one person and injuring eight others. The attack came three days after a failed attempt to bomb Leicester Square, the heart of London's entertainment district. The latter device had been hidden in a telephone booth and was set to go off at lunchtime. However, a coded warning phoned in by PIRA tipped off the police as to its whereabouts, and the device was successfully deactivated. Although several people were arrested in connection with the incident, none were charged.

The third attack occurred on March 9, when an IED in a recycling bin exploded outside Brompton Cemetery. Although there were no injuries, the blast broke windows and damaged several homes in Earl's Court and South Kensington. There was no advance warning, but PIRA later admitted responsibility. The following month, on April 17, a bomb exploded in the Boltons—an upscale residential area in western London. Again there were no casualties (PIRA had phoned in a warning 30 minutes prior to the blast), with damage limited to houses in the immediate vicinity.

Six days later, two Semtex-based bombs planted under Hammersmith Bridge malfunctioned. Although the detonators went off, the main charges failed to explode. There were no injuries, and no damage was caused. It has been suggested that undercover British intelligence agents who had infiltrated the PIRA Active Service Unit (ASU) planning the operation had managed to spike the devices.

On July 15, the Metropolitan Police found bomb components at a number of addresses in the Tooting and Peckham sections of the city. Authorities speculated the equipment was going to be used in attacks on utility installations in London and the southeast of England. Seven residents were immediately arrested; a man and a woman were later detained in Birmingham.

Finally, on September 23, police antiterrorist squads conducted dawn raids at PIRA hideouts in western London, confiscating 10 tons of Semtex and fertilizer-based explosives as well as three Kalashnikov assault rifles and two handguns; one Provo gunman was fatally shot during the exchange. Several trucks were also seized, suggesting that the materiel was be readied to make large VBIEDs.

In reaction to these events, British Prime Minister John Major threatened to call off all contact with Sinn Féin, which he had agreed in 1994 to include in talks for a political solution to the conflict in Northern Ireland. He also insisted that the Provos reinstate their previous cease-fire (begun in 1994 but broken in February 1996), which the group duly did in July 1997.

See also: Baltic Exchange Bombing; Bishopsgate Bombing; Good Friday Agreement; Manchester City Bombing; Provisional Irish Republican Army (PIRA)

Further Reading

Mickolus, Edward, and Susan Simmons. *Terrorism 1996–2001: A Chronology.* Vol. 1 Westport, CT: Greenwood, 2002.
Moloney, Ed. *A Secret History of the IRA.* New York: W. W. Norton, 2002.
Oppenheimer, A. R. *IRA: The Bombs and the Bullets: A History of Deadly Ingenuity.* Dublin: Irish Academic Press, 2009.

Donna Bassett

CLUB EL NOGAL BOMBING

On February 7, 2003, a 440-pound (200-kilogram) car bomb detonated in the interior-parking garage of the exclusive Club El Nogal complex in northern Bogotá. The explosion occurred at 8 P.M. when the facility was packed with nearly 600 people; 36 were killed and more than 200 wounded. The explosion also destroyed several of the building's 10 floors.

Although no group took responsibility for the attack, Colombian vice president Francisco Santos was quick to blame the Marxist rebel group Fuerzas Armadas Revolucionarias de Colombia (FARC, or the Revolutionary Armed Forces of Colombia). He alleged the club was targeted because it was popular with right-wing paramilitary members.

FARC denied responsibility for the attack, claiming that it had carried out a thorough internal investigation of the organization and that no evidence had come to light pointing to involvement by any of its members. Instead, FARC asserted that elements within the government of Colombia were behind the incident and that the bombing had been carried out in order to mobilize the country against the group. Officials in Bogotá denied these accusations.

Others speculated that the bombing could have been carried out by right-wing paramilitaries associated with the Autodefensas Unidas de Colombia (AUC) or United Self Defense Forces of Colombia, competing drug traffickers, other militant groups, or disaffected military elements.

On February 15, press reports surfaced that Colombian police had carried out raids on four FARC locations in the city of Neiva. Authorities said the operations had been conducted after a tip that the group was planning to kill President Alvaro Uribe by shooting down his plane while he was en route to attend a security briefing in Neiva. During the course of the raids, which led to the discovery of detonating devices at two locations, an explosion occurred at one suspect house, destroying the building, damaging 30 others, and killing 16 people. Although the exact cause of the blast remained uncertain, the head of the local prosecutor's office, Hernando de Valenzuela, said it had been caused by the "mortars [the militants planned to use] to shoot down the presidential plane."

Subsequent sting operations against FARC in January 2005 led to the arrests of several of the group's members in Nicaragua, where they were trying to procure high-tech weaponry. Just over two years later, a Syrian arms dealer by the name of Monser al-Kassar was also arrested in Spain. He was linked to FARC as well as various narcotics-trafficking and terrorist movements.

Authorities in Bogotá claimed that these detentions were evidence that FARC was actively seeking to attack civilian venues in major Colombian cities and was probably responsible for the Club El Nogal attack. However, a body of evidence that conclusively linked the group to the 2003 incident had yet to emerge.

To buttress its case that FARC was behind the bombing, the government released several documents in 2008 that had been recovered from the computer of the slain top commander in the group, Raúl Reyes. One of the electronic files included a February 13, 2003, message that specifically mentioned the Club El Nogal attack, characterizing it as a "formidable act" and commenting on the "political convenience of denying" responsibility for the incident.

Many regarded this as hard evidence of FARC's culpability in the attack. Others remained unconvinced, however. The skeptics pointed out that although Reyes clearly acknowledged the scale of the attack, he never directly took responsibility for it. They also pointed out that it was unclear whether the comment referring to the "political convenience of denying responsibilities" was made in relation to FARC or the Colombian government. At the time of this writing, no one had been detained or prosecuted for the bombing.

See also: Autodefensas Unidas de Colombia (AUC); Fuerzas Armadas Revolucionarias de Colombia (FARC)

Further Reading

Bergquist, Charles, Ricardo Peñaranda, and Gonzalo Sánchez G., eds. *Violence in Colombia 1990–2000: Waging War and Negotiating Peace.* Wilmington, DE: SR Books, 2001.

Cragin, Kim, and Bruce Hoffman. *Arms Trafficking and Colombia.* Santa Monica, CA: RAND, 2003.

"Interpol's Forensic Report May 2008." http://www.interpol.int/Public/ . . . /pdfPR200817/ipPublicReportNoCoverEN.pdf, accessed August 8, 2011.

Rabasa, Angel, Peter Chalk, Kim Cragin, Sara Daly, Heather Gregg, Theodore Karasik, Kevin O'Brien, and William Rosenau. *Beyond al-Qaeda: The Outer Rings of the Terrorist Universe, Part 2.* Santa Monica, CA: RAND, 2006.

Donna Bassett

COLOMBO WORLD TRADE CENTRE BOMBING

On October 15, 1997, the separatist Liberation Tigers of Tamil Eelam (LTTE) detonated a container truck laden with explosives in the financial district of Colombo, Sri Lanka. The primary target of the attack was the newly constructed Colombo World Trade Centre (WTC), Sri Lanka's tallest building and the symbolic center of its economy. After this initial blast, the fleeing LTTE suicide team overtook Lake House, the publishing center of the state-run newspapers, and held 20 employees hostage in a standoff that ended with commando raids that killed the remaining Tiger cadres. The final toll of the attack was 18 fatalities, over 100 wounded, and millions of dollars in damages.

Suicide terrorism was a tactic the LTTE, or Tamil Tigers, had pioneered and continuously employed against the Sri Lankan government during their conflict for statehood that began in 1982. By the mid-1990s the LTTE had evolved organizationally into a proto-state with a semiconventional armed force, and their ability to control territory in northeastern Sri Lanka gave them a sanctuary to coordinate and launch increasingly sophisticated attacks against the government.

The government countered this threat by accelerating military operations against these rebel-controlled areas in the northeast. This began a new iteration of the conflict, where the LTTE would retaliate against government offensives with the increased use of suicide terrorism in Colombo, Sri Lanka's capital, located in the south of the country. In January 1995, the Sri Lankan military had recaptured the Jaffna Peninsula from the LTTE, forcing the LTTE into a strategic withdrawal deep into the jungles in the Wanni. The Sri Lankan military hoped to capitalize on this stunning success by launching operation Jaya Sikurui—Sure Victory—in May 1997 to regain control of the A-9 highway and to connect government-held territory with the newly liberated Jaffna Peninsula.

Jaya Sikurui was the largest military operation of the conflict to that point, and it placed an enormous amount of pressure on the LTTE. During previous offensives, the LTTE had utilized suicide terrorism as a diversionary tactic, and since 2005 they had increased the number of soft-target attacks on Colombo. It was in this context that the LTTE launched an attack on the WTC complex in October 1997.

The newly built WTC complex was located in the heart of Colombo's financial district, an area that had become a high-security zone after a devastating LTTE suicide attack against the Central Bank in January 1996 killed over 91 and wounded over 1,400. By 1997 the commercial district, known as the Fort, was heavily fortified with barricades, checkpoints, and numerous security personnel.

The WTC complex itself was heavily protected on three sides. However, the southern portion of the complex, adjacent to the parking lot of the Galadari Hotel, was virtually open, the only barrier being a security booth manned by a few unarmed guards employed by the hotel. The Galadari Hotel was not the symbolic target of the attack.

Inadequate security present at the site allowed the LTTE suicide team nearly unfettered access to an adjacent high-security zone. By exploiting this security gap, the LTTE suicide team was able to launch an attack on the WTC complex only three days after it had been inaugurated.

The coordinated LTTE attack began at approximately 7 A.M. on October 15, 1997, as five cadres from the elite Black Tiger suicide unit drove a truck filled with bags of rice and explosives into the financial district. Each member was dressed in dark clothing that resembled army uniforms and carried T 56 rifles. As the driver pulled up to the entrance of the Galadari Hotel, the four remaining Tiger cadres converged on the security booth and killed three unarmed security guards on duty. With the compound breached, the LTTE suicide team drove the truck up to the rear wall of the WTC complex.

Minutes later, a massive explosion ripped through the heart of the financial district. The truck had been packed with between 300 and 350 kilograms (661–771 pounds) of explosives to achieve maximum infrastructural damage; the detonation was much larger than the 200 kilograms (400 pounds) used in the Central Bank attack in 1996. The most substantial damage occurred at the WTC complex and Galadari Hotel. However, splintered and broken glass in surrounding buildings, including the Presidential Secretariat, became the major source of injuries suffered in the attack.

The LTTE suicide team had taken cover as the bomb exploded and ran along Lotus Road on foot. Passing by the Sambuddahloka Viharaya temple complex, the LTTE cadres desecrated the building with small-arms fire and threw a grenade into the compound, killing the incumbent Buddhist monk. By then the army had mobilized its Quick Reaction Team, a new specialized armed motorcycle unit. This squad was able to kill one of the fleeing Black Tiger cadres as the suicide team made its way across the railroad tracks toward Lake House, the state-run publishing compound. Three of the Black Tigers entered Lake House through the production area, while the fourth cadre, who had been wounded by the Quick Reaction Team's fire, attempted to escape into a growing crowd of spectators. Government forces intercepted and killed the fourth cadre before he could detonate his suicide vest.

In Lake House, the remaining three cadres took 20 employees hostage while the army cordoned off the area. Minutes later, a group of soldiers under the command of Lieutenant Colonel Deepal Subasinghe advanced into the building and freed the hostages as the Black Tiger cadres retreated deeper into the interior of the building. Unsure of the situation, the army called in four-man teams of commandos to sweep and clear Lake House. The first team made contact with the remaining LTTE cadres among the newspaper stacks in a windowless room. Two of the Black Tigers were able to detonate suicide vests, killing one solider and injuring Captain Chinthaka Dissanayake. The third and final Black Tiger was killed before he could detonate himself. At 5:30 P.M. the government announced that all five members of the LTTE suicide team had been killed, and the WTC bombing was officially over.

The primary objective of the attack on October 15, 1997, was not to target civilians but rather the Sri Lankan economy. Unlike the Central Bank bombing in 1996, the attack on the WTC had low casualties since October 15 coincided with a religious holiday, *poya,* and the Fort was almost entirely deserted. This was a calculated decision by the LTTE to reduce collateral damage in an effort to prevent the further tarnishing of their human rights record. The WTC bombing was primarily undertaken as part of a larger strategy of economic attrition adopted by the LTTE in 1995 to destabilize the Sri Lankan economy and make the costs of the war untenable.

In the past this strategy had been extremely effective. In 1997 the Sri Lankan economy had only begun to recover from a devastating LTTE attack in January 1996, when LTTE suicide squads drove a truck bomb into the Central Bank. This attack had resulted in nearly 1,500 casualties, caused enormous collateral damage to the financial district, and produced a climate of insecurity. The Central Bank attack also generated significant international media attention and, as a result, crippled foreign and domestic investment and economic growth and caused tourism to fall by nearly 25 percent.

When the WTC complex was inaugurated on October 12, 1997, it served as the new epicenter for Sri Lankan commerce and banking, housing the Central Bank, the Board of Investment, and the Colombo Stock Exchange. At the time, the LTTE leadership hoped that attacking the WTC complex would deal a symbolic blow to the financial district and further undermine the credibility of Colombo's security, thereby deleteriously affecting business and investment, development, and tourism.

A secondary objective of the WTC bombing was to create an environment of insecurity in Colombo that would divert attention and resources away from the ongoing conflict in the Wanni. By 1995 the LTTE had embarked on a revolutionary strategy that utilized terrorism against soft targets in an effort to shift the battle space to government-controlled areas in southern Sri Lanka. Previously, the majority of LTTE terrorist operations had been leveraged against military and political targets. However, as conventional military operations escalated in the north, the LTTE began the systematic use of diversionary suicide terrorism to undermine the significant territorial gains being made by the Sri Lankan military.

The WTC bombing was an extension of the larger Operation Do or Die, an LTTE counteroffensive that sought to overextend the Sri Lankan military. Ideally, an attack on the WTC complex would underscore the Sri Lankan government's inability to adequately defend its own territory. This would further bring the conflict home to millions of Sri Lankans and invariably create an environment of insecurity that the LTTE hoped would subvert politics, hinder commerce, and necessitate the creation of robust and expensive security countermeasures. Ultimately, the LTTE wanted to undermine the efficacy of military operations in the North by forcing the government to make Colombo part of its defensible space at a great cost in resources, personnel, and operational flexibility.

In the aftermath of the WTC bombing, the Sri Lankan government vowed to defend the capital like a citadel. Initially, there were fears that two more undetected Black Tiger squads were operating in Colombo. As a result, the government diverted thousands of troops and police in late October 1997 to begin a sweep and cordon of Tamil neighborhoods that led to the detention of thousands of Tamils in Colombo. However, throughout 1997 the government's ability to combat LTTE terrorism in government-controlled territory remained significantly limited due to the efficacy of the LTTE's Operation Do or Die counteroffensive.

The LTTE's success was partially due to the government's misuse of vital intelligence resources. The military apparatus had shifted its mission focus to targeting cadres, so that by mid-1995 there was an inadequate infrastructure for monitoring and combating the infiltration of LTTE operatives into government controlled-areas. As a result, larger numbers of cadres were able to move freely and conduct far-reaching operations throughout Sri Lanka. Having inadequate intelligence resources, the government was forced to adopt draconian measures to identify infiltrated cadres.

The use of coercive measures did not immediately reduce the tactical reach of LTTE; the LTTE continued to conduct spectacularly devastating soft-target attacks in Colombo and southern Sri Lanka throughout 1999 that left hundreds dead, symbolically destroyed the Temple of the Tooth relic. It nearly succeeded in the assassination of Sri Lankan president Chandrika Kumaratunga. The legacy of the WTC attacks demonstrated to the LTTE that terrorism in Colombo was a useful tool for opening up multiple theaters. Over the next 12 years of the conflict, the LTTE were largely able to prevent the Sri Lankan military from concentrating and mobilizing its full security apparatus against the North. The use of such tactics throughout the war resulted in staggering economic costs, including material terms, opportunity costs, per capita income, investments, and revenues from tourism—all of which were vulnerable to the renewal of LTTE terrorist activity.

The WTC bombing was extremely successful for the LTTE tactically, but in the long run it strategically undermined the organization. The attack underscored for the Sri Lankan government the critical importance of preventing terrorism in Colombo. The devastation of the attack demonstrated the limited efficacy of the Quick Reaction Team, which had nevertheless saved countless lives, and fundamentally demonstrated that the new security measures that had been developed following the 1996 Central Bank bombing were inadequate. As a result, the government was forced to include Colombo as a secondary operative theater, and it continued to respond to the threat of LTTE terrorism by improving the security apparatus in Colombo at a rapid pace. Colombo adopted a *defensible space policy*—the creation of barriers to hinder terrorism from reaching the population—and sought to methodically separate Tamils from the LTTE and prevent infiltration through enhanced security zones, checkpoints, surveillance, curfews, and preventive detention. As a result, the LTTE's ability to carry out deadly surprise bombings was severely curtailed by a combination of increased security measures and the government's deliberate targeting of their own resources.

The WTC bombing also greatly enhanced the ability of the Sri Lankan government to interdict LTTE funds and target their overseas operations. Foremost, the attack presented the government with an opportunity to build a stronger international consensus against the LTTE. Not only had Britain, Germany, and France issued stronger travel advisories after 38 foreigners were injured in the attack, but each government also strongly condemned the LTTE, which signaled a shift away from neutrality. Similarly, Washington chose to annually renew its ban on LTTE and after 9/11 expanded its counterterrorism cooperation with the Sri Lankan government. This had significant implications in the post-9/11 environment, as previously more than 80 percent of the annual LTTE budget passed through international networks and financial systems. This coupling of international condemnation with enhanced counterterrorism coordination would ultimately be the biggest blow to the LTTE after 2005. As a result, the organization's political, financial, and military activities were devastatingly hampered, movement of its overseas leadership was severely restricted, and overseas operations were eventually forced to go underground.

See also: Central Bank (Colombo) Bombing; Liberation Tigers of Tamil Eelam (LTTE)

Further Reading

Athas, Iqbal. "Operation Twin Towers: How and Why the LTTE Did It." *The Sunday Times, Situation Report,* October 19, 1997.

Gunaratna, Rohan. "Bankrupting the Terror Business." *Jane's Intelligence Review,* August 2000.

Gunaratna, Rohan. "Sri Lanka: Another Lost Opportunity for Peace?" *Jane's Terrorism and Security Monitor,* February 2001.

Harris, Paul. "Asia, State of Insecurity: Sri Lanka and the War That Lost Its Way." *Jane's Intelligence Review* 11, no. 5 (May 1999).

Jeyaraj, D.B.S. "Deadlines to Meet." *Frontline Magazine* 15, no. 1 (January 1998).

Manoharan, N. *Counterterrorism Legislation in Sri Lanka: Evaluating Efficacy.* Policy Study 28. Washington, DC: East West Center, 2006.

Rajeswari, R. "US Policy on Terrorism—Part II Cases of Hizbollah and Liberation Tigers of Tamil Eelam." Institute for Defense Studies and Analysis. http://www.idsa-india.org/an-nov8–7.html, accessed January 24, 2012.

Singh, Ajit Kumar. "Targeting LTTE's Global Network." *South Asia Intelligence Review.* 6, no. 41 (April 2008).

Sri Lanka Tourist Development Authority. "Tourist Arrivals in Sri Lanka from 1966–2010, Annual Statistics Report 2010." http://www.sltda.lk/statistics, accessed January 30, 2012.

Tan, B. C., and John Solomon. "Feeding the Tiger: How Sri Lankan Insurgents Fund Their War." *Jane's Intelligence Review,* September 2007.

"Truck Bomb Blasts Colombo." *Sri Lanka Monitor,* October 1997. Available online at http://brcslproject.gn.apc.org/slmonitor/october97/truck.html, accessed January 30, 2012.

Vittachi, Imran (with reporting by M. Ismeth, Shelawi De Silva, Arshad Hadijirin, Dilrukshi Handunnetti, Christopher Kamalendrun, and Chamintha Tilklekerante). "Maradana Mayhem." *Sunday Times: Special Assignment,* March 8, 1998.

Ryan McKinstry

CONTINUITY IRISH REPUBLICAN ARMY (CIRA)

The Continuity Irish Republican Army (CIRA) is an Irish republican paramilitary organization that claims to be a direct descendant of the Irish Republican Army (IRA) of 1918 and consequently the only legitimate heirs of authentic Irish republicanism. The IRA of the time was also known as the Oghlaigh naEirrean (Volunteers of Ireland), and this name is sometimes used today by the CIRA when claiming responsibility for attacks. The group advocates the use of physical force in pursuit of its aims and together with the Real Irish Republican Army (RIRA) formed a dissident faction of the militant republican movement that continued to carry out attacks after the 1998 Good Friday Agreement.

Over its operational life, the IRA underwent several fractures as Irish Catholics split away to form their own groups and pursue what they viewed as the real aims and objectives of violent republicanism. In this way the Provisional Irish Republican Army (PIRA) broke away from what become known as the Official IRA (OIRA) in 1969, and in turn the CIRA broke away from PIRA in 1986.

CIRA came into existence largely as a result of a ruling by PIRA's Army Council to contest and take up seats won in elections to the Irish Parliament (Dail Eireann). This position, known as *abstentionism,* was rejected by a group of PIRA radicals, who viewed it as an unacceptable softening of the accepted "bullet and ballot box," in that the latter was now being favored at the expense of the former. When PIRA's political wing, Sinn Féin, endorsed the Army Council's decision, the rebels—soon to be known as Republican Sinn Féin (RSF)—walked out of the meeting. The formation of an armed wing associated with RSF occurred over the next few months, and in turn it became known as the CIRA.

CIRA carried out its first significant attack on July 14, 1996, when they used an improvised explosive device (IED) to destroy the Killyhelvin Hotel near Enniskillen. The ramifications of the bombing were especially marked as it occurred at the height of a very tense period arising from an Orange Order march at Drumcree. A second major attack decimated much of the small village of Markethill on September 16, 1997. The attack again involved a powerful IED that had been placed in a car, and the apparent aim was to destabilize the ongoing peace process between the Unionists and the Republicans.

CIRA vigorously denounced the Good Friday Agreement and in a direct challenge to PIRA refused to either hand over or decommission any of its weapons stocks. The group continued to engage in sporadic attacks following the turn of the millennium and has been implicated in at least one police killing—the assassination of Constable Stephen Carroll in March 2009. A member of the newly configured Police Service of Northern Ireland, he was the first officer to die in a terrorist attack in Northern Ireland since 1998. CIRA remains active and has exhibited no willingness to negotiate an end to its campaign of violence.

See also: Good Friday Agreement; Irish Republican Army (IRA); Provisional Irish Republican Army (PIRA); Real Irish Republican Army (RIRA)

Further Reading

Allen, Nick. "Pc Stephen Carroll Shooting: How a Routine Night Shift Ended in Murder." *Telegraph.co.uk,* March 11, 2009. http://www.telegraph.co.uk/news/uknews/northerni reland/4969207/Pc-Stephen-Carroll-shooting-How-a-routine-night-shift-ended-in-murder.

"Continuity Irish Republican Army." *Global Security.org.* http://www.globalsecurity.org/mil itary/world/para/cira.htm.

"Ex-Sinn Fein Politician Charged with Killing Cop." Associated Press, March 26, 2009.

Quinn, Eeamon, and John Burns. "After Killings Linked to I.R.A. Factions, Northern Ireland Defends Its Fragile Peace." *New York Times,* March 11, 2009.

Taylor, Peter. *Provos, the IRA and Sinn Fein.* London: Bloomsbury, 1998.

Lindsay Clutterbuck

CORSICAN NATIONALIST TERRORISM

Modern Corsican terrorism has its roots in the 1960s and 1970s, when Corsican farmers became increasingly angry at the perceived advantages of the Pied Noir settlers from Algeria. In particular, they were resentful over the impact the migrants were having on tourism and the number of mainland French owning property and beach areas. Matters came to a head with the Aleria farm siege of August 1975, when a group of militant Corsican farmers led by Dr. Edmond Simeoni occupied a settlers' farm cooperative to protest the owner's complicity in the so-called adulteration of wine and the "colonization" of the island by the Pied Noir. When gendarmes stormed the buildings, two officers were killed in an exchange of fire, and several others were injured. In turn, a subversive movement developed, named the Frontu di Liberazione Naziunalista Corsu (FLNC, or Corsican National Liberation Front).

The FLNC's first violent action occurred in May 1976 when the group attacked 22 different locations on both Corsica and the mainland. This was then followed by what became infamously known as the *nuit bleue,* a series of quasi-simultaneous explosions predominantly aimed at buildings and detonated overnight. Since that time, the Corsican nationalist movement has shown itself to be extremely fissiparous, leading to the creation of several small, atomized splinter factions, each with its own associated political groupings.

By 1990 the Corsican nationalist movement had divided into three main streams. The FLNC—Canal Habituel, led by Alain Orsoni, was more politically oriented and eventually abandoned armed struggle in 1997. The FLNC—Canal Historique, a more militant group led by Francois Santoni and Charles Pieri, subsequently became the armed branch of a third stream based around the Resistenza, a small clandestine group of Corsican radicals. There then followed a period of fratricide as the Canal Historique, Canal Habituel, and other factions battled among themselves, leading to the deaths of a number of leading nationalists.

In November 1999 the FLNC—Canal Historique regrouped with the remnants of Resistenza (now the FLNC du 5 Mai 1996), the Fronte Ribellu, and Clandestinu to form a new movement, the FLNC—Union des Combattants, with Charles Pieri as its head. While this group currently poses the main threat to French security forces and property on Corsica, smaller splinter organizations are constantly being created. These include the FLNC—22nd October, which split from the Union des Combattants in 2002, claiming to contain the most radical elements, and the small extremist group Sampieru, which was linked to the one of the most significant terrorist attacks on Corsica, the February 1998 assassination of Claude Erignac, the island's prefect in Ajaccio.

Further Reading

Baud, J. *Encyclopedie des Terrorismes et Violences Politiques.* Paris: Lavauzelle, 2003.
Farrugia, E., and P. Serf. *Corse: Le Terrorisme.* Paris: Diffusion International Edition (DIE), 2004.
Follorou, J., and V. Nouzille. *Les Parrains Corses: Leur Histoire, leurs Reseaux, leur Protections.* Paris: Fayard, 2004.
Hostettler, N. "Corsican Nationalists' Terrorist Struggle against France." In Martha Crenshaw and John Pimlott, eds., *International Encyclopedia of Terrorism.* London: Fitzroy Dearborn, 1997.
Janke, P. *Guerilla and Terrorist Organisations: A World Directory and Bibliography.* Brighton, UK: Harvester, 1983.

Richard Warnes

COTABATO CITY BOMBINGS

Five people were killed and 44 wounded on July 5, 2009, during a Sunday morning bombing of a church in the southern Philippines. The attack involved an improvised explosive device (IED) that detonated at around 8:45 A.M., just as people were leaving the second Mass at the Immaculate Concepción Cathedral in Cotabato City. According to Father Froi Cordero, a priest who helped take the wounded to the hospital, many of the victims were women and children. Archbishop Orlando Quevedo of the Archdiocese of Cotabato condemned the latest attack in central Mindanao and called it a sacrilege.

Officials later determined that a mobile phone had been used to trigger the IED, which had been placed underneath a row of food stalls across the street from the church. The scene of the actual explosion was less than 300 meters (984 feet) from the headquarters of the army's anticrime task force. Although no organization claimed responsibility for the attack, Major General Alfredo Cayton, the Army 6th Infantry Division commander, quickly blamed the Moro Islamic Liberation Front (MILF), one of the main Islamist insurgent groups fighting in the southern Philippines. However, MILF spokesman Eid Kabalu denied the military's allegations and called for an independent investigation to determine who was responsible.

The identity of the perpetrators soon became a vexing mystery. While eyewitnesses claimed to have seen an individual wearing a MILF uniform at the blast site just hours before the explosion, they also said this same individual had later entered the base of the 54th Infantry Battalion at Barangay Gumbay in Datu Piang. Although the authorities announced they would study closed-circuit cameras at the nearby Bangko Sentral ng Pilipinas (Central Bank of the Philippines) to try to determine the movements of people at the attack site, no definitive perpetrator could be pinpointed.

Eventually, speculation arose that a rogue member of the MILF had carried out the attack. Cerge Remonde, the press secretary for President Gloria Macapagal-Arroyo, said that if this was the case, he would do all he could to ensure that the bombing would not derail then ongoing talks between the government and the Muslim group. He further stressed that the Arroyo administration was committed to the peace process and that he expected negotiations with the MILF to resume within a month.

Terror attacks targeting churches are nothing new in Mindanao, but this was one of the first in years. Indeed, the bombing followed directly on the heels of another explosion the previous day in Datu Piang, Maguindanao. No one was reported killed in that blast, but three people were injured. An intact 81-millimeter mortar was also discovered near the scene of the blast, which an army ordinance disposal team later disarmed.

Further Reading

Abuza, Zachary. *Militant Islam in Southeast Asia: Crucible of Terror.* Boulder, CO: Lynne Rienner, 2003.

Donna Bassett

CUBANA AIRLINES BOMBING

On October 6, 1976, a bomb exploded on Cubana Airlines Flight 455 at 2:30 P.M. just after it took off from Georgetown, Guyana. The pilot radioed that he was trying to return to the airport, but the plane crashed into the ocean, killing all 73 people aboard. Most of the dead (58) were Cuban and included 16 members of the country's national fencing police.

Shortly after the Cubana plane crashed, two separate groups took credit for the bombing—although the most concerted claim was from the anti-Castro Coordination of United Revolutionary Organizations (CORU). Police in Port of Spain, Tobago, also reported detaining two Venezuelans who left the plane in Barbados. One of those held was Hernan Ricardo Losano, who said he had planted the bomb on the plane. The other was Freddy Lugo, who Cuban, U.S., and Venezuelan investigators concluded had participated in preparing and hiding the device.

On October 14, Venezuelan authorities arrested Luis Clemente Foustino Posada Carriles in connection with the attack. Born on February 15, 1928, in Cuba, he was a former Central Intelligence Agency (CIA) agent who once headed part of the Venezuelan secret police, the Direccion de Servicios de Inteligencia Policial (DISIP). He ran a detective agency that employed both Losano and Lugo in Caracas. In addition to Carriles, CORU leader Orlando Bosch and three other Venezuelans were apprehended.

On November 2, Carriles, Bosch, Losano, and Lugo were indicted for murder. The evidence against them was thin. A military prosecutor withdrew the charges on September 17, 1980, although Carriles and Losano remained in jail pending a

A diver lifts a piece of a Cubana airliner from the Caribbean Sea off Barbados, October 6, 1976. The four-jet DC-8 plunged into the sea while trying to return to Barbados after an on-board explosion. None of the 73 passengers survived. (AP/Wide World Photos)

civilian trial. On August 8, 1982, they escaped from prison and sought asylum at the Chilean embassy, which subsequently handed them over to Venezuelan authorities.

Carriles remained incarcerated waiting for the prosecutor to appeal his second acquittal. He said his successful jailbreak had been arranged and financed by Jorge Mas Canosa, who had close links to the Reagan administration in the United States and who was then the head of the Cuban American National Foundation. Carriles also claimed that Canosa had arranged for him to meet and work with CIA operative Felix Rodriguez in El Salvador and that U.S. Major General Richard Secord paid him $3,000 a month to help send supplies and arms to the American-financed contras who were fighting the Sandinistas in Nicaragua.

Much of this information was verified during investigations into the so-called Iran-Contra affair—a clandestine plan to use the proceeds from arms sales to Tehran (ostensibly made to secure the release of American hostages held in Lebanon) to finance illegal weapons shipments to the contra rebels in Nicaragua. Following the congressionally mandated hearings, which involved testimony by Secord, Rodriguez, and Oliver North—a decorated marine who was part of Washington's National Security Council (NSC)—Carriles left El Salvador and became a security advisor for the government in Guatemala. While there he suffered a serious gunshot wound. Although the attacker was never found, Carriles wrote in his memoirs that Secord and the Cuban American National Foundation paid his medical expenses.

Much of Carriles's recovery was spent in Honduras, where U.S. authorities alleged he planned and orchestrated over 40 bombings in Cuba. Carriles has admitted responsibility for many of these incidents, saying they were designed to damage the country's growing tourism industry. He also asserted that he tried to obtain support from the Honduran government to conduct the attacks but that it refused.

On November 17, 2000, the authorities arrested Carriles in Panama City when they found him with 200 pounds of explosives. Three other Cuban exiles were also arrested, including Gaspar Jimenez of the Cuban American National Foundation in Miami. They were accused of plotting to blow up Fidel Castro when he visited Panama. Although Carriles was jailed for the crime, outgoing president Mireya Moscoso pardoned him—an action many believed was the result of pressure from Washington (which never condemned the alleged assassination).

In 2005 Texan authorities detained Carriles for entering the United States illegally. Following his arrest the Caracas government immediately sought his extradition for the Cubana Airlines bombing. In response, Carriles applied for political asylum and although this was denied, a U.S. immigration judge subsequently ruled that Carriles could not be deported, citing the likelihood that he would be tortured if returned to Venezuela. Cuba and Venezuela were furious over the decision, noting that the 1971 Convention for the Suppression of Unlawful Acts against the Safety of Civil Aviation essentially required the United States to either prosecute or extradite him.

In 2006 the Federal Bureau of Investigation (FBI) investigated Carriles's role in a series of 1997 bombings in Havana. However, instead of using the information to prosecute him, law enforcement officials leveraged it to secure the conviction of the so-called Miami Five, five Cuban intelligence officers convicted of conspiracy to commit espionage and murder in the United States.

Carriles himself remained in prison on charges of entering the United States illegally. He was released on bail and placed under house arrest in April 2007 after a federal appeals court rejected a Justice Department request that this be denied. The following month a federal court dismissed seven counts of immigration fraud against him. This ruling was overturned in mid-2008, and two new charges were subsequently added: one for committing perjury by lying in his citizenship application about how he entered the United States and one for obstructing a federal terrorism investigation. However, this same indictment cleared Carriles of all involvement in the Cubana Airlines bombing.

During his trial, Carriles's defense team argued that his relationship to the CIA—from his work against the Castro regime to his anticommunist activities in Venezuela and Central America—was relevant in the case. His lawyers also asserted that the U.S. government has been involved with terrorist bombings in Cuba. On April 8, 2011, Carriles was found innocent of all charges. Although he was never convicted for terrorism, the exile community in Mexico where he now lives continues to refer to him as the "godfather" of anti-Cuban violence.

Further Reading

Cotayo, Nicanor León. *Crime in Barbados.* Budapest: Interpress, 1978.
"Cuba Anger at US Posada Carriles Verdict." *BBC News,* April 9, 2011. http://www.bbc.co.uk/news/world-latin-america-13026870, accessed December 19, 2011.
Kornbluh, Peter, and Yvette White, eds. "Bombing of Cuban Jetliner 30 Years Later, National Security Archive Electronic Briefing Book no. 202." National Security Archive, George Washington University, Washington, D.C., October 5, 2006. Available online at http://www.gwu.edu/~nsarchiv/NSAEBB/NSAEBB202/index.htm, accessed December 19, 2011.
Mickolus, Edward F. *Transnational Terrorism: A Chronology of Events, 1968–1979.* Westport, CT: Greenwood, 1980.

Donna Bassett

CURCIO, RENATO

Renato Curcio was a left-wing agitator who founded the Brigate Rosse (BR) or Red Brigades, a terrorist group that operated across Italy during the 1970s and 1980s. He was born in Monterotondo and attended Catholic high school in the town of Albenga. He studied sociology at the University of Trentino, where he became enamored with the political treatises of Karl Marx, Vladimir Lenin, and Mao Tse-tung. Profoundly influenced by these writings, Curcio urged his fellow students to form a new proletarian movement and reject the revisionist philosophy of the Italian Communist Party.

In 1966 Curcio became involved in protests against U.S. involvement in the Vietnam War and three years later refused to accept a degree from the University of Trentino. He married a fellow left-wing agitator, Margherita Cagol, and instead went to Milan, where he and his wife joined a violent extremist organization, the Metropolitan Political Collective. Embracing the idea of armed revolt against the state, Curcio, Cagol, and Alberto Franceschini formed the BR.

Under Curcio's leadership, the BR engaged in an intensive campaign of violence that included bombings, robberies, kidnappings, and maimings. He was arrested in September 1974 after masterminding the abduction of Judge Mario Sossi but was subsequently freed in a commando-like rescue operation led by his wife.

Police activity against the BR intensified in 1976 following the kidnapping of industrialist Vallarino Gancia on June 5. In rapid succession the Carabinieri (Italian paramilitary police) freed Gancia, killed Cagol, and captured Curcio. Imprisoned in 1976, he remains in jail, although in 1994 he was allowed to take up day work as a publisher in Rome, infuriating many Italians.

See also: Brigate Rosse (BR)

Further Reading

"Inside the Red Brigades." *Newsweek,* May 15, 1978.
Meade, Robert C., Jr. *Red Brigades: The Story of Italian Terrorism.* New York: St. Martin's, 1990.

Moss, David. *The Politics of Left-Wing Violence in Italy, 1969–1985.* New York: St. Martin's, 1989.

Neurberger, Luisella de Cotaldo, and Tiziana Valenti. *Women and Terrorism.* New York: Macmillan, 1992.

"The Red Brigades." http://www.americacallsitaly.org/Italia%20life/red%20Brigade.htm.

"Renato Curcio." *Encyclopedia Britannica 2010.* http://www.britannica.com/EEcheched/topic/146807/Renato-Curcio.

Edward F. Mickolus

D

DAHAB BOMBINGS

On April 24, 2006, three brutal explosions tore through the resort town of Dahab on the Gulf of Aqaba in Egypt's Sinai Peninsula. The attacks scattered Egyptians and tourists alike down the beachfront promenade, curtailing the festivities under way in recognition of Sham al-Nasim (Spring Festival) and Sinai Liberation Day. Although the circumstances surrounding the bombings were uncertain, Egyptian authorities eventually tied responsibility to the North Sinai Islamist organization Jama'at Tawhid wa Jihad (Oneness and Struggle).

Detonating at 7:15 P.M. on a busy holiday weekend, the explosions were deliberately set to occur when the streets were almost certainly going to be crowded. The bombs also targeted prime establishments along Dahab's main thoroughfare: the popular Al Capone restaurant, the Ghazala market, and a pedestrian footbridge. The timing and venue ensured a large casualty count, with between 18 and 23 people killed and at least 80 wounded. The victims were mostly Egyptians but also included at least 30 nationals from other countries such as Germany, Lebanon, the United States, the United Kingdom, Israel, and France.

Given the psychological impact of the blasts, their likely negative impact on tourism, and the authorities' own strict compartmentalization of information, initial reports following the attacks were contradictory. While the South Sinai governor proclaimed the attacks to be the work of suicide terrorists, the Egyptian interior minister believed that timed improvised explosive devices (IEDs) packed with nails had been planted. Subsequent investigations eventually tied the explosions to a militant martyr squad who had allegedly manufactured their weapons from materials procured from the abandoned minefields in Sinai, remnants of the wars between Egypt and Israel.

The question of culpability, however, has been more ambiguous. Given Osama bin Laden's call to Muslims to wage jihad, issued only a day prior to the Dahab attack, many analysts both within and outside Egypt thought an Al Qaeda–affiliated group was the most likely culprit. It was also pointed out that the nature of the bombings—simultaneous explosions—was a characteristic trait, if not a hallmark, of the group. That said, Al Qaeda never claimed responsibility, and many other radical Islamist organizations outwardly condemned the attacks, as did several Muslim countries, including Palestine.

After further investigation, the Egyptian government ultimately accused Jama'at Tawhid wa Jihad of carrying out the bombings—the same group that had been tied to the two prior Sinai attacks in Taba and Sharm el-Sheikh. Based in the North Sinai town of al-Arish, Tawhid wa Jihad was predominantly comprised of native Bedouin who sought to target the Mubarak regime for its years of discrimination against the local tribesmen. Police reports also cited apparent connections between Tawhid wa Jihad and Palestinian Islamists, who had evidently provided training in preparation for the attack. The Palestinian Authority (PA) staunchly denied any such ties, noting that if links did exist, they were only between individuals, with no official endorsement. Many Bedouin communities also distanced themselves from the attack, emphasizing that disruption of tourism in the region would dramatically curtail their own economic livelihood.

It is difficult to determine whether the Egyptian government's accusations are accurate as it strictly controlled media reports and official documentation. Irrespective, the Mubarak regime quickly set up checkpoints across the Sinai in the days following the attacks and arrested (and probably tortured) countless Bedouin, many of whom were thought to be innocent. The suspected leader of Tawhid wa Jihad, Nasr Khamis al-Mallahi, was killed in an Egyptian raid on May 9, 2006, and his close aide Muhammad 'Abdallah Elian was captured and interrogated. Other suspected associates were eventually detained, but it is unclear if anyone was officially charged.

The official line was that Tawhid wa Jihad perpetrated the Dahab attacks to retaliate against the government for its previous security crackdowns and suppression of Bedouin freedoms. Some Egyptian officials also believed that group members may have been attempting to revenge the seemingly indiscriminate wave of detentions and torture that swept through Sinai after previous attacks. Moreover, the timing of the bombings on a date of symbolic historical significance was deemed a snub at the Egyptian government—a demonstration of defiance through disruption of official holidays. The fact that the explosions targeted a resort frequented by the wealthier members of Egyptian society additionally seemed to constitute a reaction against the stark inequality between the rural communities of North Sinai and the more posh South Sinai getaways.

See also: Sharm el-Sheikh Bombings

Further Reading

"Dahab Residents Definat." *Al-Ahram Weekly* (Egypt), April 27–May 3, 2006. http://weekly. ahram.org.eg/2006/792/fr1.htm, accessed January 29, 2012.

"Egypt Ties Dahab Attacks to Other Attacks." *CNN*, April 26, 2006. Available online at http://web.archive.org/web/20060624043947/http://www.cnn.com/2006/WORLD/ meast/04/26/egypt.blasts/index.html, accessed January 29, 2012.

International Crisis Group. *Egypt's Sinai Question.* Middle East/North African Report no. 61, January 30, 2007.

Matthew, Jennie, and Jailan Zayan. "Egypt Arrests 10 over Dahab Bombings." *Mail&Guardian Online,* April 25, 2006. http://mg.co.za/article/2006-04-25-egypt-arrests-10-over-dahab-bombings, accessed January 29, 2012.

Mayton, Joseph. "Cairo's Response to Dahab Attacks Raises Fears That Reform Efforts May Suffer." *Washington Report on Middle East Affairs,* July 2006. http://www.wrmea.com/

component/content/article/284-2006-july/6039-cairos-response-to-dahab-attacks-raises-fears-that-reform-efforts-may-suffer.html, accessed January 29, 2012.
"30 Arrested in Egypt Resort Attack." *USA Today*, April 25, 2006.

Alexa Hoyne

DALLAS SKYSCRAPER PLOT

On September 24, 2009, Hosam Maher Husein Smadi, a 19-year-old Jordanian, was arrested and charged with attempting to bomb the Wells Fargo Bank office tower, a 60-story skyscraper near Fountain Place in downtown Dallas, Texas. The Federal Bureau of Investigation (FBI) had been monitoring his movements and activities ever since he had been discovered communicating with an online group of extremists. Between March and September, undercover agents interacted more than 60 times with the Jordanian, during which times he made clear his intention to act as a "soldier" for Osama bin Laden and conduct violent jihad.

According to sworn testimony presented in court, Smadi had initially wanted to target the Dallas/Fort Worth International Airport. However, he abandoned this plan because the facility was too strong and well protected. On July 16 he allegedly contacted one of the undercover FBI agents and said he was going to bomb the building containing the bank in order to further disrupt the economy, which was already shaken and weak, in Texas and the United States.

Eventually Smadi and the undercover agent had a meeting where it was decided that a vehicle-borne improvised explosive device (VBIED) would be used for the attack. Federal agents then built a dummy bomb and placed it in a 2001 Ford Explorer Sport Trac. According to documents filed on September 24, 2009, Smadi knowingly took possession of the vehicle believing that it contained an active weapon of mass destruction. The indictment went on to say that he drove the Ford to Dallas, parked it at 1445 Ross Avenue (the address of the Wells Fargo Bank office tower), and activated a timer device connected to the bomb. He apparently then left the truck and departed from the scene in a car with an undercover law enforcement agent.

Smadi pleaded guilty on May 26, 2010, to one count of attempted use of a weapon of mass destruction. On October 19, 2010, U.S. District Court Judge Barbara M. G. Lynn sentenced him to 24 years in prison. Assistant Attorney General David Kris said the court's ruling should send a clear message of the serious consequences to be paid by those willing to carry out acts of violence in the United States to further the terrorist cause.

See also: Al Qaeda; Brooklyn Bridge Bomb Plot; Millennium Plots; Sears Tower Bomb Plot; Times Square Bomb Plot

Further Reading
Emerson, Steven. *Jihad Incorporated: A Guide to Militant Islam in the US.* Foreword by Peter Hoekstra. Amherst, NY: Prometheus Books, 2006.

"Jordanian Man Pleads Guilty in Dallas Bomb Plot." *CBS News,* May 6, 2010. http://www.cbsnews.com/stories/2010/05/26/national/main6522078.shtml, accessed May 2, 2011.

Morrow, Stacy, and Elvira Sakmari. "FBI Arrests Man in Dallas Skyscraper Bomb Plot." *NBC News,* September 25, 2009. http://www.nbcdfw.com/news/local-beat/FBI-Arrests-Man-Accused-in-Skyscraper-Bomb-Plot—61272512.html, accessed May 2, 2011.

"Terror Plot Foiled: Inside the Smadi Case." Federal Bureau of Investigation, Washington, D.C., November 5, 2010. http://www.fbi.gov/news/stories/2010/november/terror-plot-foiled/terror-plot-foiled, accessed May 2, 2011.s

Donna Bassett

DANISH EMBASSY (ISLAMABAD) BOMBING

An Al Qaeda suicide car bomb detonated in front of the Danish embassy in Islamabad, Pakistan, on June 2, 2008, killing 6 people and wounding 27 others. The blast damaged the Dutch ambassador's residence, the Australian defense attaché's residence, and the building housing the United Nations (UN)–funded Devolution Trust for Community Empowerment. The attack was in revenge for a Danish newspaper's reprinting of a 1905 cartoon of the Muslim prophet Muhammad.

The dead included three Pakistanis (two policemen and a cleaner at the embassy), a child, a foreign national, an individual with dual Pakistani-Danish citizenship, and a security guard at the neighboring UN building. Mustafa Abu al-Yazid, an Al Qaeda operative, claimed credit for the bombing and warned that further attacks would occur if Denmark did not apologize for publishing the cartoon.

The bomb was packed in a white Toyota Corolla and was detonated in front of the embassy. The vehicle had managed to gain access to the facility because it had diplomatic license plates that turned out to be false. The device itself was thought to be a combination of fertilizers and diesel fuel boosted by a small amount of high explosives, with an overall weight of around 25 kilograms (55 pounds).

The embassy had received threats as recently as a month before the bombing. The Pakistani media had run several stories asserting that various groups were intending to blow up the mission, and one and a half months before the attack Al Qaeda's deputy operations chief, Ayman al-Zawahiri, urged Muslims to hit Danish targets.

On September 25, 2010, a Pakistani court convicted three men of charges in connection with the bombing. The suspects had been arrested a few months after the attack in a separate case and admitted their complicity under questioning.

See also: Al Qaeda; Zawahiri, Ayman al-

Further Reading

Atwan, Abdel Bari. *The Secret History of al Qaeda.* Berkeley: University of California Press, 2008.

Buruma, Ian. *Murder in Amsterdam: The Death of Theo van Gogh and the Limits of Tolerance.* New York: Penguin, 2006.

Rabasa, Angel, Peter Chalk, Kim Cragin, Sara A. Daly, Heather S. Gregg, Theodore W. Karasik, Kevin A. O'Brien, and William Rosenau. *Beyond al-Qaeda. Part 1: The Global Jihadist Movement.* Santa Monica, CA: RAND, 2006.

Rashid, Ahmed. *Descent into Chaos: The United States and the Failure of Nation Building in Pakistan, Afghanistan, and Central Asia.* New York: Viking, 2008.

Donna Bassett

DAOUD, MUHAMMAD

Muhammad Daoud (also known as Mohammed Daoud Oudeh) was born in the Jerusalem suburb of Siluan (Silwan) on May 16, 1937. He was first an operative and then the leader of the Black September Organization (BSO), a group formed to avenge the expulsion of the Palestine Liberation Organization (PLO) from Jordan in 1970.

Daoud sprang to infamy after masterminding the BSO commando raid on the compound housing the Israeli national team participating in the 1972 Munich Summer Olympic Games. The operation eventually led to the deaths of 11 athletes and coaches (and 1 police officer) following a botched rescue attempt by German security forces. Immediately following the attack, Daoud went to Eastern Europe. He was arrested late that same year while leading a team into Jordan with the goal of taking hostage the Jordanian prime minister and other members of the cabinet. They were to be exchanged for Palestinians imprisoned for actions committed during Black September (the name given to commemorate the PLO's expulsion from Jordan). Daoud was convicted and sentenced to death in March 1973. King Hussein commuted Daoud's sentence to life in prison and later released him along with 1,000 other prisoners in a September 1973 general amnesty. Daoud then moved to Lebanon and remained there until the onset of the civil war in 1975, at which time he returned to Amman.

In January 1977 Daoud was arrested in Paris. Although the Jerusalem Magistrates Court issued a warrant on January 10 seeking Daoud's extradition on charges stemming from the Munich attack, a French court released him when the government of the Federal Republic of Germany failed to expeditiously request his extradition. Daoud then returned to Jordan again. He was allowed to move from Jordan to the West Bank city of Ramallah in 1993, following the Oslo Accords. Daoud became a member of the Palestinian National Council in 1996, and in 1999 he publicly and unrepentantly admitted his role in the Munich attack—which he claimed had been personally sanctioned by Yasser Arafat—in his autobiography "Palestine: From Jerusalem to Munich" (which was never published).

Daoud's admission led to the issuance of a German arrest warrant that resulted in the revocation of his Israeli VIP travel card. He was subsequently denied reentry into the Palestinian Authority (PA) territories on June 13, 1999, after which he moved to Syria, the only country that would allow him residence. He currently lives a low-profile life in Damascus, though he occasionally visits his wife in Amman, Jordan.

See also: Black September Organization (BSO); Munich Olympic Games Massacre

Further Reading

Douad, Abu. *Memoirs of a Palestinian Terrorist*. New York: Arcade, 2002.

Jonas, George. *Vengeance: The True Story of an Israeli Counter-Terrorist Team*. New York: Simon & Schuster, 2005.

Klein, Aaron. *Striking Back: The 1972 Munich Olympics Massacre and Israel's Deadly Response*. New York: Random House, 2005.

Mackinnon. Ian. "Article: I Do Not Regret Athletes' Deaths, Says Munich Massacre Plotter." *Times Online* (UK), December 28, 2005. http://www.timesonline.co.uk/tol/news/world/middle_east/article782946.ece

Roman, Michael. *Black September*. Orlando, FL: Northwest, 1995.

Richard Evans

DAVIES (RODGER) ASSASSINATION

On August 19, 1974, members of the Ethnike Organosis Kypriakou Agonos (EOKA, or National Organization for Cypriot Fighters) fatally shot the U.S. ambassador to Cyprus, Rodger P. Davies, and a Greek Cypriot embassy secretary. The assassinations took place during a riot in Nicosia triggered by protests over the alleged pro-Turkish stance of U.S. government policy toward the Greek-Turkish conflict over Cyprus.

In the attack firebombs were thrown at the U.S. embassy and official residence, destroying several cars, including that of the defense attaché. Nearly 100 bullets also ripped into Davies's office from two angles, leading police to conclude that the ambassador was the intended target. Davies's secretary died as she came to his assistance.

The U.S. embassy received word of impending trouble on the morning Davies was killed. Officials alerted the Nicosia police, who dispatched 30 to 40 law enforcement personnel to the ambassador's residence. Shortly after noon some 300 to 600 demonstrators arrived, carrying anti-American placards and banners. They threw rocks at the building and, climbing over the eight-foot spiked iron fence surrounding it, tore down the U.S. flag and burned it. They then set 10 cars on fire in the embassy parking lot and on the street outside.

Some reports claimed that American intelligence services managed to identify the killers just one hour after the attack, benefiting from television footage that a local film crew had taken of the demonstration. Three defendants were shown shooting automatic weapons into the office, while another trio were firing in other directions.

After years of American pressure, the six suspects were finally arrested on February 4, 1977, and charged with belonging to EOKA. Three were also indicted for murder—Ionnis Ktimatis (a former policeman serving a prison term for illegal possession of firearms), Loizos Savva (another ex-policeman), and Neoptolemos Leftis—and arraigned seven days later. On June 3, 1977, a Cypriot court threw out the homicide charges against Ktimatis and Leftis, citing lack of evidence. The decision effectively ensured that the two would not be able to testify in court about any links between the gunmen and EOKA leaders who might have planned and ordered the assault as well as held government posts.

Two of the other defendants were acquitted, one on a technicality, while the other two were sentenced to a few months in jail after pleading guilty. On June 20, 1977, Ktimatis and Leftis were both convicted, the former for illegal use and possession of firearms, riot, and property damage, the latter for illegal possession of firearms and riot. They were respectively sentenced to seven and five years in jail.

See also: Ethnike Organosis Kypriakou Agonos (EOKA)

Further Reading

"Death of an Ambassador." *Time,* September 2, 1974. http://www.time.com/time/magazine/article/0,9171,943727,00.html, accessed May 2, 2011.

Mickolus, Edward F. *Transnational Terrorism: A Chronology of Events, 1968–1979.* Westport, CT: Greenwood, 1980.

Donna Bassett

DAWSON'S FIELD HIJACKINGS

On September 6, 1970, members of the Popular Front for the Liberation of Palestine (PFLP) carried out three well-coordinated hijackings of aircraft flying from Europe to the United States. The first was a TWA Boeing 707, which was seized over Belgium; the second was a Swissair DC-8, which was taken over France; the third was a Pan Am jet, hijacked over Holland. An attempted fourth hijacking, of an El Al Boeing 707, was thwarted by an Israeli sky marshal who shot dead one of the perpetrators and captured the other, Leila Khaled.

The first two planes, respectively carrying 155 and 151 passengers and crew, were diverted to Dawson's Field, a former Royal Air Force (RAF) desert landing strip in Zerka, Jordan. The third was flown first to Beirut and then to Cairo, where, after telling those on board to "get out fast," the terrorists blew the aircraft up.

With more than 300 hostages and two aircraft in their possession, the Palestinians demanded the release of three PFLP members being held in West Germany for an attack on an airline bus in Munich on February 10, 1970; of three imprisoned in Switzerland for a February 18, 1969, attack on an El Al plane in Zurich that had resulted in the killing of the copilot; of Leila Khaled (who had been transferred to the United Kingdom after the failed hijacking of the El Al Boeing); and of an unspecified number of fedayeen incarcerated in Israeli prisons. The terrorists threatened to blow up the two planes and their passengers by 3 A.M. on Thursday, September 10, if their demands were not met.

Commandos immediately surrounded the aircraft, flanked by troops from Jordan's army as well as 50 tanks and armored cars. Official negotiations began, with the Swiss and German governments initially being willing to deal unilaterally with terrorists to free their own nationals. However, the British prime minister, Edward Heath, called on all five governments to take a common position, and, hence, on September 8 the Berne Five was formed. Working through the International Committee of the Red Cross (ICRC), the multilateral body managed to secure the release of 127 passengers, mostly women and children, who were allowed to

Palestinian guerrillas celebrate the blowing up of a Boac Airliner hijacked to Dawson's Field, a desert airstrip north of Amman, Jordan, in September 14, 1970. The hijacking was one of a series of incidents that prompted Jordan's King Hussein to order his Bedouin Army to expel the guerrillas from Jordan. (AP/Wide World Photos)

go to two hotels in the Jordanian capital. The remaining hostages—all men from West Germany, the United Kingdom, Israel, and the United States—were forced to remain.

On September 9, the PFLP captured another plane, a British VC-10, which was also flown to Dawson's Field, adding a further 125 passengers to their hostage list. Meanwhile, the ICRC representative, Andre Rochat, informed the PFLP leadership (based in Jordan) that they would free the seven prisoners held in West Germany, Britain, and Switzerland upon the release of all passengers from the hijacked planes. This partially satisfied the terrorists, and on September 11 (one day after the stated deadline), two more Americans were allowed to leave. Eighteen others, however, were secretly taken to Zerka and hidden in homes, because the attack squad wanted extra insurance in the event of a double cross.

Although its own nationals had been abducted in the attacks, the Israeli government preferred to remain an observer in the Berne Five, and thus the ICRC was named by only four of the members as their intermediary. A three-member liaison group of officials was subsequently sent to Amman to confer with PFLP members. On September 11, an Iraqi military radio broadcast picked up the following communiqué made by the PFLP Central Committee: "The committee has decided the following: 1. To transfer all passengers to Amman; 2. To release all passengers of various nationalities with the exception of Israelis of military capacity. These passengers will be released when an official statement is issued by the foreign countries concerned that they are ready to free the Palestinian girl and other fedayeen held . . . in Western Germany, Switzerland, and Britain. 3. To release the three aircraft and their crews as soon as the fedayeen in question arrive in Jordan or in any other Arab country. . . . 4. To hold the [Zionist] passengers of military capacity in Amman until an agreement is reached in the current negotiations with the Red Cross on the release by the Zionist authorities occupying Palestine of a number of Palestinian men and women fedayeen imprisoned in enemy jails."

The next day, the PFLP terrorists announced that all the women and children who had been transferred to the hotels in Amman would be released. They then evacuated the three planes at Dawson's Field, which were subsequently destroyed by PFLP explosives experts. This left 58 hostages, including the 18 who were being secretly held in Zerka.

The PFLP's activities on Jordanian territory proved too much for King Hussein to tolerate, and he ordered the military to commence raids on Palestinian fedayeen in the country. A series of bloody battles ensued, during which an estimated seven thousand died (an event that was to become known as Black September). Negotiations quickly became of secondary importance to the embattled PFLP leadership, and hostages were rescued sequentially. On September 25, 16 Swiss, German, and British were found in the Wahdat refugee camp near Amman, apparently abandoned by their Palestinian guards. The next day 32 U.S. captives being held in Amman were released to the ICRC. The final 6 Americans—three members of the U.S. government, two rabbis, and one teacher—were handed over to the ICRC four days later. On September 29, the Swiss government announced that the seven Arab militants imprisoned in Switzerland, West Germany, and the United Kingdom would be allowed to leave jail once all the Americans had safely departed from Jordan. They also called on Israel to release 10 Lebanese soldiers and two Algerians taken from an airliner on August 14 as a humanitarian gesture. On September 30, a British RAF Comet flew Khaled out of the United Kingdom to Cairo. The plane traveled via Munich and Zurich, where it picked up the other PFLP members set free by the German and Swiss governments.

See also: Black September Organization (BSO); Popular Front for the Liberation of Palestine (PFLP); Zurich Airport Attack

Further Reading

"Dawson Field Hijackings." *Zurich.* http://www.reference.com/browse/Dawson's_Field_hi jackings, accessed February 11, 2011.

"On This Day: Hijacked Jets Destroyed by Guerrillas." *BBC News,* September 12, 1970. http://news.bbc.co.uk/onthisday/hi/dates/stories/september/12/newsid_2514000/2514929.stm, accessed February 11, 2011.

Rosie, George. *The Directory of International Terrorism.* Edinburgh: Mainstream, 1986. Pp. 95–96.

Edward F. Mickolus

DE PUNT TRAIN SIEGE

At 8:30 A.M. on May 23, 1977, terrorists from the Vrije Zuidmolukse Jongeren (VZJ) seized control of a commuter train en route from Rotterdam to Groningen in the northern Netherlands. Halting the train at De Punt, the hijackers issued a statement calling on the Dutch government to immediately exert diplomatic and political pressure on Indonesia to grant independence to their homeland of South Molucca. They also demanded the release of several of their comrades held in prison for earlier offenses and requested that a Boeing 747 be made available to fly them out of the country from Amsterdam's international airport, Schiphol. The terrorists warned that unless these demands were met, they would start to execute their hostages; to show that they were serious, the hijackers shot and killed the train driver, dumping his body on the rail tracks.

Subsequent negotiations between the Dutch government and the VZJ dragged on for days. A South Moluccan doctor initially acted as a spokesman for the authorities, but his true loyalties soon became suspect out of concern that he was secretly feeding information to the terrorists on the train. Matters came to a head on June 10 when the hijackers said they had run out of patience and gave a deadline of 24 hours for their demands to be met. Confronted with a situation that it was now clearly impossible to resolve peacefully, the authorities made the decision to storm the train using a unit from the Royal Netherlands Marine Corps elite counterterrorism force, the Bijzondere Bijstand Eenheid (BBE, or Special Backup Unit). In fact, members of the BBE had already engaged in several intelligence-gathering sorties, placing listening devices on the body of the train at night and disguising themselves as Red Cross workers who were delivering food trolleys to the hijackers. These preparations proved vital in helping the authorities identify the locations of the hostages and the carriages where the terrorists spent most of their time.

Two BBE attack teams were readied—one to storm the train and one to provide covering fire to separate the hijackers from their captives. At 4:53 A.M. on June 11, a flight of F-104s screamed over the train with full afterburners alight to distract the terrorists from the marine assault force. The tactic worked well, disorienting the South Moluccans, who had no time to recover their senses prior to the initiation of the rescue operation. The covering platoon unleashed a fusillade of fire into the carriages that held most of the hijackers, while the main attack team raided the train. In the ensuing confrontation (which lasted no more than a minute), two captives were fatally shot (largely because they failed to comply with the command "get down"), and six terrorists were killed and another seven captured. With the exception of one trooper who was slightly injured by flying debris, the marines suffered no casualties.

A year later the VZJ staged another attack—this time against government offices in Drenthe, near Assen, demanding the release of their comrades captured at De Punt in exchange for the release of 71 hostages. During the incident six civilians were killed before the marines once again freed the captives. This was the last major act attributed to the group, with the Dutch government successfully blunting the organization's campaign of violence through a combination of harsh prison sentences and economic aid aimed at improving the conditions of the South Moluccan community in the Netherlands. By the 1980s, the aspiration of creating an independent state in the Indonesian archipelago had been formally abandoned by the VZJ leadership.

See also: Beilen Train Siege

Further Reading

Foster, Nigel. "Sending in the Marines." *The Elite* 5 (1986).
"1977: Dutch Children Held Hostage." *BBC on This Day.* http://news.bbc.co.uk/onthisday/
    hi/dates/stories/may/23/newsid_2503000/2503933.stm, accessed October 30, 2009.
"Terrorists: The Commandos Strike at Dawn." *Time Magazine,* June 20, 1977.

Peter Chalk

DEMOCRATIC FRONT FOR THE LIBERATION OF PALESTINE (DFLP)

In 1969 Nayef Hawatmeh and Yasser Abed Rabbo broke off from the Popular Front for the Liberation of Palestine (PFLP), headed by George Habash. They believed the PFLP focused too narrowly on military concerns. Their new organization was known as the Popular Democratic Front for the Liberation of Palestine (PDFLP), but in 1974 it changed its name to the Democratic Front for the Liberation of Palestine (DFLP).

Hawatmeh headed the organization as its secretary-general and its chief representative to the Palestine Liberation Organization (PLO). Arab nationalist and Marxist in orientation, the DFLP was known as the most intellectually oriented of the Palestinian resistance groups. Publicly, the DFLP called for a democratic, unified, and unitary Palestinian state that would allow "both Arabs and Jews to develop their national culture." Originally, the DFLP believed this state could be achieved only through the political activation of the masses and a "people's war." Gradually, however, the organization shifted to a slightly more moderate stance. Although it condemned attacks carried out outside of Israel, such as airline hijackings by the PFLP, at the same time the DFLP refused to give up armed struggle, and it mounted a number of small-scale raids against Israeli targets. Its largest and most notorious operation was the so-called Ma'alot Massacre on May 17, 1974, in which 26 Israelis were killed and another 60 wounded.

In 1974 the DFLP was struggling with factionalism from within its ranks and the PLO in general. Four years later, it joined the Rejectionist Front. Beginning in the early 1980s, the DFLP was known as the leading pro-Soviet and pro–People's Republic of China (PRC) organization within the PLO. The collapse of the Soviet Union and a subsequent reduction in Chinese aid cost the DFLP some of its popular support. Although the DFLP leadership supported PLO chairman Yasser Arafat's efforts to begin peace negotiations with Israel, many of the organization's rank and file did not. The party also suffered with the rise of Hamas in the 1980s.

In 1991 the DFLP split when cofounder Abed Rabbo supported the negotiations in Madrid that led to the formation of the Palestinian Authority (PA). The faction led by Abed Rabbo constituted itself as the Al-Ittihad al-Dimuqrati al-Filastini (FIDA, or Palestine Democratic Union). It rejected terrorist activities in favor of negotiations and also turned its back on Marxism in favor of the democratization of Palestinian society. There were reports of armed clashes between the two factions during this split. The DFLP tended to retain control of the foreign branches, while the FIDA secured most of the membership within the Left Bank.

The other faction of the DFLP opposed the Declaration of Principles signed in 1993, claiming that the Oslo negotiations had led to an agreement that denied the Palestinians their legitimate rights. The DFLP had little influence in the Second (al-Aqsa) Intifada, which broke out in 2000.

The DFLP continues to support military activities but insists that these be confined to targets only in the so-called occupied territories and not within the Green Line. It argues that Palestinians should fight only against the occupation rather than against Israeli citizens. Although the DFLP retains considerable influence within the PLO, it did not do well in either the PA presidential election in 2005 or the Palestinian Legislative Council elections of 2006. In the former, its candidate, Taysir Khalid, won only 3.5 percent of the vote. In the latter election, the DFLP won only 2.8 percent of the popular vote and 2 seats in the 132-person council. Active among Palestinians primarily in Syria and Lebanon, and with only a limited presence in the West Bank and the Gaza Strip, the DFLP is believed to receive some financial and military support from Syria.

See also: Arafat, Yasser; Oslo Accords; Palestine Liberation Organization (PLO); Popular Front for the Liberation of Palestine (PFLP)

Further Reading

Gresh, Alain. *The PLO: The Struggle Within.* London: Zed, 1988.

Nassar, Jamal R. *The Palestine Liberation Organization: From Armed Struggle to the Declaration of Independence.* New York: Praeger, 1991.

Rubin, Barry, and Judith Colp Rubin. *Yasir Arafat: A Political Biography.* New York: Oxford University Press, 2003.

Said, Edward W. *The Question of Palestine.* New York: Vintage Books, 1992.

Spencer C. Tucker

DERA ISMAIL KHAN BOMBING

On February 20, 2009, a suicide bomber attacked a funeral procession that was being held in Dera Ismail Khan (often abbreviated to DI Khan) in Pakistan for a local Shi'a Muslim leader, Sher Zaman. The blast injured at least 175 people. Police said the terrorist detonated his device at approximately 10:05 A.M. near the Shobra Hotel and had deliberately targeted the mourners.

The identity of the bomber was unknown, but local authorities reported that his head and foot had been found. According to eyewitnesses he appeared to be 20 years old and had a crew cut and a light beard. A bomb-disposal official said that the bomb consisted of at least 14 kilograms (30 pounds) of explosives, and a task force was formed to investigate the incident.

Although President Asif Ali Zardari, Prime Minister Yousuf Raza Gilani, and the governor of Punjab, Slamaan Taseer, condemned the attack in the strongest terms, it triggered an immediate and violent response. An angry mob coalesced and began setting fire to property. The rioting escalated and soon became so intense that local authorities were compelled to call in the military to restore order. Shoot-on-sight orders were issued, and a curfew was imposed that lasted for at least two days.

On February 19 the police announced that they had arrested three of the four individuals suspected of murdering Zaman. The Tehrik-e-Taliban Pakistan (TTP, or Pakistani Taliban) subsequently took credit for the February bombing, justifying it as a means of pressuring Islamabad to put an end to an offensive in the Federally Administered Tribal Areas (FATA).

The TTP had already emerged as an increasingly visible and dangerous entity and had been linked to a previous high-profile attack on August 21, 2008, when it targeted the Pakistan Ordnance Factory in Wah. The incident killed at least 70 people, mostly civilian workers, and left more than 100 wounded.

The February bombing was very similar to two previous attacks. The first took place in August 19, 2008, when a suicide terrorist targeted a hospital waiting room. Victims there included seven police officers who were assigned to protect Basit Ali Zaidi, a local Shi'a leader who had been shot earlier in the day. The perpetrator killed at least 14 members of the victim's family and wounded many others. The second occurred on November 21, 2008. In this case, a suicide bomber targeted mourners attending the funerals of Allama Nazir Hussain Shah and Shah Iqbal Hussain, two Shi'a religious leaders who had been shot and killed that same month. The attack killed 9 and wounded 39.

Drive-by shootings and bombings have reportedly killed dozens of individuals in Dera Ismail Khan. The district borders on the South Waziristan tribal district of Afghanistan. Tensions between the Sunni majority and Shi'a minority Muslim populations seem to account for the majority of the civilian violence. Attacks on police and security forces have largely been blamed on Taliban militants.

See also: Pakistan Ordnance Factory Bombing; Tehrik-e-Taliban Pakistan (TTP)

Further Reading

Rashid, Ahmed. *Descent into Chaos: The United States and the Failure of Nation Building in Pakistan, Afghanistan, and Central Asia.* New York: Viking, 2008.

Donna Bassett

DEVRIMCI HALK KURTULUS PARTISI/ CEPHESI (DHKP/C)

Along with other threats, Turkey has countered political terrorism from extreme left groups, including the Devrimci Halk Kurtulus Partisi/Cephesi (DHKP/C), or Revolutionary People's Liberation Party/Front. Originally founded as Devrimci Sol, or Dev Sol (itself a splinter of Dev Genc), Dursun Karatas renamed the group in 1994. It is a Marxist-Leninist splinter movement that opposes the Turkish regime, which it sees as controlled by the "imperialist" West, particularly the United States and NATO, and its funding comes from leadership and cadres located in Europe.

The DHKP/C and its predecessor Dev Sol have assassinated serving and retired Turkish police, army and security officials, members of the judiciary, academics, and politicians. They have also targeted banks, businesses, and NATO and U.S. military bases and personnel in Turkey. In 2001 the DHKP/C escalated the scale of their violence, carrying out suicide strikes against Turkish police and security force personnel in addition to continuing with conventional bombings of venues linked to the United States. The frequency of these acts increased following the coalition invasion of Iraq in 2003. A major attack was narrowly averted on June 24, 2004, when a bomb exploded onboard a bus close to Istanbul's University, killing 4 passengers and injuring a further 10. Investigations subsequently revealed that one of those killed, Semira Polat, was a wanted DHKP/C terrorist and that she had been planning to bomb a NATO conference in the city but that the explosive device she was carrying had detonated prematurely.

Since 2004, arrests of its members have dented the strength of the DHKP/C, reflected by a significant drop in its activities. That said the group continues to benefit from a strong prison network and together with its armed wing remains operational.

Further Reading

Aktan, Gunduz, and Ali Koknar. "Turkey." In Yonah Alexander, ed., *Combating Terrorism: Strategies of Ten Countries.* Ann Arbor: University of Michigan Press, 2002.
Alexander, Yonah, and Dennis Pluchinsky. *Europe's Red Terrorists: The Fighting Communist Organizations.* London: Frank Cass, 1992.
Mango, Andrew. *Turkey and the War on Terror: For Forty Years We Fought Alone.* London: Routledge, 2005.

Richard Warnes

DIZENGOFF SHOPPING CENTER BOMBING

On March 4, 1996, a suicide cadre from Hamas's Izz ad-Din al-Qassam Brigades set off 20 kilograms (44 pounds) of TNT near a bus parked close to the entrance to the Dizengoff shopping center, the largest mall in Tel Aviv, Israel. The attack left 13 people dead, including several children, and another 163 wounded. The bomber had apparently attempted to detonate his device in the heart of the enclosed center but instead activated it at a crosswalk outside the building, fearing that security guards would discover the bomb.

Subsequent investigations revealed that Sa'id Husayn Sulaymani, a 45-year-old Israeli Arab from Manshiya-Zabda, had picked up the suicide operative in Gaza and drove him to Tel Aviv for $1,100. The bomber hid in a crate that had been left in a grocery truck and then walked to the mall. Sulaymani was arrested on March 4 and remanded into custody until the 20th of that month.

Palestinian Authority (PA) security forces in Ramallah later arrested Mohammed Abu Wardeh, a 21-year-old student at an Islamic teachers college, who was believed to be the mastermind behind the attack as well as two other bombings. He was convicted for recruiting terrorists and sentenced to a life of hard labor (which Yasser Arafat, the chairman of the Palestine Liberation Organization [PLO] approved).

On March 9, 1996, an anonymous Arabic-speaking caller told Israel Television Channel One that the bomber was 'Ummar Siyam, a Palestinian from Gaza's Sabra neighborhood. However, a week later *Qol Yisra'el* quoted Palestinian sources as identifying the perpetrator as Ramiz 'Abd-al-Qadir Muhammad, an Islamic radical from Khan Yunus.

The Palestinian Islamic Jihad (PIJ), the Pupils of Ayash, and the Izz ad-Din al-Qassam Brigades all claimed credit for the attack, although it is the latter that most people think was behind the atrocity. The group acts as the armed wing of Hamas and is named after the Syrian-Palestinian Islamist imam and agitator Sheikh Izz ad-Din al-Qassam. The size of the organization is not known, but its website claims that over 800 of its members have been killed. On the basis of this figure, one can surmise that the organization is probably several thousand strong. Israeli intelligence sources have given an estimated figure of 8,000 cadres, with the number in the wider Hamas movement upwards of 20,000.

The Izz ad-Din al-Qassam Brigades and other groups have been expanding in Gaza ever since the territory was taken over by Hamas. Iran is thought to be one of the organization's main backers, providing both weapons—which are smuggled via an intricate network of underground tunnels—and training.

See also: Ben Yehuda Shopping Mall Bombing; Hamas (Islamic Resistance Movement); Jerusalem Bus Attacks (1996); Palestinian Islamic Jihad (PIJ)

Further Reading

Levitt, Matthew. *Hamas: Politics, Charity, and Terrorism in the Service of Jihad.* Foreword by Dennis Ross. New Haven, CT: Yale University Press, 2006.

Milton-Edwards, Beverley, and Stephen Farrell. *Hamas: The Islamic Resistance Movement.* Malden, MA: Polity, 2010.

Mishal, Shaul, and Avraham Sela. *The Palestinian HAMAS: Vision, Violence, and Coexistence.* New York: Columbia University Press, 2000.

Donna Bassett

DOWNING STREET MORTAR ATTACK

During a rare London snowstorm on February 7, 1991, the Provisional Irish Republican Army (PIRA) fired three mortar rounds at 10 Downing Street, the British prime minister's office and residence, while the United Kingdom's cabinet was holding a meeting there. One detonated in Prime Minister John Major's garden,

15 feet from the rear of the building, and two others landed in Mountbatten Green near the neighboring Foreign and Commonwealth Office (one exploded and the other disintegrated without blowing up). The blasts shattered windows in the adjacent Downing Street residences of Chief Whip Richard Ryder and Chancellor of the Exchequer Norman Lamont, and flying glass slightly injured a cabinet official and two policemen. A white Ford Transit van, with the license plate A862 NAR and bought with cash, was used to launch the mortars.

Immediately after the attack (which occurred at 10:08 A.M.), hundreds of police officers sealed off a large area in Central London that extended from the Houses of Parliament to Trafalgar Square. Tourists were kept away from their hotels inside the zone until 6 P.M. as forensic and weapons experts combed the streets looking for pieces of the weapons, and employees at 10 Downing Street and the nearby Foreign Office were locked in all day behind security gates.

Those present at the cabinet meeting included John Major, Chief Treasury Secretary David Mellor, Conservative Party elder statesman Douglas Hurd, Conservative Member of Parliament Tom King, Conservative Member of Parliament Norman Lamont, Social Security Secretary Peter Lilley, Conservative Member of Parliament John Wakeham, Cabinet Secretary Robin Butler, Defense Staff Chief David Craig, Attorney General for England and Wales and Northern Ireland Patrick Mayhew, Chairman of the Joint Intelligence Committee Percy Cradock, the prime minister's private secretary Charles Powell, and Gus O'Donnell, the United Kingdom's executive director to both the International Monetary Fund and the World Bank.

The attack was the first use of mortars by the PIRA outside of Northern Ireland and came about despite a major overhaul of security at Downing Street three years earlier. The original plan was to assassinate Margaret Thatcher, John Major's predecessor, with a car bomb. However, the PIRA's Army Council ruled this out due to the risk of civilian casualties and the politically counterproductive effect this would have generated. Instead, the PIRA leadership sanctioned a mortar attack, and by the time the scheme was ready to be put into effect Major had replaced Thatcher as the head of government.

Planning for the plot commenced in mid-1990. Two PIRA members familiar with the construction and trajectory of mortars traveled to London to prepare the groundwork. They liaised with a PIRA coordinator who procured the explosives and materials needed for the manufacture of the mortars. An active service unit (ASU) was mobilized and given the task of purchasing a van and renting a secure garage where the vehicle could be retrofitted with the weapons. Once this had been completed the two PIRA members returned to Northern Ireland to avoid any risk of being arrested after the attack.

In November 1990 Margaret Thatcher unexpectedly resigned from the government, but the PIRA Army Council decided the planned attack should still go ahead, targeting her successor John Major instead. It was decided that the mortars should be launched when Major and his ministers were likely to be meeting at Downing Street, and February 7 was set as the date of the attack.

The PIRA team worked out the firing range and angle from scale maps and photographs of the location during a dummy run. One operative then drove the white van to Downing Street. Three one-meter (three-feet)-long Mark-10 mortars—incorporating Semtex supplied from Libya—had been installed in the back of the vehicle. This rocket had already achieved notoriety at least a decade before the Downing Street incident, when it was used in an April 1980 attack on a Northern Ireland police station near Corry Square, in Newry. A subsequent assault on a Royal Ulster Constabulary barracks in February 1985, again in Corry Square, killed 9 officers and wounded 37 people, including 25 civilians.

The Mark-10s were equipped with a short-fuse timing device and launched through a hole cut in the van roof that was hidden by a special covering and paint. Seconds before the mortars fired, the driver of the vehicle ran off and escaped on a waiting motorcycle. A preset incendiary device, designed to destroy any forensic evidence, then ignited and destroyed the van.

The trajectory of the bombs sent them over the roofs of the Horse Guards building, and two were just five degrees off target. Indeed, the mortar that landed in the garden failed to go straight into the cabinet room only because it hit a tree. Major later wrote that if it had been 10 feet closer, half of the cabinet could have been killed.

In a statement issued in Dublin, Ireland, and released in Belfast, Northern Ireland, the PIRA said, "On Feb. 7, 1991 an ASU . . . had successfully breached the greatly enhanced wartime security surrounding 10 Downing Street by launching a mortar attack in the heart of the British establishment." The communiqué went on to warn that while "nationalist people in the six counties are forced to live under British rule, the British Cabinet will be forced to meet in bunkers." PIRA justified the attack on the grounds that it was aimed at initiating a process that would ultimately lead to British withdrawal from Northern Ireland and thereby create the conditions for establishing a true democracy throughout Ireland.

In response, John Major told the House of Commons that "our determination to beat terrorism cannot be beaten by terrorism. The IRA's record is one of failure in every respect, and that failure was demonstrated yet again today. It's about time they learned that democracies cannot be intimidated by terrorism, and we treat them with contempt."

Peter Gurney, the army official who defused the unexploded mortar that had landed in Mountbatten Green, later observed that the attack team had achieved a remarkably good aim, considering that the bomb was fired from 250 yards away with no direct line of sight. His published statement said, "Technically, it was quite brilliant and I'm sure that many army crews, if given a similar task, would be very pleased to drop a bomb that close. You've got to park the launch vehicle in an area that is guarded by armed men and you've got less than a minute to do it."

The British Security Service, MI5, was equally "laudatory" in its postattack assessment: "The positioning of the [mortar] baseplate at the firing point was done with remarkable precision and the range calculations had clearly been carried out with extreme care. It was no mean feat to place one round on target, which argues for the presence of a highly experienced and capable operator."

See also: Brighton Bombing; Irish Republican Army (IRA); Mountbatten (Lord) Assassination; Provisional Irish Republican Army (PIRA)

Further Reading

Coogan, Tim. *The Troubles: Ireland's Ordeal 1966–1995 and the Search for Peace.* London: Hutchinson, 1995.

McKittrick, David, and David McVea. *Making Sense of the Troubles.* London: Penguin Books, 2000.

Oppenheimer, A. R. *IRA: The Bombs and the Bullets: A History of Deadly Ingenuity.* Foreword by Richard English. Dublin: Irish Academic Press, 2009.

"Provisional IRA's History of Violence." *BBC News,* September 1, 1998. http://news.bbc.co.uk/2/hi/events/northern_ireland/paramilitaries/162714.stm, accessed May 2, 2011.

Whitney, Craig. "I.R.A. Attacks 10 Downing Street with Mortar Fire as Cabinet Meets." *New York Times,* February 8, 1991. http://query.nytimes.com/gst/fullpage.html?res=9d0ce7da123bf93ba35751c0a967958260, accessed May 2, 2011.

Donna Bassett

DOZIER (JAMES) KIDNAPPING

On December 17, 1981, the Italian Brigate Rosse (BR, or Red Brigades), considered one of Europe's most ruthless and violent terrorist organizations, kidnapped American General James Lee Dozier, who at the time was deputy chief of staff for logistics and administration at NATO's headquarters in southern Europe. Dozier was a graduate of West Point and had received the Silver Star due to his service in Vietnam. Friends would describe Dozier as a "soldier's soldier" who was "low key and efficient." The kidnapping was particularly notable in that it was the first time the BR had targeted a prominent non-Italian.

Dozier's kidnappers accessed the general's apartment (in Verona, Italy) by posing as plumbers who claimed they needed to fix a leak. As they entered, one of the terrorists struck Dozier on the head with a pistol butt; his wife was subsequently seized and then tied up, with her eyes and mouth fastened with adhesive tape. The kidnappers placed the general in a small refrigerator box, dragged him out of the apartment, and put him into a van. They then drove 50 miles to a safe house on the outskirts of Padua.

For roughly six weeks, Dozier was kept in a single location, chained to a steel cot positioned under a small tent. He was forced to endure constant lighting and to listen to loud music, which he would later blame for hearing loss. While Dozier was held captive, the BR aired various statements to the public that detailed their demands or particular grievances. The first communiqué, issued only days after the kidnapping, made no specific reference to a ransom but rather addressed particular matters of interest to the BR and paid tribute to a fellow red terrorist organization, the German Red Army Faction (Rote Armee Fraktion, or RAF). Other communiqués followed, which again were notable for their lack of specific demands (monetary or otherwise) for Dozier's release. By this time, however, Italian authorities had gained critical information from an informant and were able to launch a successful rescue under the auspices of the Nucleo Operativo Centrale di Sicurezza (NOCS, or Central Security Operations Service).

General Dozier, who had been held for 42 days, would later report that as police stormed the apartment, one of his captives was "leveling a gun at his head."

After this rescue, the BR experienced further defections of their members, who in turn acted as informants for the government. Back in the United States, Dozier received a hero's welcome and was celebrated by President Ronald Reagan at the annual National Prayer Breakfast, following which both men traveled in a motorcade to the White House, where they posed for pictures.

Dozier continued his army career and was promoted two years later to the rank of major general. In 2006 he addressed a conference on terrorism sponsored by the U.S. Air Force and told the group that many of the lessons he learned from his experience with the BR were still applicable to contemporary terrorist groups.

See also: Brigate Rosse (BR); Rote Armee Fraktion (RAF)

Bearded Brig. Gen. James L. Dozier is photographed at police headquarters in Padua, Italy, after Italian police commandos freed him from his kidnappers. The rescue ended the American general's six-week ordeal in a "peoples prison." (AP/Wide World Photos)

Further Reading

"Dozier Kidnap Defendant Says Bulgaria Sought Role." *Gazette News Service*, March 17, 1982. Available online at http://news.google.com/newspapers?nid=1946&dat=1982 20317.

"1982: US General Rescued from Red Brigades." *BBC*, January 28, 1982. *BBC on This Day*. http://news.bbc.co.uk/onthisday/hi/dates/stories/jawag/28/newsid-4202000/4202723.

Philipps, Thomas. "The Dozier Kidnapping: Confronting the Red Brigades." *Air and Space Power Journal*, February 7, 2002. http://www.airpower.maxwell.af.mil/airchronicles/cc/philipps.html.

Smith, Paul. *The Terrorism Ahead: Confronting Transnational Violence in the Twenty-First Century.* Armonk, NY: M. E. Sharpe, 2008. Pp. 33–34.

Wilson, George. "Kidnapped Officer Seen as a 'Soldier's Soldier.'" *Washington Post,* December 18, 1981, p. A52.

Paul Smith

DUJANA, ABU

Abu Dujana was born in Cianjur, West Java, and raised in central Java. He has close family connections to Darul Islam, a Muslim militant movement founded in 1942 that is generally considered to be the predecessor of Jemaah Islamiyah (JI).

Much of Abu Dujana's early education was overseen by Dadang Hafidz, who would later assist with procuring weapons and providing support for JI operatives in Indonesia. After overseeing his study of the Koran, Hafidz selected Abu Dujana to travel to Pakistan for additional religious instruction. Abu Dujana remained in that country until 1988; while there, he met Abu Rusdan—a future JI leader—and Nurjaman Riduan Hambali (also known as "Hambali"), Al Qaeda's main link to militants in Southeast Asia.

In 1988 Abu Dujana went to Afghanistan, where he was trained in tactics, small arms, and bomb making. It was there that he befriended Aris Sumarsono (also known as Zulkarnaen), who would become JI's military chief, and made first contact with Osama bin Laden. Abu Dujana's fluency in Arabic facilitated relationships with other Islamic extremists and more than likely assisted in fostering the ties that would form between JI and Al Qaeda.

Shortly after 1991, Abu Dujana returned to Southeast Asia. He worked for a time as a teacher at Lukmanul Hakiem, an Islamic boarding school founded by JI in Johor, Malaysia. In 1996 he is believed to have traveled to the southern Philippines, where he assisted in training recruits at an Islamist camp in Mindanao. Two years later the JI leadership dispatched Abu Dujana to coordinate the group's activities in the Malukus and Central Sulawesi (both of which were experiencing severe religious communal violence), where he remained until 2001. During this time Abu Dujana solidified his reputation in JI and rose through its ranks. By 2000 he had become the secretary of Mantiqi II, a subdivision of the organization that oversaw operations in Indonesia (except Sulawesi and Kalimantan) and was responsible for leadership and recruitment.

Abu Dujana served as the personal secretary to Abu Bakar Bashir, JI's emir until October 2002 (when Bashir was arrested on charges of rebellion in connection with the Bali bombings). He was then appointed as the direct aide to Abu Rusdan, Bashir's replacement. Abu Dujana remained in this position until Rusdan's arrest a year later, after which he assumed the leadership of JI.

Abu Dujana played an active role in plotting and executing some of JI's most infamous attacks on Western targets in Indonesia. It is believed that he met with Zulkarnean the day before coordinated bombings killed 202 people in Bali, the majority of them Australian tourists. He also met with operatives shortly before a suicide bomber detonated his explosives outside the Marriott Hotel in Jakarta in 2003.

Despite being placed on the 10-most-wanted list by Indonesian authorities in 2003, Abu Dujana avoided capture for many years. He was eventually arrested in June 2007 in central Java and is currently serving a 15-year prison sentence.

See also: Bali Bombings (2002); Bashir, Abu Bakar; Jemaah Islamiyah (JI); Marriott Hotel (Jakarta) Bombing (2003)

Further Reading

Abuza, Zachary. "Abu Dujana: Jemaah Islamiyah's New al-Qaeda Linked Leader." *Terrorism Focus,* April 4, 2006. http://jamestown.org/terrorism/news/article.php?articleid= 2369948.

Brummitt, Chris. "Indonesian Militant with Close al-Qaeda Links Now Leads Jemaah Islamiyah." Associated Press, March 22, 2006. Available online at http://www.signon sandiego.com/news/world/20060322-1313-indonesia-militantleader.html.

"Indonesia Holds Extremist Leader." *BBC News,* June 13, 2007. http://news.bbc.co.uk/2/hi/6747253.stm.

"Indonesian Court Sentences Key Militant." *CNN.com,* April 21, 2008. http://www.cnn.com/2008/WORLD/asiapcf/04/21/indonesia.militant/.

"Key Leader Profile: Abu Dujana." Terrorism Knowledge Base, Memorial Institute for the Prevention of Terrorism. http://www.tkb.org/KeyLeader.jsp?memID=6370.

"New JI Leader 'Has al-Qaeda Link.'" *BBC,* March 22, 2006. http://news.bbc.co.uk/2/hi/asia-pacific/4832380.stm.

Edward F. Mickolus

DWIKARNA, AGUS

Agus Dwikarna was the commander and founder of Laskar Jundullah, the militia of the Komite Pengerakan Syariat Islam (KPSI, or Committee to Uphold Islamic Law), which fought to evict Christians from several central Indonesian islands in late 2000. The group established a terrorist camp in the dense jungle near the port city of Poso and helped train two dozen Filipino members of the Moro Islamic Liberation Front, several cadres of the Malaysian Mujahideen Group (which is affiliated with Jemaah Islamiyah [JI], an Al Qaeda–linked group that planned to bomb several Western embassies in Singapore), and scores from the Middle East, Europe, and North Africa. The camp was dismantled soon after the September 11 attacks.

Dwikarna was active in several radical groups, including the Majelis Mujahideen of Indonesia (MMI), which is led by Abu Bakar Bashir—the cleric accused by Malaysia and Singapore of being the ideological leader of JI. He is alleged to have provided alibis to several hundred foreigners traveling in Southeast Asia by giving them documents with the letterhead of the Muslim charity for which he worked: the Committee to Overcome Crisis. Regional intelligence authorities also believe he worked with Parlindungan Siregar, a Muslim living in Spain who helped arrange for several hundred Al Qaeda operatives from Europe to travel to Indonesia for training.

Dwikarna was arrested at Manila International Airport on March 13, 2002, while attempting to board a plane for Bangkok. He was detained along with two other Muslims after plastic explosives and a detonation cable were found in his luggage. Police subsequently found that his computer contained the name of Omar al-Farouq, a known Al Qaeda financier and operative, who was tracked down three months later and handed over to U.S. authorities for interrogation in Afghanistan. Dwikarna claimed that Indonesian intelligence agents had fabricated the whole episode and that he and his traveling companions were simply on a business trip.

The two colleagues, Abdul Jamal Balfas and Tamsil Linrung, were released in April 2002 because Philippine prosecutors did not have enough evidence to charge them. However, Dwikarna was found guilty and sentenced to 17 years in prison on July 12.

See also: Bashir, Abu Bakar; Farouq, Omar al-; Jemaah Islamiyah (JI)

Further Reading

Abuza, Zachary. "Al Qaeda Comes to Southeast Asia." In Paul Smith, ed., *Terrorism and Violence in Southeast Asia.* London: M. E. Sharpe, 2005. P. 48.

International Crisis Group. *Indonesian Backgrounder: Jihad in Central Sulawesi.* Asia Report, no. 74, February 3, 2004.

"Philippines Frees Terror Suspects." *CNN World,* April 19, 2002. http://articles.cnn.com/2002-04-19/world/phil.suspects_1_al-ghozi-ghozi-al-qaeda-network?_s=PM:asiapcf, accessed February 11, 2011.

"South-East Asia's Terror Clampdown." *BBC News,* September 23, 2002. http://news.bbc.co.uk/2/hi/asia-pacific/1937478.stm, accessed February 11, 2011.

Edward F. Mickolus

E

EARTH LIBERATION FRONT (ELF)

The Earth Liberation Front (ELF) represents an extreme and violent fringe of the American environmental movement that seeks to restore the environment in its entirety and recreate ecosystems that have been despoiled by the immoral and selfish actions of the human race. This is to be achieved by adopting an uncompromising stance on the environment and by emphasizing direct action over lobbying and legal forms of protest.

The ELF has employed a variety of tactics in pursuit of its objectives. Principal attack modalities have included arson, product contamination, tree spiking, monkey wrenching, destruction of logging infrastructure (monkey wrenching), basic vandalism, and (in conjunction with animal rights extremists) and the mailing of booby-trapped letters.

The bulk of the ELF's violent actions have taken place in the Pacific Northwest given the volume of logging and wilderness leisure development that characterizes that part of the country. However, the group has also demonstrated a capacity to act on a national basis, carrying out attacks in California, Colorado, New York, Michigan, Minnesota, Pennsylvania, and Indiana. This latter willingness and ability reflects the ELF's

- highly decentralized, flat structure, which has provided a useful militant "force multiplier" that draws on the resources of individuals across the country;
- extremely close contacts with animal rights activists, which have led to the development of a common, nationwide antihumanist operational agenda; and
- affinity with the general imperatives of antiglobalization, which is contributing to the emergence of a radical populist movement prepared to act in any "theater" representative of or derived from the contemporary free-market capitalist system.

An inevitable consequence of the ELF's close identification with the goals and imperatives of antiglobalization and animal rights has been a target menu that covers an extremely broad spectrum of corporate, public, and private sector interests. Principal targets—chosen both for their symbolic value and for ease of attack—have included (1) logging companies, forestry stations, wilderness recreational firms, and urban developers; (2) facilities and businesses deemed to be detrimental or degrading to animal welfare; and (3) perceived symbols of global capitalism and corporate greed.

ELF attacks have caused substantial economic damage. U.S. law enforcement calculates the group has caused anywhere between US$35 and US$45 million in damage to property since first emerging as a visible militant entity in 1996.

Estimates of the costs resulting from monkey-wrenching tactics alone run to roughly US$25 million a year, while in 2003 so-called antisprawl operations—arson directed at urban housing projects—are thought to have generated losses in excess of US$2 million. If one factors in indirect multiplier effects (which are inherently difficult to measure), the true fiscal consequences of ELF actions would be far greater.

Further Reading

Chalk, Peter, Bruce Hoffman, Robert Reville, and Anna-Britt Kasupski. *Trends in Terrorism: Threats to the United States and the Future of the Terrorism Risk Insurance Act.* Santa Monica, CA: RAND, 2005. Pp. 47–52.

Davidson-Smith, Tim. "Single Issue Terrorism." *CSIS Commentary* 74 (1998). http://www.csis-scrs.gc.ca/eng/comment/com74_e.html.

Eagan, Sean. "From Spikes to Bombs: The Rise of Eco-terrorism." *Studies in Conflict and Terrorism* 19 (1996).

Lee, Martha. "Violence and the Environment: The Case of Earth First!" *Terrorism and Political Violence* 7, no. 3 (1995).

Makarenko, Tamara. "Earth Liberation Front Increases Actions across the United States." *Jane's Intelligence Review,* September 2003.

Nauess, Arne. "Deep Ecology and Ultimate Premises." *Ecologist* 18, nos. 4–5 (1998).

Peter Chalk

EGYPT AIR HIJACKING

Following the arrest of four members of the Palestine Liberation Front for the October 1985 hijacking of the Italian cruise ship *Achille Lauro,* many Palestinian groups blamed Egypt for its covert assistance in the capture of the terrorists. The following month the Abu Nidal Organization (ANO) launched a reprisal, in which three of its members hijacked Egypt Air Flight 648, a Boeing 737 flying from Athens to Cairo.

As the three terrorists moved through the aircraft collecting passengers' passports, an armed Egyptian sky marshal shot and killed one of the hijackers. A brief firefight then erupted between the two remaining hijackers and two other sky marshals, both of whom were subsequently killed. During this exchange, bullets punctured the aircraft fuselage, causing the plane to fall 20,000 feet before the pilot regained control. He performed an emergency landing at Luqa Airport, Malta, where the aircraft was surrounded by government troops. After releasing 11 female hostages and two female members of the crew, the two terrorists demanded the release of the *Achille Lauro* hijackers and the immediate refueling of the aircraft. The Maltese authorities, however, refused to comply, and the hijackers began shooting hostages, deliberately singling out two Israelis and three Americans, who were dumped onto the tarmac. Miraculously, only one of these five, Nitzan Mendelson, actually died.

While these events had been occurring, the Egyptians had dispatched a C-130 Hercules aircraft with a team from its elite counterterrorist unit, Force 777, to Luqa Airport. It appears, however, that the Force 777 members failed to either interview the released hostages regarding the number, location, weaponry, and mindset of the terrorists or carry out a detailed reconnaissance of the hijacked aircraft and its surroundings.

After hours of fruitless negotiation, the Force 777 squad launched its rescue bid on the morning of November 24, 1985. Rather than using the doors of the 737 aircraft as entry points as had been successfully done in other plane hostage situations, the main assault team planned to blow a hole through the floor of the aircraft from the cargo hold and use this as a means of both entry and distraction. Unfortunately the charge killed nearly 20 passengers sitting above it. The second wave of commandos entered from above the aircraft wings throwing smoke grenades. This added to the lack of visibility and confusion in the now-burning aircraft, with a number of hostages cut down in the ensuing cross fire. Having turned off the airport lights prior to the assault, Force 777 snipers providing cover shot a number of hostages as they attempted to exit the aircraft. Consequently, while one terrorist was killed and the other captured, 57 of the 90 hostages also died in the operation.

See also: Abu Nidal Organization (ANO); Larnaca Airport Attack

Further Reading

Davies, Barry. *Terrorism: Inside a World Phenomenon.* London: Virgin Books, 2003.
Griffiths, John. *Hostage: The History, Facts and Reasoning behind Hostage Taking.* London: Andre Deutsch, 2003.
Harclerode, Peter. *Secret Soldiers: Special Forces in the War against Terrorism.* London: Cassell, 2002.
Seal, Patrick. *Abu Nidal: A Gun for Hire.* London: Random House, 1992.

Richard Warnes

EGYPTIAN EMBASSY (ISLAMABAD) BOMBING

On the morning of November 19, 1995, a truck bomb exploded at the Egyptian embassy in Islamabad, Pakistan, killing 19 people and wounding more than 80 others. Five of the dead were Egyptians; one was an Afghan. The attack occurred on the 18th anniversary of President Anwar Sadat's historic 1977 visit to Jerusalem and took place sometime between 10:00 and 11:00 A.M.

The Egyptian fatalities included Second Secretary Ahmad Numayr Ahmad Bin-Khalil; embassy counselor Hisham 'Abd-al-Mun'im Abu-Al-Wafa; security guards Ayman Muhammad 'Ali, Husayn Mahmud Fahmi, and Mahmud 'Abd-al-Maqsud; and two administrative attachés. The injured were Pakistani visa applicants, locally hired employees of the embassy, and the driver of the small Mazda that carried 1,000 pounds of explosives. The Egyptian ambassador, Noman Jalal, was in the residential section of the compound and was unhurt

The bomb severely damaged the two-story building and threw metal 700 yards away. The windows of Grindley's Bank and the Japanese, Indonesian, Swiss, and French embassies were also broken, injuring several people. Some reports said a second explosion also occurred in the booby-trapped vehicle, although this was never confirmed.

On November 21, Egyptian Islamic Jihad (EIJ) announced that two of its members, 'Isam al-Qamari and Ibrahim Salamah, had carried out the operation. The group said one of the two dead set off explosives wired to his torso, destroying the embassy gate; this allowed the second member to drive directly into the compound, where the bomb was detonated. Another report gave a slightly different description of the attack. According to this account, two men in a vehicle approached the embassy at approximately 9:30 A.M. and killed its security detail with guns and grenades. They then rammed the outer gates and detonated a 250-pound bomb. The breach permitted a Jeep with a second, larger device to enter the embassy grounds; it exploded three minutes later.

It is now known that Ayman al-Zawahiri planned the attack in 1994, shortly after aligning himself with Osama bin Laden. He later said that al-Jihad had wanted to target the American embassy, but it was too heavily fortified. Although the operation was successful, bin Laden apparently disapproved of it, as it alienated the host of the embassy, Pakistan, which acted as a crucial gateway to Afghanistan. However, al-Zawahiri later justified the attack on the grounds that it was integral to countering Cairo's expanding campaign against Egyptian fundamentalists outside the country. The bombing itself was al-Jihad's fourth attack on external Egyptian targets and followed on the heels of the attempted assassination of Mubarak in the Ethiopian capital of Addis Ababa.

The first person to be arrested in connection with the attack was a Canadian citizen, Ahmed Said Khadr. He was apprehended on November 27, 1995, after information surfaced that his son-in-law, Khalid Abdullah, may have purchased the truck used in the bombing. However, he was released the following March due to a lack of evidence indicating he had any involvement.

Over the next three years, several other people were detained for aiding and abetting the attack, including Syed Ahmed and Bashir Bahar Qadim (arrested in Faisalabad in April 1996); Hasan Ahmed Rabi (captured in Kuwait in May 1999 and extradited to Egypt); and Mahmoud Jaballah (caught in Canada in 1999 and also charged with complicity in the 1998 bombings of the U.S. embassies in Kenya and Tanzania).

In 2001 Egyptian forces again moved to arrest Khadr after new evidence emerged tying him to the planning of the attack. However, before he could be apprehended, Pakistan's Inter Services Intelligence (ISI) Directorate contacted the Taliban, which dispatched a diplomatic car to pick up Khadr and take him to Afghanistan.

Finally, in 2002 Khaked Abul el-Dahab confessed to Egyptian interrogators that he had funded the attack on orders from bin Laden. Subsequent investigations revealed a money trail that linked a bank in California with one in Pakistan, and it was there that the money for the bombing had originated.

See also: Zawahiri, Ayman al-

Further Reading

Jehl, Douglas. "Islamic Militants War on Egypt." *New York Times,* November 20, 1995.
McGirk, Tim. "Bomb Kills 14 at Egyptian Embassy." *The Independent* (UK), November 20, 1995.

Nachman, Tal. *Radical Islam in Egypt and Jordan.* Sussex, UK: Sussex Academic Press, 2005.
"Pakistan Arrests 10 in Embassy Bombing." *New York Times,* November 24, 1995.

Donna Bassett

EGYPTIAN ISLAMIC JIHAD (EIJ)

Egyptian Islamic Jihad (EIJ) emerged in the late 1970s as a group dedicated to overthrowing the Egyptian government. Founded by Muhammad abd-al-Salam Faraj in 1979 as an offshoot of the Muslim Brotherhood, the group's philosophical roots are best understood through Faraj's pamphlet *The Neglected Duty.* In this text Faraj argued, "We have to establish the Rule of God's Religion in our own country first, and to make the Word of God supreme." EIJ established a *majlis al-shura* (consultative council) by the fall of 1980; Faraj and Karam Zuhdi, the founder of al-Gama'a al-Islamiyya (Islamic Group), were both council members and collaborated to form the Cairo and Saidi branches of the organization.

On October 6, 1981, members of EIJ assassinated President Anwar Sadat—an action that marked it for the first time as one of Egypt's foremost terrorist organizations. At their trial, the perpetrators justified the murder on the grounds that Sadat had not effectively enacted sharia law to ensure the emergence of a true Islamic regime in Egypt. After the assassination, EIJ's northern and southern factions split, with Ayman al-Zawahiri taking over the helm of the former.

A wounded Egyptian soldier, foreground, is carried away on a stretcher after President Anwar Sadat was assassinated in Cairo, Egypt, on October 6, 1981. Sadat was shot by members of the Egyptian Islamic Jihad who opened fire from a truck during the military parade commemorating the Arab-Israeli War of October 1973. (AP/Wide World Photos)

Some 1,536 suspects were arrested in connection with Sadat's slaying, a majority of whom were found guilty and given prison sentences. On April 15, 1982, the assassin Khaled Ahmed Shawki Islambouli, Faraj, and 22 others were executed. While Omar Abdel-Rahman, a radical inspirational cleric to both EIJ and al-Gama'a al-Islamiyya (and more commonly known as the "Blind Sheik"), evaded a death sentence, he leveraged the publicity of his trial to defend Islamist ideologies against his depictions of an insufficiently Islamic, and therefore evil, governing system. From the courtroom Abdel-Rahman addressed Egypt and the Muslim world in its entirety about dutiful obedience to Allah; photographs of him encaged with other "members of the faithful" were transmitted throughout the Middle East. The Blind Sheik further strengthened his position by suing the state for torture during his imprisonment, for which he received $10,000 in damages. In short, Abdel-Rahman had cemented himself as the premier spiritual leader of the new generation of Egyptian jihad.

When the net positions of both the government and the jihadi movements are assessed in the aftermath of Sadat's assassination, however, it becomes clear that despite all the publicity Abdel-Rahman was able to generate, EIJ and al-Gama'a al-Islamiyya had both been dealt substantial blows. Egyptian counterterrorism measures were swift and brutal, resulting in the deaths of, or heavy jail sentences for, many key members, including al-Zawahiri. Others went into hiding or were driven into exile. Combined, these losses made future operations incredibly difficult to plan and carry out.

That said, Sadat's successor, Hosni Mubarak, failed to fully douse the terrorist organizations' *raisons d'être* and, by attempting to court certain radical Islamist entities in an effort to boost his own legitimacy, may have actually served to sustain them. This latent ideology would once again come to set the country ablaze in the early 1990s. Moreover, the prison experience cemented the resolve of many. This was especially true of al-Zawahiri, who once released in 1984 was generally recognized as the hardened leader of EIJ. On attaining his freedom he immediately left Egypt for Saudi Arabia to plan the next stages of the jihad.

While he was in exile—a time that coincided with the Soviet invasion of Afghanistan—al-Zawahiri began interacting with Osama bin Laden. It has been suggested that the intent of these interactions was to gain the latter's backing for EIJ and Faraj's vision of the "near jihad." Over time, a distinctly *takfir* ideology (or "purging" mentality within Islam, globally defined) began to take hold in both men's heads, and after al-Zawahiri won an internal power struggle within EIJ, he increasingly moved to intertwine his group with Al Qaeda. The relationship between the two movements was formalized in 1998 with the signing of the now-infamous Khost fatwa against Zionists and Crusaders. In June 2001, EIJ effectively merged with Al Qaeda, with al-Zawahiri assuming the mantle of second in command.

While EIJ is arguably most well known for its intimate allegiance with Al Qaeda, it should be noted that while it existed as an independent organization, its capacity for incredibly destructive and murderous terrorist activity—predominantly through armed attacks and bombings—was significant. Despite a brutal counterterrorist effort within Egypt in the years following Sadat's assassination, EIJ managed to remain in existence. Although degraded and arguably sidelined by al-Gama'a al-Islamiyya, the group continued to perpetrate a number of incidents and, indeed, in 1993 nearly succeeded in assassinating Egyptian prime minister Atef Sedky and interior minister Hassan al-Alfi. EIJ also staged a number of high-profile attacks abroad, including the bombing of Cairo's embassy in Islamabad in 1995, an unsuccessful attempt to assassinate President Mubarak in Addis Ababa, Ethiopia, that same year, and a failed strike on the U.S. embassy in Albania in 1998.

On March 25, 1999, al-Gama'a al-Islamiyya, by then long the dominant domestically operating Egyptian terrorist organization, formally announced that it would be suspending all future armed and violent activity. Members of EIJ strongly rebuked this annulment of hostilities and refused to abide by any cease-fire. Accordingly, while the Egyptian government rewarded al-Gama'a al-Islamiyya by freeing some 2,000 of its members from prison, it continued its crackdown on EIJ. As noted, however, by this point, al-Zawahiri and bin Laden had forged a close alliance that largely focused on fighting the "far" enemy, namely, the United States and its Western allies, effectively eliminating the domestic threat posed by the group within Egypt.

See also: Abdel-Rahman, Omar; Al Qaeda; al-Gama'a al-Islamiyya; bin Laden, Osama; Zawahiri, Ayman al-

Further Reading

Al-Jihad al-Islami Backgrounder. Monterey, CA: Monterey Institute of International Studies (nda).

Boyer Bell, J. *Murders on the Nile: The World Trade Center and Global Terror.* San Francisco: Encounter Books, 2003.

EIJ Backgrounder. Washington, DC: Council on Foreign Relations.

Tal, Nachman. *Radical Islam in Egypt and Jordan.* Brighton: Sussex Academic/Jaffee Center for Strategic Studies, 2005.

Wright, Lawrence. *The Looming Tower: Al-Qaeda and the Road to 9/11.* New York: Knopf, 2006.

Michael E. Orzetti

EGYPTIAN TOURIST RESORT BOMBINGS

On October 7, 2004, bombs struck three Egyptian Sinai resorts popular with Israelis, killing at least 37 people and wounding more than 198. Intelligence officials with Shin Bet had warned of possible attacks as far back as the previous August and had advised tourists to stay away during the harvest season of Sukkot. After this warning, Israel moved troops into the Gaza Strip, which borders on Egypt, in an effort to stop militant Palestinians from Hamas and Palestinian Islamic Jihad (PIJ) from shooting rockets into Israel. Hamas had vowed retaliation against Israel and Israelis for the assassination of two of its leaders.

Most of the casualties occurred at the five-star Taba Hilton located just five miles from the Israeli border, a venue that had often been used for Middle East peace negotiations. The building was rammed with a Peugeot sport-utility vehicle packed with an estimated 440 pounds of explosives. In that attack, 31 people died, and another 159 were injured. The force of the blast was sufficient to rip the face off the 10-story hotel.

Although around 150 of the hotel guests could not be immediately accounted for, Israeli officials posited that many of them had fled back to Israel across the border near the resort town of Eilat. Other witnesses supported this position, claiming that panicked Israelis had rushed the frontier post yelling at soldiers and police that their belongings and documents were still in the burning hotel. Guards apparently fired into the air in an effort to disperse the fleeing civilians before shutting down the crossing point temporarily. They then blocked the road, leaving other vacationing Israelis trapped in their hotels. The Israeli deputy defense minister, Zeev Boim, said the bomb appeared to be the work of Al Qaeda. "It's not the kind of attack that we know comes from Palestinian terror organizations," he said.

The second incident involved at least one suicide bomber driving a taxi that was similarly laden with 440 pounds of explosives. The vehicle detonated at 10 P.M. near the dining room of the Moon Island Resort in Ras Shytan (Ras al-Sultan), 30 miles south of Taba. The attack killed 5 and wounded another 38. A second device blew up outside the gates of Mobarak, the camp next door, although there were no casualties.

One man who was eating at the restaurant described the scene to Israeli television in the following terms: "The electricity went out and rocks were jolted by the blast. We then saw a second explosion not far from the first blast; it was a ball of fire higher on the mountain. We immediately drove over to the site and found wounded people on the ground. There were Israelis among them. They were bleeding in the sand and there was no one there to help them."

The third strike targeted the Nuweia Resort, 40 miles south of Taba. Again the strike took the form of a vehicle bomb made up of an estimated 440 pounds of explosives. Although the device was similar to the ones employed in the previous attacks, there were no reports of either deaths or serious injuries.

Officials subsequently discovered that the three cars used in the bombings had been stolen and that the explosives had been scavenged from artillery shells across various Sinai battlefields. The timers had all come from washing machine parts. Three days after the incidents a Bedouin tribesman confessed to selling explosives, some of which might have been used in the bombings. He said he was told they would used in the Palestinian territories.

Two weeks later, Egyptian police announced that five people had been arrested for planning the bombings. Authorities also named the notional attack leader as Ayad Said Salah, claiming that he had been accidentally killed in one of the explosions. In addition, they identified the terrorist who had carried out the Taba bombing as an Egyptian national named Suleiman Ahmed Saleh Flayfil. In November 2006, three Egyptians, Younes Mohammed Mahmoud, Osama al-Nakhlawi, and Mohammed Jaez Sabbah, were sentenced to death for their roles in the bombings.

See also: Al Qaeda; Sharm el-Sheikh Bombings

Further Reading

Kepel, Gilles, *Muslim Extremism in Egypt: The Prophet and Pharaoh.* Berkeley: University of California Press, 1993.

Mickolus, Edward F., with Susan L. Simmons. *Terrorism 2002–2004: A Chronology.* Vol. 2. Westport CT: Praeger Security International, 2006.

Zayyat, Montasser al-. *The Road to Al-Qaeda: The Story of Bin Lāden's Right-Hand Man.* Sterling, VA: Pluto, 2004.

Donna Bassett

EJÉRCITO DE LIBERACIÓN NACIONAL (ELN)

The Ejército de Liberación Nacional (ELN, or National Liberation Army) is a Colombian left-wing rebel group that was founded in 1964. Unlike the Marxist-oriented, peasant-based leadership of the Fuerzas Armadas Revolucionarias de Colombia (FARC, or Revolutionary Armed Forces of Colombia), the ELN was mostly composed of intellectuals and students from the University of Santandar who were adherents of Cuban-style revolutionary thought. At its height the ELN could count on around 5,000 cadres who operated from five *frentes de guerra* (war fronts) mostly concentrated in an extended region that stretched from the middle Magdalena Valley to the Venezuelan border.

Aside from its Castroite component, the ELN attracted radicalized Catholics who blended religious teachings on social justice with Marxist ideology. The most notable of these recruits was Father Camilo Torres, a Louvian-educated priest from a prominent Colombian family. He joined the rebel group in October 1965 but was killed four months later in an encounter with the army.

The ELN originally operated in a restricted geographic area—the northern departments of Santandar, Antioquia, and Bolivar—which it sought to turn into a Colombian version of the Sierra Maestra, Fidel Castro's mountain stronghold in Cuba. As a military organization, the ELN initially failed to mount any operations of consequence, both due to a lack of popular support in the country (the group was mostly urban based) and on account of internal ideological divisions that the ELN's supreme commander, Fabio Vasquez Castano, failed to reconcile.

The group reemerged as a more credible force in the 1980s, however, under the guidance of another guerrilla priest, Father Manuel Perez (also known as *el curra*). The new leader (who died of malaria in 1998) proved successful in bridging the rifts between different factions within the group and, just as important, garnering more grassroots backing beyond the cities. The ELN quickly grew from just 800 fighters in 1986 to 3,000 in 1996 to between 3,000 and 5,000 in 2000. Militant operations focused on acts of urban sabotage, hit-and-run attacks on the security forces, and the abduction or assassination of local political and civil leaders. The group was also linked to a number of civilian bombings, although these were not nearly as frequent as those attributed to FARC.

Virtually all of the ELN's financing has been derived from criminality. Traditionally the bulk of revenue came from kidnap for ransom and the extortion of protection money from energy firms (oil, coal, and gas) and mining companies (gold and emeralds). By the turn of the millennium the group was thought to have earned approximately $150 million from these two endeavors, 30 percent from the former and 70 percent from the latter. Over the last several years the ELN has also sought to fund its operations on the back of the highly lucrative South American drug trade (which under Perez's leadership had been strictly off-limits). The group has been relatively successful in this regard and is now thought to control several coca-growing areas along Colombia's northern Pacific coast—although it remains unclear exactly how much it earns from taxing production (the organization is not thought to have made any decisive inroads into narcotics trafficking per se, which is still dominated by stronger and better-connected FARC and paramilitary rivals).

These resources have allowed the ELN to develop a relatively sophisticated and diverse arms pipeline that delivers everything from pistols, assault rifles, and ammunition to heavy machine guns, mortars (60, 81, and 82 millimeters), and rocket-propelled grenades. Reports of surface-to-air missiles have not been confirmed and, to the extent that they exist, are thought to lie within the inventory of FARC. The majority of weapons are sourced from Central America, with El Salvador and Nicaragua playing a particularly important role. Munitions are smuggled through Panama into Colombia by both land and sea. In the former case, shipments run via the Gulf of Uraba or the Gulf of San Miguel, while in the latter case, routes follow a logistic bridge of between 40 and 50 jungle footpaths through the Darien Gap.

Although the ELN remains a viable force in Colombia, its overall strength has declined as a result of defections and successful army infiltration that has resulted in the capture of several top leaders. The group currently lacks the capacity to execute large-scale tactical (much less strategic) attacks and is generally confined to carrying out strikes against soft targets as and when the opportunity arises. Several commentators have also suggested that the ELN's growing interest in the drug trade reflects a militant agenda that has become progressively weaker and is now systematically degenerating into straight criminality.

See also: Autodefensas Unidas de Colombia (AUC); Fuerzas Armadas Revolucionarias de Colombia (FARC)

Further Reading

Chalk, Peter. *The Latin American Drug Trade: Scope, Dimensions, Impact, and Response.* Santa Monica, CA: RAND, 2011.

Maullin, Richard. *Soldiers, Guerrillas and Politics in Colombia.* Santa Monica, CA: RAND, 1971.

Rabasa, Angel, and Peter Chalk. *Colombian Labyrinth.* Santa Monica, CA: RAND, 2001.

Tickner, Arlene. "Colombia: Chronicle of a Crisis Foretold." *Current History* 97, no. 616 (1998).

Edward F. Mickolus

EJÉRCITO REVOLUCIONÁRIO DEL PUEBLO (ERP)

The Ejército Revolucionário del Pueblo (ERP, or People's Revolutionary Army) was the armed wing of the Argentinian Trotskyist Partido Revolucionario de los Trabajadores (PRT, or the Workers' Revolutionary Party), an affiliate of the Fourth International. It launched an urban guerrilla insurgency against military dictator Juan Carols in July 1970.

With an estimated 5,000 members, the ERP was smaller than the Montoneros—another left-wing rebel group active in Argentina at this time—but better organized. The group carried out numerous assassinations, targeting police officials, soldiers, moderate trade union leaders, and foreign corporate executives. It also engaged in widespread criminal activity to raise money. Authorities credited the group with at least 166 bank robberies and 185 kidnappings, which earned it an estimated $76 million.

Politically, the ERP soon came to reject the urban-centered ideology of Trotskyism as too restrictive and in 1973 formally severed its links with the PRT. Under the guidance of Mario Robert Santucho, the group then shifted to a rural guerrilla strategy that was focused on the northwestern province of Tucumán, where it had about 100 guerrillas and a 400-person support network. Although Santucho quickly controlled a third of the province, his fighting force never exceeded 300.

Following Juan Perón's death in 1974, the administration of Isabel Martínez de Perón moved to counter the ERP's base of operations in the northwest. The new president sent some 3,500 elite troops under Brigadier General Acdel Vilas to the Tucumán Mountains, backing them with an additional 1,500 soldiers from the 4th Airborne Brigade and the 8th Mountain Infantry Brigade.

Vilas focused on eradicating the ERP's support network in the towns and by the end of the year had eradicated Santucho's headquarters, killed many of the group's top leaders, and scattered its forces. In May 1975 the army captured Amilcar Santucho, a senior ERP representative who provided the authorities with critical information that helped to further erode the organization's fighting strength.

Despite these setbacks, the ERP still managed to carry out a number of attacks. On October 5, 1975, the group hit the 29th Mountain Infantry Regiment, following this up with a raid against a military supply base in the Buenos Aires suburb of Monte Chingolo in December. That same month an ERP bomb killed six senior officers at the Buenos Aires Argentine Army headquarters. Overall, 137 members of the security forces died at the hands of the group during 1975.

In March 1976 the military staged a coup, setting the scene for the notorious "dirty war" of repression that followed. Within four months the army had killed Santucho and destroyed ERP's elite Special Squad. Although the group limped along for a while under the leadership of Enrique Gorriaran Merlo, it was effectively eradicated as a viable entity by the end of 1977.

See also: Montoneros

Further Reading

Crenshaw, Martha, ed. *Terrorism in Context.* University Park: Pennsylvania State University Press, 1995.
Dobson, Christopher, and Ronald Payne. *The Terrorists: Their Weapons, Leaders and Tactics.* New York: Facts on File, 1979.

Fauriol, Georges, ed. *Latin American Insurgencies.* Washington, DC: Georgetown University Center for Strategic and International Studies, 1985.

Spencer, David E. *From Vietnam to El Salvador: The Saga of the FMLN Sappers and Other Guerrilla Special Forces in Latin America.* Westport, CT: Praeger, 1996.

Donna Bassett

EL AL HIJACKING

On July 22, 1968, three members of the Popular Front for the Liberation of Palestine (PFLP) hijacked an Israeli El Al Boeing 707 on its way from Rome to Israel's Lod Airport in Tel Aviv. The two Palestinians and one Syrian attacked 20 minutes after takeoff, threatening to blow up the plane with grenades. They then fired shots into the cockpit and demanded the surrender of the pilot, Captain Oded Abarbanel, who duly complied. One of the skyjackers took control of the plane and flew it, together with its 10 crewmembers and 38 passengers, to Algiers's Dar al-Bayda Airport. Upon landing they demanded the release of an unspecified number of Arabs from Israeli jails.

An aide to PFLP leader George Habash, who had arrived in Algiers the night before, asked a high Algerian security official to demand full diplomatic and material support for the group. Although the actions of the trio were initially lauded, they were subsequently refused exit visas and held at a military camp. The Algerians immediately released 23 non-Israeli passengers, flying them to Paris, France, aboard an Air Algerie plane. However, the 10 remaining Jewish crew members and 12 other Israeli civilians, including four women and three children, were taken and held in a barracks near the airport. Five days later, the women, children, and three stewardesses were allowed to fly to Geneva, Switzerland, and on to Israel.

The Palestine Liberation Organization (PLO) and al-Fatah sent a six-man delegation to Algiers to demand that the other hostages be held until 1,200 Arabs were released from Israeli jails. Algerian President Houari Boumédienne was caught in the middle of an increasingly complex diplomatic standoff. Many Middle Eastern states strongly supported the PLO position and also started to add their own requests: Iraq demanded the return of a MIG-21 that had been stolen and flown to Israel in 1965, and Egypt, Jordan, and Syria all requested the return of captured territory, respectively, the Sinai Peninsula, the old city of Jerusalem, and the Golan Heights.

At the same time, international pressure against the continued detention of the hostages also grew. The International Federation of Air Line Pilots' Associations announced on August 13 that it would begin a boycott of Algeria on August 19. Swissair, Alitalia, and Air France made similar plans, and various African states threatened to boycott an upcoming summit conference in the country.

On August 17, the boycott was called off when it was learned that negotiations were taking place via the Italian consulate in Algiers. On September 1, the hostages were flown to Rome on an Italian jet piloted by a French crew. On September 2, Israel's information minister told the International Committee of the Red Cross (ICRC) that 16 Arabs captured prior to the June 1967 war would be released as a humanitarian gesture. While the deal ended the crisis, the PFLP strongly criticized Algeria for releasing the hostages without consulting them.

It was subsequently learned that the skyjackers had been studying passenger manifests and El Al logistics in Rome since mid-July, hoping to seize General Ariel Sharon, commander of the armored forces in Sinai during the Arab-Israeli Six-Day War. The group believed he was on the hijacked flight because one of them had seen a stewardess give what appeared to be a diplomatic pouch to the pilot. However, Sharon had actually taken a direct flight from Paris after arriving from the United States.

Two of the terrorists would go on to engage in future actions. Yousef Khatib led a group of skyjackers in a February 22, 1972, Indian incident, and Ali Shafik Ahmed Taha (also known as Captain Rafat) participated in a Black September Organization hijacking on May 8, 1972.

See also: Palestine Liberation Organization (PLO); Popular Front for the Liberation of Palestine (PFLP)

Further Reading

Mickolus, Edward F. *Transnational Terrorism: A Chronology of Events, 1968–1979.* Westport, CT: Greenwood, 1980.

St. John, Peter. *Air Piracy, Airport Security and International Terrorism: Winning the War against Hijackers.* Westport, CT: Quorum Books, 1991.

Wilkinson, Paul, and Brian M. Jenkins. *Aviation Terrorism and Security.* Portland, OR: Frank Cass, 1999.

"World: Drama of the Desert: The Week of the Hostages." *Time,* September 21, 1970. http://www.time.com/time/magazine/article/0,9171,942267,00.html, accessed May 2, 2011.

Donna Bassett

ENTEBBE HOSTAGE RESCUE

At around noon on June 27, 1976, terrorists commandeered Air France Flight 139, en route from Tel Aviv to Paris with 246 passengers and 12 crew. The hijacking, which occurred shortly after a brief stopover in Athens, Greece, was co-led by Wilfred Bose, a member of the West German Rote Armee Fraktion (RAF, or Red Army Faction), and Fayez Abdul-Rahim Jaber of the Popular Front for the Liberation of Palestine (PFLP).

The hijacked plane left the Athens radar screen and flew to a preplanned stop in Libya, a nation that had long harbored terrorists. As the aircraft refueled at the Benghazi airport, one passenger, an Israeli woman claiming to be pregnant, was freed. Departing Libya around 9:30 P.M., Flight 139 flew to Entebbe Airport in Uganda, in accordance with the hijacking plan. It arrived at 3:15 A.M. on June 28, at which time three terrorists joined the attack team.

All evidence suggests that the Ugandan government was complicit in the hijacking of Flight 139 from the very beginning and that President Idi Amin Dada assisted the terrorists once they arrived in the country. Although the mercurial leader visited the hostages several times during their ordeal and claimed he was doing all he could to negotiate their release, he did not discourage the terrorists' actions and, indeed, seemed to be pushing their demands. Throughout the crisis, he also allowed Ugandan troops at Entebbe Airport to assist with the guarding of the Jewish captives.

A mother and her daughter embrace when the latter arrived at Tel Aviv's Ben Gurion Airport after Israeli paratroopers freed her and other hostages aboard an Air France jet at Uganda's Entebbe Airport earlier in the day, July 4, 1976. (AP/Wide World Photos)

On June 29 the hijackers issued their demands, which included the release of 40 Palestinians held by the Israelis and another 13 terrorists languishing in jails in France, Germany, Switzerland, and Kenya. As a sign of "good faith," the terrorists agreed to a two-stage release of some of their captives, who were then flown to Paris. Another 105 Jewish passengers, however, continued to be held, along with the entire Air France crew (who volunteered to stay with the hostages).

An extremely distressed Israeli cabinet initially rejected any hope of mounting a military rescue operation, largely due to the enormous distances involved— 2,000 air miles one way. In addition, the government faced added pressure from relatives of the hostages, who demanded that a deal be concluded at the earliest opportunity. In response, Prime Minister Yitzhak Rabin quickly dispatched a team of diplomats to France to investigate the feasibility of negotiating a terrorists-for-hostages swap in either Paris or Djibouti.

Meanwhile, the Israeli defense minister, Shimon Peres, ordered the Israeli Defense Force (IDF) to review any reasonable military option. Under the direction of Chief of Staff Mordechai Gur and Israeli Air Force chief Benny Peled, a planning committee led by General Dan Shomron began to investigate the suitability of an armed rescue. The initial planning was done in great secrecy, while Rabin continued to use diplomatic channels to negotiate a possible end to the situation.

To better determine the feasibility of a military solution, a massive intelligence effort was instituted to learn everything possible about Entebbe Airport. Israeli agents traveled to Paris to interview the released hostages, who provided sharp insights into both the hostage and the terrorist situation.

On July 1 a final plan was presented to the IDF General Staff and Defense Minister Peres, and two days later a somewhat reluctant Rabin gave his endorsement after gaining approval from the cabinet. Four C-130 aircraft subsequently left Israel just after noon on July 3, arriving at Entebbe at 11:00 P.M. that same evening. The rescue force was commanded by Lieutenant Colonel Jonathan Netanyahu, brother of future prime minister Benjamin Netanyahu.

The rescue operation consisted of five teams. The first, led by Netanyahu, was charged with seizing the old terminal building and releasing the hostages. The second was to commandeer the air traffic control center while the third prepared emergency beacons for the runways. A fourth team was left to refuel the C-130s, and a final squad was given the task of destroying any Ugandan planes on the ground that might threaten the Israelis' escape. In addition to the ground assault force, two aircraft were dispatched to Kenya (which vehemently opposed the Amin regime and hence was willing to cooperate). The first was deployed to Nairobi to assist in the medial care of the hostages and any wounded IDF personnel; the second was charged with flying sorties over Lake Victoria to provide airborne surveillance and electronic support to the rescuers.

The main assault team quickly managed to gain control of the old terminal after duping guards by driving up to the building in an exact replica of the black Mercedes-Benz used by President Amin. During the ensuing firefight, however, Netanyahu was fatally wounded. The first C-130, carrying the hostages, left the airport within 40 minutes, followed by the remaining planes. By midday on July 4, even before the former hostages had reached Israel, most of the world was aware of the successful rescue. The entire operation had lasted less than an hour, and around half of the Ugandan Air Force had been destroyed.

At least six terrorists involved in the hijacking, and approximately 20 to 40 Ugandan soldiers supporting the terrorists, were killed. Three hostages died during or shortly after the operation, and apart from the death of Netanyahu, the IDF suffered only one other casualty. Following the raid, four air traffic controllers and one sick hostage who had been taken to a local hospital prior to the rescue, Dora Bloch, were executed, allegedly on Amin's orders.

See also: Popular Front for the Liberation of Palestine (PFLP); Rote Armee Fraktion (RAF)

Further Reading

Ben-Porat, Yeshayahu, Eitan Haber, and Zeev Schiff. *Entebbe Rescue.* New York: Delacorte, 1977.
Hastings, Max. *Yoni, Hero of Entebbe.* New York: Bantam Books, 1979.
Herzog, Chaim. *Heroes of Israel: Profiles of Jewish Courage.* London: Little, Brown, 1989.
Netanyahu, Iddo. *Yoni's Last Battle: The Rescue at Entebbe.* Jerusalem: Gefen Books, 1976.
Stevenson, William. *90 Minutes at Entebbe.* New York: Bantam, 1976.

Ralph Martin Baker

EPANASTATIKI ORGANOSI 17 NOEMVRI (EO17N)

The Epanastatiki Organosi 17 Noemvri (EO17N, or Revolutionary Organization 17 November) was a small extreme left Greek terrorist organization. It was named after the events of November 14–17, 1973, when 34 student protestors were killed at the hands of the police while demonstrating at the Athens Polytechnic against the Greek military "Colonel's Regime." EO17N espoused a Marxist-Leninist ideology and sought to act as the vanguard for a wider revolution in Greek society. Its targets included anyone seen as complicit in the exploitation of the Greek masses, NATO and U.S. military personnel, and those who argued for the country's membership in the European Union and/or closer ties with Turkey.

The EO17N first came to prominence on December 23, 1975, when it fatally shot Richard Welch, the Central Intelligence Agency (CIA) station Chief for Athens. Over the next 30 years, the group took responsibility for more than 23 killings, many of which took the form of carefully planned assassinations carried out with the same Colt .45 caliber pistol. In each case, the group justified the murders in carefully crafted communiqués, often written on the same typewriter.

The nature of EO17N attacks changed in 1985 when the group started to use explosives. In November of that year it bombed a police bus, killing 1 and injuring 14; two similar strikes against buses carrying American military personnel quickly followed but did not result in any loss of life. Three years later, a remote-controlled car bomb was used to assassinate the U.S. defense attaché, Navy Captain William Nordeen, as he left his home. In 1990, EO17N again hanged tactics when it commenced a campaign of violence using vintage but functioning World War II vintage rocket. Targets included the Athens office of British Petroleum in 1991 (as a protest against the First Gulf War), the U.S. embassy, and European Union buildings.

EO17N stepped up its level of activity in 2000 following NATO's intervention in Kosovo. One of the most prominent attacks at this time was the assassination of British defense attaché Brigadier Stephen Saunders, who was shot dead by gunmen on a motorcycle as he drove to work during the morning rush hour in Athens.

Despite the lengthy period of its activities and dozens of operations, the Greek authorities had very little success in countering EO17N or even identifying its members. This failure led many to speculate that the group was either a phantom entity or was being deliberately protected by left-wing elements within the government and political parties. The group was finally exposed in 2002 when one of its leading members, Savvas Xeros, was arrested after a bomb he was attempting to plant in the Piraeus area near Athens exploded prematurely, severely injuring his hands. His apprehension led police investigators to a cache of weapons and documents, including the Colt .45 used in many of the EO17N assassinations. A wave of subsequent arrests ensued, which after the seizure of Alexandros Giotopoulos—a Greek academic who had been the leader of the organization—effectively crippled its organizational structure. Although EO17N no longer exists as a viable operational entity, remnants of the group appear to have reorganized under the guise of the Revolutionary Struggle. The new entity appears to have assumed the mantle of EO17N and has been implicated in several assassinations, bombings, and mortar attacks since 2008.

See also: Saunders (Stephen) Assassination

Further Reading

Bossis, Mary. "The Mysteries of Terrorism and Political Violence in Greece." In Marianne van Leeuwen, ed., *Confronting Terrorism: European Experiences, Threat Perceptions and Policies*. The Hague: Kluwer Law International, 2003.

Gourdoumbas, Athena. "Modern Greek Terrorism." In Martha Crenshaw and John Pimlott, eds., *International Encyclopedia of Terrorism*. Chicago: Fitzroy Dearborn, 1997.

Kassimiris, George. *Europe's Last Red Terrorists: The Revolutionary Organization 17 November*. New York: New York University Press, 2001.

Richard Warnes

ETHNIKE ORGANOSIS KYPRIAKOU AGONOS (EOKA)

The Ethnike Organosis Kypriakou Agonos (EOKA, or National Organization of Cypriot Fighters) was a Greek Cypriot military group that fought to end British rule in Cyprus and unite the island with Greece. The group was active between 1955 and 1959 and had both a military and political component. George Grivas, a former Greek army officer who served in both World Wars, led the former, while Archbishop Michail Christodolou Makarios (born Michail Christodolou Mouskos) oversaw the latter.

At the height of the military campaign, EOKA had a total membership of around 1,250, which included about 250 guerrillas and 1,000 active underground cadres. Although the group did not enjoy the benefit of an entrenched revolutionary environment (widespread poverty, unemployment, and popular alienation), it did have the support of the Greek government in the form of arms, money, and propaganda. This assistance proved vital in terms of sustaining the struggle against the British, who eventually conceded to a presidential election in 1959 that was easily won by Makarios.

EOKA commenced its military campaign on April 1, 1955, with simultaneous attacks launched on the British-controlled Cyprus Broadcasting Station in Nicosia, the British Army's Wolseley barracks, and various targets in Famagusta. Subsequent strikes over the course of the next four years left 156 members of the security forces dead. An unknown number of expatriates, colonial officers, and civilian police officers were also killed, while assassination operations against Greek Cypriots resulted in at least 148 fatalities.

As a counterweight to EOKA, the island's Turkish population formed a rival guerrilla force in 1957. Known as the Turk Mukavemet Teskilati (TMT, or Turkish Resistance Organization), the group quickly moved to target Greek Cypriots in reprisal attacks—setting the scene for rapidly escalating intercommunal violence that peaked in 1958 with over 100 civilian deaths.

EOKA's activity continued until December 1959, when a cease-fire was declared. This paved the way for the Zurich agreement, which provided for presidential elections that same year. EOKA achieved its primary goal when Cyprus became an independent state on August 16, 1960, with the exception of two British military bases. The settlement ruled out any union with either Greece or Turkey, with Ankara, Athens, and London all committing to equally guarantee the island's sovereignty.

Grivas vehemently rejected the Zurich agreement because it did not include any roadmap for Cyprus's eventual unification with Greece. In 1971 he formed EOKA-B to overthrow President Makarios (who had been reelected in 1968) and achieve *enosis* (the union of Greece and Cyprus) through violent means. While Grivas was in an ideal position to create a new organization (which he oversaw until his death in January 1974) given his role as commander of the Greek Cypriot National Guard, his movement did not have any widespread popular support. Unlike the original EOKA, EOKA-B had no anticolonial anchor to justify its existence and indeed was largely perceived as a renegade outfit that was a threat to both Greeks and Turks on the island.

Despite this, the military junta in Athens saw Grivas's group as a potentially useful proxy for achieving complete Greek control over Cyprus. On July 15, 1974, with the tacit blessing of Dictator Dimitrios Ioannides and the help of the National Guard, EOKA-B tried to overthrow Makarios. The attempted coup failed and left some 3,000 people dead. Turkey invaded five days later—an intervention that most authorities held to be legal—leading to the partition of Cyprus that holds to this day.

Further Reading

Asprey, Robert B. *War in the Shadows: The Guerrilla in History*. New York: Doubleday, 1975.

Barker, Dudley. *Grivas: Portrait of a Terrorist*. Dallas, TX: Harcourt, Brace, 1960.

Brogan, Patrick. *The Fighting Never Stopped: A Comprehensive Guide to World Conflict since 1945*. New York: Random House, 1989.

Byford-Jones, W. *Grivas and the Story of EOKA*. London: Robert Hale, 1959.

Donna Bassett

EUSKADI TA ASKATASUNA (ETA)

Euskadi Ta Askatasuna (ETA, or Basque Homeland and Freedom) is a separatist movement group that seeks the establishment of an independent Basque state in the Western Pyrenees on the border between Spain and France. The group, which is designated as a terrorist organization by the European Union, the United States, and the United Nations, has caused more than 820 deaths over the last 40 years (58 since 2000) despite declaring several cease-fires—the most recent of which, announced in 2011, remains in effect.

A militant youth section of the Basque Nationalist Party (Partido Nacionalista Vasco) formed ETA in 1959 out of frustration with their parent movement's rejection of armed resistance. Over the course of the 1960s, the group developed a distinctly Marxist-Leninist revolutionary ideology and emerged as a fierce opponent of the Franco regime, which banned the Basque language and suppressed any attempt to promote the region's culture. ETA carried out its first planned assassination in 1968, killing the police chief of San Sebastián, Meliton Manzanas. This was followed up with a car bomb attack on Prime Minister Luis Carrero Blanco in 1973, a murder that some credit with speeding the end of the Franco regime, as the dictator no longer had a clear successor.

The Basque separatist group ETA announces a cease-fire with Spain in a March 22, 2006, video. The declaration was one of several made by the group, which were then renounced. ETA finally suspended all military activities in 2011, ending a violent campaign for independence that left over 800 people dead. (AP/Wide World Photos)

During the transition to democracy that began after Francisco Franco's death in 1975, the Basque territories in Spain achieved home rule. Despite this, ETA did not put down its arms, pursuing a policy of full independence that saw almost 100 people killed in 1980 alone. The group's escalating campaign of violence cost it public support, however, with opposition becoming particularly marked after it claimed responsibility for the kidnapping and murder of Miguel Angel Blanco, a young Basque town councilor. The incident led to mass protests across the country and triggered widespread demands for an end to violence. According to a poll conducted by the Spanish Universidad del País Vasco, by 2004 over 71 percent of Basques said they "totally rejected" ETA.

While ETA has been at the forefront of trying to coerce political change in Spain through violence, arguably the biggest impact on the country's internal governing situation resulted from an attack that it did not carry out. On March 11, 2004, ten improvised explosive devices (IEDs) were set off in Madrid trains—an event that has since come to be known as 3/11—killing 191 and injuring another 1,800. President Jose Maria Aznar, who himself was targeted by an ETA car bomb in 1995, was quick to blame the group for the bombings. However, it soon became clear that Al Qaeda was behind the incident, which the opposition claimed was directly related to Spain's presence in Iraq. The public agreed and four days later voted Aznar out of office.

ETA's hierarchy has traditionally been predicated on three pillars: political, military, and logistical. The first is charged with planning and executing attacks, the second with coordinating and harmonizing political directives, and the third with financially underwriting the needs of the group's "commandos"—mainly through robbery and the imposition of a "revolutionary tax" on Basque businesses. ETA altered this structure in 2004, creating two new branches under the control of the Zuba, or Zuzendaritza Batzordea ("directory committee"): one to handle foreign relations and one to oversee prisoner activity.

ETA has declared several cease-fires since its creation, including, notably, one in 1998 that lasted 14 months and one in March 2006 that the organization affirmed would be permanent. In December of that year, however, ETA bombed Madrid's airport. The attack, which left two people dead, was quickly followed up by a formal communiqué that the group was resuming its campaign of violence. In 2010 ETA announced yet another cease-fire, declaring it would not carry out any "armed actions." Former United Nations secretary-general Kofi Annan and Sinn Féin (the political arm of the Provisional Irish Republican Army) leader Gerry Adams, among others, subsequently sponsored a conference in October 2011, the outcome of which was a resolution calling on ETA to renounce violence and on Spain and France to open talks. Quickly thereafter the group issued a statement that it was definitively ceasing all armed activity but would continue to pursue the goal of Basque independence. At the time of writing, ETA continued to abide by this commitment.

See also: Adams, Gerry; Carrero-Blanco (Luis) Assassination; Madrid Commuter Train Bombings

Further Reading

Aviles, Juan. *El Terrorismo en España: De ETA a Al Qaeda.* Madrid: Arco/Libros, 2011.

Clark, Robert. *The Basque Insurgents: ETA, 1952–1980.* Madison: University of Wisconsin Press, 1984.

Gallego, Carlos. *ELN: una historia contada a dos voces: entrevista con "el cura" Manuel Pérez y Nicolás Rodríguez Bautista, "Gabino."* Bogota: Rodriguez Quito Editores, 1996.

Larranaga, Roberto. *Guerrilla y terrorismo en Colombia y Espana: ELN y ETA.* Bucaramanga, Colombia: Editorial UNAB, 2003.

Drew Bazil

F

FADL, JAMAL AL-

American intelligence received its first full disclosure about the capabilities of Al Qaeda from a series of interviews with Jamal al-Fadl beginning in 1996. He had been a low-level member of Al Qaeda before he defected to the Americans. Al-Fadl asserted he had important information to pass to American intelligence in a series of interviews with American intelligence officials in Eritrea. These officials decided that al-Fadl would be a reliable and valuable source of intelligence and sent him to the United States. His interrogation over the next five years produced a gold mine of information about Al Qaeda and its operations up to 1996.

Al-Fadl was a Sudanese from a relatively affluent family. He was born in 1963 in Rufaa City, Sudan, near Khartoum. After graduation from high school, he went to Saudi Arabia, where he lived on the fringes of society. His roommate was apprehended for possession of marijuana, after which al-Fadl looked to move to another country. He immigrated to the United States in 1986. In his new country, al-Fadl held two jobs: working in a grocery store in Brooklyn, New York, and raising funds for the al-Kifah Refugee Services Office, where his boss was Mustafa Shalabi. Another, unofficial part of his job was to recruit fighters for the Afghan side in the war against the Soviets in Afghanistan.

In time, it was al-Fadl's turn to go to Afghanistan to fight the Soviets. He traveled to Afghanistan, where he attended an Al Qaeda training camp at Khalid ibn Walid. His 45 days there were filled with weapons training and religious indoctrination. Next, al-Fadl was sent to other camps for further training. It was about this time that al-Fadl met Osama bin Laden. After completing his training, he joined a combat unit in Afghanistan.

Most of al-Fadl's later training was aimed at turning him into an administrator. As the war in Afghanistan drew to an end with the withdrawal of the Soviet forces, his responsibilities had increasingly transformed his job into an administrative one. Al-Fadl was present at the meeting in the fall of 1989 when the establishment of Al Qaeda was announced by Abu Ubaidah al-Banshiri, head of the military committee of the Shura (Consulting) Council. Al-Fadl was the third signatory of the document on which the participants pledged their allegiance to Al Qaeda.

Al-Fadl carried out a variety of tasks for Al Qaeda. Besides performing routine courier work, al-Fadl was also appointed as the point man for bin Laden's move from Afghanistan to Sudan. Because al-Fadl was a Sudanese citizen, it was easy for him to buy property for Al Qaeda in his native country. Another one of his crucial missions was to inquire about the availability of chemical weapons in the international underground market. Finally, he was given the task of finding out the availability of weapons-grade uranium. Both of these missions ended in failure.

By the early 1990s al-Fadl was becoming increasingly discontent with his role in Al Qaeda. He believed that others were being rewarded more for their work than he was. He made his feelings known to bin Laden; however, his complaints fell on deaf ears, with bin Laden simply telling him to get back to work. Al-Fadl's salary as an officer in Al Qaeda was $700 a month with health benefits. Others in the organization with similar responsibilities made much more. In retaliation, al-Fadl began to skim funds off the top of the deals he made on behalf of the organization. He was able to accumulate $250,000 before his peers in Al Qaeda caught on to his scheme in 1995. Al-Fadl promised restitution, but he then went into hiding. Uncertain of his fate if he stayed in Al Qaeda, al-Fadl took the first opportunity to turn himself over to American intelligence officers in Eritrea.

Al-Fadl was too low ranking a member to have useful information about possible future terrorist plots, but his information regarding the inner workings of Al Qaeda has been invaluable. Al Qaeda's terrorist campaign started in 1995, and al-Fadl was already on the outs with the organization by that time. What he did have knowledge about was the organization of Al Qaeda, its leadership structure, and its philosophy. The 9/11 plot had not yet been contemplated by Al Qaeda, but al-Fadl's testimony showed that Al Qaeda was capable of almost anything.

Al-Fadl has remained under the protection of the U.S. government. He pled guilty to multiple counts of conspiracy against the United States, charges that carried a maximum prison sentence of 15 years. Ultimately, the Federal Bureau of Investigation (FBI) kept him under house arrest for nearly two years before moving him and his family into the Witness Protection Program. Al-Fadl testified against Wadih el Hage with respect to Hage's role in the bombings of the U.S. embassies in Nairobi, Kenya, and Dar es Salaam, Tanzania. Since September 11, al-Fadl has been in constant demand by intelligence organizations for his extensive knowledge of the operations of Al Qaeda.

See also: Al Qaeda; bin Laden, Osama

Further Reading

Miller, John, Michael Stone, and Chris Mitchell. *The Cell: Inside the 9/11 Plot and Why the FBI and CIA Failed to Stop It.* New York: Hyperion, 2002.

Naftali, Timothy. *Blind Spot: The Secret History of American Counterterrorism.* New York: Basic Books, 2005.

Stephen E. Atkins

FAROOQI, AMJAD HUSSEIN

Amjad Hussein Farooqi was an Islamist militant who was a chief suspect in the murder of *Wall Street Journal* reporter Daniel Pearl in February 2002. He was also tied to the overthrow of Afghan president Mohammad Najibullah in 1992, the subsequent formation of the Taliban, and two failed assassinations on Pakistani President Pervez Musharraf in December 2003.

Born in 1972 in Punjab, Pakistan, Farooqi was known by the alias Amjad Hussaid. He joined the Sunni sectarian extremist group Sipah-e-Sahaba Pakistan (SSP) at the age of 18 and was present when Kabul fell to a coalition of Afghan mujahideen forces in 1995. That same year he took up a position in Jaish-e-Mohammed (JeM)—a jihadi *tanzeem* (outfit)created and sponsored by Pakistan's InterService Intelligence (ISI) Directorate—to fight against Indian troops in the disputed province of Jammu and Kashmir. As a member of JeM Farooqi allegedly participated in the 2002 murder of Pearl, a suicide bombing of the U.S. consulate in Karachi—also in 2002—that killed 12 Pakistanis, and the attempts on Musharraf in 2003.

A massive manhunt for Farooqi began in May 2004, with authorities in Islamabad offering a 20 million rupee ($330,000) reward for information leading to his capture. He was eventually killed during a two-hour gun battle in Pakistan's southern Sindh province on September 26, 2004.

It is alleged that the army could have captured Farooqi alive but did not lest he reveal embarrassing details about the role of Pakistani civilian and military officials in the killing of Pearl and attacks against American and French targets. According to one senior policeman, who was never named, Farooqi was the key link between the foot soldiers and those who ordered the journalist's murder. Another Pakistani official, who again remained anonymous, asserted that although Khalid Sheikh Mohammed did the actual killing, Farooqi was the real "anchor" in the case.

Apart from his activities in JeM, it is thought that Farooqi played a leading role in Lashkar-e-Jhangvi (LeJ)—the armed wing of Sipah-e-Sahaba Pakistan—and also worked closely with the Libyan Abu Faraj al-Libi, a senior member of Al Qaeda who was captured in Pakistan on May 2, 2005.

See also: Jaish-e-Mohammed (JeM); Lashkar-e-Jhangvi (LeJ); Libi, Abu Faraj al-

Further Reading

Lévy, Bernard-Henri. *Who Killed Daniel Pearl?* Translated by James X. Mitchell. Hoboken, NJ: Melville House, 2003.

Rabasa, Angel, Peter Chalk, Kim Cragin, Sara A. Daly, Heather S. Gregg, Theodore W. Karasik, Kevin A. O'Brien, and William Rosenau. *Beyond al-Qaeda. Part 1: The Global Jihadist Movement.* Santa Monica, CA: RAND Corporation, 2006.

Rashid, Ahmed. *Descent into Chaos: The United States and the Failure of Nation Building in Pakistan, Afghanistan, and Central Asia.* New York: Viking Books, 2008.

Donna Bassett

FAROUQ, OMAR AL-

Omar al-Farouq was born in Iraq on May 24, 1971. He was raised in Kuwait but moved to West Java, where he married Mira Augustuina and had two children. While in Indonesia he became one of Al Qaeda's top lieutenants in Southeast Asia, serving as a primary intermediary between Osama bin Laden's organization and Jemaah Islamiyah (JI) until his death on September 25, 2006. An explosives expert, he is believed to have developed plans for bombing U.S. embassies throughout Southeast Asia.

Al-Farouq joined Al Qaeda in the early 1990s and trained in Afghanistan for three years. While there, he volunteered for a suicide mission in the Philippines but failed to carry out the mission after unsuccessfully attempting to enroll in a flight school.

In 2002 al-Farouq was arrested in Indonesia and turned over to American authorities. He was subsequently detained in a military prison in Bagram, Afghanistan, but managed to escape along with three other Al Qaeda suspects three years later.

At some point between his escape from Bagram and his death in September 2006, al-Farouq made his way back into Iraq. Here he is believed to have initially stayed in Zubair, a Sunni enclave near Basra, where he went by the assumed name Mahmoud Ahmed. He was killed on September 25, 2006, when more than 200 British troops launched a predawn operation to arrest him in Basra.

See also: Al Qaeda; Jemaah Islamiyah (JI)

Further Reading

"Profile: Omar al-Farouq." *BBC News,* September 26, 2006. http://news.bbc.co.uk/go/pr/fr/-/2/hi/middle_east/5379604.stm.
Senggotro, Moerkekaq. "Al Farouq, al-Qaeda Leader in Southeast Asia, Is Dead." *Asianews.it,* September 27, 2006. http://www.asianews.it/view.php?l=en&art=7325.
"Top Al-Qaeda Leaders Shot Dead." *World News Australia,* September 26, 2006. http://www9.sbs.com.au/theworldnews/region.php?id=131500&region=6
"UK Troops Kill Fugitive al-Qaida Leader." *The Guardian* (UK), September 26, 2006.

Horacio Trujillo

FAZUL, ABDULLAH MOHAMMED

Abdullah Mohammed Fazul was born in 1972 in Moroni, the capital of the Comoros Islands. In 1990 he studied briefly in Saudi Arabia and then Pakistan but soon quit school to move to Afghanistan, where he began training with Al Qaeda. He then traveled to Sudan and the Horn of Africa, where he joined fellow Al Qaeda operative Mohammed Saddiq Odeh in recruiting Somali militants for combat against U.S. and UN forces. Both men reportedly participated in the 1993 Battle of Mogadishu, in which Odeh boasted that he provided the rocket launchers and rifles that brought down two American helicopters (the infamous Blackhawk Down incident). Fazul and his associates were credited with introducing two Al Qaeda tactical hallmarks to the Somali insurgency: suicide bombings and roadside improvised explosive devices (IEDs).

By 1996 Fazul was living in Nairobi with Wadih el Hage, the former personal secretary of Osama bin Laden and the head of Al Qaeda's East Africa cell. Together they planned and executed the 1998 U.S. embassy bombings in Kenya and Tanzania. The operation, which involved the detonation of trucks loaded with TNT, left 224 people dead and thousands more wounded. The day marked Al Qaeda's first attack on an American target and was one of the most devastating since Hezbollah's 1983 suicide assault on the Marine barracks in Beirut, Lebanon. Following the bombings, the Federal Bureau of Investigation (FBI) included Fazul in a list of 22 most wanted terrorists, issuing a $5 million bounty for information leading to his capture.

In 2001 Fazul traveled to Liberia with Ahmed Khalfan Ghailani, another suspect in the 1998 embassy attacks. There, the two reportedly established financing deals in illegally traded diamonds to fund future Al Qaeda operations. Fazul returned to Nairobi in August 2002, when he began planning another mission. Carried out in November of that year, the attack involved synchronized assaults on Israeli targets in Mombasa: one against a charter jet as it took off from Moi International Airport and one against the Israeli-owned Paradise Hotel. The first, which involved surface-to-air missiles, failed; however, the second, which took the form of a suicide attack, killed 16 and injured 80.

When the Ethiopian army ousted Somalia's Council of Islamic Courts (CIC) in 2007, Fazul was believed to be living in Mogadishu. The following year he ventured to the Kenyan resort town of Mandali to be treated for a kidney condition. When intelligence reports revealed he was in the country, Kenyan officials raided his residence. He narrowly escaped and made his way back to Somalia. He continued to lead the Islamist insurgency, becoming a military commander for al-Shabaab, the youth movement of the CIC. In November 2009 Fazul was inaugurated as Al Qaeda's top commander in East Africa in the Somali town of Kismayo, following the death of his predecessor, Saleh Ali Saleh Nabhan.

In June 2011, Fazul and another operative lost their way in northwestern Mogadishu and accidentally drove into a checkpoint manned by troops of Somalia's Transitional Federal Government. When the two men refused to identify themselves, the soldiers opened fire and killed them both. After the shoot-out, the soldiers searched the vehicle and discovered $40,000 in cash, laptop computers, and other equipment. U.S. officials confirmed Fazul's identity after carrying out DNA tests on his corpse, and Secretary of State Hillary Clinton announced his death as "a significant blow to Al Qaeda, its extremist allies, and its operations in East Africa."

See also: Mombasa Attacks; U.S. Embassy (East Africa) Bombings

Further Reading

"Attack against al-Qaeda Continue in Somalia." *MSNBC News,* September 1, 2007. http://www.msnbc.msn.com/id/16531987/#.TzsPiphPaao, accessed February 14, 2012.

"Elusive Al-Qaeda Operative Was 'Real Deal.'" *CBS News,* February 11, 2009. http://www.cbsnews.com/stories/2007/01/10/world/main2347258.shtml, accessed February 14, 2012.

Gatsiounis, Ioannis. "Somali Terror Group Curtailed." *Washington Times,* July 10, 2011.

Mango, Caroline, Paul Gitau, and Cyrus Ombati. "Top al-Qaeda Man Now Back in Africa." *Africa Press International,* August 4, 2008. http://africanpress.me/2008/08/04/top-al-qaeda-man-now-back-in-kenya/, accessed February 14, 2012.

Omar, Hamsa. "Somali Soldier Who Killed al-Qaeda Leader Is Injured in Retaliatory Attack." *Bloomberg News,* August 17, 2011. http://www.bloomberg.com/news/2011-08-17/somali-soldier-who-killed-al-qaeda-leader-is-shot-in-retaliation.html, accessed February 14, 2012.

Prestholdt, Jeremy. "Phantom of the Forever War: Fazul Abdullah Mohammed and the Terrorist Imaginary." *Public Culture* 21, no. 3 (Fall 2009).

"Profile: Fazul Abdullah Mohammed." *New York Times,* June 13, 2011.

Rajan, Karim, and Fred Mukinda. "Two Arrested as Top Terror Suspect Flees." *Daily Nation* (Kenya), August 30, 2008. http://www.nation.co.ke/News/-/1056/446582/-/tj2yrs/-/index.html, accessed February 14, 2012.

Roggio, Bill. "Al-Qaeda Names Fazul Mohammed East Africa Commander." *Long War Journal,* November 11, 2009.

"US African Embassy Bomber Fazul Muhammed Dead." *BBC News,* June 11, 2011. http://www.bbc.co.uk/news/world-africa-13737942, accessed February 14, 2012.

Elinor Kasting

FORT DIX PLOT

On May 7, 2007, agents from the Federal Bureau of Investigation (FBI) arrested six Muslim extremists, originally from the Middle East, after two tried to buy automatic weapons from an undercover officer in a plot to attack the Fort Dix military base in New Jersey. They were charged and convicted for trying to kill military personnel and, although not connected to Al Qaeda, were alleged to have been inspired by Osama bin Laden and his concept of jihad in the defense of Islam.

The group included three brothers: Dritan Duka, 28; Shain Duka, 26; and Eljvir Duka, 23. The trio were ethnic Albanians from Debar in the Republic of Macedonia and had first entered the United States illegally in 1984. Between 1996 and 2006, police had charged Dritan and Shain with a number of traffic citations and minor offenses, including marijuana possession. Court records show they were fined amounts varying from $20 to $830.

The other three were Agron Abdullahu, 24, an Albanian from Kosovo who was living legally in New Jersey and who gave the group weapons training; Mohamad Ibrahim Shnewer, 22, Dritan's brother-in-law and a Palestinian cab driver from Jordan who became a naturalized U.S. citizen; and Serdar Tatar, 23, born in Turkey, who resided in Philadelphia legally and who had worked at a Super Mario Pizza, owned by his family.

The six men trained on firing semiautomatic weapons at a Gouldsboro, Pennsylvania, shooting range and used cell phones to video-record their sessions while shouting in Arabic, "God is great." On January 31, 2006, the group went to a Circuit City store in Mount Laurel, New Jersey, to convert the electronic images into a DVD. However, they failed to effectively screen the cell phone from outside purview, and after store employee Brian Morgenstern saw the content, he contacted authorities.

The FBI then began a 16-month investigation and infiltrated the group with two paid informants who recorded the members planning their attacks. Additional incriminating evidence was extracted from their cell phones, which clearly indicated they wanted to kill as many Americans as possible at the military base. According to U.S. attorney Christopher J. Christie, the members all seemed to feed off each other and obviously had aspirations to be jihadists.

The 26-page indictment showed that the group had no formal military training, no apparent connection to Al Qaeda or other foreign terrorist organizations, no clear ringleader (although some reports cited Shnewer as the main commander), and very little chance of actually succeeding in pulling off that operation. Court records said the cell had first considered attacking Fort Monmouth in New Jersey, Delaware's Dover Air Force Base, and the U.S. Coast Guard Building in Philadelphia. However, the six settled on Fort Dix because Tatar had delivered pizzas there from his family's Super Mario Pizza and had a map of the installation.

A conversation involving members of the group, recorded by one of the informants, revealed that the cell planned to hit four, five, or six Humvees; rampage through the base, killing people as they went; and then completely retreat without suffering any losses. To do this they had attempted to purchase weapons from an undercover FBI agent, including AK-47s, M16s, M60s, and rocket-propelled grenades.

On May 11, 2007, all six were ordered held without bail at the federal detention facility in Philadelphia. Their trial opened the following October, and after a month the following convictions were handed down: the Duka brothers and Shnewer all received life sentences; Tatar was imprisoned for 23 years; and Abdullahu accepted a plea bargain deal for five years in jail.

See also: Al Qaeda

Further Reading

Emerson, Steven. *Jihad Incorporated: A Guide to Militant Islam in the US.* Foreword by Peter Hoekstra. Amherst, NY: Prometheus Books, 2006.

Lawrence, Bruce. *Messages to the World: The Statements of Osama bin Laden.* London: Verso, 2005.

Temple-Raston, Dina. *The Jihad Next Door: The Lackawanna Six and Rough Justice in the Age of Terror.* New York: Perseus Books, 2007.

Donna Bassett

FRENCH EMBASSY (THE HAGUE) ATTACKS

On September 13, 1974, three members of the Japanese Red Army (JRA) attacked the French Embassy in The Hague, Netherlands. They took 11 people hostage, including the French ambassador, and triggered a siege that lasted 101 hours.

The JRA team, which consisted of Haruo Wako, Junzo Okudaira, and Jun Nishikawa, threatened to kill their hostages, including Ambassador Jacques Senard, unless their demands were met. These included the release of Furuya Yataka (also known as Yoshiaki), a JRA member who had been arrested at the Orly Airport south of Paris on July 21 during the group's aborted Operation Translation.

The Netherlands' government immediately deployed a counterterrorist squad, as well as a military platoon, to surround the barricaded French embassy. On the third day of the crisis, the terrorists released three ill Dutch women. They also demanded a $1 million ransom, which the French refused to pay. The trio reduced the sum to $300,000, which was paid by the Dutch government and subsequently reimbursed by Paris.

The French also gave in to the demand for a plane to take the terrorists to a Middle Eastern country but, not wishing to endanger any more nationals, did not provide a crew. In exchange, Paris demanded that the hostages be released and that the terrorists surrender their weapons.

According to some reports, two women hostages were freed on September 16, 1974, and the other nine on September 17, 1974, after Yataka was freed (who had initially refused to join the JRA team for fear of being subjected to reprisals for failing in his mission). Three of the hostages were left at the embassy, with the other six being freed at the airport.

The terrorists were first flown to Lebanon, where they were refused landing rights. South Yemen did, however, grant them admission; there, the plane was refueled for a final trip to Damascus. Once they arrived in Syria, the Assad government agreed to grant the terrorists safe conduct out of the country in exchange for surrendering both their weapons and money. Initially, the JRA members refused but finally agreed and handed over both, with the ransoms returned to the Dutch. It is alleged that the hijackers were then handed over to an official with the Palestine Liberation Organization (PLO), one of the main groups represented in the umbrella movement that had had contacts with the JRA in the past but which denied any involvement in the incident.

The Japanese government, which was consulted by the Dutch, arrested Jun Nishikawa in Stockholm, Sweden. He was indicted on May 2, 1975, and charged with attempted murder and unlawful arrest and confinement. Fusako Shigenobu, Kazuo Yoshimura, and Nishikawa's two partners in The Hague were placed on an international wanted list as accomplices.

There is some evidence that Ilich Ramirez Sanchez (alias Carlos the Jackal), a freelance terrorist with close connections to the Popular Front for the Liberation of Palestine (PFLP), may have been involved in the attack. Shortly after the attack, French police arrested Taketomo Takahashi, who had become a Paris JRA leader. He had apparently tried to swallow a piece of paper that had two code names: "Acheme" and "Jean Baptiste." The latter was document forger Andrew Haberman, who was subsequently identified as Antonio Perera Carvalho, a Brazilian who held messages for the Japanese but was also listed in a notebook belonging to Carlos's assistant, under the alias Felipe Fereira. Carlos also apparently went to Amsterdam the day before the embassy attack and changed a substantial amount of money, much of which he gave to Acheme for safekeeping.

See also: Japanese Red Army (JRA); Sanchez, Ilich Ramirez (Carlos the Jackal)

Further Reading

Farrell, William R. *Blood and Rage: The Story of the Japanese Red Army.* Lexington, MA: Lexington Books, 1990.

Smith, Colin. *Carlos: Portrait of a Terrorist.* New York: Holt, Rinehart and Winston, 1976.

Yallop, David. *Tracking the Jackal: The Search for Carlos, the World's Most Wanted Man.* New York: Random House, 1993.

Donna Bassett

FRONT DE LIBÉRATION DU QUEBEC (FLQ)

The French-Canadian separatist group Front de Libération du Quebec (FLQ) should not be seen as a single structured organization. Rather, it existed as a loosely associated milieu of individuals linked by a similar ideological objective aimed at securing the independence of Quebec. Despite the FLQ's amateurism, it was implicated in a number of violent acts between 1963 and 1973, leading to seven deaths, injuries, armed robberies, and the destruction of property.

In February 1963, the original FLQ was formed as a splinter of the Reseau de Resistance (RR) by Georges Schoeters, Gabriel Hudon, and Raymond Villeneuve. Initially, the group launched attacks against targets that symbolized English domination, particularly those of a commercial nature. After Schoeters, Hudon, and Villeneuve were arrested, Hudon's younger brother established a six-man sabotage squad, which carried out a number of bank robberies before he too was apprehended. Francois Schirm then took over the leadership of the FLQ but again this was short-lived. In 1965 he was sentenced for murder along with four colleagues. Despite these setbacks, the FLQ continued to instigate a low-level campaign of violence, bombing venues in Montreal and Ottawa during the autumn of 1968.

However, the peak of FLQ activity occurred with Operation Liberation in October 1970. This incident involved two kidnap teams, one led by Jacques Lanctot and one by Paul Rose. The first abducted British diplomat James Cross on October 5, the second Pierre Laporte, Quebec's deputy premier, on October 10. Their demands included publicity, the release of FLQ prisoners, and sanctuary abroad. In response to the October Crisis, the Canadian government invoked the War Measures Act of 1942, swamping Quebec with troops who conducted a wave of searches and arrested up to 250 separatist suspects. Although the terrorists murdered Laporte, Cross was later released. The draconian nature of the Canadian response generated considerable criticism within Canada and was directly responsible for several constitutional and legislative reforms and changes. That said, the stringent measures effectively broke the back of the FLQ and the cause of Quebecois independence has since been pursued through legitimate political channels.

Further Reading

Charters, David. "The Amateur Revolutionaries: A Reassessment of the FLQ." *Terrorism and Political Violence* 9, no. 1 (1997).

Crelinsten, Ronald. "The Internal Dynamics of the FLQ during the October Crisis of 1970." In D. Rapoport, ed., *Inside Terrorist Organisations*. London: Frank Cass, 2001.

Davidson-Smith, Tim. "Canada's Counter-Terrorism Experience." *Terrorism and Political Violence* 5, no. 1 (1993).

Ross, Jeffrey Ian. "The Rise and Fall of Quebecois Separatist Terrorism: A Qualitative Application of Factors from Two Models." *Studies in Conflict and Terrorism* 18, no. 4 (1995).

Richard Warnes

FRONT DE LIBÉRATION NATIONALE (FLN)

The Front de Libération Nationale (FLN) was an Algerian nationalist movement committed to armed revolt against France in the pursuit of complete independence. In the course of the 1954–1962 war of liberation, the FLN employed a mixture of terrorist, guerrilla, and conventional military tactics.

The FLN revolt began on November 1, 1954, with largely unsuccessful attacks directed against police stations, military outposts, government infrastructure, and the property of wealthy European civilians. In April 1955, however, the group significantly expanded its target set to include Muslim "collaborators" and by the summer of that year had escalated its campaign further by launching total war against French civilians. The FLN was subsequently tied to the brutal Philippeville massacres in which 37 European civilians were killed, some of whom were literally hacked to pieces.

Late 1956 saw the FLN shift its emphasis to urban attacks, and over the course of four months the group conducted a series of high-profile civilian-orchestrated operations in Algiers. Notable incidents included a wave of bombings in the heart of the city's European sector (collectively killing 18 and injuring over 140); the assassination of the city's mayor, Amedee Froger; an attempted massacre of the cortege accompanying the stricken leader's funeral procession; killings of several other high-ranking officials in the colonial administration; and the staging of a

Members of the Algerian National Liberation Front pose with their World War II surplus machine guns in the mountains of Algeria on March 1, 1957. The rebel group was formed by Ahmed Ben Bella and other nationalists in 1954 to fight for Algerian independence from France. That goal was realized in 1962 after eight years of war. (AP/Wide World Photos)

general strike that seriously disrupted the capital's postal, telegraph, and railway services for a number of days.

In response, the French called out the elite 10th Parachute Division, granting it full authority to do whatever was necessary to restore order in the capital. Triggering what subsequently became known as the Battle of Algiers, the decision proved to be one of great import. Rationalizing that extreme circumstances warranted extreme countermeasures, the unit's commander in chief, General Jacques Massau, authorized wholesale roundups of entire neighborhoods (enacted under a system of *quadrillage* in which the city was divided into controlled "squares"— each one conforming to a regional command) in addition to extrajudicial preemptive detentions of FLN suspects, who were then subjected to what amounted to an institutionalized regime of torture. Overall, it is thought that almost 40 percent of the Casbah (Arab quarter) were arrested or detained during the course the four months, some 3,000 of whom were never heard of again.

While Massau's actions were instrumental in crushing the FLN's terror-based operations, they elicited widespread international debate and consternation. Just as significant, they destroyed the middle ground of Muslim political compromise—driving formerly passive Algerians, if not directly into the ranks of the FLN, at least away from the colonial administration—as well as polarized and undercut domestic public opinion and support in France itself.

Following the (draconian) restoration of order in Algiers, the French devised a more nuanced, two-pronged doctrine of pacification that focused on (1) obtaining the support of the population and (2) "starving" the FLN of vital external support and internal territorial control. To accomplish the first task, Paris moved to provide humanitarian and material support to local Muslim communities, pledged full protection for those who sided with the army, and through the notion of "association" guaranteed that the colony would be recognized as a constituent part (though not an integral component) of the French Republic, with concomitant rights guaranteed for all its citizens. The ultimate goal was to sideline the FLN by demonstrating that stability, security, and socioeconomic and political development would best be secured if Algeria remained under France's constitutional authority rather than seeking to attain its own sovereign statehood.

Simultaneously, the army moved to stop the external flow of humanitarian support to the FLN by reestablishing control over Algeria's land borders. To this end, an electrified barbed-wire fence complete with minefields, radar, and patrol zones for armed elements was constructed along the colony's external boundaries with Morocco and Tunisia. The barrier was intended to act as a "fishnet" that security-force interdiction units could then use to "trawl" Algeria's frontier regions, both to catch rebels covertly crossing into the country and to identify the routes they were taking. It was so efficient that infiltration became essentially suicidal, prompting FLN cadres in Morocco and Tunisia to deliberately abandon their home-based comrades. Having stymied this important source of overseas support, the military then sought to rout the group internally by initiating regionally coordinated search-and-cordon operations against known FLN strongholds. Again, the stratagem was a great success, to the extent that by 1960 the rebels had no more than

5,000 members, no firm area from which to conduct and plan offensive attacks, and no objective beyond survival.

While the second strand of France's pacification strategy worked well, Massau's brutal campaign to break the FLN's terror infrastructure in Algiers during 1958 undercut the first. Revelations of torture and summary executions generated revulsion throughout France and growing domestic and overseas pressure for a definitive end to the conflict. Combined, these factors eventually forced President Charles de Gaulle, who had come to power in 1958 on a distinct pro-French Algerian policy, to reverse his stance and concede to a negotiating stance that explicitly recognized the possibility of colonial self-determination and majority rule.

The president's U-turn sparked a major insurrection among the colonial population in Algeria, who in conjunction with hard-line elements in the army (which were adamant that they would not repeat in North Africa their earlier ignominious retreat from Indochina), established the Organisation Armeé Secréte (OAS)—an overtly terrorist entity that intended to assassinate de Gaulle; unleash a civil war against the metropolitan government, police, and army; and ignite an ethnic war against Muslims.

Although the OAS carried out a wave of bloody attacks that at its height averaged 120 bombings a day, the rebellion was contained (largely because the bulk of the military remained loyal to de Gaulle), allowing negotiations to take place between the FLN and Paris that culminated with the signing of the Evian Agreements on March 19, 1962. These provided for a cease-fire, the granting of a full range of civil, political, economic, and cultural rights for all Algerians, and the holding of a popular referendum to decide whether the territory should remain a constitutional component of France or become a sovereign state in its own right. Although the OAS attempted to destroy the accord through a last-ditch campaign of urban terrorism, a vote on the future status of the colony was taken on July 1, 1962. This returned a nearly unanimous result in favor of independence, which was legally conferred to Algeria two days later. The FLN quickly moved to seize power and after outlawing opposition parties formed a one-party state in which it became the only legal and ruling party.

Further Reading

Hoffman, Bruce. *Inside Terrorism.* London: Victor Gollancz, 1998.
Horne, Alistair. *A Savage War of Peace: Algeria 1954–1962.* New York: New York Review Books, 2006.
Martin, Giles. "War in Algeria: The French Experience." *Military Review,* July–August 2005.
Rosie, George. *Directory of International Terrorism.* Edinburgh: Mainstream, 1986.

Gregory Wyatt

FUERZAS ARMADAS REVOLUCIONÁRIAS DE COLOMBIA (FARC)

The Fuerzas Armadas Revolucionárias de Colombia (FARC, or Revolutionary Armed Forces of Colombia) is a Colombian-based Marxist-Leninist terrorist-guerrilla organization that was established in 1966 under the leadership of

Manuel Marulanda (also known as "Sureshot"). The group's purported aim is to seize national power through a protracted people's war, although the bulk of its agenda has tended to focus on more pragmatic goals such as land redistribution, reform of the security forces, and empowerment of the rural poor. Kidnappings for ransom and taxation of the illegal drug trade have traditionally been FARC's main sources of revenue. However, gold mining has become increasingly important, particularly in recent years as the price of the precious metal has risen dramatically.

FARC is the largest and oldest insurgent-terrorist entity in the Americas. Estimates of its membership vary. According to the Colombian Armed Forces commander Admiral Édgar Cely, the group had 18,000 members in 2010, half of them armed fighters with the remainder working in the areas of intelligence and logistics. Other commentators claim this figure is inflated and does not reflect the generally weakened state of the organization since President Álvaro Uribe took office in 2002.

FARC has existed alongside two other substate militant groups in Colombia: the Ejército de Liberación Nacional (ELN, or National Liberation Army) and the Autodefensas Unidas de Colombia (AUC, or United Self-Defense Forces of Colombia). The former is still active; the latter agreed to demobilize in 2006 (although many have since returned to arms as a result of dissatisfaction with the peace dividend). At their height these three organizations controlled anywhere from 35 to 45 percent of the country, with FARC's main source of strength concentrated in southeastern Colombia's 193,000 square miles of jungle and plains.

FARC's roots go back to the murder of the populist politician Jorge Eliecer Gaitan in 1948. His killing triggered the so-called *La Violencia* (The Violence), an era that lasted until 1958 and saw some 200,000 people lose their lives. Marulanda began his guerrilla career at the outset of this period, joining a liberal insurgent band in the Department of Tolima, an epicenter of the violence. In 1964 he helped form a communist-oriented "independent republic" in Marquetalia, a remote area in southern Tolima. It was one of several such "republics" established in southern Colombia. In June 1964 the army attacked and captured the Marquetalia group, although Marulanda managed to escape. Two years later, the guerrillas reorganized themselves as FARC with Marulanda as chief of staff.

FARC expanded slowly over the next decade. However, by 1982 the group had grown into a semi-quasi regular army thanks to revenue derived from taxing coca production in areas under its control and training in Vietnam and Russia. This transformation allowed FARC to significantly enhance the scale and tempo of its operations, which increased from small hit-and-run raids in the countryside to major offensives against the military and strikes on middle-sized cities.

Between 1984 and 1987, FARC took advantage of a cease-fire with the government of President Belisario Betancur to further consolidate its presence in resource-rich regions. Prominent were the eastern plains (cattle), the middle Magdalena Valley (oil), Antioquia (gold), and Urabá (commercial agriculture). During the 1990s FARC also moved to increase its involvement in Colombia's booming cocaine business, using profits to purchase a wide array of weapons and expand its guerrilla force to between 7,000 and 10,000 combatants.

In the hope of negotiating a peace settlement with a now extremely forceful internal threat, President Andres Pastrana granted FARC a 42,000-square-kilometer (26-square-mile) safe haven (*zona despeja*) on November 7, 1998. This sanctuary was systematically exploited to build up the group's strength, attract new members, and access outside training. The latter became a subject of international focus on August 11, 2001, when two members of the Provisional Irish Republican Army (PIRA, or the "Provos") were arrested in Bogotá along with a Sinn Féin representative stationed in Cuba. All three were subsequently convicted for imparting bomb-making skills to FARC in the *zona despeja* as well as traveling on false passports. However, before they were imprisoned, they disappeared while on bail and fled to Ireland. The incident came just months after the U.S. House Foreign Affairs Committee had released a report alleging a long relationship between FARC and the PIRA. According to the document, the Provos had been providing advanced urban terrorist training to the Colombian group since at least 1998, receiving at least $2 million in drug money for this instruction.

Mainly as a result of the PIRA affair, Pastrana suspended the peace talks on February 21, 2002, and ordered the army to retake the *zone despeja*. This sparked a return to violence that during the course of the next year saw FARC attack 10 large ranches in Meta, which were captured, occupied, and then redistributed to the local peasantry.

By this time Álvaro Uribe had assumed the presidency. With the active backing of the United States, the new Colombian leader commenced a major offensive against the interrelated challenges of drugs and insurgency. By 2008 these efforts had paid dividends, with FARC losing an estimated 17,274 combatants—5,316 through voluntary demobilizations and the remainder through captures and casualties. That same year the group suffered a series of major losses, including the death (through natural causes) of Marulanda; the killings of Luis Edgar Devia-Silva (also known as Raúl Reyes, the group's international spokesman and main ideologue) and Manuel Muñoz-Ortiz (also known as Iván Ríos, head of the Central Block); and the capture of Gerardo Aguilar (also known as César, a senior figure in FARC's secretariat).

These setbacks have caused FARC to systematically degenerate into a largely criminally based entity with profit rather than ideology as the main motivational drive. The group is now involved in all aspects of the cocaine trade—from production through refining to trafficking—and is presently thought to earn between $200 and $300 million from these activities. Several alleged FARC members have also been linked to a smuggling and passport forgery ring thought to be supplying Colombian identity and nationality documents to individuals from Pakistan, Jordan, Iraq, Egypt, and other countries. FARC's more acute interface with crime is consistent with the arguments of those who maintain that the group no longer has the capacity to confront Bogotá as a concerted insurgent entity and that its members have concluded that their militant skills represent a commodity to be marketed for profit and power, not just for the good of a cause.

See also: Autodefensas Unidas de Colombia (AUC); Club El Nogal Bombing; Ejército de Liberación Nacional (ELN)

Further Reading

Bergquist, Charles, Ricardo Peñaranda, and Gonzalo Sánchez G., eds. *Violence in Colombia 1990–2000: Waging War and Negotiating Peace.* Wilmington, DE: SR Books, 2001.

Byman, Daniel, Peter Chalk, Bruce Hoffman, William Rosenau, and David Brannan. *Trends in Outside Support for Insurgent Movements.* Santa Monica, CA: RAND, 2001.

Chalk, Peter. *The Latin American Drug Trade: Scope, Dimensions, Impact and Response.* Santa Monica, CA: RAND, 2011.

Cragin, Kim, and Bruce Hoffman. *Arms Trafficking and Colombia.* Santa Monica, CA: RAND, 2003.

Kirk, Robin. *More Terrible than Death: Violence, Drugs, and America's War in Colombia.* New York: Public Affairs, 2004.

Donna Bassett

G

G-20 PLOT

On February 27, 2009, British security officials warned that thousands of demonstrators were planning to stage a series of protests during the G-20 summit that was to be held on April 1. Antiwar, antiglobalization, and environmental activists had referred to the event as "Financial Fool's Day" and were allegedly organizing various marches, rallies, and sit-ins to coincide with the meeting.

The G-20 is a gathering of the leaders of the world's wealthiest countries. The summit was to be held at the ExCeL arena in London's Docklands. At least 3,000 police officers were scheduled to provide security at the event, which was expected to attract as many as 100,000 demonstrators. The authorities were determined to avoid a repeat of a 1999 protest that triggered fighting between city workers and anarchists and left 46 people injured and caused some £2 million in property damage.

The Metropolitan Police summed up their concerns as follows: "We have said that we are seeing an unprecedented level of activity amongst protest groups not seen since the late 1990s, involving some individuals we have not seen on the protest circuit for some time. However, while these individuals are talking about what they would like to happen, we are unsure of how much of this is achievable or simply aspiration."

On March 30, 2009, police officials announced the arrest of three men and two women from Plymouth and the surrounding area. They were charged with planning to disrupt the summit using homemade explosives manufactured from fireworks. These items were later characterized as flares that were intended to cause panic and chaos rather than human fatalities. In addition to the devices, the police said they found fake handguns and a fake Kalashnikov.

All of those arrested were between the ages of 16 and 25. Four were British citizens, and one was identified as an international student. They were not known to have been affiliated with any particular terrorist group but were motivated by radical antiglobalist/environmental sentiments. Their plot was disrupted after the oldest member of the group, a 25-year-old male, was arrested for spray-painting a wall in the Plymouth city center. An initial search of the man's apartment led to the detention of the three others on unrelated drug offenses. The discovery of the fake firearms, the "suspicious devices," and anarchist literature led to the further arrest of another individual on March 29. All were held for offenses under the Terrorism Act in Cornwall.

As the investigation progressed, the alleged terrorist plot was downgraded to "a small scale stunt." Police indicated that the protestors had intended to cause "disruption," not death or injury, and characterized the rest of the protests as largely peaceful in nature.

See also: Earth Liberation Front (ELF)

Further Reading

Adapting to Protest: G20 Final Report. London: Her Majesty's Chief Inspector of Constabulary, 2009. http://www.hmic.gov.uk/sitecollectiondocuments/ppr/ppr_20090706.pdf, accessed July 22, 2011.

Lewis, Paul. "Five Held over Suspected Plot to Disrupt G20 Summit with Explosives Stunt." *The Guardian,* March 30, 2009.

Rogers, Paul. *Losing Control: Global Security in the Twenty-First Century.* London: Pluto, 2002.

Vullamy, Ed, and Richard Rogers. "The Voices in G20's Chorus of Protest." *The Guardian,* March 8, 2009.

Donna Bassett

GANDHI (RAJIV) ASSASSINATION

On May 21, 1991, a Liberation Tigers of Tamil Eelam (LTTE) suicide bomber detonated her suicide bomb vest next to Rajiv Gandhi, the former Indian prime minister, killing him (and herself) instantly. The attack occurred as Gandhi was attending a political rally in Sriperumbudur in India's Tamil Nadu state to support a fellow Congress Party candidate who was preparing for upcoming general elections. The assassination, undertaken in revenge for Gandhi's termination of support to the LTTE and subsequent deployment of an Indian Peace-Keeping Force (IPKF) to the Jaffna Peninsula in 1987, was one of the few instances when the LTTE specifically targeted a foreigner outside Sri Lanka.

Although the LTTE leadership is believed to have made the decision to assassinate Gandhi in the late 1980s, it was not until 1990 that the LTTE actually began tactical preparations. Velupillai Prabhakaran, the supreme commander of the LTTE, reasoned that security arrangements for Gandhi, as an opposition candidate, would be less stringent than those provided to an actual serving prime minister (Gandhi's term as India's prime minister ended on December 2, 1989). On September 12, 1990, the LTTE deployed its first team to India, consisting of three operatives. Their core function was to set up safe houses and establish support networks near the target site. A second team, also consisting of three persons, arrived later that same month to establish an additional forward operating base in a more rural location. Other smaller groups began to arrive during subsequent weeks.

The tactical leader for the Gandhi operation was a man named Sivarasan. An Indian Supreme Court finding would later determine: "Among the conspirators, nobody else seems to have played a greater role on the Indian soil than what Sivarasan had played." Sivarasan traveled to India in December 1990, although he also shuttled between India and Sri Lanka to receive advice and provide updates to the LTTE leadership. The core assassination squad arrived in India on May 1,

1991. This nine-member team included Dhanu (the suicide bomber who would assassinate Gandhi), Suba (Dhanu's close friend), and seven others. For the first few days while in India, Sivarasan sheltered Dhanu and Suba in a safe house established by one of the advance LTTE groups. He then arranged a dummy run at an actual campaign rally featuring former prime minister V. P. Singh. During this rehearsal Dhanu was able to get close to her intended target, which helped to instill confidence that a successful operation against Gandhi could be achieved.

On May 19, 1991, local newspapers published Gandhi's itinerary, highlighting that he would be speaking at a rally in Sriperumbudur; the LTTE team decided this would be the venue for the assassination. On the day of the attack, the operatives began their final preparations. Sivarasan acquired a pistol, pre-

A gun carriage bearing the remains of former Indian prime minister Rajiv Gandhi leaves the grounds of Teen Murti in New Delhi, May 24, 1991. Gandhi was assassinated by the Liberation Tigers of Tamil Eelam (LTTE) while campaigning in southern India. Teen Murti is the family museum. (AP Photo/Mark Lennihan)

sumably to kill Gandhi in the event the suicide bomb failed. He then traveled back to the safe house where Dhanu and her friend Suba were staying, equipping the former with an explosive vest consisting of ball bearings, a battery, and a detonation switch. After this he escorted the two girls and another native from Tamil Nadu (Nalini) to a local Hindu temple, where Dhanu offered her final prayers. Finally, he met with Haribabu, who would photograph the assassination. The attack team then proceeded to Sriperumbudur, where Gandhi was scheduled to speak. Sivarasan asked Nalini to provide "necessary cover" to Dhanu and Suba so that their Sri Lankan accents would not betray their identities. After arriving at the rally site, Sivarasan escorted Dhanu toward the rostrum where she could be near Gandhi. Dhanu subsequently found herself standing next to a small girl (Kokila) and her mother (Latha Kannan), who were waiting to recite a poem for the former prime minister. As Gandhi advanced toward the group, he saw the girl and walked toward her to hear her poem.

At that time, at 10:19 P.M., Dhanu detonated her bomb, killing herself, Gandhi, and 18 others (including Kokila and her mother). Three of the original core team members (Sivarasan, Suba, and Nalini) were able to escape. Haribabu, the photographer, also perished in the attack, although pictures from his camera depicting the LTTE operatives survived and played a critical role in helping unravel the origins of the plot. Despite vigorous denials of any involvement in the assassination, the LTTE was held directly responsible for the incident, and 41 people (including Prabhakaran) were later charged with complicity in murder. The choice of Dhanu as the primary suicide bomber has raised a number of questions as to why the LTTE would be inclined to select a young, relatively inexperienced, unmarried woman for this role. First, the LTTE may have believed that a female martyr (or "Black Tiger") would be less likely to arouse suspicion from Indian security personnel. Just as important, a female operative could pass herself off as being pregnant, which would both help to explain the bulkiness caused by the explosive vest and limit the intrusiveness of any pursuant personal body search. A third explanation could be that Dhanu specifically volunteered for the mission in order to exact revenge for being sexually assaulted by Indian peacekeepers during the IPKF's tenure in Sri Lanka from 1987 to 1990.

Following the attack, the government established an inquiry known as the Jain Commission (named after Chief Justice Milap Chand Jain, who chaired the commission) to investigate the events leading up to and surrounding the assassination. The commission's report, which reached 17 volumes (5,280 pages), was heavily critical of the quality of security provided to Gandhi, the competence of relevant government authorities, and the failure of Indian intelligence. It also raised troubling questions about the possible involvement of co-conspirators beyond the LTTE. Overall, the assassination of Gandhi was a traumatic event for India and the world. It galvanized a considerable hardening of Delhi's attitude toward the LTTE, with the government consistently rejecting any peace deal that did not specifically provide for Prabhakaran's extradition to stand trial for murder. It also triggered the beginning of the international community's delegitimization of the Tamil struggle, which would become even more marked following the assassination of Sri Lankan president Ranasinghe Premadasa in 1993 and the bombing of the Colombo World Trade Center in 1996.

See also: Liberation Tigers of Tamil Eelam (LTTE)

Further Reading

O'Rourke, Lindsey. "What's Special about Female Suicide Terrorism." *Security Studies* 18, no. 681 (December 2009).

Stack-O'Connor, Alisa. "Lions, Tigers and Freedom Birds: How and Why the Liberation Tigers of Tamil Eelam Employs Women." *Terrorism and Political Violence* 19 (2007).

State through Superintendent of Police. *CBI/SIT Appellant vs. Nalini and Others, Respondents, in the Supreme Court of India, Criminal Appellate Jurisdiction* (Justice K.T. Thomas, May 11, 1999). http://www.cbi.gov.in/judgements/thomas.pdf.

Paul Smith

GEMAYEL (BASHIR) ASSASSINATION

On September 14, 1982, a 77-pound improvised explosive device (IED) killed Lebanese Bashir Gemayel, a senior politician, militia commander, and president-elect, at his Christian Phalangist Party headquarters in East Beirut. In addition to Gemayel, the bomb killed 25 others, including Phalangist Party head John Nazir. Fifty people were injured by the blast.

Habib Shartouni, a member of the Syrian Social Nationalist Party, confessed to planting the IED in his sister's apartment above the room Gemayel was in. After calling and telling her to evacuate the building, he detonated the bomb from a few miles away. When Shartouni came back to check on his sister, he was immediately arrested. He later justified his actions on the grounds that Gemayel "had sold the country to Israel." He was imprisoned for eight years until Syrian troops took over Lebanon at the end of the war and freed him on October 13, 1990.

Prior to the assassination, Israeli defense minister Ariel Sharon had informed Gemayel that the Jewish state was going to invade Lebanon to root out the Palestine Liberation Organization (PLO). Gemayel, who had already angered many Lebanese Muslims and leftists by working with the Israeli political and military establishment, accepted the notification and duly warned the main Palestinian spokesman in the country that his organization should immediately leave or be wiped out. The representative refused, and in the summer of 1982 Israel invaded, successfully driving out the PLO. The casus belli was the attempted assassination of Israeli ambassador Shlomo Argove by Abu Nidal Organization (ANO) members in London on June 4, 1982.

Following the invasion and Gemayel's subsequent election, Israeli prime minister Menachem Begin demanded that the new Lebanese leader sign a peace treaty in return for Israel's earlier support of his Lebanese forces. If Gemayel did not comply, Begin warned that Israel would stay in South Lebanon indefinitely. Infuriated, Gemayel said that he had not fought for seven years to rid Lebanon of the Syrian Army and the PLO so that Israel could take their place. Begin relented and agreed that Israel's troops would cooperate with the Lebanese Army to force out the Syrian Army and then depart from the country. Begin also accepted that Gemayel needed to mend Lebanon's internal conflicts before he could consider signing a peace accord. The 1982 assassination abruptly ended those plans.

Following Gemayel's death, his brother Amin was elected as president. Although Amin was a member of parliament and an experienced political operator, he lacked Gemayel's charisma, did not inherit control of the armed forces, and failed to win the support of the Maronite community. He was largely dependent on the support of the Israelis, who liked him less than his brother, and on the United States and a narrow domestic power base. This did not provide him with the necessary personal authority to either heal Lebanon's fractious internal conditions or consolidate a peace agreement with Israel.

See also: Palestine Liberation Organization (PLO)

Further Reading

Fisk, Robert. *Pity the Nation: The Abduction of Lebanon.* New York: Touchstone, Simon & Schuster, 1990.
Oren, Michael B. *Power, Faith, and Fantasy: America in the Middle East 1776 to the Present.* New York: W. W. Norton, 2007.
Parker, Richard B. *The Politics of Miscalculation in the Middle East.* Bloomington: Indiana University Press, 1993.
Tyler, Patrick. *A World of Trouble: The White House and the Middle East—from the Cold War to the War on Terror.* New York: Farrar Straus Giroux, 2009.

Donna Bassett

GERESHK BOMBING

On September 10, 2007, a suicide bomber blew himself up at a market in the Afghan town of Gereshk, Helmand province. The attack left at least 26 people dead and 24 wounded, some seriously. According to eyewitness reports, a single terrorist was involved in the incident. He apparently detonated an explosive belt while walking up to a truck that was carrying policemen, 13 whom were killed in the ensuing blast. Subsequent forensic evidence supported these accounts.

Although the reason for the attack was unknown, it came on the heels of the assassination of Taliban leader Mullah Dadullah, who had been killed in a joint operation involving U.S., NATO, Afghan, and British special forces on May 12, 2007. Asadullah Khalid, governor of Kandahar province, described Dadullah as "the backbone of the Taliban" and one of the movement's most brutal commanders. It is reasonable to speculate that the bombing was in revenge for Dadullah's death.

On September 8, the United Nations (UN) announced that there had been 103 suicide bombings in the first eight months of 2007. This figure represented a 69 percent increase over the same period of time in 2006 (which saw a total of 123 martyr attacks during the year). The UN had received reports from former Taliban leaders that at least half of the current crop of suicide bombers had entered Afghanistan from North or South Waziristan, where many had been recruited and trained. It was alleged that a large number of these cadres were originally identified and recruited in Pakistani madrassas.

The September 2007 attack was part of a larger trend of terrorist violence that was increasingly targeting civilians and police as opposed to soldiers. Indeed, all of the casualties at Gereshk were noncombatants, while ordinary Afghans accounted for half the fatalities. This shift in focus seemed designed to discourage local populations from supporting foreign military forces and to coerce them to continue cultivating poppies (a principal source of income for the Taliban).

In many ways, however, these tactics were backfiring on the Taliban. According to Haji Maulavi Mokhta, a senior mullah in Lashkar Gah, while Afghans were suspicious of foreigners due to the Soviet occupation in the 1980s, they were certainly not favorably inclined toward Mullah Omar's movement: "The Taliban don't dig any canals, they don't pave roads, they can't rebuild hospitals or mosques. All they do is commandeer people's property without paying. They ask for food, for money, for cars and motorbikes. Why would anyone join them or support them, of their own free will?" That said, the Taliban were clearly benefiting from the civilian toll taken by indiscriminate Allied bombing campaigns, which was generating considerable opposition and anger. The Taliban skillfully manipulated this resentment to recruit bombers who would be willing to offer their lives in the manner that occurred at Gereshk.

See also: New Baghlan Bombing; Taliban

Further Reading

Allen, Charles. *God's Terrorists: The Wahhabi Cult and the Hidden Roots of Modern Jihad.* Cambridge, MA: Da Capo, 2006.
"ISAF Treat Afghan Civilians Injured in Gereshk Suicide Bombing." International Security Assistance Force (ISAF) Press Release, September 10, 2007. Available online at http://www.nato.int/isaf/docu/pressreleases/2007/09-september/pr070910-635.html, accessed July 22, 2011.
Peters, Gretchen. *Seeds of Terror: How Heroin Is Bankrolling the Taliban and al Qaeda.* New York: St. Martin's, 2009.
Rashid, Ahmed. *Descent into Chaos: The United States and the Failure of Nation Building in Pakistan, Afghanistan, and Central Asia.* New York: Viking Books, 2008.
Rohde, David. "Suicide Bombing Kills at Least 26 in Southern Afghan Market." *New York Times,* September 11, 2007.

Donna Bassett

GERMAN HYDROGEN PEROXIDE BOMB PLOT

On September 4, 2007, two white converts to Islam, Fritz Martin Gelowicz and Daniel Schneider, and a Turkish national, Adem Yilmaz, were arrested in Germany for conspiring to cause a series of terrorist bombings against U.S. military bases. Had these attacks succeeded, they would have ranked among the most serious extremist atrocities to have ever taken place on German territory. It is believed that at the time of their apprehension the three militants were within days of executing their operation.

Nine months earlier, on January 1, 2007, Gelowicz was apparently observed carrying out a reconnaissance mission on a U.S. military base in Hannau near Frankfurt. Following this incident, Gelowicz, Schneider, and Yilmaz were all placed under surveillance. Code-named Operation Alberich, this effort involved several hundred German police, who were reportedly assisted by members of the U.S. Central Intelligence Agency (CIA). Details of a major plot soon emerged.

Officials first learned that the trio had procured 1,650 pounds of hydrogen peroxide, a chemical precursor used in the construction of the explosives triacetone triperoxide and hexamethylene triperoxide diamine. They then became aware that the group had managed to obtain Syrian-made military detonators and that during 2006 at least two had received explosives training in camps run by the Islamic Jihad Union (IJU) within the tribal areas of Pakistan. These revelations generated considerable concern, not least because the IJU—a splinter of the Islamic Movement of Uzbekistan (IMU)—was known to have links with the wider Al Qaeda network and had previously been linked to attacks on U.S. and Israeli diplomatic locations in Uzbekistan before expanding into Pakistan.

Continuing to observe the group, the authorities learned that the suspects had extensive funding at their disposal, which they used to travel around the country, hire vehicles, and rent properties. Police also traced the trio to a villa in the Black Forest; it was there that they stored the hydrogen peroxide; if properly prepared, this material had the potential to produce around 1,000 pounds of TNT. By this time German officials were convinced that a significant terrorist attack was in the making and decided to take some preemptive action. Hence, while Gelowicz, Schneider, and Yilmaz were away, bomb-making specialists broke into the villa and replaced the hydrogen peroxide with a more diluted version less suited for the manufacture of explosives.

As Operation Alberich continued, more intelligence about the plot emerged. Phone taps revealed the group was being coordinated by two individuals in Pakistan, who were pushing for attacks against the U.S. Air Force base at Ramstein, various American military social venues in Germany, and Frankfurt International Airport. On September 4, 2007, the three suspects were observed transferring the hydrogen peroxide from the Black Forest villa to a rented house in Oberschledorn, located near U.S. airbases in Westphalia. Given the information that was emerging on an imminent attack, the proximity to potential targets, and the forthcoming sixth anniversary of 9/11, the German authorities decided to intervene.

On September 4, members of Grenzschutzgruppe 9 (GSG 9), the elite German hostage-rescue and counterterrorist unit, stormed the house in Oberschledorn, immediately restraining and apprehending two of the suspects. The third member of the group tried to escape through a bathroom window but was quickly overpowered during a struggle with a pursuing officer (who was slightly wounded in the altercation). Following the arrests, another seven individuals associated with the conspiracy were detained and dozens of addresses searched. It later transpired that the police were seeking nearly 50 additional suspects, some in Germany but others in France, Turkey, and Pakistan.

While Germans were surprised at the amount of potential explosives and the scale of the conspiracy, they were particularly shocked at the core involvement of two white citizens. No less surprising was the participation of Yilmaz. For many years the public had believed that their predominantly Turkish Muslim minority was largely immune to radicalization and not nearly as likely to foster the type of violence extremism seen in other European Islamic communities such as France and the United Kingdom. These assumptions rapidly changed in the wake of the hydrogen peroxide conspiracy, generating real concerns that younger members of the German Turkish diaspora might have been indoctrinated to carry out acts of terrorism through the burgeoning network of independent mosques that had sprung up across the country.

Further Reading

Boyes, Roger. "Muslim Converts Target Germany." *The Times* (London), September 6, 2007.

Kaiser, Simone, Marcel Rosenbach, and Holger Stark. "Operation Alberich: How the CIA Helped Germany Foil Terror Plot." *Der Spiegel* (English version), September 10, 2007.

Landler, Mark. "German Police Arrest 3 in Terrorist Plot." *New York Times,* September 6, 2007.

Landler, Mark, and Nicholas Kulish. "Turkish Connection Shakes Germans." *International Herald Tribune,* September 8–9, 2007.

Paterson, Tony. "Bomb Threat against US Base in Germany." *The Independent* (London), September 12, 2007.

Richard Warnes

GHOZI, FATHUR ROHMAN AL-

Fathur Rohman al-Ghozi was an Indonesian demolitions expert and explosives trainer who served as the main liaison between Jemaah Islamiyah (JI) and the Moro Islamic Liberation Front (MILF). In this capacity he was also the chief instructor at a JI training facility in the southern Philippines, Camp Hudaibiyah, located at MILF's headquarters in the Maguindanao province of Mindanao. He was killed in October 2003.

Al-Ghozi was born in East Java on February 17, 1971. He spent most of his early life in Malaysia, where he worked as a contractor near the Lukmanul Hakiem pesantren (Islamic boarding school). He served time in prison for alleged links to Komando Jihad, a radical Islamist group accused of seeking the overthrow the modern and Western-leaning government in Kuala Lumpur.

After reportedly being recruited into JI by the Indonesian imam Zainal Arifin, he traveled to Afghanistan for training and graduated from Camp Ngruki in 1989. Subsequently, he served as a leader at Camp Torkham in eastern Afghanistan, where he met and trained various members of the MILF. This exposure placed him well to take on the task of setting up and running JI's Camp Hudaibiyah—a move that Abdullah Sungkar felt necessary given the internal chaos in Afghanistan.

According to al-Ghozi's own testimony, he arrived in the Philippines in December 1996. Although members of the MILF have reportedly claimed that al-Ghozi invited the organization to join JI, which they turned down, it is likely that the relationship remained more symbiotic in nature, with the latter providing assistance to the former in exchange for accommodation at Camp Abubakar.

In 2002 al-Ghozi was arrested in the Philippines and pled guilty to the possession of explosives that were to have been shipped to Singapore the year before. These munitions had originally been procured to carry out attacks against several high-profile targets in the country, including a U.S. warship docked at the port of Changi, the subway system, commercial complexes housing some 250 Western business interests, the Australian and British high commissions, and the U.S. and Israeli embassies. During his arrest, al-Ghozi also acknowledged playing a role in the attempted assassination of the Philippine ambassador to Indonesia in August 2000 as well as the Rizal Day bombing of a commuter train in Manila that killed 22 people in December 2000.

Al-Ghozi was sentenced to 17 years in prison. However, he escaped from the maximum-security facility in which he was being held in July 2003, an event many still believe was carried out with the direct assistance of internal authorities. His newfound freedom was to prove short-lived, however, as four months later he was killed in a gun battle with members of the Philippine National Police who had been dispatched to recapture him.

See also: Jemaah Islamiyah (JI)

Further Reading

International Crisis Group. *Jemaah Islamiyah in Southeast Asia: Damaged but Still Dangerous.* Asia Report no. 63, August 26, 2003.

Maitem Jeoffrey. "Al-Ghozi Invited MILF to Join JI but Offer Turned Down." *MindaNews,* October 15, 2003. http://www.intellnet.org/news/2003/10/15/20641-1.html.

"Manila: Key Terror Suspect Killed." *CNN.com,* October 12, 2003. http://edition.cnn.com/2003/WORLD/asiapcf/southeast/10/12/ghozi.killed/index.html.

"Profile: Fathur Rohman al-Ghozi." *BBC News.com,* October 13, 2003. http://news.bbc.co.uk/go/pr/fr/-/2/hi/asia-pacific/3064345.stm, accessed December 2006.

Horacio Trujillo

GIESSEN COMMUTER TRAIN PLOT

On the June 31, 2006, a pair of Lebanese students in Germany, Youssef Mohammed el-Hajdib and Jihad Hamid, placed two suitcases on separate commuter trains leaving Cologne Station, the first going to Dortmund and the second to Koblenz. Packed in each piece of luggage was an improvised explosive device (IED) made out of a propane tank, a container of gasoline and diesel fuel, nails (to enhance lethality), and a simple triggering mechanism based on an alarm clock and electronic devices. Both bombs were set to explode at the same time at around 2:30 P.M.— around 10 minutes before the trains reached their respective destinations. However, while both detonators were triggered, they failed to ignite the main charge due to technical faults in the electronic wiring. The suitcases were subsequently recovered by the authorities, along with a shopping bag, a receipt for the components used in the devices, and some Arabic script.

The two would-be bombers alleged that they based their IEDs on designs they had accessed via the Internet, and it soon became apparent that the devices failed only sbecause of minor technical faults. The German authorities later claimed that had the bombs exploded as planned, they would have generated fireballs that in the confined space of a railway carriage would have killed dozens and possibly hundreds. This was of particular concern for the government given that the country has well over 5,000 stations that cater for four and a half million train passengers a day. Providing comprehensive security for such a dense rail transportation network would have been almost impossible.

El-Hajdib had arrived in Germany in 2004 to study at Kiel Technical University, and it was here that he met Hamid. Apparently while living together in the same house in Cologne, they became increasingly radicalized. The two later claimed their actions were motivated by the publication in German newspapers of cartoons lampooning the Prophet Muhammad, which had originally appeared in the Danish paper *Jyllands-Posten.* It has also been suggested that their actions may have been in response to the killing of Abu Musab al-Zarqawi, the leader of Al Qaeda in Iraq, on June 7, 2006, and German military involvement in Afghanistan.

El-Hajdib was arrested in August after German authorities released video footage from Cologne Station that showed the two (as yet unidentified) terrorists transporting their cases and placing them on the trains. He was detained at Kiel Central Station while apparently trying to leave the country for Denmark. Hamid had meanwhile fled to his native Lebanon, but he gave himself up after hearing of el-Hajdib's arrest in Germany. He was tried in Lebanon and, having been found guilty in December 2007, he was sentenced to 12 years in prison. Roughly a year later a German court convicted el-Hajdib to life imprisonment for attempted murder.

Subsequent investigations in the wake of the failed attack led Lebanese authorities to identify four others believed to have been linked to the plot. Notably, these included Saddam el-Hajdib, the brother of Youssef and a leading member of Fatah al-Islam—a Sunni Islamist group that purportedly draws its inspiration from, and has links to, Al Qaeda. Saddam el-Hajdib allegedly helped plan the attacks, but before he could be tried, he was killed (in 2007) during clashes between Fatah al-Islam and the Lebanese Army. Given these links and the similarity to other mass-casualty attacks by movements affiliated with the wider Al Qaeda network, there continues to be suspicion that the German operation was part of a larger conspiracy. El-Hajdib and Hamid have always denied this, insisting they acted alone.

See also: German Hydrogen Peroxide Bomb Plot; Tanzom Qa'idat al-Jihadi Bilad al-Rafidyan (QJBR)

Further Reading

Boyes, Roger. "Train Bomb Plot Brings Fear of Terrorism to Germany." *The Times* (London), August 21, 2006.

"Germany Train Bomb Trial Begins." *BBC News,* December 18, 2007. http://news.bbc. co.uk/1/hi/world/europe/7149644.stm.

"New Arrests in German Train Plot." *BBC News,* August 25, 2006. http://news.bbc.co.uk/1/hi/world/europe/5285662.stm.

Whitlock, Craig. "Student Gets Life in German Train-Bombing Plot." *Washington Post,* December 10, 2008.

Richard Warnes

GLOBAL WAR ON TERROR

The Global War on Terror is a term used to describe the military, political, diplomatic, and economic measures employed by the United States and other allied governments against organizations, countries, or individuals that are committing terrorist acts, might be inclined to engage in terrorism, or support those who do commit such acts. The Global War on Terror is an amorphous concept and a somewhat indistinct term, yet its use emphasizes the difficulty in classifying the type of nontraditional warfare being waged against U.S. and Western interests by various terrorist groups that do not represent any nation. The term was coined by President George W. Bush in a September 20, 2001, televised address to a joint session of the U.S. Congress, and it has been presented in official White House pronouncements, fact sheets, State of the Union messages, and National Security Council (NSC) position papers such as the *National Security Strategy* (March 2006) and the

National Strategy for Combating Terrorism (February 2003 and September 2006 editions). Since 2001 the Global War on Terror has been directed primarily at Islamic terrorist groups but has also been expanded to include actions against all types of terrorism. During the Bush administration, Secretary of Defense Robert Gates also called it the "Long War."

As with the Cold War, the Global War on Terror is being waged on numerous fronts, against many individuals and nations, and it involves both military and nonmilitary tactics. President Bush's September 20 announcement of the Global War on Terror was in response to the September 11, 2001, terror attacks against the United States, which led to the deaths of some 3,000 civilians, mostly Americans but including civilians from 90 different countries.

Although the war constitutes a global effort, stretching into Asia, Africa, Europe, and the Americas, the Middle East remains a focal point of the effort. The ongoing conflict and the manner in which it has been waged have been the source of much debate. There is no widely agreed-on estimate of the number of casualties during the Global War on Terror because it includes the invasion of Afghanistan in 2001 and the war in Iraq, as well as many acts of terrorism around the world. Some estimates, which include the invasion of Afghanistan in 2001 by a U.S.-led coalition and the invasion of Iraq in March 2003, claim that well over two million people have died in the struggle.

Following the September 11 terror attacks, the United States responded quickly and with overwhelming force against the organizations and governments that supported the terrorists. Evidence gathered by the U.S. government pointed to the Al Qaeda terrorist organization. Al Qaeda at the time was being given aid and shelter by the Taliban regime in Afghanistan. On September 20, President Bush announced to a joint session of Congress that the Global War on Terror would not end simply with the defeat of Al Qaeda or the overthrow of the Taliban but only when every terrorist group and terrorist-affiliated government with a global reach had been defeated. These broad aims implied attacks on countries known to support terrorism, such as Iran and Syria. Bush further assured the American people that every means of intelligence, tool of diplomacy, financial pressure, and weapon of war would be used to defeat terrorism. He told the American people to expect a lengthy campaign. Bush also put down an ultimatum to every other nation, stating that each had to choose whether it was with the United States or against it. There would be no middle ground. Clearly Bush's pronouncements were far-reaching, yet the enemies were difficult to identify and find.

Less than 24 hours after the September 11 attacks, the North Atlantic Treaty Organization (NATO) declared the terrorist attacks of 9/11 to be against all its member nations, the first time the organization had made such a pronouncement since its inception in 1949. On October 7, 2001, U.S. and coalition forces (chiefly British) invaded Afghanistan to capture Osama bin Laden (the head of Al Qaeda), to destroy his organization, and to overthrow the Taliban government that supported him. Eventually, Canada, Australia, France, and Germany, among other nations, joined that effort. However, when a U.S.-led coalition invaded Iraq in March

2003, there was considerable international opposition to this campaign being included under the rubric of the Global War on Terror. One problem for national leaders who supported President Bush's policies was that many of their citizens did not believe that the overthrow of Iraqi dictator Saddam Hussein was really part of the Global War on Terror and questioned the other reasons the Bush administration gave to justify the U.S.-led invasion. International opinion polls have shown that support for the War on Terror has consistently declined since 2003, likely the result of opposition to the Bush administration's preemptive invasion of Iraq in 2003 and later revelations that Iraq possessed neither ties to Al Qaeda nor weapons of mass destruction.

The Global War on Terror has also been a sporadic and clandestine war since its inception in September 2001. U.S. forces were sent to Yemen and the Horn of Africa to disrupt terrorist activities, while Operation Active Endeavor is a naval operation intended to prevent terror attacks and limit the movement of terrorists in the Mediterranean. Terrorist attacks in Pakistan, Indonesia, and the Philippines led to the insertion of coalition forces into these countries as well and to concerns about the situation in other Southeast Asian countries. In the United States, Congress has also passed legislation intended to help increase the effectiveness of law enforcement agencies in their search for signs of terrorist activity. In the process, however, critics claim that Americans' civil liberties have been steadily eroded, and government admissions that the Federal Bureau of Investigation (FBI) and other agencies have engaged in wiretapping of international phone calls without requisite court orders and probable cause have caused a storm of controversy, as have the methods used to question foreign nationals.

The Bush administration also greatly increased the role of the federal government in the attempt to fight terrorism at home and abroad. Among the many new government bureaucracies formed is the Department of Homeland Security, a cabinet-level agency that counts at least 210,000 employees. The increase in the size of the government, combined with huge military expenditures—most of them going to the Iraq War, added to the massive U.S. budget deficits.

Proponents of the Global War on Terror believe that proactive measures must be taken against terrorist organizations to effectively defeat global terrorism. They believe that to meet the diverse security challenges of the 21st century, a larger, global military presence is needed. Without such a force, they argue, terrorist organizations will continue to launch strikes against innocent civilians. Many of the people argue that the United States, Great Britain, Spain, and other countries that have been the victims of large-scale attacks must go on the offensive against such rogue groups and that not doing so will only embolden the attackers and invite more attacks. Allowing such organizations to gain more strength may allow them to achieve their goal of imposing militant Islamist rule.

Critics of the Global War on Terror claim that there is no tangible enemy to defeat, as there is no single group whose defeat will bring about an end to the conflict. Thus, it is virtually impossible to know if progress is being made. They also argue that terrorism, a tactic whose goal is to instill fear into people through violent actions, can never be truly defeated. There are also those who argue against the justification for preemptive strikes, because such action invites counterre-sponses and brings about the deaths of many innocent people. Many believe that the Iraqi military posed no imminent threat to the United States when coalition forces entered Iraq in 2003, but the resultant war has been disastrous for both the Iraqi and American people. Civil rights activists contend that measures meant to crack down on terrorist activities have infringed on the rights of American citizens as well as the rights of foreign detainees. Furthermore, critics argue that the war and the amount of spending apportioned to military endeavors negatively affects the national and world economies. Others argue that the United States should be spending time and resources on resolving the Arab-Israeli problem and trying to eradicate the desperate conditions that feed terrorism. As support for the Global War on Terror effort has diminished, the debate over its effectiveness has grown. Terrorist attacks have continued, and the deliberation over the best way to ensure the safety of civilian populations around the world likewise continues.

The administration of Barack Obama chose not to use the terms *Global War on Terror* or *Long War*, instead using the phrase *Overseas Contingency Operations*. White House press secretary Robert Gibbs explained that the name change was made "in order to denote a reaching out to many moderate parts of the world that we believe can be important in a battle against extremists." However, the term *Global War on Terror* is still widely used in the media and in public discourse.

See also: Al Qaeda; Bali Bombings (2002); Bali Bombings (2005); bin Laden, Osama; London Underground Bombings; Madrid Commuter Train Bombings; Operation Enduring Freedom (OEF); Taliban

Further Reading

Bacevich, Andrew J. *The New American Militarism: How Americans Are Seduced by War.* New York: Oxford University Press, 2005.
Mahajan, Rahul. *The New Crusade: America's War on Terrorism.* New York: Monthly Review, 2002.
Woodward, Bob. *Bush at War.* New York: Simon and Schuster, 2002.

Gregory W. Morgan

GOLDEN TEMPLE MASSACRE

In 1984 Indian Army troops in the city of Amritsar attacked hundreds of Sikh sepa-ratists who had taken up positions in the Golden Temple, one of the most important shrines of Sikhism. The event led to the deaths of 300 people and was directly re-sponsible for the assassination of Indira Gandhi, India's president at the time.

Amritsar holds a long history of resistance and tragedy. It is located in the Pun-jab state, close to Pakistan. The Golden Temple is surrounded by the sacred Amrita Saras, or the Pool of Immortality, which serves as a vessel of spiritual purification. Because of its religious significance, this site is often used for religiously based po-litical protest. The year 1919 saw a violent clash between British troops and impe-rial protesters that is known as the Amritsar massacre. In 1947 the Golden Temple was the site of demonstrations against the division of Punjab between Pakistan and India.

In the early 1980s, Sikh terrorists began enacting a campaign of terror in support of separatist, autonomous intentions concerning the Punjab state. Although not specifically headquartered in the Golden Temple, the Sikh separatists used the site as a protective refuge. On June 4, 1984, the government of India, headed by Indira Gandhi, sent in troops to take the terrorist stronghold by force. Code-named Blue Star, the operation left over 100 people dead, including the Sikh fundamentalist leader Jamail Singh Bhindranwale. Although the Golden Temple was retaken, the event was to prove catastrophic for Gandhi: in revenge for the killings, two of her bodyguards—Satwant Singh and Beant Singh—assassinated the prime minister four months later on October 1.

Within the next week, nearly 3,000 more Indian citizens died. Most of the killing took place in Delhi, where mobs pulled civilians from trains, rousted them from homes, and attacked them in the streets. Eyewitness reports suggest the Delhi police often stood on the sidelines, inactive, and sometimes participated in the violence. A prominent author, V. N. Narayanan, noted in his book *Tryst with Terror* that the first week of November "completed the cycle of tragedy and trauma of 1984. The Indian nation was at its worst in displaying anti-Sikh barbarity and at its best in expressing shock and outrage at the savagery. . . . The Government and the ruling party let loose the barbarians, but ordinary people tried to protect the innocent targets."

Today, many who participated in the violence are in jail, many go unpunished, and many suffer the memories of the past. As Narayanan's quote suggests, India saw its worst face, and its best, that year.

Further Reading

"Assassination in India: A Leader of Will and Force; Indira Gandhi, Born to Politics, Left Her Own Imprint on India." *New York Times*, November 1, 1984. *New York Times On This Day.* http://www.nytimes.com/learning/general/onthisday/bday/1119.html.

Bran, K. S. *Operation Blue Star: The True Story.* Delhi: South Asia Books, 1993.

"Indira Regretted Operation Blue Star Decision, Say Aides." *Times of India,* October 30, 2009. http://timesofindia.indiatimes.com/india/indira-regretted-Operation-Bluestar-decision-say-aides/articleslow/5179509.cms.

"1984: Assassination and Revenge." *BBC News*, November 1, 1984. *On This Day: BBC News.* http://news.bbc.co.uk/onthisday/hi/witness/oct31/news_id3961000/3961851.stm.

Stacy Kowto

GOLDSTEIN, BARUCH

Dr. Baruch Goldstein, an ultranationalist Jew and member of the extremist Kahane Khai organization, was born in Brooklyn in 1957. Academically bright and serious minded, he graduated a year early from high school and attended the Yeshiva University in Manhattan. Here he became a disciple of the radical Rabbi Meir Kahane, founder of the Jewish Defense League (JDL) and the right-wing Israeli party Kach, or "Thus." It was through these links that Goldstein met his wife in Jerusalem, being married by Rabbi Kahane prior to the latter's assassination in New York on November 5, 1990 (Kahane was gunned down by El Sayyid Nosair, an Egyptian extremist linked to the group that later launched the 1993 bombing of the World Trade Center).

In 1983, having graduated from medical college, Goldstein emigrated to Israel and, shortly after arriving, completed his compulsory military service as a conscript doctor within an artillery battalion in Lebanon. Here, various incidents occurred where he rejected the concept of the Hippocratic oath, refusing to treat Arabs and other non-Jews, including Druze soldiers serving in his battalion. He justified his position on religious grounds, citing teachings from Rabbi Kahane. While senior military officers sought to have him court-martialed and expelled from the army, the influence of powerful lobbies in the Jewish religious parties and settlers groups meant he was instead transferred to the Jewish settlement of Kiryat Arba in the Arab town of Hebron. Known to its Palestinian residents as al Khalil, the almost exclusively Arab town of Hebron also had religious significance for Jews, and the settlement of Kiryat Arba allowed religiously committed Jews to live near the ancient town.

Here, Goldstein worked as an Israeli Army doctor while becoming active in the local Kiryat Arba Council as the representative of Kahane Khai, or "Kahane Lives." This right-wing party continues the teachings and goals of Rabbi Kahane, having been established by Binyamin Kahane after his father's death. Goldstein became increasingly bitter through his experience of having to treat wounded Jewish settlers who had been attacked by Palestinian extremists. Along with many other ultra-Orthodox Jews and radical settlers, he bitterly opposed the peace talks between Prime Minister Yitzhak Rabin and Yasser Arafat of the Palestine Liberation Organization (PLO). The final straw for Goldstein appears to have been on the evening of February 24, 1994, when he went to pray at the Tomb of the Patriarchs in Hebron, a site sacred to Judaism, Christianity, and Islam. While Goldstein attended the Jewish side of the shrine, Arab youths on the Muslim side apparently shouted abuse.

The following morning, Goldstein, dressed in his army uniform and carrying an assault rifle and a full supply of magazines, entered the mosque on the Muslim side of the shrine, which was packed with morning worshippers. Taking careful aim, he began selectively shooting at Muslim worshippers, causing pandemonium. The shooting went on for around 10 minutes until Goldstein was rushed by a mob (while changing a magazine on his rifle) and beaten to death.

A frantic scramble ensued to convey the wounded to the hospital, but ultimately Goldstein's actions led to the deaths of some 29 Palestinian worshippers and the serious injury of 125 others. While the vast majority of Israelis were appalled by the slaughter, Goldstein was a hero to elements of the extreme right among the ultra-Orthodox and radical settlers. Although the Israeli authorities subsequently outlawed Kahane Khai and arrested some of its leaders, Goldstein's grave became a shrine and site of pilgrimage for the extreme right in Israel.

See also: Hebron Mosque Massacre; Jewish Defense League (JDL)

Further Reading

Juergensmeyer, Mark. *Terror in the Mind of God: The Global Rise of Religious Violence.* Berkeley: University of California Press, 2001.

Kushner, Harvey. *Encyclopedia of Terrorism.* Thousand Oaks, CA: Sage, 2003.

Shahak, Israel, and Norton Mezvinsky. *Jewish Fundamentalism in Israel.* New ed. London: Pluto, 2004.

Richard Warnes

GOOD FRIDAY AGREEMENT

The Good Friday Agreement (GFA) goes by a number of names including the Agreement, the Belfast Agreement, and the Stormont Agreement. After years of multiparty talks on the status of Northern Ireland, the negotiators agreed to the final terms on April 10, 1998. The population of Northern Ireland and the Republic of Ireland (ROI) then ratified the accord in a simultaneous referendum held on May 22, 1998. The language of the agreement is flush with promises to respect the equality and diversity of all people in Northern Ireland.

Five key provisions are laid out in the agreement. First, it stipulates that the people of Northern Ireland possess the power to determine their status within the United Kingdom. They may join the ROI if the majority of both communities choose to become reunited via a referendum. They may also elect to become an independent country if they so wish. The second key stipulation is that the executive body of Northern Ireland will be comprised of both Unionists and Republicans in a power-sharing arrangement. In the legislature of Northern Ireland, major laws that affect both communities cannot be passed without a majority of each community's representatives voting in favor of it. This measure is aimed at

Votes are counted at Dublin's Royal Horticultural Halls where referendum "YES" votes are registered in favor of the Northern Ireland Good Friday Agreement, May 23, 1998. To cheers of jubilation and sighs of relief, Chief Electoral Officer Pat Bradley said that 71 percent had voted yes in that day's referendum. (AP Photo/John Cogill)

preventing the majority (Protestants/Unionists) from imposing its will on a minority (Catholics/Republicans).

The next major clause of the agreement provides for cross-border councils for the mutual benefit of all communities involved. They include groups composed of representatives from Northern Ireland and the ROI, Britain and Northern Ireland, and Britain and the ROI. These bodies do not take up contentious issues but rather look for ways to work with each other for mutual benefit, like promoting trade, travel, and tourism. The fourth critical provision was that the agreement stipulated that the ROI change its constitution to reflect that it alone does not have sovereignty over the six counties of Northern Ireland. The final important part of the GFA was the requirement that the Provisional Irish Republican Army (PIRA), the main nationalist paramilitary group, begin decommissioning its stockpiles of weapons once the government of Northern Ireland was formed.

The Republican and Unionist communities that came together to negotiate the GFA had been fighting one another since 1968, the beginning of what has been termed "the Troubles." In 1973 an accord known as the Sunningdale Agreement was finalized in an effort to end the conflict, which by then had been raging for five years. This proposal was largely similar to the GFA, with cross-border councils and power-sharing agreements, but it collapsed within a year, and violence broke out once again. The immediate predecessor to the GFA was the Anglo-Irish Agreement of 1985. This second attempt at a negotiated settlement failed because of opposition from the Unionists, who at the time refused to recognize the ROI's role in the Northern Irish affairs.

The GFA was the first time that all parties to the conflict in Northern Ireland, political and paramilitary, were involved in the peace talks. This was an important development as it helped to ensure that whatever agreement eventuated would, as far as possible, reflect the wishes and concerns of relevant stakeholders. Ultimately, only the Democratic Unionist Party refused to support the GFA. However, two crucial entities, the PIRA and Sinn Féin, did accept the accord, with the former also committing to cease its armed terrorist campaign.

As had happened after many previous attempts at peace, some members of the PIRA chose to splinter from the mainstream group and continue the resistance. The remaining dissidents, who number fewer than 100, have formed several groups including the Real IRA (RIRA), Oghlaigh na Eireann, and the Continuity IRA (CIRA). An entity responsible for attacks in April 2011 has simply donned the name the Irish Republican Army. All groups contend they are the rightful heirs of the original IRA, which emerged from the Irish War of Independence.

It took over a year to put the GFA into action. By December 1999, an assembly and an executive had been formed, but, problematically, PIRA failed to begin the process of disarmament. As a result, the government of Northern Ireland was suspended until May 2000, after which the decommissioning process finally began. Another setback occurred in 2002 when the main Unionist party resigned from the government due to concerns over continued Republican violence. Ongoing talks on how best to reform the government failed to reach any consensus for a number of years. In the absence of a formal elected government in Northern

Ireland, the UK Parliament assumed the responsibility of passing legislation—much of which was at the most basic level—to keep Northern Ireland from descending into renewed chaos. All parties finally came together in 2006 with the St. Andrews Agreement, which is largely seen as an addition to the GFA. It restored the assembly and executive of Northern Ireland on the condition that the Police Service of Northern Ireland be devolved from the United Kingdom to the executive of Northern Ireland.

The GFA had a slow and uncertain start, but as time has passed from its initial ratification, the main tenants it put forth have become ingrained in the culture and politics of Northern Ireland. As of 2012, there remains widespread optimism that the peace brokered with the agreement will hold into the foreseeable future. The political rhetoric has shifted from focusing on how the government should be structured and who should hold power to how the assembly and executive of Northern Ireland can best spur economic growth and create more jobs.

See also: Adams, Gerry; Continuity Irish Republican Army (CIRA); Provisional Irish Republican Army (PIRA); Real Irish Republican Army (RIRA)

Further Reading

Bew, Paul. *The Making and Remaking of the Good Friday Agreement.* Dublin: Liffey, 2008.
Cox, Michael, Adrian Guelke, and Fiona Stephen, eds. *A Farewell to Arms? Beyond the Good Friday Agreement.* 2nd ed. Manchester, UK: Manchester University Press, 2006.
Mitchell, George. *Making Peace: The Inside Story of the Making of the Good Friday Agreement.* London: William Heinemann, 1999.

Jonathan Tabb

GRAND MOSQUE SEIZURE

The Grand Mosque seizure of 1979 refers to the takeover of the Masjid al-Harem in the city of Mecca, Saudi Arabia, during the annual hajj of that year. A radical Saudi antiroyalist group led by Juhayman Sayf al-Otaibicarried out the attack, which lasted from November 20 to December 4 and resulted in the death of over 255 pilgrims and Saudi security forces, with another 500 injured. The siege highlighted rejectionist themes that were later echoed by other violent Islamist groups, as well as Riyadh's occasionally dangerous embrace of conservative and fundamentalist strands of the Muslim faith.

Juhayman's group consisted of approximately 400 to 500 members who subscribed to a Salafist interpretation of Islam. Many had studied at the Islamic University of Medina, where they were heavily influenced by Abd al-Aziz bin Baz, Muhammad Nasir al-Din al-Albani, and other conservative scholars. Students were encouraged to engage in proselytization and enforcement of religious laws. One faction mentored by bin Baz was particularly active—the al-Jama'a al-Salafiya al-Muhtasiba (JSM).

Juhayman's followers constituted a radical offshoot of JSM that advocated violent action to reverse trends of modernity that they believed corrupted Islam. They also believed that the Saudi government, which was expanding social services and encouraging the adoption of technology, was corrupt and were highly critical of senor clerics (ulema) for being subservient to the wishes of the royal family. By 1974 Juhayman and his adherents had split from JSM over the issue of using force to topple the kingdom. They subsequently moved to Riyadh, where they engaged in proselytism and distributed antiroyal propaganda, growing to more than 200 members (including Egyptians, Kuwaitis, Pakistanis, and Yemenis). Although senior clerics in Medina (including bin Baz) were concerned about Juhayman's views, they concluded that his critiques were both justified and theologically sound.

Intelligence officials who were monitoring Juhayman and his followers were less sympathetic. A raid in the fall of 1978 disrupted the group's activities, although Juhayman himself remained free thanks to a tip from sympathizers within the security forces. However, many members of his movement were captured and imprisoned under extremely harsh conditions. Following the arrests, bin Baz moved quickly to exert his considerable influence with Medina's civil authorities to gain their release. He was eventually successful in this endeavor, convincing them that the young radicals were well intentioned and harmless.

Emboldened by bin Baz's support and further radicalized by their severe treatment in detention, Juhayman's followers began to pursue a more apocalyptic goal. Convinced by his interpretation of Islamic religious history that the Mahdi's (12th Imam) return was imminent, the group made plans to anoint Juhayman in the Grand Mosque. As the militants stockpiled weapons and practiced their marksmanship, Juhayman searched for the Mahdi and was eventually convinced in a dream that his brother-in-law, Muhammad Abdullah al-Qahtani, was the redeemer.

The seizure itself was timed to coincide with the first day of the new century of the Islamic calendar. Juhayman's group quickly gained control of the Grand Mosque during prayers on November 20 by overpowering the few guards present. After releasing some pilgrims, Juhayman's adherents began to fortify the compound with the help of other worshippers who were convinced that the Mahdi had arrived. The security forces' initial attempts to retake the building were repelled by snipers positioned in the Grand Mosque's minarets. For two weeks, the Saudis tried in vain to dislodge the militants, suffering numerous casualties with every attempt. News of the events in Mecca spread throughout the Islamic world, prompting much speculation and turmoil. In Pakistan, students stormed the American embassy in Islamabad on November 21 and burned it to the ground after hearing rumors that the United States was involved in the siege. Washington's mission in Tripoli was also attacked and set on fire by demonstrators fueled by similar rumors.

On November 24, the ulema gave permission for more forceful means to be used against the mosque. The Saudi military subsequently deployed armored vehicles and antiarmor weapons and initiated a full offensive on the building. However, the well-entrenched militants managed to resist the onslaught and, indeed, inflicted significant casualties on the attackers. The siege continued to drag on for several weeks and showed signs of ending only after the army killed al-Qahtani. Dismayed and demoralized by the death of the supposed redeemer, Juhyaman and his stalwarts took refuge in the catacombs underneath the Grand Mosque (known as the Qaboo). With advice from France's elite Groupe d'Intervention de la Gendarmerie Nationale (GIGN), Saudi commandos eventually forced the surrender of Juhayman and 67 of his followers through the extensive use of explosives and by pumping tear gas into the Qaboo.

Juhayman and the surviving members of his movement were tried and executed in January 1980. In the following months, Saudi officials engaged the ulema to denounce Juhayman's claims as absurd. The government was especially keen to draw public attention away from the group's criticism of the royal family's modernist reform initiatives, as these were integral to maintaining the kingdom's alliance with the United States. This particular relationship had taken on greater salience with the Soviet invasion of Afghanistan, which Riyadh saw as part of a concerted communist effort to destroy Islam. Despite these efforts, Juhayman's views on the dysfunctional Saudi stewardship of Mecca continued to resonate within certain radical sectors and would eventually be taken up by other extremist groups.

Further Reading

Coll, Steve. *The Bin Ladens: An Arabian Family in the American Century.* New York: Penguin, 2008.

Hegghammer, Thomas, and Stephane Lacroix. "Rejectionist Islamism in Saudi Arabia: The Story of Juhayman al-'Utaybi Revisited." *International Journal of Middle Eastern Studies* 39 (2007).

Rasheed, Madawi al-. *A History of Saudi Arabia.* New York: Cambridge University Press, 2002.

Teitelbaum, Joshua. *Holier than Thou: Saudi Arabia's Islamic Opposition.* Washington, DC: Washington Institute for Near East Policy, 2000.

Trofimov, Yaroslav. *The Siege of Mecca: The Forgotten Uprising in Islam's Holiest Shrine and the Birth of Al Qaeda.* New York: Doubleday, 2007.

Jonathan Wong

GROUPE ISLAMIQUE ARMEÉ (GIA)

The Groupe Islamique Armeé (GIA, or Armed Islamic Group) emerged in 1992 after the Algerian military annulled elections that the Islamic Salvation Front (FIS) was set to win. The group quickly initiated a highly violent campaign of terrorism to restore the FIS to power, marking its arrival with the bombing of the Algiers airport terminal in August 1992, which killed nine and wounded dozens. This set the scene for a wave of similar attacks by the GIA and other militant Islamist groups that targeted the Algerian police and security forces. The continuing violence in the country escalated to the level of a civil war, ultimately leading to the deaths of more than 100,000 people in just five years, impacting other countries in the Maghreb, and spilling over into acts of terrorism on French territory.

By the autumn of 1993, it had become clear that the GIA was the most violent and extreme of the various Islamist groups operating in Algeria, sometimes targeting even its own rivals. After murdering two French surveyors near Sidi Bel Abbes in September of that year, the GIA announced it would kill any foreigners who remained in Algeria after the end of November. Although a number of countries responded to the threat by withdrawing their diplomatic staff, many overseas nationals remained in the country. By 1997 over a hundred had been killed, including French citizens living in Algeria, Western tourists, Eastern European workers, foreign oil company staff, and priests and members of Catholic religious orders.

The Algerian regime responded to GIA attacks with a draconian, and at times highly abusive, counterterrorism strategy. In 1992 the government introduced antiterrorist legislation that sanctioned mass roundups of Muslims in "sweep operations," the administrative detention (without trial) of Islamists in prison camps, and the introduction of "special-jurisdiction courts" with the executive power to execute suspected terrorists without appeal. In addition, the regime formed death squads that were implicated in both extrajudicial killings and, allegedly, the massacre of civilians, which were then blamed on Islamist extremists.

The GIA reacted to these measures by stepping up its own level of violence. The group engaged in an increasingly indiscriminate campaign of terrorism that targeted the general public as well as more specific locations. Car bombs emerged as the main weapon of choice, and a number of these attacks resulted in high casualty counts:

- On June 29, 1994, two car bombs were detonated during a republic parade, killing 2 and wounding 64.
- On January 30, 1995, a car bomb exploded in Algiers, killing 40 and wounding over 200.
- In March 1995, a car bomb exploded outside the Algiers Central Police Station, leaving more than 40 people dead.
- On August 31, 1995, a bombing of the General Office of National Security killed 9 and wounded 100.
- In September 1996, a car bomb was used to destroy the Hotel d'Angleterre in Algiers.

Primarily due to France's close ties with the Algerian regime as well as its status as the former colonial power, the GIA also used terrorism against French targets. On August 3, 1994, a car bomb in Algiers killed three gendarmes and two French diplomatic staff. Four months later, the group hijacked an Air France jet at Algiers International Airport with the apparent plan to fly the plane to Paris and detonate it over the city. Before they were able to complete the mission, however, French commandos stormed the jet while it was being refueled in Marseille. During the summer of 1995, the GIA claimed responsibility for a wave of bombings against metro stations and TGV trains in Paris and Lyon, which left 12 dead and wounded hundreds. In March 1996, the group kidnapped seven French monks from their monastery at Tibehrine, southwest of Algiers, and killed them, following this up with the assassination of Pierre Claverie, the archbishop of Oran, on August 1. Overall, around 19 predominantly French clergy were killed by the GIA between 1993 and 1998.

The level of GIA violence in Algeria had by now expanded to include the massacre of whole rural villages seen as loyal to the government or supporting the "Patriots" civilian militia. Extreme brutality was frequently used in these attacks, which included the murder of the elderly, women, and children. The absolute and largely unrestrained nature of these actions generated misgivings among certain elements of the GIA, eventually leading to a split in its ranks and the formation of a rival entity, the Groupe Salafiste pour la Prédication et Combat (GSPC, or Salafist Group for Preaching and Combat). The new group, which was led by Hassan Hattab and later would become closely aligned with Al Qaeda, rejected the mass targeting of innocents, proclaiming that its aggression would be focused only on members of the military and police.

The formation of the GSPC dealt a significant blow to the GIA. A major government offensive in 1997 further weakened the group, and the effects of this were compounded by a 1998 amnesty deal that many of its members accepted. By the turn of the millennium, the GIA had essentially disappeared as a viable organization, with the Islamist struggle in Algeria now effectively championed by the GSPC. The latter group would go on to systematically expand the contours of its own campaign of violence and eventually form a close alliance with Al Qaeda.

See also: Air France Hijacking; Groupe Salafiste pour la Prédication et le Combat (GSPC); Paris Metro Bombings

Further Reading

Barker, Trevor. "Islamic Fundamentalism and Terrorism in Algeria." In Martha Crenshaw and John Pimlott, eds., *International Encyclopedia of Terrorism.* Chicago: Fitzroy Dearborn, 1997.
Kepel, Gilles, ed. *Jihad: The Trail of Political Islam.* New York: I. B. Tauris, 2006.
Lutz, James, and Brenda Lutz. *Global Terrorism.* London: Routledge, 2004.
Stora, Benjamin. *Algeria 1830–2000: A Short History.* Ithaca, NY: Cornell University Press, 2001.
Whittaker, David, ed. *The Terrorism Reader.* London: Routledge, 2001.

Richard Warnes

GROUPE ISLAMIQUE COMBATTANT MAROCAIN (GICM)

The Groupe Islamique Combattant Marocain (GICM) emerged sometime during the late 1990s. According to the U.S. State Department, the group came into being in 1999, with its founding members coming from the same circles as the London-based Al Qaeda ideologue Abu Qatada. Others contend that its origins trace back to Afghanistan when the Taliban were in power and that it had established a number of European bases by 1998, many of which were used for the purposes of gunrunning and document forgery.

The GICM advocates a hard-line Wahhabist ideology and seeks to replace the secular regime in Rabat with a theocracy that adheres to sharia law in all aspects of daily life. However, it also espouses a wider agenda that goes well beyond Morocco and identifies with the broader aims of the international jihadist movement. The current emir of the group is not known, although Mohamed Guerbouzi, Taeb Bentizi, and Abdelaziz Benyaich have all at various times been identified as leaders.

The GICM has been closely linked to Al Qaeda; as with other North African terrorist groups, ties appear to have been the product of personal contacts forged in the crucible of Afghanistan. It is unclear, however, whether the group operates as a loosely affiliated franchise of Al Qaeda or as a more integrated constituent element.

The GICM first gained public notoriety in May 2003 when it carried out a series of car bombings that struck several foreign interests in Casablanca, including a Spanish social club, a Jewish community center, and a hotel and restaurant popular with Israeli tourists. The attacks resulted in more than 40 fatalities, with another 65 injured. The operation, overseen by Mohamed Omari and Abdelhaq Bentassir, was ordered by Abu Musab al-Zarqawi (then head of al-Tawhid, part of the wider Al Qaeda movement), was financed to the tune of $50,000–$70,000 by Osama bin Laden and executed with the assistance of "professional" externally based specialists.

The GICM is now also thought to have played a prominent role in the March 11, 2004, bombings of commuter trains in Madrid, which left 191 people dead; that attack remains one of the most destructive acts of terrorism ever carried out in Europe. Investigations following the attacks revealed that one of the main individuals involved in the planning, Jamal Zougam, had traveled to North Africa on several occasions and in 2003 had met with senior GICM leader Benyaich, apparently to test cellular devices that could set off explosives similar to the ones used in Madrid.

Although the GICM has benefited from financial backing from Al Qaeda for certain attacks, such as the Casablanca bombings, much of its activity is self-financed from organized crime. The group has carried out numerous robberies to sustain its operational and logistic capital, supplementing this with extortion money derived from threats against private citizens and property in Morocco.

Following the Casablanca bombings, the Moroccan government instituted a major crackdown against entities identifying with radical ideologies. This has since resulted in widespread arrests and detentions across the country. These actions served to significantly deplete the GICM's experienced and trained cadres, creating a middle-management personnel void the group has never really recovered from. Although the GICM continues to exist in name, it has suffered from a severely restricted operational space at home and has been systematically eclipsed by other jihadist groups in terms of championing the transnational Islamist cause across the Maghreb.

See also: Al Qaeda; Casablanca Bombings; Madrid Commuter Train Bombings; Zarqawi, Abu Musab al-

Further Reading

"Bomb Carnage Shocks Morocco." *BBC News,* May 17, 2003. http://news.bbc.co.uk/2/hi/africa/3037157.stm, accessed February 27, 2006.

Darif, Mohammed. "The Moroccan Combat Group (ARI)." *Analisis del Real Instituto,* March 30, 2004.

Finn, Peter, and Keith Richburg. "Madrid Probe Turns to Islamic Cell in Morocco." *Washington Post,* March 20, 2004.

"In the Spotlight: Moroccan Combatant Group (GICM)." Center for Defense Information (CDI), Washington, D.C., May 21, 2004. http://www.cdi.org/program/document.cfm?DocumentID=2227, accessed January 6, 2012.

Rabasa, Angel, Peter Chalk, Kim Cragin, Sara A. Daly, Heather S. Gregg, Theodore W. Karasik, Kevin A. O'Brien, and William Rosenau. *Beyond al-Qaeda. Part 1: The Global Jihadist Movement.* Santa Monica, CA: RAND, 2006. Pp. 119–24.

Soudan, Francois. "Paris Magazine Reports on Terrorist Networks Responsible for May 16 Attacks." *Paris Jeune Africque-L'Intelligent,* July 6, 2003.

Edward F. Mickolus

GROUPE SALAFISTE POUR LA PRÉDICATION ET LE COMBAT (GSPC)

The Groupe Salafiste pour la Prédication et le Combat (GSPC, or the Salafist Group for Preaching and Combat) emerged in 1996 as an offshoot of the Groupe Islamique Armeé (GIA, or Armed Islamic Group) with the aim of establishing a theocratic state in Algeria. The organization split from its parent movement in protest over the latter's systematic targeting and slaughter of Algerian civilians, arguing that these actions were hurting the national Islamist cause. Estimates of the GSPC's size vary from a few hundred to several thousand. The current leader is Abu Musab Abdel Wadoud, who assumed the position of national emir after the former commander, Nabil Sahraoui, was killed in a shoot-out with the Algerian Army in June 2004.

Although the GSPC was initially founded as an organization committed to jihadist struggle in Algeria, it has gradually morphed into a full Al Qaeda affiliate. In October 2003, Sahraoui issued a communiqué asserting the group was operating at the behest of and in full accordance with Osama bin Laden and Taliban leader Mullah Omar. In line with this statement, the GSPC is alleged to have sent significant numbers of combatants to fight alongside Al Qaeda in Iraq (AQI) as foot soldiers, suicide bombers, and midlevel commanders. Overall, it is thought that about 9 percent of all foreigners participating in the Iraq conflict hailed from Algeria, most of whom were shuttled to the country by Adil Sakir al-Mukni.

In a 2005 interview Wadoud specifically lauded the actions of Abu Musab al-Zarqawi—then the leader of AQI—following this up with a declaration of solidarity with Islamist extremists in the Palestinian territories, Iraq, Somalia, and Chechnya. These vocal statements were given concrete expression in 2007 when the GSPC officially changed its name to Al Qaeda in the Islamic Maghreb (AQIM).

AQIM employs conventional terrorist tactics including ambushes, bombings, shootings, and suicide strikes. While many of the group's attacks have been relatively ineffectual, some have resulted in significant casualties. In April 2007, the group killed 23 people with twin bombings in Algiers (one of which detonated outside the prime minister's office). The following December, AQIM carried out a double suicide bombing, again in the capital, that left 41 people dead, including 17 employees of the United Nations. The organization has also demonstrated an ability to decisively hit military targets. In June 2009, for instance, 24 members of the army died after two improvised explosive devices detonated as their convoy drove by.

Despite being one of the weakest of Al Qaeda's various affiliates, AQIM retains a significant network of Islamic extremists across Europe, Africa, and Canada. These hubs have been tied to a number of attempted high-profile anti-Western attacks, including a 2002 plot to conduct a chemical bombing against the U.S. embassy in Rome. The group is also largely self-sufficient, deriving most of its income from criminal activities such as credit card theft, passport fraud, and ransoms from kidnappings (in 2003, the group received between $5 and $10 million for the release of 32 European tourists traveling in the Algerian Sahara). Finally, it may yet benefit from the tumultuous events of the so-called Arab Spring. AQIM quickly moved to endorse the popular Libyan uprising against Colonel Muammar el-Qaddafi, and should the new government fail to deliver, it could become a beacon of support for dissatisfied Muslim radicals in the country.

See also: Al Qaeda; Algiers Bombings; Tanzom Qa'idat al-Jihadi Bilad al-Rafidyan (QJBR); United Nations Headquarters (Algiers) Bombing; Zarqawi, Abu Musab al-

Further Reading

Bennhold, Katrin, and Craig Smith. "Tally in Algiers Attacks Uncertain." *New York Times,* December 13, 2007.

Crumley, Bruce. "The Algeria Bombings: Target Europe?" *Time World,* April 11, 2007. http://www.time.com/time/world/article/0,8599,1609181,00.html, accessed January 6, 2012.

Hansen, Andrew, and Lauren Vriens. *Al-Qaeda in the Islamic Maghreb.* Washington, DC: Council on Foreign Relations, July 21, 2009. http://www.cfr.org/north-africa/al-qaeda-islamic-maghreb-aqim/p12717, accessed January 6, 2012.

Philipps, Mark. "Italy: Cops Thwart Terror Attack." *CBS News,* February 20, 2002. http://www.cbsnews.com/stories/2002/02/20/attack/main329974.shtml, accessed April 3, 2006.

Rabasa, Angel, Peter Chalk, Kim Cragin, Sara A. Daly, Heather S. Gregg, Theodore W. Karasik, Kevin A. O'Brien, and William Rosenau. *Beyond al-Qaeda. Part 1: The Global Jihadist Movement.* Santa Monica, CA: RAND, 2006. Pp. 75–76.

Smith, Craig. "At Least 67 Dead in Algiers Bombings." *New York Times,* December 12, 2007.

Walsh, Courtney. "Italian Police Explore Al Qaeda Links in Cyanide Plot." *Christian Science Monitor,* March 7, 2002.

Donna Bassett

GRUPO DE RESISTENCIA ANTIFASCISTA PRIMERO DE OCTUBRE (GRAPO)

Although now posing only a limited threat, the Grupo de Resistencia Antifascista Primero de Octubre (GRAPO, or First of October Antifascist Resistance Group) is a small urban terrorist group that emerged in 1975 as the armed wing of the outlawed Spanish Reconstituted Communist Party. Motivated by its Marxist-Leninist ideology, the organization committed assassinations, bombings, kidnappings, and numerous violent robberies of banks and security vans. Around 700 such incidents were linked to the group between 1975 and 2003; these caused over 80 fatalities.

As well as Spanish military and judicial officials and businessmen, GRAPO has assassinated a number of police officers, notably in 1975, when it killed four officers in its first attack; in 1989, when it killed two officers in Gijon; and in 2000, when a further officer was murdered. In one of its worst attacks, GRAPO was responsible for the 1979 bombing of Cafeteria California-47, which killed 8 and injured more than 50. While the majority of its targets are Spanish, it has also attacked U.S. interests, as it opposes Spain's involvement in NATO and any American presence in the country.

Despite its ideological strength, the organization has been weakened to a point where it is now essentially nonexistent as a viable terrorist threat. GRAPO's remaining membership is aging, and it has proved difficult to recruit new younger members. However, the main factor undermining GRAPO has been the wave of arrests by both the Spanish and French authorities. In November 2000, the entire Central Committee of the PCE (r)-GRAPO was detained in Paris, and its explosives and forgery structures were disbanded. Nearly two years later, 12 members of a reconstituted Central Committee were apprehended, 8 in Paris and 4 in Madrid. The arrests dealt a crippling blow to the leadership command structure of GRAPO that it is unlikely to recover from.

Further Reading

Alexander, Yonah, and Dennis Pluchinsky. *Europe's Red Terrorists: The Fighting Communist Organisations.* London: Frank Cass, 1992.

Schmid, Alex, and Ronald Crelinsten. *Western Responses to Terrorism.* London: Frank Cass, 1993.

Schmid, Alex, and Albert Jongman. *Political Terrorism.* New Brunswick: Transaction, 2006.

Richard Warnes

GUZMÁN, ABIMAEL

Abimael Guzmán was the leader of Peru's Maoist Sendero Luminoso (SL, or Shining Path) terrorist group. He developed a powerful cult of personality that attracted significant support from the nation's indigenous Andean population as well as from Spanish-speaking city dwellers. Guzmán was captured and imprisoned in 1992. After two retrials, he was eventually sentenced to life imprisonment for "aggravated terrorism."

Abimael Guzmán Reynoso was born in 1934 in the southeastern city of Arequipa. A member of a middle-class family, he received a law degree and a PhD in philosophy from Arequipa's St. Augustin National University. Upon completing his studies, Guzmán took a job teaching philosophy at Ayacucho's progressive University of Huamanga, a position he held until 1975.

Guzmán developed a strong interest in radical politics, joining the Communist Party of Peru toward the end of the 1950s but leaving it in 1964 to become a member of the Maoist Bandera Roja. He spent time in China during the Cultural Revolution, attending a military academy where he became a strong advocate of Mao Tse-tung's theory of the "people's war." Soon after returning to Peru he was expelled from the Bandera Roja for doctrinal heresy, whereupon he founded the SL. Guzmán was arrested in 1979 and after a brief period of detention went underground. The following year, SL launched its devastating terrorist campaign against the Peruvian government, which was to last for over a decade.

Guzmán's ideological thinking embraced not only the concept of a "people's war" against the government and the right wing but also the need to eliminate any entity on the left that sought to use nonviolent methods to improve the plight of the poor. This expansive definition of the enemy led SL to kill a great many Peruvian peasants and civilians as well as international aid workers who had come to the country to try to help those afflicted by war and the increasingly perilous national economic condition. In the province of Puno alone, the government estimated that by 1991 the group's actions had put an end to more than $100 million worth of foreign developmental aid.

Following his election in 1990, President Alberto Fujimori suspended the constitution and unleashed a highly brutal counterterrorist campaign against SL. Although criticized for their detrimental impact on human rights and democratic freedoms, the government's actions served to greatly weaken the group and eventually resulted in the arrest of Guzmán and three of his top aides on September 12, 1992. In the military trial that followed, SL was found guilty of being complicit in the deaths of more than 25,000 civilians and the destruction of some $22 billion in property, and the four arrested members were sentenced to life imprisonment. Guzmán's capture and conviction triggered a violent response from his hard-core supporters, who by this time were said to number around 15,000.

In 2003 the Supreme Court declared that Guzmán's military trial had been unconstitutional and ordered a new, civilian hearing. The first retrial that year resulted in chaos and delays, while a second one in 2004 collapsed after two judges resigned. A third trial eventually upheld Guzmán's life sentence on October 13, 2006—marking the end of the rebel leader's career and the effective demise of his organization. At the same hearing, SL's second in command, Elena Iparraguirre, was also jailed for life, and another 10 defendants received sentences of 24 to 35 years. Guzmán is currently serving his term in virtual isolation on San Lorenzo Island, a naval base off the Lima coast.

See also: Sendero Luminoso (SL)

Further Reading

"Profile: Peru's Shining Path." *BBC News,* November 5, 2004. http://news.bbc.co.uk/2/hi/america/3985659.stm.

Ross, Oakland. "A New Outrage for Shining Path Leader." *Toronto Star* (Canada), September 20, 2009. http://www.thestar.com/news/world/artice/698285.

Shakespeare, Nicholas. *The Dancer Upstairs.* Vancouver, WA: Vintage Books, 2007.

"Shining Path Militant Leaders Given Life Sentences in Peru." *CBC News,* October 13, 2006. http://www.cbc.ca/world/story/2006/10/13/shining-path-peru.html.

Peter Chalk

H

HABASH, GEORGE

George Habash (1926–2008) was a Palestinian who founded the Arab Nationalist Movement (ANM) and later, in 1967, the Popular Front for the Liberation of Palestine (PFLP). Habash spent his formative years in Lebanon, enrolling at Beirut's American University in 1944. He was deeply influenced by the mass expulsion of Palestinians in 1948 following the United Nations' partition solution that set the stage for the creation of Israel.

During his second year in medical school, Habash began attending seminars (comprised of politically active students) organized by Professor Constantine Zurayk, who espoused Arab nationalism and resistance. In June 1948, Habash returned to Lydda (now Lod, Israel), where he obtained a position at the city's hospital, serving as an assistant to Dr. Mustafa Zahlan. During this time, he witnessed firsthand the carnage associated with Jewish efforts to expel Palestinians from the area. However, it was two specific events that were to have a profound effect on Habash's outlook. The first was the death of his older sister as a direct result of Jewish/Palestinian violence. The second was witnessing the killing of a neighbor's son as he was passing an Israeli checkpoint on the outskirts of the city. The young boy had refused to be searched by a Jewish soldier and was subsequently shot.

Later, Habash and his family moved to Ramallah, then Amman, and finally back to Lebanon where he continued his medical studies. While in Lebanon, he became progressively more politically active, joining a student political movement comprised of radicals from across the country. Among his fellow peers were Hanadi al-Hindi and Wadi Haddad, who would subsequently become operational commander of the PFLP, as well as Habash's right-hand man. Along with Haddad, Ahmad al-Khatib, and Hanadi al-Hindi, Habash formed the Kata'ib al-Fida al-Arabi (Arab Commando Battalions), which would later evolve into the ANM. The organization's ideology was based on the ideas of Zurayk and Sati al-Husari, known as the father of Arab nationalism.

Following the 1967 Six-Day War, Habash turned to Marxism, primarily as a result of his imprisonment in Syria. During a period of roughly 10 months of solitary confinement, he was able to read the collected works of Marx, Engels, Lenin, Ho Chi Minh, and Mao Tse-tung. After this period of self-education, Habash wrote the declaration of the PFLP's second national convention. Central to his agenda was the argument that Israel's devastating military defeat of Arab forces in the 1967 war necessarily required that Palestinians adopt guerrilla tactics, similar to the military tactics being used by North Vietnamese forces. The leftist orientation of the PFLP would later facilitate fruitful relations with the Soviet Union, which provided the group with logistic and moral support. Further cementing ties with Moscow was the Komitet Gosudarstvennoy Bezopasnoti's (KGB, or Committee for State Security) assessment that Habash and the PFLP were far more reliable than Yasser Arafat and his al-Fatah organization. Often informed of planned PFLP attacks in advance, the KGB is widely known to have provided advice and intelligence to assist the perpetration of these acts and influence the manner in which they were carried out.

Habash was instrumental in internationalizing the PFLP's agenda and contacts. He forged relationships with like-minded leftist-oriented groups in Western Europe, such as the German Rote Armee Fraktion (RAF, or Red Army Faction), and also consolidated ties with the Japanese Red Army, inviting its members to attend PFLP training camps throughout the Middle East. In addition, he expanded his ideological goals beyond a sole focus on Israel. Fusing his Marxist revolutionary and nationalist outlooks, he proclaimed a goal of destroying "the troika of Zionism, imperialism and Arab reaction." He became as much concerned about corrupt and bourgeois Arab governments, existing under the "remnants of Western imperialism," as Israeli oppression of Palestinians.

Under the influence of Haddad, his chief of operations, Habash oversaw the PFLP's tactical decision to initiate a systematic campaign of airline hijackings to bring publicity to their cause. He would later tell a German newspaper that "when we hijack a plane it has more effect than if we kill a hundred Israelis in battle." On December 26, 1968, the PFLP attacked an El Al plane in Athens, which resulted in one death and two injuries. On February 18, 1969, three PFLP terrorists fired on an El Al jet that was positioned to take off from Zurich en route to Tel Aviv. The pilot and three crew members were killed. On September 6, 1970, the PFLP conducted its most visible and famous hijacking operation when it hijacked multiple airliners, flying three of them to Dawson's Field in Jordan. The incident received widespread international media attention and greatly embarrassed King Hussein and the Amman government. In reaction, Jordan immediately expelled the exiled Palestine Liberation Organization (PLO) from the country—a move that subsequently led to the creation of the Black September Organization (BSO), the movement behind the 1972 massacre of Israeli athletes at the Munich Olympic Games.

Habash fled to Lebanon following the Jordanian military action in 1970. Two years later he decided to cease hijacking operations, although he remained wholly unrepentant about their effect. Any belief that this signaled a softening of his stance was nullified in 1974, however, when he withdrew the PFLP from the PLO's Executive Committee in opposition to Arafat's moratorium on acts of terrorism outside Israel and the Occupied Territories and willingness to explore a Middle East settlement plan.

Following the Israeli invasion of Beirut in 1982, Habash took refuge in Syria, where he continued to denounce what he deemed to be corrupt Arab governments. However, his immediate visibility dropped as a result of increasingly serious health problems. In September 1980, Habash underwent brain surgery to remove a benign tumor, which although successful caused him to suffer partial paralysis. In 1992 Habash suffered a stroke and was briefly allowed to receive medical treatment at a Paris hospital. The decision generated a great deal of controversy throughout the country, not least because the PFLP had been linked to several hijacking incidents involving French targets. Habash eventually died of a heart attack in Amman, Jordan, on January 26, 2008. He was 82 years old.

See also: Black September Organization (BSO); Dawson's Field Hijackings; El Al Hijacking; Palestine Liberation Organization (PLO)

Further Reading

"George Habash." *Daily Telegraph* (UK), January 27, 2008. http://www.telegraph.co.uk/news/obituaries/1576681/George-Habash.html.

Ginat, Rami, and Uri Bar-Noi. "Tacit Support for Terrorism: The Rapprochement between the USSR and Palestinian Guerrilla Organizations following the 1967 War." *Journal of Strategic Studies* 30, no. 2 (April 2007): 255–284.

Habash, George. "George Habash: The Future of the Palestinian National Movement." *Journal of Palestine Studies* 14, no. 4 (Summer 1985).

Habash, George, and Mahmoud Soueid. "Taking Stock" An Interview with George Habash." *Journal of Palestine Studies* 28, no. 1 (Autumn 1998).

"PFLP Founder George Habash Dies." *Aljazeera.net,* January 27, 2008. http://english.aljazeera.net/news/middleeast/2008/01/200852512350233223.html.

Paul Smith

HAIFA RAID

On March 11, 1978, 11 members of the al-Fatah faction of the Palestine Liberation Organization (PLO) killed 46 Israeli civilians, including 13 children, and wounded 85 others during a raid on Haifa in northern Israel. The operation, code-named Martyr Kamal Adwan, was planned by Abu Jihad (Khalil al-Wazir) and primarily designed to disrupt the nascent Middle East peace process.

Thirteen terrorists carried out the raid. They left Lebanon by ship armed with automatic weapons and high explosives and sailed a pair of rubber boats south toward Israel. Two of the gunmen drowned en route, but the remaining 11 men landed just north of Tel Aviv. After coming ashore, they found an American woman walking on the beach and asked her where they were. The female, Gail Rubin, was a 39-year-old photographer and relative of U.S. Senator Abraham Ribicoff; she gave them directions, whereupon the terrorists shot and killed her.

The attack team walked less than a mile up to a four-lane highway, where they began shooting at passing cars and hijacked a white Mercedes taxi, which they initially used to drive toward Tel Aviv. The group subsequently decided the car was too small for their purposes, so they stopped and abducted a coach carrying families on an outing.

As they drove, the terrorist shot at and threw grenades at passing automobiles, tossing at least one body out of their vehicle. They then transferred the hostages to a second bus, which was finally stopped at Herzliya. A shoot-out with the police ensued, during which several of the passengers died. Although it was initially claimed that the hostages had been deliberately killed by the terrorists, a postincident investigation revealed that many had, in fact, been caught in the wild cross fire of the police. The finding triggered widespread criticism of the authorities, who were also questioned as to why security was so lax that such an attack could have occurred at all.

On March 15, three days after the massacre, Israel launched Operation Litani against PLO bases in southern Lebanon. A government spokesman rejected claims that this had been undertaken in retaliation for the Haifa raid. Rather, he asserted it was aimed at external bases of al-Fatah and the PLO, who were using Lebanese territory as a pad for launching attacks against Israel and its citizens.

It later transpired that the terrorists' original intention was to scuttle peace talks between Menachem Begin and Egypt's Anwar Sadat by hijacking a bus traveling toward Tel Aviv, capturing a luxury hotel, and taking tourists and foreign ambassadors hostage, who would then be used as leverage to demand the release of Palestinian prisoners. The plan was dropped in favor of the raid because it was deemed too complex and costly.

See also: al-Fatah; Palestine Liberation Organization (PLO)

Further Reading

Becker, Jillian. *The PLO: The Rise and Fall of the Palestine Liberation Organization.* New York: St. Martin's, 1984.

Fisk, Robert. *Pity the Nation: The Abduction of Lebanon.* New York: Touchstone, Simon & Schuster, 1990.

Livingstone, Neil C., and David Halevy. *Inside The PLO: Covert Units, Secret Funds, and the War against Israel and the United States.* New York: William Morrow, 1990.

"Middle East: A Sabbath of Terror." *Time,* March 20, 1978. http://www.time.com/time/magazine/article/0,9171,919454,00.html, accessed August 8, 2011.

Donna Bassett

HAMAS (ISLAMIC RESISTANCE MOVEMENT)

Hamas, also known as Harakat al-Muqawima al-Islamiyya (Islamic Resistance Movement), was founded on December 16, 1987. The group formally emerged after the beginning of the First Intifada and through its military wing, the Izz ad-Din al-Qassam Brigades, quickly became one of the most active resistance movements fighting the Israeli government. It presently governs Gaza and is the chief rival to al-Fatah in the West Bank.

Sheikh Ahmad Yasin was considered the spiritual leader of Hamas. A nearly blind paraplegic, he was a member of the Palestinian Muslim Brotherhood (MB) and founded the al-Mujamma' al-Islami Islamic (AMAI) Center in 1973. Yasin registered AMAI in Israel five years later and in 1979 gained a license to run it as an accredited Islamic association. AMAI is generally considered to be the organizational forerunner of Hamas and the principal source of the movement's eventual founders: Isa al-Nashshar, Dr. Ibrahim al-Yazuri, Abdulfattah Doukhan, Dr. Abdel-Aziz al-Rantissi, Mohamad Hassan Shama'a, and Salah Shehade. In May 1989, the Israeli government arrested Yasin, after which leadership passed to Abdel-Aziz al-Rantissi and Ismail Abu Shanab. Although sentenced to life imprisonment, Yasin was released in 1997 in exchange for two Mossad agents who had been arrested in

Jordan. He resumed control of Hamas and immediately called for increased attacks on Jewish targets using all means possible, including suicide strikes. Yasin was eventually assassinated by an Israeli helicopter gunship on March 22, 2004. An estimated 200,000 Palestinians attended his funeral.

Hamas has several subsets. The most important of these is its armed division, the Izz ad-Din al-Qassam Brigades (also called the Issadin Kassem Brigades, al-Qassam Brigades, Izz al-Din al-Kassam squad, Ezzedin al-Kassam). The wing, which owes its name to Sheikh Izz ad-Din al-Qassam (also spelled Kassam)—a Syrian-born Islamic militant who was killed while fighting Jewish and British forces in 1935—was created by Yahya Ayyash (who was killed in 1996) with the primary ob-

Palestinian Hamas activists burn a poster of Palestinian president Mahmoud Abbas, and other Fatah officials, January 27, 2011. (AP Photo/Hatem Moussa)

jective of building a coherent military wing to support and further the goals of Hamas. It has conducted operations in Gaza and the West Bank as well as Israel proper and is listed as a terrorist organization by the United States, the European Union, Australia, and the United Kingdom. The Izz ad-Din al-Qassam Brigades' current leader is thought to be Mohammed Deif, who remains at large and is thought to have survived at least five assassination attempts.

Hamas's ideology, in common with many radical movements in the Arab world, is firmly grounded in the teachings of Egypt's MB—particularly the emphasis on promoting traditional Islamic values and reducing Western influence. There are, however, key differences in the ideological outlooks of Hamas and the MB, notably the use of violence in addition to passive resistance and the strong emphasis on Palestinian nationalism. The latter aspect is generally taken as one of the main reasons why the organization never formally allied itself with the Al Qaeda network.

Hamas demands the establishment of an Islamic Palestinian state on all land presently occupied by Israel; this necessarily means the group denies the right of the latter to exist. Although Hamas's commitment to ensuring a future homeland for the Palestinian people has earned it a strong following, it is perhaps the provision of food as well as other critical social services such as schools, orphanages, hospitals, transportation, and law and order that has been the main factor accounting for the movement's success. This has been especially true in Gaza, which suffers from dire poverty and chronic unemployment (measured at 45 percent in 2010). Hamas has adroitly exploited this popular support to both consolidate its position as an alternative to the Palestinian Authority (PA) and as a base from which to launch terrorist attacks against Israel.

A key component of Hamas's campaign of violence has been the employment of suicide bombings. Attacks have been directed at a range of targets, including buses, shopping malls, cafés, and pedestrian markets. The most intensive use of suicide tactics occurred during the first two years of the al-Aqsa Intifada (2000–2002) when the group's leaders internally concluded that this particular weapon had the potential to achieve results that were simply not possible with other modalities. In making the strategic decision to engage in so-called martyrdom, Hamas was clearly influenced by the example of Hezbollah's success in evicting Israel from Lebanon. As the movement's Khaled Meshal told the British Broadcasting Corporation (BBC) in 2000: "Like the Intifada in 1987, the current intifada has taught us that we should move forward normally from popular confrontation to the rifle to suicide operations. This is the normal development. . . . We always have the Lebanese experiment before our eyes. It was a great model of which we are proud."

In pursuing martyrdom as a principal form of struggle, Hamas has sought and been remarkably successful in bestowing positive social connotations on suicide operations. The group has achieved this by fostering an inverted sense of normality among the Palestinian communities from which it enlists bombers, who view suicide attacks as not only necessary but as the ultimate expression of heroism and selflessness. To give an added incentive, Hamas indoctrination routinely stresses that martyrs will feel no pain in the prosecution of their acts, which will, in turn, earn them the eternal gratitude of Allah and guarantee 70 members of their family an automatic right to enter heaven.

Hamas has also been highly pragmatic in its use of suicide terrorism, only resorting to such tactics when the benefits were perceived to outweigh the costs. In adopting this policy of "controlled violence," the movement has shown that the employment of "human bombs," far from being irrational or mindless (the common picture painted in the media), was in fact a reasoned and calculated instrument of war. In addition, the group has gone to great lengths to explain the tactical advantages of suicide terrorism—not least its ability to decisively level the battlefield against a far stronger enemy—in order to circumvent potential opposition from the Palestinian community, which has at times been highly critical of these types of attacks (especially when they have generated draconian Israeli responses such as blockading the West Bank and Gaza).

Key to Hamas's early development of suicide terrorism was 'Ayyash, also known as "the Engineer." He acted as the group's chief bomb maker as well as the commander of the Izz ad-Din al-Qassam Brigades. During his career, he was credited with killing at least 130 Israelis and wounding another 500. Ayyash was eventually assassinated on January 5, 1996, when a booby-trapped cell phone exploded as he was making a call. Approximately 100,000 people attended his funeral, and he continues to be a venerated hero among many Palestinians, who have named streets and other locales after him.

In common with other terrorist movements such as the Provisional Irish Republican Army (PIRA), Hezbollah, and Euskadi Ta Askatasuna (ETA, or Basque Homeland and Liberty), Hamas has also been prepared to accompany violence with participation in the political process, the so-called bullet-and-ballot-box approach. Again the group has been successful in this endeavor, and in January 2006 its Change and Reform Party won an outright majority (74 seats out of 132) in the Palestinian Legislative Council. The victory reflected a highly sophisticated and disciplined election campaign that effectively exploited mass dissatisfaction with the PA on account of its nepotism, corruption, and willingness to make too many concessions in negotiations with Israel.

Hamas's win triggered a brief conflict with al-Fatah, which had expected to be returned as the governing party. The violence was curtailed only by the intervention of Saudi Arabia, which played host to critical negotiations between the two factions of the PA in February 2007. The following month Hamas and al-Fatah announced the formation of a new Palestinian National Unity Government. It was agreed that Ismail Haniya would represent the former as the prime minister and Mahmoud Abbas the latter (as well as other non–Hamas-related elements of the PA) as the president.

Renewed tension erupted when Hamas claimed that al-Fatah was planning to stage a coup in Gaza. Although Abbas strongly denied the charge, a major battle broke out between the two groups between June 7 and June 15, 2007, leaving at least 118 dead and wounding more than 550. The conflict resulted in the dissolution of the National Unity Government, a Hamas military takeover of Gaza, and the effective partition of the PA, with al-Fatah retaining control of the West Bank. Despite various rounds of reconciliation talks, this division remained in place at the time of writing, suggesting a widening, perhaps irreconcilable, rift within the wider Palestinian movement. Problematically, for Hamas to be recognized as a legitimate partner of al-Fatah in a newly reconfigured unity government, it would have to renounce violence and recognize Israel's right to exist—neither of which is likely to be forthcoming in the near to medium term.

Hamas has been linked to a wide variety of militant groups over the years. They include the 15 May Group (May 15 Group), Epanastatiki Organosi 17 Noemvri (EO 17N), Abu Nidal Organization (ANO), Abu Sayyaf Group (ASG), Al Qaeda (joint operations with Heroes of the Islamic Jihad), al-Gama'a al-Islamiyya, al-Jihad al-Islami, al-Muqawamah al-Mu'minah (the Faithful Resistance, Faithful Amal), al-Nahdah, Tala'I al-Fatah (Vanguards of Conquest), Armed Front of the Islamic Jihadists in Algeria, Armenian Secret Army for the Liberation of Armenia (ASALA), Association of Guidance and Reform, Egyptian Islamic Jihad (EIJ; al-Jihad), Front Islamique du Salut (FIS, or Islamic Salvation Front), Groupe Islamique Armeé (GIA; Armed Islamic Group of Algeria), Hezbollah (also written Hizballah; Party of God), Islamic Army for the Liberation of Palestine, Moro Islamic Liberation Front (MILF), Muslim Brotherhood, Palestine Liberation Organization (PLO), Palestinian Islamic Jihad (PIJ), Popular Front for the Liberation of Palestine (PFLP), Sabab (International Muslim Brotherhood), Taliban, Tanzim, and Unified National Leadership of the Uprising.

Hamas was also involved with what came to be called the Rejectionists, or the Rejectionist Front. The majority of these groups were Palestinian militant organizations that refused to make peace or otherwise negotiate with Israel and were often highly hostile to the PLO and elements of al-Fatah. One such group was Damascus 10, which included the Democratic Front for the Liberation of Palestine (DFLP), the PIJ, al-Saiqa Forces (Organization of the People's Liberation War Vanguards), the Palestine Liberation Front, the Syrian branch of the PLO, Palestinian National Forces Coalition, Palestinian National Liberation Movement, Palestinian National Salvation Front, Palestinian Peoples' Party Revolutionary (Revolutionary PPP), and PFLP.

See also: Al Qaeda; Ashdod Port Attack; Ayyash, Yahya; Beersheba Bus Bombings; Ben Yehuda Shopping Mall Bombing; Dizengoff Shopping Center Bombing; Jerusalem Bus Attacks (1996); Jerusalem Bus Attacks (2003); Netanya Restaurant Bombing; Palestine Liberation Organization (PLO)

Further Reading

Abu-Amr, Ziad. *Islamic Fundamentalism in the West Bank and Gaza: Muslim Brotherhood and Islamic Jihad.* Bloomington: Indiana University Press, 1994.

Chalk, Peter, and Bruce Hoffman. *The Dynamics of Suicide Terrorism: Four Case Studies of Terrorist Movements.* Santa Monica, CA: RAND, 2005.

Levitt, Matthew. *Hamas: Politics, Charity, and Terrorism in the Service of Jihad.* New Haven, CT: Yale University Press, 2006.

Milton-Edwards, Beverley, and Stephen Farrell. *Hamas: The Islamic Resistance Movement.* Malden, MA: Polity, 2010.

Mishal, Shaul, and Avraham Sela. *The Palestinian HAMAS: Vision, Violence, and Coexistence.* New York: Columbia University Press, 2000.

Donna Bassett

HAMBURG CELL

A group of radical Islamists in Hamburg, Germany, formed a terrorist cell affiliated with Al Qaeda. This cell began when Mohamed Atta, Ramzi bin al-Shibh, and Marwan al-Shehhi began rooming together on November 1, 1998, in an apartment at 54 Marienstrasse in Hamburg. They were members of a study group at the al-Quds Mosque run by Mohammad Belfas, a middle-aged postal employee in Hamburg who was originally from Indonesia. Both in the study group and at the apartment they began talking about ways to advance the Islamist cause. Soon the original three attracted others of a like mind. The nine members of this cell were Mohamed Atta, Said Bahaji, Mohammad Belfas, Ramzi bin al-Shibh, Zakariya Essabor, Marwan al-Shehhi, Ziad Jarrah, Mounir el-Motassadeq, and Abdelghani Mzoudi. At first, Belfas was the leader of the group, but he was soon replaced by Atta and left the cell. Atta then became the formal leader of the Hamburg Cell, but bin al-Shibh was its most influential member because he was better liked in the Muslim community than the dour Atta.

At first the members of the Hamburg Cell wanted to join the rebels fighting against the Russians in Chechnya. Before this move could take place, the leaders of the cell met with Muhammad Heydar Zammar, a key Al Qaeda operative in Duisburg, Germany, who advised that they undertake military and terrorist training in Afghanistan first. Atta, bin al-Shibh, Jarrah, and al-Shehhi traveled to Kandahar, Afghanistan, where they underwent extensive training in terrorist methods. They also met with Osama bin Laden, at which time Atta, Jarrah, and al-Shehhi were recruited for a special martyrdom mission to the United States.

Bin al-Shibh was to have been a part of this mission, but he was never able to obtain a visa to travel to the United States. Instead, bin al-Shibh stayed in Hamburg, serving as the contact person between the Hamburg Cell and Al Qaeda. He also served as the banker for the September 11 plot.

The most dedicated members of the Hamburg Cell participated in the September 11, 2001, plot. Other members of the group, however, provided moral and technical support. Mamoun Darkanza was the money man for the Hamburg Cell. What made those in the Hamburg Cell so important was that they were fluent in English, well educated, and accustomed to the Western lifestyle, so they could fit in any of the Western countries. They also had the capability to learn how to pilot a large aircraft with some training.

Bin al-Shibh shut down the Hamburg Cell as soon as he learned the date of the attacks. He made certain that anyone connected with the Hamburg Cell was forewarned so that they could protect themselves. Bin al-Shibh destroyed as much material as possible before leaving for Pakistan. Only later did German and American authorities learn of the full extent of the operations of the Hamburg Cell.

German authorities had been aware of the existence of the Hamburg Cell, but German law prevented action against the cell's members unless a German law was violated. This restriction did not prevent a veteran Central Intelligence Agency (CIA) officer attached to the American consulate in Hamburg, Thomas Volz, from attempting to persuade the German authorities to take action against the Islamist extremists in the Hamburg Cell. Volz had become suspicious of several members of the Hamburg Cell and their connections with other Muslim terrorists. He hounded the German authorities to do something until his actions alienated them to the point that they almost had him deported from Germany.

After the September 11 attacks, German authorities began a serious investigation of the Hamburg Cell and its surviving members. By this time there was little to examine or do except to arrest whoever had been affiliated with it. German authorities learned the extent to which Al Qaeda had been able to establish contacts in Germany and elsewhere in Europe.

See also: al-Quds Mosque; Atta, Mohamed; bin al-Shibh, Ramzi; September 11 (2001)

Further Reading

Bernstein, Richard. *Out of the Blue: The Story of September 11, 2001, from Jihad to Ground Zero.* New York: Times Books, 2002.

McDermott, Terry. *Perfect Soldiers: The 9/11 Hijackers: Who They Were, Why They Did It.* New York: HarperCollins, 2005.

Posner, Gerald. *Why America Slept: The Failure to Prevent 9/11.* New York: Ballantine Books, 2003.

Sageman, Marc. *Understanding Terror Networks.* Philadelphia: University of Pennsylvania Press, 2004.

Stephen E. Atkins

HANGU BOMBING

On February 9, 2006, a suicide bomber killed 30 people during a procession through the bazaar in the town of Hangu (Hanga) in Pakistan's Northwest Frontier Province (NWFP). The attack occurred on Ashura—the holiest day of the year on the Shia calendar—and sparked at least two days of sectarian violence with Sunnis that claimed 43 lives, injured 143 people, and destroyed 60–70 percent of the Muslim shops in the bazaar (although some believe this unrest had more to do with trying to gain control over trafficking routes for Afghan opium). Two weeks before the attack, national security officials had issued a threat assessment regarding pending terrorist strikes in the Hangu area. Given this specific warning, many expressed surprise that local officials had not been better prepared.

There were reports of a second explosion, but police later said this was probably caused by stored bottles of gas in a nearby shop. That explanation is supported by the fact that only one crater was found at the scene of the attack.

No group claimed responsibility for the bombing. However, the incident was consistent with previous Sunni strikes designed to spark sectarian unrest—an operational trait often linked to organizations associated with Al Qaeda.

Following the bombing, the police and Frontier Corps set up patrols for the market and placed the area under an indefinite curfew. However, one-on-one revenge attacks—involving both heavy machine guns and mortars—as well as looting and arson continued to be widespread. Both sides also blatantly ignored the pleas of the district government to cease fire, with the intensity of the fighting so great that it prevented giving last rites to many of the dead. Unrest additionally spread beyond Hangu to affect Koi Bagh, Mohallah Bahadur Garhi, Mohallah Chashma Masjid, and Pass Kali.

About 3,000 protesters turned out in the streets of Karachi over the killings. Shia cleric Allama Mehdi Najfi told the Associated Press "this attack has spread anger among our people throughout the country, but I appeal [to] them not to clash with any member of other sects." A judicial inquiry into the attack and the spread of the violence was also ordered.

On February 12, 2006, a 24-member peace committee made up of elders from both religious sects held its first meeting to put a cease-fire in place. They agreed on a number of measures, including setting up subcommittees to restore peace and assess the damage.

See also: Pakistani Sectarian Violence

Further Reading

Jones, Seth G., and Christine C. Fair. *Counterinsurgency in Pakistan.* Santa Monica, CA: RAND, 2010.

Rabasa, Angel, Peter Chalk, Kim Cragin, Sara A. Daly, Heather S. Gregg, Theodore W. Karasik, Kevin A. O'Brien, and William Rosenau. *Beyond al-Qaeda. Part 1: The Global Jihadist Movement.* Santa Monica, CA: RAND, 2006.

Rashid, Ahmed. *Descent into Chaos: The United States and the Failure of Nation Building in Pakistan, Afghanistan, and Central Asia.* New York: Viking Books, 2008.

Donna Bassett

HANJOUR, HANI SALEH HUSAN

Hani Saleh Husan Hanjour was the leader and probable pilot of the terrorist group that seized American Airlines Flight 77 and crashed it into the Pentagon on September 11, 2001. He was a last-minute recruit because the September 11 conspirators needed one more pilot. Although Hanjour was a terrible pilot, he had enough skill to guide an airliner into a stationary target.

Hanjour had advantages in life, but he lacked the abilities to capitalize on them. He was born on August 30, 1972, in Ta'if, Saudi Arabia. His father was a successful food-supply businessman in Ta'if. Hanjour was a devout Muslim, and it colored all of his conduct. Because he was an indifferent student, Hanjour was only persuaded to stay in school by his older brother. This older brother, who was living in Tucson, Arizona, encouraged him to come to the United States. Hanjour arrived in the United States on October 3, 1991. He stayed in Tucson, where he studied English at the University of Arizona. After completing the English program in three months, Hanjour returned to Ta'if. He spent the next five years working at his family's food-supply business. In 1996 he briefly visited Afghanistan. Following this visit, Hanjour decided to move back to the United States. He stayed for a time with an Arab American family in Hollywood, Florida. Then, in April 1996, Hanjour moved in with a family in Oakland, California. This time he attended Holy Names College and attended an intensive course in English. Hanjour decided to become a pilot and fly for Saudi Airlines. Hanjour also enrolled in a class at Sierra Academy of Aeronautics, but he withdrew because of the cost. After leaving Oakland in April 1996, he moved to Phoenix, Arizona. This time he paid for lessons at CRM Flight Cockpit Resource Management in Scottsdale, Arizona, but his academic performance there was disappointing. His instructors found him to be a terrible pilot, and it took him a long time to master the essentials of flying. While in Phoenix, he roomed with Bandar al-Hazmi. In January 1998, Hanjour took flying lessons at Arizona Aviation, and after a three-year struggle, he earned his commercial pilot rating in April 1999. Hanjour was unable to find a job as a pilot. His Federal Aviation Administration (FAA) license expired in 1999 when he failed to take a mandatory medical test.

Frustrated in his job hunting, Hanjour traveled to Afghanistan. He arrived there just as Khalid Sheikh Mohammed's men were looking for another pilot for the September 11 plot. Hanjour was made to order. After being recruited by Al Qaeda, he returned to the United States. In September 2000, when he moved to San Diego, California, Hanjour met up with Nawaf al-Hazmi. Hanjour returned to Phoenix to continue his pilot training at the Jet Tech Flight School. He was so inept as a flyer, and his English was so bad, that the instructors contacted the FAA to check whether his commercial license was valid. The FAA confirmed that his commercial license was indeed valid. Hanjour spent most of his time there on the Boeing 737 simulator. Next, he moved to Paterson, New Jersey, in the early spring of 2001. There, he met several times with other members of the September 11 conspiracy. On September 11, 2001, Hanjour was the hijackers' pilot on American Airlines Flight 77. Despite his lack of ability, he managed to fly that aircraft into the Pentagon.

See also: Mohammed, Khalid Sheikh; September 11 (2001)

Further Reading

Graham, Bob. *Intelligence Matters: The CIA, the FBI, Saudi Arabia, and the Failure of America's War on Terror.* New York: Random House, 2004.

McDermott, Terry. *Perfect Soldiers: The Hijackers: Who They Were, Why They Did It.* New York: HarperCollins, 2005.

Stephen E. Atkins

HARAKAT UL-JIHAD AL-ISLAMI (HUJI)

Harakat ul-Jihad al-Islami (HuJI, or Islamic Struggle Movement) is a Pakistan-based terrorist group that adheres to the Deobandi sect of Islam and espouses a virulent anti-Indian, anti–United States, and anti-Pakistani government agenda. Conflicting reports exist regarding the precise date of HuJI's founding and its creators; however, most sources agree that the organization was established during the Afghan jihad to fight against occupying Soviet forces and that Qari Saifullah Akhtar and Maulana Irshad Ahmed were prominent early members. Following Moscow's withdrawal from Kabul in 1989, HuJI refocused its efforts toward fighting Indian rule in the predominantly Muslim state of Jammu and Kashmir with the prominent support and backing of Pakistan's InterServices Intelligence (ISI) Directorate.

HuJI suffered an early setback when a ranking member named Fazlur Rehman Khalil broke away from the group to establish his own militant organization, the Harakat-ul-Mujahideen (HuM, or Holy Warriors' Movement). At the behest of militant Deobandi clerics and the ISI, the two agreed to reunite in 1993 under the banner of Harakat-ul-Ansar (HuA, or Helpers' Movement). Three years later the new entity staged a series of international kidnappings that resulted in the deaths of five Western tourists. The abductions led the United States to proscribe the HuA as a foreign terrorist organization, which subsequently prompted HuM and HuJI to terminate their merger and revert to their own independent existence.

HuJI developed strong ties with the Taliban government in Afghanistan during the late 1990s, and several sources suggest that by this time Akhtar was serving as a political advisor to Mullah Omar. HuJI relocated much of its training infrastructure to Afghanistan, establishing a major training camp in Rishkot, and assisted the Taliban in combat operations against the Northern Alliance—eliciting perhaps the first known use of the term *Punjabi Taliban.* HuJI's leadership was also reportedly close to Al Qaeda and is believed to have been a principal force in helping to solidify links between Osama bin Laden and Mullah Omar.

Following the fall of the Taliban in late 2001, much of the group's membership relocated to Pakistan, establishing a strong presence in the Federally Administered Tribal Areas (FATA) and the Northwest Frontier Province (NWFP; now known as Khyber-Pakhtunkwha). The group also set up various smaller branches in other parts of the country. Akhtar reportedly fled from Afghanistan first to South Waziristan, then to Saudi Arabia, and finally to Dubai. He was deported to Pakistan in 2004 following suspicions of his involvement in two foiled plots to assassinate then president Pervez Musharraf and was held in custody until 2007, when he was evidently released.

Following the storming of the Lal Masjid mosque, HuJI was suspected of involvement in a number of high-profile terrorist attacks in Pakistan. These included, notably, two assassination attempts against Benazir Bhutto in 2007—the second of which proved successful—and the bombing of a Marriott hotel in Islamabad in 2008. At this time Akhtar moved to Waziristan, where under his auspices HuJI continued to foster links to Al Qaeda as well as the newly formed Tehrik-e-Taliban Pakistan (TTP, or Pakistani Taliban). Until his death in June 2011, HuJI's operational commander, Ilyas Kashmiri, emerged as a top commander for joint operations conducted by his group, Al Qaeda, the TTP, and other Deobandi terrorist outfits. HuJI itself has been tied to an assault on the Pakistani Army's general headquarters in 2009, a plot to attack a Danish newspaper that had published offensive cartoons of the prophet Muhammad, and the assassination of Khalid Khwaja, an ex-ISI squadron leader, in 2010 (the latter being claimed under the name Asian Tigers)

Despite these operations, HuJI's overall level of activity has declined in recent years as the group has been eclipsed by other terrorist organizations based in Pakistan. HuJI's current infrastructure in India is unknown at the present time, although its affiliate in Bangladesh—Harakat-ul-Jihad-Islami Bangladesh (HuJI B)—is thought to retain a strong network in the country, particularly in the state of West Bengal.

See also: Al Qaeda; Harakat-ul-Mujahideen (HuM); Tehrik-e-Taliban Pakistan (TTP)

Further Reading

"Harakat_ul-Ansar (now known as Harakar-ul-Mujahideen): Evolution of the Outfit." South Asia Terrorism Portal (SATP). http://www.satporg/satporgtp/countries/india/states/jandk/terrorist_outfits/harakat_ul_ansar_or_harakat_ul_jehad_e_islami.htm.
"Harakat-ul-Jihad-al-Islami." Investigative Project on Terrorism, nda. http://www.investigativeproject.org/profile/147.
"HuJI Chief behind EX-ISI Man's Killing?" *Times of India,* May 2, 2010.
Roul, Animesh. "HuJI Operations Expand beyond the Indian Subcontinent." *Global Terrorism Analysis,* April 29, 2010. http://www.jamestown.org/programs/gta/single/?tx_ttnews%5Btt_news%5D=36327&cHash=77e57144d9, accessed February 20, 2012.

Ben Brandt

HARAKAT-UL-JIHAD-ISLAMI BANGLADESH (HUJI B)

Harakat-ul-Jihad-Islami Bangladesh (HuJI B) is an extremist Islamist entity in Bangladesh. The organization's roots date back to 1992, but it has emerged as a prominent terrorist group in its own right only since 2000. Shaquat Osman (also known as Maulana or Sheikh Farid) leads the movement, overseeing an operational cadre that is believed to number 15,000; of these, 2,000 are described as hard-core. Most of these members are recruited from the proliferating web of radical unlicensed madrassas that have sprung up in the country and are based in cells that are scattered along a stretch of coastline that runs from the port city of Chittagong south through Cox's Bazar to the Burmese border.

HuJI B's purported goal is to overthrow the central government in Dhaka and institute a theocratic state based on sharia law. Indian intelligence sources, however, claim this is only part of the group's overall aim and that its long-term objective is to spark an Islamic revolution in India's northeast by working with like-minded extremists in Kashmir and Assam, including Harakat-ul-Mujahideen, Jaish-e-Mohammed, and the United Liberation Front of Asom.

There is widespread suspicion that, besides working in tandem with Indian groups, HuJI B is closely aligned with Al Qaeda. Members of the organization are known to have accessed training camps run by Osama bin Laden when the Taliban was in power in Afghanistan, while Shaikh Abdur Rahman—the leader of the umbrella Jama'at ul-Mujahideen Bangladesh (JMB, or Jihad Movement in Bangladesh) to which Harakat belongs—was one of the original signatories of the 1998 Khost "Declaration of Jihad against Jews and Crusaders." Many of the fundamentalist Bangladeshi religious institutions to which HuJI B belongs are also open about their support of Al Qaeda, while the group itself has frequently exhorted the dual refrain of "Ambra Sobai Hobo Taliban Bangla Hobe Afghanistan" ("We will all be Taliban, and Bangladesh will be Afghanistan").

HuJI B derives a considerable amount of its funding from overseas, especially donations from Pakistan, Kuwait, the United Arab Emirates, Qatar, Oman, and Saudi Arabia. It is believed that this money is channeled into the country via the Saudi-based al-Haramain Foundation and Bangladeshi nongovernmental organizations and charities such as Adsara Kutir, the Al Faruk Islam Foundation, Hataddin, and the Servants of Suffering and Humanity International. Financial backing for the group is also believed to flow from Pakistan's Inter Services Intelligence (ISI) Directorate, which is alleged to underwrite the organization as part of its proxy war against India.

HuJI B is thought to operate at least six dedicated training camps in Bangladesh, which were reportedly set up with the direct assistance of the ISI on the condition that they were made available to anti-Indian groups. According to one former Burmese guerrilla, three located just outside of Cox's Bazar have a combined capacity of at least 2,500 cadres, with the largest comprising a complex of 26 interconnected bunkers built under a three-meter (10-feet)-high false floor. The facilities reportedly have kitchens, lecture halls, telephones, and televisions, and all have access to a wide array of weapons, including AK-47 assault rifles, heavy machine guns, pistols, rocket-propelled grenades, mortars, mantraps, and mines.

HuJI B has been linked to several acts of terrorism in Bangladesh. The group was the prime suspect in a plot to assassinate then prime minister Sheikh Hasina in 2000 and was thought to be behind several bombings in 2005. The group was also tied to twin blasts at a Hindu temple and railway station at Varanasi on March 7, 2006.

Dhaka banned HuJI B in October 2005, three months after a series of 500 explosions struck 63 of Bangladesh's 64 town districts, killing two people and injuring hundreds. Although subsequent investigations traced the attacks to the umbrella JMB, HuJI B was thought to have played a direct role in facilitating the operation. The United States proscribed HuJI B as a foreign terrorist organization in March 2008.

See also: Al Qaeda; Bangladesh Bombings; Harakat ul-Jihad al-Islami (HuJI); Jaish-e-Mohammed (JeM); Jama'at ul-Mujahideen Bangladesh (JMB); United Liberation Front of Asom (ULFA)

Further Reading

Datta, Sreeradha. "Bangladesh's Political Evolution: Growing Uncertainties." *Strategic Analysis,* April–June 2003.

Perry, Alex. "Deadly Cargo." *Time Asia,* October 21, 2002.

Rabasa, Angel, Peter Chalk, Kim Cragin, Sara Daly, Heather Gregg, Theodore Karasik, Kevin O'Brien, and William Rosenau. *Beyond al-Qaeda. Part 1: The Global Jihadist Movement.* Santa Monica, CA: RAND Corporation, 2006.

Raman, B. "HuJI B and the Varanasi Blasts." South Asia Analysis Group Paper 1762, April 6, 2006. http://www.southasiaanalysis.org/%5Cpapers18%5CPaper1762.htm, accessed January 7, 2012.

"Terrorist Outfits, Bangladesh: Harakat-ul-Jihad-al-Islami (HuJI)." South Asia Terrorism Portal (SATP). http://www.satp.org/satporgtp/countries/bangladesh/terroristoutfits/Huj.htm, accessed February 21, 2006.

Donna Bassett

HARAKAT-UL-MUJAHIDEEN (HUM)

Harakat-ul-Mujahideen (HuM, or Holy Warriors' Movement) is a Pakistan-based Islamic terrorist group that is affiliated with the Deobandi sect of Islam and espouses an anti-Indian agenda. It is one of several jihadist outfits that have fought in the disputed territory of Jammu and Kashmir (J&K) and is known to have received the active backing and support of Pakistan's InterServices Intelligence (ISI) Directorate. Farooq Kashmiri currently leads the group, taking over from its longtime emir, Fazlur Rehman Khalil, in February 2000. HuM has several hundred armed supporters in Pakistani Occupied Kashmir (POK, or Azad Kashmir), Pakistan, India's southern Kashmir and Doda regions, and the Kashmiri Valley. Similar to Lashkar-e-Taiba (LeT) and Jaish-e-Mohammed (JeM), the Pakistani government banned HuM in 2002; since then the group has operated under various names, including Jamiat ul-Ansar (JuA, literally Group of Helpers) and Harakat ul-Mujahideen al-Aalami (HuMA). HuM is frequently described as being politically aligned with the Pakistani Deobandi political party Jamiat-i-Ulama-i-Islam-Fazlur (JUI-F), is known to recruit personnel from the apolitical Deobandi missionary organization Tablighi Jamaat, and has set up booths at Tablighi Jamaat's annual *ijtema* (gathering) in Raiwind, Pakistan.

HuM first originated as a splinter faction of the Harakat ul-Jihad al-Islami (HuJI) when Khalil broke away from the parent movement after he was denied the position of emir (in preference for Qari Saifullah Akhtar). HuJI and HuM reunited in 1993, reportedly at the urgings of militant Deobandi clerics and the ISI, in the guise of Harakat-ul-Ansar (HuA). The new group suffered a major setback shortly after its founding, however, when Indian security forces arrested three of its senior members in 1993–1994. HuA unsuccessfully attempted to gain their release by staging the kidnapping and murder of several Western nationals under the alias al-Faran. The United States retaliated by designating HuA as a foreign terrorist organization in 1997, at which point the group split again and HuJI and HuM went their separate ways.

HuM established ties with Al Qaeda during the 1990s and set up training camps in Afghanistan. The tight links between the two groups first became apparent in 1998, following Washington's retaliatory missile strikes in Afghanistan, launched in reaction to the suicide bombings of the U.S. embassies in Kenya and Tanzania. Several of those killed in two Al Qaeda camps were subsequently identified as HuM cadres. Khalil also allegedly represented the group in 1998 when Osama bin Laden signed the now-infamous "Declaration of Jihad against Jews and Crusaders." According to Indian sources, Khalil maintained a close working relationship with Al Qaeda following the Khost meeting and systematically sought to refine HuM's ideological focus to one that was more internationalist and anti-Western in orientation.

In 1999 several members of HuM staged a hijacking of Air India Flight 814 to secure the release of the ranking militants captured in 1993–1994; the endeavor proved successful, and Maulana Masood Azhar, a senior member of HuM, was released. Shortly after his release, Azhar established a new Islamist group named Jaish-e-Mohammed (JeM) with the approval of both senior militant Deobandi clerics and the ISI. JeM subsequently drew away a large number of HuM members, and the two groups engaged in armed clashes over the disposition of property claimed by both.

HuM's operations in J&K were adversely affected by the loss of personnel and material to JeM, which also frequently eclipsed its parent organization by staging high-profile suicide attacks in India. Indian efforts to effectively monitor the Line of Control with Pakistan further curtailed HuM's ability to operate in the disputed territory, although the group still retains an active presence there.

As with other Deobandi militant groups, an increasing number of HuM members became interested in targeting American and Western interests as well as the Pakistani state following the coalition invasion of Afghanistan in 2001 (Operation Enduring Freedom [OEF]). It was within this context that an offshoot of the group emerged in 2002. Calling itself Harakat ul-Mujahideen al-Aalami (HuMA), the new entity was reportedly responsible for a string of attacks in Karachi, which included a failed assassination attempt on then president Pervez Musharraf and bombings of the U.S. consulate and the Sheraton Hotel. HuMA's activities largely ceased, however, with the capture of the group's commander and deputy chief in July 2002, although it was accused of staging a series of strikes Shell gas stations in Karachi in 2003. Analysts continue to debate whether HuMA was a true splinter faction of HuM or merely a rubric designed to allow the group to engage in anti-state violence without fear of retribution. Given that Khalil is currently free and that the Punjabi Taliban have explicitly denounced HuM as a proxy of the ISI, it appears that HuMA may represent a genuine splinter faction.

In addition to the activities of its splinter faction, the mainline HuM has continued to target Indian security forces in J&K and is widely suspected of sending militants to battle coalition forces in Afghanistan. Khalil himself was arrested in 2004 on charges of training and deploying militants to fight alongside the Taliban, though several sources in Pakistan claim the arrest was merely a ploy to defuse U.S. criticism and insulate the HuM leader from interrogation at the hand of the Federal Bureau of Investigation (FBI). Evidence to support these allegations arguably came in 2006 when Khalil was released from detention and allowed to travel to mosques and exhort Muslims to fight in Afghanistan under the aegis of Mullah Omar.

Despite its extensive losses of personnel and material resulting from the split with JeM, HuM is thought to retain training facilities in both Mansehra and Muzaffarabad and continues to benefit from ongoing recruitment drives at madrassas and public schools. In addition, the group is believed to have a relatively secure line of financing as a result of donations from Pakistan and the Middle East and profits garnered from legitimate businesses in the areas of real estate, commodities trading, and manufacturing. It is unclear whether the ISI provides the group with funding at the present time.

See also: Al Qaeda; Harakat ul-Jihad al-Islami (HuJI); Jaish-e-Mohammed (JeM)

Further Reading

"Harakat ul-Mujahideen Dossier." Federation of American Scientists (FAS) Intelligence Program. http://www.fas.org/irp/world/para/hum.htm, accessed February 20, 2012.

Howenstein, Nicholas. "The Jihadi Terrain in Pakistan: An Introduction to the Sunni Jihadi Groups in Pakistan and Kashmir." Pakistan Security Research Unit, Report no. 1 (February 5, 2008). Available online at http://spaces.brad.ac.uk-8080/download/attachments/748/resrep1.pdf, accessed February 20, 2012.

"Jamiat ul-Ansar." Australian Department of the Attorney General, November 6, 2008. http://ag.gov.au/agd/WWW/nationalsecurity.nsf/Page/What_Governments_are_doing_Listing_of_Terrorism_Organisations_Jamiat_ul_Ansar.

Mir, Amir. "The Pakistanis Training in Al Qaeda Camps." *COBRA Post.* http://www.cobrapost/documents/Training/AlQaeda.htm, accessed February 20, 2012.

Rana, Mohammad Amir. *A to Z of Jehadi Organizations in Pakistan.* Lahore, Pakistan: Mashal Books, 2004.

Ben Brandt

HARIRI (RAFIQ) ASSASSINATION

On February 14, 2005, a roadside bomb in Beirut killed the Lebanese prime minister Rafiq Hariri. His assassination galvanized Lebanese society and led to the Cedar Revolution, which resulted in the withdrawal of Syrian troops from Lebanon.

Hariri began his career as a businessman and engineer and gained acclaim for his reconstruction work in Beirut after the 1982 occupation by Israel. He quickly developed close ties with King Fahd of Saudi Arabia, who selected him as his delegate to the proceedings that produced the 1989 Ta'if Accord ending the Lebanese Civil War. Hariri also worked to create educational programs to provide scholarships for Lebanese students to study abroad. Even before his own entry into politics, Hariri was well connected with influential governments in both the West and the Middle East. He maintained a particularly close friendship with French leader Jacques Chirac and cultivated relationships with the United States, Syria, and Saudi Arabia. These prominent connections helped to internationalize the Lebanese conflict.

By 1990 Hariri was regarded as a rising power broker in Lebanese politics and was, accordingly, placed in charge of forming a new parliament following the end of the country's civil war. Hariri was elected prime minister in 1992 and would serve until 1998. His first term started optimistically; he enjoyed a high level of support from the Lebanese Sunni population and was instrumental in helping to rally the faltering economy. However, by 1997 fiscal growth and development had slowed significantly, a setback for which Hariri was squarely blamed. Compounding his difficulties was a complex and increasingly frayed relationship with the Shia militia Hezbollah, which suspected that the Lebanese government was working to erode its military arm (which remained intact despite the provisions of the Ta'if Accord that required all militias to disarm).

In 1998 Hariri called for renewed reform of the Lebanese political, legal, and bureaucratic system, but his attempts at change served only to deepen internal criticism. As a result, Hariri was forced to withdraw from nomination as prime minister in 1998. However, dissatisfaction with the Saleim al-Hoss government that followed allowed for Hariri's quick return to the Lebanese premiership, which he held from 2000 to 2004. During his second term, Hariri fell out of favor with a contingent of pro-Syrian government officials, and possibly with Damascus itself, which pushed to extend the term of President Emile Lahoud. The incident damaged Hariri's relationship with Syria and may have led to his resignation in 2004.

On February 14, 2005, a roadside bomb detonated as Hariri's motorcade passed the St. George Hotel in Beirut, killing him, 8 of his aides, and 14 additional civilian bystanders. Shortly after the explosion, an unidentified individual called the Al Jazeera television network and claimed credit for the assassination on behalf of a group called Victory and Jihad in Greater Syria (Nasra Group). A similar claim was made to Reuters.

In the wake of Hariri's death his family organized a massive funeral procession. Many of those in attendance vocally criticized the government's lethargic response to the assassination and expressed animosity toward Syrian involvement in Lebanon. Subsequent protests led to additional demonstrations against the government of Umar Karame, which had taken power after Hariri's resignation. Karame eventually capitulated and tendered his resignation in late February 2005.

On March 14, approximately 1.5 million Lebanese citizens, or about one-third of the country's total population, gathered for an unprecedented demonstration in Central Beirut to demand the dissolution of the remaining Karame government and the removal of all Syrian troops. The string of demonstrations, which came to be referred to as the Cedar Revolution, achieved its goals. By the end of April 2005, Damascus had withdrawn its forces from the country, and a new cabinet had been formed to oversee elections and the establishment of a new government.

On April 7, 2005, the United Nations (UN) Security Council convened an International Independent Investigation Committee (UNIIIC) to investigate Hariri's assassination and identify those responsible for carrying it out. Among the commission's findings was an assertion that several Lebanese and Syrian security officials were involved in the plot and that the prime minister's telephones had been wiretapped to track his movements leading up to the attack. It also found no evidence of the existence of the Nasra Group, which had originally claimed responsibility. In August 2005, the committee released the results of its investigation, and four senior pro-Syrian officials in the Lebanese security and intelligence apparatus named in the plot were incarcerated. Several others were forced to resign.

In December 2005, the Lebanese government formally requested additional UN assistance to further investigate events surrounding Hariri's death as well as other assassinations that took place in the country during the same period. A Special Tribunal for Lebanon (STL) was subsequently established and, although separate from the UNIIIC, was informed by the findings of its predecessor. In August 2011, the STL indicted four alleged supporters of Hezbollah on several counts related to the killing of Hariri. In its report, the tribunal asserted that the perpetrators took steps to cover evidence of Hezbollah's involvement, including making the false claim of responsibility on behalf of the fictitious Nasra Group.

After the unsealing of the indictments, Hezbollah leader Hassan Nasrallah vehemently denied his group's involvement in the crime, dismissed the STL's findings as speculative, and denounced the tribunal as a tool of the United States and Israel. To date, Hezbollah has refused to hand over the individuals named in the STL's indictment, and efforts to locate them have failed. In February 2012, the STL announced it would proceed with trying the subjects in absentia.

See also: Hezbollah (Party of God)

Further Reading

Blanford, Nicholas. *Killing Mr. Lebanon: The Assassination of Rafik Hariri and Its Impact on the Middle East.* New York: I. B. Tauris, 2009.
Iskandar, Marwan. *Rafiq Hariri and the Fate of Lebanon.* San Francisco: Saqi, 2006.
Rabil, Robert G. *Religion, National Identity, and Confessional Politics in Lebanon: The Challenge of Islamism.* New York: Palgrave Macmillan, 2011.
Special Tribunal for Lebanon. *Indictment in the Case of Ayyash et al* (STL-11-01). http://www.stl-tsl.org/en/the-cases/stl-11-01, accessed February 8, 2012.

Kate Mrkvica

HARRODS BOMBING

At 12:44 P.M. on December 17, 1983, a branch of the Samaritans charity organization in London received the following message: "This is the IRA (Irish Republican

Army). Car bomb outside Harrods. Two bombs in Harrods. One in Oxford Street. One in Littlewood's [a department store], Oxford Street." Ninety minutes later, a 25-pound improvised explosive device (IED) hidden in a car parked on Hans Crescent at the rear entrance of Harrods detonated as police approached.

The blast killed six, including three civilians and three policemen. The fatalities included Philip Geddes (journalist), 24; Kenneth Salvesen, 28; Jasmine Cochrane-Patrick, 25; Police Sergeant Noel Lane, 28, and Police Constable Jane Arbuthnot, 22. Police Inspector Stephen Dodd, 34, was injured and died on December 24, 1983. Police Constable Jon Gordon survived but lost both legs and part of a hand in the explosion.

The bomb also wounded 90 people, including 77 civilians and 13 policemen, damaged all five floors of Harrods, and sent a shower of glass fragments onto Christmas shoppers and people in the street. The other IEDs mentioned by the caller were a hoax to throw the police off. Hundreds of extra police and mobile bomb squads were drafted into London to protect the public from further attacks. Harrods reopened three days later despite the damage. Its owners said the store would not be defeated by acts of terrorism.

The bomb had been left in a 1972 blue Austin 1300 GT. It was parked outside the side entrance of Harrods and set to be detonated by a timer. The man who called the Samaritans specified the vehicle's registration number as KFP 252K.

The aftermath of the Provisional Irish Republican Army (PIRA) car bombing of Knightsbridge department store Harrods. Six people died in the explosion in London, England, on December 17, 1983. (Express/Getty Images)

At about 1:21 P.M. four policemen in a patrol car, a dog handler, and an officer on foot approached the Austin. When the IED went off, the squad car absorbed much of the blast, probably reducing other casualties.

On December 18, 1983, the Provisional Irish Republican Army (PIRA, or the "Provos") issued a communiqué that claimed dissident members of the group had carried out the bombing without the authority of the PIRA's High Command. The statement apologized for the civilian deaths and said there would be no further incidents of its kind. In March 1984 Paul Kavanagh, a 29-year-old resident of Northern Ireland, was arraigned in Belfast, Northern Ireland, for carrying out the bombing. Three months later,

Natalino Christopher Francis Vella, 30, also of Northern Ireland, was charged with plotting the attack.

The Harrods bombing came at a time when Sinn Féin, the political wing of the PIRA, was starting to attract more electoral support and international backing. The attack was therefore a public relations disaster for the party and necessitated a strong statement from Martin McGuinness, by then an established Sinn Féin politician. He declared that all PIRA Active Service Units (ASUs) in Britain, as in Ireland, were aware of the need to avoid civilian casualties. He also said that although the Harrod's incident had never been endorsed by the PIRA's High Command, the coded warning issued 40 minutes prior to the IED detonation showed that there was no intention to kill or injure members of the public.

Despite McGuinness's statement, the Harrods bombing (and the later October 12, 1984, attack on the Conservative Party's annual conference in Brighton) did a great deal to erode the contacts that Sinn Féin had been trying to build with socialist parties and movements in Britain. Outright support from the broad left could never have been expected as long as PIRA's violence continued, but the sympathy of at least some of those in this stratum might have been preserved if the PIRA had waged a more restrained campaign.

Although the far left never extended its influence into government during the 1980s, such contacts could still have proved a useful bridgehead into British politics. Clumsy attacks like the Harrods incident placed sympathizers in a moral quandary over whether or not to support a movement that continued to engage in operations that killed civilians. Meanwhile, the Brighton bomb had the inadvertent effect of strengthening the Conservative government's public image, an anathema to the radical socialist parties and something guaranteed to ensure their contempt for Sinn Féin.

The Harrods attack also generated considerable condemnation in the United States, which through the Northern Irish Aid Committee (NORAID) was an important source of financial assistance for the PIRA. This caused considerable problems for the Provos, who increasingly had to turn to the Middle East and Europe for money and arms. One state that was to become particularly important as a PIRA backer was Libya. Among the more prominent attacks carried out with the plastic explosives imported from the North African state were the Enniskillen massacre, which killed 11 at a Remembrance Day service in November 1987; the 1989 midair destruction of Pan Am Flight 103 over Lockerbie in December 1989, which killed 270; and the August 1998 bombing in Omagh, which resulted in 29 fatalities and 220 injuries. As of June 2010, Colonel Muammar Qaddafi had paid as much as £2 billion in compensation for PIRA terrorism carried out with explosives supplied by Libya, including £5 million to the family of each victim aboard Pan Am Flight 103.

In January 1993, Harrods was once again targeted by PIRA. This time, a package containing one pound of Semtex exploded in a litter bin at the front of the store in Brompton Road. Four people were injured. The IED smashed windows but did no internal damage. Those responsible were Patrick Taylor, a 51-year-old former corporal in the British Army, and Jan Hayes, a 41-year-old computer programmer. In March 1993, police captured them at Hayes's home in Stoke Newington, North London. They each received prison sentences of 30 years.

See also: Adams, Gerry; Brighton Bombing; Pan Am/Lockerbie Bombing; Provisional Irish Republican Army (PIRA)

Further Reading

Doughty, Steven. "IRA Victims Killed with Libyan Semtex to Get £2bn in Compensation from Colonel Gaddafi." *Daily Mail* (UK), June 13, 2010. http://www.dailymail.co.uk/news/worldnews/article-1286302/Colonel-Gaddafi-pay-2bn-compensation-IRA-victims-killed-semtex.html, accessed May 02, 2011.

"1983: Harrods Bomb Blast Kills Six." *BBC*, December 17, 1983. http://news.bbc.co.uk/onthisday/hi/dates/stories/december/17/newsid_2538000/2538147.stm, accessed May 02, 2011.

Oppenheimer, A. R. *IRA: The Bombs and the Bullets: A History of Deadly Ingenuity.* Foreword by Richard English. Dublin: Irish Academic Press, 2009.

Smith, M.L.R. *Fighting for Ireland? The Military Strategy of the Irish Republican Movement.* New York: Routledge, 1995.

Donna Bassett

HATSHEPSUT (LUXOR) TEMPLE MASSACRE

On November 17, 1997, six men dressed in black sweaters opened fire on foreign tourists at the 3,400-year-old temple of Hatshepsut in Luxor, Egypt. At least 62 people were killed, including 58 foreigners, of whom 36 were Swiss. Among the dead were two policemen. The shooters were armed with six machine guns, two pistols, ammunition, and two bags of homemade explosives. Witnesses said some of the militants wore red bandannas with black lettering that read, "We will fight until death." Local shopkeepers reported the presence of two additional participants who wore faded blue denim jackets and jeans. They disappeared after the attack.

At 8:45 A.M. the gunmen approached the entry to Hatshepsut and shot the guard, wounding him in the elbow and leg. They then killed the remaining security personnel before making their way to the main temple complex, which was crowded with tourists. The terrorists opened fire in a massacre that lasted 45 minutes, during which the attackers reportedly slit the throats of the wounded and sliced off their ears and noses. The youngest victim was six years old.

Meanwhile, a bus driver, Hagag al-Nahas, who was returning to pick up the 30 Swiss tourists he had dropped off earlier that morning (all but 8 were now dead), drove up to the temple and stopped. The terrorists, seeing an opportunity, boarded the vehicle and demanded that al-Nahas take them to another tourist site so they could "shoot more people."

The driver bravely drove in circles for 30 minutes, hoping to give security forces time to arrive. When none came, he headed toward a police checkpoint near an access road to the Valley of the Queens at Gourna, a half mile away from the crime scene. Realizing they had been tricked, one of the militants struck al-Nahas in the chest with his rifle butt. The other terrorists then abandoned the bus and began shooting at the three startled officers. The ensuing gunfight wounded two of the policemen and one of the militants, who was subsequently shot by his associates before they fled to nearby hills.

What happened next remains a mystery. Egypt's Interior Ministry announced that the "criminal group" had been killed during a two-hour gunfight in Dayr al-Muharib. Although the bodies of the gunmen were indeed discovered at a cave in the area, local witnesses from Gourna said that the only member of the security forces who could have followed the gunmen was the unwounded officer at the checkpoint, and he did not give chase. Furthermore, the wounds found on the militants' bodies were inconsistent with a shoot-out.

Another version of the story claimed that villagers from the Valley of the Queens chased down the men and killed them. This is supported by the fact that some locals did indeed follow the militants into the hills. However, they did not have guns, and all of the bodies in the cave had gunshot wounds. Others speculated that the militants had killed themselves or that their handlers had executed them and then staged the scene to make it look like suicide.

On November 20, a communiqué claimed the attack in the name of two al-Gama'a al-Islamiyya leaders who had left Egypt for Sudan and Afghanistan: Rifai Taha and Mustafa Hamza. Both were students of Sheikh Omar Abdel-Rahman and Hamza, and each had been linked to the attempted assassination of Egyptian president Hosni Mubarak in Ethiopia (June 26, 1995). The statement said the operation had been carried out to acquire hostages who would then be used as leverage to demand the release of Sheikh Omar Abdel-Rahman (who was imprisoned in the United States for his involvement in the 1993 bombing of the New York World Trade Center) and 65 other Egyptian Islamic Jihad (EIJ, or al-Jihad) cadres on trial in Cairo for conspiracy to commit murder.

However, the communiqué was inconsistent with the evidence and witness reports. The gunmen had clearly come to kill tourists, not acquire hostages. It later became evident that the claim of responsibility had been prepared for another attack that had been scheduled to take place in October during a gala hosted by President Mubarak at Luxor. This incident never occurred due to the heavy security presence at the event. Thus, the EIG statement was consistent with the plot that never happened, not the operation that actually occurred.

On November 24, members of Tala'I al-Fatah (Vanguards of Conquest), a militant wing of the EIJ, took credit for the massacre. They said that orders had "already been given for attacks against Americans and Zionists not only in Egypt but elsewhere." The spokesman also claimed to be related to Takfir wa Hijra (Repentance and Holy Flight), another extremist faction of the EIJ that had been linked to the assassination of Egyptian president Anwar Sadat on October 6, 1981.

Further complicating the investigation was evidence that local police had been arming vigilantes in the region. These bands had been originally tasked with rooting out Islamic militants but had progressively degenerated into criminal bands that acted as a law unto themselves. Members of these militias typically dressed in jeans similar to those worn by the two men seen in the marketplace who disappeared after the temple massacre.

Another odd incident involved the treatment of witnesses. On January 17, 1998, local police entered the village of Gourna and opened fire on villagers, killing 4 and wounding 29. Officials claimed they had been trying to enforce a government edict to remove homes built too close to an archaeological site and had met with armed resistance. It was later revealed that the police had acted without authority and that the villagers had no firearms.

Many viewed the massacre at Luxor as a humiliation on par with the 1967 defeat of the country by Israel during the Six-Day War. However, the impact of the massacre went far beyond the issue of national pride or international reputation, directly affecting the economy by disrupting tourism. Within a week, visits to archaeological sites in Luxor had dropped by 90 percent. This represented an unprecedented loss to a venue that had typically attracted two million foreigners a year.

An assessment of security failures associated with the Hatshepsut site and the poor response to the massacre led to a major internal disciplinary tribunal. On June 28, 1998, Luxor police chief Major General Medhat Shanawami was fired, as was his deputy, Major General Abul-Ata Youssef. Both were determined to have ignored security warnings specific to an attack on tourist sites in Luxor.

On March 10, 2000, Swiss authorities formally announced that they had been forced to abandon their inquiry into the massacre. According to the federal police, the Egyptian authorities had failed to return personal possessions belonging to the victims, had taken six months to respond to requests for legal assistance, had provided insufficient information to carry out a comprehensive investigation, and had generally been uncooperative.

Although the true identities of those who carried out the Hatshepsut massacre have yet to be determined, the EIG remains the prime suspect—not least because the group had previously warned all tourists to leave Egypt and had been involved in attacks on buses transporting foreign sightseers on day excursions. In October 2001, Rifai Taha was arrested at Damascus Airport in Syria after fleeing the post-9/11 invasion of Afghanistan. He was quietly extradited to Egypt and, according to government authorities, executed soon after arrival.

See also: Abdel-Rahman, Omar; al-Gama'a al-Islamiyya; Egyptian Islamic Jihad (EIJ); Sadat (Anwar) Assassination; World Trade Center (New York) Bombing

Further Reading

"Al-Qaida: Dead or Captured." *MSNBC,* June 22, 2005. http://www.msnbc.msn.com/id/4686228/, accessed July 28, 2011.

Boyer Bell, J. *Murders on the Nile: The World Trade Center and Global Terror.* San Francisco, CA: Encounter Books, 2003 2003.

"Egypt's Most Wanted." *Al-Ahram Weekly Online,* no. 556, October 18–24, 2001. http://weekly.ahram.org.eg/2001/556/11war3.htm, accessed July 28, 2011.

Kepel, Gilles. *Jihad: The Trail of Political Islam.* Translated by Anthony F. Roberts. Cambridge, MA: Belknap Press of Harvard University Press, 2002.

Weaver, Mary Anne. *A Portrait of Egypt: A Journey through the World of Militant Islam.* New York: Farrar, Straus and Giroux, 2000.

Zayyat, Montasser al-. *The Road to Al-Qaeda: The Story of Bin Lāden's Right-Hand Man.* Sterling, VA: Pluto, 2004.

Donna Bassett

HAZMI, NAWAF AL-

Nawaf bin Muhammad Salim al-Hazmi was one of the hijackers of American Airlines Flight 77, which crashed into the Pentagon on September 11, 2001. He was intended to be one of the team pilots, but he lacked the skills to fulfill that role. Instead, al-Hazmi worked behind the scenes to provide logistic support to all the teams.

Al-Hazmi became an Islamist militant at an early age. He was born on August 9, 1976, in Mecca, Saudi Arabia. His father was a grocer. An older brother was a police chief in Jizan, Saudi Arabia. As a teenager, al-Hazmi had traveled to Afghanistan. In Afghanistan, he met Khalid al-Mihdhar. They joined the Muslims in Bosnia to fight against the Serbian Bosnians in 1995. Then, along with his brother Salem al-Hazmi, al-Hazmi and al-Mihdhar returned to Afghanistan in time to fight with the Taliban against the Afghan Northern Alliance. Next, al-Hazmi traveled to Chechnya in 1998 to fight with the Chechen rebels. Returning to Saudi Arabia in early 1999, al-Hazmi decided to go to the United States with al-Mihdhar and his brother Salem. They easily obtained visas.

By 1999 al-Hazmi had been recruited by Al Qaeda for a special mission. The original plans called for him to become a pilot, but he lacked the necessary competency in English and the ability to pass pilot's training. He teamed with al-Mihdhar to provide logistic support for the September 11 plot. On September 11, 2001, al-Hazmi was part of the American Airlines Flight 77 hijacker team. He provided security while the airliner was crashed into the Pentagon.

See also: September 11 (2001)

Further Reading

McDermott, Terry. *Perfect Soldiers: The 9/11 Hijackers: Who They Were, Why They Did It.* New York: HarperCollins, 2005.

Stephen E. Atkins

HEADLEY, DAVID

David Coleman Headley, formerly known as Daood Sayed Gilani, is a Chicago-based Pakistani American who worked with Lashkar-e-Taiba (LeT) in planning the November 26, 2008, attacks in Mumbai, India. He was also tied to a plot to target a Danish newspaper in Copenhagen that published anti-Muslim cartoons.

Headley was born in the United States on June 30, 1960. His father worked for Voice of America (VoA) but also served for a time as a diplomat at Islamabad's embassy in Washington, D.C., where his mother was employed as a secretary. After his parents split up in the mid-1960s, Headley went with his father to Pakistan and attended the Hasan Abdal Cadet College, a preparatory boy's high school for the military. Following an army coup in 1977, he returned to America and moved in with his mother, who was now living in Philadelphia.

Headley married a Penn State University student in 1985, but the couple divorced two years later due to cultural differences. He then opened two video rental stores in New York City and apparently fell in with drug gangs. He was arrested on narcotics charges in 1987 but agreed to cooperate with the Drug Enforcement Administration (DEA) in exchange for a reduced sentence. Headley was detained for a second time in 1997 for smuggling Pakistani heroin into the United States. He again collaborated with the DEA, which earned him a much lighter period of jail time: 15 months in prison followed by five years of supervised release. The latter was never completed, and in November 2001 a U.S. attorney applied to have him discharged so he could conduct undercover surveillance operations for the DEA in Pakistan.

While overseas, Headley attended LeT camps and met with the group's spiritual leader, Hafiz Muhammad Saeed. Accepting LeT's Ahl-e-Hadith tradition, Headley completed five training stints with the organization. In 2006 he was interviewed by Pakistan's Inter-Services Intelligence (ISI) Directorate and offered financial compensation for helping to plan terrorist strikes in India. Headley accepted and underwent a basic course of intelligence instruction in Lahore. Between 2006 and 2008 he traveled to Mumbai on several occasions to scout potential targets and was provided with $25,000 to set up a front company in the city as cover while conducting surveillance. It was largely his information that led to the selection of the key sites that were hit in the Mumbai assaults—the Chhatrapati Shivaji train terminus, Nariman House (a commercial-residential complex run by the Jewish Chabad Lubavitch movement), the Oberoi-Trident Hotel, and the Taj Mahal Palace Hotel.

In 2009 Headley traveled to Europe with another accomplice, Tahawwur Hussain Rana, to help plan attacks on the headquarters of the *Jyllands-Posten,* the Danish newspaper that had published denigrating cartoons of the prophet Muhammad, and a nearby synagogue. He was arrested in October of that year at Chicago's International Airport while en route to Pakistan.

Headley was charged with planning terrorist attacks in Copenhagen, conspiring to bomb targets in Mumbai, providing material support to LeT, and facilitating the murder of U.S. citizens. He pleaded guilty to all counts on March 18, 2010, and faces life in prison as well as a $3 million fine. At the time of writing, U.S. authorities had urged leniency during sentencing because Headley had provided valuable evidence linking both the Pakistani Army and the ISI to LeT.

See also: Lashkar-e-Taiba (LeT); Mumbai Attacks (2008)

Further Reading

Burke, Jason. "Pakistan Intelligence Services 'Aided Mumbai Terror Attack.'" *The Guardian* (London), October 18, 2010.

Clarke, Ryan. *Lashkar-i-Taiba: The Fallacy of Subservient Proxies and the Future of Islamist Terrorism in India.* Carlisle, PA: U.S. Army War College, Strategic Studies Institute, March 2010. http://www.strategicstudiesinstitute.army.mil/pdffiles/pub973.pdf, accessed August 1, 2011.

Fair, Christine C. "Antecedents and Implications of the November 2008 Lashkar-e-Taiba (LeT) Attack upon Several Targets on the Indian Mega-City of Mumbai. Testimony presented before the House Homeland Security Committee, Subcommittee on Transportation, Security and Infrastructure Protection, Washington DC, March 11, 2009.

Peters, Gretchen. *Seeds of Terror: How Heroin Is Bankrolling the Taliban and al Qaeda.* New York: St. Martin's Press, 2009.

Posner, Gerald. "The Making of a Terrorist." *The Daily Beast,* December 8, 2009. http://www.thedailybeast.com/blogs-and-stories/2009-12-08/making-of-a-terrorist/full, accessed December 01, 2011.

Rabasa, Angel, Robert Blackwill, Peter Chalk, Kim Cragin, Christine C. Fair, Brian Jackson, Brian Jenkins, Seth Jones, Nate Shestak, and Ashley Tellis. *The Lessons of Mumbai.* Santa Monica, CA: RAND, 2009.

Rotella, Sebastian. "Key Witness in Chicago Trial Offers More Details on 2008 Mumbai Attacks." *Washington Post,* May 24, 2011.

Donna Bassett

HEATHROW LIQUID BOMB PLOT

In August 2006, United Kingdom (UK) authorities arrested 24 individuals alleged to have been plotting to detonate a number of explosive devices aboard transatlantic commercial aircraft while in flight from Heathrow airport to a number of destinations in the United States and Canada. British and American authorities claimed this plot had strong links to Al Qaeda militants based in Pakistan. Those arrested were said to have intended to utilize a novel form of liquid explosives to attack passenger aircraft; as a result of this plot, a range of new airport security measures were introduced.

The leader of the cell, Ahmed Abdullah Ali, was identified as a person of interest by UK authorities as part of investigations into potential violent extremists following the July 2005 underground bombings in London. When Ali returned from a trip to Pakistan in June 2006, his luggage was covertly searched, and a bottle of powdered soft drink (Tang) and a large number of batteries were discovered. Concern over this discovery led the authorities to begin a large-scale surveillance operation targeting Ali and his associates; it has also been reported that a member of the British Security Service (MI5) penetrated the group. In June 2005, intelligence officials learned that members of the apparent homegrown terror cell had made a cash purchase of an apartment on Forest Road, London. The property was subsequently searched, and video and listening devices installed. During this and later covert searches, officers found what appeared to be bomb-making equipment including batteries and chemicals. As the surveillance operation continued, the scale of the alleged plot became apparent, and it is thought up to 19 attackers may have been involved (mirroring the number of hijackers involved in the 9/11 attacks).

Surveillance of the London cell may have continued for considerably longer than was the case if it had not been for the detention in Pakistan of Rashid Rauf, a British-born Pakistani thought to have been a key player in the plot. This arrest apparently took the UK authorities by surprise and compelled the security forces to move against the alleged plotters earlier than may have been planned. It was alleged at the time of the apprehensions that the U.S. and UK authorities had disagreed over when to act. Reportedly, the British wished to continue to observe the terrorists, while the Americans were pushing for an early intervention to bring the plot to a halt. Rauf subsequently escaped from Pakistani custody, although he was later killed in 2008 during a U.S. air strike.

Of the 25 individuals initially arrested, 8 were eventually charged with conspiring to cause explosions with intent to endanger life and conspiring to cause explosions on board passenger aircraft. Several other men were accused of lesser terrorism offenses. During their trials those involved claimed that their preparations were part of an elaborate publicity stunt rather than an attempt to destroy a number of aircraft in flight.

The key individuals in the case were the following.

- Ahmed Abdullah Ali, the alleged ringleader of the plot, who claimed that the intention had been to plant a number of small explosive devices at Heathrow to draw attention to UK foreign policy and that there was no intention to endanger life. Ali admitted to having researched over the Internet how to construct an explosive device using a drink bottle, batteries, and bleach.
- Assad Sarwar, described during the trial as the cell's quartermaster responsible for buying and concealing bomb-making materials. Reported to have met Ali while volunteering at a refugee camp in Pakistan, Sarwar admitted to having learned how to make explosives in Pakistan.
- Tanvir Hussain, who was already known to the UK authorities and who had been approached by MI5 prior to the emergence of this plot. Despite this, he persisted in his involvement and helped manufacture the devices to be used in the attacks. He also recorded a "living will" or martyr video that was recovered and formed a key element in the prosecution's case.
- Arafat Waheed Khan, who also recorded a martyr video and was alleged to have helped procure bomb-making materials for the attack. Khan had been at school with Ali and had failed a business course at Middlesex University. He was reportedly approached by the security service to act as an informant but refused to cooperate.
- Waheed Zaman, who claimed he only wanted to raise public awareness of the oppression of Muslims and denied he knew what Ali had been planning.
- Ibrahim Savant, a convert to Islam who also recorded a martyr video. He later claimed that he had done so at Ali's behest and did not adhere to the radical statements made in the video.
- Umar Islam, another convert to Islam and a close associate of Ali and Sarwar. He helped in refugee camps in Pakistan and recorded a video in which he stated, "I say to you disbelievers that as you bomb, you will be bombed. As you kill, you will be killed. And if you want to kill our women and children then the same thing will happen to you. This is not a joke."
- Adam Katib, who was described as being Ali's lieutenant and had conducted research into the chemicals to be used in the manufacture of detonators.
- Mohammed Gulzar, who was accused of being an international terrorist and of being the superintendent of the plot.

At the end of the original trial in September 2008, Ali, Sarwar, and Hussain were found guilty of conspiring to commit murder, but no verdict was reached on the charges that they intended to detonate an explosive device on an aircraft. Khan, Zaman, Savant, and Islam all pleaded guilty to conspiracy to commit a public nuisance—the jury was unable to reach a verdict on the charges of murder.

In September 2009, a second trial found Ali, Sarwar, and Hussain guilty of attempting to cause explosions in passenger aircraft and convicted Islam of conspiracy to commit murder. However, the jury was unable to reach a verdict on the remaining defendants. A third trial found Savant, Khan, and Zaman guilty of conspiracy to murder in July 2010. Gulzar was cleared on all charges. Those convicted were sentenced to serve between 20 and 36 years in prison.

Prior to deciding on their final targets, the cell appeared to have looked into the feasibility of attacking other venues. During searches following the arrest of the plotters, a diagram of the layout of the Bacton gas terminal in Norfolk was discovered, along with plans of the Coryton oil refinery in Essex. During the trial Sarwar, alleged to have been the chief target scout for the cell, admitted he had also conducted research on the Internet into possible targets, including the Houses of Parliament and the Heathrow, Gatwick, Stansted, and Birmingham airports. Further evidence of potential alternate targets emerged with the discovery of CD-ROMs containing photographs of the area around a pedestrian tunnel under the Thames, along with photographs of a nearby university campus and closed-circuit television camera locations.

A notable aspect of this plot was the plan to utilize a novel explosive device to circumvent the stringent security procedures instituted at airports in light of the 9/11 attacks in the United States. The plotters' intent was to use a peroxide-based liquid explosive, which would be injected into sealed plastic soft drink bottles. A second element of the device was a disposable camera containing a small quantity of hexamethylene triperoxide, which would be triggered by the camera's flash unit. When held beside the bottle of liquid explosive, this would act as a detonator for the main explosive charge. As part of the evidence for the various trials, British government technical experts claimed to have replicated the devices and found that they would have been viable if properly constructed and executed. It was alleged that the cell was on the verge of conducting a dummy run, aimed at testing airport security to see if the liquid explosives could be successfully smuggled aboard the aircraft without detection. Parallels have been drawn between this attempt and the mid-1990s Bojinka plot, which sought to use a series of small nitroglycerine-based devices to bring down commercial aircraft in flight.

The cell had apparently also given consideration to the possibility of using other measures to get their devices through security. Specifically, Ali had suggested that the alleged bombers should take pornographic magazines and condoms in their hand luggage to allay any suspicions security staff might have. It has also been claimed that the plotters discussed bringing their wives and children with them for the attacks.

The innovative use of liquid explosives in this plot led to the introduction of a range of new security measures at North American and European airports. These included a ban on any liquids or gels over three ounces (100 milliliters) in passengers' carry-on luggage and the institution of more stringent search and screening procedures. The new rules remained in place at the time of writing.

See also: Al Qaeda; Bojinka Operation

Further Reading

Bennett, Brian, and Douglas Waller. "Thwarting the Airline Plot: Inside the Investigation." *Time,* August 10, 2006.

"Bomb Plot—The al-Qaeda Connection." *BBC News,* September 9, 2008. http://news.bbc.
co.uk/2/hi/uk_news/7606107.stm.

"Details Emerge in British Terror Case." *New York Times,* August 28, 2006.

"In '06 Bomb Plot Trial, a Question of Imminence." *New York Times,* July 15, 2008.

"Profiles: Operation Overt." *BBC News,* September 8, 2008. http://news.bbc.co.uk/2/hi/
uk_news/7604808.stm.

"The Terrorists Who Changed Air Travel Forever." *The Independent* (UK), September 9,
2008.

Greg Hannah

HEBRON MOSQUE MASSACRE

On February 25, 1994, a lone Israeli gunman massacred 29 Palestinian Muslims at the Mosque of Abraham in Hebron, located in the Judean region of the West Bank. Also known as the Cave of the Patriarchs or Tomb of the Patriarchs, the mosque site is held holy by both Muslims and Jews. The attack occurred during a period of religious holidays that saw both Jews and Muslims using the site for their observances. For Muslims, the event was Ramadan, the monthlong period of prayer, fasting, charity, and introspection. The Jews were observing Purim, a remembrance of Jews in Persia who had escaped a scheme to murder them en masse, as told in the book of Esther.

Divided into two sections—one Muslim and one Jewish—the Cave of the Patriarchs includes Isaac Hall, which is reserved for Muslims, and Jacob and Abraham Halls, used by Jews. On February 25, 1994, at 5:00 A.M., a group of some 750 Palestinian Muslims entered the complex to pray. Israeli security forces were supposed to be guarding the mosque, but that morning they were significantly understaffed. Shortly after the early-morning prayers commenced, a lone gunman, Baruch Goldstein, dressed in an Israeli Army uniform and carrying an assault rifle, got past the security detail and entered Isaac Hall. As he placed himself in front of the lone exit and immediately in back of the Muslim worshippers, he began firing randomly into the crowd. Pandemonium ensued, and before the gunfire stopped, 29 Palestinians had died, many of gunshot wounds but some trampled to death as the crowd tried to flee the hall. An additional 125 Palestinians were injured in the attack.

Goldstein, who was wrestled to the floor and then killed by his would-be victims, was an American-born Orthodox Jew who had immigrated to Israel in the mid-1980s. He was also a member of the radical Jewish Defense League and was a follower of Rabbi Meir David Kahane, an extremist American-born Jew who advocated open warfare against all Arabs and who vehemently opposed the Israeli-Palestinian peace process.

The Hebron Mosque massacre shocked Israelis and the world and cast dark shadows over the emergent Israeli-Palestinian peace process, which had gained momentum only during the previous year via the Oslo Accords. Not surprisingly, the event sparked protests in many Arab nations, with subsequent rioting claiming the lives of another 26 Palestinians as well as 9 Jews in the West Bank and other occupied territories. Protests in Jordan turned particularly violent, and a British tourist in Amman died at the hands of an unruly mob.

Immediately following the carnage, the Israeli government and all the mainstream political parties roundly condemned Goldstein and his deed. The Israelis offered compensation to the victims of the massacre and stepped up efforts to disarm and detain would-be Jewish terrorists. Polls in early March showed that the vast majority of Israelis denounced the killings and considered them nothing less than a cowardly act of terrorism.

Within weeks, Israeli prime minister Yitzhak Shamir convened a formal inquiry into the Hebron Mosque Massacre headed by Judge Meir Shagmar, then head of the Israeli Supreme Court. Shagmar's committee determined that Goldstein had acted alone and had not shared his plans with anyone else, that security forces had not appropriately interacted with other local officials or Israeli national forces such as the Israel Defense Forces (IDF), and that gunfire alone had caused the deaths. (Many Palestinians charged that grenades had been used as well.) Few Palestinians were assuaged by the findings of the committee, however, and the entire episode clearly showed the continued precariousness of the peace process.

See also: Goldstein, Baruch

Further Reading

Crown-Tamir, Hela. *How to Walk in the Footsteps of Jesus and the Prophets: A Scripture Reference Guide for Biblical Sites in Israel and Jordan.* Jerusalem: Gefen, 2000.
Friedman, Robert I. *The False Prophet: Rabbi Meir Kahane, from FBI Informant to Knesset Member.* Westport, CT: Lawrence Hill, 1990.

Paul G. Pierpaoli Jr.

HERRHAUSEN (ALFRED) ASSASSINATION

On November 30, 1989, the Wolfgang Beer Commando of the Rote Armee Fraktion (RAF or Red Army Faction) terrorist organization assassinated Alfred Herrhausen, chairman of the Deutsche Bank and personal advisor to the German chancellor Helmut Kohl. His killing was justified in a RAF communiqué on the grounds that as head of one of the largest banks in Europe, he was responsible not only for capitalism in Europe but also for third world exploitation. In addition, with the recent collapse of the Berlin Wall, Herrhausen was likely to play an increasingly critical role in the economic reintegration of the former East German state, which had provided support and sanctuary to the RAF, into a revitalized and unified Germany.

On the morning of November 30, Herrhausen left his Bad Homburg home in an armored chauffer-driven Mercedes 500 limousine, heading for his office in the Deutsche Bank tower in Frankfurt. Bodyguards in vehicles escorted his car, but rather than varying its timing or route, the convoy took its usual direction in its normal formation. Unknown to the protection team, a sophisticated seven-kilogram (15-pound) bomb had been planted around half a kilometer (0.3 miles) from Herrhausen's fortified house the previous night. The improvised explosive device (IED) was hidden in a satchel on a bicycle that had been strategically placed at a critical position by the side of the road. A command wire ran from the IED through a channel in the road to an initiator held by an RAF member in a nearby children's playground next to a local park.

When Herrhausen's convoy approached, the bomber initiated a carefully positioned infrared light, which sent a beam across the road and armed the IED. As the first vehicle broke the beam, a time delay ensured the device fired horizontally into the following vehicle containing Herrhausen. When the bomb detonated, a thin concave copper disk sitting on top of the IED turned into a projectile of molten copper, which was blasted across the road at thousands of yards per second. This slammed into Herrhausen's limousine, killing him immediately. The RAF assassin then crossed the park to a waiting vehicle and made off, leaving behind the group's trademark motif—a five-pointed star and MP5 submachine gun.

While the nature of the attack and its technical sophistication have led to various conspiracy theories, two days later the RAF issued a detailed communiqué claiming responsibility, and the German authorities named Horst Meyer and Christoph Seidler of the RAF as possible suspects. Nevertheless, it has been suggested that the assassination may have been assisted by former members of the East German Ministerium für Staatssicherheit (the Stasi) who were opposed to German reunification.

See also: Baader-Meinhof Gang; Rote Armee Fraktion (RAF)

Further Reading

Alexander, Yonah, and Dennis Pluchinsky. *Europe's Red Terrorists: The Fighting Communist Organizations.* London: Frank Cass, 1992.
Hollington, Kris. *How to Kill: The Definitive History of the Assassin.* London: Century, 2007.
Merkl, Peter. "West German Left Wing Terrorism." In Martha Crenshaw, ed., *Terrorism in Context.* University Park: Pennsylvania State University Press, 1995.
Peters, Butz. *Tödlicher Irrtum: Die Geschichte der RAF.* Frankfurt: Fischer Taschenbuch, 2007.

Richard Warnes

HEZB-E-ISLAMI-GULBUDDIN (HIG)

Hezb-e-Islami-Gulbuddin (HIG, or Gulbuddin's Party of Islam), named for its leader Gulbuddin Hekmatyar, is an Islamist political organization that operates in Afghanistan and Pakistan. Its main goals are to unite Afghanistan and restructure society based on a rigid interpretation of the Koran with Hekmatyar as the emir. Unsatisfied with the political strategy of Jamaat-e-Islami (JeI), a Pakistan-based radical party seeking to overthrow the Daoud Khan regime in Afghanistan, HIG was founded in 1977 under the name Hezb-e-Islami. Based on the Ikhwan model, it was structured in a cellular fashion, offered both ideological indoctrination and military training, and was characterized by secrecy. In 1979 Hezb-e-Islami split into two factions: Hezb-e-Islami Khalis (HIK) and HIG. The latter has since remained under the command of Hekmatyar, a Ghilzai Pashtun from Konduz Province and a ruthless leader who has shown no hesitation in using violence to advance his power and the goals of his movement.

HIG gained significant influence as a result of its active role in resisting the Soviet occupation of Afghanistan during the 1980s. The group benefited from the patronage of Saudi Arabia and the United States and received millions of dollars in financial backing channeled through Pakistan's Inter-Service Intelligence (ISI) Directorate. In 1984 Hekmatyar and the leaders of six other resistance groups formed an alliance known as the Peshawar Seven to drive the USSR out of Afghanistan—an endeavor they achieved five years later.

After Moscow's withdrawal and the collapse of Mohammad Najibullah Ahmadzai's puppet communist government, HIG was one of several competing factions that emerged during the civil war of the 1990s. Hekmatyar capriciously forged and broke alliances with other former mujahideen commanders in an attempt to seize power, which he was briefly able to do in 1993 and then again in 1996. HIG's enduring legacy from this period was the indiscriminate shelling of Kabul in April 1992, which caused enormous destruction to the capital city.

Following the Taliban's ascension and subsequent consolidation of power in 1996, the HIG effectively collapsed, with its members either joining Mullah Omar's movement or relocating to Pakistan. Hekmatyar himself fled to Iran, where he remained until he was expelled in 2002. Returning to the Afghan-Pakistan border region, he aligned himself with the Taliban and took up arms against American and allied NATO forces. In 2004 several ex-HIG commanders entered the new administration of Hamid Karzai (using their original nomenclature of Hezb-e-Islami), but Hekmatyar disavowed them and went into hiding in the southwest of the country. Four years later he resurfaced with a new band of HIG fighters that took credit for many bloody attacks against coalition and Afghan government troops. The reconfigured group was tied to an attempt on Karzai's life on April 27, 2008; the shooting down of at least two U.S. helicopters; and the bombing of a police station in Kabul that killed 10 people. Hekmatyar has said he will continue his campaign until all foreign forces leave Afghanistan.

HIG has not been listed on the U.S. State Department list of foreign terrorist organizations, although it has been designated as a "group of concern." The U.S. State Department and Treasury Department both declared Hekmatyar a "global terrorist" in 2003.

See also: Taliban

Further Reading

Coll, Steven. *Ghost Wars: The Secret History of the CIA, Afghanistan, and bin Laden, from the Soviet Invasion to September 10, 2001.* New York: Penguin, 2004.

Jones, Seth G. *In the Graveyard of Empires: America's War in Afghanistan.* New York: W. W. Norton, 2010.

Rashid, Ahmed. *Taliban: Militant Islam, Oil and Fundamentalism in Central Asia.* New Haven, CT: Yale University Press, 2010.

Roy, Olivier. *Afghanistan: From Holy War to Civil War.* Princeton, NJ: Darwin, 1995.

Tahir, Muhammad. "Gulbuddin Hekmatyar's Return to the Afghan Insurgency." *Jamestown Terrorism Monitor* 11, no. 6 (2008).

Michael McBride

HEZBOLLAH (PARTY OF GOD)

Hezbollah (the Party of God) is a Lebanese Shiite Islamic group with ideological and strategic ties to Iran. It officially came into being with the promulgation of its first manifesto, the 1985 "Open Letter." Today it acts simultaneously as a vast social services provider, a recognized political party with elected representation in the Lebanese National Assembly, an illegal armed militia, and a terrorist organization implicated in a variety of global criminal enterprises. The group's objectives upon its creation were to end the Israeli invasion of Lebanon, oppose any "imperial" occupation in that same country, and ultimately create a representative Lebanese government with a noted commitment to Shiite Islam. As a resistance movement conducting asymmetrical warfare against Israel, Hezbollah was one of the first Islamist organizations to employ tactical suicide attacks in the Middle East. The organization is listed, in whole or in part, as a terrorist organization by the United States, Israel, the United Kingdom, Australia, Canada, Bahrain, Egypt, and the Netherlands.

Hezbollah's foundations can be traced back to the early 1960s, when Lebanon and the entire Arab world were exposed to a revival of Islamism in the political and cultural scenes. The movement was largely a result of widespread disillusionment with the failure of Gamal Abdel Nasser's pan-Arabism to both create a unifying identity in the Middle East and defeat Israel. Greatly inspired by the teachings

Shiite Muslim members of Hezbollah beat their chests during a procession organized by the movement in the southern Lebanese town of Nabatiyeh on May 7, 1998. (AP/Wide World Photos)

of clerics such as Ayatollah Imam Musa al-Sadr and Ayatollah Sayyed Muhammad Hussein Fadlallah, as well as the 1979 Iranian Revolution, the group's founding members sought to create a united Islamic organization whose objectives would rest on three pillars: (1) Islam, to provide the structure and guiding principles for managing the intellectual, religious, ideological, and practical aspects of personal and public life; (2) resistance against Israel's occupation of Lebanon through jihad; and (3) the jurisdiction and the unquestionable authority of the Jurist-Theologian (Wilayat al-Faqih)—the successor of the Prophet and the imams—to guide the faithful toward a nation of Islam. These pillars resonated with Lebanese Shiites, many of whom felt excluded from and underrepresented in the country's Sunni-Maronite-dominated political system, despite having become the largest confessional group by the early 1980s.

Initially, Hezbollah's organizational apparatus served largely as an umbrella movement in which different Islamic and extremist cells acted independently or under Iranian supervision. As such the movement's leadership had little, if any, institutional control over the actions of regional commanders and international cells. However, since 1989, Hezbollah's structure has consolidated itself into a more centralized form of command. This shift was largely a result of the group's acceptance of the 1989 Ta'if Accords between the differing religious confessions in Lebanon and its own integration into Lebanese politics as a legitimate actor. In 1989 Hezbollah officially split into two structures: a political wing ruled by a 15-member Majlis Shura (Consultative Assembly) and a military al-Muqawama al Islamiyya (Islamic Resistance). It still boasts a large worldwide network of cells engaged in fundraising, media campaigning, and logistic planning but maintains a hierarchical centralized form of command that forbids these various cells from planning or executing operations independently.

Hezbollah's organizational structure derives from the religious leaders, the ulema, who represent the supreme authority from which all decisions derive to the community. The leader of Iran is the ultimate clerical authority that provides the Hezbollah leadership with guidance and directives in case of dissent. The decision-making bodies of Hezbollah are divided as such:

1 The Consultative Assembly, or Majlis Shura, composed of 12 clerical members who oversee Hezbollah's activity within Lebanon and all related tactical decisions. It also has responsibility for the functioning of seven subcommittees that tackle ideological, military, political, financial, judicial, and social matters within Hezbollah.
2 The Deciding Assembly, or Majlis al-Shura al-Karar, again composed of 12 clerical members (headed by Fadlallah) who take charge of all strategic decisions.

According to the Gulf Research Centre, Hezbollah's military force is estimated at approximately 1,000 full-time members and between 6,000 and 10,000 volunteers. Its military arsenal includes long-range and antitank guided missiles, as well as surface-to-air and antiship missiles.

As a political organization, by the latter half of 2011 Hezbollah held 12 of the 128 seats in the Lebanese parliament and 2 of the 30 seats in the cabinet. As a social services organization, it runs a number of construction companies, a minimum of four hospitals, 12 clinics, 12 schools, and three agricultural centers. Militarily, it has evolved from the use of terrorist tactics in the 1980s to highly professional guerrilla warfare tactics, as was demonstrated in its confrontation against the Israel Defense Forces (IDF) in 2006.

Hezbollah relies on a number of sources for financing, among which Iran is one of the more substantial. It is estimated that the group receives roughly $100 million every year from Tehran, although some sources have placed the figure as high as $200 million. In addition to financial assistance, Iran helped with the early development of Hezbollah by dispatching a contingent of the Iranian Revolutionary Guard (al Quds) to the Lebanese Bekaa Valley to set up and run training camps for the organization.

Hezbollah also receives significant financial support from expatriates living in the United States, Latin America, and African countries with large wealthy Lebanese Shiite communities. These funds are transferred directly to the group, sent via front charity organizations, or smuggled into the country by human couriers.

Hezbollah has also been known to link itself to various global criminal enterprises, including drug trafficking, "blood" diamond smuggling, and fraud networks. Although the group engages in these pursuits in the Americas, Africa, and the Middle East, it is the Tri-border Area of South America that has been the most important to Hezbollah, providing it with an annual income thought to be in the range of $10 million. The group has also profited financially and operationally from the growth of and trade in hashish (poppy crop) in the Lebanese Bekaa Valley itself.

Domestically, Hezbollah has undergone a series of metamorphoses in its identity, which is largely a function of the changing political and security conditions in Lebanon. In its development from its foundations within the Islamic movement of social and political protest (1978–1985), to a social movement (1985–1991), to a parliamentary political party (1992–present), the group has expanded its framework beyond a purely military wing dedicated to resisting the Israeli presence to a broader movement aimed at supporting the Lebanese Shiite community through the provision of health care, social services, educational services, and monetary and communal assistance. Stepping up in areas traditionally neglected by the Lebanese government, such as South Lebanon and the Bekaa Valley, Hezbollah has made use of its social leverage to transition into the political sphere as a representative of the Shiite community. In May 2008, Hezbollah for the first time managed to obtain sufficient votes to secure veto power in the Lebanese cabinet, thus greatly enhancing its political role.

Internationally, Hezbollah has so far successfully walked the fine line between preserving its Islamic identity and recognizing and working within the confines of the Lebanese state. The organization maintains its strategic ideological alliance with Iran and continues to enjoy a political partnership with Syria. With regards to the relationship with Tehran, Hezbollah initially served as a proxy organization, with the Majlis al-Shura deferring to the Ayatollah as its supreme clerical authority on all matters of contention, and Hezbollah's military wing training directly under the Iranian Revolutionary Guard. The relationship seems to have taken a step down over the years toward more of a partnership as Hezbollah has sought to further integrate itself into Lebanese politics and adapt its ideology within a more nationalistic sphere.

The United States has placed Hezbollah on its list of foreign terrorist organizations. A 2003 U.S. court decision ruled that the Islamic Jihad Organization (IJO) and Hezbollah were one and the same. The IJO is a terrorist organization that was responsible for a number of suicide attacks in Lebanon and Europe, including bombings in Beirut, Lebanon, that targeted the U.S. embassy and the American Marines (and French Paratrooper) military barracks in 1983. The latter attacks were especially destructive and have only been superseded by Al Qaeda's strike on September 11, 2001, in terms of American casualties. However, given the organizational structure of Hezbollah at the time, it remains unclear just how much involvement and operational control the group's leadership had over the attacks. It has been argued that at the time, the group's external security organization operated independently of the party and reported directly to Iranian intelligence. The 2011 Hezbollah Anti-Terrorism Act was passed in the U.S. Congress, ensuring that no American aid to Lebanon reach Hezbollah. Hezbollah does not figure on the European Union's terrorist list.

In July 2006, a confrontation between Hezbollah members and an Israeli border patrol, and the subsequent abduction of two members of the IDF, prompted Israeli air strikes and artillery fire against Lebanese infrastructure. This incident triggered a 33-day war between Israel and Hezbollah that in many ways saw the latter emerge as the victor. The conflict was a testimony to Hezbollah's guerrilla warfare capabilities and considerable military arsenal.

In 2008 an attempt by the Lebanese government to shut down Hezbollah's telecommunications network and remove Beirut International Airport's chief of security, Wafic Shkeir, because of his alleged ties to Hezbollah spurred fighting in Beirut on May 7. Hezbollah fighters took over a number of neighborhoods in the west of the city of Beirut, which they then handed over to the Lebanese Army. The conflict ended with the signing of the May 21 agreement between rival government factions, ending what had become an 18-month political feud between government and opposition forces.

In 2009 the United Nations Special Tribunal for Lebanon, investigating the assassination of former prime minister and multimillionaire Sunni tycoon Rafiq Hariri in 2005, reportedly uncovered evidence potentially linking Hezbollah to the murder. To date, Hezbollah vehemently denies any involvement in the incident, with Hassan Nasrallah maintaining that he and the former prime minister were in the process of overcoming ideological differences and were moving to draft a unifying vision for Lebanon in an unprecedented Sunni-Shiite exchange prior to Hariri's death. According to Hezbollah, the two leaders frequently met at Nasrallah's headquarters in the southern suburbs of Beirut for late-night chats, the last of which occurred a mere two days before the explosion. Despite Hezbollah's protestations, the special tribunal investigating Hariri's death issued a warrant for the arrest of four senior Hezbollah members on June 30, 2011. Those named were

Mustafa Badr el-Din, Salim al-Ayyash, Assad Sabra, and Hassan Unaisi. Nasrallah has stated that these individuals will not be arrested under any circumstances.

See also: Jewish Community Center (Buenos Aires) Bombing

Further Reading

Alagha, Joseph. *Hezbollah's Documents: From the 1985 Open Letter to the 2009 Manifesto.* Amsterdam: Pallas, 2001.

Blanford, Nicholas. *Killing Mr. Lebanon: The Assassination of Rafik Hariri and Its Impact on the Middle East.* New York: I. B. Tauris, 2006.

Hamzeh, Ahmed Nizar. *In the Path of Hezbollah: Modern Intellectual and Political History in the Middle East.* Syracuse, NY: Syracuse University Press, 2004.

Jackson, Michael. *Hezbollah: Organizational Development, Ideological Evolution, and a Relevant Threat Model.* Washington, DC: Georgetown University Press, 2009.

Levitt, Matthew. "Hezbollah Finances: Funding the Party of God." In Jeanne Giraldo and Harold Trinkunas, eds., *Terrorism Financing and State Responses: A Comparative Perspective.* Stanford, CA: Stanford University Press, 2007.

Norton, Augustus Richard. *Hezbollah: A Short History.* Princeton,. NJ: Princeton University Press, 2007.

Qassem, Naim. *Hezbollah.* London: SAQI, 2005.

Taylor, Paul. "Latin American Security Challenges: A Collaborative Inquiry from North and South." Newport Paper, no. 21. Newport, RI: Navy War College, 2004.

Yara Zogheib

HILTON HOTEL (LONDON) BOMBING

On September 5, 1975, an improvised explosive device (IED) detonated in the crowded lobby of the London Hilton Hotel in Park Lane. The device destroyed the front entrance, killing a man and a woman, and injuring 63 others—7 of them seriously. There were about 100 people in the lobby at the time of the blast. A coded warning of the impending attack was received by the Associated Newspaper Group, Ltd., owners of the *Daily Mail* and the *Evening News.*

One eyewitness who was making a telephone call at the time of the bombing said he did not know what was happening because his back was toward the blast and the sound was muffled. Initially, he thought something was wrong with the phone. When he turned around he saw a small fire in the middle of the lobby, strewn debris, and bodies on the floor.

Guests at the 28-story Hilton property were asked to stay in their rooms, while customers were evacuated from the lobby and coffee shop. The hotel was fully reopened an hour after the explosion, although nearby streets in the West End remained closed.

Some witnesses said the police arrived only five minutes before the blast. However, the duty manager, George Ashou, contradicted these statements, saying the device detonated a full 40 minutes after detectives and members of the bomb squad had commenced their search. He went on to explain that staff and guests had not been evacuated because warnings of the kind phoned in to the Associated Newspaper Group were common, and many turned out to be hoaxes.

The Provisional Irish Republican Army (PIRA) took responsibility for the attack, which was the first in Britain since the Birmingham pub bombings 10 months previously. The incident was to mark the start of a renewed terrorist campaign on the mainland.

The Hilton had been the target of a previous attack in December 1973 when two small incendiary devices in cigarette packets went off, one in a side entrance to the hotel, the other in the trunk of a car nearby. Only minor damage was caused.

A violent PIRA unit that became known as the Balcombe Street Gang was operating in and around London during this period. It carried out at least 50 bombings and shootings between 1974 and 1975. The group was believed to have been responsible for at least 15 deaths and numerous injuries. The members of the gang were tried and convicted for the murders of two policemen and sentenced to life. They were later released on April 9, 1999, as part of the Good Friday Agreement.

See also: Birmingham Pub Bombings; Good Friday Agreement; Provisional Irish Republican Army (PIRA)

Further Reading

McKittrick, David, and David McVea. *Making Sense of the Troubles.* London: Penguin Books, 2000.
Oppenheimer, A. R. *IRA: The Bombs and the Bullets: A History of Deadly Ingenuity.* Foreword by Richard English. Dublin: Irish Academic Press, 2009.
Smith, M.L.R. *Fighting for Ireland? The Military Strategy of the Irish Republican Movement.* London: Routledge, 1995.

Donna Bassett

HILTON HOTEL (SYDNEY) BOMBING

On February 13, 1978, a bomb exploded in a garbage bin outside the Hilton Hotel in Sydney, Australia. The building was the site of a meeting of Asia Pacific leaders of the Commonwealth group of nations. The blast killed 3 people and wounded 11 others in what is commonly regarded as Australia's first domestic act of terrorism since World War II.

The device detonated early in the morning, killing two workers who had just picked up the trash can and were loading it into their garbage truck. A policeman on duty outside the hotel also died in the blast. All the injured were law enforcement officers on duty to guard the visiting officials.

No one claimed responsibility, although Indian prime minister Morarji Desai blamed the attack on Ananda Marga Pracaraka Samgha (AMS, or Path of Bliss), an Indian religious cult whose members had been demonstrating outside the hotel. The group arrived in Australia in 1973 and began attracting acolytes by the hundreds. It had been under close scrutiny for several years.

In June 1978, three adherents of the AMPS cult were charged with conspiracy to murder in an incident unrelated to the Hilton bombing. Although they were all pardoned by a judicial inquiry in 1985, one of the trio, Tim Anderson (who acted as the group's purported national spokesman), was rearrested on May 1989 in connection with the Hilton bombing. Immediately following his detention, an ex-AMPS member, Evan Pederick, confessed to the attack and alleged Anderson was the main planner.

During his trial Pederick claimed to have placed 20 sticks of gelignite in the bin outside the Hilton. He was found guilty in September 1989 and sentenced to 20 years in prison. Pederick later testified in the hearing against Anderson, and his evidence was largely responsible for the latter's conviction in October 1990, which resulted in a 14-year jail term. Anderson's sentence was overturned on appeal the following year, and he was released. After eight years behind bars Pederick was also freed in November 1997. There continues to be considerable doubt as to whether he really was the Hilton bomber.

Conspiracists allege that someone in authority knew about the bomb in advance but decided it would be politically expedient to allow security to discover it on-site. According to this account, the device was never discovered and exploded before it could be recovered. The theory remains unproven, as does the true identity of the perpetrator.

The AMPS was ostensibly founded as a yoga society in Bhar, India, in 1955. The group's leader, Shrii Prabhat Ranjan Sarkar, was imprisoned in 1971 for conspiracy to murder (the sentence was overturned seven years later), and the movement itself was banned between 1975 and 1977. In 1978 three AMPS members were convicted of stabbing an Indian government employee and plotting to assassinate the Indian high commissioner in London.

Although the Supreme Court of India affirmed the legal status of AMPS in 1996, the movement was subsequently tied to the 1995 Purulia arms drop case. This incident involved a British mercenary and was purportedly linked to a plot designed to implicate left-wing rebels in illegal weapons consignments in order to justify the imposition of presidential rule in West Bengal. These allegations remain unproven.

Further Reading

Government of New South Wales (NSW), Australia. "Parliament Hansard: Hilton Bombing Inquiry Proposal." Sydney, NSW: March 16, 2008. http://www.parliament.nsw.gov.au/prod/parlment/hansart.nsf/V3Key/LA19950921010, accessed May 20, 2011.

Hills, Ben. "The Hilton Fiasco." *Sydney Morning Herald* (Australia), February 12, 1998. http://www.benhills.com/articles/articles/SCM38a.html, accessed May 2, 2011.

"Hilton Bombing." Australian Broadcasting Corporation (ABC), September 20, 2004. http://www.abc.net.au/gnt/history/Transcripts/s1202891.htm, accessed May 2, 2011.

Hudson, Phillip. "Hilton Bombing Sets Off Battle of Tactics." *Sydney Morning Herald* (Australia), January 1, 2009. http://www.smh.com.au/news/national/hilton-bombing-sets-off-battle-of-tactics/2008/12/31/1230681578363.html, accessed May 2, 2011.

Donna Bassett

HIPERCOR SUPERMARKET BOMBING

The 1987 bombing of the Hipercor Shopping Center Supermarket was not only the deadliest attack in the history of the Basque terrorist organization Euskadi Ta

Askatasuna (ETA, or Basque Fatherland and Freedom) but also one of its most indiscriminate. The attack left several civilians dead, including children, and generated widespread condemnation of ETA in Spain.

A three-man terrorist cell working under the orders of a senior ETA leader, Santiago Arrospide Sarasola, carried out the Hipercor bombing. The trio, Rafael Caride Simon, Domingo Troitino, and Josefa Ernaga, settled on the venue, which was located on Avenue Meridiana in Barcelona, mainly because the underground parking lot was exposed and devoid of any concerted security measures. The team concluded that the best method of attack would be an improvised explosive device (IED) left in a vehicle and timed to explode during the busy Friday afternoon shopping hours. The group used a stolen Ford Sierra, which was packed ammonium nitrate, TNT, aluminum powder, and gasoline mixed with glue and soap flakes to create a large napalm-type blast incendiary.

On Friday June 19, 1987, the ETA cell drove the vehicle to the shopping center and left it in the subterranean car park. At approximately 4:10 P.M. a timer device detonated the IED, which exploded just as shoppers were completing their purchases prior to the weekend. The bomb blew a hole through the ground floor of the center, sparking a major toxic fire. The blast and ensuing conflagration killed 21 people, injuring over 30. ETA acknowledged responsibility for the attack, claiming that sufficient notice of the bombing had been given to clear the shopping complex. The police, however, quickly rejected this, arguing the warning had arrived too late to allow them time to respond and evacuate the building.

Following the incident, there was almost universal condemnation, and an estimated 750,000 people marched through Barcelona in protest. More significant, many traditional supporters of Basque separatism turned their back on ETA, denouncing the indiscriminate killing of women and children out shopping.

It did not take the Spanish authorities long to identify the perpetrators and in September 1987 Ernaga and Troitino were arrested. Following a trial in October 1989 both were sentenced to life in prison. Six years later Simon was detained in France, which was and still is used as an ETA safe haven. He was subsequently extradited to Spain and charged along with Sarasola for the Hipercor bombing. Both received life sentences.

See also: Euskadi Ta Askatasuna (ETA)

Further Reading

Alexander, Yonah, Michael Swetnam, Herbert Levine. *ETA: Profile of a Terrorist Group.* Ardsley, NY: Transnational, 2001.
Elorza, Antonio, ed. *La Historia de ETA.* Madrid: Temas de Hoy, 2000.
San Sebastian, Isabel. *Los Años de Plomo: Memoria en Carne Viva de las Victimas.* Madrid: Temas de Hoy, 2003.
Woodworth, Paddy. *Dirty War Clean Hands: ETA, the GAL and Spanish Democracy.* New Haven, CT: Yale Nota Bene, 2002.

Richard Warnes

HOLSWORTHY BARRACKS BOMB PLOT

On August 4, 2009, Australian authorities reported that they had thwarted a plot to attack an army barracks in Sydney. According to the statement, over 400 law enforcement and security officers had raided 19 properties and made four arrests. The operation was the climax of seven months of surveillance. According to Australian Federal Police (AFP) Commissioner Tony Negus, those arrested had been planning to stage a suicide attack on a defense establishment within the country and were heavily armed with automatic assault weapons.

The five men, all Australian citizens of Somali or Lebanese descent, were identified as Wissam Fattal, Saney Aweys, Nayef El Sayed, Yacqub Khayre, and Abdirahman Ahmed. They were between 22 and 26 years of age and were members of the Preston Mosque in the northern suburbs of Melbourne but had recently been attending the 8 Blacks prayer hall. The quartet were accused of plotting to carry out a violent attack in Australia and with having ties to Al Qaeda and al-Shabaab.

Just over a year later, the Victorian Supreme Court began hearing the case, which by this time had expanded to include a fifth man, Abdirahman Ahmed. During the proceedings, prosecutors played several recorded messages that the police had intercepted and that specifically discussed Holsworthy Barracks as an attractive target due to its relative lax base security. Closed-circuit television recordings were also presented showing at least one of the alleged plotters in the vicinity of the military compound.

Commissioner Negus testified that "the men's intention was to actually go into the army barracks and to kill as many soldiers as they could until they themselves were killed." Federal prosecutor Nicholas Robinson claimed that the accused were angry because there were Australian troops in Iraq and Afghanistan. Events in Chechnya were also a subject of concern.

After a seven-month trial, three of the five were eventually found guilty of plotting a shooting rampage at the Holsworthy Army Base in Sydney. The jury found that the men planned the attack as payback for Australia's participation in the Iraq and Afghan wars and as revenge for the jailing of other Muslim men on terrorism-related charges. Their two co-accused were acquitted of the same offense.

Authorities responded to the alleged plot by ordering a review of security at all military bases and the preparation of a national security white paper, for release by 2009. The government also listed al-Shabaab as a terrorist organization. Prior to this incident, the group had done nothing domestically to warrant this formal designation.

Australia has traditionally experienced little serious domestic terrorism. The most serious incident in modern times was the bombing of the Sydney Hilton Hotel in 1978, which killed three people. However, there have been a number of serious incidents outside the country, including, notably, the 2002 Bali bombings and the suicide strike against the Australian embassy in Jakarta (2004). Jemaah Islamiyah (JI), an Indonesian-based organization with purported ties to Al Qaeda, carried out both attacks as part of its self-defined agenda to create a pan-regional Islamic caliphate across Southeast Asia.

See also: Australian Embassy (Jakarta) Bombing; Bali Bombings (2002); Hilton Hotel (Sydney) Bombing; Jemaah Islamiyah (JI)

Further Reading

"Al Qaeda in Yemen and Somalia: A Ticking Time Bomb: A Report to the Committee on Foreign Relations United States." 111th Congress, 2nd Session, January 21, 2010. Committee on Foreign Relations. http://www.gpoaccess.gov/congress/index.html; http://foreign.senate.gov/imo/media/doc/Yemen.pdf, accessed February 20, 2012.

Colvin, Mark. "Three Found Guilty of Holsworthy Terror Plot." *ABC News,* December 23, 2010. Available online at http://www.hiiraan.com/news2/2010/dec/three_found_guilty_of_holsworthy_terror_plot.aspx, accessed July 23, 2011.

Heller, Claude. "Letter Dated 10 March 2010 from the Chairman of the Security Council Committee Pursuant to Resolutions 751 (1992) and 1907 (2009) concerning Somalia and Eritrea Addressed to the President of the Security Council." United Nations Security Council. 10-24689 (E) 110310, S/2010/91, page 32, item 104.

Lauder, Simon. "Base Attack Plotters 'Wanted Maximum Body Count.'" *ABC News,* September 13, 2010. http://www.abc.net.au/news/2010-09-13/base-attack-plotters-wanted-maximum-body-count/2257942, accessed July 23, 2011.

Schanzer, Jonathan. *Al-Qaeda's Armies: Middle East Affiliate Groups and the Next Generation of Terror.* Foreword by Dennis Ross. Washington, D.C.: Washington Institute for Near East Policy, 2005.

Donna Bassett

INDIAN EMBASSY (KABUL) BOMBING

On July 7, 2008, a suicide car bomb exploded at the entrance of the Indian embassy in Kabul, killing 58 people and injuring another 141. The attack took place at the height of the morning rush hour. Among the dead were an Indian defense attaché, a political information officer, two Indian security officials, and nine police officers.

The car used in the bombing, an explosives-packed Toyota Camry, was rammed into two Indian diplomatic vehicles entering the embassy and detonated at approximately 8:30 A.M. on a busy street outside the diplomatic mission where people usually line up to apply for visas. The *Times of India* later reported that the suicide operative was Hamza Shakoor, 22, of the Gujranwala district in Pakistan.

India had been raising the issue of security for its law enforcement and diplomatic staff in Afghanistan for months. The government's consulate in Jalalabad had already been attacked twice by hand grenades in 2007, while a Taliban ambush on the Indo-Tibetan Border Police (ITBP) a month prior to the embassy bombing left one officer dead and four others injured. In the aftermath of the second incident, Delhi's Home Ministry issued a warning to the ITBP (an elite force that had been deployed to Afghanistan to protect Indian nationals and projects) to take necessary precautionary measures and remain on guard against possible suicide attacks; it also noted that the security provided by the Afghan police was not up to the mark.

On August 1, 2008, just a month after the bombing, U.S. authorities leaked to the *New York Times* that Islamabad's InterServices Intelligence (ISI) Directorate planned and coordinated the attack. Their conclusions were based on intercepted communications between Pakistani intelligence officials and the perpetrators before the attack as well as statements from an ISI officer inside Afghanistan. That same day, the *Washington Post* reported that American security agencies had reason to believe the ISI had provided logistic assistance to the bombers, who were in turn linked to Jalaluddin Haqqani, a Pashtun and pro-Taliban insurgent leader.

The news stories were consistent with revelations that Central Intelligence Agency (CIA) deputy director Stephen R. Kappes had visited Islamabad just before the attack. The reason for his trip was to present senior Pakistani officials with information that members of the ISI were actively supporting militant Islamist groups and that this was both known and sanctioned by their superiors.

Following the bombing, questions were raised about Pakistan's reliability as an ally in the U.S.-led war on terror. President George W. Bush confronted Pakistani prime minister Yousuf Raza Gilani in Washington, D.C., with evidence that the ISI

Afghan policemen stand guard at the site of a suicide attack in Kabul, Afghanistan, on Monday, July 7, 2008. A suicide car bomb exploded near the Indian Embassy in central Kabul, killing 58 people and wounding 141. (AP/Wide World Photos)

had at least known about, if not been directly involved in, the attack and that serious action would be taken if another bombing occurred.

The embassy bombing occurred in the context of a rapidly strengthening Indo-Afghan partnership post-2001. During Operation Enduring Freedom (OEF), Delhi had offered intelligence and other logistic support to Allied forces to help overthrow the Taliban. In 2002 India established diplomatic relations with the newly elected government in Kabul and provided aid and workers to help with the country's reconstruction efforts. By 2007 India had pledged $850 million in development assistance and support, the largest amount from any country without a military presence in Afghanistan.

Bilateral ties further strengthened in the wake of Afghanistan's deteriorating relationship with Pakistan over charges that the government was not only harboring militants in the Federally Administered Tribal Areas (FATA), including the Taliban, but also doing nothing to halt cross-border jihadi infiltration. India was keen to capitalize on this to gain influence in Central Asia as well as to keep a check on Kashmiri militants that it alleged were operating in Afghanistan.

This has caused growing consternation in Pakistan, which has been equally keen to exert its own presence in Afghanistan to gain strategic depth and offset India's economic, military, and demographic superiority—all of which are viewed as a direct threat to the country's national security. Moreover, Delhi's penetration into Afghanistan has upset pro-Taliban elements, many of which are suspected of acting as ISI proxies. According to one editorial in the London *Times,* with the

United States and other NATO members increasingly unwilling to sustain long-term commitments to Afghanistan, the Taliban see India as the only regional enemy capable of resisting them.

Further Reading

"Bomb Rocks Indian Embassy in Kabul." *BBC News,* July 7, 2008. http://news.bbc.co.uk/2/hi/7492601.stm, accessed May 15, 2011.
"Indian Embassy Bomb Kills 41 in Kabul." *The Telegraph* (UK), July 7, 2008. http://www.telegraph.co.uk/news/worldnews/asia/afghanistan/2261882/Indian-embassy-bomb-kills-41-in-Kabul.html, accessed May 15, 2011.
Miller, Frederic. *2008 Indian Embassy Bombing in Kabul.* Mauritius: Vdm, 2010.

Donna Bassett

INDIAN MUJAHIDEEN (IM)

The Indian Mujahideen (IM) is an indigenous terror group that spearheads India's jihadist movement. The organization has to date claimed responsibility for at least nine terror strikes in the country, targeting major cities such as New Delhi, Bangalore, Ahmedabad, Jaipur, and Varanasi. The exact moment of IM's inception remains unknown, but its founding members possibly met as early as 2001. It was then that the Students Islamic Movement of India (SIMI)—the student wing of the Jamaat-e-Islami Hind (JIH)—held its last public convention and called on its adherents to engage in jihad. From IM cadre confessions, however, it is now clear that SIMI was not the group's mother organization, merely a place for activists to gather.

The IM announced its formal emergence to the world on November 23, 2007, with simultaneous bombings in three cities (Varanasi, Faizabad, Lucknow) across the state of Uttar Pradesh. In May 2008 it struck the western tourist city of Jaipur, detonating nine improvised explosive devices that killed over 60 people. In July of that same year, IM commenced what came to be coined Operation B-A-D, which involved attacks in Bangalore, Ahmedabad, and (New) Delhi over a two-month period; the most serious of these incidents was the strike in Ahmedabad, which involved a series of more than 16 synchronized bombings across the city. Indian intelligence agencies also believe IM helped Lashkar-e-Taiba (LeT) conduct the November 2008 Mumbai assault that left 170 people dead. By now the group had demonstrated that it was a formidable force to be reckoned with.

Before each of its strikes, the IM sends out e-mails to media organizations declaring its intentions. Authorities who have examined these electronic messages remain undecided as to whether the group's sole aim is to establish a theocratic caliphate in India. Many of the e-mails slam Delhi and state governments for failing to protect the rights of the country's Muslim minority and regularly criticize the practices and anti-Islamic discrimination that Hindutva (an ideology of chauvinistic Hinduism) groups are accused of engaging in. Prominent events such as the Babri Masjid demolition of 1992, the Mumbai riots of 1993, and the Gujarat pogroms of 2002 are also widely quoted, and calls are made for Muslims to rise up and target "evil" politicians and "wicked" police officials. At times the e-mails use abusive language that analysts claim mirrors that employed by the mafia.

What makes the IM a particularly intimidating concern for the security forces is that all its members are Indian. For a long time Delhi's domestic and foreign intelligence services denied that the group existed as an indigenous entity and stressed that its members worked in tandem with Pakistani and Bangladeshi terrorist outfits under the direction of Islamabad's Inter-Services Intelligence Directorate. However, this supposed international dimension has been contradicted by statements from captured IM militants, who deny ties to foreign groups and position their movement as a fully homegrown terrorist outfit.

The IM's leadership has been traced to Abdul Subhan Qureshi, a former Mumbai resident and the group's suspected chief bomb maker. He is thought to oversee a core nucleus of six senior commanders, all of whom are reported to have fled to Pakistan or Bangladesh after the Delhi serial blasts in 2008. Mumbai's Crime Branch has identified these individuals as Amir Reza Khan, Riyaz Shahbhandar, and Iqbal Shahbhandari (nicknamed the Bhatkal brothers as they hail from the town of Bhatkal in the southern state of Karnataka), Muhammad Khalid, Shahzad Ahmed, and Ariz Khan. Amir Reza Khan is also wanted by Interpol for his role in the attack on the U.S. cultural center in Kolkata (2002).

On an operational, tactical level IM is divided into four "brigades":

1 Shahabuddin Ghouri Brigade: Responsible for the planning and execution of attacks in southern India, headquartered in Kerala
2 Muhammad Ghaznavi Brigade: Responsible for the planning and execution of terror strikes in northern India
3 Shaheed-al-Zarqawi Brigade: Responsible for the targeting of political and other important personalities of the country as well as organizing suicide attacks
4 Media Wing: Headquartered in Pune, Maharashtra; most of its members were arrested after the New Delhi blasts in 2008

The majority of IM cadres belong to the more prosperous lower- and middle-class families of India. Only an exceptionally small number are madrassa educated or versed in the Quran. Many are well-educated youth employed in the private sector. Arrested IM terrorists have included, for instance, information technology professionals, engineers, and dentists. One of those implicated in the Ahmedabad and New Delhi bombings, Mohammed Mansoor Asgar Peerbhoy (also known as Munawar or Mannu), was the head of IM's media wing and worked at Yahoo! where he earned an annual salary of US$45,000. The group's recruiting pool is thus extremely diverse, extending well beyond the economically deprived to sections of the Indian Muslim youth who feel mistreated or marginalized by their Hindu counterparts. The arrest of IM cadres from various locations across the nation has also demonstrated the spread of its terror network—although a crackdown on the group's activities post-2008 does appear to have weakened its influence in certain parts of the country.

The Indian government formally banned IM on June 4, 2010. The United States followed suit in September 2011, adding the group to its list of foreign terrorist organizations. This designation allows Washington to freeze its assets and prevents individuals from supporting its activities.

See also: Ahmedabad Bombings; Jaipur Bombings; New Delhi (2008) Bombings; Mumbai Attacks (2008); Students Islamic Movement of India (SIMI)

Further Reading

Fair, Christine C. *Students Islamic Movement of India and the Indian Mujahideen: An Assessment.* Seattle, WA: National Bureau of Asian Research, January 2010.

"Indian Mujahideen Declared a Terrorist Outfit." *Decaan Herald,* June 4, 2010. http://www.deccanherald.com/content/73373/indian-mujahideen-declared-terrorist-outfit.html, accessed February 15, 2012.

Kumar, Hari, and Alan Cowell. "At Least 64 Die in Bombings in a Northeastern Indian State." *New York Times,* October 31, 2008.

Nanjappa, Vicky. "Revealed: Indian Mujahideen's Two Pronged Terror Strategy." *Rediff.com,* July 29, 2008. http://www.rediff.com/news/2008/jul/29ahd4.htm, accessed February 15, 2012.

Sen, Sudhi. "What Is the Indian Mujahideen?" *NDTV,* July 27, 2008. http://www.ndtv.com/convergence/ndtv/mumbaiterrorstrike/Story.aspx?ID=NEWEN20080058894&type=News, accessed February 15, 2012.

Siddique, Haroon, and Barry Neild. "Mumbai Blasts." *The Guardian* (UK), July 13, 2011.

"US Places Indian Mujahideen on Terror List." *International Herald Tribune,* September 15, 2011.

Sumitha Narayanan Kutty

INDIAN NATIONAL PARLIAMENT ATTACK

An ordinary day of business in the Indian Parliament turned into a bloody nightmare on December 13, 2001, when five men stormed into the complex and opened fire on unsuspecting lawmakers and journalists gathered at the building's main entrance. Hundreds of individuals were in the Parliament at the time of the attack, and the terrorists had intended to target all those present but failed to do so. All five intruders were gunned down, but nine security personnel and a journalist were also killed. Investigators later determined that the perpetrators were linked to two Pakistan-based terrorist groups, Lashkar-e-Taiba (LeT) and Jaish-e-Mohammed (JeM).

Maulana Masood Azhar and Hafiz Saeed, the respective leaders of JeM and LeT, masterminded the operation, allegedly on orders from Islamabad's Inter-Services Intelligence (ISI) Directorate. Responsibility for executing the attack fell to Ghazi Baba, who worked closely with a Kashmiri, Mohammad Afzal Guru, to procure arms, explosives, and a laptop computer. It appears that initially Baba kept his options open as to possible venues to target, considering both the UK and U.S. embassies as well as the New Delhi International Airport. However, after conducting thorough surveillance on all these sites, he eventually settled on the Parliament.

On December 13, 2001, the five terrorists drove a white Ambassador car to the complex. Baba had instructed Guru to monitor television stations and keep them abreast of the status of proceedings inside the building; however, he was unable to do so as there was no electricity at the hideout in Delhi. Baba's team initiated the operation without waiting for information from Guru, apparently unaware that the session had adjourned. While the terrorists attempted to park near Gate 11 of the parliament, they hit the main car of the vice president's motorcade. In the commotion that ensued, the gunmen got out of their vehicle and began firing indiscriminately while running toward the building. The security forces, once alerted, retaliated, and the siege was over in about half an hour. Baba and his colleagues were all killed; no parliamentarian was injured during the standoff.

Authorities subsequently arrested four men in connection with the attack. Two were acquitted in August 2005 for lack of evidence. The remaining two were Guru and his cousin, Shaukat Hussain. The latter, who had helped to supply Baba's team with food and provisions, received a reduced prison term. However, Guru was found guilty of conspiracy and sentenced to death, which sparked widespread protests, especially in the state of Jammu and Kashmir. In his confession Guru confirmed the operation's genesis in Pakistan and asserted that Baba and his team had used cell phones to stay in touch with their ISI handlers—located across the border—through the whole duration of the attack. He also claimed he was the principal point person between JeM and the five terrorists and admitted to having received weapons training from members of the Jammu and Kashmir National Liberation Front in 1990.

The biggest fallout from the Parliament attack was that it brought the rival nations India and Pakistan to the brink of war. Even as investigations into the incident proceeded, diplomatic niceties between Delhi and Islamabad were all but abandoned. Addressing the Parliament a week after the attack, Indian prime minister Atal Bihari Vajpayee asserted that his government was "keeping all its options open" in the fight against terrorism and its sponsors. Delhi subsequently expelled all Pakistani diplomats from the country, recalled military personnel on leave, and deployed hundreds of thousands of troops along the 1,800-mile border (Operation Parakram). Islamabad responded in kind and began preparations to mobilize and reposition its own troops.

With the nuclear-armed neighbors on the verge of a military confrontation, the international community—specifically, the United States—stepped in to defuse the situation. The Bush administration embarked on a frantic diplomatic effort to soothe tensions, urging India to exercise restraint and pressuring Pakistan to forcibly crack down on the two terrorist outfits responsible for the assault. The lobbying worked. President Pervez Musharraf arrested the leaders of JeM and LeT, shut their offices, and froze their bank accounts (although both Saeed and Azhar were only placed under house arrest and their respective organizations would later resume operations under different names). In return, Vajpayee began to demobilize troops along the border and after 10 months formally suspended Operation Parakram.

See also: Jaish-e-Mohammed (JeM); Jammu and Kashmir National Liberation Front (JKNLF); Lashkar-e-Taiba (LeT)

Further Reading

Mukherji, Niarmalangshu. *Terror over Democracy.* New Delhi: Promilla, 2005.

Parasuram, T.V. "US Declares Lashkar, Jaish as Terrorist Outfits." *Rediff News,* December 27, 2001. http://in.rediff.com/news/2001/dec/26parl1.htm.

"Parliament Attack: 10 Years On." *Wall Street Journal,* December 13, 2011. http://online.wsj.com/article/SB10001424052970203518404577095821784640002.html#slide/1, accessed February 16, 2012.

"Parliament Attack Suspect Indicts Pakistan on Television." *Rediff News,* December 20, 2001. http://in.rediff.com/news/2001/dec/20parl10.htm, accessed February 14, 2012.

Sahay, Tarah Shankar. "India, Pakistan Dangerously Close to the Brink." *Rediff News,* December 20, 2001. http://in.rediff.com/news/2001/dec/20parl.htm, accessed February 14, 2012.

Schaffer, Michael, and Thomas Omestad. "India and Pakistan Become the Powder Keg Next Door." *U.S. News & World Report,* January 14, 2002.

Tkacik, John. "Kashmir: A 50 Year Controversy—Threat of War." *The World & I,* May 2002. Available online at http://www.highbeam.com/doc/1G1-86396674.html, accessed February 16, 2012.

Sumitha Narayanan Kutty

INTERNAL MACEDONIAN REVOLUTIONARY ORGANIZATION (IMRO)

The Internal Macedonian Revolutionary Organization (IMRO), also known by its Bulgarian name Vatreshna Makedonska Revoluzionna Organizazia (VMRO), was an ethnonationalist liberation movement that operated in the Southern Thracian and Macedonian geographic regions of the Balkans in the late 19th and early 20th centuries. IMRO emerged in response to the Congress of Berlin of 1878 when the Great Powers amended the San Stefano Treaty of March 3, 1878, between the Russian Empire and Ottoman Empire at the end of the Russo-Ottoman War (1877–1878). As a result of the Congress of Berlin, the Bulgarian tsardom, newly liberated from Ottoman rule, was divided into two territories, the Bulgarian Khanate and Eastern Rumelia. Large parts of the Bulgarian territories in the Macedonian and Thracian geographic regions, whose populations were predominantly of Bulgarian ethnic background, were returned to the sultan.

IMRO was established on October 13, 1893, in the city of Solun (the Slavic name for the city of Thessaloniki in modern-day Greece) by a group of Bulgarian intellectuals: Hristo Tatarchev, Damian Gruev, Ivan Hadjinikolov, Petar Poparsov, Hristo Batandjiev, and Andon Dimitrov. The primary goal of the organization was to liberate the Macedonian and Thracian regions from the Ottoman Empire by inciting a popular uprising and creating an autonomous state, with the ultimate goal of unification with the Bulgarian Khanate. The latter objective was a long-term goal and remained secondary to the physical liberation from the Great Porte because of the fear that a potential unification could lead to intervention by the Great Powers, as had happened in 1878. It was further feared that the territories would be divided between Serbia, Greece, and the Ottoman Empire so as to prevent the rise of a strong Balkan state that could challenge European interests in the region.

At its zenith during the Ilinden-Preobrazhenie Uprising of 1903, IMRO could muster 15,000 guerrillas, also known as Chetnici in Bulgarian. The organization was financed by membership dues, donations from wealthy Bulgarians, and direct funding by the Bulgarian government. IMRO also resorted to criminal activities to raise additional funds, including kidnappings for ransom. One of the group's most prominent abductions was that of the American protestant missionary Ellen Stone.

After the declaration of Bulgarian independence from the Ottoman Empire on September 22, 1908, Sofia's support for the organization grew. In 1911 and 1912, numerous paramilitary formations were launched from Bulgaria into the Ottoman-controlled Macedonian geographic region. Administrative buildings, railroads, and other symbols of Turkish authority were targeted using weapons and explosives smuggled across the Bulgarian-Ottoman border by mules. The Ottoman authorities responded with massive and brutal retaliations against civilians, which ultimately caused the outbreak of the First Balkan War.

During World War I, Bulgaria moved its forces into the Macedonian and Thracian regions, seeking to use the structural organization of IMRO to govern the territories. The group cooperated fully, and some of its members were appointed to leading positions within the administration. For a few years during the war, it seemed that IMRO's ultimate objective of Bulgarian unification had been achieved.

However, Bulgaria (which was allied to Germany) was defeated in World War I, and Macedonia and Southern Thrace were divided between Serbia, Greece, and Turkey. This caused IMRO to assume a more distinct communist ideological identity, with the group gradually transforming itself from a national liberation movement into a covert political tool aimed at securing a left-leaning Macedonian nation. Bulgaria banned the organization in the wake of the country's military coup on May 19, 1934.

A short list of IMRO's most prominent acts of terrorism included the sinking of the ship *Vashkapu* in 1903, which left 28 people dead; the assassination of the Bulgarian prime minister Dimitar Petkov on February 26, 1907; the murder of Bulgarian foreign and defense minister Aleksandar Dimitrov on October 22, 1921; the attempted killing of Bulgarian prime minister Aleksandar Stamboliiski on February 2, 1923; and the slayings of Yugoslav tsar Alexander I and French foreign minister Louis Barthou in 1934.

Further Reading

Perry, Duncan. *The Politics of Terror: The Macedonian Liberation Movements, 1893–1903*. Durham, NC: Duke University Press, 1988.

Sherman, Laura Beth. *Fires on the Mountain : The Macedonian Revolutionary Movement and the Kidnapping of Ellen Stone*. New York: Columbia University Press, 1980.

Dimitar Georgiev

INTERNATIONAL RED CROSS HEADQUARTERS (BAGHDAD) BOMBING

On October 27, 2003—the first day of Ramadan of that year—a series of bombs ripped through downtown Baghdad in a coordinated string of attacks unprecedented in both scale and scope. Among the targets of the bombings was the headquarters of the International Committee of the Red Cross (ICRC), located in central Baghdad. The attack on the ICRC came on the heels of a number of high-profile bombings targeting other civilian entities in Iraq such as the Jordanian embassy and the offices of the United Nations (UN). Still, it sent shock waves through nongovernmental organizations operating in Iraq and prompted most of those that had not already left the country to further scale back their operations or withdraw altogether.

The months preceding the ICRC bombing saw substantial changes in the overall security environment in Iraq. In the immediate aftermath of the March 2003 U.S.-led invasion, looting posed a serious problem, and an Iraqi nationalist and ex-Baathist insurgency was percolating. While there were some portentous developments—the July 22, 2003, killing of a Sri Lankan ICRC employee and a handful of attacks on members of Iraqi civil society—the vast majority of attacks took the form of ambushes, roadside bombings, and improvised explosives primarily targeting U.S. forces. In effect, through the spring and midsummer of 2003, there was still reason for optimism about the future of Iraqi security.

By the late summer of 2003, however, the security environment in Iraq had changed drastically. On August 7, 2003, a car bomb detonated in central Baghdad outside the headquarters of the Jordanian embassy, killing 18 and wounding scores more. Less than two weeks later, on August 19, 2003, the headquarters of the UN Assistance Mission in Iraq were rocked by a suicide car bombing that decimated the UN staff and killed the UN's special envoy, Sergio Vieira de Mello, a veteran with 33 years of experience working in some of the world's toughest conflict zones. The UN bombing was followed a mere 10 days later by a car bomb attack on a crowd outside the Imam Ali shrine in the southern city of Najaf on August 29, 2003. This incident marked the first major sectarian attack of the Iraq War and left 83 people dead, including the influential Shi'ite Ayatollah Muhammad Baqir al-Hakim. The attack also wounded 500 others. In sum, these three bombings loudly announced the presence of foreign jihadists within Iraq and obliterated any notion of an insurgency strictly characterized by Saddam Hussein loyalists and ex-Baathists.

Despite this violence, Iraq still had not seen anything near the scope, scale, and coordination of the attacks that took place on October 27, 2003. Beginning at roughly 8:30 A.M. local time, a flurry of coordinated suicide attacks rocked Baghdad. First, a suicide bomber detonated his explosives-laden vehicle at Dora patrol station in Baghdad's Bayaa neighborhood. The attack killed at least 15 people, including one U.S. soldier. Just minutes after this explosion, a suicide bomber in a Peugeot ambulance marked with the emblem of the Red Crescent—the Muslim equivalent of the Red Cross and the type of vehicle ubiquitous in post-invasion Iraq—sped toward the ICRC headquarters. Approximately 30 meters

(98 feet) from the organization's offices, the bomber slammed into the protective barrier surrounding the building, which was comprised of little more than loosely strung together oil barrels filled with sand. The collision detonated the explosives.

The blast was devastating. Its impact created a hole 21 feet deep by 53 feet wide, tore a 129-foot hole in the sandbag-reinforced front wall of the building, and caused extensive damage to the interior of the building. The explosion sent shrapnel flying hundreds of feet in all directions and ultimately killed 12 people and wounded 22. Among the dead were two ICRC staff members. Both were unarmed security guards, and both were Iraqis. Given that the blast occurred early in the morning, the death toll at the organization would have been substantially higher had the staff not been instructed to arrive one hour later because of Ramadan. It is believed that as few as 10 staff members were inside the ICRC's offices at the time of the attack.

In the immediate aftermath of the ICRC bombing, U.S. forces arrived on the scene to cordon off the area and assist those wounded in the explosion. Immediately after their arrival, however, a series of three other coordinated blasts occurred at police stations scattered throughout downtown Baghdad. A fifth attempted suicide bombing on a police station was foiled when Iraqi police forces shot and wounded the driver, who was caught in a Toyota Land Cruiser filled with approximately 400 pounds of TNT and three 120-millimeter mortar rounds. His capture was a boon for the Iraqi security services as it shed substantial light on the identity of those behind the October 27, 2003, bombings. Claiming at first to be a Syrian national and possessing a Syrian passport, the bomber later told authorities he hailed from Yemen.

Even without the knowledge of the exact nationality of the bomber, the tactics and the targeting of the bombings bore the mark of sophisticated foreign jihadists. First, the fact that the bombings were so closely coordinated revealed significant technical and operational expertise on behalf of the perpetrators. Routes to the police stations were carefully planned out in advance, and eyewitness reports suggested that the vehicles used were either stolen police cars or, in the case of one vehicle, a truck painted with the exact same color scheme as an Iraqi police vehicle. Moreover, all of the bombings were specifically timed to take place within a span of only 45 minutes. Second, the choice of weapon, a suicide vehicle-borne improvised explosive, was another tactical hallmark of Al Qaeda. Finally, the fact that the attackers targeted an international organization such as the ICRC, which had operated in Iraq for 23 years and through three separate wars, suggested the work of foreign jihadist elements rather than Iraqi nationalists.

Nonetheless, some still believed the bombings were connected to Saddam Hussein loyalists. Specifically, the Iraqi Governing Council, an interim Iraqi transitional government that operated in parallel to the U.S.-led Coalition Provisional Authority, partly blamed the attack on former Baathists. These allegations were echoed by Iraq's deputy minister of the interior. Similar allegations followed the Jordanian embassy bombing and the suicide bombing on the UN. In all three cases, they were, however, incorrect.

Indeed, the ICRC bombing and the attacks on the Iraqi police stations were widely believed to have been carried out by Abu Musab al-Zarqawi's network, Jamaa al-Tawhid wa'a Jihad (JTJ). JTJ would later merge with Al Qaeda to form Tanzom Qa'idat al-Jihadi Bilad al-Rafidyan (QJBR), or, as it is more commonly known, Al Qaeda in Iraq (AQI). Displaying impressive operational capability and a much greater threshold for civilian bloodshed than some of their Iraqi nationalist insurgent counterparts, JTJ represented a newer, deadlier threat. As evidenced by their choice to deliberately target a neutral, respected international organization like the ICRC, JTJ was determined to oust not only the United States from Iraq but all Western elements.

In some senses, JTJ succeeded in this aim with their October 27, 2003, attacks. The ICRC bombing sent shock waves through the community of international organizations operating in Iraq. On October 30, 2003, the UN announced that it would pull out all remaining international staff from the country, though most of its employees had already been withdrawn following the August 19 bombing and a second, smaller attack on September 22, 2003. Doctors without Borders largely withdrew to Amman, reducing its expatriate staff to a mere three people. In the days following the attack, the ICRC surprisingly insisted that it would remain in Iraq but still chose to withdraw the vast majority of its international staff and adopt more stringent security measures. Yet on November 8, 2003, citing no letup in violence since the October attacks, the ICRC announced that it was shutting down its offices in Baghdad and Basra. It left behind only a small office in the northern Iraqi city of Irbil, effectively closing down much of its operations inside of Iraq.

Overall, the ICRC bombing, like the UN bombing and the Jordanian embassy bombing, is remembered as a substantial turning point in the Iraqi insurgency. In concert, the three blasts violently proclaimed that no entity, no matter how well regarded by Iraqis or the international community, was safe in Iraq. With the attack, foreign jihadists announced that they would ruthlessly kill civilians in their efforts to oust any Western presence from Iraq and topple the Iraqi government.

See also: Jamaa al-Tawhid wa'a Jihad (JTJ); Jordanian Embassy (Baghdad) Bombing; United Nations Headquarters (Baghdad) Attack; Zarqawi, Abu Musab al-

Further Reading

Chandrasekaran, Rajiv. "Car Bombs Kill at Least 35 in Baghdad." *Washington Post,* October 28, 2003.

Filkins, Dexter, and Alex Berenson. "Suicide Bombers in Baghdad Kill at Least 34." *New York Times,* October 28, 2003.

Hanley, Charles J. "36 Killed in Bomb Attack upon Baghdad Red Cross Headquarters, Police Stations." Associated Press, October 27, 2003.

Labbe, Theola, and Keith B. Richburg. "Decades of Good Deeds Provide No Armor; Red Cross Reassesses Its Presence in Iraq." *Washington Post,* October 28, 2003.

Nate Shestak

INTERNATIONAL SIKH YOUTH FEDERATION (ISYF)

The International Sikh Youth Federation (ISYF) was one of several Sikh terrorist organizations that emerged with the aim of creating an independent Sikh homeland, Khalistan (Land of the Pure), in what is now the Indian Punjab. Lakhbir Singh Rode established the organization in the United Kingdom in 1984 shortly after Operation Blue Star—the code name for India's storming of the Golden Temple to flush out militant Sikh separatists. This episode, which left at least 439 people dead (some sources put the figure in the thousands), inflamed the Sikhs, with many interpreting it as a direct assault on their culture and beliefs. It was also directly responsible for the assassination of Indira Gandhi, who had ordered the raid.

Apart from its main base of strength in the Punjab, the ISYF created branches in Canada, Germany, and the United States. It also worked closely with other militant Sikh movements such as Babbar Khalsa (BK), the Khalistan Liberation Force (KLF), and the Khalistan Commando Force (KCF). The ISYF primarily used bombings, assassinations, and kidnappings and targeted Indian officials and nonsupportive Sikhs. Members of the group may also have been involved in the bombing of Air India Flight 301 in June 1985 (329 killed), but their involvement was never proven. Attacks began dropping in 1992 after Delhi gave the police chief of the state, K.P.S. Gill, a largely free hand to rein in Sikh extremists. The subsequent campaign was highly brutal and, although it crippled rebel groups in the Punjab, is regarded as one of the bloodiest in the country's history. By 1999 ISYF's operational activity had largely petered out.

In February 2001, the United Kingdom proscribed the ISYF under new antiterrorist legislation. The following year the Canadian wing disbanded as a result of its terrorist group status. The ISYF was listed as a prominent Sikh terrorist organization by the U.S. State Department in 1999, although not officially a designated foreign terrorist organization. It was then placed on the U.S. Terrorist Exclusion List in 2004.

Although the ISYF was crushed in the Punjab, the Indian government still had some concerns that Sikh groups abroad would try to revive Sikh militancy and separatism on the back of the ISYF's international branches. Delhi accordingly banned the group in 2002 and continued to keep a very close watch for any sign of renewed activity. As of 2011, however, the group's global presence appears to have become largely defunct, with most of its original leaders now exiled in Pakistan.

See also: Babbar Khalsa (BK); Golden Temple Massacre; Khalistan Commando Force (KCF)

Further Reading

Fair, Christine C. "Diaspora Involvement in Insurgencies: Insights from the Khalistan and Tamil Eelam Movements." *Nationalism and Ethnic Politics* 11, no. 1 (2005).

Mahmood, Cynthia Keppley. *Fighting for Faith and Nation: Dialogues with Sikh Militants.* Philadelphia: University of Pennsylvania Press, 1996.

Razavy, Maryam. "Sikh Militant Movements in Canada." *Terrorism and Political Violence* 18, no. 1 (2006).

Kathy Alexeef

IRANIAN BOMBINGS

On June 12, 2005, four bombs killed 11 people and wounded at least 87 in the space of two hours in Avhaz, Khuzestan (Khouzestan). With a largely ethnic Arabic population, the oil-rich province has had a history of unrest. The targets were apparently linked to the government and the media, and most believed that the proximity of the bombings to upcoming presidential elections in Iran was no coincidence. Following the attacks, leading reformist presidential candidate Mostafa Moeen accused unspecified far-right "elements" of leveraging the explosions as a means of frightening people into voting for hard-line candidates.

The attacks were part of a series that took place in Iran that day. In Tehran, a bomb concealed in a trashcan close to Imam Hussein Square (Hoseyni Square) killed 2 people, wounding 12 others. A second device exploded soon afterward in Vali Asr Square, also in the capital. No casualties were reported in the latter incident. Authorities located and defused three additional bombs and arrested one suspect.

The Supreme National Security Council (SNSC) initially blamed the explosions in Avhaz on separatists linked to Iraq, implicating the People's Mojahedin (Mujahedin-e-Khalq, or MeK) and vestiges of the Baath Party. The MeK later denied the accusation.

The Iranian Labor News Agency subsequently released a copy of a communiqué published on an unidentified Internet site by an alleged terrorist group calling itself the Brigades of Revolutionary Martyrs of al-Ahwaz (BRMA). The statement said it was boycotting the upcoming elections and asked others to do the same "in order to show the Iranian occupiers that we will win." The declaration was similar to releases previously put out by the Democratic Popular Front of Ahwazi Arabs (DPFA, also known as the Popular Democratic Front of Ahvazi). The DPFA denied any responsibility for the attacks in Avhaz (and Tehran) and instead blamed the BRMA.

Interior Ministry spokesman Jahanbaksh Khanjani was less specific: "Whoever is responsible for this, the target of the blasts is to undermine Friday's presidential elections." Others accused "British spies and soldiers" of encouraging the violence. The UK government vehemently denied the accusation.

Two men were later arrested and privately tried for their role in the bombings. They were publicly hanged in March 2006. Prior to the executions, nine individuals confessed on Iranian television to their involvement in the attack. One, Ali Afravi, claimed he had been in contact with foreign separatists groups based in Canada and the United Kingdom that were seeking to destabilize Iran. He was also hung.

See also: Mujahedin-e-Khalq (MeK)

Further Reading

"Explosions in Ahwaz, at Least 7 Killed, 70 Wounded, 5 in Tehran." *Iran Press Service,* June 12, 2005. http://www.iran-press-service.com/ips/articles-2005/june-2005/ahwaz-explosions-12605.shtml, accessed May 2, 2011.

"Hundreds Arrested in Iran Clashes." *BBC,* April 18, 2005. http://news.bbc.co.uk/2/hi/mi
  ddle_east/4457777.stm, accessed May 2, 2011.
"Iranians Hang Two Ahwaz Bombers." *BBC,* March 2, 2006. http://news.bbc.co.uk/2/hi/mi
  ddle_east/4765962.stm, accessed May 2, 2011.
"'Unrest' in Iran Arabic Province." *BBC,* November 5, 2005. http://news.bbc.co.uk/2/hi/mi
  ddle_east/4410506.stm, accessed May 2, 2011.

Donna Bassett

IRANIAN EMBASSY (LONDON) SIEGE

On April 30, 1980, a team of six Iranian Arabs seized the Iranian embassy in South Kensington, London. The group took 23 diplomatic staff and three British citizens hostage and demanded political reforms from Tehran. The crisis ended when the British Special Air Service (SAS) retook the embassy by force on May 5, rescuing the hostages and killing all but one of the terrorists. The incident took place shortly after the Iranian Revolution of 1979 and highlighted some of the internal ethnic tensions with the potential to destabilize Iran, as well as the growing counterterrorism capabilities of British security forces in the early 1980s.

The hostage takers claimed to be members of the Democratic Revolutionary Front for Arabistan and said they belonged to a larger community of Khuzestani separatists. The group's goal was to gain autonomy for the oil-rich Iranian province of Khuzestan. Long suppressed by the Iranian state prior to the 1979 Iranian Revolution, the ethnically Arab Khuzestani were marginalized economically and politically by the Persian-dominated government. The fact that Tehran benefited enormously from the province's oil reserves while neglecting the indigenous population was especially galling to the Khuzestani.

In the last days of Mohammad Reza's rule in Iran, the Khuzestani felt that they could take advantage of the political instability then gripping the country. A major strike by the province's oil workers in 1978 contributed to the growing opposition against the shah, culminating in the 1979 revolution. Although the Khuzestani initially aligned with the new leadership in Tehran, they soon realized that the Islamic Republic under Ayatollah Ruhollah Khomeini intended to enforce the same policies of economic, political, and social marginalization as the previous regime and would not accede to demands for autonomy for Khuzestan. The issue came to a head on May 29, 1979, when a Khuzestani protest in Khorramshahr was violently suppressed by the Revolutionary Guards.

It was in this environment that the Democratic Revolutionary Front for Arabistan chose to act. Inspired by the siege of the American embassy in Tehran and angered by the events at Khorramshahr, Awn Ali Mohammad decided to draw maximum attention to the Khuzestani cause by attacking the Iranian diplomatic mission in London. After recruiting several followers, Mohammad and his group began to plan the attack. Arriving in London on March 31, 1980, the group acquired weapons and finalized preparations for the operation.

At 11:30 A.M. on April 30, Mohammad and his group overpowered Metropolitan Police constable Trevor Lock and forced their way into the embassy. The charge d'affaires Gholam Ali Afrouz attempted to jump to safety but was apprehended by

Sim Harris, sound man of the BBC, who was among the hostages held by gunmen at the Iranian Embassy, climbs along the balcony from the embassy to make his escape following two explosions at the embassy in London, May 5, 1980. Flames can be seen shooting from the embassy, top left. (AP/Wide World Photos)

the hostage takers. Two other embassy staffers managed to reach the safety of the adjacent Ethiopian embassy.

After establishing contact with the London Metropolitan Police, Mohammad's team demanded that 91 Khuzestani prisoners in Iran be released and delivered to London, where they would accompany the hostage takers to a friendly Arab country. The terrorists set a deadline for noon the next day and threatened to kill the captives if their demands were not met. The Iranian reaction to the crisis was to refuse to cooperate with the hostage takers, as well as with the British government. Khomeini denounced the siege as an attempt by the Iraqi, British, and American governments to discredit his revolutionary regime.

With British prime minister Margaret Thatcher away on a trip, Home Secretary William Whitelaw led the British crisis response in London (while regularly conferring with Thatcher via car phone). Since the Tehran government was unwilling to cooperate, the government decided that the incident had to be handled under British law, even though the embassy was technically Iranian territory. The government also alerted the SAS, the elite wing of the British Army, and instructed it to start making contingency plans to retake the embassy by force.

As noon approached on May 1, police negotiators managed to persuade the hostage takers to extend their deadline by two hours. They also gambled that the terrorists would probably not carry out their threats to kill their captives, and, indeed, the second time limit (2 P.M.) passed without violence. Instead, Mohammad changed his list of ultimatums and merely called for the British Broadcasting Corporation (BBC) to air a statement of Khuzestani grievances. He also demanded to have an ambassador from an Arab country negotiate their safe passage out of the country.

With these new developments, the British government believed that the siege could end peacefully, although security officials were ordered to continue refining their plans to retake the embassy if necessary. The SAS was assisted in this endeavor when the terrorists released a seriously ill hostage, who was able to provide vital intelligence on the size, composition, and disposition of Mohammad's team. After conferring with several Middle Eastern ambassadors, Whitelaw's crisis group also decided not to involve a third-party Arab government. As it was, only the Jordanians were even willing to entertain the prospect. By May 3, the SAS team was in place in a building adjacent to the embassy, ready to execute a rescue if needed.

After the BBC broadcast a truncated version of the group's manifesto, Mohammad began to realize that the UK government was stalling. On the morning of May 5, he demanded to speak with an Arab ambassador and threatened to kill a hostage if this request was not met. After the British allowed the deadline to pass, the hostage takers killed chief press officer Abbas Lavasani and pushed his body through the front door of the embassy.

This action prompted Whitelaw to initiate military action to retake the embassy. Within 20 minutes the SAS had executed their rescue plan, killing all but one of the hostage takers (two captives also died in the ensuing firefight). The surviving terrorist, Fowzi Badavi Nejad, was later sentenced to life imprisonment. Although Khomeini's regime expressed its gratitude to the British for carrying out the successful operation, it continued to claim that the whole episode was an Iraqi and Western plot designed to discredit Iran.

In the aftermath of the siege, the Khuzestani issue gained some attention, but the 1981 Iran-Iraq War eventually drowned out their message, and they remain a marginalized group. The SAS raid, carried out in full view of the world's television cameras, persuaded many governments, including the United States, to invest in specialized counterterrorism training and expertise.

See also: U.S. Embassy (Tehran) Hostage Crisis

Further Reading

Campbell, John. *Margaret Thatcher.* Vol. 2, *The Iron Lady.* London: Jonathan Cape, 2003.

Daniel, Elton L. *The History of Iran.* Westport, CT: Greenwood, 2001.

Fremont-Barnes, Gregory. *Who Dares Wins: The SAS and the Iranian Embassy Siege, 1980.* Oxford: Osprey, 2009.

O'Toole, Pam. "Iran and the Hostage-Takers." *BBC News World Edition,* April 26, 2000. http://news.bbc.co.uk/2/hi/in_depth/uk/2000/iranian_embassy_siege/720640.stm, accessed February 7, 2012.

Thatcher, Margaret. *The Downing Street Years.* BBC Television Mini-Series, 1993. http://www.margaretthatcher.org/document/109119, accessed May 2, 2011.

Jonathan Wong

IRAQI, ABU MAYSARA AL-

Abu Maysara al-Iraqi is considered the top spokesperson of Tanzom Qa'idat al-Jihadi Bilad al-Rafidyan (QJBR, commonly referred to as Al Qaeda in Iraq) and is in charge of posting statements on the Internet and claiming responsibility for attacks carried out by the group. While the name Abu Maysara al-Iraqi is almost certainly a pseudonym, authorities believe he is indeed of Iraqi descent. Little is known for sure about Abu Maysara, however. In fact, users of jihadist Internet sites and chat rooms have posted numerous personal questions to Abu Maysara, yet none has been definitively answered.

Abu Maysara's name first appeared around January 2004 in jihadist chat rooms, specifically Muntada Al-Ansar and Islah, sites that are password protected and restricted to individuals who support extremist activity. According to the *Washington Post,* Abu Maysara initially claimed responsibility for several attacks against coalition forces and confirmed Abu Musab al-Zarqawi's presence in Iraq. His statements are said to be full of half sentences, ellipses, and religious references. He reportedly posts messages so that information "does not become lost in the media blackout that America imposes in order to deceive its people and its allies."

Abu Maysara used various websites and technologies to carry his messages in order to hinder intelligence agencies working to limit his reach. In the fall of 2004, he began using a technology originally developed to allow users to share files, called YouSendIt. With YouSendIt Abu Maysara is able to transfer files, such as videos and other media, quickly and anonymously to supporters. The process is such that authorities are unable to effectively hinder Abu Maysara's distribution of material that they find inspires hate and support Iraqi insurgents.

In January 2006, Abu Maysara announced the formation of the Mujahideen Shura Council of Iraq, an umbrella group for various insurgent factions (the group has since changed its name to the Islamic State of Iraq). According to the Memorial Institute for the Prevention of Terrorism, Abu Maysara can be considered a spokesman for the coalition as well.

See also: Tanzom Qa'idat al-Jihadi Bilad al-Rafidyan (QJBR); Zarqawi, Abu Musab al-

Further Reading

Cha, Ariana Eunjung. "From a Virtual Shadow, Messages of Terror." *Washington Post,* October 2, 2004.

"Key Leader Profile: Al-Iraqi, Abu Maysarah." Memorial Institute for the Prevention of Terrorism's Terrorism Knowledge Base, Oklahoma City, OK. http://www.tkb.org/Key Leader.jsp?memID=6270, accessed January 27, 2007.

Edward F. Mickolus

IRAQI MINISTRY OF THE INTERIOR BOMBING

On January 26, 2010, a suicide terrorist driving a truck with explosives attacked the Iraqi Ministry of the Interior's forensics division, killing at least 38 people. The bomb detonated on a traffic circle near a security checkpoint on Al Taharyiat

Square, setting cars ablaze and spraying glass through an assortment of nearby restaurants and shops. The incident took place a day after coordinated explosions targeted three landmark hotels in the city catering to foreigners, journalists, and expatriate businessmen. The combined casualty toll over the two days was 75 dead and over 150 injured.

No group claimed responsibility, although suspicion immediately fell on Tanzom Qa'idat al-Jihadi Bilad al-Rafidyan (QJBR, or Al Qaeda in Iraq [AQI]), which had carried out numerous similar attacks in an effort to topple the U.S.-backed Shi'ite-led central administration in Baghdad and generally make the country ungovernable as the American military prepared to withdraw.

According to General Ray Odierno, Washington's top commander in Iraq, AQI had morphed into a loosely coordinated band of terrorists controlled by 5 to 10 highly educated individuals with backgrounds in engineering and science. The attacks were indicative of this flatter configuration and probably reflected the work of small, well-trained cells based in the city.

Others speculated that the bombings could have been in revenge for the recent execution of Ali Hassan al-Majid. Colloquially known as "Chemical Ali," he had been a senior lieutenant in former regime of President Saddam Hussein and a revered figure among Baathist extremists.

The hotel and Ministry of the Interior attacks threatened to undermine faith in Prime Minister Nouri Kamal al-Maliki, who had staked his reputation on being able to protect the country's civilian population. They also fueled anger over a widening scandal involving British-made handheld explosive-detection devices that the U.S. military had determined were "totally useless." It was believed that the Iraqi government had paid $18,000 for each device under a contract worth $850 million. A British Broadcasting Corporation (BBC) report just prior to the bombings had found that they cost no more than $250 apiece to manufacture and used the same simple sensors as in anti-shoplifting tags.

See also: Tanzom Qa'idat al-Jihadi Bilad al-Rafidyan (QJBR)

Further Reading

Arraf, Jane, and Sahar Issa. "US Blames al Qaida in Iraq for Baghdad Bombing Spree." *Christian Science Monitor,* January 26, 2010.
Leland, John, and Anthony Shadid. "Blast Hits Central Baghdad as Attacks Accelerate." *New York Times,* January 27, 2010.
Mizher, Qais, Leilel Fadel, and Ernesto Lonono. "Bomber Kills 38 in Iraq a Day after Hotel Attacks." *Washington Post,* January 27, 2010.

Peter Chalk

IRAQI SECTARIAN ATTACKS

Following the U.S.-led invasion of Iraq in 2003, a wave of sectarian violence devastated the country and its people. At its peak in late 2006, sectarian violence claimed well over 2,000 Iraqi lives per month. As sectarian tensions mounted, attacks inevitably begat reprisal attacks. Group abductions, execution-style killings, and the unearthing of torture rooms made daily headlines. Dead bodies were dumped out in the open, scattered throughout Iraq's urban mixed-sect neighborhoods. This vicious descent into sectarian violence left many observers wondering whether an all-out civil war had broken out in the country. Beginning in 2007, however, sectarian violence began to recede with the advent of the U.S. "surge" of troops, the blows dealt to the Shi'ite militias driving much of the violence, and the overall decline of Tanzom Qa'idat al-Jihadi Bilad al-Rafidyan (QJBR; more commonly known as Al Qaeda in Iraq [AQI]). Nonetheless, sectarian tensions and sectarian violence still pose a major threat to Iraq's future as of this writing.

In the months immediately following the U.S.-led invasion of Iraq, sectarian violence was largely absent from the country. Widespread looting and other forms of criminal activity were commonplace, and Iraq saw the growth of a loyalist or Sunni nationalist insurgency. Nonetheless, there was relatively little evidence of the serious sectarian clashes that would soon engulf the country. That said, two key trends during this time period laid the foundation for sectarian violence. First, Iraq's Interim Governing Council—while balanced in terms of its sectarian composition—largely ignored Sunni Arab political leaders who had not been in exile during Saddam Hussein's rule. This structure effectively excluded indigenous Sunni voices, which only drove more Sunnis to either tacitly or actively support the then inchoate insurgency within the country. It also played a role in codifying Iraq's demographic landscape along sectarian lines. Second, the run-up to the March 2003 invasion and the spring and summer of 2003 witnessed the steady inflow into Iraq of Sunni salafist jihadist foreign fighters. Many of these fighters were led by Jordanian militant Abu Musab al-Zarqawi, the future founder of AQI and the man who would play a critical role in striking the match that would ultimately set the country's sectarian landscape aflame.

On August 29, 2003, a car bomb ripped through a crowd outside of the Imam Ali mosque in Najaf, a Shiite holy city. The blast killed at least 83, including the spiritual leader of the Supreme Council of the Islamic Revolution in Iraq, Ayatollah Muhammad Baqir al-Hakim, in addition to wounding 500 others. The attack devastated the country's Shi'a. While some observers believe that the blast was tied to the Iranian Revolutionary Guard Corps, most attribute it to al-Zarqawi's network, then operating under the name of Jamaa al-Tawhid wa'a Jihad.

A torrent of attacks against Iraq's Shi'ites soon followed the Imam Ali mosque bombing. On March 2, 2004, suicide bombers targeted Shi'ite mosques in Baghdad and Karbala in a series of coordinated attacks that killed at least 181 people and wounded over 500 others. On April 21, 2004, five nearly simultaneous bombings left 73 dead and wounded 200 others in the predominantly Shi'ite city of Basra. On June 28, 2004, bombs detonated outside a mosque in the predominantly Shi'ite city of Hillah, killing 40 and wounding 22. On August 26, 2004, a mortar attack on the al-Kufah mosque in Najaf killed 40 and wounded 60, including many supporters of Muqtada al-Sadr, an extremely influential Shi'ite cleric whose followers would soon enter the country's sectarian conflict. Finally, on December 19, 2004, a car bomb detonated in the midst of a funeral procession in

Najaf, killing at least 50 and wounding 91 in an attack that occurred very close to the Imam Ali shrine.

While most point to 2005 or early 2006 as the time when sectarian violence truly accelerated in Iraq, as the aforementioned attacks illustrate, there was already considerable sectarian violence aimed at the country's Shi'a by the end of 2004. It is widely believed that al-Zarqawi's network was behind the majority of these attacks since he openly endorsed a strategy of driving a wedge between the country's Sunni and Shi'a. Still, throughout 2004, Shi'a retaliation had been relatively minor. While elements of the Badr Organization, a Shi'ite militia, targeted former regime officials in the aftermath of the U.S. invasion, and southern Baghdad saw some sectarian clashes, the country's Shi'ites had not entered the internecine conflict en masse. However, it was not long before the Shi'a responded, and the country devolved into brutal sectarian clashes.

Beginning in 2005, national elections swept Shi'ites into power, shifting the political landscape of the country. This, in turn, allowed the Ministry of the Interior to become infiltrated with members of the Badr Organization. From within the ministry, these groups co-opted large segments of the national police, in effect turning them into sectarian death squads that undertook wholesale abductions and executions of Sunni males. In one particularly egregious incident on August 22, 2005, armed men wearing uniforms from the Ministry of the Interior kidnapped 22 Sunni men in Baghdad's Iskan neighborhood. Their bodies, bound with ropes and handcuffs, were found outside the town of Kut a little over one month later. This incident was preceded by a massacre of at least 40 Sunnis in Baghdad's Jihad neighborhood only a few weeks earlier, carried out by gunmen believed to be affiliated with Jaish al-Mahdi (JAM).

Similar attacks became commonplace throughout the country. Sunni attacks begat reprisal killings, many of which ostensibly targeted Sunni belligerents but in reality were simply indiscriminate campaigns of violence against Sunnis. Checkpoints were set up throughout Baghdad where drivers would be killed on the basis of whether they possessed a common Sunni or Shi'ite name. Generally, Shi'ites tended to engage in targeted killings, mass abductions, torture, and executions. While the Sunnis used similar tactics, some Sunni extremists (chiefly those associated with al-Zarqawi's network) would respond with suicide bombings targeting large-scale Shi'ite gatherings. By the end of 2005, overall security in the country plummeted to previously unseen levels.

Sectarian violence would only continue to escalate in 2006. On February 22, 2006, armed men dressed in military uniforms detonated a series of bombs inside the al-Askariya mosque in Samarra, one of the most important Shi'ite religious sites in the world. While the attack itself did not directly result in any fatalities or injuries, the blast destroyed the mosque's northern wall and collapsed its dome. The retaliatory attacks were devastating. Because al-Zarqawi—believed to be the orchestrator behind the attack even though he widely denied involvement—issued a declaration of war against the Shi'a in September 2005, Iraq's Shi'ites viewed the attack as the opening volley of a sectarian war. The country erupted in violence. Angry Shi'ites destroyed a slew of Sunni mosques, and hundreds were killed in the days following the attack, setting the tone for what was then the most violent year in the war. By early 2006, the United States had concluded that Shi'ite militias were killing more Iraqis than their Sunni rivals, eclipsing them as the greatest threat to the Iraqi state. Enmeshed in a seemingly endless cycle of violence, the country teetered on the precipice of civil war.

The human toll of sectarian conflict left Iraq reeling. At the height of the violence, thousands of Iraqis were being killed in sectarian clashes each month. Displacement surged; roughly two million Iraqis found themselves internally displaced, and about another two million fled the country to live as refugees, mostly in neighboring Syria and Jordan. Sectarian cleansing dramatically redrew the demographic maps in many mixed-sect cities, especially Baghdad. Shi'ites and Sunnis abandoned mixed-sect neighborhoods for areas primarily inhabited by members of their own sect. By the end of 2006, sectarian violence had left Iraq in shambles.

It is important to note that violence was not limited to attacks between Iraq's two main sects but also took place within these sects. Indeed, both intra-Shi'ite killing and intra-Sunni killing were common in Iraq. In the case of the former, Shi'ite rivals JAM and the Badr Organization (which was backed by the Supreme Council of the Islamic Revolution in Iraq [SCIRI]) battled frequently in Iraq's south as they jockeyed for political power and control over different funding streams. Fueled in part by Iran, this conflict raged on unabated until the United States and the al-Maliki government convinced JAM to agree to a cease-fire. In the case of the latter, the Sunni organization QJBR gained notoriety for its violent intimidation tactics, whose victims were often the very same Iraqi Sunnis that were hosting the group. QJBR's draconian application of sharia law against these Sunnis led to a number of violent punishments. QJBR also carried out assassinations and targeted killings of members of rival Sunni insurgent groups, including both secular nationalist organizations, such as the 1920s Revolution Brigades, and also other like-minded jihadist groups, like Ansar al-Sunnah.

Violence in Iraq also claimed non-Muslim victims as well. The country's religious minorities, such as the Christians and Yazidis, were frequently targeted. In fact, as of this writing, the single deadliest attack of the Iraq War took place on August 14, 2007, near Mosul, when a series of coordinated bombs essentially leveled the towns of Qahtaniya and Jazeera, killing at least 500 Yazidis. It is widely believed that QJBR was responsible for the attack. However, such violence against these minority religious groups was relatively overlooked, compared to the more high-profile Shi'ite-on-Sunni or Sunni-on-Shi'ite violence.

The year 2007 saw a dramatic decrease in the level of sectarian violence plaguing Iraq. Sectarian killings were at an all-time high at the start of the year but by the year's end had plunged to below their pre-2005 levels. While the aforementioned sectarian cleansing that took place likely played a role in this drop, a number of other key factors led to the dramatic turnaround. Chief among them were an expanded U.S. military presence, the disruption of the QJBR network, and the weakening of JAM, a key Shi'ite militant group.

First, the United States ordered an increase of over 20,000 military forces to provide more security in Iraq, paying attention to the country's urban centers, especially Baghdad. Given that many of these centers had the highest proportions of mixed Sunni-Shiite neighborhoods and the highest levels of violence in the country, the move helped reduce the levels of violence. The surge also coincided with a change in U.S. strategy. U.S. forces increasingly embedded with their Iraqi counterparts, moving out of their large forward operating bases and living closer to the Iraqi population, whom they were tasked with protecting. Overall, the surge helped to usher in a dramatic drop in violence, including sectarian violence. However, most doubt it would have had such a level of success if it did not occur in concert with two other factors: the weakening of JAM and the decline of QJBR.

The weakening of JAM, a key combatant in the country's sectarian conflict, proved crucial in reducing sectarian violence throughout the country. With the increase in U.S. military forces, JAM elements were increasingly confronted and targeted in an effort to rein in the group's overall influence. After a couple of cease-fires and a successful battle against JAM by the Iraqi government in Basra in March 2008, JAM's strength had been greatly reduced. The movement's leader, Muqtada al-Sadr, ultimately announced a freeze on his militia's activities. JAM's decline led to a large-scale decrease in the number of roving Shi'ite death squads as well as fewer excuses for Shi'ite reprisal attacks. It also came alongside a crackdown within the Ministry of the Interior, which had essentially become an incubator for many of the Shi'ite militants undertaking sectarian killings throughout the country.

The drop in violence also coincided with a series of devastating blows to QJBR. After al-Zarqawi's death in 2006, the group continued to experience serious setbacks. Chief among these was the loss of support among the tribes in Anbar province, the group's base. The tribes tired of the group's strict enforcement of sharia law, its trampling of their smuggling routes, its assassination of local tribal leaders, and its widespread attacks on Iraqi civilians. In short, al-Zarqawi's strategy of sowing the seeds of sectarian conflict backfired, and the movement lost much of its local support. This loss of support, in conjunction with numerous devastating attacks on its leadership and midlevel fighters by U.S. and Iraqi forces, led to a greatly diminished QJBR.

The sum of these three developments in the country resulted in an environment much less permissive to sectarian violence. As a result, such violence plummeted. Most estimates place the decline in sectarian violence somewhere between 80 and 90 percent by September 2009. The specter of major sectarian conflict still looms in the country as JAM remains a powerful extra-state Shi'ite adversary, and QJBR still maintains the operational capability to undertake mass-casualty bombings aimed at Shi'ite targets, as in April 2010, when they struck a number of Shi'ite mosques and funeral processions, killing nearly 70 people. In effect, while Iraq's sectarian landscape has become significantly more peaceful, it remains both fragile and volatile.

See also: Jamaa al-Tawhid wa'a Jihad (JTJ); Mahdi Army; Tanzom Qa'idat al-Jihadi Bilad al-Rafidyan (QJBR); Zarqawi, Abu Musab al-

Further Reading

Baker, James A., III, and Lee H. Hamilton. *The Iraq Study Group Report.* New York: Vintage Books, 2006.

Cordesman, Anthony H. "Iraq's Sectarian and Ethnic Violence and the Evolving Insurgency." Center for Strategic and International Studies, Washington, D.C., January 26, 2007.

Fearon, James D. "Iraq's Civil War." *Foreign Affairs* 86, no. 2 (March–April 2007).

Hashim, Ahmed S. "Iraq's Civil War." *Current History* 106, no. 696 (January 2007).

International Crisis Group. *The Next Iraqi War? Sectarianism and Civil Conflict.* Middle East Report no. 52, February 27, 2006.

Pirnie, Bruce R., and Edward O'Connell. *Counterinsurgency in Iraq (2003–2006): RAND Counterinsurgency Study.* Vol. 2. Santa Monica, CA: RAND, 2008.

Nate Shestak

IRGUN TSVAI LEUMI

The Irgun Tsvai Leumi (National Military Organization) was a right-wing paramilitary Zionist underground movement that existed in Palestine from 1931 to 1948. It was better known later as Etzel, for its contracted Hebrew initials. Irgun became renowned for launching immediate and harsh retaliatory attacks on persons or organizations that had initiated violence against the Jewish community in Palestine (Yishuv). It was also known for its advocacy of military action against the British, who held a mandate over Palestine until May 1948. The British categorized Irgun as a terrorist organization, and the Jewish Agency for Palestine, Haganah, and Histadrut declared many of its operations to be acts of terrorism.

Even as the British slowly shifted their support to Palestine's Arab population in the 1930s, the leadership of the Jewish Agency for Palestine, in particular David Ben-Gurion, continued to work closely with the British to promote the interests of the Jewish population in Palestine. Haganah supported this position through its self-defense and military strategy of *havlaga,* or self-restraint. But not all of the Haganah membership agreed with a restrained response to the perceived British pro-Arab bias. This political and policy disagreement, coupled with Haganah's prevailing socialist ideology, caused a minority of its members, led by Avraham Tehomi, to leave Haganah in 1931 and form Irgun. The group was based on premises formulated by Vladimir Jabotinsky, who had led the Jewish Legion when it had fought with the British to remove the Ottoman Turks from Palestine in World War I. He believed strongly that swift, retaliatory action would forestall Arab attacks on the Yishuv.

By 1936 Irgun was little more than a pawn of the extreme nationalist Revisionist Zionists (Revisionist Party), led by Jabotinsky. The Revisionists had seceded from the World Zionist Organization (WZO) and were advocating the creation by force of a Jewish homeland spanning both banks of the Jordan River. In 1937 Haganah again split into right-wing and left-wing factions. The right-wing faction joined

Irgun, and some of the members of Irgun, including Tehomi, rejoined Haganah. Until this time, Irgun had been little more than a small and ineffective irritant in the region.

When Arab attacks during the Arab Revolt of 1936–1939 killed some 400 Jews, Irgun began launching retaliatory attacks, utilizing car bombs in areas of high Arab concentration. These endured until the beginning of World War II and killed as many as 250 Arab civilians. Irgun, which considered the British mandatory government to be illegal under international law, also directed acts of terrorism and assassination against the British. When the British White Paper of 1939 openly shifted British support away from the Jews to the Arabs by severely restricting Jewish immigration, settlement, and land purchases in Palestine, Irgun focused on targeting British military installations and interests. Irgun's rationale for the attacks was that the new, more severe British restrictions on Jewish immigration from Europe were contributing to the Nazi genocide of Jews in Germany, an event soon to become known as the Holocaust. To back up its claim, Irgun demonstrated that immigration to Palestine had saved approximately 18,000 European Jews prior to the shift in British policy, which began in earnest in early 1940.

During 1940–1943, Irgun suspended its attacks on British interests and supported the Allies against Germany and its Arab allies in the Middle East. However, a small militant faction known as the Stern Gang (the Fighters for the Freedom of Israel, or Lehi) separated from Irgun in 1941 under the leadership of Avraham Stern and continued to attack the British in Palestine during this period. The Irgun's own respite proved to be short-lived, and under the command of Menachem Begin it (1943–1948) once again declared war against the British and Arab villages in February 1944.

On November 6, 1944, Walter Edward Guinness, the resident British minister in the Middle East, was assassinated in Cairo. The murder was carried out by Lehi, allegedly in retaliation for the 1939 White Paper's restrictions on Jewish immigration that were contributing to the deaths of Jews in the Holocaust. At that point, Haganah and the Jewish Agency for Palestine launched an active campaign against Irgun and Lehi, which under the name Sezon (Hunting Season) successfully turned over a number of members and leaders to the British. Ultimately around 1,000 Irgun and Lehi cadres were arrested and jailed.

In an attempt to fight more effectively against the continuing British restrictions on Jewish immigration, Irgun, Lehi, and Haganah joined together in October 1944–July 1945 under the collective banner of the Jewish Resistance Movement. This alliance promptly ended in August 1945, however, after Irgun bombed the King David Hotel in Jerusalem, killing 91 soldiers as well as scores of British, Arab, and Jewish civilians. Although Begin and Irgun claimed to have issued three separate warnings in an attempt to limit casualties, the attack was viewed as a premeditated act of terrorism and the British arrested, tried, convicted, and hanged several members of Irgun. When the latter responded by hanging two British sergeants, the executions stopped, although British arrests of Irgun members continued. However, 251 of these prisoners were freed on May 5, 1947, when Haganah and Irgun combined forces to breach the wall of the supposedly secure British prison at Akko (Acre).

In anticipation of and following the United Nations (UN) partition of Palestine in 1947, Irgun and Haganah increasingly coordinated their forces. Irgun's greatest victory and largest operation was the capture of the Arab city of Jaffa. On May 28, 1948, the provisional government of the newly declared State of Israel transformed Haganah into its national military, the Israel Defense Forces (IDF). In doing so, it outlawed all other armed forces. In September 1948 Irgun's military activities were folded into the IDF. Begin, meanwhile, adapted what remained of the movement into a political party that was the precursor of the Herut (Freedom) Party, which merged in 1965 with the Liberal Party to form the Gahal Party. Gahal served as the foundation for the present-day Likud Party.

See also: King David Hotel Bombing; Stern Gang

Further Reading

Begin, Menachem. *The Revolt: The Story of the Irgun.* Jerusalem: Steimatzky, 1977.

Ben Ami, Yitshaq. *Years of Wrath, Days of Glory: Memoirs from the Irgun.* New York: R. Speller, 1982.

Boyer Bell, J. *Terror out of Zion: Irgun Zvai Leumi, Lehi and the Palestine Underground, 1929–1949.* New York: St. Martin's, 1979.

Hoffman, Bruce. *Inside Terrorism.* London: Victor Gollancz, 2006.

Hoffman, Bruce. *Jewish Terrorist Activities and the British Government in Palestine, 1939–1947.* PhD diss., Oxford University, 1986.

Irgun Zeva'I Le'umi. "The National Military Organization (Etzel, IZL)." Jewish Virtual Library, 2000. http://jewishvirtuallibrary.org/jsource/History/irgun.html, accessed January 19, 2010

Levine, David. *The Birth of the Irgun Zvai Leumi: The Jewish Resistance Movement.* Jerusalem: Gefen, 1996.

"Struggle for the Establishment of the State of Israel." Jewish Agency to Israel. http://www.jewishagency.org/JewishAgency/English/Jewish+Education/Compelling+Content/Eye+on+Israel/120/Chapter+Eight+The+Struggle+for+the+Esatblishment+of+the+State+of+Israel.htm, accessed January 19, 2010.

Tavin, Eli, and Yonah Alexander, eds. *Psychological Warfare and Propaganda: Irgun Documentation.* Wilmington, DE: Scholarly Reserves, 1982.

Richard M. Edwards

IRISH NATIONAL LIBERATION ARMY (INLA)

The Irish National Liberation Army (INLA) was established on December 8, 1974, with the aim of ousting the United Kingdom from Northern Ireland and then forming a 32-county socialist republic in Ireland. The group's principal founder, Seamus Costello, espoused an agenda that mixed traditional republican militarism with a Marxist-oriented ideology. During the 1970s and 1980s the INLA developed a relatively robust terrorist infrastructure in Northern Ireland, much of it based out of western Belfast, and also worked through legitimate channels via its political wing, the Irish Republican Socialist Party. The organization declared a cease-fire in August 1998 and eventually renounced all violence on October 11, 2009.

The INLA opened its violent campaign with the murder of Airey Neave—a Conservative Member of Parliament and one of Margaret Thatcher's closest political supporters—on March 30, 1979. Thereafter it claimed responsibility for a series of explosions, assassinations, and attempted assassinations, the vast majority of which took place in Northern Ireland. One of the most serious incidents occurred on December 6, 1982, when the group bombed a nightclub frequented by British troops (the Droppin' Well Bar) in Ballykelly, County Londonderry. The attack left 17 people dead (12 soldiers and 5 civilians).

Most of the INLA's weaponry was obtained from the Middle East, especially Libya and sympathetic Palestinian movements. However, the group also drew on sources in Eastern Europe and Australia, as well as, to a certain extent, Irish suppliers in the United States (organized through Northern Irish Aid, or NORAID). The INLA inventory primarily consisted of firearms, including handguns of various types, AK-47 assault rifles, and Uzi and Skorpion submachine guns. Unlike the Provisional Irish Republican Army (PIRA, or the "Provos"), the organization did not have a large stock of military-grade explosives such as Semtex, although it did have the capacity of produce homemade fertilizer-based devices. Operational and organizational financing was derived almost exclusively from criminality, particularly bank robberies.

The INLA claimed to have an organizational structure as disciplined as that of Provisional Irish Republican Army (PIRA, or the "Provos") and like the latter it organized its militant cells into so-called Active Service Units (ASUs). In reality, however, the group was a highly divided entity and suffered enormously from internal splits and factionalism. Several INLA members also provided state's evidence against their comrades in return for money, protection, and immunity from prosecution (instituted through the British government's so-called super-grass scheme).

The schisms and distrust were so endemic within the INLA that it eventually led Jimmy Brown and Gerard Steenson to set up an entirely new movement, the Irish People's Liberation Organization (IPLO). In 1987 the two groups engaged in a bitter feud for supremacy that left 16 people dead. A truce was eventually negotiated, after which the IPLO essentially degenerated into a straight drug-dealing syndicate; it was eventually put out of existence by PIRA in 1992. The IPLO was not the only faction to emerge out of the INLA. Other splinters included the Irish Revolutionary Brigade (established in 1987 under the leadership of Dessie O'Hare) and the INLA/General Head Quarters (INLA/GHQ, under the command of John Fennell).

Apart from its militant activities, the INLA achieved widespread publicity in 1980–1981 when several of its members participated in the Maze Hunger Strikes, carried out in an effort to galvanize recognition of the political status of paramilitary prisoners. Three of the group's members died as a result of these protests—Patsy O'Hara, Kevin Lynch, and Michael Devine—along with seven from PIRA.

Weakened by defections and infighting, and overshadowed by the larger and more influential PIRA, the INLA declared a cessation of hostilities on August 22, 1998. In announcing its cease-fire, the group acknowledged the many "faults and grievous errors" it had made in the prosecution of the republican war and admitted "its actions as liberation army fell far short of what they should have been." While the INLA rejected the 1998 Good Friday Agreement, it did accept the will of the Irish people as "clear" and did not call for a return to armed struggle.

Despite this positive development the INLA refused to disarm and for much of the next 10 years became heavily involved in organized crime, including narcotics trafficking, extortion, money laundering, and fuel smuggling. The group was also implicated in a number of murders, most of which appear to have been aimed at weakening the influence of rival drug gangs.

On October 11, 2009, the INLA eventually issued a communiqué that it would permanently renounce violence, asserting that the political environment in Northern Ireland was such that the group could now pursue its goals through peaceful and democratic means. Four months later the organization professed it had put all its weapons beyond use, a claim that General John de Chastelain of the Independent International Commission on Decommissioning subsequently confirmed.

Overall, the INLA is thought to have been responsible for around 113 killings between 1974 and 2009. The group has never formally apologized for these deaths or its role in the Northern Ireland conflict, and it continues to oppose the current status quo. The INLA remains a proscribed terrorist group in the United Kingdom and an illegal organization in the Republic of Ireland.

See also: Good Friday Agreement; Neave (Airey) Assassination; Provisional Irish Republican Army (PIRA)

Further Reading

Hanley, Brian, and Scott Millar. *The Lost Revolution: The Story of the Official IRA and the Worker's Party.* Dublin: Penguin Books, 2009.

Holland, Jack, and Henry McDonald. *INLA: Deadly Divisions.* Dublin: Poolbeg, 1996.

"INLA Ends Campaign of Violence." *RTÉ,* October 11, 2009. http://www.rte.ie/news/2009/1011/inla.html, accessed October 11, 2009.

"Northern Ireland INLA Paramilitaries Dump Terror Cache." *BBC News,* February 6, 2010. http://news.bbc.co.uk/hi/northern_ireland/8504932.stm, accessed February 6, 2010.

O'Regan, Michael, and Gerry Moriarty. "INLA Has 'Ended Armed Struggle' Says Statement from Organization." *Irish Times,* October 12, 2009.

Greg Hannah

IRISH REPUBLICAN ARMY (IRA)

The Irish Republican Army (IRA) has the distinction of being one of the longest-surviving nonstate groups dedicated to achieving its aims through violence. The name IRA was first used in 1866 on dispatches sent by the commander of a U.S.-based group of Irish republicans who had made an incursion into Canada, then part of the United Kingdom. In 2005 the main contemporary manifestation of the IRA, the Provisional IRA (PIRA), put its weapons beyond use as part of the Anglo-Irish peace process and by 2008 had, for all practical purposes, disbanded itself as an active militant organization.

The antecedents of Irish republicanism are to be found in the 19th century and were promulgated by a plethora of groups, of which the Fenian Brotherhood,

British soldiers stand guard as a department store goes up in flames in the center of Londonderry, Northern Ireland, January 4, 1972. The fire followed the explosion of a bomb planted in the building by Provisional Irish Republican Army (PIRA) terrorists. (AP/Wide World Photos)

the Irish Republican Brotherhood, and Clan na Gael were the most prominent. However, the IRA did not crystallize into a concrete entity until 1916, when it filled the void created by the arrest and execution of leading members of the Irish Volunteers and Irish Republican Brotherhood who participated in the Easter Rising against British rule. Three years later, after the election of the first Irish parliament (Dail Eireann) in 1919, the IRA was officially proclaimed as the army of the new Irish Republic. Subsequent attacks designed to overthrow direct rule from Westminster finally erupted into a wider insurgency, coming to an end only in 1921 when London signed a negotiated treaty with the Irish government. Under its terms, Ireland was partitioned into Northern Ireland, which continued to be part of a wider United Kingdom, while the south gained its independence as the Irish Free State (IFS).

The Irish republican movement then split into factions, led by Michael Collins, who had negotiated the treaty, and Eamonn de Valera, who opposed it. The majority of the IRA supported de Valera's position and in 1922 commenced a violent campaign against the IFS. Known as the Irregulars, they were militarily defeated by the Irish government, and in 1923 the IRA called a unilateral cease-fire. The group did not employ violence again until 1939, when they carried out numerous small-scale bombings on the British mainland. These attacks culminated in August 1939 when an improvised explosive device detonated in the center of Coventry, killing 5 people and injuring 60. Activity continued into the early 1950s with a series of major arms thefts in England, followed by the launching of a "Border campaign" in 1956 when three IRA "flying columns" crossed into Northern Ireland with the objective of attacking British targets and rousing the local Irish population to their side. It was not a success, and by 1959 the renewed attacks had dwindled into insignificance.

The rise of the civil rights movement in Northern Ireland and the repressive actions the Unionist government took to quell it led to increasing sectarian violence that culminated with the outbreak of mass rioting in 1969 and the dispatching of British troops to Northern Ireland. This provided the IRA with the opportunity to position itself as the defender of the minority Catholic and republican community, but initially the group was ill prepared to capitalize on it.

In December 1969, the IRA split on ideological grounds, with the new PIRA rejecting what it saw as the failure of the established "Official" IRA (OIRA) to act strongly enough in defense of the Catholic community in Northern Ireland. From 1970 until the signing of the Good Friday Agreement in 1998, PIRA was to form the major driving force behind the republican terrorist campaigns in Northern Ireland, on the British mainland, and against UK targets in various European countries. The group's dominance within republicanism was reflected from the 1990s onward when PIRA dropped the word *Provisional* and increasingly began to refer to itself just as the IRA.

OIRA itself went on to carry out a limited number of violent actions, the most serious of which was the 1972 bombing of the Parachute Regiment's headquarters in retaliation for the deaths on Bloody Sunday. The attack, which killed six civilian workers and a Catholic padre, was one of the group's last, and in May of that year the leadership declared an indefinite cease-fire. OIRA continued to exist in name but in 1975 suffered a further split in its ranks when a dissident faction broke away to form the Marxist-oriented Irish National Liberation Army. Since then it has been largely moribund and essentially sidelined by PIRA as the main representative of the Irish republican cause.

See also: Irish National Liberation Army (INLA); Provisional Irish Republican Army (PIRA)

Further Reading

Alonso, Rogelio. *The IRA and Armed Struggle*. New York: Routledge, 2006.
Coogan, Tim. *The IRA*. London: Palgrave Macmillan, 2002.
English, Richard. *Armed Struggle: The History of the IRA*. New York: Pan Books, 2004.
Smith, M.L.R. *Fighting for Ireland? The Military Strategy of the Irish Republican Movement*. New York: Routledge, 1995.

Lindsay Clutterbuck

ISLAMIC ARMY OF ADEN (IAA)

The Islamic Army of Aden (IAA) operated as an Al Qaeda regional affiliate in southern Yemen. The group's name references the alleged revelation of the prophet Muhammad that "twelve thousand will appear from Aden Abyan who will aid God and His Messenger." The IAA emerged in the mid-1990s as one of several loosely connected organizations established by Afghan-Soviet War veterans and various local and international Islamic jihadists. The battlefield experience of the former mujahideen, combined with the extraordinarily large number of weapons available in Yemen (estimated at three firearms to each resident), expedited the creation of a formidable movement.

The IAA emerged under the leadership of Zein al-Abidin al-Mihdar (aka Abu al-Hassan) against the backdrop of civil unrest following the shaky unification of North and South Yemen in 1990. The group called for the overthrow of the government in Sana'a and the removal of all U.S. and British ambassadors from the country. Despite this dual-track agenda, the IAA targeted only foreigners, never the Yemeni government itself.

The IAA gained notoriety through statements applauding the 1998 U.S. embassy attacks in Kenya and Tanzania and the group's subsequent kidnapping of 16 Western tourists, who were seized in the name of Osama bin Laden. Yemeni forces captured Abu al-Hassan in an operation to free the hostages, four of whom were killed. He was executed and succeeded by Hatem bi Fareed.

The IAA set up a training camp in the mountains of Abyan and adjusted its strategy to focus on high-visibility targets. In coordination with local Al Qaeda members, the organization carried out a failed attack on USS *The Sullivans* and took credit for the bombings of USS *Cole* and the *M/V Limburg* (although primary responsibility for these strikes has always lain with Al Qaeda). The day after the *Cole* incident, another IAA member was charged with throwing a hand grenade into the British embassy.

The IAA issued most threats and statements through Abu Hamza al-Masri, a British-Egyptian dual-national cleric known for preaching a violent and politicized interpretation of Islam. The Bush administration froze his assets in 2002 on the grounds that he was a primary financier for the IAA, and the UK government revoked his citizenship a year later after he was determined to be a threat to national security. Al-Masri was arrested in London on May 27, 2004, and has since been fighting deportation to both Yemen and the United States.

The IAA itself has suffered from a number of setbacks as a result of heightened counterterrorist efforts since 9/11. In 2002 an unmanned missile from a U.S. Predator aircraft struck a car carrying four suspected IAA members along with an Al Qaeda regional commander and a Yemeni-American recruiter. The next year Yemeni forces stormed one of its main compounds, killing several senior members. Following the raid Abd al-Nabi accepted President Ali Abdullah Saleh's offer of a full pardon for all insurgents who surrendered to the government. Deprived of its leader, the IAA effectively collapsed, and there is little evidence that the group has been active since 2003. That said, there have been periodic reports of ex-IAA militants joining jihadist extremists in Yemen, Iraq, and elsewhere.

See also: Al Qaeda; Al Qaeda in the Arabian Peninsula (AQAP); *Limburg* Bombing; USS *Cole* Bombing

Further Reading

Cook, David. *Paradigmatic Jihadi Movements.* West Point, NY: Combating Terrorism Center, 2006. http://www.ctc.usma.edu/posts/paradigmatic-jihadi-movements, accessed February 10, 2012.
McGregor, Andrew. "Strike First." *The World Today* 58, no. 12 (2002).

Schanzer, Jonathan. "Behind the French Tanker Bombing: Yemen's Ongoing Problems with Islamist Terrorism." *Columbia International Affairs Online,* October 21, 2002. http://www.ciaonet.org/pbei/winep/policy_2002/2002_670.html, accessed January 31, 2012.
Schanzer, Jonathan. "Yemen's War on Terror." *Orbis* 43, no. 3 (2004).
"Yemen: Coping with Terrorism and Violence in a Fragile State." *ICG Middle East Report* 8 (2003).

Julie Manning

ISLAMIC JIHAD ORGANIZATION (IJO)

The Islamic Jihad Organization (IJO), more commonly known as Islamic Jihad, was a Shia underground guerrilla group that was formed in 1983 as a resistance movement to the deployment of French and American peacekeepers to Lebanon. It was primarily based out of Baalbek in the Bekaa Valley and was an active participant in the Lebanese Civil War (1975–1990). IJO's leader was Imad Mughniyah, a former cadre of al-Fatah's Force 17 and since 1990 a key member of Lebanese Hezbollah. At its zenith the organization could muster around 200 militants who were funded, trained, and supported by the Revolutionary Guard of post-1979 Iran. The organization is mostly known for its intimate ties to Hezbollah, its attacks on American targets inside Lebanon, and the extensive use of suicide bombings to advance its objectives. This latter tactic was to inspire a number of later terrorist groups, including Al Qaeda.

IJO's inaugural attack occurred on April 18, 1983, when a vehicle-borne improvised explosive device detonated outside the U.S. embassy in Beirut. The ensuing blast claimed the lives of 63 people, including 17 American nationals. Just over six months later, on October 23, the group claimed credit for one of the most successful and well-known strikes against Western interests in Lebanon, the bombing of the Multinational Force barracks in Beirut. Involving two trucks packed with close to 12,000 pounds of TNT, the twin explosions killed 299 international service members: 241 U.S. Marines, 18 Navy personnel, and 3 Army soldiers as well as 58 French paratroopers. The 241 Marines killed represented the highest single-day death toll of American Marines since the Battle of Iwo Jima during World War II. It remains unclear as to whether these two attacks were the work of IJO as an independent organization or as a precursor for Hezbollah, which did not officially exist at the time.

While the bombing of the Multinational Force barracks in Beirut precipitated a limited French air campaign against targets of the Islamic Revolutionary Guard in the Bekaa Valley, the American response was virtually nonexistent. Indeed, in February 1984, just four months after the attack, President Ronald Reagan withdrew all U.S. forces from Lebanon. This decision was widely viewed by militant jihadists as a direct result of the bombings and has been taken as evidence (ultimately flawed) of the country's lack of resolve when hit decisively by its enemies.

IJO continued its campaign of terrorism into 1984 and 1985. Prominent incidents attributed to the group included the murder of Malcolm Kerr, president of the American University in Beirut (January 18, 1984); a suicide attack against Washington's embassy annex in East Beirut, which left 14 dead and dozens injured

(September 20, 1984); the bombing of the El-Descanso restaurant, a Spanish eatery frequented by American servicemen that resulted in 18 fatalities; and the attempted assassination of Kuwaiti emir Jaber al-Ahmad al-Jaber al-Sabah (May 25, 1985).

In the closing years of the Lebanese Civil War, IJO began to lose much of its purpose as a dedicated movement in its own right. Indeed, with the departure of U.S. soldiers in 1985, the organization had achieved its main goal and defining raison d'être. The group's strong ties with the Lebanese Shi'a community made it a natural ally of Hezbollah (which had formally emerged in 1985), and by 1992 the two movements had effectively morphed into one, with Mughniyah appointed as chief of their combined overseas security apparatus. He was later to be tied to the bombing of the Israeli embassy in Buenos Aires.

IJO's relationship with Hezbollah has long been a subject of considerable conjecture. Many analysts have argued that they were one and the same—allowing the latter to distance itself from mass-casualty attacks by claiming responsibility in the name of the former. It is also noted that the organizations were both founded by Iran and received extensive military support, training, financial backing, organizational aid, and other forms of assistance. Given this common external backing and the existence of virtually identical long-term goals, it becomes clear that IJO and Hezbollah certainly had more in common than just being different Shia organizations pursuing similar ideas at the same time.

That said, the religious and communal complexities that underscored the internal violence wracking Lebanon at this time made it extremely difficult to unify the Shia community under the banner of a single organization. In this regard, the two groups *did* have different immediate objectives. Hezbollah was the successful creation of Revolutionary Iran to unite the Shia population in such a way as to advance its foreign-policy goals. By contrast, IJO focused on the immediate goal of physically driving Western military forces out of Lebanon.

See also: Hezbollah (Party of God); Israeli Embassy (Buenos Aires) Bombing

Further Reading

Deeb, Marius. *Militant Islamic Movements in Lebanon: Origins, Social and Ideology.* Washington, DC: Georgetown University, 1986.
Goldberg, Jeffrey. "In the Party of God." *New Yorker,* October 14, 2002.
Ranstorp, Magnus. *Hizb'allah in Lebanon.* New York: Palgrave Macmillan, 1996.
Shatz, Adam. "In Search of Hezbollah." *New York Review of Books,* April 29, 2004. http://www.nybooks.com/articles/archives/2004/apr/29/in-search-of-hezbollah/, accessed February 7, 2012.
Wright, Robin. *Sacred Rage.* New York: Simon and Schuster, 2001.

Dimitar Georgiev

ISLAMIC MOVEMENT OF UZBEKISTAN (IMU)

The Islamic Movement of Uzbekistan (IMU or Harakatul Islamiyyah Uzbekistan) was founded in 1996 as a coalition of militants drawn from Uzbekistan and several other Central Asian regions, including Chechnya, Afghanistan, Pakistan,

Kyrgyzstan, and Tajikistan. It is a large and well-funded terrorist organization that seeks to overthrow the secular and authoritarian regime of Islom Karimov and its replacement with a fundamentalist Muslim state based on the full implementation of sharia law. The group has a close relationship with the Afghan Taliban, and until the overthrow of Mullah Omar's government by the United States in 2001, many of its fighters were based in and trained at camps controlled by the IMU.

Under the leadership of Takhir Yuldashev, the IMU declared a jihad on Uzbekistan in 1999 and commenced a systematic campaign of kidnappings, assassinations, random shootings, and bombings. That same year the group's military commander, Juma Namangani, launched two successful offensives into the heart of Uzbek territory, projecting the group into the spotlight of regional and international publicity.

The IMU has been implicated in a number of terrorist attacks in Uzbekistan, including a 1999 car bomb in Tashkent that killed 16 civilians (and only narrowly missed Karimov); the 1999 abduction of a group of Japanese geologists; the August 2000 kidnapping of four U.S. mountain climbers; and various violent acts against civilian targets that reportedly have little to do with the rebels' ostensible cause. In September 2000, the United States proscribed the group as a designated foreign terrorist organization.

While much of the group's early activity was orchestrated out of the contested Fergana Valley—where it reportedly controls several Central Asian drug-smuggling routes—it has increasingly reoriented its operational focus to regions located in Pakistan's Federally Administered Tribal Areas. These militants continue to espouse a highly fundamentalist agenda and are known to have participated in Taliban attacks directed against Allied forces in Afghanistan as well as in Al Qaeda and Tehrik-e-Taliban Pakistan (TTP) suicide bombings in the Northwest Frontier and Singh provinces. Although the IMU does retain a presence in Fergana, most of these combatants now act as straight narco-syndicates, merely using religion as a justification for their criminal activities.

In November 2000, Namangani was sentenced to death in absentia for the 1999 Tashkent bombing. By then, he had reportedly fled to Afghanistan, where he was a close associate of Osama bin Laden. In November 2001, press sources reported that Namangani had been killed during fighting between Taliban soldiers and the U.S.-backed Northern Alliance in Mazar-e Sharif, Afghanistan. Yuldashev continued to lead the IMU from a hideout along the Pakistani-Afghan border until his death from a U.S. drone attack in October 2009.

See also: Al Qaeda; Tehrik-e-Taliban Pakistan (TTP)

Further Reading

Burgess, Mark. "Terrorism—The Islamic Movement of Uzbekistan." Center for Defense Information, Washington, D.C., March 25, 2002. http://cdi.org/terrorism/imu.cfm.

Child, Greg. *Over the Edge.* New York: Villand, 2002.

Christian, Caryl. "In the Hot Zone." *Newsweek* (Atlantic ed.), October 8, 2001.

Rotar, Igor. "The Islamic Movement of Uzbekistan: A Resurgent IMU?" *Jamestown Terrorism Monitor* 1, no. 8 (2003).

Yakubov, Oleg. *Pack of Wolves.* Moscow: Veche, 2000.

Edward F. Mickolus

ISRAELI EMBASSY (BUENOS AIRES) BOMBING

On March 17, 1992, a suicide terrorist detonated a truck with 220 pounds of explosives at the Israeli embassy in Buenos Aires. The ensuing blast, which was heard three miles away, killed 29 people—among them four staffers and five local Jews—and injured 292 others. The bomb demolished the diplomatic mission (a five-story structure on the corner of Arroyo and Suipacha streets) and severely damaged the surrounding buildings including a church, retirement home, and school.

Shortly after the attack, a statement from a group in Beirut, Lebanon, bearing the name of the "Pro-Iranian Group Islamic Jihad" claimed responsibility and released a surveillance videotape of the Israeli embassy taken prior to the operation. The organization claimed that the bombing was "one of our continuing strikes against the criminal Israeli enemy in an open-ended war, which will not cease until Israel is wiped out of existence." It also disclosed that the perpetrator was a Muslim convert named Abu Yasser, who was motivated by his desire to avenge the death of Sayyid Abass Musawi—the secretary general of Hezbollah (who was killed the same year when an Israeli helicopter gunship ambushed his motorcade in southern Lebanon). Islamic Jihad additionally claimed responsibility for the assassination of the chief of security at the Israeli embassy in Ankara, Turkey, 10 days earlier.

Following the embassy bombing, several foreign intelligence organizations conducted their own independent inquiries in conjunction with the investigation led by the local Argentinean authorities. Israel sent Mossad and Shin Bet teams (which were in charge of the security of Israeli legations abroad) to Buenos Aires as well as police explosives and ballistics experts. The Mossad worked closely with the American Central Intelligence Agency (CIA), which also dispatched teams from its Counter Terrorist Center (CTC) and conducted its own internal inquiry. According to one of the Israeli agents who participated in the operation, "the attack had seriously embarrassed the local authorities, who were in a hurry to wrap it all up quickly and quietly."

These independent investigations provided strong evidence of Iranian and Hezbollah involvement. The CIA intercepted a message sent from Tehran's embassy in Moscow three days before the bombing (which was not translated in real time) that indicated an attack on an Israeli embassy in South America was imminent. Two other dispatches from Iranian embassies in Buenos Aires and Brasilia also contained coded signals about an impending operation. In addition, information gleaned by the U.S. National Security Agency identified Hezbollah operatives Imad Mughniyah and Talal Hamiyah as the principal planners behind the attack. In a recorded conversation between the two, Hamiyah rejoiced over "our project in Argentina" and mocked the Shin Bet for its failure to thwart the bombing. The

American investigation, led by Dr. Stanley Bedlington of the CTC, concluded that Iran was responsible for the operation but that Hezbollah had carried it out to shield Tehran from direct involvement.

The Argentinean intelligence agency (Secretaría de Información del Estado [SIDE]) also produced transcripts of an exchange that took place in the residence of an Iranian diplomat after the attack. In the middle of a noisy family quarrel, the embassy official's wife threatened her husband that she would tell everything she knew about his part in "what happened to the offices of the Zionists." Like the CIA, the SIDE eventually placed direct responsibility for the bombing on Iran, its leaders, and its intelligence service, as well as Hezbollah.

Further Argentinean, American, and Israeli investigations showed that financing for the bombing had come from sympathetic elements of the Shi'ite community in Ciudad del Este, Paraguay—an area located in what is known as the tri-border area (TBA). The perpetrators of the attack also allegedly came from the TBA, and two were eventually charged with direct involvement: Salman el-Reda, who was accused of transporting the explosives used in the bombing, and Assad Ahmad Barakat, Hezbollah's military operations chief and fund-raiser in the TBA. The latter had apparently made several trips to Tehran between 1990 and 1991, during which he reportedly met with high-ranking officials of the Islamic Republic's government.

In the aftermath of the attack, a debate arose within Israel on how to respond. The foreign minister, David Levi, publicly warned that those responsible would receive a "painful punishment." Members of the intelligence community also advocated strong action, asserting that anything else would inevitably encourage further attacks. Others, however, argued knee-jerk reprisals would dangerously escalate tensions between Israel and Iran and could trigger criticism from the international community given the absence of incontrovertible evidence linking Tehran to the incident. Interestingly, Shabtai Shavit, at the time the director of the Mossad, similarly rejected proposals for a forceful response—though on the grounds that his agency had "more important things to do."

Two years later, a second, more devastating attack occurred in the Argentinean capital, this time against a Jewish community center, leaving 85 dead and 151 injured. Various experts indicated that the bombings involved identical methods and suggested that the success of the first operation was almost certainly instrumental in influencing the decision to carry out the second. Prosecutors eventually linked Hezbollah members in Ciudad del Este and Foz do Iguaçu (on the Brazilian side of the TBA) to the 1994 incident and issued additional arrest warrants for Barakat and Mughniyah.

In May 1998, the Argentinean government announced that it had "convincing proof" of Iran's involvement in the Israeli embassy attack and expelled seven diplomats from the country. In a decision presented on December 23, 1999, the Supreme Court in Buenos Aires determined that the operation was the work of the Islamic Jihad Organization (IJO), which it described as the deniable "armed wing" of the Hezbollah. For its part, Iran has consistently rejected any claim it either knew about or took part in the bombing.

See also: Hezbollah (Party of God); Islamic Jihad Organization (IJO); Jewish Community Center (Buenos Aires) Bombing

Further Reading

Bergman, Ronen. *The Secret War with Iran: The 30-Year Clandestine Struggle against the World's Most Dangerous Terrorist Power.* New York: Free Press, 2008.

"Hezbollah: Profile of the Lebanese Shiite Terrorist Organization, of Global Reach Sponsored by Iran and Supported by Syria, the Bombing of the Jewish Community Center in Argentina (1994)—an Example of the Modus Operandi of Hezbollah's Overseas Terrorist Apparatus." Intelligence and Terrorism Information Center, Israel, July 2003. http://www.terrorism-info.org.il/malam_multimedia/html/final/eng/bu/hizbullah/pb/app5.htm, accessed February 5, 2012.

Hudson, Rex. *Terrorist and Organized Crime Groups in the Tri-border Area (TBA) of South America.* Washington, DC: Federal Research Division, Library of Congress, July 2003.

Knight-Ridder. "Group: Israeli Embassy Bombed for Revenge." *Chicago Tribune,* March 19, 1992.

Long, William. "Islamic Jihad Says It Bombed Embassy, Toll 21." *Los Angeles Times,* March 19, 1992.

Office of the Coordinator for Counterterrorism. *Patterns of Global Terrorism: 1992, The Year in Review.* Washington, DC: U.S. Department of State, April 30, 1993.

Gilard Stern

ISTANBUL AIRPORT ATTACK

On August 11, 1976, at around 7:30 P.M. local time, two terrorists aligned with the Popular Front for the Liberation of Palestine (PFLP) opened fire and set off a series of explosives in the El Al boarding area of Yesilkoy International Airport in Istanbul, Turkey. The attack left four dead: Harold Rosenthal, a foreign-policy aide to U.S. senator Jacob K. Javits of New York; Yutako Hirano of Japan; and Solomon Weisbeck and Ernest Elias of Israel. Approximately 20 others were injured. The perpetrators, who intended to hijack El Al Flight 582, a Boeing 707 flying from Bucharest to Tel Aviv via Istanbul, struck as passengers were boarding the plane and as Israeli security officials were screening luggage for weapons. The melee ended after an exchange of gunfire between the attackers and Turkish airport authorities after they had attempted to take a Turkish policewoman hostage. The El Al jet itself was undamaged and departed for Tel Aviv with six wounded passengers on board.

The terrorists, Mahdi Muhammed and Muhammed al-Rashid, were themselves ticketed on a Pakistani International Airlines flight bound for Baghdad. They had traveled on Kuwaiti passports from Tripoli to Istanbul by way of Rome. The pair had intended to gain entry to the El Al plane but opened fire in the terminal as the boarding process was still under way. The two attackers were in transit, which suggests they had hoped to bypass security screening procedures in Istanbul. El Al Airlines, however, had implemented a series of enhanced measures, including checks on all passengers and their baggage immediately prior to boarding.

Upon their arrest, Muhammed and al-Rashid told authorities they were members of the George Habash organization, a reference to the founding father of the PFLP. They were apparently instructed to kill as many Jewish passengers as possible in reprisal for the Israeli raid in Entebbe, Uganda. The latter event had taken place in June 1976 and involved a daring commando raid to free an Air France jet that had been hijacked by a team of seven PFLP terrorists—all of whom were killed. Turkish officials initially sentenced Muhammed and al-Rashid to death in November 1976, but their sentences were later reduced to life imprisonment

The Istanbul airport incident was one in a series of related PFLP attacks conducted during the late 1960s and 1970s that targeted civilian planes and infrastructure. The purpose of these operations was both to elicit international publicity for the group's cause and to coerce the release of captured Palestinian terrorists held in various countries around the world. The most infamous of these assaults occurred in September 1970 when five passenger jets were simultaneously hijacked and re-routed to Dawson's Field in Jordan. The governments of the United Kingdom, the Netherlands, Israel, the United States, and Switzerland all eventually became embroiled in lengthy negotiations for the release of the captives, which the PFLP claimed was tantamount to official recognition of its political agenda. Another dramatic case took place in 1972. In this episode, two members of the Japanese Red Army (JRA)—acting on behalf of Habash's organization—struck Lod Airport in Tel Aviv and murdered 28 passengers who had just arrived on an Air France flight.

While the PFLP was prepared to attack any civilian aircraft, El Al was the preferred target as it was the national carrier of Israel and many of its pilots were former officers in the country's air force. By striking against the airline, the PFLP was able to portray itself as a meaningful force that had the capacity to take the battle directly to the heart of the Jewish state.

See also: Dawson's Field Hijackings; Entebbe Hostage Rescue; Lod Airport Massacre; Popular Front for the Liberation of Palestine (PFLP)

Further Reading

Black, Ian, and Benny Morris. *Israel's Secret Wars: A History of Israel's Intelligence Services.* New York: Grove, 1991.

Byman, Daniel. *A High Price: The Triumphs and Failures of Israeli Counterterrorism.* New York: Oxford University Press, 2011.

"El Al Passengers at Istanbul Attacked; Guerillas Seized; 4 Dead, 20 Wounded." *New York Times,* August 12, 1976.

Mickolus, Edward F., and Susan L. Simmons. *The Terrorist List.* Santa Barbara, CA: Praeger, 2011.

"Turkey to Ask Death for 2 Guerillas after Attempt to Hijack El Al Jetliner." *New York Times,* August 12, 1976.

Austin C. Imperato

ISTANBUL BOMBINGS

On November 15, 2003, suicide terrorists detonated two vehicle-borne improvised explosive devices (VBIEDs) at Neve Shalom and Beth Israel synagogues in Istanbul, Turkey, killing 29 and injuring more than 300 others. Five days later the city was hit again when VBIEDs blew up at the headquarters of the Hong Kong and Shanghai Banking Corporation and the British consulate, leaving 32 dead and over

400 wounded. The attacks were part of an orchestrated Al Qaeda strategy designed to terrorize Turkey's Jewish population, expose Ankara's links to Israel, and "punish" London for its willing collusion in the U.S. occupation of Iraq.

Initially, Al Qaeda had designated the Incirlik Air Base, Israeli ships docked in Istanbul, and the U.S. consulate as primary targets. However, the local planners shifted their focus to "softer" venues when they concluded that the original sites were too well protected. The synagogue attacks were originally scheduled for November 8 but for reasons unknown were called off at the last minute and delayed for a week.

The bombings were carried out using commercial vans and explosive ingredients purchased on the open market. The VBIEDs were based on ammonium nitrate and detonated using trigger mechanisms installed on each of the vehicles. The entire operation is thought to have cost no more than $150,000, although surveillance and planning are thought to have lasted well over a year.

The key plotters all came from the southeastern city of Bingol and belonged to a group known as the Union of Imams. The group served as a local Al Qaeda cell, and its members are known to have received terrorist training in Afghanistan. It was organized around four concentric circles. The first were the "imams," who provided leadership and coordination. Key personalities in this circle were Habib Aktas, who was in charge of operational planning and recruiting; Azad Ekinci,

Police forensic officers examine and collect evidence in front of the ruined Neve Shalom Synagogue in Istanbul, Turkey, November 15, 2003. The attack was one part of a coordinated strike that also targeted the Beth Israel Synagogue. A total of 29 people died in the explosions, with more than 300 injured. (AP Photo/Burhan Ozbilici)

who oversaw logistics and vehicle procurement; and Gurcan Bac, who acted as the main bomb maker.

Below the imams were the suicide bombers, who were required to take a martyrdom oath and pledge allegiance to the organization's leaders. The third circle consisted of financiers, most of whom worked in textile firms. Finally, there were recruiters, who networked among small businessmen and in mosques, inviting potential cadres to attend fortnightly religious house meetings.

Following the bombings the Turkish authorities arrested 74 people. Three of those detained, Harun Ihan, Loai al-Saqa (whom Jordanian authorities had already tried in absentia for participating in the 2002 failed chemical attack in Amman), and Hamid Obysi, admitted their own complicity and identified several other key players involved. These included Aktas, who oversaw the operation; Muhammad Atet, Al Qaeda's liaison to the Union of Imams; Bac and Yusuf Polt, who were both responsible for surveillance and reconnaissance; and the four suicide terrorists who detonated the VBIEDs: Mesut Cabuk (at Beth Israel), Gokhan Elaltuntas (Neve Shalom), Ilas Kuncak (HSBC Bank), and Feridun Ugurlu (British consulate).

Aktas and Bac were both thought to have fled the country immediately after the attacks and escaped the dragnet. Aktas was later reportedly killed during a U.S. raid in Fallujah, Iraq in September 2004. Bac's whereabouts are unknown, although there is some speculation that he is hiding in Syria.

On February 16, 2007 a Turkish court convicted al-Saqa, Polt, Ihan, and five others to life imprisonment for their role in the attacks. Obysi was sentenced to 12.5 years for being a member of Al Qaeda. Ten militants received jail terms of three years and nine months for aiding and abetting terrorism, and 26 were acquitted.

See also: Al Qaeda; Amman Toxic Chemical Bomb Plot

Further Reading

"Istanbul Rocked by Double Bombing." *BBC News,* November 20, 2003. http://news.bbc.co.uk/2/hi/europe/3222608.stm, accessed October 8, 2011.

"Seven Jailed for Turkey Bombings." *BBC News,* February 17, 2007. http://news.bbc.co.uk/2/hi/europe/6370117.stm, accessed October 8, 2011.

"Turks Bust Alleged Qaeda Plotter." *CBS News,* December 19, 2003. http://www.cbsnews.com/stories/2003/12/17/terror/main588982.shtml, accessed October 8, 2011.

Vick, Karl. "Al Qaeda's Hand in Istanbul Plot." *Washington Post,* February 13, 2007.

Edward F. Mickolus

JAIPUR BOMBINGS

On May 13, 2008, seven improvised explosive devices (IEDs) were detonated across Jaipur, India, killing 64 people and injuring more than 150. The bombs, which went off in a space of 15 minutes commencing around 1:45 P.M., were strategically placed in crowded marketplaces and outside Hindu temples. They were composed of high-grade C-4 plastic explosive (RDX) packed in containers along with nitrate compounds, ball bearings, and iron pipes. The devices were strapped to bicycles and triggered using simple alarm clocks. The blasts constituted the 23rd act of terrorism on Indian soil since 2005.

The attacks sought to cripple the tourism industry in Jaipur. The city is a popular holiday destination, the capital of the northwestern state of Rajasthan, and the center of what is known as India's tourism golden triangle (Agra and Delhi being the other two hubs). The attacks were clearly designed to inflict maximum damage. One IED exploded close to Jaipur's most famous landmark, the historic Hawa Mahal (palace of winds), while others targeted busy intersections and bazaars thronged with shoppers. In addition, the day of the blasts—a Tuesday—is an auspicious day for Hindus, and at least one device went off in front of a temple to the god Hanuman, which was packed with worshippers.

Indian Mujahideen (IM)—a little-known terrorist movement at the time—claimed responsibility for the blasts in an e-mail sent to media outlets the next day. Apart from taking credit, the group declared "war" on the central government in Delhi and threatened it was planning more attacks. Investigators initially dismissed IM's touted complicity, rejecting the idea that any domestic extremist organization was operating in the country and casting blame on external Pakistani groups such as Harakat ul-Jihad al-Islami (HuJI) or Lashkar-e-Taiba (LeT). However, the Rajasthan police managed to successfully recover the serial number of one of the bicycles used in the attacks, confirming it was the same as one listed in the IM e-mail. This authenticated the group's claim.

The Jaipur bombings and IM's involvement came as huge shock to the Indian security community, which had yet to take seriously the existence of a homegrown extremist movement. The lack of any prior intelligence led to blame games between federal agencies and the Rajasthan state police and calls for the establishment of an effective counterterrorist network to monitor potential internal threats. There were also demands for a strong response, and hundreds of suspects were detained for questioning. Dozens were picked up on highly circumstantial evidence, and many were released. As of September 2011, nine accused have been named in the charge sheet by the Rajasthan Anti-terrorism Squad. The investigation has yet to reach its conclusive end. Delhi banned the IM in June 2010, and the United States placed the group on its list of foreign terrorist organizations in September 2011.

See also: Indian Mujahideen (IM)

Further Reading

Chengappa, Raj, and Sandeep Unnithan. "How We Can Stop it." *India Today,* May 13, 2008. http://indiatoday.intoday.in/story/How+we+can+stop+it/1/8303.html, accessed February 17, 2012.

Herman, Steve. "Bangladeshis Questioned about Jaipur Blasts." *VOA News,* 2008. http://www.voanews.com/english/news/a-13-2008-05-15-voa22.html, accessed February 17, 2012.

"India Seeks Bombers Who Killed 45." *International Tribune,* July 28, 2008.

Mehta, Ashish. "Jaipur Blast: NIA Unhappy with Raj ATS progress." *Times of India,* September 8, 2011. http://articles.timesofindia.indiatimes.com/2011-09-08/jaipur/3012 9875_1_jaipur-blasts-rajasthan-ats-rajasthan-anti-terrorist-squad, accessed February 13, 2012.

Nanjappa, Vicky. "Report Exposes How the Police Botched Up the Jaipur Serial Blast Probe." *Rediff News,* January 12, 2012. http://www.rediff.com/news/report/report-exposes-how-police-botched-up-jaipur-blasts-probe/20120125.htm, accessed February 13, 2012.

Sengupta, Somini. "Curfew in Indian City after Blasts." *New York Times,* May 13, 2008.

Sumitha Narayanan Kutty

JAISH-E-MOHAMMED (JEM)

Jaish-e-Mohammed (JeM, or the Army of Mohammed) is a Pakistan-based Islamic terrorist group espousing the Deobandi sect of Islam. The group was founded in 2000 by Maulana Masood Azhar, then general secretary of the militant group Harakat-ul-Mujahideen (HuM), following his release from an Indian prison after the hijacking of Air India Flight 814 by members of HuM. Azhar recruited heavily among members of HuM to build his new organization and received extensive support in this endeavor from both militant Deobandi clerics and Pakistan's InterServices Intelligence (ISI) Directorate. A dispute broke out regarding the disposition of HuM property claimed by JeM, leading to armed clashes between members of the two groups before a settlement was negotiated by Deobandi clerics.

Like HuM, JeM espoused a primarily anti-Indian agenda at its outset and developed a reputation for high-profile suicide attacks, including so-called fedayeen-style assaults where heavily armed members would attempt to infiltrate military encampments, fortify themselves in place, and then kill as many soldiers as possible before succumbing to counterattack. JeM staged what is believed to have been the first suicide bombing in Jammu and Kashmir in 2000. The group was also involved in the October 2001 attack on the legislative assembly in Jammu and Kashmir, which left 31 people dead, as well as a joint operation with Lashkar-e-Taiba (LeT) against the Indian national parliament three months later in December 2001 (which nearly precipitated a war between Delhi and Islamabad). In addition to its relationship with ISI, JeM established strong ties with various violent Deobandi sectarian groups, including Sipah-e-Sahaba and Lashkar-e-Jhangvi (LeJ).

JeM was also closely affiliated with Al Qaeda. The group operated joint training camps in Afghanistan when the country was under Taliban rule and is also known to have used its al-Akhtar Trust to help provide financial and medical support to Al Qaeda.

JeM was banned by the Pakistani government in January 2002 following its attack on the Indian parliament, and Azhar was placed under house arrest. However, Azhar was later released from his detention, and the group continued to operate freely. The U.S. invasion of Afghanistan had a strong impact on JeM, and many of the group's members became increasingly interested in targeting American and other Western interests in response to Operation Enduring Freedom (OEF). Then president Pervez Musharraf, who had continued the long-standing Pakistani government policy of supporting terrorist groups operating against India, was also vilified for his support of Washington's self-declared global war on terrorism.

In 2003 Azhar ousted a dozen ranking members of JeM including Maulana Abdul Jabbar after revelations that they had organized attacks against Western and Christian targets in Pakistan without his authorization. This caused a major schism within JeM ranks, with hard-liners deserting Azhar and joining the expelled members to form Jamaat ul-Furqaan (JuF); the mainline faction of JeM under Azhar was renamed Khuddam-al-Islam. Both groups were banned in November 2003 and were heavily monitored by Pakistani security forces following assassination attempts against Musharraf in December 2003, one of which involved a suicide bomber affiliated with JuF.

Despite Azhar's attempts to maintain the group's ties with the Pakistani government and retain JeM's focus on operations against India, numerous members of the group have been linked to Al Qaeda and attacks/plots outside the subcontinent. These include Rashid Rauf, a relative of Azhar by marriage who helped organize the 2006 liquid explosives plot against transatlantic flights from Europe to the United States; Ahmed Omar Saeed Shaikh, who was released from prison in India alongside Azhar and helped orchestrate the kidnapping of Daniel Pearl; Shezad Tanweer, one of the principal perpetrators implicated in the 7/7 bombings of the London Underground in 2005; and Mohammed Rehan, who is believed to have assisted Times Square bomber Faisal Shahzad travel to Peshawar prior to his training in Waziristan.

JeM has also been linked to the Tehrik-e-Taliban Pakistan (TTP, or Pakistani Taliban), hosting its members when they visit the Punjab. Breakaway JeM members—possibly affiliated with JuF—have additionally been linked to attacks on Pakistani security forces. According to some sources, members of the group fought alongside the Tehrik-e-Nefaz-e-Shariat-e-Mohammadi (TNSM) to repel military offensives in Swat and have increasingly joined forces with the TTP and Al Qaeda in Pakistan's tribal areas, helping stage attacks throughout the Punjab as part of what is frequently called the Punjabi Taliban.

It is unclear at the present time what level of control Azhar is able to exert over JeM. As the preceding examples indicate, members of the group continue to freely associate with and assist Al Qaeda and other terrorist groups that advocate an anti-American and anti–Pakistani government agenda. The current status of JeM's relationship with ISI is also unclear. While the group is allowed to continue operations in Pakistan and remains active in the Indian state of Jammu and Kashmir, its association with attacks directed against Islamabad and the West neither accords with, and is almost certainly not sanctioned (at least directly) by, the intelligence services.

JeM operates several Urdu- and English-language publications such as *Haftroza Al-Qalam* and retains a vast network of mosques, madrassas, training camps, legitimate businesses (such as commodity trading and real estate), and religious trusts throughout Pakistan, particularly in Punjab, Sindh, and Kashmir. The group controls an expansive training facility in Balakot (in Khyber-Pakhtunkhwa) and has extremely close links with several prominent mosques and madrassas in Karachi that are suspected of acting as a major source of recruits. Azhar currently resides in Model Town, Bahawalpur, where the group maintains a massive compound.

See also: Harakat-ul-Mujahideen (HuM); Indian National Parliament Attack; Jamaat ul-Furqaan (JuF); Lashkar-e-Taiba (LeT); Tehrik-e-Taliban Pakistan (TTP)

Further Reading

Fair, Christine C. and Peter Chalk. *Fortifying Pakistan: The Role of US Internal Security Assistance.* Washington, DC: U.S. Institute of Peace, 2006. Pp. 15–18.

Foster, Peter, and Nasir Malick. "Suicide Bombers Flew to Pakistan Together." *Daily Telegraph* (UK), July 19, 2005.

Haqqani, Husein. "The Gospel of Jihad." *Foreign Policy,* September–October 2002, 72–74.

Harding, Luke, and Rosie Cowan. "Pakistan Militants Linked to London Attacks." *The Guardian* (UK), July 19, 2005.

"Jaish-e-Muhammad: Profile." South Asia Terrorism Portal. http:// http://www.satp.org/satporg/countries/Indian/states/jandk/terrorist_outfits/jaish-e-mohammad_mujahideen_e_tanzeem.html.

Rabasa, Angel, Peter Chalk, Kim Cragin, Sara A. Daly, Heather S. Gregg, Theodore W. Karasik, Kevin A. O'Brien, and William Rosenau. *Beyond Al Qaeda. Part 1: The Global Jihadist Network.* Santa Monica, CA: RAND, 2006.

Rana, Muhammad. *A to Z of Jehadi Organizations in Pakistan.* Lahore: Mashal, 2004.

Sciolino, Elaine, and Don Van Natta. "2004 British Raid Sounded Alert on Pakistani Militants." *New York Times,* July 14, 2005.

Ben Brandt

JAMAA AL-TAWHID WA'A JIHAD (JTJ)

Jamaa al-Tawhid wa'a Jihad (JTJ), whose name translates to Monotheism and Jihad, was a Sunni salafist-jihadist group operating in Iraq during the early stages of the Iraq War. One of the most violent and disruptive insurgent movements in post-invasion Iraq, the group was founded and led by Abu Musab al-Zarqawi. Al-Zarqawi would ultimately pledge allegiance to Osama bin Laden and formally rebrand the group as Tanzom Qa'idat al-Jihadi Bilad al-Rafidyan (QJBR), more commonly known as Al Qaeda in Iraq (AQI). As the successor to JTJ, QJBR currently operates in Iraq as of this writing under the name of its umbrella organization, the Islamic State of Iraq.

While the exact date of JTJ's founding is unknown, one can trace its roots through the life of al-Zarqawi and his relationship to various militant groups, portions of whose cadres would ultimately form JTJ. Following a short stint in prison for sexual assault, al-Zarqawi left Jordan in 1989 to participate in jihad against the Soviets in Afghanistan. While he arrived too late to take part in the heavy fighting, this visit provided al-Zarqawi with his first chance to forge ties with veterans of the Afghan jihad. After he returned to Jordan, he fell in with the Jordanian militant group Bayat al-Imam, led by al-Zarqawi's mentor Abu Muhammad al-Maqdisi, many of whose members were Jordanian veterans of the Afghan jihad. Al-Zarqawi was thrown into prison a second time for plotting against the Jordanian state in 1994. This stint in jail merely served as a chance for al-Zarqawi to make connections and mature into a leader, for he was admired by fellow prisoners for his religious discipline and ultimately supplanted al-Maqdisi. Upon his release as part of King Abdullah's amnesty program in 1999, al-Zarqawi took part in the millennium bomb plot, which aimed to bomb a series of luxury hotels in Jordan. However, the plot was uncovered, and al-Zarqawi fled to Afghanistan via Pakistan.

It was in Herat, Afghanistan, that al-Zarqawi began to truly forge the core leadership of what would ultimately become JTJ. Drawing on his previous connections to various jihadist groups, he set up camp in Herat province in the northwestern part of the country. Before doing so, he first had to receive permission from bin Laden. Al-Zarqawi founded his organization as a wholly separate entity from bin Laden's Al Qaeda organization, chiefly because al-Zarqawi believed in first targeting the "near enemy" (Arab regimes deemed to be apostates), while bin Laden believed jihadist efforts should be targeted at the "far enemy" (the United States and other Western regimes). In spite of these differences, al-Zarqawi was permitted to remain in the country and run his camp out of northwestern Afghanistan in 1999.

The U.S.-led invasion of Afghanistan in 2001 disrupted al-Zarqawi's network. While al-Zarqawi and his cadres briefly participated in the fighting, he and his network were ultimately forced to flee from his base in Herat to Iraq, via northern Iran. In Iraq, al-Zarqawi was able to link up with members of Ansar al-Islam (AaI), a Kurdistan-based Iraqi militant group, in early 2002. As a charismatic figure with extensive ties to Arab jihadist networks in the region, al-Zarqawi quickly broadened beyond AaI and eventually branched off to form his own independent organization, JTJ. Under al-Zarqawi's guidance JTJ engaged in international terrorism. The group assassinated Laurence Foley, an American employee of the U.S. Agency for International Development, outside of his home in Amman in 2002. It also was implicated in plots involving the use of ricin in France and Europe. However, perhaps owing to al-Zarqawi's emphasis on the near enemy, JTJ maintained a focus on Iraq, basing itself in the country's Sunni triangle, already home to a number of different Sunni insurgent movements.

Following the U.S. invasion of Iraq, JTJ blossomed. It executed a number of deadly attacks on Western targets. As a successful facilitator of foreign fighters, al-Zarqawi helped to send a steady stream of suicide bombers for a wave of attacks he unleashed on the country. Among the most devastating was the August 7, 2003, car bombing at the Jordanian embassy, which marked the first major attack of the war against a non–Coalition Forces target and set the tone for the rampant violence that would soon engulf the country. JTJ then followed this attack with the August 19, 2003, suicide car bombing at the headquarters of the United Nations (UN) Assistance Mission in Iraq, located in Baghdad's Canal Hotel. The attack proved especially devastating as it killed Sergio Vieira de Mello, the UN special representative for Iraq, and ultimately prompted the UN to withdraw from Iraq altogether. JTJ's descent into infamy reached its high-water mark a few months later when on May 7, 2004, it beheaded American businessman Nicholas Berg. The videotaped beheading, which allegedly included al-Zarqawi personally wielding the knife, made for gruesome international headlines. This act was but one of a number of beheadings JTJ carried out in post-invasion Iraq.

While JTJ might be best known for these high-profile attacks on international targets, the bulk of its operations targeted and killed Iraqis. The group is believed to have been behind numerous attacks on police recruiting centers, including a series of five coordinated blasts on October 27, 2003, which killed potential police recruits and civilian bystanders alike. JTJ also intentionally targeted the country's Shi'a, both because al-Zarqawi viewed them as apostates and because he saw strategic value in sowing the seeds of sectarian war between the country's Sunni and Shi'a. With this goal in mind, JTJ carried out a number of high-profile attacks against the Shi'a. Its first major attack took place on August 29, 2003, when it targeted the Imam Ali mosque in the Shi'ite holy city of Najaf in a bombing, killing a prominent Shi'ite cleric and 83 others. Though some sources allege that Iran had a hand in the attack, most attribute it to JTJ. The group then followed the Najaf bombing with a spate of other bombings in the Shi'ite-dominated cities of Karbala and Basra that left thousands of Iraqi Shi'a dead.

By mid-2004, these attacks catapulted the group to prominence as arguably the most important jihadist insurgents operating in the country. As one of the core elements of the Sunni insurgency, JTJ ultimately attracted U.S. attention. The United States conducted a number of air strikes in Fallujah aimed at JTJ targets in August 2004 and ultimately launched the second Battle of Fallujah partly in an effort to oust al-Zarqawi's network (alongside many Sunni nationalist groups) from what was perceived to be his main base of operations. U.S. efforts also included targeted raids on members of al-Zarqawi's network throughout central, western, and northern Iraq.

JTJ survived these onslaughts, which further fueled the reputation of al-Zarqawi and his network. At the same time, JTJ saw an opportunity to expand its role in Iraq by leveraging the broader Al Qaeda network. Following eight months of lengthy negotiations, al-Zarqawi officially pledged allegiance to bin Laden in October 2004, renaming JTF as QJBR. This alliance was somewhat unexpected because al-Zarqawi had had the opportunity to join Al Qaeda upon his arrival in Afghanistan in 1999 and chose not to do so, chiefly over the differences as to whether to prioritize attacking the near enemy or the far enemy.

Nonetheless, in 2004, al-Zarqawi felt he could overlook these differences since official Al Qaeda affiliation offered JTJ a number of advantages. The move allowed al-Zarqawi greater access to Al Qaeda's technical and operational expertise. Most important, Al Qaeda offered al-Zarqawi both a brand name and a larger platform from which he could draw recruits. Already a successful facilitator of foreign fighter inflows, Zarqawi now had much greater pool of personnel resources from which he could draw. Overall, these benefits outweighed the strategic differences between al-Zarqawi and bin Laden, and thus JTJ evolved to become QJBR. In its new form, the group would go on to become an even more brutal insurgent jihadist organization than its predecessor.

See also: International Red Cross Headquarters (Baghdad) Bombing; Iraqi Sectarian Attacks; Jordanian Embassy (Baghdad) Bombing; Tanzom Qa'idat al-Jihadi Bilad al-Rafidyan (QJBR); United Nations Headquarters (Baghdad) Attack; Zarqawi, Abu Musab al-

Further Reading

Fishman, Brian. "Zarqawi's Jihad: Inside the Mind of Iraq's Most Notorious Man." Working paper, Combating Terrorism Center, West Point, NY, April 26, 2006.

International Crisis Group. *Jordan's 9/11: Dealing with Jihadi Islamism.* Middle East Report no. 47, November 23, 2005.

Michael, George. "The Legend and Legacy of Abu Musab al-Zarqawi." *Defence Studies* 7, no. 3 (September 2007).

Raphaeli, Nimrod. *'The Sheikh of the Slaughterers': Abu Mus'ab Al-Zarqawi and the Al-Qaeda Connection.* Washington, D.C.: The Middle East Media Research Institute. Inquiry and Analysis Series Report no. 23. July 1, 2005.

Nate Shestak

JAMAAT UL-FURQAAN (JUF)

Jamaat ul-Furqaan (JuF) is a splinter faction of the Deobandi terrorist group Jaish-e-Mohammed (JeM) that formed in 2003 after JeM's emir, Masood Azhar, purged a dozen ranking cadres from his organization in June 2003. The expelled members had conducted attacks on Western and Christian targets within Pakistan in 2002 without Azhar's authorization, killing two U.S. citizens in the process. Following the fissure, both groups reportedly fought over control of mosques and sought the blessing of senior jihadist clerics, with members of JuF accusing Azhar of corruption and nepotism and belittling him as beholden to his "masters in the Pakistani intelligence agencies."

Led by Maulana Abdul Jabbar (who reportedly served as JeM's liaison to Al Qaeda and the Taliban prior to 9/11) and Maulana Abdullah Shah Mazhar, JuF is considered the dominant faction of JeM and is believed to have forged close ties with the Tehrik-e-Taliban Pakistan (TTP, or the Pakistani Taliban) and Lashkar-e-Jhangvi (LeJ). Some reports also allege that the group works through a charitable entity named al-Asr Trust. JuF was banned along with Azhar's faction of JeM in November 2003, and Jabbar was taken into custody following assassination attempts against President Pervez Musharraf; he was eventually released in August 2004, reportedly after providing information on militants who could have helped plan the attacks.

JuF has been linked to a number of high-profile terrorist incidents in recent years. In 2005 three JuF members were arrested on suspicion of being involved in a suicide attack against then prime minister Shaukat Aziz the previous year. In

2007 the group actively supported the Tehrik-e-Nefaz-e-Shariat-e-Mohammadi (TNSM) in its fighting with the Pakistani Army, taking up positions and setting checkpoints in the Swat Valley. A number of reports have alleged that Rashid Rauf, the mastermind behind the 2006 liquid explosives plot to target transatlantic flights between Europe and the United States, was a member of JuF; similar accusations have been made against Osama Nazir, who reputedly met with Shezad Tanweer, one of the main architects of the July 2005 bombings on the London Underground.

Although the current status of JuF is difficult to pinpoint with any real degree of accuracy given the porous and constantly changing nature of jihadi outfits operating out of Pakistan, the group is widely considered to be an integral component of the so-called Punjabi Taliban, which is based in the southern part of Punjab and also includes among its membership LeJ and Lashkar-e-Taiba (LeT). JuF is also thought to have attracted recruits from other militant organizations disgruntled by the Pakistani government's support of the United States and has been tied to attacks staged in conjunction with the TTP. According to one knowledgeable local source, Mazhar presently lives in Karachi, while Jabbar is in North Waziristan, where he operates a small network of fighters in Afghanistan. This same commentator also claims that Jabbar has been increasingly critical of the TTP and had voiced opposition to the movement's then emir, Baitullah Mehsud, prior to his death. If accurate, this would seem to suggest that JuF may have developed a schism of its own regarding the issue of targeting Pakistani security forces.

See also: Heathrow Liquid Bomb Plot; Jaish-e-Mohammed (JeM); London Underground Bombings; Mehsud, Baitullah; Tehrik-e-Taliban Pakistan (TTP)

Further Reading

Benjamin, Yobie. "The Top 15 Terrorist Organizations in Pakistan and Afghanistan." U.S. Labor Against the War. http://www.uslaboragainstwar.org/article.php?id=2046.
"Bojinka II: The Transatlantic Liquid Bomb Plot." NEFA Foundation Report 15, April 2008. http://www.nefafoundation.org/miscellaneous/FeatureDocs/Bonjinka2LiquidBombs.pdf, accessed February 29, 2012.
"Jammat-ul-Furqa." *BasicsProject.org.* http://www.basicsproject.org/islamist-etrrorism/islamist_terror_organizations/islamist_terrororganizations.html#Jammat-ul-Furqua.
"The Politics of Jamaat-ul-Furqan." *Intrepid Truth,* October 31, 2005. Available online at http://politicsofcp.blogspot.com/2005/10/jamaat-ul-furqan.html.

Ben Brandt

JAMA'AT UL-MUJAHIDEEN BANGLADESH (JMB)

The Jama'at ul-Mujahideen Bangladesh (JMB, or the Bangladesh Assembly of Holy Warriors) was reportedly formed in 1998 in Jamalpur; however, its origin is still somewhat vague. The group aims to establish a system of Islamic *hukumat* (rule) in Bangladesh through the force of arms and is vigorously opposed to Western-style democracy. It has been linked to Al Qaeda, although a concrete association between the two organizations has never been proven. Indian sources also allege that the organization works in conjunction with various Kashmiri *tanzeem* (outfits) and benefits from training, intelligence, and logistical assistance imparted by Pakistan's main spy service, the InterServices Intelligence (ISI) Directorate.

JMB has about 10,000 full-time and 100,000 part-time members, many of whom have been recruited from a proliferating web of radical mosques and unlicensed madrassas (known as *Dars-e-Nizami*) throughout the country. These individuals come from a wide spectrum of social and professional backgrounds and are known to have included university teachers. Different wings of the group handle finances, public relations, external links, and recruitment. The latter is reportedly the largest. A relatively small division is responsible for military training and intelligence as well as overseeing cells that have infiltrated various political and nongovernmental organizations.

JMB has reportedly received funds from wealthy benefactors in Kuwait, the United Arab Emirates, Bahrain, Pakistan, Saudi Arabia, and Libya. The authorities believe money is sent either directly or channeled through established Middle Eastern nongovernmental organizations such as Revival of Islamic Heritage, Doukatelis Kuwait, Al Fuzaira, Khairul Ansar Al Khairia, Doulatul Bahrain, and the Al Haramaine Islamic Institute. Additional sources of income come from investments in legitimate shrimp farms and cold-storage plants, most of which are based in the southwestern region of Bangladesh, as well as money-laundering rackets run in Dhaka, Jessore, and Chittagong.

JMB first gained publicity on May 20, 2002, when eight members were arrested in the Dinajpur district of India. According to the authorities, those apprehended had 25 petrol bombs and were planning unspecified attacks to further the extremist Islamist cause on the subcontinent. The following February the group allegedly set off seven improvised explosive devices that wounded three people in the Chhoto Gurgola area of Dinajpur town.

Two years later, in August 2005, 500 bombs detonated in 300 locations, hitting 63 out of Bangladesh's 64 districts. JMB claimed responsibility for the explosions, affirming in a written statement, "We're the soldiers of Allah. We've taken up arms for the implementation of Allah's law the way Prophet, Sahabis and heroic Mujahideen have done for centuries. . . . It is time to implement Islamic law in Bangladesh. There is no future with man-made law." These attacks were followed by suicide bombings at courthouses in Gazipur and Chittagong on November 29, 2005—the first to have ever occurred in Bangladesh—which killed 9 people and wounded over 65.

The events of 2005 came as a major shock to government authorities in Dhaka, who until that time had dismissed domestic Islamists as irrelevant and of no consequence to national security. JMB was immediately banned, as was another organization that was also believed to have played a supporting role in the August bombings, Harakat-ul-Jihad-Islami Bangladesh (HUJI B). Bangladesh's elite Rapid Action Battalion (RAB) later captured Maulana Abdur Rahman and Siddiqul Islam—respectively, the supreme and deputy commanders of JMB and the suspected masterminds behind the bombings. Both were executed, along with four other militants who were tied to the attacks against the courthouses, on March 30, 2007.

After Abdur Rahman's death, Maulana Saidur Rahman took over the leadership of the JMB. Other senior figures include Maulana Akram-uzzaman, Abdur Rouf, Maulana Shahidul Islam, Maulana Mahadi, Sheikh Maulana Noman, and Maulana Manjur Ahmed. Most of these men were allegedly trained in Afghanistan. Maulana Fariduddin Masud, a former director of the government-run Islamic Foundation, is also alleged to be a top JMB leader. He was arrested on August 22, 2005.

Although Bangladesh has come to appreciate the potential threat posed by JMB, the group's early development and subsequent expansion are largely owing to the lax and casual attitude of the central administration in Dhaka. As noted, prior to 2005 the authorities blithely ignored the group, despite several incidents that should have alerted them to a budding extremist network. Several members have been granted bail, and a number of investigations have been allowed to stall due to the loss of key documents. Moreover, JMB directly benefited from the political bargaining that led to the election of a National Party–led coalition in 2001. A key partner in the new government of Prime Minister Khaleda Zia was Jamaat-e-Islami—the parent organization of Islami Chhatra Shibir, a student wing that also includes many JMB members.

See also: Bangladesh Bombings; Harakat-ul-Jihad-Islami Bangladesh (HuJI B)

Further Reading

"Bangladesh Gets Its First Taste of Suicide Attacks." *New York Times*, November 30, 2005.

Karlekar, Hiranmay. *Bangladesh: The Next Afghanistan?* New Delhi: Sage, 2005.

Montero, David, and Somini Sengupta. "Bangladesh Blast Kills One and Hurts 30." *New York Times,* December 2, 2005.

Rabasa, Angel, Peter Chalk, Kim Cragin, Sara A. Daly, Heather S. Gregg, Theodore W. Karasik, Kevin A. O'Brien, and William Rosenau. *Beyond al-Qaeda. Part 1: The Global Jihadist Movement.* Santa Monica, CA: RAND, 2006.

Rashid, Ahmed. *Descent into Chaos: The United States and the Failure of Nation Building in Pakistan, Afghanistan, and Central Asia.* New York: Viking Books, 2008.

Donna Bassett

JAMMU AND KASHMIR NATIONAL LIBERATION FRONT (JKNLF)

The Jammu and Kashmir National Liberation Front (JKNLF) served as the main insurgent organization in the disputed territory of Jammu and Kashmir (J&K) during the 1990s. The group's principal demand was that India and Pakistan give up control of J&K—half of which makes up Delhi's only Muslim-majority state—and let the area establish its own geopolitical identity. Failing this, the JKNLF would accept Kashmir's incorporation into Pakistan, India's Muslim neighbor.

The roots of the present J&K struggle date back to 1947. In this year the princely state's last Hindu maharaja, Hari Singh, formally elected to join India in return for military assistance to help suppress a Muslim tribal invasion that had allegedly been orchestrated by Pakistan at the time of the subcontinent's partition. Islamabad vigorously rejected the validity of this Instrument of Accession, arguing that

Singh had been coerced into signing an agreement of union on terms dictated by Delhi and supported by Britain, the ex-colonial power. Pakistan quickly moved to consolidate control over that part of the state that had fallen to Muslim hands, which it has since referred to as Azzad Jammu o-Kashmir (AJK, or Free Jammu and Kashmir). A year of subsequent fighting led to intervention by the United Nations (UN), which determined that the state's future should be decided on the basis of a plebiscite held under international supervision (UN Resolutions of August 13, 1948, and January 5, 1949). This popular referendum never materialized, generating two more Indo-Pakistani wars in 1965 and 1971. In 1972 a 740-kilometer (459-mile) Line of Control (LoC) was delineated from Sangar to map reference NJ9842, which effectively set the division between J&K (administered by India) and AJK (administered by Pakistan) that exists today.

J&K's Muslim majority has always been at odds with the predominantly Hindu orientation of the Indian polity. However, Delhi's lamentable rule in the region has also been a major factor in triggering and entrenching local perceptions of alien and unresponsive rule. The central government has consistently denied outside arbitration and adjudication in determining the state's future and repeatedly refused to allow Kashmiri leaders passports to travel and confer with their counterparts in AJK. Widely documented human rights abuses (especially during the 1980s), corruption, a lack of development, and insufficient employment opportunities have merely confounded the situation, playing a key role in radicalizing the sentiments of a population that by the late 1980s had become bitter, sullen, and disillusioned.

The specific catalyst for militant violence in J&K was state elections of 1987, which were contested by antigovernment groups under the banner of the Muslim United Front (MUF). Following an impressive showing at the polls, Delhi annulled the results of several constituencies that the MUF had won to ensure the return of a pro-Indian administration under the auspices of Farooq Abdullah's National Conference, which has retained the state's seat of government ever since. It was from the ranks of these cheated victors that the JKNLF was born. The group specifically eschewed the middle ground of political compromise in favor of more direct, militant actions, commencing armed operations in 1989 to achieve full and complete independence for the Kashmiri people.

The JKNLF initially served as the main vehicle for the anti-Indian insurgency in J&K and at its height had roughly 5,000 cadres in place throughout the Kashmir Valley region. By the mid-1990s, however, the JKNLF had largely ceased to exist as a viable militant force, its demise stemming from the interaction of several factors, including the loss of Pakistani patronage, the capture of its top leadership, and a growing acceptance that Indian rule could not be defeated through the force of arms. From 1995 on, the broad character of the Kashmiri conflict underwent a dramatic change, evolving from one that was primarily indigenously and nationally based to one that was defined in far more explicit religious and transnational terms. While this transformation certainly began with the void created by the fall of the JKNLF, it is owed, more intrinsically, to decisions taken within Islamabad's Inter Services Intelligence (ISI) Directorate, which has deliberately fostered the infusion of foreign jihadist elements in an attempt to replicate the success of the anti-Soviet mujahideen campaign it oversaw in Afghanistan during the 1980s.

Further Reading

Ashraf, Fahmida. "State Terrorism in Indian-Held Jammu and Kashmir." *Strategic Studies* 1 (Spring 2001).

Choudry, Shabir. "Why I Said Goodbye to JKLF?" *CounterCurrents.org,* July 25, 2008. http://www.countercurrents.org/choudry250708.htm.

"Jammu and Kashmir Liberation Front." *Globalsecurity.org.* http://www.globalsecurity.org/military/world/para/jklf.htm.

"Jammu and Kashmir Liberation Front." South Asia Terrorism Portal (SATP). http://www.satp.org/satporgtp/countries/india/states/jihadk/terrorist_outfits/jammu_&_kashmir_liberation_front.htm.

Peter Chalk

JAMRUD MOSQUE BOMBING

On March 27, 2009, a suicide bomber carried out an attack on a two-story mosque in Jamrud in the Khyber Pass Agency of the Federally Administered Tribal Areas (FATA) in northwestern Pakistan. The region, part of the Hindu Kush range, is one of the principal routes for resupplying NATO (North Atlantic Treaty Organization) forces in Afghanistan. Jamrud is sometimes referred to as the "doorway" to the pass, and its general importance has generated violence between rival tribes, countries, and criminals.

At least 51 individuals were killed in the attack, and approximately 150 wounded, at least 20 seriously. Some estimated that the final death toll was as high as 70. The strike took place during Friday prayers. An estimated 250 individuals were in the mosque at the time of the attack, and the force of the blast was powerful enough to cause the upper floor of the building to collapse onto worshippers below. Among the casualties were 11 tribal policemen (Khasaders) and four paramilitary soldiers from the adjacent Bhagyari checkpost. This led some to speculate that it, rather than the mosque, was the primary target.

Although no one claimed responsibility for the bombing, regional administrator Tariq Hayat Khan blamed local members of Tehrik-e-Taliban Pakistan (TTP) for the attack. Pakistani officials also claimed that local rebels belonging to a TTP chapter known as Tehrik-e-Taliban Khyber had warned they would carry out an attack if security forces did not abandon security checkpoints in the Khyber Pass by February 20, 2009. Locals in the village of Bhagyari were more specific. They told journalists that TTP commander Nazeer Afridi, from the Sepah tribe in Bara, had threatened violence if NATO convoys were not stopped from using the Peshawar–Torkham route into Afghanistan.

A series of related incidents appeared to support these claims. The Bhagyari post had already come under fire from three gunmen in February, one of whom was killed; the other two were arrested. The March 27 mosque bombing also occurred just one day after an attack on a restaurant in the Jandola district of South Waziristan that left 11 dead and was immediately followed by an assault on a supply base for NATO troops.

Counterterrorism operations carried out after the incident led to the arrest of 39 alleged militants and the discovery of an assortment of weapons, including heavy and small arms, light artillery, mortars, and a cache of explosives marked with an Indian insignia. Narcotics were also found, including a quantity of hashish. These items were put on display at a press conference. Afridi avoided capture. However, the authorities demolished his house.

See also: Tehrik-e-Taliban Pakistan (TTP)

Further Reading

Farah, Douglas. *Blood from Stones: The Secret Financial Network of Terror.* New York: Random House, 2004.
Kelly, Robert, Jess Maghan, and Joseph Serio. *Illicit Trafficking.* Santa Barbara, CA: ABC-CLIO, 2005.
Peters, Gretchen. *Seeds of Terror: How Heroin Is Bankrolling the Taliban and al Qaeda.* New York: St. Martin's, 2009.
Valentine, Simon Ross. "The Tehrik-i-Taliban Pakistan: Ideology and Beliefs." Bradford: Pakistan Security Research Unit (PSRU) Brief 49, September 8, 2009.

Donna Bassett

JAPANESE AMBASSADOR RESIDENCE (LIMA) SEIZURE

On December 17, 1996, 14 members of the Moviemiento Revolucionario Tupac Amaru (MRTA, or Tupac Amaru Revolutionary Movement) seized the residence of the Japanese ambassador to Peru during a diplomatic reception celebrating the birthday of Emperor Akihito. The group, which had previously been thought suppressed by the counterterrorism policies of President Alberto Fujimori, captured several hundred prominent Peruvian and Japanese government, military, and business leaders. The purpose of the attack was to demand the release of MRTA prisoners and to draw attention back to the flagging movement. After a 126-day siege, the Peruvian military successfully rescued most of the hostages in a raid on April 22, 1997. The hostage crisis highlighted the harsh counterterrorism measures that the Peruvian government took to suppress MRTA and its Maoist counterpart, Sendero Luminoso (SL, or Shining Path).

MRTA originated in the early 1980s in response to severe social and economic inequalities that crippled Peru after two decades of coups and government instability. Lima's inability to address skyrocketing debt, drug violence, and other socioeconomic ills inspired many to seek alternative, mostly leftist, ideologies. MRTA and SL were a manifestation of this environmental context and emerged as the most significant threats to the Peruvian government at the time.

MRTA's ideology was Marxist, populist, and nationalistic in tone and substance. Emphasizing land reform, popular democracy, administrative morality, and a socialist economy, it ultimately sought a more leftist identity for Peru. The group pursued violent means but was less apocalyptic than SL. Unlike that more notorious Maoist group, MRTA did not advocate completely wiping out the existing political and social structure of the country. Rather, it believed that progressive

Special forces conducting surveillance on the Japanese Ambassador residence in Lima, Peru. The building had been seized by 14 members of the Tupac Amaru Revolutionary Movement (MRTA) on December 17, 1996, and was held for 126 days until troops retook it, successfully rescuing most of the hostages inside. (AP/Wide World Photos)

societal elements, including some sympathetic clergy, could be persuaded to align with the group and used to build a popular leftist consensus that would subsequently allow it to gain representation in the government.

However, despite carrying out a string of successful attacks during the 1980s, MRTA was never able to mobilize significant popular support. On the one hand, the group's violence nullified claims that it answered to a higher moral authority. At the same time, its stance of relative moderation (at least compared to SL) was not extreme enough to attract a hard-core following. Over time, the MRTA's operational tempo slowed as it struggled to maintain its support base. From a high of over 400 actions in 1987, MRTA attacks dropped to fewer than 300 by 1990. The group's fortunes suffered an additional blow that same year with the election of Fujimori. Assuming the country's leadership on a platform of delivering security, the new president suspended the constitution, dismissed Congress, and reorganized the courts to grant him what amounted to dictatorial powers. Fujimori subsequently initiated a highly draconian counterterrorist response that saw many MRTA (and SL) members either killed or detained and indefinitely incarcerated.

By 1996 many considered that MRTA had been fully suppressed, as a result of both government offensives and also infighting and clashes with SL. However, the group's leader, Nestor Cerpa, refused to relinquish his struggle and continued to look for opportunities to break MRTA out of its position of isolation and stagnation.

Cerpa concluded that a spectacular operation was needed to reinvigorate MRTA's base of support and highlight its cause. He surmised that the Japanese ambassador's residence was an ideal target for these purposes. Since the emperor's birthday was the highlight of Tokyo's diplomatic social calendar, he was certain that many high-profile individuals would be present, making significant media attention all but inevitable. After several months of recruitment and training, Cerpa and his cell made their way to Lima. They finalized their plans, and the operation was put into effect on December 17. At roughly 8 P.M. the terrorists stormed into the residence grounds and herded several hundred shocked guests, who were gathered in a large tent (where the party was being held), into the compound's main building. Government security forces responded almost immediately and began shooting at the MRTA team. After an exchange of 40 minutes Cerpa forced the Japanese ambassador, Morihisa Aoki, to order the guards to stop firing, and the hostage crisis settled into a siege.

Early on, Cerpa released all females and individuals with no connection to the administration in Lima, including President Fujimori's mother and sister. Several days after letting these hostages go, however, Cerpa threatened he would start killing those still being held unless talks were initiated to free approximately 450 MRTA prisoners languishing in Peruvian jails. After the deadline he set came and passed with no bloodshed, the government decided to pursue a two-pronged approach of engaging in dialogue while planning to retake the compound by force.

President Fujimori allowed the Peruvian Red Cross and several released hostages to act as intermediaries. Negotiations went on through the winter with halting progress. In the meantime, Peruvian commandos meticulously planned and rehearsed a raid using mock-ups of the compound. They also dug a complex series of tunnels that stretched from the outer perimeter of the embassy to the ambassador's residence, laboriously removing the soil in bags that were transported by car to a nearby landfill.

As the weeks passed and negotiations failed to produce results, the MRTA fighters began to drop their guard. Some started to play indoor soccer during the afternoon; others organized card games while guarding the hostages. Cerpa himself attempted to engage the captives. He tried to convince them of the rightness of his cause and reiterated his beliefs that MRTA was benevolent in its goals and debated the merits of socialism.

With negotiations at a virtual standstill, President Fujimori authorized a military raid on April 22. Attacking from the roof and the garden, as well as through the lattice of tunnels below the residence, Peruvian commandos executed a meticulously rehearsed operation, successfully rescuing all but one of the hostages while killing the entire MRTA terrorist squad.

Although the Peruvian public lauded the rescue, there were some misgivings about President Fujimori's motives and methods. Some argued that he never intended to end the siege peacefully and merely engaged in negotiations to buy time for the raid. It was also later discovered that some of the hostage takers had been summarily executed after they attempted to surrender. In this manner the episode highlighted some of the heavy-handed tactics used by the Fujimori government to suppress domestic terrorist groups—measures that would ultimately play a central role in his ouster from power in 2000.

See also: Sendero Luminoso (SL)

Further Reading

Giampietri, Luis, Bill Salisbury, and Lorena Ausejo. *41 Seconds to Freedom: An Insider's Account of the Lima Hostage Crisis, 1996–97.* New York: Ballantine, 2007.

Goldfield, David J. *The Ambassador's Word: Hostage Crisis in Peru, 1996–1997.* Manotick, ON, Canada: Penumbra, 2007.

Poole, Deborah, and Gerardo Rénique. *Peru: Time of Fear.* London: Latin American Bureau, 1992.

Schemo, Diana Jean. "How Peruvian Hostage Crisis Became Trip into the Surreal." *New York Times,* April 26, 1997.

Jonathan Wong

JAPANESE RED ARMY (JRA)

During the late 1960s and early 1970s, mirroring developments in Western Europe, several extremist left-wing groups emerged in Japan. Preeminent among these was the Nippon Sekigun, or Japanese Red Army (JRA). The group strongly opposed defense treaties between Tokyo and Washington, the stationing of American military forces on Japanese soil, and Israeli Zionism. It championed itself as a revolutionary vanguard working on behalf of the urban masses and claimed close solidarity with other fighting communist organizations such as the Rote Armee Fraktion, Brigate Rosse, and Action Directe.

In 1970 following the hijacking of a Japan Airlines aircraft that was forced to fly to North Korea, the JRA divided into two main factions. The first was the Rengo Sekigun, or United Red Army (URA), which was led by Mori Tsuneo and merged with the Keihin Joint Struggle Committee. The URA believed it should concentrate its activities within Japan and vigorously enforced a strict internal code of conduct. Indeed, in 1972 the leadership executed 14 of its members for "deviationism." However, this action merely brought the URA to the attention of the local police, forcing its main constituent component to flee. These members seized a holiday chalet and took its female owner hostage. After a weeklong siege in which two police officers were killed and the woman released, the majority of the remaining members were arrested, effectively putting an end to the URA and its actions.

The other faction, comprising around 50 activists, continued to call itself the JRA. Fusako Shigenobu led the group and sought to align its actions with those of other international social revolutionary and Palestinian terrorist organizations. She forged particularly close ties with the Popular Front for the Liberation of Palestine (PFLP) and relocated with her followers to its camps in Lebanon.

In May 1972 the PFLP called a summit meeting with the intention of furthering international cooperation between extreme left and Palestinian groups. Representatives at the summit included Abu Iyad and Fuad Shemali of the Black September

Organization (BSO), Andreas Baader of the Rote Armee Fraktion (RAF, or Red Army Faction), and Shigenobu of the JRA. Several other terrorist entities also allegedly attended the meeting, including the Provisional Irish Republican Army (PIRA), South American groups, and the Turkish People's Liberation Army, a forerunner to the current Devrimci Halk Kurtulus Partisi/Cephesi. Three weeks later, in a demonstration of this international solidarity, the JRA carried out its most infamous attack—the attack on Israeli's Lod Airport, undertaken on behalf of the PFLP.

The strike team for the Lod operation consisted of three members: Kozo Okamato (the leader), Takeshi Ukudaira, and Yasuiki Yashuda. All three had undergone training in the use of automatic weapons and grenades at a PFLP camp near Baalbek. The trio flew from Beirut to Paris on May 23, 1972, traveling on to Frankfurt and then Rome, where they met Shigenobu on May 30. She briefed them on their forthcoming mission and provided the three terrorists with false passports, Czech VZ58 assault rifles, and fragmentation grenades. That same evening, Okamato, Ukudaira and Yashuda caught an Air France flight to Lod Airport, Tel Aviv, checking bags that contained their weaponry.

Upon arrival, the three JRA operatives waited in the arrivals area and calmly collected their suitcases. They then opened their luggage and indiscriminately opened fire and threw fragmentation grenades at the 300 or so passengers around them. During the course of their attack, Okamato and his JRA colleagues managed to kill 25 people, wounding another 72. Ukudaira and Yashuda died in the attack, and Israeli security forces captured Okamato. He was subsequently sentenced to life imprisonment but released on medical grounds in 1985, having become mentally ill.

In 1982 Shigenobu announced that the JRA had rejected terrorism and the use of violence, justifying the decision on the grounds that the group had failed to win any international support. Over the next five years the group suffered from the arrest of several of its members and by 1987 had become essentially moribund. Despite a brief comeback in 1988, when the JRA took responsibility for the bombing of U.S. Officers Club in Naples, little more was heard from the organization, and in 2001 Shigenobu formally announced that the JRA had disbanded.

See also: Action Directe (AD); Popular Front for the Liberation of Palestine (PFLP); Rote Armee Fraktion (RAF)

Further Reading

Farrell, William. *Blood and Rage: The Story of the Japanese Red Army.* Lexington, MA: Lexington Books, 1990.
Harclerode, Peter. *Secret Soldiers: Special Forces in the War against Terrorism.* London: Cassell, 2002.

Richard Warnes

JARRAH, ZIAD SAMIR

Ziad Samir Jarrah was one of the 19 suicide skyjackers on September 11, 2001. He had been recruited by Ramzi bin al-Shibh at al-Quds Mosque. Less religious than the other members of the Hamburg Cell, Jarrah still joined the September 11 conspiracy. He was the hijackers' pilot on United Airlines Flight 93.

Jarrah came from a prosperous Lebanese family. He was born on May 11, 1975, in Beirut, Lebanon, into a wealthy and influential family. His father held a high-ranking post in the Lebanese social security system, and his mother taught school. Although the family lived in a prosperous area of Beirut, the Lebanese Civil War that began in 1975 made this Sunni neighborhood less than secure. Jarrah attended the best private Christian schools in Beirut, but he was never more than an indifferent student. His family claimed he was more interested in girls than his studies. He flunked his high school finals and only graduated two years later. Members of his family were secular Muslims who paid little attention to religion. After he finished his schooling, the family sent him to study biochemistry in Greifswald, Germany, in the spring of 1996. His parents subsidized his education by sending him at least $2,000 dollars a month. In Germany, Jarrah met Aysel Sengün, a young Turkish student studying dental medicine, and they became a couple.

Jarrah was a happy-go-lucky person until he returned to Lebanon for a winter break in 1997. He returned with a much more serious outlook on life, and he began to have trouble with his girlfriend. Jarrah wanted her to conform to a more traditional Muslim form of behavior. Searching for a career, Jarrah decided to study aeronautical engineering at Hamburg University of Applied Science. Jarrah joined the al-Quds Mosque in Hamburg, and he became a militant Islamist. Bin al-Shibh was his chief contact at the mosque, and Jarrah had little contact with Mohamed Atta. Jarrah was never an active member of the Hamburg Cell, but he shared most of its orientation. As religion became a more important part of his life, his relationship with his girlfriend deteriorated to the point that she was unable to understand him. They still intended to marry at a future time.

Jarrah was a follower, not a leader, in the September 11 plot. In some respects, he was the weak link among the leaders of the plot. He was intelligent enough to pass the qualifying tests as a pilot, but he lacked some of the other characteristics of a dedicated terrorist, such as ruthlessness. An American psychological profile pointed out character flaws: "indecisive and impulsive as well as immature, unstable, and unprofessional." Nevertheless, he trained at an Al Qaeda camp beginning in November 1999, along with Atta. He was with Atta and Marwan al-Shehhi when they met and talked with Osama bin Laden in Kandahar. It was at this time that bin Laden asked them to swear allegiance to him and to be part of a suicide mission. Jarrah agreed with the others to do both. He then received a briefing from Mohammad Atef, the military chief of Al Qaeda, on the general outlines of the September 11 operation. Jarrah returned to Germany with the others to prepare for their mission.

Jarrah entered the United States on June 27, 2000, on a Delta flight from Munich. He trained at the Florida Flight Training Center in Venice, Florida. His flight instructor considered him an average pilot who needed more training to become a proficient pilot. Jarrah left the school without a commercial pilot's license. In an October 2000 note, Jarrah wrote about his longing for paradise.

In January 2001 Jarrah returned to Germany. Then, in April 2001, Jarrah was back in the United States, living in Hollywood, Florida. While there, Jarrah took martial arts lessons at the U.S. 1 Fitness Club, working with Bert Rodriguez. Rodriguez held eight black belts in the martial arts, and he considered Jarrah a good student. Jarrah made one last trip to Germany to see his girlfriend, leaving on July 25 and returning on August 4. Later, in August 2001, Jarrah moved to an apartment in Lauderdale-by-the-Sea. While still in Germany, Jarrah had received notification that he had qualified for a commercial license to fly single-engine aircraft. After his return from Germany, Jarrah began to study the manuals on flying Boeing 757 and 767 aircraft. In the weeks before September 11, Jarrah lived with Ahmed al-Haznawi. Throughout late August and September, Jarrah traveled frequently from South Florida to the Washington, D.C., area. On September 7, 2001, Jarrah made a flight from Fort Lauderdale to Newark, New Jersey, on Continental Airlines with al-Haznawi. Jarrah reappeared in the Washington, D.C., area when he received a speeding ticket on Interstate 95 in Maryland. Jarrah and two of his fellow conspirators checked in at the Newark Airport Marriott soon after midnight on September 11. Before boarding a United Airlines flight, Jarrah made a last phone call to Sengün in Germany.

Jarrah was the leader and pilot of the hijack team of United Airlines Flight 93. Team members had some trouble passing through security at Dulles International Airport, but they all made it. Once in the air, the hijackers seized control of the aircraft. Jarrah assumed the role of pilot. He began turning the aircraft around to head to the Washington, D.C., area. There were only three hijackers to control the crew and passengers. Soon, passengers learned through cell phone calls that the aircraft was to be used as a flying bomb. They revolted and attempted to regain control of the plane. When it became apparent that the hijackers were about to be overpowered by the passengers, Jarrah crashed the aircraft into the ground near Shanksville, Pennsylvania. Jarrah followed instructions to destroy the aircraft if the mission did not have a chance of success.

See also: al-Quds Mosque; Atta, Mohamed; Hamburg Cell

Further Reading

Bernstein, Richard. *Out of the Blue: The Story of September 11, 2001, from Jihad to Ground Zero.* New York: Times Books, 2002.
Longman, Jere. *Among the Heroes: United Flight 93 and the Passengers and Crew Who Fought Back.* New York: Perennial, 2003.
McDermott, Terry. *Perfect Soldiers: The 9/11 Hijackers: Who They Were, Why They Did It.* New York: HarperCollins, 2005.

Stephen E. Atkins

JEMAAH ISLAMIYAH (JI)

Jemaah Islamiyah (JI) is an active jihadist terrorist group with purported historical links to Al Qaeda. The group currently enjoys a concerted presence in Indonesia and, to a lesser extent, the Philippines and is known to have had established cells in Malaysia and Singapore. The United States designated JI a foreign terrorist organization in October 2002, shortly after the first Bali attacks. The group was subsequently added to the United Nations' (UN) list of proscribed entities, a move that requires all member states to freeze its assets, deny it access to funding, and prevent its cadres from entering or traveling through their territories.

JI was established as a dedicated entity in 1998, having been directly inspired by the militant breakaway wing of the Muslim Brotherhood in Egypt, which went by the same name. The group itself formally came into being at Camp Saddah, the mujahideen training camp set up in Afghanistan by Abdul Rasul Sayyaf, a close confidant of Osama bin Laden. JI's actual genesis, however, is far more historical in nature, tracing its heritage to Darul Islam (DI)—a movement established in the 1940s and committed to the creation of a full-fledged Islamic state in Indonesia (the Negara Islam Indonesia). JI's aims are essentially the same as those of DI but are shaped by a more explicit regional perspective and a stronger sense of jihadist ideology. The immediate goal is the Islamization of Indonesia, which is enshrined as a fundamental component of a broader ideological vision that views Daulah Islamiyah (an Islamic state) as the necessary catalyst for the restoration of Islamic governance across Southeast Asia (according to chapter 5 of the group's ostensible manifesto, *Pedoman Umum Perjuangan Al-Jama'ah Al-Islamiyyah* [or, General guidelines for the struggle of JI], referred to as PUPJI and written in the 1990s).

According to PUPJI, such an outcome can be achieved only via a two-step process: first, the development of a puritanical organization whose members have a strong sense of religious, social, political, and (most important) military identity, and second, the use of this group as a platform from which to launch armed jihad (*jihad musallah*) against "infidels, polytheists, apostates, atheists, and the [morally] corrupt" in order to create a theocratic, pan-regional caliphate.

Much of JI's initial operational activity was aimed at fanning anti-Christian violence in Maluku and Sulawesi. The group worked primarily with other Indonesian jihadist organizations created to defend Muslim interests in this part of the archipelago, operating under the collective banner of Laskar Mujahidin (LM). By July 1999 there may have been as many as 500 LM members on the ground in the central Maluku islands of Ceram, Saparua, Haruku, and Ambon. The bulk of these cadres were "deployed" for between 6 and 12 months and were organized into small groups of up to a dozen fighters who specialized in carrying out either precision or hit-and-run attacks against priests and Christian businessmen, community leaders, and churches.

Apart from participating in communal fighting, JI also carried out three significant terrorist strikes between 2000 and 2001: the attempted assassination of the Philippine ambassador to Indonesia in August 2000, simultaneous attacks on 38 churches across the Indonesian archipelago on December 24, 2000, and the bombing of the Atrium Mall in East Jakarta in August 2001.

The most audacious and lethal strikes attributed to JI, however, date from October 2002 on and include the Bali bombings of 2002, suicide strikes against the Marriott Hotel (2003) and Australian embassy (2004) in Jakarta, and repeat attacks in Bali in 2005. These operations, all of which demonstrated considerable skill in terms of bomb construction, pre-attack planning, and target surveillance, were mostly justified under the twin umbrellas of fighting the "far enemy" (the United States, its allies, and adherents to capitalist-led development) and fostering the supremacy of Islam across Southeast Asia.

Although unquestionably spectacular, JI's post-2002 activities generated considerable controversy within the movement. Not only did the bombings galvanize concerted counterterrorist action that led to the arrest of some 300 of the group's cadres, but many in the movement were also highly uncomfortable with the large number of Muslim casualties that resulted from the blasts (something that was particularly true of the Marriott hotel and Australian embassy attacks in Jakarta). Strategically, the operations were also deemed counterproductive, not least because they directly contributed to increased pressure on Jakarta to crack down on JI's main territorial base in Indonesia.

Growing disunity in JI's ranks as a result of these attacks has effectively seen the movement split into opposing factions: a minority pro-bombing group, which advocates fast-tracking the goal of a pan-regional Islamism by engaging in a sustained campaign of suicide bombings across Southeast Asia (irrespective of whether this results in Muslim casualties), and a larger, more traditionalist bloc (known as the "bureaucrats"), which asserts that indiscriminate attacks are not sanctioned by PUPJI and that JI's end state can be brought about only by returning to the movement's DI roots and entrenching a more conservative religious order in Indonesia.

Despite this rift, the general thrust of JI's ideological approach can still be summed up as one aimed at Islamizing Indonesia in the expectation that this will positively alter the religious balance in Southeast Asia and ultimately foster the creation of a wider caliphate. The adoption of force is commonly viewed as an integral means of successfully achieving this outcome. Although differences of opinion exist over how quickly JI's end state can be achieved, the long-term goal of instituting a cross-border caliphate, as well as the emphasis on appropriately developing the resources and capabilities of JI cadres to engage in concerted armed violence, is largely shared by the movement's wider membership.

See also: Australian Embassy (Jakarta) Bombing; Bali Bombings (2002); Bali Bombings (2005); Bashir, Abu Bakar; Marriott Hotel (Jakarta) Bombing (2003)

Further Reading

Chalk, Peter, Angel Rabasa, William Rosenau, and Leanne Piggott. *The Evolving Terrorist Threat to Southeast Asia: A Net Assessment.* Santa Monica, CA: RAND, 2009, Chapter 5, "The Regional Dimension: Jemaah Islamiya."

International Crisis Group. *Al-Qaeda in Southeast Asia: The Case of the "Ngruki Network" in Indonesia.* Asia Briefing no. 20, August 8, 2002.

International Crisis Group. *Indonesia: Jemaah Islamiyah's Current Status.* Asia Briefing no. 63, May 3, 2007.

International Crisis Group. *Indonesia Backgrounder: How the Jemaah Islamiyah Terrorist Organisation Operates.* Asia Report no. 43, December 11, 2002.

International Crisis Group. *Recycling Militants in Indonesia: Darul Islam and the Australian Embassy Bombing.* Asia Report no. 92, February 22, 2005.

Jones, Sidney. "Arrested Development." *Jane's Intelligence Review,* August 2007.

Singapore Ministry of Home Affairs. *The Jemaah Islamiyah Arrests and the Threat of Terrorism.* White paper, January 7, 2003.

Suryhardy, Irfan, ed. *Perjalana Hukum di Indonesia: Sebuah Gugatan.* Yogykarta: Ar-Risalah, 1982.

Peter Chalk

JERUSALEM BUS ATTACKS (1996)

A total of 44 people were killed and 90 others wounded in a series of suicide bombings on buses in Israel during the early months of 1996. Two of these attacks occurred in Jerusalem and Ashkelon (Ashqelon) on February 25, 1996, with the third taking place on March 3, 1996.

The first bomb exploded at about 6:45 A.M. on the Number 18 Egged bus as it was waiting at a red light in Jerusalem, killing 23 people, including two Americans, and injuring 49. According to authorities and eyewitness accounts, a passenger at the front of the bus carried out the attack, detonating a large kit bag that police said contained a 10–20 kilogram (22–44 pound) improvised explosive device (IED) that contained nails, bullets, and ball bearings.

Prime Minister Shimon Peres, like Yitzhak Rabin before him, was forced to take a macabre walking tour of the bomb scene. The attack was to serve as a severe blow to the nascent peace talks between Israel and the Palestinians that were then unfolding.

Police and investigators work at the scene of a suicide bomb attack on a bus in the French Hill neighborhood of Jerusalem, May 18, 2003. At least eight people were killed in the attack, with another 20 wounded. (AP Photo/Oded Balilty)

The second IED went off around 7:35 A.M. at an Ashkelon hitchhiking post for soldiers, killing 2 people and injuring 31. A Palestinian militant wearing an Israeli Army uniform and an earring allegedly detonated the device.

The Izz-ad-Din al-Qassam Brigades, the military wing of Hamas, took credit for the attacks. The group said the twin bombings were in revenge for the January 5 assassination of Yahya Ayyash (the Engineer)—Hamas's chief explosives expert—and claimed responsibility in the name of the Squads of the New Disciples of Martyr Yehiya Ayash. Additional grievances used to justify the mass murders were the February 25, 1994, killings of 29 Muslims by a Jewish settler in Hebron and the October 26, 1995, shooting death of Palestinian Islamic Jihad leader Fathi al-Shaqaqi.

Fearing that the bombers had come from Gaza, Yasser Arafat, chairman of the Palestine Liberation Organization (PLO), ordered his police and secret service to conduct a massive search in order to show the world—particularly the Israeli public—that his movement was doing its share to fight terrorism. Throughout that afternoon and evening, PLO forces detained 250 Palestinian activists, although it later turned out that the bombers were not from Gaza but instead the Al-Fatwa refugee camp near Hebron.

Investigators believed that the man behind the attacks in Jerusalem and Ashkelon was another Hamas hero named Mohiyedine Sharif, known in Izz-ad-Din al-Qassam circles as "the Electrician." Originally from Hebron, Sharif was one of Ayyash's prized pupils and protégés, organizing numerous cells in and around his hometown as well as in East Jerusalem.

The third IED exploded at 6:25 A.M., again on a Number 18 Egged bus that was traveling between the central post office and police headquarters in Jerusalem. The bomb killed 19 and wounded 10 more and was similarly justified as revenge for the death of Ayyash. On March 8, Israeli soldiers blew up the two-room house belonging to the family of Raed Shaghnoubi, who carried the bomb onto the bus.

By March 10, Palestinian security forces had arrested three of the main members of Hamas suspected of complicity in the string of bombings: Abdel Fatah Satari, Salem Abu Marouf, and Kamal Khalifa. The alleged ringleader, Mohammed Dief, however, remained at large.

See also: Hamas (Islamic Resistance Movement)

Further Reading

Levitt, Matthew. *Hamas: Politics, Charity, and Terrorism in the Service of Jihad.* Foreword by Dennis Ross. New Haven, CT: Yale University Press, 2006.

Milton-Edwards, Beverley, and Stephen Farrell. *Hamas: The Islamic Resistance Movement.* Malden, MA: Polity, 2010.

Mishal, Shaul, and Avraham Sela. *The Palestinian HAMAS: Vision, Violence, and Coexistence.* New York: Columbia University Press, 2000.

Donna Bassett

JERUSALEM BUS ATTACKS (2003)

In mid-2003 Hamas launched a campaign of suicide bombings against bus facilities in Israel, most of which were directed at targets in Jerusalem. The strikes, which occurred at a critical juncture in evolving peace talks with the Palestine Liberation Organization (PLO), left 52 people dead and wounded another 140.

The bombing spree began at 6 A.M. on May 18, 3003. An Arab dressed as a religious Jew boarded the Number 6 Egged commuter bus in Jerusalem's northeastern French Hill area. Despite arousing the suspicion of several passengers, including the American-born Steve Averbach, he was able to detonate his explosive vest before anyone could intercept him. Eight people were killed and 20 wounded in the ensuing blast.

Thirty minutes later and just a few miles from the site of the first attack, a second bomb detonated at a major road junction. There were no casualties. The Izz al-Din al-Qassam Brigades, the military wing of Hamas, took credit for both attacks.

After a short lull, the bombings resumed on June 11, 2003, when a suicide cadre, later identified as the 18-year-old Abdel Muati Shaban, destroyed Bus 14 in downtown Jerusalem at the peak of the rush hour. In addition to himself, he murdered 17 people and wounded at least 70 others. Hamas claimed responsibility for the attack, claiming it was carried out to avenge the attempted assassination of Abdel-Aziz al-Rantissi—a senior member of the group—the previous day. Among the victims was Sari Zinger, the daughter of U.S. Representative Robert Zinger.

Later that same month Israeli authorities arrested Samar Atrash and Omar Sharif. The two men lived in eastern Jerusalem and admitted to gathering intelligence for Hamas. Both were subsequently charged with complicity in the May 18 and June 11 bombing attacks as well as providing information on senior military and government officials, including Prime Minister Ariel Sharon.

On August 19, a third suicide terrorist detonated a 12-pound device loaded with ball bearings and shrapnel on the Number 2 Egged bus in Jerusalem. The explosion occurred across from the Synagogue of the Jews of the Caucasus on Shmuel Hanavi Street in Jerusalem's Beit Israel neighborhood. This was the most lethal of the attacks, with 21 fatalities and over 100 injuries. Among those murdered were five Americans and six children, one of whom was only 11 months old. The driver of the bus, Hasser Hirbawi, a 40-year-old Israeli Arab and father of six, sustained severe wounds that made him unfit for work. Another victim, who was hit in the eyes by shrapnel, was the 21-year-old son of an Israeli parliamentarian. Hamas and Palestinian Islamic Jihad claimed credit for the attack.

Two final bombings took place on September 9. The first targeted a bus stop near the Tzrifin military base in Tel Aviv, killing 7, including three women, and wounding 15. The second occurred at 11:19 P.M. at Café Hillel in Jerusalem, resulting in 7 deaths and 30 injuries. The perpetrators were distant cousins, both members of Hamas.

See also: Hamas (Islamic Resistance Movement); Palestinian Islamic Jihad (PIJ)

Further Reading

Levitt, Matthew. *Hamas: Politics, Charity, and Terrorism in the Service of Jihad.* New Haven, CT: Yale University Press, 2006.

Mickolus, Edward F., and Susan Simmons. *Terrorism 2002–2004: A Chronology.* Vol. 1. Westport, CT: Praeger, 2006.

Milton-Edwards, Beverley, and Stephen Farrell. *Hamas: The Islamic Resistance Movement.* Malden, MA: Polity, 2010.

Donna Bassett

JEWISH COMMUNITY CENTER (BUENOS AIRES) BOMBING

At 9:53 A.M. on July 18, 1994, an enormous explosion rocked the Argentinean capital of Buenos Aires in what was to become the worst terror attack in the country's history. The target of the bombing was the Argentinean Asociación Mutual Israelite Argentina (AMIA, or Jewish Community Association), a seven-story building located in the heart of the city. The perpetrator was Ibrahim Hussein Berro, who drove a Renault van to the entrance of the center and then detonated some 660–880 pounds (300–400 kilograms) of explosives. The ensuing blast collapsed the facade of the AMIA and severely damaged surrounding buildings, killing 86 and wounding an additional 151. The bombing occurred two years after a similar attack on the Israeli embassy in Buenos Aires (on March 17, 1992), which left 29 people dead and injured 292. The homologous nature of the two incidents suggested they were linked.

Shortly after the AMIA strike, various other bombings occurred against Jewish and Israeli targets. On July 19, a plane from Colon City to Panama City, Alas Chiricanas Flight 00901, exploded shortly after takeoff, killing all 21 passengers on board—12 of whom were Jews. On July 27, two devices detonated in London, one near the Israeli embassy and another targeting a Jewish charity center. The explosions injured 14 people and caused severe damage to both buildings.

On July 23, the Lebanese newspaper *Al-Nahar* published a communiqué from an unknown organization named Ansar Allah claiming responsibility for both the AMIA and Alas Chiricanas incidents. Authorities believed that the organization was fictitious and was actually a front for Hezbollah. Indeed, this same method had been used after the Israeli embassy bombing in 1992 when Islamic Jihad took credit, which again turned out to be a cover for Hezbollah.

The reasons for the attacks were never made clear. Various sources assumed that both the 1992 and 1994 bombings were carried out in revenge for the assassination of Hezbollah's leader, Secretary General Sayyid Abbas Musawi, who was killed by Israeli gunship helicopters in 1992. Other analysts suggested that they were a response to the abduction of Lebanese religious leader Mustafa Dirani on May 21 as well as the shelling of the Ayn Dardara training camps in the Bekaa Valley. Operationally, terrorism experts pointed out that Hezbollah ran an extensive logistic network in the Tri-border Area (TBA) of Argentina, Paraguay, and Brazil that could be easily leveraged to conduct a large-scale attack in Buenos Aires. While the Argentinean authorities acknowledged these reasons as plausible, the official explanation for the terror strike was the "government's unilateral decision to terminate the nuclear materials and technology supply agreements that had been concluded some years previously . . . [with] Iran."

The Argentinean probe into the AMIA bombing (as well as the earlier Israeli embassy attack) was harshly criticized for its lack of professionalism. Local forensic teams failed to conduct proper DNA tests at the site of the attack, and the police accidentally dumped Berro's head into a bin. More serious was the general ineptitude of the postincident investigation, which not only failed to solve the case but was also replete with controversies that reached to the very highest echelons of state power. Most notable were allegations made against President Carlos Menem, who together with senior officials was accused of intentionally hindering the inquiry in exchange for receiving a $10 million payment from Iran (although the charges were never proven). The federal judge who conducted the investigation, Juan Jose Galeano, was also caught on video offering $400,000 to one of the suspects to persuade him to convict his fellow accomplices. As result of this misconduct, Galeano was impeached, all of those being held in connection with the bombing were released, and their testimonies were sacked. President Nestor Kirchner, who stepped into office in 2003, later claimed that the whole affair was a "national disgrace."

Despite these egregious shortcomings, the various probes conducted by the Argentinean intelligence service (Secretaría de Inteligencia de Estada [SIDE]), the Mossad, and the Central Intelligence Agency (CIA) provided overwhelming evidence linking Hezbollah and Iran to the attack. A detailed report issued by the Argentinean attorney general revealed that the decision to carry out the operation was made during a meeting of the Supreme Iranian National Security Council on August 14, 1993, in the city of Mashhad, a year before the bombing took place. The report also directly linked the Israeli embassy and AMIA incidents, saying that the modus operandi of the two attacks was "identical."

Subsequent evidence from the investigations led authorities to the TBA, where an arms-and-money logistic network that was in constant communication with Iran and Hezbollah was found to exist. It was additionally discovered that Berro was himself a resident of Foz do Iguaçu on the Brazilian side of the TBA and had phoned his family just hours before conducting the attack to tell them that he was "about to join his brother"—a reference to As'ad Hussein Berro, who had died in a suicide strike against the Israeli Defense Forces on August 9, 1989.

It was clear, however, that Berro did not act alone in the TBA, and the intelligence services later identified Assad Ahmad Barakat as a central player in both the Israeli embassy and AMIA bombings. He allegedly served as Hezbollah's military operations chief in the TBA as well as the group's principal fund-raiser in the Southern Cone. Barakat had made several trips to Tehran between 1990 and 1991, where he had reportedly met with high-ranking officials of the Islamic Republic. Another individual tied to the attack was Samuel Salman, who had lived in Argentina since 1987 and left the country just a week after the bombing to return to Lebanon. He was suspected of helping to coordinate Hezbollah members' stays in Argentina and allegedly assisted in gathering crucial information for the attack.

According to the Argentinean attorney general's report, the supreme spiritual leader of Iran, Ali Hoseyni Khamenei, issued a fatwa (religious decree) for the attack. The decision was conveyed to Ali Fallahian, at the time Iran's intelligence minister, who was given the responsibility for executing the mission. To attain plausible deniability, Fallahian asked Hezbollah to plan and actually carry out the bombing, with all operational tasks falling to Imad Mughniyah, the group's second in command and leader of its military wing. Argentinean authorities also asserted that Syria was at least aware of the impending attack, if not more directly involved.

In addition to Fallahian and Mughniyah, the inquiry named other key officials who had participated in the Mashhad meeting, including the Iranian president, Ali Akbar Rafsanjani; the foreign minister, Ali Akbar Velayati; the commander of the Revolutionary Guards, Mohsen Rezai; the head of the al-Quds Force (and current defense minister), Ahmad Vahidi; a Shi'ite cleric and iman at the At-Tauhid Mosque in Buenos Aires, Mohsen Rabbani; and the third secretary of Iran's embassy in Argentina, Ahmad Reza Asghari. Of these individuals, Rabbani appeared to have been most closely associated with helping to lay the groundwork for the bombing. He both made inquiries into the purchase of a Renault van—the same vehicle used for the attack—and acted as a financial conduit through which to disburse funds (to the tune of US$150,812) sent from Tehran.

In the two decades after the attack, further information has continued to leak out suggesting the direct complicity of Iran in the bombing. In July 1998, the Jordanian General Intelligence Department infiltrated and broke up a Hezbollah cell led by Abu al-Foul that was about to conduct an attack in Europe. One of those caught, Yousuf Aljouni, admitted during questioning that he and his cell were directly involved in helping to organize attacks in Buenos Aires in 1992 and again in 1994. As proof he provided details of the attacks' planning and execution. Despite numerous requests, neither al-Foul nor Aljouni was ever extradited to Israel or Argentina—allegedly out of Jordan's concern that if it acceded to these demands, the country would become a target of retaliatory Hezbollah terrorism. The members of the so-called al-Foul cell were eventually released from custody in December 1998.

On October 26, 2000, Argentina's embassy in Riyadh, Saudi Arabia, received a telephone message claiming responsibility for an unspecified past explosion in Buenos Aires. Argentinean judicial sources believe that the callers were referring to the 1994 AMIA incident. Just over two years later, SIDE presented a 500-page report on the bombing that confirmed the C4 explosives used in the attack had come from Ciudad del Este—a prominent center of Hezbollah support in Paraguay—and that two or three Lebanese men had facilitated the transportation of the material into Argentina.

International arrest warrants were eventually issued for Mughniyah and seven other senior Iranian officials, including former president Rafsanjani. Although legal proceedings were not initiated against Supreme Leader Ali Khamenei, the Argentinean attorney general's report determined that he was directly involved in the decision to carry out the attack. Despite the accumulating evidence, Hezbollah and Iran have repeatedly denied they were involved in either the Israeli embassy or AMIA bombings, labeling the accusations a "Zionist plot."

See also: Hezbollah (Party of God); Israeli Embassy (Buenos Aires) Bombing

Further Reading

"Argentina Accuses Iran of Responsibility for the Hezbollah Terrorist Attack Which Destroyed Jewish Community Center in Buenos Aires, 1994." Intelligence and Terrorism Information Center, Israel, November 14, 2006. http://www.terrorism-info.org.il/malam_multimedia/English/eng_n/pdf/argentina_amia_e.pdf, accessed February 17, 2012.

"Argentina: Iranian's Property Seized." *New York Times,* December 16, 2008.

Bergman, Ronen. *The Secret War with Iran: The 30-Year Clandestine Struggle against the World's Most Dangerous Terrorist Power.* New York: Free Press, 2008.

"Bombing in London Hits Israeli Embassy." *New York Times,* July 27, 1994. http://www.nytimes.com/1994/07/27/world/bombing-in-london-hits-israeli-embassy.html, accessed February 19, 2012.

"Buenos Aires Bomber 'Identified'." *BBC News,* November 10, 2005. http://news.bbc.co.uk/2/hi/americas/4423612.stm, accessed February 17, 2012.

Byman, Daniel. *A High Price: The Triumphs and Failures of Israeli Counterterrorism.* Oxford: Oxford University Press, 2011.

"Flashback: Argentina Bomb." *BBC News,* August 25, 2003. http://news.bbc.co.uk/2/hi/americas/3179861.stm, accessed February 17, 2012.

"Hezbollah: Profile of the Lebanese Shiite Terrorist Organization, of Global Reach Sponsored by Iran and Supported by Syria, the Bombing of the Jewish Community Center in Argentina (1994)—an Example of the Modus Operandi of Hezbollah's Overseas Terrorist Apparatus." Intelligence and Terrorism Information Center, Israel, July 2003. http://www.terrorism-info.org.il/malam_multimedia/html/final/eng/iran.htm#table, accessed February 17, 2012.

Hudson, Rex. *Terrorist and Organized Crime Groups in the Tri-border Area (TBA) of South America.* Washington, DC: Federal Research Division, Library of Congress, July 2003 (revised December 2010).

"Iran Denies Argentina Bomb Charge." *BBC News,* October 26, 2006. http://news.bbc.co.uk/2/hi/middle_east/6089788.stm, accessed February 17, 2012.

"1994: Israel's London Embassy Bombed." *BBC News,* July 26, 2005. http://news.bbc.co.uk/onthisday/hi/dates/stories/july/26/newsid_2499000/2499619.stm, accessed February 17, 2012.

Pertossi, Mayra. "Argentina Orders Detention of Colombian in Bombing." *The Guardian,* (UK), June 9, 2009.

"UK Refuses to Extradite Iranian." *BBC News,* November 13, 2003. http://news.bbc.co.uk/2/hi/middle_east/3266011.stm, accessed February 17, 2012.

Yapp, Robin. "Iran Defense Minister Forced to Leave Bolivia over 1994 Argentina Bombing." *The Telegraph* (UK), June 1, 2011.

Gilard Stern

JEWISH DEFENSE LEAGUE (JDL)

The Jewish Defense League (JDL) was formed by Rabbi Meir Kahane in New York in 1967. It is a Jewish nationalist organization with the stated purpose of fighting against anti-Semitism. The Federal Bureau of Investigation (FBI) describes the JDL as "a right-wing terrorist group," while the Southern Poverty Law Center refers to it as a "hate movement" that actively propagates "anti-Arab terrorism."

Initially, the JDL focused its attention on the USSR and the plight of Soviet Jews, who were barred from leaving the country to emigrate and resettle in Israel if they wished to. While the group mostly engaged in propaganda and lobbying efforts, it was also connected to a number of violent attacks. These included a bombing outside the Manhattan offices of Aeroflot on November 29, 1970; an attack on the Soviet Cultural Center in Washington, D.C., on January 8, 1971; and an alleged firing spree against the USSR's mission to the United Nations in 1971.

In 1975 U.S. authorities accused Kahane, the JDL's founder and leader, of trying to kidnap a Russian diplomat and bomb the Iraqi embassy in Washington, D.C. He was sentenced to one year in jail for violating probation on another conviction.

Apart from the USSR, the JDL also targeted neo-Nazis, Holocaust deniers, and other individuals and groups viewed as enemies of the Jewish people. One notable incident attributed to the group was the October 11, 1985, murder of American-Arab Anti-Discrimination Committee regional director Alex Odah.

Following the fall of the Soviet Union in 1989, the JDL redirected the thrust of its activity toward Middle Eastern states opposed to Israel. This brought the group more squarely into the crosshairs of Arab and Palestinian militants, which culminated in November 1990 when El Sayyid Nosair, an Egyptian American, shot and killed Kahane in front of an audience at a Manhattan hotel. Nosair was later convicted to life imprisonment for murder as well as for participating in the 1993 bombing of the World Trade Center in New York.

In 1994 former JDL member Baruch Goldstein slaughtered 29 Palestinians while they were praying and wounded another 125 at the Tomb of the Patriarchs in the West Bank. The JDL lauded the attack, proclaiming on its website that it was "not ashamed to say that Goldstein was a charter member of the Jewish Defense League."

In 2004 the JDL had an internal dispute over legal control of the organization and split into two factions. The groups operated as independent entities for two years before reunifying in the guise of B'nai Elim. Other extremist groups associated with the JDL over the years have included Kach, Eyal, Kahane Khai, the Jewish Task Force, and the Jewish Resistance Movement.

See also: Goldstein, Baruch; Hebron Mosque Massacre; Kahane Khai; World Trade Center (New York) Bombing

Further Reading

Friedman, Robert I. *The False Prophet: Rabbi Meir Kahane, from FBI Informant to Knesset Member.* Westport, CT: Lawrence Hill Books, 1990.
Gorenberg, Gershom. *The End of Days: Fundamentalism and the Struggle for the Temple Mount.* New York: Oxford University Press, 2000.
Kahane, Rabbi Meir. *The Story of the Jewish Defense League.* Radnor, PA: Chilton, 1975.

Donna Bassett

JORDANIAN EMBASSY (BAGHDAD) BOMBING

On August 7, 2003, a massive truck bomb exploded outside the Jordanian embassy in Baghdad. At the time of the incident, it represented the highest-profile attack of the Iraq War. In total, the explosion killed 18 people and wounded at least 60 others. Carried out by members of Abu Musab al-Zarqawi's network, the bombing marked a dramatic turning point in the Iraq War as it was the most massive terrorist attack on a soft target following the U.S. invasion. Not long after the incident, the country would see a slew of other attacks on soft targets, including the bombing of the headquarters of the United Nations (UN) Assistance Mission in Iraq a mere 12 days later and the bombing of the offices of the International Committee of the Red Cross (ICRC) on October 29, 2003. In effect, the Jordanian embassy bombing ushered in a new era in the Iraq War and foreshadowed the maelstrom of violence that would soon engulf the country.

In the immediate aftermath of the U.S.-led invasion in March 2003, Iraq saw little in the way of extreme violence. While widespread looting posed a serious problem, major attacks were virtually unheard of. Yet by early summer of that year, an inchoate insurgency began to rear its head. Relatively small-scale attacks against U.S. military and other coalition forces targets were on the rise, including a climbing number of improvised explosive device attacks and roadside bombings. In hindsight, security in Iraq was beginning to deteriorate. At the time, however, these relatively small-scale incidents were perceived by some to be manifestations of the last throes of Saddam Hussein's Baathist regime. Believed by many to be Saddam Hussein loyalists or Iraqi nationalists, U.S. secretary of defense Donald Rumsfeld famously referred to the militants thought to be behind these attacks as "dead-enders."

This view would be shattered by the events that took place on August 7, 2003. On that day, at roughly 11:00 A.M. local time, a large green truck laden with roughly 250 pounds of explosives pulled up in front of the Jordanian embassy, located in central Baghdad. The driver parked the vehicle, exited, and left the scene. Moments later the explosives—believed to be Saddam-era munitions acquired from an unsecured arms cache—were detonated by remote control.

The ensuing blast tore a ten-yard hole in the facade of the embassy and reportedly even tossed a vehicle onto the roof of a nearby building. Shrapnel was sent flying hundreds of yards in all directions in the wake of the blast. Numerous cars outside the building were left smoldering. The explosion killed one Jordanian and 17 Iraqis, including five Iraqi police officers. Surprisingly, those working inside the embassy sustained only minor injuries.

Following the blast, crowds of angry Iraqis arrived at the scene and began to loot the embassy, tarnishing portraits of Jordan's King Abdullah II and his father, King Hussein. Media reports later wondered whether the motive for the attack could be connected to Jordan's recent decision to offer asylum to two of Saddam Hussein's daughters and their children. Perhaps related to this anger, the day before the attack, the embassy received a vague threat in the form of a letter whose contents were never disclosed. However, the embassy did not increase its security following the threat. In any event, U.S. personnel quickly arrived on the scene and cordoned off the area. Victims were rushed to the hospital, and a security perimeter was established. The United States aided with the response to the bombing, but many of the wounded would succumb to their injuries.

In the days following the attack, suspicion immediately fell on Saddam Hussein loyalists. Some even posited that perhaps Saddam himself could have been behind the bombing. However, more credible speculation also hovered over the possibility that the attack was the work of foreign terrorist elements that had infiltrated the country. Iraq had long been home to groups such as Ansar al-Islam, an Islamist separatist group fighting secular Kurdish political parties in semiautonomous Iraqi Kurdistan. While the group had been decimated by U.S. Special Forces and Kurdish paramilitaries during the invasion of Iraq, some of its remnants had survived the assault and slipped across the border into Iran. In the wake of the bombing, many feared that these elements had regrouped and reentered the country, poised to attack the Iraqi state.

These fears about the potential jihadist identity of the perpetrators proved to be true. The plotters of the Jordanian embassy attack were part of al-Zarqawi's terrorist network Jamaa al-Tawhid wa'a Jihad (JTJ). A former affiliate of Ansar al-Islam (AaI), al-Zarqawi derived some of the membership of JTJ from his connections to AaI. He would later merge JTJ with Al Qaeda and found Tanzom Qa'idat al-Jihadi Bilad al-Rafidyan (QJBR), more commonly known as Al Qaeda in Iraq (AQI). Al-Zarqawi's orchestration of the attack meant that the United States simply was no longer dealing with Saddam-era loyalists or "dead-enders." Now, it found itself pitted against a radical and violent adversary willing to target civilians in a quest to drive out not only the United States but also other Arab elements, such as the Jordanian monarchy, which had supported the U.S. invasion and which al-Zarqawi deemed to be apostate. This new jihadist adversary brought newer and drastically more violent tactics and capabilities, alongside an utter disregard for civilian lives.

In this sense, the attack marked a serious and sobering turn in the Iraq War. Apart from a handful of small attacks targeting a UN convoy and a few members of Iraqi civil society, most attacks had focused on the U.S. military prior to August 7, 2003. As the first major attack targeting a non-U.S. military or coalition forces target, the Jordanian embassy bombing represented the opening salvos of a new stage of the Iraq War, one in which the Iraq would be forced to confront salafi-jihadist terrorism and one that would devour much of the country in the years that followed. In effect, the bombing loudly announced that terrorist elements had thrust themselves into the conflict and that they would no longer simply be targeting U.S. forces but rather anyone they deemed to be complicit in the invasion of Iraq.

In January 2005, captured al-Zarqawi associate Abu Ahmad Umar al-Kurdi confessed to rigging the explosives for the bombing. According to later court documents, another al-Zarqawi aide, Muammar Ahmad Jaghbir, was told to monitor the embassy for three days. Al-Zarqawi and Jaghbir instructed that the car should be filled with explosives and driven to the site. Jaghbir would be sentenced to death in 2007 for his role in the attack. Al-Kurdi, who also helped plot the attack on the UN headquarters and construct the bombs used in it, was sentenced in 2006 and executed the following year.

Unlike the UN, the Jordanians would remain in Iraq after the attack. The embassy was threatened again the following year, but there have been no further attacks against it.

See also: Ansar al-Islam (AaI); Jamaa al-Tawhid wa'a Jihad (JTJ); United Nations Headquarters (Baghdad) Bombing; Zarqawi, Abu Musab al-

Further Reading

Chandrasekaran, Rajiv. "Car Bomb Kills 11 in Baghdad; Subsequent Attack on Humvee Injures 2 Soldiers, Ignites Firefight." *Washington Post,* August 8, 2003.
Filkins, Dexter, and Robert F. Worth. "After the War: Iraq; 11 Die in Baghdad as Car Bomb Hits Jordan's Embassy." *New York Times,* August 8, 2003.
Whitaker, Brian. "Baghdad Bombing: Bomb Type and Tactics Point to al-Qaida." *The Guardian,* August 21, 2003.

Nate Shestak

JUNDALLAH

Jundallah is an Iranian terrorist group based in Baluchistan that emerged sometime around 2003. It claims to be fighting for the rights of the country's Sunni Muslims and is thought to have a wider membership that numbers in the thousands. The group has carried out numerous attacks in Iran that are thought to have left at least 154 people dead and another 320 injured. The group's founder, Abdolmalek Rigi, was captured and executed in 2010. Muhammad Dhair Baluch is believed to have replaced him as the group's acting leader.

Jundallah denies it has any foreign links and dismisses the charge that it is pursuing a separatist agenda aimed at the creation of a separate Baluchi state. Rather, it says its one and only goal is to end discrimination against the Iranian Sunni minority and to improve their day-to-day lives. Tehran, however, alleges that the organization was set up with the direct support of the United States and various other foreign elements in Pakistan, Saudi Arabia, the United Kingdom, and Israel to wage a proxy war against Iran in collaboration with the Mujahedin-e-Kalq (MeK). For its part Washington has always denied providing any type of support to Jundallah, with the Obama administration pointing out that besides Iran the United States is the only other country to have designated the group as a foreign terrorist organization.

Jundallah's ideology appears to be based on an idiosyncratic mixture of Sunni Islamist fundamentalism, salafist jihadism, and religious conservatism. Some of these tenets bear a close affinity to Al Qaeda, although, as with charges that it receives support from foreign governments, the group insists it has no links to the global movement. Most of the organization's attacks take place in areas of Balochistan that lie close to the border with Pakistan, and many have been aimed at Shiite mosques in Zahedan. Two of the most serious occurred in 2010. On December 14, a pair of suicide bombers targeted a group of Shiite worshippers in Chah Bahar, leaving at least 39 dead. The next day a lone operative killed 39 people and wounded many more. Both strikes appears to have been timed to coincide with Ashoura, the mourning period leading up to the death of Immam, the grandson of the Prophet Muhammad.

Other major incidents attributed to the group include an attempted assassination of President Mahmoud Ahmadinejad (2005), the slaughter of 21 civilians in an ambush on a road near Tasooki (2006), the mass abduction of 21 Iranian truck drivers near Chah Bahar (2007), and two additional bombings in Zahedan (2009 and 2010) that resulted in a total of 51 fatalities.

See also: Mujahedin-e-Khalq (MeK)

Further Reading

Black, Ian. "Iran Accuses US and UK of Supporting Group behind Mosque Attacks." *The Guardian* (UK), July 16, 2010.

Hersh, Seymour. "Annals of National Security: Preparing the Battlefield." *New Yorker,* July 7, 2008.

Shipman, Tim. "Bush Sanctions 'Black Ops' against Iran." *Daily Telegraph* (UK), May 27, 2007.

Stockman, Farah. "Anti-Iran Militia Faces Terrorist Designation: US Is Weighing Conciliatory Step." *Boston Globe,* May 30, 2009.

Yong, William. "Bombings Kill Dozens near Mosque in Iran." *New York Times,* December 16, 2010.

Edward F. Mickolus

JUSTICE COMMANDOS OF THE ARMENIAN GENOCIDE (JCAG)

The Justice Commandos of the Armenian Genocide (JCAG), along with the more widely known Armenian Secret Army for the Liberation of Armenia (ASALA), was an Armenian terrorist organization active during the 1970s and 1980s that predominantly targeted Turkish diplomatic personnel. Like ASALA, it sought publicity, an independent Armenian homeland, and Turkish recognition of the deaths of up to a million and a half Armenians during forced deportations in 1915. However, while ASALA was motivated by Marxism-Leninism and had links to Palestinian groups and the Soviet Union, JCAG was more right-wing and nationalist, linked to the Armenian Dashnak Party, with funding from the wider Armenian diaspora.

During its attacks between 1975 and 1985, JCAG, and its successor, the Armenian Revolutionary Army (ARA), killed 20 Turkish diplomats or their family members, including Danis Tunaligil, the Turkish ambassador to Vienna (October 1975); the Turkish consul general to Sydney (December 1980); and the Turkish consul general in Los Angeles (January 1982). In addition, JCAG claimed responsibility for the bombing of the Turkish United Nations Mission in New York on October 12, 1980, while in March 1985 the ARA killed a security guard in an attack on the Turkish embassy in Ottawa, Canada.

Unlike the more indiscriminate ASALA—and despite the international venues for many of its operations—JCAG-ARA did not wish to alienate Western public opinion and deliberately limited its attacks to Turkish diplomatic staff and buildings. These attacks ceased in the mid-1980s following Armenian internecine feuds and killings in Lebanon, which resulted in the deaths of Apo Ashjian and Sarkis Aznavourian, the respective leaders of JCAG and ARA.

See also: Armenian Secret Army for the Liberation of Armenia (ASALA)

Further Reading

Gunter, Michael. *Transnational Armenian Activism.* Conflict Studies 229. Research Institute for the Study of Conflict and Terrorism, London, 1990.

Lang, David Marshall, and Christopher Walker. *The Armenians.* The Minority Rights Group, Report 32. London: Minority Rights Group, 1987.

Shafritz, Jay, E. F. Gibbons, and Gregory Scott. *Almanac of Modern Terrorism.* New York: Facts on File, 1991.

Richard Warnes

K

KABUL DIPLOMATIC QUARTER BOMBING

On October 8, 2009, the Indian embassy in Kabul was hit by a suicide bombing that left 17 people dead and another 63 wounded. The attack occurred amid debate in NATO (the North Atlantic Treaty Organization) about sending more troops to Afghanistan.

The bomber struck at about 8:30 A.M. when the street on which the embassy is located is normally busy with pedestrians. He detonated a car loaded with explosives outside the building's perimeter—but blast walls constructed in the aftermath of a major bombing the year before deflected much of the force of the explosion. Although doors and windows were smashed, there were no casualties inside the mission itself. In a grimly familiar pattern, most of the dead were ordinary Afghans, many of them merchants trading at a market that had been refurbished in recent months. Only a few Indian security personnel suffered injuries in the attack, none of which were serious.

The Taliban claimed responsibility for the bombing within hours of the attack. A spokesman for the movement said the perpetrator was an Afghan who had used a sport-utility vehicle for the operation. G. Parthasarathy, a former diplomat and analyst at the Center for Policy Research, believed the incident was designed to "punish" India for its economic assistance to Afghanistan, which was viewed as complementary to American strategic objectives.

The attack followed another major bombing against the Indian embassy the previous July that killed 58 and wounded 141. That attack was the largest to have occurred in the Afghan capital since 2001. U.S. intelligence officials concluded that Pakistan's InterService Intelligence (ISI) Directorate had planned the operation—a charge Islamabad denied. Nevertheless, then American president George W. Bush confronted Pakistani prime minister Yousuf Raza Gilani with evidence, warning him that in the case of another large-scale incident the United States would be forced to take serious action.

The two bombings on the Indian embassy were the latest in a series of Taliban-instigated attacks in Kabul, including

- The storming of a luxury hotel near the presidential palace in January 2008 (six dead)
- The attempted assassination of President Hamid Karzai in April 2008, which he survived but which left three others dead
- A suicide bombing outside the Information Ministry in October 2008
- Another suicide bombing outside the German embassy in November 2008 (three dead)

- Attacks on the Justice Ministry and two other government buildings in February 2009
- A bombing outside NATO headquarters in August 2009 (7 dead, 90 injured)
- An assault by gunmen on a bank just south of the presidential palace that same month
- A suicide car bombing at the entrance to a NATO military base inside Kabul's only airport in September 2009 (several Afghans dead)
- Another car bombing on the road between Kabul's airport and the U.S. embassy that same month (10 Afghan civilians killed)

See also: Indian Embassy (Kabul) Bombing

Further Reading

"Afghan Bombs Strike India Embassy." *BBC News,* October 8, 2009. http://news.bbc.co.uk/2/hi/8296137.stm, accessed May 15, 2011.

Faiez, Karim, and Mark Magnier. "Taliban Claims responsibility for Kabul Embassy Attack." *Los Angeles Times,* October 9, 2009. http://articles.latimes.com/2009/oct/09/world/fg-afghanistan-bomb9, accessed May 15, 2011.

Taversine, Sabrina. "17 Die in Kabul Bomb Attack." *New York Times,* October 8, 2009. http://www.nytimes.com/2009/10/09/world/asia/09afghan.html, accessed May 15, 2011.

Donna Bassett

KACZYNSKI, TED

Theodore John "Ted" Kaczynski is an American mathematician who engaged in a mail-bombing campaign over 17 years that killed 3 people and injured 23 others. Many of his victims were university professors and airline employees, which earned him the moniker "Unabomber"—a combination of "university and airline bomber." Kaczynski was the subject of one of the Federal Bureau of Investigation's (FBI) most costly investigations and was eventually captured after his brother tipped off federal authorities in 1995.

Kaczynski was motivated by an idiosyncratic mixture of neo-Luddite and anarchist convictions that modern technology requiring large-scale organization was working to fundamentally erode human freedom. He claimed that his bombings were necessary to draw attention to this malaise and to curtail and ultimately roll back industrial technology. Basing himself out of a remote cabin without electricity or running water in Lincoln, Montana, he mailed or hand-delivered 16 letter bombs between 1978 and 1995. Most of his devices were handcrafted and made with both metal and wooden parts. The initial bomb—sent to an engineering professor at Northwestern University in 1978—adopted a highly primitive triggering mechanism involving a nail tensioned by rubber bands. Over time, however, the sophistication of the detonation techniques improved and would eventually take the form of a combination of batteries and filament wire.

While most of Kaczynski's attacks targeted individuals, on at least one occasion he attempted to blow up a passenger plane—American Airlines Flight 444 flying from Chicago to Washington, D.C., in 1979. Only a faulty timing mechanism

Theodore Kaczynski, known as "The Unabomber," is escorted in handcuffs from the federal courthouse in Helena, Montana, on April 4, 1996. (AP/Wide World Photos)

prevented the bomb—which had been placed in the cargo hold—from detonating. According to the authorities, had the device been properly wired, it would have obliterated the aircraft.

As aviation sabotage is a federal crime, the FBI assumed responsibility for the postincident inquiry. The agency code-named the ensuing investigation UNABOM and formed a joint task force with the Bureau for Alcohol, Tobacco, and Firearms and the U.S. Postal Inspection Service. Overall, 150 full-time employees were assigned to the case, and a $1 million reward was also posted for anyone who could provide information leading to the Unabomber's arrest.

Despite these measures Kaczynski avoided capture and indeed over the next 15 years carried out attacks that left three people dead: Hugh Scratton, the owner of a computer store in California; Thomas Malder, a senior executive with the national advertising firm Burson-Masteller; and Gilbert Murray, the president of the timber industry lobbying group California Forestry Association. There is speculation that the latter two murders were undertaken in support of the wider radical environmental movement. Following Murray's death, Kaczynski reportedly wrote a letter to Earth First! acknowledging responsibility under the rubric of the "Freedom Club." Following his arrest he also admitted to killing Malder after reading an article by the same group charging that Burson-Masteller was guilty by association for the Valdez 1989 oil spill in Alaska, as it had advised the company that owned the vessel at the heart of the accident, Exxon-Mobil.

In 1995 Kaczynski sent a letter to the *New York Times* and promised to desist from further acts of violence if that paper or the *Washington Post* agreed to publish a 35,000-word statement of his beliefs and objectives—*Industrial Society and Its Future.* The FBI pressed the *Times* and *Post* to jointly run the so-called manifesto piece in the hope that a reader would identify the author. The move paid off as David Kaczynski recognized the style of writing and beliefs as those of his brother. His wife, Linda, pushed him to alert the authorities that Ted was in fact the Unabomber, and after a search he was eventually traced to the cabin in Lincoln on April 3, 1996. Combing the premises, agents discovered a wealth of bomb-making components, 40,000 handwritten journal pages, one live bomb, and what appeared to the original manuscript of the manifesto.

In a bargain to avoid the death penalty Kaczynski pleaded guilty to all the government's charges on January 22, 1998. He is currently serving a life sentence without the possibility of parole at the Federal Administrative Maximum Facility supermax near Florence, Colorado. David Kaczynski donated the reward money, less expenses, to the families of his brother's victims.

See also: Earth Liberation Front (ELF)

Further Reading

"Excerpts of the Unabomber Manifesto." *USA Today,* November 13, 1996. http://www. usatoday.com/news/index/una6.htm, accessed January 10, 2012.

Ottley, Ted. "Ted Kaczynski: The Unabomber." *Crime Library.com,* 2005. http://www. crimelibrary.com/terrorists_spies/terrorists/kaczynski/1.html?sect=1, accessed June 12, 2005.

"Post, Times Publish Unabomber Manifesto." *CNN News,* September 19, 1995. http:// www-cgi.cnn.com/US/9509/unabomber, accessed June 12, 2005.

Taylor, Bron. "Religion, Violence and Radical Environmentalism: From Earth First! to the Unabomber to the Earth Liberation Front." *Terrorism and Political Violence* 10, no. 4 (Winter 1998).

Edward F. Mickolus

KAHANE KHAI

Kahane Khai (also known as Kahane Chai or Kahane Lives) broke away from the Israeli far-right Kach ("Thus") Party after the latter's founder, Rabbi Meir Kahane (Martin David Kahane), was assassinated on November 5, 1990, in New York. Although the Western Emanation Group (Majmu'at al-Shu'a' al-Gharbi) claimed responsibility for his murder, the prime suspect in the attack was El Sayyid Nosair (El Sayyid Abdulaziz El Sayyd). Nosair was later linked to the February 26, 1993, attack on the World Trade Center and is alleged to have been involved in a plot to assassinate six prominent New Yorkers. Several of those targeted had been involved in the extradition of an Abu Nidal Organization (ANO) member from Venezuela to Israel who was wanted for an attack on a bus carrying settlers to the West Bank on April 12, 1986.

Kahane Khai was originally based in Kfar Tapauch (Tupuah) and came under the leadership of Binyamin Ze'ev Kahane, Rabbi Kahane's son. The group shares members with Kach and other far-right Israeli organizations such as the Jewish Defense League (JDL, also founded by Meir Kahane) and Eyal. All these movements espouse a common vision: the restoration of a "greater Israel" and the eviction of all Palestinians from within those borders. While the specific definition of this geographic area varies, most extremists typically take it to incorporate the West Bank, the Gaza Strip, and Lebanon, as well as parts of Egypt, Jordan, and Syria.

Groups associated with the original Kach movement, including Kahane Khai, have claimed credit for several attacks carried out against Palestinians and moderate Israelis. One of the most infamous was the February 1994 massacre of 29 Palestinians at the Cave of the Patriarchs (Ibrahimi Mosque) in Hebron. The perpetrator was Baruch Goldstein, a Jew born in Brooklyn, New York, who appeared to have acted out of opposition to the Oslo peace accords. Hamas, the al-Aqsa Martyrs' Brigades, and various other militant groups responded by carrying out a series of suicide strikes in Israel.

Kahane Khai was banned in 1994, whereupon it officially disbanded and formed an advocacy group known as the Kahane Movement. The United States claims this is just a front organization for the original group as well as Kach and lists it as a foreign terrorist organization. In January 1995 Washington froze assets belonging to 12 groups and 18 individuals, including the Kahane Movement. All were accused of trying to use terrorism to disrupt the peace process. Later that same year, Yigal Amir assassinated former Israeli prime minister Yitzhak Rabin. He was a member of Eyal and is alleged to have had strong ties to both Kach and the Kahane Movement.

In 2000 Binyamin Kahane was convicted of sedition after being arrested for distributing pamphlets that advocated violence against Palestinians. However, both he and his wife were killed in an ambush in December 2000. It remains unknown whether they were specifically targeted. Kahane Khai supporters and related entities continue to carry out fund-raising operations in the United States.

See also: Goldstein, Baruch; Hamas (Islamic Resistance Movement); Hebron Mosque Massacre; Jewish Defense League (JDL); Nosair, El Sayyid; Oslo Accords; World Trade Center (New York) Bombing

Further Reading

Gorenberg, Gershom. *The End of Days: Fundamentalism and the Struggle for the Temple Mount.* New York: Oxford University Press, 2000.

Kahane, Rabbi Meir. *The Story of the Jewish Defense League.* Radnor, PA: Chilton, 1975.

Karpin, Michael, and Ina Friedman. *Murder in the Name of God: The Plot to Kill Yitzhak Rabin.* New York: Metropolitan Books, 1998.

Sprinzak, Ehud. *Brother against Brother: Violence and Extremism in Israeli Politics from Altalena to the Rabin Assassination.* New York: Free Press, 1999.

Donna Bassett

KHALAF, SALAH

Salah Khalaf was a Palestinian nationalist leader and one of the original founders of the Fatah organization (where he was known as Abu Iyad). Born in Jaffa, Palestine, on August 31, 1933, he fled with his family to Gaza in 1948 after Jewish militants captured Jaffna during the Israeli War of Independence. As a student at Cairo University, he met and became a close friend of Yasser Arafat and in 1952 helped found the Association of Palestinian Students. Twelve years later the Palestine Liberation Organization (PLO) was created, and Khalaf was appointed its chief of security.

Following the 1967 Six-Day War, Khalaf moved to Syria and played an integral role in extending Fatah's low-intensity guerrilla campaign into Jewish territory in what became known as the War of Attrition (1967–1970). In reprisal, Israel launched a series of large-scale bombing raids on PLO positions inside Jordan; one of these attacks, against the Karameh refugee camp on March 21, 1968, nearly killed Khalaf and Arafat. Reconsidering the wisdom of hosting Palestinians on its soil, the Jordanian government expelled the PLO in September 1970 (Black September) and arrested, tried, and sentenced to Khalaf to death. His execution was never carried out, however, largely due to pressure from Egypt and the Arab League.

Now more opposed than ever to Israel, Khalaf helped to found the even more militant Black September Organization (BSO). Under his leadership, the group took responsibility for the assassination of Jordanian prime minister Wasfi Tal in Cairo on November 28, 1971; the destruction of an oil storage facility in Italy; the infamous 1972 Munich Olympics Massacre; the seizure of the Israeli embassy in Bangkok, Thailand; and the taking of the U.S. embassy in Khartoum, Sudan (during which three diplomats, two Americans and a Belgian, were slain). Besides these known cases, it has been alleged but never proven that Khalaf ordered the assassination of four members of the Maronite Phalange militia in Lebanon in December 1975 on what became known as Black Sunday.

By the mid-1970s Khalaf was reportedly the third highest-ranking member in the Fatah hierarchy, answering only to Arafat and Khalil al-Wazir. His senior status was reflected by the personal charge that he was given to ensure the unity of the PLO and prevent any fracturing of its constituent elements. One high-placed individual who was pressing to leave was Abu Nidal (Sabri Khalil al-Banna). The future founder of the Abu Nidal Organization (ANO), this renegade was to emerge as one of the most violent and fanatical Palestinian terrorists during the 1980s. Although Abu Nidal had been a close confident of Khalaf (both had been closely involved with the founding of the BSO), strong enmity developed between the two militants, largely due to the former's rejection of the latter's willingness to work with Arafat and support the more explicitly politically oriented direction he was taking the PLO. Following the Israeli invasion of Lebanon in 1982, Khalaf relocated to Tunis with the rest of the PLO leadership. He was subsequently assassinated in Tunis on January 14, 1991, by an operative of the Abu Nidal Organization.

See also: Abu Nidal Organization (ANO); Black September Organization (BSO); Palestine Liberation Organization (PLO)

Further Reading

Musallam, Sami. *The Palestine Liberation Organization: Its Organization and Structure.* London: Amana, 1990.

Nassar, Jamal R. *The Palestine Liberation Organization: From Armed Struggle to the Declaration of Independence.* New York: Praeger, 1991.

Seale, Patrick. *Abu Nidal, a Gun for Hire: The Secret Life of the World's Most Notorious Arab Terrorist.* New York: Random House, 1992.

Tibi, Bassam. *Arab Nationalism: Between Islam and the Nation-State.* New York: St. Martin's, 1997.

Spencer C. Tucker

KHALISTAN COMMANDO FORCE (KCF)

In June 1984 Indian troops backed up with tanks attacked Sikhs at the Golden Temple in Amritsar. In the assault, code-named Operation Bluestar, 83 soldiers and anywhere from 492 to as many as 1,500 civilians were killed. The government alleged that those inside were separatists who were amassing weapons in preparation for a campaign of violence aimed at securing Khalistani independence. The incident led to an uproar among Sikhs around the world and was directly responsible for the assassination of Indira Gandhi on October 31, 1984. Two years later Manbir Singh Chaheru, Harjinder Singh Jinda, Sukhdev Singh Sukha, Gurdev Singh Debu, Mathra Singh, and Tarsem Singh Kuhaar established the Khalistan Commando Force (KCF) to avenge those killed in Operation Bluestar and take up the cause of Sikh secession. Chaheru was subsequently declared the group's military leader.

Just months after KCF's formation, Chaheru participated in a jail break that resulted in the deaths of six Punjabi prison guards. He was arrested on August 8, 1986, and disappeared while in custody. Thereafter, Sukhdev Singh Sukha (also known as Sukha Sipahi), a former police officer, took command of the KCF. He changed his name to Labh Singh and assumed the title of "general." Under his tenure the KCF killed General Arun Vaidya, the commander of Operation Bluestar (the two assassins, Harjinder Singh Jinda and Sukhdev Singh Sukha, were both hanged on October 9, 1992), and conducted attacks against tobacco and liquor sellers in the Punjab. Singh's leadership was to prove short-lived, however, as police fatally shot him on July 12, 1988.

The loss of Singh was a major blow to the organizational unity of the KCF, which subsequently split into a number of factions led by Wassan Singh Zaffarwal, Paramjit Singh Panjwar, and Gurjant Singh Rajasthani. Singh's death also weakened the KCF alliance with another Sikh extremist movement, Babbar Khalsa (BK), as he had been largely responsible for forging ties between the two groups.

Despite this, the KCF managed to maintain a sporadic, if visible, operational tempo. In June 1991 the group attacked a train in northwestern Punjab, killing about 50 passengers, mostly Hindus. This was followed in September 1993 with a bombing in New Delhi that left eight people dead, including Indian Youth Congress president Maninderjeet Singh Bitta.

A concerted, if not draconian, antiterrorist drive eventually crushed the KCF and other Sikh extremist groups. Coming under the direction of Kanwar Pal Singh (KPS) Gill, the director general of police, the campaign ran from 1991 to 1995 and resulted in the deaths and detentions of thousands of suspects. Although the campaign was welcomed in India, with many seeing Gill as a hero, the methods used to crush these groups were the subject of considerable international controversy and led to widespread accusations of human rights abuses.

While essentially destroyed, the KCF has continued to periodically attract the headlines. In June 2006, Kulbir Singh Barapind, a member of the main KCF Panjwar faction, was extradited from the United States to India for belonging to a terrorist organization and entering America on a false passport. He was wanted for 32 felonies but was arrested for only three murders in the early 1990s. After his detention, Barapind said he would seek to renew the Khalistan movement through peaceful means.

More recently, in 2008, Punjabi authorities announced they had foiled a KCF plot to kill Gurmeet Rahim Singh, head of the Dera Sacha Sauda (a nonprofit spiritual organization based in Haryana). Police said they had seized arms, drugs, and counterfeit currency, which they maintained had been smuggled into the country from Pakistan. The KCF remains a banned organization in India.

See also: Babbar Khalsa (BK); Golden Temple Massacre

Further Reading

Crenshaw, Martha, ed. *Terrorism in Context.* University Park: Pennsylvania State University Press, 1995.

Ganguly, Sumit, and David Fidler, eds. *India and Counterinsurgency: Lessons Learned.* London: Routledge, 2009.

McLeod, W. H. *The Sikhs: History, Religion, and Society.* New York: Columbia University Press, 1989.

Pettigrew, Joyce. *The Sikhs of the Punjab: Unheard Voices of State and Guerrilla Violence.* London: Zed Books, 1985.

Donna Bassett

KHOR AL-AMAYA OIL TERMINAL ATTACK

Suicide bombers sailing three small boats rigged with explosives charged the Khor al-Amaya and al-Basra oil terminals on April 24, 2004. The audacious sea assault killed three members of a U.S. security boarding party and wounded at least four others.

While the overall damage to the terminals was relatively minor, the attack disrupted Iraqi petroleum exports and cost the country the loss of almost one million barrels of crude in the first day alone. More important, perhaps, the assault generated a heightened sense of vulnerability that had a disquieting effect on world markets, especially in those sectors related to oil and gold.

Witnesses said that as the first of the three boats approached the two-mile exclusion zone (approximately 3,700 meters) around the Khor al-Amaya oil terminal, a coalition patrol ship sent an eight-member boarding team to investigate, as was standard security practice at the time. The unidentified vessel was a type known locally as a dhow. It is commonly used for fishing. Once the boarding party came alongside the craft, the militants detonated their bomb. The explosion flipped the security team's inflatable craft, killing two U.S. sailors and wounding five others. One of the injured, a member of the U.S. Coast Guard, died later that evening.

Approximately 20 minutes later after the first explosion, another pair of small boats approached the second oil terminal at al-Basra. Again security teams were sent to intercept, but the attackers proved to be far more elusive than the squad that had hit the Khor al-Amaya facility and managed to maneuver their dhow to within 50 yards of their intended target. One of the ships then self-detonated, severely damaging the terminal, which temporarily could no longer service tankers.

Although the Khor al-Amaya terminal was up and working again by April 25, officials estimated speculated that the al-Basra terminal would not be fully operational until at least April 26. This represented a significant disruption as the latter accounts for 700,000 of the roughly 1.6 million barrels of oil that Iraq exports daily.

A team of experts was subsequently sent to investigate the incidents, which occurred on a day of considerable violence elsewhere in the country. U.S. military officials said that it was especially important to determine whether the point of origin for the bombings was Iraq or neighboring Iran or Kuwait. To date this issue remains unresolved, at least publicly.

In a statement posted on the Arabic Muntada al-Ansar Islamic website on April 26, Abu Musab al-Zarqawi claimed credit for the attacks. He said that those who carried out the coordinated operations had been inspired by "what their brothers, the lions of al-Qaeda, did against the destroyer USS *Cole* in the Gulf of Aden" in 2000, further affirming that the strike was specifically intended to target "sensitive points of the infidels' economy." Al-Zarqawi signed the communiqué as "emir of the Jamaat al-Tawhid wa'l-Jihad" (Monotheism and Jihad, Monotheism and Holy War, Unity and Jihad Group).

The names of the targeted terminals used in al-Zarqawi's declaration, Mina al-Amiq and Mina al-Bakr, were no longer in use at the time of the attack. Mina al-Amiq had been changed to Khor al-Amaya (also once known as Khor al-Abdullah) and Mina al-Bakr to the al-Basra terminal (also called the Bakr terminal) in 2003.

Al-Zarqawi and his group have links to Ansar al-Islam (AaI; Partisans of Islam or Followers of Islam), a group with a complex history dating back to 1991 that evolved to forge initial ties with Al Qaeda sometime in 2001. A U.S. counterterrorism official noted at the time, however, that it would be a mistake to equate the al-Zarqawi group with Al Qaeda, alleging that the two groups had parted ways in early 2004. Whatever the true nature of this on-again, off-again relationship, it seems to have been resolved by mid-October 2004, when al-Zarqawi posted a note on an Islamist website pledging full allegiance to Osama bin Laden

Ahmad al-Khafaji, a senior Iraqi security official, warned that oil installations would likely continue to be subjected to sabotage unless the country's neighbors did more to stop the infiltration of foreign extremists. The U.S.-led coalition was also concerned about repeat attacks and quickly moved to restructure security around these platforms in what became known as "defense in depth."

See also: Al Qaeda; Ansar al-Islam (AaI); Jamaa al Tawhid wa'a Jihad (JTJ); USS *Cole* Bombing; Zarqawi, Abu Musab al-

Further Reading

"Blasts Target Iraqi Oil Terminals." *BBC News,* April 25, 2004. http://news.bbc.co.uk/2/hi/middle_east/3656481.stm, accessed May 2, 2011.

"Coalition Maritime Forces Revise Iraqi Oil Terminal Protection Procedures." Commander, Joint Forces Maritime Component Commander/Commander, U.S. Naval Forces Central Command/Commander, U.S. 5th Fleet Public Affairs, May 6, 2004. http://www.navy.mil/search/display.asp?story_id=13177, accessed May 2, 2011.

"Jordanian Claims Suicide Attacks on Iraqi Terminal." *NBC News,* April 26, 2004. http://www.msnbc.msn.com/id/4829643/ns/world_news-mideast/n_africa/Jordanian claims_suicide_attacks_on_Iraqi_terminal, accessed May 2, 2011.

Pyke, Nicholas. "Suicide Bomber Boats Explode in Attack on Basra Oil Terminal." *The Independent,* April 25, 2004. http://www.independent.co.uk/news/world/middle-east/suicide-bomber-boats-explode-in-attack-on-basra-oil-terminal-756454.html, accessed May 2, 2011.

Donna Bassett

KING DAVID HOTEL BOMBING

On July 22, 1946, a 350-kilogram (771-pound) bomb exploded in the basement of the King David Hotel, which at the time housed the headquarters of the British Army and the secretariat of the Palestinian government. The blast killed 91 people, including 17 Jews, and injured 45. It was the deadliest terrorist act directed at the British during the Mandate era (1920–1948).

The Irgun Tsvai Leumi (IZL, also known as Irgun, Irgun Zeva'i Le'umi, Etzel, or the National Military Organization [NMO]) claimed responsibility for the attack, declaring that it was in retaliation for a June 29, 1946, British raid on the Jewish Agency (JA) for Palestine—the pre-state authority that had been instituted prior to the establishment of an independent Israel. That sweep had netted a large quantity of information detailing the JA's operations and links with violent groups, and this material was then taken to the King David Hotel.

The Irgun made three phone calls prior to the bombing. The first was to the hotel operator, who ignored it. The second went to French consulate. The call was taken seriously, and the hotel staff subsequently went through the building opening windows and closing curtains to lessen the impact of any potential blast. The third went to the *Palestine Post* newspaper, which alerted the police.

The King David Hotel housed the British secretariat in its southwestern section, while the remainder of the property continued to function as a hotel and the social center of the Mandate. Irgun decided that the easiest way to carry out the attack was to first cause a distraction and then smuggle the bomb into the building through kitchen deliveries. In line with this plan, the group detonated two small improvised explosive devices to the south and north of the hotel. They were designed to draw attention away from the building as well as scare away pedestrians.

While this was happening, a commercial truck turned into the hotel drive from the north and went down to the basement entrance. Thirteen men and one woman exited the vehicle and began unloading seven milk churns, each stuffed with a TNT-gelignite mixture. A British officer who noticed something suspicious demanded to know what was going on and was shot by an Irgun member. Three policemen who heard the retort of the weapon rushed toward the kitchen, alerting Inspector J. C. Taylor at the control center that something was wrong, who then issued a general alarm.

By this time the seven milk churns containing the explosives were in place around the central pillars under the southwestern section of the hotel, and the Irgun assault group had departed. At exactly 12:37 P.M. the milk churns detonated. The walls at the southwestern corner of the hotel bulged outward, and the entire southwestern wing began to crumble, one story collapsing into the next. With a final crash, the secretariat became a huge pile of rubble.

The immediate British response was to declare martial law and initiate a house-to-house search that resulted in the detention of 133 men and 10 women. The UK government then enacted widely unpopular restrictions on the civil liberties of Jews in Palestine, which included military curfews, roadblocks, and mass arrests. The measures shifted British public opinion further against the Mandate system and alienated the Jewish populace, which had been Irgun leader Menachem Begin's intention from the beginning.

See also: Irgun Tsvai Leumi

Further Reading

Boyer Bell, J. *Terror Out of Zion: Irgun Zvai Leumi, Lehi and the Palestine Underground, 1929–1949.* New York: St. Martin's, 1979.
Clarke, Thurston. *By Blood and Fire: July 22, 1946: The Attack on Jerusalem's King David Hotel.* New York: Putnam's Sons, 1981.

Donna Bassett

KONGRA-GEL

Kongra-Gel was the name adopted by the Partiya Karkeren Kurdistan (PKK), otherwise known as the Kurdistan Workers Party, from October 2003 through April 2005. During the PKK's unilateral cease-fire, which stretched from 1999 through 2004, the group experimented with a number of name changes, most likely in an effort to distance itself from its terrorist past and improve its image in the wake of the September 11, 2001, attacks. The PKK settled on Kongra-Gel Kurdistan, which translates to the People's Congress of Kurdistan, in October 2003.

Under the banner of Kongra-Gel, the group ended its unilateral cease-fire with Turkey in June 2004. The decision to dissolve the cease-fire likely emanated from a takeover by the group's militant wing in February 2004. Frustrated by Turkey's failure to accede to Kongra-Gel's demands for greater Kurdish autonomy and by Turkey's repeated attacks on Kongra-Gel targets during the cease-fire, Abdullah Ocalan, the group's imprisoned leader, directed his movement to resume its operations in southeastern Turkey. The ensuing wave of attacks on Turkish military targets killed hundreds. Kongra-Gel also launched a number of bombings of oil installation targets throughout Turkey. In addition, a hard-line splinter of the group, the Kurdistan Freedom Falcons, carried out a series of deadly attacks on civilian targets in western Turkey, including a handful of bombings targeting tourist sites and hotels that catered to Westerners. As a result of the group's violent activities, Kongra-Gel was swiftly labeled as a terrorist organization by both the European Union and the United States. Perhaps because of this designation, by April 2005, the group had opted to revert to its original name, the PKK. Under its original moniker, the PKK continues its attacks on Turkey as of this writing.

See also: Ocalan, Abdullah; Partiya Karkeren Kurdistan (PKK)

Further Reading

"Kongra-Gel (KGK)." National Counterterrorism Center, West Virgina. http://www.nctc.gov/site/groups/kgk.html, accessedJune 25, 2010.

Marcus, Aliza. *Blood and Belief: The PKK and the Kurdish Fight for Independence.* New York: New York University Press, 2007.

"Terrorist Organization Profile: PKK/KONGRA-GEL." MIPT Terrorism Knowledge Base. http://www.start.umd.edu/start/data/tops/terrorist_organization_profile.asp?id=4179, accessed June 25, 2010.

Nate Shestak

KOSOVO LIBERATION ARMY (KLA)

The Kosovo Liberation Army (KLA or Ushtria Clirimtare e Kosoves) was a guerrilla force that fought for Kosovo's independence from Yugoslavia, and later from Serbia. Most of the group's members were ethnic Albanians, who make up approximately 90 percent of Kosovo's two million people. Although the KLA officially disbanded in July 1999, many of its commanders and fighters joined forces with the National Liberation Army in Macedonia and other satellite organizations to continue their fight for an independent Kosovo.

The KLA formed around 1990 as a small band of peasants committed to the liberation of Kosovo. The province had been an autonomous region from 1974 to 1989, and its degree of home rule was virtually equivalent to that of any republic of the former Yugoslav federation. However, Kosovo's autonomy was rescinded in 1989 by then Yugoslav president Slobodan Milosevic, who cited a need to suppress separatism and protect non-Albanian ethnic minorities living in the province. For several years, most Kosovar Albanians followed a policy of nonviolence in their efforts to restore a degree of local independence. As severe repression against ethnic Albanians by Serbian police and Yugoslav Army forces continued unabated through the mid-1990s, however, the KLA began to carry out well-planned attacks against carefully chosen Serbian targets. Unrest culminated at the beginning of 1997 when open clashes erupted between KLA rebels and government forces.

In 1998 Milosevic launched a crackdown on the KLA and also on ethnic Albanian villages throughout the province suspected of providing assistance to the rebels' cause. The crackdown merely drove Kosovars into the arms of the KLA, and the group's membership expanded to an estimated 35,000 fighters. In early 1999 the Serbs began a heightened military campaign to destroy the organization, burning entire villages, driving tens of thousands of civilians from their homes, and causing many civilian casualties. The North Atlantic Treaty Organization (NATO)

Kosovo Liberation Army (KLA) fighters running to battle with Serbian police in the town of Junik, Kosovo, June 22, 1998. Although the group officially disbanded in 1998, many of its fighters joined with the National Army of Macedonia to continue the fight for an independent Kosovo. (AP Photo/Santiago Lyon)

responded to this aggression by launching air strikes against Yugoslavia to help prevent further attacks on Kosovar Albanians.

By the onset of the NATO air strikes, the KLA's force had dwindled to roughly 3,000 fighters. However, by June 1999, the organization had swelled to 17,000 as a result of an influx of volunteer refugee fighters and foreign militants mostly drawn from Albania but also from the United States, Sweden, Belgium, the United Kingdom, France, and Croatia. Although the KLA remained far outnumbered by the heavily armed Yugoslav military, the NATO air war hindered the mobility of Milosevic's forces, helping to somewhat equalize the battlefield. On June 9, NATO and Yugoslav officials signed the Military-Technical Agreement, which reaffirmed Belgrade's sovereignty over Kosovo but also paved the way for a complete withdrawal of Serbian troops and the demilitarization of the province.

Following the agreement, the KLA was transformed into the Kosovo Protection Corps, which worked alongside United Nations (UN) forces to patrol the province. However, renegade factions within the organization remained unwilling to disarm under any peace plan negotiated with the Yugoslav government and moved to form a rival entity known as the Armed Forces of the Republic of Kosovo, led by Bujar Bukowski. The new splinter group continued to call for full independence and as part of this effort carried out numerous, albeit sporadic, attacks against both Serbian and NATO troops.

The ongoing unrest eventually resulted in a round of UN-sponsored peace talks commenced in 2006 but failed to elicit a final settlement on the status of Kosovo. The province's Albanian leaders reacted by proposing a unilateral declaration of independence on November 28, 2007, which despite UN and Russian disapproval was officially announced on February 27, 2008. A constitution of the Republic of Kosovo was proclaimed four months later and immediately denounced by Serbia.

Further Reading

Bissett, James. "War on Terrorism Skipped the KLA." Center for Research on Globalisation, November 13, 2001. http://www.globalresearch.ca/articles/BISIIIA.html.

Huggler, Justin. "KLA Veterans Linked to Latest Bout of Violence in Macedonia." *The Independent* (UK), March 12, 2001.

"Kosovo Liberation Army." GlobalSecurity.org. http://www.globalsecurity.org/military/world/para/kla.htm.

Perritt, Henry. *Kosovo Liberation Army: The Inside Story of an Insurgency.* Chicago: University of Illinois Press, 2008.

Edward F. Mickolus

KU KLUX KLAN (KKK)

The Ku Klux Klan (KKK) is a series of white supremacist organizations that claim direct lineal descent from the original KKK, which emerged in the South after the Civil War of the 1860s. The latter defined itself as a violent secret society dedicated to rolling back the political rights and freedoms that had been bestowed on African Americans after the abolition of slavery. Members disguised themselves in white robes and hoods and became infamous for torching their victims and their property. The first KKK was short-lived, fading out in response to federal legislation that cracked down on the group and its activities.

New organizations bearing the name KKK sprang up again in the 1910s and 1920s, adding foreigners, Jews, Catholics, and organized labor to their lists of enemies. During this era, the Midwest constituted the main stronghold of the KKK, where it enjoyed a wide membership base and a significant amount of political power. This manifestation of the KKK declined during the Depression of the 1930s and came to a complete end in 1944.

The KKK was revived again, however, during the 1950s as the fear of communism gripped the United States. The organization continued to exist in opposition to the civil rights movement of the 1960s and was responsible for unleashing tremendous violence against African Americans and any who supported them, including whites. The bulk of its actions were concentrated in the South, and it was able to operate with effective impunity before being brought under some control by the federal government under President Lyndon B. Johnson.

The different KKK organizations that exist today have in common a belief in the inequality of separate races and a desire to promote what they see as the "supreme" interests of the white American community. They are secretive, fraternal entities that claim extreme patriotism and loyalty to their own idiosyncratic definition of the national identity. Klan groups still use methods of hatred and violence, and some are closely tied to far-right militias and the U.S. Nazi movement.

One of the more prominent KKK groups is the Knights of the Ku Klux Klan, first established in Tuscaloosa, Alabama, in 1956. By the 1960s the organization had a membership of around 5,000 and was later galvanized by the teachings and influence of David Duke, who emerged as a prominent Klansman in 1974. The Knights claim that the federal government is controlled by Jews and has explicitly sought the destruction of the white race by abandoning the defining principles enshrined in the U.S. Constitution.

The Knights of the KKK are led by an imperial wizard and a national chaplain and hold an annual convention every October in Harrison, Arkansas. The organization includes the Klan Youth Corps and a publishing arm that has benefited tremendously from the expansion of the Internet. In 1983 the Knights joined with the New Order Knights of the KKK and the White Knights to form a single "confederacy" aimed at coordinating, and thereby enhancing, their influence and national reach.

Another major Klan faction is the Invisible Empire of the Knights of the Ku Klux Klan, which split from the Knights in 1975. This latter group named itself after an organization that had been founded in 1915 but had died out in the 1960s. According to its manifesto, the Invisible Empire claims to be dedicated to the "protection and maintenance of distinctive institutions, rights, privileges, principles, and ideals of pure Americanism and to the defense and preservation of the Constitution as originally written." The group has educational programs and maintains a youth corps and a publishing wing.

There exist a number of other regional KKK groups across the country, all of which similarly define themselves along racist and white patriot lines. The ideas of these entities have resonated with xenophobic and racist elements in many other countries, and Klan organizations have been founded in Canada, Australia, Denmark, Germany, and Britain.

Further Reading

Bridges, Tyler. *The Rise of David Duke.* Jackson: University of Mississippi, 1994.

George, John, and Laid Wilcox. *American Extremists: Militias, Supremacists, Klansmen, Communists and Others.* Amherst, NY: Prometheus Books, 1996.

Kelly, Robert. "The Ku Klux Klan: Recurring Hate in America." In Robert Kelly and Jess Maghan, eds., *Hate Crime: The Global Politics of Polarization.* Champaign: Illinois University Press, 1998.

Moffatt, John. *The New Ku Klux Klan: A Study of the American Mind.* New York: Russell and Russell, 1963.

Rice, Arnold. *The Ku Klux Klan in American Politics.* Washington, DC: Public Affairs, 1962.

Edward F. Mickolus

L

LA BELLE DISCOTHEQUE BOMBING

On April 4, 1986, a bomb placed near the dance floor of the packed La Belle Discotheque in West Berlin exploded, killing 3 people and wounding 231 others, including 79 Americans. In response, the U.S. government launched a retaliatory strike on Libya (Operation El Dorado Canyon), which was widely suspected to have provided financial and logistical assistance for the attack.

The improvised explosive device blew a hole through the club's floor and ceiling, causing the walls to collapse inward. Two people died at the scene: Sergeant Kenneth Terrance Ford from the U.S. Army and Nermine Haney, a 28-year-old woman from Turkey. A third person, Staff Sergeant James E. Goin, succumbed to his wounds four days later.

A self-proclaimed spokesman for the Anti-American Liberation Front phoned a West German news agency in West Berlin and took credit for the attack. Another person told a London news agency that the Holger Meins Commando—an offshoot of the Rote Armee Fraktion (RAF, or Red Army Faction)—was behind the bombing. A third caller made contact with a West Berlin news agency and said the RAF was responsible.

On April 7 Richard Burt, the U.S. ambassador to West Germany, asserted in an interview on the *Today Show* that there was very clear evidence of Libyan involvement in the attack, alleging the perpetrators operated out of the Libyan People's Bureau in East Berlin. Although the White House rebuked Burt for his outspoken comments, it did confirm that there were grounds to suspect that Tripoli had played some role in the incident.

During a press conference on April 9, U.S. president Ronald Reagan declared that the United States was prepared to retaliate militarily if there was proof definitively linking Libya to the discotheque bombing. Two days later, German chancellor Helmut Kohl phoned Reagan confirming the country's complicity.

On April 12 Vernon Walters, the U.S. ambassador to the United Nations (UN), was secretly dispatched to obtain European support for a U.S. strike against Libya. British prime minister Margaret Thatcher backed the request, saying that Washington could launch the raid using its UK-based F-111s. France, Spain, Italy, and Greece all refused to support a strike and also denied permission for American fighters to fly over their airspace.

On April 14 U.S. aircraft took off from Britain. After flying around France and Spain, they passed through the Strait of Gibraltar and launched a missile assault on Tripoli. The attack killed at least 15 civilians, including the 15-month-old adopted daughter of Libyan leader Colonel Muammar Qaddafi, and injured more than 2,000.

A week after the strike, West German police arrested Ahmed Nawaf Mansour Hasi, 35, as a prime suspect in the La Belle Discotheque attack. Although he denied playing a role in the incident, he did admit to bombing the Arab-German Friendship Society on March 29, 1986. His confession led to the arrests of two others, Farouk Salameh and Fayez Sahawneh, both of whom were later convicted as accomplices in the March 29 operation.

More than a month after the bombing, authorities unearthed evidence that a terrorist-for-hire group called the Jordanian Revolutionary Movement for National Salvation had been involved in the attack. The group had ties to Libya, Syria, and the Abu Nidal Organization (ANO). It was also connected to the Hindawi clan, which had risen to prominence on April 17, 1986, when its leader, Nezar Hindawi, had tried to use his pregnant Irish girlfriend to unwittingly smuggle a bomb aboard an El Al flight to Tel Aviv. The 3.25-pound bomb was found by security. It was subsequently reported that Hindawi was already married and had apparently concluded that the best way to rid himself of his girlfriend and unwanted child was to use them to carry out a terrorist attack.

In 1996 three men and a woman were convicted of planning La Belle Discotheque bombing. Two of the males, Musbah Eter and Ali Chanaa, worked for the Libyan embassy in East Berlin and doubled as spies for the Stasi. They were found guilty of aiding and abetting murder and sentenced to 12 years in prison. The third man, the alleged ringleader of the team, Yassar al-Shuraidi, received a 14-year jail term for multiple counts of homicide, as did Verena Chanaa, the German ex-wife of Ali Chanaa.

The judge said it was not clear whether Qaddafi or Libyan intelligence had actually ordered the attack, or not, though the speculation was that they had. Two weeks before the La Belle Discotheque blast, U.S. forces had sunk a Libyan patrol boat in the Mediterranean, killing 35 seamen. The presumed wisdom was that the operation in Germany was to avenge this incident. Whatever the truth of the matter, the U.S. raid on Tripoli served to galvanize anti-American sentiment in Libya and was almost certainly the trigger for the 1988 bombing of Pan Am Flight 103 over Lockerbie, which killed all 259 passengers and crew on board as well as 11 people on the ground.

See also: Abu Nidal Organization (ANO); Pan Am/Lockerbie Bombing

Further Reading

Davis, Brian. *Qaddafi, Terrorism, and the Origins of the U.S. Attack on Libya.* New York: Praeger, 1990.

"Four Jailed for Berlin Disco Bombing." *BBC,* November 13, 2001. http://news.bbc.co.uk/2/hi/europe/1653575.stm, accessed September 14, 2011.

Mickolus, Edward, Todd Sandler, and Jean M. Murdock. *International Terrorism in the 1980s: A Chronology of Events.* Vol. 2, *1984–1987.* Ames: Iowa State University Press, 1989.

Stanik, Joseph T. *El Dorado Canyon: Reagan's Undeclared War with Qaddafi.* Annapolis, MD: Naval Institute Press, 2003.

Donna Bassett

LAGHMANI (ABDULLAH) ASSASSINATION

On September 2, 2009, a suicide bomber assassinated Abdullah Laghmani, the deputy head of the Afghan National Directorate of Security. An ethnic Pashtun in his 40s, he was the country's second-highest intelligence official and a close ally of President Hamid Karzai.

In addition to himself and Laghmani, the terrorist killed 17 others. The final casualty count was 19 dead and 56 wounded. Among the fatalities were two senior Laghman Province officials, a leading local religious figure, and three women. The attack took place at about 9:30 A.M. as Laghmani left the main mosque in the center of Mehtar Lam (Mehtarlam), the capital of Laghman Province, 60 miles east of Kabul. He was just about to climb into his armored sport-utility vehicle when the suicide bomber ran toward him and detonated his explosives.

Taliban spokesman Zabihullah Mujahid claimed responsibility for the assassination within hours of the incident. He said Laghmani was a marked man on account of the numerous detentions and jailings of the group's members that he had overseen in Kandahar Province.

The attack was not just an assassination; it represented a security disaster. Laghmani, one of the most powerful members of Afghanistan's national security organization, had been murdered in broad daylight during the holy month of Ramadan as he left a prominent mosque in his hometown while surrounded by armed guards. Furthermore, the murder occurred in a city where the Taliban had not operated on this scale before.

General Nur ul-Haq Ulumi (retired), a member of the Afghan Parliament's defense committee, called Laghmani's death a "big loss" for the country and especially for the security sector. He went on to remark that losing people of his stature underscored the sheer vulnerability that many officials continued to be exposed to. Indeed, just a few days prior to Laghmani's assassination, another senior Afghan intelligence officer had been killed in Kunduz Province. Police speculated that the two murders were possibly related.

Laghmani had served with the Northern Alliance during the 1990s, playing a key role in its conflict against the Taliban. Following Operation Enduring Freedom (OEF) and the subsequent overthrow of Mullah Omar's regime in 2001, he joined the Directorate of Security and was based in Kandahar. He was later appointed deputy chief in charge of operations in eastern Afghanistan.

Laghmani was particularly knowledgeable about the Taliban and their Pakistani backers. In 2008 he uncovered a direct link between Islamabad's Inter-Services Intelligence (ISI) Directorate and the suicide bombers who attacked the Indian embassy in Kabul. He had also been instrumental in tying militant border crossings into Afghanistan to safe havens in Pakistan's Federally Administered Tribal Areas (FATA)—infiltration that he consistently claimed was being facilitated by the ISI. This led many to speculate that elements within Pakistan's security and intelligence community, possibly working with foreign extremist groups such as Al Qaeda, had a role in his assassination. Laghmani was a popular figure in Afghanistan and a prominent member of Karzai's inner circle. It is likely that he would have occupied a key post in any new government had he not been killed.

See also: Indian Embassy (Kabul) Bombing; Taliban

Further Reading

Farrell, Stephen, and Sangar Rahimi. "Deputy Chief of Intelligence Is Slain in Afghanistan." *New York Times,* September 2, 2009. http://www.nytimes.com/2009/09/03/world/asia/03afghan.html?_r=1, accessed August 8, 2011.

Peters, Gretchen. *Seeds of Terror: How Heroin Is Bankrolling the Taliban and al Qaeda.* New York: St. Martin's, 2009.

Rabasa, Angel, Peter Chalk, Kim Cragin, Sara A. Daly, Heather S. Gregg, Theodore W. Karasik, Kevin A. O'Brien, and William Rosenau. *Beyond al-Qaeda. Part 1: The Global Jihadist Movement.* Santa Monica, CA: RAND, 2006.

Rashid, Ahmed. *Descent into Chaos: The United States and the Failure of Nation Building in Pakistan, Afghanistan, and Central Asia.* New York: Viking, 2008.

Donna Bassett

LAHORE POLICE ACADEMY ATTACK

The attack on the Manawan Police Training Academy in Lahore took place on the morning of March 30, 2009. The incident followed a previous assault by heavily armed gunmen against the Sri Lankan cricket team (also in Lahore) on March 3 and appears to have been in revenge for the 2007 storming of the Lal Masjid, a Deobandi institution in Islamabad connected to Islamist extremism. The two strikes created considerable shock in Lahore, which had hitherto been largely spared militant violence, and led to growing fears of "Talibanization" throughout Pakistan.

The attack on the Manawan Academy was carried out by an estimated 14 terrorists armed with assault rifles, grenades, claymore mines, and rocket-propelled grenades and dressed in a combination of police and civilian clothes. The operation against commenced at 7:30 A.M. when the perpetrators drove up to the school and killed the security guards monitoring the compound's rear entrance. They then advanced to the main parade ground and opened fire on some 750 unarmed recruits who were conducting calisthenics. Following the initial assault approximately 35 people were taken hostage and held in an interior barracks room, precipitating an eight-hour siege.

Pakistani security forces responded approximately 90 minutes after the violence began, cordoning off the training school and moving in hundreds of commandos from the Rangers as well as members from the Punjabi police and army. The security forces temporarily shut down live feeds from local news cameras in order to deprive the terrorists' handlers of a potential source of information, blew up part of the perimeter wall surrounding the academy, fired tear gas into the compound, and staged an air assault using military helicopters (at least one of which was damaged by ground gunfire). Despite severe resistance the offensive proved successful, and the school was retaken. During the rescue, eight terrorists were killed—two of whom detonated suicide vests to avoid capture—and six were taken alive. Thirty-four police recruits and civilians also lost their lives, with an additional 90 wounded.

The attack on the Manawan Academy generated considerable controversy in Pakistan. The school was heavily criticized for failing to improve its security

Hostage police officers are freed by their colleagues as the fire continues inside the compound of a police training school on the outskirts of Lahore, Pakistan, March 30, 2009. A group of 14 gunmen attacked the facility and rampaged through it for hours throwing grenades, seizing, and killing at least 34 recruits. (AP Photo/Emilio Morenatti)

despite receiving a warning from the Criminal Investigation Department of potential terrorist threats to police offices and training facilities. Among other lapses highlighted were a lack of sufficient automatic weapons to deal with an assault, insufficient foot patrols around the compound's perimeter, inexperienced gate security guards (all of whom were police cadets), and an absence of checkpoints on roads leading to the school. Several observers also criticized the slow response time of the security forces following the outbreak of violence and noted that the terrorists were far better trained, physically conditioned, and equipped than regular police forces. In addition, a number of commentators pointed out that the incident graphically illustrated the ease with which police uniforms could be obtained in Pakistan, casting doubt on government claims that shops selling these clothes are closely monitored and regulated to ensure that all purchasers are identified and verified as bona fide law enforcement personnel.

On March 31, then-emir of the Tehrik-e-Taliban Pakistan (TTP) Baitullah Mehsud claimed credit for the attack, stating that it was intended to punish President Asif Ali Zardari's adherence to U.S. policies and his willingness to allow drone attacks in FATA. However, several eyewitnesses also reported that the militants had shouted slogans during the operation indicating that they were avenging Islamabad's operation against the Lal Masjid two years earlier. Pakistani Interior Minister Rehman Malik later confirmed that Mehsud had organized the attack, although he went on to allege that a "foreign hand" may have additionally been involved. The statement was a thinly veiled reference to India, whose government denied complicity and offered its sympathies.

The Manawan Academy would be struck again on October 15, 2009, in the run-up to the Pakistani Army's invasion of South Waziristan, resulting in the deaths of nine police officers and four terrorists. The second attack, which coincided with terrorist assaults on the regional headquarters of the Federal Investigation Agency (FIA) and on the headquarters of the elite Special Services Group (SSG), involved tactics strikingly close to those utilized in the first operation: an early-morning assault, perpetrators wearing military uniforms and suicide vests, initial targeting of perimeter gate guards, and the subsequent storming of the compound using a combination of automatic weapons and grenades. The Amjad Farooqi Group, a TTP-affiliated organization organized by Ilyas Kashmiri from the ethnic Punjabi Harakat ul-Jihad al-Islami (HuJI), claimed credit for the second attack. The choice of venue, similarity of tactics, and use of Punjabi fighters in both incidents suggests that the Amjad Farooqi Group may have executed the first assault on behalf of the TTP as well.

See also: Tehrik-e-Taliban Pakistan (TTP)

Further Reading

Abbas, Hassan. "Defining the Punjabi Taliban Network." *CTC Sentinel* 2, no. 4 (April 2009).

Roggio, Bill. "Terrorists Storm Lahore Academy, Kill More than 30." *Long War Journal,* March 30, 2009. http://www.longwarjournal.org/archives/2009/03/terrorist_storm_laho.php.

Sahi, Aoun. "Tragedy or Victory." *Encore,* April 2009. http://jang.compk/thenews/apr2009-weekly/nos-05-04/2009/enc.htm, accessed February 1, 2012..

Tahir, Zulquarnain, Ahemd Fraz, and Zaheer Mamood. "Police Interrogate Suspects after Lahore Attacks." *Dawn.com,* October 16, 2009. http://www.dawn.com/wps/wcm/connect/dawn-content-library/dawn/news/pakistan/metropolitan/09-gunmen-fire-at-fia-office-in-lahore—szn04+, accessed July 12, 2011.

Tavernise, Sabrina, Waqar Gillani, and Salman Masood. "Rampage in Pakistan Shows Reach of Militants." *New York Times,* March 30, 2009.

Ben Brandt

LAKKI MARWAT BOMBING

On January 1, 2010, a suicide bomber driving a Mitsubushi Pajero sport-utility vehicle (SUV) packed with explosives detonated his vehicle during a volleyball match taking place in the village of Shah Hasan Khel in the Lakki Marwat District of Pakistan's Khyber-Pakhtunkwha. The attack killed 105 people and injured over 100. It was the deadliest act of terrorism in the country since a bombing in Peshawar the previous October that left 120 people dead.

Targeting sports events is an unusual occurrence in Pakistan, and no group immediately claimed responsibility. However, authorities speculated that the village was selected because the local residents had formed a pro-government militia to rid the area of Islamist militants. In the weeks leading up to the attack, the Taliban had threatened death to any person joining these types of self-defense forces. Others also argued that the operation was likely prompted as a response to ongoing military offensives that were taking place to rid North and South Waziristan of extremist elements. This region forms an extended rebel belt that insurgents had frequently used to mount attacks across northwestern Pakistan as well as into Afghanistan.

Approximately 400 people were present at the match at the time of the attack. The perpetrator drove his SUV into a nearby playground and detonated the vehicle while a game between local male teams was in progress. The truck was estimated to contain around 600 pounds of explosives, and the ensuing blast ripped through the watching crowd. Among the dead were six children, five paramilitary soldiers, and members of a local peace committee who were meeting in a nearby mosque. The explosion also destroyed more than 20 surrounding houses and was apparently felt from more than 11 miles away.

Pakistani president Asif Ali Zardari and the prime minister both denounced the bombing, as did Altaf Hussain, the chief of the Muttahida Qaumi Movement, calling the blast an attempt to deliberately worsen the already tense domestic situation in the country. The Khyber-Pakhtunkwha announced that it would pay compensation to the families of those killed or injured in the attack at the respective rates of US$35,000 and US$1,200 per victim.

See also: Taliban

Further Reading

Magnier, Mark, and Ali Zulfiqar. "Pakistan Suicide Bomb Kills at Least 75." *Los Angeles Times,* January 2, 2010.

Marwat, Ghulam. "Bomber Rams Car into Volleyball Venue." *The Nation* (Pakistan), January 2, 2010.

"Pakistan Suicide Bomb Kills Scores at Volleyball Match." *BBC News,* January 1, 2010. http://news.bbc.co.uk/2/hi/south_asia/8437114.stm, accessed January 1, 2010.

"Pakistani Tribal Elders Defiant against Taliban." *CBC,* January 1, 2010. http://www.cba.ca/world/story/2010/01/02/pakistan-bombing-taliban002.html, accessed January 1, 2010.

Peter Chalk

LARNACA AIRPORT ATTACK

During the late 1970s, in part because of Cairo's peace negotiations with Israel, Egypt came under increasing threat from both radical Palestinian terrorist organizations and some of its Arab neighbors. As a consequence, the government formed a small 50-man hostage-rescue and counterterrorist unit in 1977. Later known as Force 777, the division was made up of volunteers from the army's As-Saiqa "Lightning" Special Forces.

It was not long before the unit saw its first action. On February 19, 1978, two members of the Popular Front for the Liberation of Palestine (PFLP) gunned down Youssef Sebai, an Egyptian newspaper editor and personal friend of President Anwar Sadat, in the Cypriot Nicosia Hilton. They then took 30 people in the hotel hostage, and a siege developed. Eventually, the Cypriot authorities conceded to the two attackers' demands that in exchange for the release of most of the hostages they would be granted safe passage out of the country. The terrorists and 11 of their captives were then taken to a Cyprus Airways DC 8. However, having taken off, they found that no country in the Middle East was willing to allow them to land, and running low on fuel they returned to Cyprus, landing at Larnaca Airport. Members of the members of the Cypriot Police and National Guard immediately surrounded the plane.

While any hostage incident on Cypriot soil involving a Cypriot aircraft would normally be considered the responsibility of the national authorities, President Sadat had other ideas. The Egyptians informed Cypriot authorities that they were flying in a team of negotiators on an Antonov transport aircraft; however, the plane was actually carrying a team of Force 777 members. During the one-hour flight from Cairo, the team prepared a plan to storm the hijacked aircraft the moment their own aircraft came to a stop. Upon arrival, the Force 777 team, dressed in civilian clothes and with many armed with AK-47 assault rifles, like those used by many terrorist groups, jumped from their aircraft and rushed toward the hijacked aircraft.

The Cypriot Police and National Guard surrounding the hijacked aircraft assumed these were fellow terrorists who had come to reinforce the hijackers and opened fire. For over an hour the Egyptians and Cypriot forces battled one another while the hijackers looked on bewildered. At the end of the exchange of hostilities, 15 members of Force 777 and 5 members of the Cypriot National Guard were dead, and many were wounded. In the meantime, as the two potential rescue forces fought one another, the Cypriot crew of the DC 8 managed to persuade the two PFLP hijackers to surrender and release their hostages. Needless to say, these events resulted in a major diplomatic row between Egypt and Cyprus, with both sides blaming the other for the deaths caused by the lack of coordination and communication.

See also: Popular Front for the Liberation of Palestine (PFLP)

Further Reading

Davies, Barry. *Terrorism: Inside a World Phenomenon.* London: Virgin Books, 2003.
Griffiths, John. *Hostage: The History, Facts and Reasoning behind Hostage Taking.* London: Andre Deutsch, 2003.
Harclerode, Peter. *Secret Soldiers: Special Forces in the War against Terrorism.* London: Cassell, 2002.

Richard Warnes

LASHKAR-E-JHANGVI (LEJ)

Lashkar-e-Jhangvi (LeJ) was founded in 1996 by a group of radical extremists—led by Muhammad Ajmal (also known as Akram Lahori)—who strongly endorsed the anti-Shi'a principles associated with Maulana Haq Nawaz Jhangvi (from whom the outfit derives its name), which stressed that the only way to effectively sanctify the Sunni faith in Pakistan was through violent means. LeJ has an estimated militant base of 300 cadres organized into semi-autonomous cells of five to eight members and retains most of its hard-core membership in the Punjab. The Pakistani government proscribed LeJ in August 2001.

LeJ has been at the forefront of sectarian violence in Pakistan—a conflict that left 1,518 dead and 2,817 injured between 2002 and 2008. Attacks perpetrated by the group frequently involve suicide bombers and have targeted Shi'a religious sites, marches, funeral processions, and those at home or even in the hospital.

Although primarily focused on prosecuting its sectarian agenda in Pakistan, LeJ is widely suspected of having established links with Al Qaeda. The group is known to have sent recruits to train at terrorist camps located near to the Sarobi Dam in Afghanistan, many of whom were subsequently retained for attacks against the Northern Alliance as well as Shi'ite enemies of the Taliban. LeJ is also thought to have benefited from the financial largesse of wealthy Gulf patrons with known sympathies for Osama bin Laden. The desert town of Rahimayar Khan in southern Punjab appears to have played a prominent role in this regard. Each year thousands of Arabs come to the region, spending several million dollars hunting local wildlife. Western officials suspect that a significant proportion of these monies have been transferred to the Sipah-ed Sahaba Pakistan (SSP) leadership, and through it to LeJ, to sustain and otherwise support anti-Shi'a activities in Pakistan.

There are also indications that LeJ has established ties to Al Qaeda through the conduit of organized crime. The group is known to have established links with drug syndicates based in the port city of Karachi, facilitating the transfer of Afghan-sourced heroin across Pakistan's western borders for both internal consumption and distribution to Asia and Europe. Profits earned from these overseas markets are widely believed to form a substantial component of Al Qaeda's war chest, which has, in return, paid LeJ with guns, explosives, and other materiel. Moreover, in common with Lashkar-e-Taiba, LeJ has been linked to Ibrahim Dawood's D-Company; Indian sources assert this international criminal enterprise retains at least residual links with bin Laden's wider jihadist network.

It is additionally believed that contacts with Al Qaeda have emerged in the context of links to Harakat-ul-Mujahideen (HuM) and the Tehrik-e-Taliban Pakistan (TTP). With regards to the former, LeJ is thought to have participated in past HuM attacks that were allegedly executed with Khalid Sheikh Mohammed's blessing. Indian sources additionally maintain they have evidence front-ranking LeJ members have consistently benefited from access to Camp Khalid ibn Walid—securing Al Qaeda training in everything from small arms handling to the preparation of improvised explosive devices. LeJ operatives also participated in the suicide bombing of the Islamabad Marriott on September 20, 2008; the attack, which left more than 60 people dead, has been directly linked to the TTP—a group with known ideological and operational sympathies with Al Qaeda.

Finally, evidence (albeit nondefinitive) of an Al Qaeda link has emerged in the testimony of Ajmal, the former leader of LeJ who was arrested in 2002. By his own admission, Ajmal has confirmed that members of his group (as well as cadres of HuM) swore an oath on the Koran to physically eliminate Pervez Musharraf at any cost. The basis for this commitment was apparently a conviction that the Pakistani president had both damaged and betrayed the true cause of jihad by siding with the United States in the post-9/11 global war on terror and was actively seeking to further a secular, Western-oriented agenda in Pakistan and throughout South Asia.

See also: Al Qaeda; Bombay Bombings (2003); Pakistani Sectarian Violence

Further Reading

Howard, Roger. "Probing the Ties That Bind Militant Islam." *Jane's Intelligence Review,* February 2000.
"Lashkar-e-Jhangvi." South Asia Terrorism Portal (SATP). http://www.satp.org/satporgtp/countries/pakistan/terroristoutfits/lej.htm.
Lawson, Alastair. "Pakistan's Evolving Sectarian Schism." *BBC News,* February 20, 2009. http://news.bbc.co.uk/2/hi/south/south_asia/7901094.stm.
Rabasa, Angel, Peter Chalk, Kim Cragin, Sara A. Daly, Heather S. Gregg, Theodore W. Karasik, Kevin A. O'Brien, and William Rosenau. *Beyond al-Qaeda Part 1: The Global Jihadist Movement.* Santa Monica, CA: RAND, 2006. Pp. 93–98.

Peter Chalk

LASHKAR-E-TAIBA (LET)

Lashkar-e-Taiba (LeT, literally, the Army of the Pure) dates back to 1993, when it was created as the military wing of the Markaz-ad-Da'awa Wal Irshad (MDI) madrassa. It is affiliated with the Ahl-e-Hadith sect of Wahhabism (which emphasizes statements attributed to the Prophet Muhammad) and was a creation of Pakistan's InterServices Intelligence (ISI) Directorate to act as a proxy force for prosecuting Islamabad's policy objectives in Jammu and Kashmir (J&K). The group is led by Hafiz Saeed (its spiritual emir) and Zaki ur-Rehman Lakhvi (its operational commander) and has a broader membership of around 150,000 cadres (including 750 insurgents on the ground in J&K). Under international pressure following the 9/11 attacks in the United States, then president Pervez Musharraf banned the group in 2002. However, it has since operated more or less openly under the name Jama'at-ud-Da'awa (which Saeed leads purportedly as an Islamic charity), although this group was also banned in 2009.

LeT possesses a robust network in India and has made strenuous efforts to cultivate ties with various extremist groups in the country, including the Students Islamic Movement of India and the Indian Mujahideen. LeT also enjoys an established international network outside South Asia, with particular strength in the Middle East and a growing presence in the United Kingdom. Financially, most of the group's funds come from diaspora contributions, earnings from legitimate businesses (such as real estate and commodity trading), the Pakistani military, and the provincial government of the Punjab (in the form of donations). Its espousal of Ahl-e-Hadith, which is considered theologically similar to the Salafi Islam practiced in Saudi Arabia, has additionally helped it procure financial support from that country.

LeT has between 100,000 and 150,000 supporters and members and enjoys an extensive infrastructure in Pakistan that includes its sprawling compound in the town of Murdike outside Lahore, training camps in Pakistani Occupied Kashmir (POK, or Azzad Jammu o-Kashmir) offices, madrassas, schools, medical clinics, and mosques. The group publishes several periodicals in Urdu and English, has operated websites and promulgated news bulletins via outlets such as Yahoo Groups, recruits openly on Pakistani university campuses, and operates the MDI madrassa (which was heavily involved in relief efforts following the devastating 2005 earthquake in POK).

Although the group was established as a *tanzeem* to fight Indian rule in J&K, most of LeT's personnel are Punjabi and Pashtun, with relatively few Kashmiris in its ranks. In addition, the group has always defined its objectives in local and regional terms, articulating a twofold ideological and operational agenda that aims to (a) exploit ethnoreligious tension in Kashmir in order to (b) trigger a wider religious revolution across the Indian state. To this end, the group has spearheaded terrorist attacks across J&K and has been directly tied to numerous assaults in India, including the attack on India's Red Fort in December 2000, the strike against the Indian National Parliament in December 2001, the Kaluchak massacre in May 2002, serial explosions in Delhi in October 2005, the Varanasi attack in March 2006, the Mumbai assaults in November 2008, and the bombing of a German bakery restaurant in Pune in February 2010. Of these, arguably the most serious and audacious were the November 2008 assaults, which were allegedly undertaken in collaboration with Ibrahim Dawood, the head of D Company (also known as the Bombay Mafia) and one of India's most wanted men.

Besides its J&K and Indian operations, there is evidence to link LeT to attacks and plots outside South Asia. Shezad Tanweer, one of the perpetrators behind the 2005 Underground bombings in London, was thought to have visited the LeT headquarters in Murdike; Willie Brigitte, who was arrested in 2003 on suspicion of planning attacks on the Lucas Heights nuclear reactor and the Pine Gap intelligence-gathering station in Australia, admitted to French authorities that he was trained by the LeT; U.S. officials have periodically claimed that LeT has been instrumental in recruiting Islamists to fight against Allied troops in Iraq; and in November 2009 four suspected operatives of LeT were arrested in Bangladesh for plotting to lead a fedayeen assault against the Indian and U.S. diplomatic missions in Dhaka to coincide with the anniversary of the 2008 attacks in Mumbai.

LeT is known for its sophisticated intelligence and operational planning capabilities. The 2008 Mumbai attacks represent a case in point. David Headley, a Pakistani American, traveled to India on several occasions to reconnoiter targets for the assault, using a fake visa-processing business to establish his cover identity. The attacks were then executed by LeT cadres trained in marine operations and equipped with automatic weapons, grenades, and delayed explosive charges. Members of the strike team used *Google Earth* to familiarize themselves with Mumbai, hijacked a fishing trawler to make the trip to India, employed modern GPS receivers to navigate, and communicated with their Pakistani handlers via satellite phones routed through the Internet. The attackers operated in small, heavily armed units, exploiting news broadcasts to ascertain the position, size, and maneuvers of the security forces. These tactics allowed 10 men to not only strike multiple locations across the city but also decisively overwhelm Mumbai's massive but poorly trained and equipped police force.

LeT is set apart from other Pakistani terrorist groups by its relative obedience to the military and ISI as well as by its espousal of the Ahl-e-Hadith sect of Islam. These traits have frequently caused friction with the major Deobandi militant entities, although it has often cooperated on an operational and logistic level with groups in India and Bangladesh. Unlike many other Kashmiri tanzeems, LeT is additionally characterized by a relatively strong sense of internal cohesion, and at the time of writing, there was little evidence to suggest that it was suffering from the type of internal hemorrhaging that has befallen groups such as Jaish-e-Mohammed and Harakat-ul-Mujahideen.

That said, speculation has arisen that certain globalized elements within LeT have moved to establish concrete ties with Al Qaeda. Fueling this concern is residual evidence linking the two organizations:

1. Abu Zubaydah, a senior Al Qaeda field commander arrested in 2002, was detained in a LeT safe house in Faisalabad.
2. LeT has been suspected of involvement in the 2005 London Underground bombings; although these attacks are not believed to have been directly ordered by Al Qaeda, they were definitely inspired and endorsed by the movement.
3. A sizable proportion of killed or captured LeT militants have been linked to radicals known to have received training in former Afghan camps run by Al Qaeda and/or the Taliban, including militant centers at Tayyba and Aqsa.
4. Indian sources have consistently claimed that Al Qaeda has supplied LeT with money—both directly and through intermediaries in Pakistan (although these assertions need to be assessed in the politically interested context in which they have been made).
5. Indian sources have additionally claimed that contacts exist between Osama bin Laden's international jihadist network and D Company—the crime syndicate that allegedly collaborated with LeT in carrying out the 2008 Mumbai attacks.
6. Pakistani commentators have periodically alleged that Al Qaeda has funneled financial support to aid Kashmiri tanzeems fighting in J&K, including LeT.
7. LeT has shown increased willingness to target Western interests in South Asia, such as the Café Leopold and Jewish Chabad Lubavitch Center, which were attacked during the 2008 Mumbai assault, and a disrupted plot to attack the U.S. and UK embassies in Dhaka in 2009.

Currently, there is no definitive evidence of an established logistic or operational link between LeT elements and Al Qaeda. However, the existence of at least residual ties cannot be discounted. LeT's ideological focus has certainly taken on a much more explicit anti-Western tenor in recent years, reflecting concerns and aspirations that, at least rhetorically, closely accord with the open-ended aims of the broader Al Qaeda jihadist network. Although the group has always promoted an international agenda (promising, for instance, to plant the Islamic flag in the capitals of the United States, Russia, and Israel), it has mostly focused its activities on the local and regional theaters. Today, as much emphasis is given to fighting Washington and allied governments supportive of (what was formerly called) the global war on terror as to staging attacks in India and J&K. This shift in focus is arguably supported by LeT's alleged involvement in the aforementioned attacks and plots in the United Kingdom, Australia, and Bangladesh.

Despite LeT's growing connections to anti-Western violence, the Pakistani government has refused to act against the group, and both the military and the ISI are considered to enjoy somewhat cordial relations with it. Indeed, reports from the Indian media indicated that Saeed was the guest of honor at an *iftar* dinner (the evening meal that breaks the daily fast during the holy month of Ramadan) hosted by the Pakistani Army's 10th Corps in 2009, shortly before he was charged with preaching jihad and raising money for terrorist activities (all of these charges have since been dropped). The general reluctance to act against LeT is considered to be a product of the army's belief that the group continues to be a strategic asset vis-à-vis Pakistan's competition with India. A number of military and intelligence officers also share LeT's religious convictions, further strengthening bonds. A number of sources in Pakistan have additionally suggested that Islamabad is fearful of the consequences of attempting a wholesale crackdown on LeT, given its size and formidable capabilities.

See also: Indian National Parliament Attack; London Underground Bombings; Mumbai Attacks (2008)

Further Reading

Bajoria, Jayshree. "Profile: Lashkar-e-Taiba." Council on Foreign Relations, January 14, 2010. http://www.cfr.org/publication/17882/profile.html.

Fair, Christine C. "Antecedents and Implications of the November 2008 Lashkar-e-Taiba (LeT) Attack upon Several Targets in the Indian Mega-City of Mumbai." Testimony given before the House Homeland Security Committee, Subcommittee on Transportation and Infrastructure, March 11, 2009. http://home.comcast.net/~christine_fair/pubs/CT-320_Christine_Fair.pdf.

Gilliani, Waqar, and Somini Sengupta. "Pakistan Court Frees a Mumbai Attack Suspect." *New York Times,* June 3, 2009.

"Lashkar-e-Toiba: Army of the Pure." South Asia Terrorism Portal. http://www.satp.org/satporgtp/countries/india/states/jandk/terrorist_outfits/lashkar_e_toiba.htm

Polgreen, Lydia, and Souad Mekhennet. "Militant Network Intact Long after Mumbai Siege." *New York Times,* September 30, 2009.

Rana, Muhammad, Amir. *A to Z of Jehadi Organizations in Pakistan.* Lahore, Pakistan: Mashal Books, 2004.

Rubin, Alissa. "Militant Group Expands Attacks in Afghanistan." *New York Times,* June 15, 2010.

Tankel, Stephen. "Lashkar-e-Taiba: From 9/11 to Mumbai." International Center for the Study of Radicalisation and Political Violence, London, April/May 2009. http://www.iscr.info/news/attachments/12408469161SRTTankelReport.pdf, accessed January 1, 2011.

Ben Brandt

LIBERATION TIGERS OF TAMIL EELAM (LTTE)

Until May 2009 the Liberation Tigers of Tamil Eelam (LTTE), popularly known as the Tamil Tigers, or simply Tigers, was Sri Lanka's largest and most militant Tamil separatist group. The organization fought for more than 30 years to create an independent state of Tamil Eelam, becoming particularly infamous for its hallmark trait of suicide bombings.

The LTTE was originally founded as the Tamil New Tigers (TNT) in 1972. Led by Chetti Thanabalasingham, the TNT embarked on a particularly intensive campaign of assassinations and violence that was variously designed to silence pro-government Tamils, eliminate informants, and disrupt police investigations into terrorist incidents and related criminal activities perpetrated in the group's name. In 1976 the TNT suffered a major blow when Thanabalasingham was arrested. His second in command, Velupillai Prabhakaran, subsequently assumed leadership, renaming the group the LTTE. Affirming the legitimacy of the Tamil struggle for independence on the basis of the Thimpu principles—and specifying that the Tigers' ideological objectives could be achieved only through violence, Prabhakaran fashioned a uniquely elite and ruthlessly efficient fighting force that emphasized selective recruitment and an unswerving dedication to the Eelam cause.

The Tamil Tigers initially benefited from Indian patronage, with Delhi using the organization as a proxy to pressure Colombo away from its increasingly close economic relationship with the West and return the country to its own nonaligned (and largely pro-Moscow) orbit. By 1986 the LTTE had gained control over much of northeastern Sri Lanka, including the strategically located Jaffna Peninsula, which was subsequently set up as the symbolic capital of a future independent state. Fearing that the LTTE's success could trigger secessionist demands by India's own Tamil population, however, India turned on its erstwhile ally in 1987 and for the next three years fought a protracted war that ultimately led to the Tigers' defeat and humiliating withdrawal from Jaffna.

From 1987 on, the LTTE quickly developed into an extremely proficient fighting force, drawing on the internalized training it had received from the Indians and supplementing this with tactical and strategic innovations of its own. The group demonstrated an ability to operate along a full combat spectrum ranging

Tamil Tiger cadres march in northeastern Sri Lanka. The group carried out a highly brutal and efficient terrorist insurgency for an independent state of Tamil Eelam before finally being crushed in May 2009. (AP Photo/Julia Drapkin)

from selective assassinations through acts of urban sabotage, civilian-directed bombings, and hit-and-run attacks to full-scale frontal assaults.

Most of the LTTE's terrorist activities were carried out by the Black Tigers (BTs), the group's highly feared suicide wing. Operations were directed against critical national infrastructure; civilians; urban complexes such as railway stations, religious shrines, and banks; and what were expansively defined as "very important persons"—elected leaders, prominent political figures, other high-level government functionaries, and senior police and intelligence commanders. The BTs carried out over 200 major suicide bombings during the LTTE's operational existence, 80 percent of which were believed to have been instrumental in achieving their primary objective. Some of the more notable missions claimed by the group included the assassinations of former Indian prime minister Rajiv Gandhi in 1992 and Sri Lankan president Ranasinghe Premadasa in 1993, the bombings of the Colombo Central Bank in 1996 and the Colombo World Trade Centre in 1997, the attempted assassination of Sri Lankan president Chandrika Kumurtunga in 1999, a strike on the Bandaranaike International Airport in 2001, and an attack on an unarmed naval transport convoy in 2006.

The LTTE was long regarded as the primary obstacle to peace between the country's restive Hindu Tamil minority and the Sinhalese Buddhist government because of its terrorist activities, hard-line position, and intolerance of dissent. However, in 2002 the group agreed to the terms of a Ceasefire Agreement with Colombo. Brokered by Norway on February 22, the accord opened the way for several rounds of talks during which the LTTE was given de facto control of an autonomous area in northeastern Sri Lanka, complete with its own tax structure, judiciary, police, and health and educational structure.

Although the Ceasefire Agreement did raise hopes that a final peace settlement could be achieved with the LTTE, repeated violations of the agreement and fears that the group was exploiting the cessation of active combat to build up its own forces eventually led to the collapse of the accord in 2006. Large-scale hostilities quickly resumed, which saw some of the bloodiest fighting of the more than three-decade-long war. By May 2009 the Tigers had been reduced to a small sliver of land in the northeast, where they made their last stand. Banning reporters from the region and reportedly ignoring the safety of Tamil civilians, the Sri Lankan army launched an all-out offensive against this rump force, capturing or killing all remaining LTTE combatants, including Prabhakaran, who reportedly died while making a final charge against troops in an armor-plated van filled with armed rebels.

The United Nations estimated that some 7,000 civilians lost their lives and more than 10,000 were wounded as the army systematically cornered the LTTE in 2009. The last two weeks of the conflict likely saw thousands more civilians killed at the hands of both the army and the rebels. After the war, the government interned more than a quarter million displaced Tamils—some for more than six months—in violation of both Sri Lankan and international humanitarian law.

See also: Central Bank (Colombo) Bombing; Colombo World Trade Centre Bombing; Gandhi (Rajiv) Assassination; Premadasa (Ranasinghe) Assassination

Further Reading

Bonner, Raymond. "Rebels in Sri Lanka Fight with Aid of Global Market in Light Arms." *New York Times,* March 7, 1998.

Chalk, Peter. "The Liberation Tigers of Tamil Eelam Insurgency in Sri Lanka." In Rajat Ganguly and Ian Macduff, eds., *Ethnic Conflict and Secessionism in South and Southeast Asia.* London: Sage, 2003.

Chalk, Peter. *Liberation Tigers of Tamil Eelam's (LTTE) International Organization and Operations—A Preliminary Analysis.* Canadian Security Intelligence Commentary 77, March 17, 2000. http://www.csis-scrs.gc.ca/eng/comment/com77e.html, accessed January 20, 2010.

Chalk, Peter, and Bruce Hoffman. *The Dynamics of Suicide Terrorism: Four Case Studies of Terrorist Movements.* Santa Monica, CA: RAND, 2005. Chapter 5, "The Tamil Tigers."

Gunaratna, Rohan. *Sri Lanka's Ethnic Crisis and National Security.* Colombo, Sri Lanka: South Asian Network on Conflict Research, 1998.

Gunaratna, Rohan. *War and Peace in Sri Lanka.* Colombo, Sri Lanka: Institute of Fundamental Studies, 1987.

Jayasekera, Shanaka. "Cornered Tigers: The LTTE Evolves as Guerillas." *Jane's Intelligence Review,* April 2009.

Joshi, Manoj. "On the Razor's Edge: The Liberation Tigers of Tamil Eelam." *Studies in Conflict and Terrorism* 19 (1996).

McDonald, Mark, and Alan Cowell. "Sri Lankans Say Rebels Crushed and Leader Killed." *New York Times,* May 19, 2009.

Rotberg, Robert, ed. *Creating Peace in Sri Lanka: Civil War and Reconciliation.* Washington, DC: Brookings Institution Press, 1999.

"Sri Lanka's Peace Process in Jeopardy." *IISS Strategic Comments* 10, no. 3 (April 2004).

Wijesekera, Daya. "The Liberation Tigers of Tamil Eelam (LTTE): The Asian Mafia." *Low Intensity Conflict and Law Enforcement* 2, no. 2 (Autumn 1993).

Peter Chalk

LIBI, ABU FARAJ AL-

Abu Faraj al-Libi was Al Qaeda's external operations chief and the organization's third-highest-ranking member before being arrested by Pakistani intelligence operatives on May 2, 2005. That year, U.S. president George W. Bush described al-Libi as a "major facilitator and chief planner for the al-Qaeda network." Many believed his arrest to be the most significant since the capture of Khalid Sheikh Mohammed—al-Libi's mentor—by Pakistani agents in March 2003.

Al-Libi traveled to Afghanistan during the 1980s to fight against the Soviets. From Afghanistan he moved to Pakistan and lived mostly in the tribal areas in the northwest for 18 years. He also lived in Lahore and Baluchistan; however, he frequently returned to Afghanistan for training in Arab-run camps. While in Pakistan, al-Libi married a Pakistani woman and learned Pashto (he could also speak Arabic and Urdu).

Al-Libi was able to maintain a relatively low profile in Pakistan, and it is believed that he moved relatively freely throughout the country. Indeed, the government's Inter-Services Intelligence (ISI) Directorate did not include his name on a most-wanted list until 2004. During that year, interrogations of militants arrested in Pakistan, particularly Salahuddin Bhatti, revealed the degree of al-Libi's involvement in Al Qaeda; intelligence agencies noted, however, that they had been keeping an eye on his activities since the arrest of Khalid Sheikh Mohammed. Naeem Noor Khan, a computer expert for Al Qaeda, and Ahmed Khalfan Ghailani, a Tanzanian suspected of involvement in the 1998 twin bombings of the U.S. embassies in Nairobi and Dar es Salaam, also stated that they had interacted with al-Libi.

Al-Libi is believed to have served as Osama bin Laden's personal assistant during the 1990s. He later took charge of Al Qaeda's activities in North Africa and worked as the top deputy and personal aide to Khalid Sheikh Mohammed—the ranking Al Qaeda member in Pakistan and the mastermind of the September 11 attacks. The relationship between the two has led some to speculate that al-Libi played a role in planning the attacks as well. Authorities believe that al-Libi took over Mohammed's duties upon the latter's arrest in 2003 and a year later also assumed responsibility for Al Qaeda's operations in the United States and Great Britain.

Al-Libi made several key contacts as a result of his work and training in Afghanistan and Pakistan. One of those was Amjad Farooqi, an Al Qaeda operative and leader of the Sunni sectarian group Lashkar-e-Jhangvi (LeJ). Farooqi is thought to have facilitated al-Libi's interactions with numerous extremists in Pakistan, a number of whom carried out attacks planned under his auspices. Notably these included two assassination attempts on then Pakistani president Pervez Musharraf, which, although unsuccessful, resulted in numerous casualties.

The attacks on Musharraf brought al-Libi to the attention of the ISI (at the time he was known only as Dr. Taufeeq), and he was subsequently captured on May 2, 2005 in Marwan, the second-largest city in the Northwest Frontier Province (NWFP). He initially attempted to avoid arrest by running into a home and holding the occupants hostage; however, he was forced out with tear gas after a 45-minute standoff. Authorities stated that they were able to confirm al-Libi's identity because of markings on his face caused by leukoderma, a disease that causes blotchiness on the skin.

The month after al-Libi's capture, President Musharraf stated that al-Libi had been handed over to American authorities for further questioning and interrogation, despite initial claims that he would be tried in Pakistan under the Anti-Terrorism Act. Sources stated that al-Libi was flown out of the country and handed over to U.S. officials on June 1, 2005. He is reported to have provided information regarding sleeper cells in several Arab states and was of particular interest because of his role in Al Qaeda's external operations.

During interrogations, al-Libi confirmed allegations that he had planned two assassination attempts against President Musharraf in December 2003; however, he said he was not a member of Al Qaeda and denied that he was linked to either Osama bin Laden or Mullah Omar, the leader of the Taliban. Al-Libi is currently being held at the U.S. detention facility at Guantánamo Bay, Cuba.

See also: Farooqi, Amjad Hussein; Lashkar-e-Jhangvi (LeJ); Mohammed, Khalid Sheikh; U.S. Embassy (East Africa) Bombings

Further Reading

"Al Libbi to Be Tried under ATA." *Dawn,* May 14, 2005.
"Burqa Trap Set for Terror Suspect." *BBC,* May 5, 2005. http://news.bbc.co.uk/go/pr/fr/-/2/hi/south_asia/4516567.stm.

"Faraj Handed over US to Purge Al Qaeda, Says Musharraf." *The News,* June 13, 2005.

"Further on Pakistan Hands Top Al-Qa'ida Suspect Al-Libi to US." Associated Press, June 6 2005.

Khan, Aamer Ahmed. "Pakistan and the 'Key al-Qaeda' Man." *BBC,* May 4, 2005. http://news.bbc.co.uk/go/pr/fr/-/2/hi/south_asia/4513281.stm.

"Libyan Al-Qa'ida Mastermind Betrayed by Skin Disorder." Associated Press, May 5, 2005.

Sengupta, Somini. "Pakistan Reports Arrest of a Senior Qaeda Leader." *New York Times,* May 5, 2005.

Tufail, Mazhar. "Libbi Confesses to Twin Attacks on President." *The News,* May 18, 2005.

Windrem, Robert. "Libyan Now Believed Responsible for U.S. & U.K. Terrorist Plans." *MSNBC,* September 7, 2004. http://www.msnbc.msn.com/id/5774446/.

Edward F. Mickolus

LIBYAN ISLAMIC FIGHTING GROUP (LIFG)

The Libyan Islamic Fighting Group (LIFG) was founded in the Green Mountain area of eastern Libya in 1990. Veterans from the war against the Soviet Union in Afghanistan created the group with the original intent to overthrow Colonel Muammar Qaddafi, whom they accused of being corrupt and un-Islamic. Initially, the LIFG maintained a relatively low-level resistance profile, mainly engaging in sporadic hit-and-run attacks against the security forces. However, in February 1996, the group elevated its operational tempo with a failed assassination attempt on Qaddafi. This galvanized a draconian response on the part of the state, which stymied much of LIFG's militant activity. Reeling from this onslaught, many LIFG members fled to Sudan, Iraq, and Afghanistan in 1998, where some joined ranks with Al Qaeda. Several leaders also resettled in the United Kingdom, which became a headquarters for the group in the latter part of the decade.

After the turn of the millennium, the LIFG became increasingly involved in transnational Islamist extremism. The group allegedly provided materials for a series of devastating suicide bombings in Casablanca in 2003, prompting the U.S. State Department to designate it as a foreign terrorist organization in 2004. That same year then Central Intelligence Agency (CIA) director George Tenet testified to the Senate Select Committee on Intelligence that the LIFG had established strong ties with Osama bin Laden, was benefiting from concerted Al Qaeda support, and represented an "immediate threat." The United States also reportedly facilitated the capture of LIFG leader Abdel Hakkim Belhaj in Malaysia, who was extradited to Libya after interrogation and held in Tripoli's infamous Abu Salim jail.

In November 2007 Al Qaeda's Ayman al-Zawahiri released an audio recording that welcomed the LIFG into the global jihad against Western powers. The message declared Qaddafi to be an "enemy of Islam" and specifically named LIFG leader Abu Laith al-Libi as an ally. In response, one of the group's exiled commanders, Norman Benotman, issued a disclaimer and urged Al Qaeda members to renounce violence against the West.

In September 2010 about 200 LIFG members were released from the Abu Salim prison under a reconciliation agreement brokered by Benotman and Qaddafi's son Saif al-Islam. After producing a 400-page theological treatise disavowing the use of terrorism and denouncing Al Qaeda, these cadres gained their freedom, and the LIFG officially disbanded.

In 2011 a new manifestation of the LIFG emerged—the Libyan Islamic Movement for Change (LIMC)—which joined with Benghazi-based rebels in the national uprising against the Qaddafi regime. Following the former dictator's fall, ex-LIFG commander Belhaj became an active political figure in Libya, appearing frequently at press conferences with other leaders of Libya's National Transitional Council. He has consistently downplayed alleged links between the LIFG and Al Qaeda, denying that the group ever actively targeted civilians. In September 2011 Belhaj explicitly renounced any connection with transnational terrorism, affirming in an interview, "Our goal was to help our people. We didn't participate in or support any action outside of Libya. We never had any link with al-Qaeda. . . . We had a different agenda; global fighting was not our goal."

See also: Al Qaeda; Casablanca Bombings; Zawahiri, Ayman al-

Further Reading

"Libyan Islamic Fighting Group." Violent Extremism Knowledge Base. http://vkb.isvg.org/Wiki/Groups/Libyan_Islamic_Fighting_Group, accessed February 26, 2012.
"Libyan Islamists 'Join al-Qaeda'." *BBC News*, November 3, 2007. http://news.bbc.co.uk/2/hi/7076604.stm, accessed February 26, 2012.
Nordland, Ron. "In Libya, Former Enemy Is Recast in Role of Ally." *New York Times*, September 1, 2011.
Pugliese, David. "One Year Later, Libya's Future Still Very Much in the Air." *Edmonton Journal*, February 18, 2012.
Robertson, Nic. "Former Jihadist at the Heart of Libya's Revolution." *CNN*, September 2, 2011.
Tawil, Camile. "The Libyan Islamic Fighting Group's Revisions: One Year Later." *Magharebia*, July 23, 2010.

Elinor Kasting

LIMBURG BOMBING

On October 6, 2002, a suicide bomber rammed an explosive-laden small boat into the side of the *Limburg,* a supertanker owned by Euronav and registered under the French flag. The blast created a 26-foot-wide hole, with edges dented inward, and ignited a huge fire, ultimately releasing between 50,000 and 90,000 barrels of crude oil into the Gulf of Aden. The vessel had been waiting for a tugboat and pilot to guide it into the Ash Shihr terminal at Al Mukallah (Yemen), 570 kilometers (353 miles) east of Aden, and was en route to Malaysia.

The blast killed a 38-year-old Bulgarian named Atanas Atanasov. His body was discovered on October 8. Of the remaining crew of 25 French and Bulgarian sailors, 12 were hospitalized in the port city of Al Mukallah. Only one had sustained serious injuries. The *Limburg* was carrying 397,000 barrels of crude oil at the time of the attack.

Witnesses on board the tanker reported seeing a small craft rapidly approaching the tanker. The boat detonated as the two ships collided. The blast was of sufficient force that it pierced both hulls, continued 7 meters (22 feet) beyond, and breached the cargo hold loaded with oil. It also ignited a fire so intense that the crew was forced to abandon ship. French authorities said the Yemenis did not have the facilities to contain such a large blaze, which burned for a full four days before it could be brought under control.

Initially, Yemeni officials stated that the incident was an accident, not an act of terrorism. The managing director of France Ship, Captain Peter Raes, contradicted this claim, saying it would be "near impossible" for an accidental explosion to have occurred. He added, "A junior officer saw a craft approaching the *Limburg*. He was of the opinion that we touched that craft then there was an explosion."

The *Limburg*'s captain, Hubert Ardillon, agreed with Raes, saying that in his opinion, "The way the explosion happened it could not be due to a technical problem." Although he conceded he had not witnessed the attack firsthand, he similarly added that a member of the crew had seen a small boat rapidly approach the tanker and that he had every confidence in the veracity of this account.

French authorities supported these views. President Jacques Chirac's spokeswoman Catherine Colonna said, "Mounting indications show that the hypothesis of a terrorist attack is very plausible," adding that "France will not let itself be intimidated." However, the Yemeni minister of sea transport, Said Yafaai (who was also in charge of the investigation), vehemently criticized the *Limburg*'s captain and crew as "irresponsible" for having publicly suggested that the incident was an act of terrorism.

On October 8, four investigators from the French Ministry of Transport, accompanied by agents from the Service de Documentation Exterieure et de Contre-Espionnage (SDECE, the external intelligence service), arrived on the scene. American counterterrorism experts were also actively engaged in carrying out inquiries. Although cautionary, these officials concluded that the incident was indeed an act of terrorism. The double-hulled ship was only two years old at the time of the explosion; weather was not an issue; the witness statements indicated an attack had taken place; and traces of explosives as well as fragments from a small boat were all found on board the *Limburg*. Similarities between the bombing and the attack on the USS *Cole* in 2000 (which left 17 American sailors dead) led many to speculate that Al Qaeda was behind the incident. However, no initial claim of credit was made at this time.

On October 14, Yemen's interior minister, Rashad al-Alimi, officially declared the incident "a deliberate act of terror carried out by an explosive-laden boat." This admission came as the antiterrorist division of France's public prosecutor began an independent investigation into the incident. Two days later, police raided a house that had been rented in Al Mukallah. It was thought that the explosives had been prepared there. By the end of the month, the authorities had detained 20 individuals suspected of having been involved in the attack.

The Islamic Army of Aden (IAA) initially took responsibility for the attack. The group sent a communiqué stating that the original target was a U.S. frigate but that when this proved impossible, they decided to attack the French tanker "because they are all infidels, and infidelity is one and the same." American and French authorities doubted that the IAA had conducted the operation, however. Not only was the group largely defunct at the time of the bombing, but its leader had already been executed for his role in the December 28, 1998, kidnapping of 16 tourists. This, and the fact that the style of the attack was so similar to the one carried out against the USS *Cole,* led officials to speculate that Al Qaeda was actually to blame.

This was later confirmed when a statement alleged to have come from Osama bin Laden was posted the Jehad.net website. The communiqué read, "By exploding the oil tanker in Yemen, the holy warriors hit the umbilical cord and lifeline of the crusader community, reminding the enemy of the heavy cost of blood and the gravity of losses they will pay as a price for their continued aggression on our community and looting of our wealth."

Authorities suspected that Abd al-Rahim al-Nashiri had planned the attack. Colloquially known Ameer al Bahr, or "Prince of the Seas," he was widely believed to be the chief architect of Al Qaeda's maritime agenda. Al-Nashiri was arrested in 2003 and transferred to a secret U.S. detention center, where he admitted to being the mastermind behind both the *Limburg* and USS *Cole* bombings. Under interrogation he also provided details of an ambitious strategy that he had planned on carrying out against Western shipping interests, which involved four main components: ramming vessels with explosive-laden zodiacs; detonating medium-sized fishing trawlers near frigates, cruise liners, or ports; crashing planes into large carriers such as supertankers; and employing suicide divers or underwater demolition teams to destroy surface platforms. Al-Nashiri is currently being held as one of the last remaining inmates at Guantánamo Bay in Cuba.

Overall, 15 militants were sentenced for their role in the *Limburg* attack, two of whom received the death penalty—Huzam Saleh Mejalli and Fawaz Yahya al-Rabeiee (also written as Fawaz al-Rabihi or Fawaz al-Rabei). The latter escaped from a Yemeni prison on February 3, 2006, but was killed in Sana'a the following October along with another Al Qaeda suspect, Mohammed Daylami.

Although the bombing of the *Limburg* did not destroy the vessel or result in a large loss of life, it did have some serious short-term economic consequences. The incident directly contributed to a brief collapse in international shipping business off the Arabian Peninsula and the Horn of Africa (both key channels to the Suez Canal), led to a $0.48 per barrel hike in the price of Brent crude oil, and tripled the war risks premiums levied on vessels calling at Aden (which resulted in a 93 percent drop in container terminal throughput at a cost of roughly $3.8 million a month in lost port revenues). The *Limburg* was eventually sold to Tanker Pacific Management in 2003 and renamed *Maritime Jewel.*

See also: Al Qaeda; Islamic Army of Aden (IAA); Nashiri, Abd al-Rahim al-; USS *Cole* Bombing

Further Reading

Burnett, John S. *Dangerous Waters: Modern Piracy and Terror on the High Seas.* New York: Penguin Books, 2002.

Chalk, Peter. *The Maritime Dimension of International Security: Terrorism, Piracy and Challenges for the United States.* Santa Monica, CA: RAND, 2006. Pp. 23–24.

Herbert-Burns, Rupert. "Terrorism in the Early 21st Century Maritime Domain." In Joshua Ho and Catherine Zara Raymond, eds., *The Best of Times, the Worst of Times: Maritime Security in the Asia-Pacific.* Singapore: Institute for Defense and Strategic Studies (IDSS), 2005. Pp. 164–65.

"People: Abd al-Rashim al-Nashiri." *New York Times,* April 21, 2011. http://topics.ny times.com/topics/reference/timestopics/people/n/abd_alrahim_al_nashiri/index.html, accessed July 23, 2011.

Richardson, Michael. *A Time Bomb for Global Trade.* Singapore: Institute for Southeast Asian Studies (ISEAS), 2004. Pp. 70–71.

Sheppard, Ben. "Maritime Security Measures." *Jane's Intelligence Review,* March 2003.

Donna Bassett

LINDH, JOHN WALKER

John Walker Lindh, commonly referred to as the "American Taliban," was born in 1981 to a middle-class family in suburban Washington, D.C. His family moved to Marin County, an affluent area in northern California, when he was 10 years old. Lindh attended Tamiscal High School, an alternative institution for "self-directed" students, and was described as hard-working and musically inclined.

At a young age Lindh was moved by the biography of Malcolm X and by 16 had converted to Islam and changed his name to Sulayman. In July 1998 he went to Yemen, where he studied classical Arabic and Islam. Lindh returned to the United States a year later and began worshipping at a San Francisco mosque, although he found the experience dull and flew back to in Yemen in February 2000. His e-mail correspondence began to take on an increasingly radical tone, and in one message sent to his parents he asserted that the Al Qaeda attack on the USS *Cole* was justified because the ship's presence in the region constituted an act of war.

Around this time, Lindh informed his mother and father that he planned to enroll in a religious school in the Northwest Frontier Province (NWFP) of Pakistan. However, he never followed through and in May 2001 began training in a camp operated by Harakat-ul-Mujahideen (HuM), a militant Kashmiri group based north of Islamabad. After 24 days Lindh decided against joining HuM and instead agreed to fight with the Taliban in Afghanistan. In a subsequent interview with CNN, Lindh stated that he came to support the movement's religious doctrine after reading its literature and speaking with supporters in the NWFP.

In late May, Lindh crossed the border into Afghanistan with a letter of introduction from HuM. He was interviewed at a Taliban recruitment center in Kabul and then sent to Al Qaeda's al-Farooq camp. He received seven weeks of training in weapons handling, topography, explosives, and battlefield operations and swore an oath of allegiance to jihad. Following the completion of the course at al-Farooq, Lindh was presented with several options. These included fighting the Northern Alliance or leaving Afghanistan to carry out an attack against an American or Israeli target. Lindh decided to stay in Afghanistan and was deployed to Mazar-e Sharif. He fled to Kunduz on foot after U.S. air strikes began in October 2001; there, he was captured along with 3,000 other Taliban fighters.

In November 2001 Lindh was interviewed by an employee of the Central Intelligence Agency (CIA) at the Qala-i Janghi compound near Mazar-e Sharif. Shortly after the session ended, several hundred prisoners staged an uprising and killed the CIA officer. Lindh heard the commotion and tried to run; however, he was shot in the leg. His companions carried him to a basement, where, after hiding from the authorities for several days, he was eventually caught and apprehended. Having been identified as an American citizen, Lindh spent several weeks being interrogated on a U.S. Navy ship in the North Arabian Sea. He was flown back to the United States on January 23, 2002.

After reaching a deal with prosecutors in 2002, Lindh pled guilty to one count of supplying services to the Taliban and carrying weapons for use against the Northern Alliance. During the trial, Lindh apologized for his actions and stated, "Had I realized then what I know now . . . I would never would have joined [the Taliban.]" He is currently serving a 20-year term in prison at a supermax facility in Florence, Colorado.

See also: Al Qaeda

Further Reading

"The Case of the Taliban American." *CNN People in the News,* December 19, 2001. http://www.cnn.com/CNN/Programs/people/shows/walker/profile.html
"Profile: John Walker Lindh." *BBC News,* January 24, 2002. http://news.bbc.co.uk/2/hi/americas/1779455.stm.
Serrano, Richard A. "Release of Lindh Again Urged." *Los Angeles Times,* April 5, 2007.
United States of America v. John Philip Walker Lindh. U.S. District Court for the Eastern District of Virginia, Alexandria Division, January 15, 2002. http://www.usdoj.gov/ag/criminal complaint1.htm.

Horacio Trujillo

LOD AIRPORT MASSACRE

On May 30, 1972, three members of the Japanese Red Army (JRA), operating on behalf of and in solidarity with the Popular Front for the Liberation of Palestine (PFLP), attacked Tel Aviv's Lod International Airport. The trio had arrived on Air France Flight 132 from Paris and Rome and had hidden Czech VZ-58 automatic rifles and six shrapnel grenades in their checked baggage. After picking up their weapons they indiscriminately opened fire on the 116 passengers that had just deplaned as well as some 300 other people who were congregating in the waiting lounge. The attack killed 28 people and wounded 76 others. Two of the terrorists died in the massacre.

Among the dead were 16 Puerto Rican Catholic pilgrims on a visit to the Holy Land; another 27 of the 68 members of the tour group were wounded. Others killed included Israeli professor Aharon Katchalsky, one of the world's foremost biophysicists. One of the terrorists, identified as Yasuyuki Yasuda, was killed accidentally by bullets from the rifle of Takeshi Ukudaira, who was blown up by a grenade. The surviving member of the squad, Kozo Okamato, ran onto the tarmac outside the terminal in an attempt to blow up an SAS plane parked outside. He was tackled with two grenades in his hands by El Al traffic officer Hannon Claude Zeiton.

Police found out that the trio had also used symbolism in their selection of passports. Okamato claimed to be Daisuke Namba, who had been executed for the attempted assassination of Crown Prince Hirohito in 1923. His birth date was given as December 7, Pearl Harbor Day. Ukudaira using the name Jiro Sugisaki, gave his birthday as February 26, 1937, when Japanese army officers had mutinied. The other dead man, Yasuda, claimed to be Ken Torio and listed his birthday as March 30, the date of the Red Army's hijacking of a Japanese airliner.

PFLP spokesman Bassam Towfik Sherif (aka Bassam Zayad), claimed credit for the attack, referring to the three by their Palestinian names: Bassem, Salah, and Ahmed. Bassam said that the attack was in reprisal for the deaths of two Black September terrorists three weeks earlier in the Sabena hijacking (May 6, 1972) in the United States.

Okamato was indicted with the military offense of political terrorism. The charge carried a death penalty under the 1945 British Emergency Regulations, which had initially been applied to Irgun members. Okamato sabotaged all of his attorney's attempts to provide a defense and tried to convince the court to sentence him to death, stating, "This was our duty, to the people I slaughtered and to my two comrades, who lost their lives. . . . I take on myself full responsibility for it."

He went on to say, "I believe that, as a means toward world revolution, I must prepare the creation of the world Red Army . . . a means of propelling ourselves onto the world stage. . . . The Arab world lacks spiritual fervor, so we felt that through this attempt we could stir up the Arab world. The present world order has given Israel power, which has been denied the Arab refugees. This is the link between the Japanese Red Army (JRA) and the Popular Front for the Liberation of Palestine (PFLP), with whom we collaborate."

Lieutenant Colonel Abraham Frisch, the presiding judge, sentenced Okamato to life imprisonment. His release was subsequently demanded in a number of subsequent incidents, including the September 5, 1972, Olympics massacre; the hijacking of a Japanese Air Lines (JAL) jet on July 20, 1973; and the Entebbe affair of July 1976. Tel Aviv's Lod International Airport was renamed Ben Gurion International Airport in 1973.

See also: Black September Organization (BSO); Japanese Red Army (JRA); Popular Front for the Liberation of Palestine (PFLP); Sabena Airlines Hijacking; Zurich Airport Attack

Further Reading

Farrell, William R. *Blood and Rage: The Story of the Japanese Red Army.* Lexington, MA: Lexington Books, 1990.

"Lebanon Seizes Japanese Rebels Sought in Terror Attacks." *New York Times,* February 19, 1972.

"1972: Japanese Kill 26 at Tel Aviv Airport." *BBC,* May 29, 1972. *BBC on This Day,* http://news.bbc.co.uk/onthisday/hi/dates/stories/may/29/newsid_2542000/2542263.stm

Schreiber, Mark. *Shocking Crimes of Postwar Japan.* New York: Tuttle, 1996.

Donna Bassett

LONDON DOCKLANDS BOMBING

The Provisional Irish Republican Army (PIRA, or the Provos) ended a 17-month cease-fire on February 9, 1996, by detonating a massive vehicle-borne improvised explosive device (VBIED) at Canary Wharf, London's largest office and apartment development. The building contained newspaper, television, and merchant bank offices.

The one-and-a-half-ton fertilizer bomb (3,306 pounds) detonated at 7:02 P.M. in the complex's underground parking garage, destroying part of the South Quay Plaza. The ensuing blast killed two news vendors, Inan Bashir and his assistant John Jefferies, and injured 106 others, 39 seriously. The damage was assessed at $127.5 million. One expert described the incident as "a chilling echo of the first Al Qaeda bomb attack on the New York World Trade Center," which took place on February 26, 1993.

Although the Provos had issued a coded warning of the impending attack to the Radio Telefis Eireann (RTE) Broadcasting Network, it was ignored as a hoax as the PIRA cease-fire was still in effect. As a result, the station failed to contact the security services for over an hour. When the alert was eventually given, police began to clear the area. However, the truck bomb detonated before the evacuation could be finished. When the VBIED exploded, office workers inside the building thought it was going to collapse. The two men killed by the blast were literally blown through two walls. One woman was so badly cut by flying glass that she required over 300 stitches.

Irish prime minister John Bruton responded to the attack by announcing that unless a cease-fire was immediately reinstated, he would refuse to meet with Gerry Adams, the leader of PIRA's political wing, Sinn Féin. He also said he would cancel the previously scheduled early release of seven Provo prisoners.

Many had feared that PIRA had merely called the cease-fire with the British and Irish governments in order to regroup and rearm. The Docklands explosion appeared to bear out this suspicion. Indeed, the incident turned out to be just the first in a string of bombings mounted on mainland England that year, with six subsequently taking place in London and a seventh in Manchester.

In the immediate aftermath of the attack, British police carried out raids on 30 locations. However, although several individuals were arrested, none was charged. A reward of $1.55 million was also offered by local communities in the hope of bringing the perpetrators to justice. This latter initiative resulted in a stream of information, which was used to convict James McArdle of conspiracy to cause explosions in June 1998. He was sentenced to 25 years in prison but released in 2000 under the terms of the 1998 Good Friday Agreement.

The Docklands VBIED was unique in many ways. It was composed of a mixture of ammonium nitrate fertilizer and fuel oil that had been packed in bags and placed around custom-made booster tubes that had been drilled and filled with five kilograms (five pounds) of Semtex (allegedly supplied by Libya). The detonating cord was made from plastic tubing (also filled with explosives) that was connected to an American-made Ireco trigger controlled by a two-hour kitchen timer. To ensure that the VBIED could not be easily disarmed, a motion-sensitive booby trap was installed and activated after the truck was parked at the target location.

Experts concluded that PIRA's South Armagh Brigade had begun construction on the bomb well before the date of the attack, probably sometime in June 1995. Intelligence officials believed that the device had been built at a farm complex (The Slab) owned by Tom Murphy at Ballybinaby near Hackballscross. The property, which the British referred to as the "IRA's Los Alamos," was in the middle of Provo bandit country and difficult, if not impossible, to penetrate. It was considered the heart of PIRA and, later, Real IRA (RIRA) bomb-making operations.

The U.S.-made detonator used in the Canary Wharf bomb was one of 2,900 that had been purchased from Ireco Inc., a mining supply company in Tucson, Arizona, in November 1989. The buyer, Kevin McKinley, a member of the South Armagh Brigade, claimed they were to be used in mining operations. The mechanisms were trucked to New York City and from there shipped across the Atlantic in crates of clothing addressed to a terminally ill AIDS patient in Ireland. The detonators were first used in Northern Ireland in 1991 and later in various London attacks, including bombings at London Bridge station (1992), Bishopsgate (1992), and the Baltic Exchange (1992). After the Canary Wharf incident, one of PIRA's chief quartermasters, Micky McKevitt, stole many of the remaining detonators and took them with him when he formed the breakaway RIRA in 1997. One of these devices was subsequently used to trigger a deadly car bomb in Omagh a year later. That attack, described as one of the worst terrorist atrocities to have ever taken place in Northern Ireland, killed 29 and wounded at least 220.

In 2009 survivors and relatives of victims of past PIRA attacks demanded that British prime minister Gordon Brown support their bid to gain compensation from Colonel Muammar Qaddafi. The Libyan leader was alleged to have provided substantial support to Irish militant groups over the years, including selling Semtex explosive that was used in at least 10 major attacks. Brown declined, saying that he did not think doing so would be "appropriate" at a time when Libya appeared to be making strident attempts to reintegrate itself into the mainstream of global political affairs. The prime minister told Jonathan Ganesh, a security guard who was badly injured in the Canary Wharf attack, that Tripoli "has genuinely become an important international partner for the UK on many levels." This came on the heels of revelations that British oil companies hoping to win lucrative oil contracts in Libya had been asked to donate funds to compensate American victims of terrorism, including the December 21, 1988, midair destruction of Pan Am Flight 103 over Lockerbie, Scotland.

See also: Baltic Exchange Bombing; Bishopsgate Bombing; Manchester City Bombing; Provisional Irish Republican Army (PIRA); Real Irish Republican Army (RIRA)

Further Reading

McKittrick, David, and David McVea. *Making Sense of the Troubles.* London: Penguin Books, 2002.

Moloney, Ed. *A Secret History of the IRA.* New York: W. W. Norton, 2002.

"1996: Dockland's Bomb Ends IRA Ceasefire." *BBC,* February 10, 1996. *BBC on This Day.* http:// news.bbc.co.uk/onthisday/hi/dates/stories/february/10/newsid_2539000/2539265.stm, accessed July 26, 2011.

Oppenheimer, A. R. *IRA: The Bombs and the Bullets: A History of Deadly Ingenuity.* Dublin: Irish Academic Press, 2009.

Tumposky, Ellen, and Don Gentile. "Blast Shatters London; Adams Presumes IRA's Responsible." *Daily News,* February 10, 1996. http://www.nydailynews.com/archives/news/ 1996/02/10/1996-02-10_blast_shatters_london__adams.html, accessed July 26, 2011.

Donna Bassett

LONDON UNDERGROUND BOMBINGS

Four simultaneous suicide bombings of London's public transportation system on July 7, 2005, killed 56 people, including the bombers, and injured more than 700. The terrorist attacks targeted three key lines on the London Underground rail system and one commuter bus, all packed with passengers during the morning rush hour. The attacks were western Europe's first-ever suicide bombings, and the largest terrorist attacks ever committed on British soil.

The three rail attackers detonated their bombs within 50 seconds of one another, at about 8:50 A.M., in trains just outside the Liverpool Street, Edgeware Road, and King's Cross stations. The bus bomb, which hit a double-decker bus in Tavistock Square, exploded at 9:47 A.M. In the ensuing chaos, London police, medical staff, and communications systems struggled to cope. Mobile phone systems were overwhelmed, and a June 2006 report investigating the response to the bombings lamented a lack of medical supplies in area hospitals. Hundreds of people were trapped underground without access to first-aid supplies.

Two weeks later, on July 21, a virtually identical attack on three Underground stations and one bus failed when the bombers' detonating devices did not work. However, the incident again plunged London's transportation system into chaos, just as it had begun to function again after extensive investigations. The attempted attack also raised questions about British security and antiterrorism efforts.

All but one of the suicide bombers responsible for the July 7 attacks were Muslims who had been raised in England. Their backgrounds and seemingly normal lives raised concerns about growing Islamic discontent within the United Kingdom. Many feared that British involvement in the Iraq War had motivated the bombers, but the writings and videos they left behind made no mention of Iraq. Instead, they noted Islamic ideals and anger toward Britain and other Western governments for their treatment of Muslims worldwide. One of the bombers, Mohammad Sidique Khan, said in a posthumous video: "Your democratically elected governments continuously perpetrate atrocities against my people all over the world. Until we feel security, you will be our targets."

Subsequent investigations into the bombings also revealed that two of the bombers, Khan and Shehzad Tanweer, had spent several months in Pakistan from November 2004 to February 2005. Both of their families had migrated to the

The aftermath of a series of coordinated terrorist bombings on July 7, 2005. At least four bombs exploded on London's subway trains and a double-decker bus, with a death toll of 56. A "homegrown" cell of Islamist militants inspired by Al Qaeda carried out the attacks. (AP Photo/Dylan Martinez)

United Kingdom from Pakistan, but investigators believe their 2004 visit included contact with, and training by, Al Qaeda operatives. Khan, who was 30, is believed to have been the mastermind behind the attacks; Tanweer was 22, and the other two bombers were 18 and 19.

A May 2006 report issued after months of investigations into the July 7 attacks blamed a lack of security resources for intelligence agencies' failure to prevent the bombings. Security agents had information about two of the four bombers but had not fully investigated them because they were understaffed and had to address "more pressing priorities," including disrupting known plans to attack the United Kingdom. Britain's domestic intelligence agency, the Security Service (MI5), has estimated that at the time of the London bombings it was investigating about 800 people who were viewed as potential threats and had possible Al Qaeda ties or sympathies. That figure rose to more than 1,000 people in 2007. With several agents needed to monitor one person, intelligence officials said they were simply overwhelmed.

See also: Jaish-e-Mohammed (JeM); Laskar-e-Taiba (LeT); London Underground Bombings (Attempted); Tanweer, Shehzad

Further Reading

Benetto, Jason, and Ian Herbert. "London Bombings: The Truth Emerges." *The Independent* (UK), August 13, 2005.
House of Commons. *Report of the Official Account of the Bombings in London on 7th July 2005.* London: Her Majesty's Stationery Office, May 11, 2006.

"Indepth London Attacks." *BBC News.* http://news.bbc.co.uk/2shared/spl/hi/uk/05/london_blasts/what_happened/html/russel_square.stm.

Intelligence and Security Committee. *Report into the London Terrorist Attacks on 7 July 2005.* London: Her Majesty's Stationery Office, May 11, 2006.

LONDON UNDERGROUND BOMBINGS (ATTEMPTED)

On July 21, 2005, four men attempted to detonate explosive devices at a number of points across London's transport network. Between 12:26 and 12:45 P.M., three small explosions occurred on the Hammersmith and City Line, the Northern Line, and the Victoria Line. Approximately an hour later a fourth bomb detonated on board a London bus on Hackney Road. In all four incidents the devices failed to function correctly, and only the detonating mechanism fired. These incidents took place against a backdrop of heightened security, following the deaths of 52 people two weeks previously in the 7 July suicide bombing attacks. The attempted attacks on July 21 bore strong resemblances to the earlier incident.

Following the failure of the attack, the perpetrators were the subjects of an intensive manhunt across the United Kingdom. As part of this manhunt, police shot and killed a Brazilian national, John Charles de Menezes, at Stockwell Underground station in the mistaken belief he was one of the suspected bombers. Police later admitted that de Menezes had no connection whatsoever to the incidents and apologized for his death.

By July 25 police had named at least two of the suspects—Muktar Said Ibrahim and Yasin Hassan Omar, both residents of the United Kingdom. Omar was arrested in Birmingham on July 27, and two days later Ibrahim and another suspect, Ramzi Mohammed, were detained at an apartment in London. Italian police apprehended a fourth alleged perpetrator, Osman Hussein, in Rome; he was eventually extradited back to the United Kingdom in December 2005. By January 2006, Omar, Ibrahim, Hussain, and Mohammed had been charged with attempted murder, possession of explosives with intent to endanger life, and conspiracy to cause explosions. A fifth suspect, Manfo Kwaku Asiedu, was charged in connection with the discovery of an unexploded bomb in a park in West London shortly after the failed attacks. It was believed Asiedu was meant to be another bomber but had changed his mind and abandoned his device. Another man, Adel Yahya, who had assisted with the preparation of the attacks, was charged with conspiracy to cause explosions.

Muktar Said Ibrahim, born in 1978, was of Eritrean origin, and his family had sought asylum in the United Kingdom in 1990. Granted UK residency in 1992, Ibrahim moved out of the family home in 1994 and did not appear to have a close relationship with them. Having dropped out of college Ibrahim survived on government benefits and by working in a market. He had a criminal record, having participated in a number of gang robberies, and had indecently assaulted a 15-year-old girl. Ibrahim had served five years at a Young Offenders' Institution. At his trial the prosecution asserted that Ibrahim had been the leader, or "emir," of the July 21 team.

Ramzi Mohammed, born in 1981, was of Somali origin. His family had spent time in a refugee camp, and in 1998 he and his brother were sent to Kenya to escape militia recruiters in Somalia. In September of that year Mohammed and his brother arrived in London and were taken in by child welfare services. At 18, Mohammed was granted a visa to remain in the United Kingdom for four years, and in 2001 he secured a job in a bar in London, while studying information technology at college. However, by 2004 Mohammed had become increasingly interested in radical Islam and had begun associating with Ibrahim and Omar and attending sermons given by the radical preacher Abu Hamza at the notorious Finsbury Park mosque. Mohammed also met a Swedish woman of Eritrean origin, and they had two children together.

Yassin Omar was born in Somalia in 1981 and moved to the United Kingdom with his sisters in 1992. He spent much of his teens in the care of the child welfare services or foster parents. Omar does not appear to have been employed, but he did study science at Enfield College in London. Friends later stated that by 2001 he had become increasingly enamored of Islamic teachings and frequently traveled to the Finsbury Park mosque to hear Abu Hamza's sermons. Five days before the July 21 attack, Omar participated in the first part of his marriage ceremony. Following the failure of the bombings, Omar escaped to Birmingham, disguised in a female burka borrowed from his mother-in-law. When armed police broke into the house he was hiding in, Omar was standing in a bath and wearing a rucksack. In the ensuing struggle he was incapacitated with a Taser.

Osman Hussein was born in Ethiopia in 1978. His family moved to Italy in 1992, and in 1996 Hamdi and his brother arrived in the United Kingdom. Here he adopted the name Hussein, claiming to be a Somali asylum seeker. There is little additional biographical detail about Hussein, but it is known he was married with three children. After the attack Hussein escaped to Italy via Paris, using his brother's passport to avoid detection. However, he was tracked to an apartment in Rome and arrested by Italian authorities.

Manfo Kwaku Asiedu (his real name is believed to be Sumaila Abubakhari), who is believed to have backed out of the July 21 attack, was a Ghanaian born in 1973. It appears he was from a relatively well-off family background and received a good education. In July 2003 he borrowed money from a relative to purchase a false Ghanaian passport and bank statements in order to apply for a UK visa under the name George Nanak Marquaye. Arriving in Britain in December 2003, he then adopted the name Asiedu and worked as a painter and decorator. Asiedu frequented a number of mosques in London, including one in Finchley, which Yassin Omar also attended. During the trial Asiedu claimed he discovered the plan to act as suicide bombers only on the morning of July 21, after which he abandoned his device and voluntarily walked into a police station.

Adel Yahya was born in Ethiopia in 1982, later emigrating with his family to Yemen. In 1991 he moved to the United Kingdom with his sister and was granted indefinite leave to remain. After leaving school, where he was a classmate of Yassin Omar, Yahya completed a course in information technology at a London college and in October 2004 began a computing degree at London Metropolitan

University. Yahya attended sermons at the Finsbury Park mosque with Omar and was said to have become increasingly distrustful of British society and the media. Yahya's role in the July 21 plot was to identify sources of hydrogen peroxide for use in the explosives. Yahya was not in the United Kingdom on July 21, having traveled to Ethiopia with his wife on July 11, 2005. He was subsequently extradited back to the United Kingdom.

The trial of these five men began on January 15, 2007, at the high-security Woolwich Crown Court. In the subsequent proceedings a detailed picture of the how the attacks had been planned emerged. Five of the defendants (Ibrahim, Hussein, Mohammed, Omar, and Yahya) all attended a so-called training camp in Cumbria in May 2004. Arranged by Mohammed Hamid (who was convicted in 2008 for organizing terrorist training and soliciting murder), the facility's regimen revolved mostly around physical fitness and instruction in military-style activities. Ibrahim was also believed to have traveled to Sudan in 2003 for weapons training, and in 2004 Ibrahim, Yahya, and Omar all went to Scotland for "team-building." Ibrahim again went overseas in December 2004, flying to Pakistan, where he stayed until March 2005. While there he is believed to have received instruction in the construction of improvised explosive devices (IEDs).

Following Ibrahim's return from Pakistan the cell members began material preparations for the attack. A key component in their plans was the use of hydrogen peroxide as a precursor for their explosives. Between May 9 and July 5, 2005, the cell members bought almost 450 liters (118 gallons) of the chemical from three London suppliers. When a retailer asked why they wanted such large quantities, the cell members claimed it was for stripping wallpaper.

The liquid was then taken to Omar's apartment in a tower block in North London, which was to serve as the cell's bomb factory. The chief explosive charge was to be a mixture of 70 percent concentrated hydrogen peroxide and chapati flour, which would act as an accelerant. The electrical components for the devices were bought from a high-street electronics shop. The main charge was placed inside a large plastic container, to which metal shrapnel was then adhered. The plastic containers were then placed in rucksacks. The detonators consisted of a tube of triacetone triperoxide (TATP), which was to have been activated by means of a flashlight bulb inside the tube, itself connected to a 9-volt battery. The IEDs were virtually identical to those used in the July 7 attacks; however, in this case they failed to function correctly.

Ibrahim claimed that the devices failed to explode because the whole incident was an elaborate hoax to protest the invasion of Iraq. However, expert witnesses suggested that the IEDs did not work due to Ibrahim's incompetence and his inability to mix the correct concentration of hydrogen peroxide. Unlike for the July 7 bombers, no martyrdom videos were discovered. However, when police arrested Ibrahim and Mohammed, they discovered a jihadist banner and headband, similar to those worn by Mohammed Siddique Khan and Shezad Tanweer—two key members of the cell responsible for the earlier July 7, 2005, London bombings that left 52 people dead (commonly referred to as the 7/7 attacks). Also, when Hussein was arrested in Rome, police found a video camera in his possession. It is therefore possible that martyrdom videos were recorded but destroyed following the failure of the attacks.

On July 20 and 21 Ibrahim and his four cell members constructed their devices at Mohammed's house. On the morning of July 21, Ibrahim, Mohammed, and Omar drove to Stockwell Underground station and entered the station. Hussein traveled alone to Westbourne Park station. At around midday, Mohammed used his cell phone to call Hussein, apparently in an effort to coordinate the timing of the attacks. Mohammed was the first to attempt to detonate his IED, at around 12:26 P.M. on board a train at Oval Underground station. The device failed to explode, and Mohammed fled under cover of the ensuing panic. At around 12:37 Omar tried to detonate his IED on board a Victoria Line train traveling between Oxford Circus and Warren Street. Again the device failed, and Omar escaped. At around the same time Osman attempted to detonate his IED on a Hammersmith and City line train traveling between Latimer Road and Sheperd's Bush stations; again the device failed to function, and he jumped onto the tracks to escape. Less than an hour later Ibrahim boarded a London bus and tried to detonate his bomb at Shoreditch High Street. When the IED failed to explode, Ibrahim fled the scene. Asiedu's target was believed to have been the White City Underground station, but he lost his nerve and abandoned his rigged rucksack in a West London park.

At the end of the trial, which took nearly seven months to complete, the jury found Ibrahim, Omar, Hussein, and Mohammed guilty of conspiracy to murder and cause explosions. Each was sentenced to a minimum of 40 years imprisonment. The jury failed to reach verdicts on Yahya and Asiedu, and they were scheduled for a retrial; however, Asiedu later pleaded guilty to conspiring to cause explosions and was sentenced to 33 years. Yahya pleaded guilty to collecting information likely to be of use in the commission of an act of terrorism and was sentenced to six years imprisonment.

At a further trial in February 2008, a number of individuals were charged in connection with the July 21 attacks. Wahbi Mohammed, Ramzi's brother, was convicted of withholding information from the police and with aiding a fugitive and was sentenced to 17 years imprisonment. Siraj Yassin Abdullah Ali, a friend of Yassin Omar, was charged with failing to alert the police about the impending attacks and with helping to clean up the bomb factory after the attacks; he was convicted and given a jail term of 12 years. Abdul Sherif, Osman Hussein's brother, was charged with helping his brother escape to Italy and received a 10-year sentence. Ismail Abdurahman was convicted of helping Hussein evade the police before escaping to Italy and was sentenced to 10 years in prison.

In June 2008 Yeshi Girma, Hussein's wife, was convicted for helping an offender and for withholding information about the bombings; she was sentenced to 15 years imprisonment. Yeshi's brother, Esayas Girma, was convicted at the same time for failing to inform the authorities about the attacks and for helping an offender; he was jailed for 10 years. Mulu Girma, their sister, was also convicted on similar charges and sentenced to 10 years in prison.

See also: Abu Hamza al-Masri (Mustafa Kamel Mustafa); Al Qaeda

Further Reading

Gardham, Duncan. "Five Who Aided July 21 Bombers Sentenced." *Daily Telegraph* (UK), February 5, 2008.

Gardham, Duncan. "July 21 Bombers Trained at Cumbria Camp." *Daily Telegraph* (UK), October 17, 2007.

Lefkowitz, Josh. *The July 21 2005 London Transport Bombings.* The NEFA Foundation, New York, December 2008. http://www.nefafoundation.org/miscellaneous/FeaturedDocs/nefa721bombings.pdf, accessed February 29, 2012.

McGrory, Daniel, Stewart Tendler, and Sean O'Neill. "Captured—All Five 21/7 Bomb Suspects." *The Times* (UK), July 30, 2005.

Oliver, Mark. "July 21 Suspects Arrested." *The Guardian* (UK), July 29, 2005.

"21 July: Attacks, Escapes and Arrests." *BBC News*, July 11, 2007. http://news.bbc.co.uk/2/hi/uk_news/6752991.stm.

"21 July Bomb Plot Trial." *BBC News*, July 11, 2008. http://news.bbc.co.uk/2/hi/in_depth/uk/2007/21_july_trial/default.stm.s

"21 July Plot Suspects: Charges in Full." *BBC News*, January 27, 2006. http://news.bbc.co.uk/2/hi/uk_news/4130420.stm.

Greg Hannah

LONDON-GLASGOW AIRPORT PLOT

Shortly after 3:00 P.M. on June 30, 2007, two men attempted to drive a sport-utility vehicle (SUV) through the entrance doors of the passenger terminal at Glasgow International Airport in Scotland, the United Kingdom. The SUV was prevented from entering the terminal by a security barrier; the two occupants then set the vehicle, which contained petrol and propane gas canisters, on fire. One of the vehicle's occupants, Kafeel Ahmed, was severely burned in the fire, while the other, Bilal Abdullah, escaped with minor injuries. Police, assisted by members of the public, quickly detained both men. The airport terminal suffered extensive external damage in the fire that resulted. It rapidly became apparent that the same two men had been involved in planting two failed vehicle bombs, which had been discovered in London the previous day.

Within a few days of the attacks, police had arrested eight individuals, including one in Australia. Several of those detained were medical personnel, which drew considerable media attention, and the attack became know as the "Doctors' Plot." Three men were initially charged: Dr. Bilal Abdullah and Dr. Mohammed Asha in the United Kingdom and Dr. Mohammed Haneef (the cousin of Ahmed) in Australia. The Australian authorities later withdrew the charges against Haneef, but Abdullah and Asha were sent to London for trial. Asha, who was charged with helping to fund the attack, was acquitted on all counts. Ahmed's brother, Sabeel, was also arrested and charged with failing to inform police of an imminent terrorist attack (Kafeel had apparently sent him an e-mail before the attack explaining his actions).

Bilal Talal Samad Abdullah was born in the United Kingdom on September 17, 1980, where his father, an Iraqi national, worked in the medical sector. In 1985 the family returned to Iraq, where Abdullah studied in Baghdad, qualifying as a doctor in 2004. Abdullah returned to the United Kingdom in the same year, undertaking further training at Addenbrookes hospital in Cambridge before registering to work as a doctor in 2006. In May 2006 he returned to Iraq for three months before moving to work as a junior house officer at the Royal Alexandria Hospital in Paisley, Scotland. At his trial Abdullah claimed to have been motivated by the destruction wrought in Iraq, both by sanctions in the 1990s and in the subsequent invasion in 2003. It has also been suggested that he was radicalized by the persecution of his family and friends by Shi'a militants in Iraq. Abdullah may also have been a member of Hizb-ut Tahrir.

Ahmed, who suffered burns on 90 percent of his body and died of his injuries, was born in Bangalore, India, on January 1, 1979. Ahmed's parents were both doctors, and the family had spent time in Saudi Arabia. Ahmed was an engineer and was studying in Cambridge for a PhD in computational fluid dynamics, not medicine (initial media reporting confused Kafeel with his brother, Sabeel, who was a doctor). Having completed a bachelor's degree in mechanical engineering in India in 2000, Kafeel is known to have been in the United Kingdom as early as 2003, when he received a master's degree in aeronautical engineering from Queen's University Belfast. Kafeel, reportedly a member of Tablighi Jamaat, was known to have a keen awareness of the conflicts in Palestine, Afghanistan, and Iraq and was reported to have frequented Islamist chat rooms on the Internet.

At Abdullah and Asha's trial, significant detail regarding the London and Glasgow attacks was revealed. The court heard that Ahmed had met Abdullah in Cambridge when he was living at a property owned by an Islamic charity. The two men reportedly began discussing the possibility of an attack in February 2007. In late April, Abdullah had rented a house in Renfrewshire, Scotland. Ahmed (Kafeel) arrived from India on May 5 and joined Abdullah. Over the following weeks they purchased components for their devices from local hardware stores and acquired the vehicles that were used in both London and Glasgow.

Both devices placed in London consisted of petrol containers, gas cylinders, and packets of nails. The intent was for the petrol vapor inside the vehicles to be ignited by an improvised detonator consisting of lightbulb filaments placed inside a bundle of matches. These were to have been initiated via a mobile phone wired to the bulb. On June 28 both men drove their vehicle bombs from Scotland to London, and early on the morning of June 29, both vehicles were placed in West London. It later emerged that multiple calls had been made to the detonators in each of the vehicles, but both failed to explode. It has been suggested that one reason for this was the lack of oxygen inside the cars, which prevented the petrol and gas vapors from igniting. The first device was made safe in situ by bomb disposal officers; the second rigged car had been towed by parking enforcement officers, who later called police because of the smell of petrol emanating from the vehicle. Ahmed and Abdullah had earlier left the scene and spent the night in a London hotel before catching a train back to Scotland on the morning of the 29th.

Realizing it was now a matter of time before the police identified and arrested them, the two men chose to conduct a hasty improvised suicide attack. Early on the morning of June 30, they loaded their SUV with gas cylinders, petrol, and nails and drove to a scenic location near Loch Lomond, where they spent eight hours praying and preparing themselves. On two occasions the police came very close to intercepting the bombers, missing them at their rented house by around an hour. The men then drove from Loch Lomond to Glasgow airport, where they tried to conduct the attack. When their vehicle became immobilized, they set fire to it and began throwing petrol bombs. After a violent scuffle with police and passersby, both men were subdued and arrested. Asha was arrested that evening as he and his wife traveled down the M6 motorway. Kafeel's brother Sabeel was arrested at the Liverpool train station.

In December 2008, the jury in Abdullah's trial found him guilty of conspiring to murder and of conspiring to cause explosions. He was sentenced to life imprisonment, with a minimum of 32 years to be served. Asha was found not guilty on the same charges and was released. Sabeel Ahmed had earlier pleaded guilty to withholding information from the police and was sentenced to 18 months imprisonment; however, as he had already spent 9 months on remand, he was immediately deported to India. After his release by the Australian authorities, Mohammed Haneef also returned to India.

Further Reading

"Behind the London-Glasgow Plot." *BBC News*, December 16, 2008. http://news.bbc.co.uk/2/hi/uk_news/7772925.stm.

Clements, Jon. "Glasgow Airport Terror Attack: Suspects Tried to Detonate Car Bomb 15 Times, Court Hears." *Daily Record*, October 21, 2008.

"Doctor Guilty of Car Bomb Attacks." *BBC News*, December 16, 2008. http://news.bbc.co.uk/2/hi/uk_news/7773410.stm.

Marsden, Sam. "Glasgow Airport Terror Attack: Doctors Created Bomb Factory in Suburban House." *Daily Record*, October 10, 2008.

O'Hare, Paul. "Glasgow Airport Terror Attack: Cops Tell of Race to Catch the Bombers." *Daily Record*, December 17, 2008.

Siddique, Haroon. "Glasgow Airport Car Bomber Jailed for 32 Years." *The Guardian* (UK), December 17, 2008.

Taylor, Matthew. "The Doctor, the Engineer and a Failed Call That Averted Disaster." *The Guardian* (UK), December 17, 2008.

Taylor, Matthew. "Just One Open Window Would Have Caused Carnage." *The Guardian* (UK), December 16, 2008.

Greg Hannah

LORENZ (PETER) KIDNAPPING

On February 27, 1975, just three days before the mayoral election in West Berlin, members of Movement 2 June (M-2) kidnapped Peter Lorenz. In addition to being a candidate in the upcoming race, he was also chairman of the Berlin Christian Democratic Union (CDU).

Two armed men and a woman stopped Lorenz's car and, after knocking out the chauffeur, drugged him. The following day M-2 demanded that six convicted militants be freed, given 8,900 marks, and flown out of the country (accompanied by the retired mayor of Berlin, Heinrich Albertz). They also insisted on the release of all those imprisoned for protesting the November 10, 1974, death of Holger

Meins, a member of the Rote Armee Fraktion (RAF, or Red Army Faction) who had died after staging a 56-day hunger strike in Treveri prison.

The West German government agreed to M-2's demands within 72 hours. Verena Becker, 22, a telephone operator serving six years for bank robbery and bombings, and Ingrid Siepmann, 30, a technical pharmaceutical assistant serving 12 years for similar crimes, were flown from West Berlin to Frankfurt along with Albertz. Upon landing, the trio was joined by another three individuals: Rolf Pohl, 33, an attorney serving six years for belonging to the Baader-Meinhof Gang; Rolf Heissler, 26, a student jailed for eight years on charges of armed robbery; and Gabriele Kröcher-Tiedemann, a member of M-2 who had been imprisoned for shooting a policeman in 1973. Horst Mahler, one of the original Baader-Meinhof four, chose to remain in detention.

The group, including Albertz, boarded a Lufthansa plane and left the country. After being turned away from Libya, Lebanon, Syria, and Jordan, the People's Democratic Republic of Yemen granted the terrorists political asylum, and they were allowed to land and deplane in Aden. Albertz was freed and flew home the following day in order to broadcast a coded message from the terrorists. Lorenz was released in a West Berlin park six hours later.

On September 14, 1975, West Berlin police arrested Fritz Teufel, 32, for the Lorenz kidnapping after he was detained in a police sweep following a bombing in Hamburg that injured 11 people. Just over three months later, Kröcher-Tiedemann accompanied Carlos the Jackal (Ilich Ramirez Sanchez) in the December 20 raid of the Organization of Petroleum Exporting Countries (OPEC) headquarters in Vienna, Austria. She shot and killed two people and the following year was suspected of involvement with the Entebbe hijacking.

Pohl was arrested in Greece on July 22, 1976. The West German government immediately requested his extradition, and after a long legal battle, the Supreme Court in Athens agreed to send him back, acknowledging any other decision could potentially "make Greece a haven for international terrorists or any fugitive on the lam." Pohl was returned to Munich on October 3, 1976.

See also: Baader-Meinhof Gang; Entebbe Hostage Rescue; OPEC Ministers Attack; Sanchez, Ilich Ramirez (Carlos the Jackal); Rote Armee Fraktion (RAF)

Further Reading

Becker, Jillian. *Hitler's Children: The Story of the Baader-Meinhof Terrorist Gang.* London: Michael Joseph, 1978.

Bougereau, Jean Marcel. *The German Guerrilla: Terror, Reaction, and Resistance: Memoirs of an International Terrorist: Conversations with Hans Joachim Klein.* Minneapolis, MN: Soil of Liberty, 1981.

Meinhof, Ulrike. *Everybody Talks about the Weather . . . We Don't: The Writings of Ulrike Meinhof.* New York: Seven Stories, 2008.

Vague, Tom. *Televisionaries: The Red Army Faction Story 1963–1993.* San Francisco: AK Press, 1994.

Donna Bassett

LOYALIST VOLUNTEER FORCE (LVF)

The Loyalist Volunteer Force (LVF) is a Protestant paramilitary group in Northern Ireland. The formation of the LVF came about in the context of the June/July 1996 Drumcree Crisis, in which Protestant Orangemen were prevented from marching along the Garvaghy Road, a predominantly Roman Catholic area. The LVF emerged during this standoff, made up of disaffected members of the Ulster Volunteer Force (UVF), notably Billy Wright (also known as "King Rat"), a self-professed born-again Christian and the UVF's Mid-Ulster "brigade commander." Wright, thought to have been responsible for the deaths of at least 30 people, was expelled from the UVF for the unsanctioned killing of a Roman Catholic taxi driver, which breached the cease-fire that the UVF and the majority of the loyalist paramilitaries had announced in response to the first Provisional Irish Republican Army (PIRA) cease-fire in 1994.

While the overwhelming majority of UVF members in Belfast remained loyal to their existing leadership, former members of a UVF unit based in Portadown formed the core of the LVF. From the outset, the LVF's objective was to thwart the possibility of reconciliation between the Nationalist and Unionist communities in Northern Ireland. To this end the group carried out a series of notably brutal murders of Roman Catholic civilians during July 1997, including the use of torture and mutilation that was reminiscent of the methods employed by the UVF's Shankill Butchers in the mid-1970s. In August 1997 the LVF also planted four small explosive devices in Dundalk in the Irish Republic, but the devices were rendered safe by the security forces.

In parallel, the LVF and their former comrades in the UVF engaged in an increasingly violent feud, with several UVF attempts to kill senior LVF members. Wright himself may have been saved from assassination in 1998 at the hands of the UVF by being sentenced to eight years in prison for witness intimidation. However, any reprieve was short-lived and on December 27, 1998, Wright was murdered within the high-security Maze prison by three prisoners from the Irish National Liberation Army (INLA) while awaiting transport inside a prison van. The INLA prisoners claimed he had been killed for waging a war on the Nationalist population from inside the high-security Maze prison.

The leadership of the LVF then passed to one of Wright's lieutenants, Mark Fulton, and in retaliation for Wright's murder the LVF stepped up their attacks against Roman Catholic targets, killing 10 civilians and a former PIRA member between December 1997 and April 1998. The LVF also sought to strengthen its position though cooperation with elements of the Ulster Defence Association (UDA)/Ulster Freedom Fighters (UFF), particularly the unit commanded by Johnny Adair. A number of the killings for which the LVF claimed responsibility in early 1998 were in fact the work of UDA gunmen. These deaths incited a response from the INLA, which retaliated with the murder of a UDA member in Belfast. The PIRA also breached its cease-fire in retaliation for the UDA/LVF campaign, killing a leading UDA man and bringing about a political crisis in the ongoing peace process. This led then secretary of state for Northern Ireland, Mo Mowlam, to visit loyalist paramilitaries in prison to ask for a cessation of the violence. Partly as a result of her intervention, and political pressure being placed on the UDA's political representatives, the group's leadership reined in its members. However, the LVF continued its killing spree. On April 29 a gunman from the group murdered a Roman Catholic council worker in Portadown, shooting him at point-blank range. The next month LVF members fatally shot a 22-year-old student near Crumlin in Antrim.

However, within a month of this last killing, the LVF announced to general surprise that it was calling its own cease-fire. The statement was formally recognized by the British government in November 1998, which entitled LVF members to the paramilitary prisoner early-release scheme installed under the Good Friday Agreement. In December 1998 the LVF became the first Irish paramilitary group to hand over weapons to the Independent International Commission on Decommissioning.

Despite this official recognition, the LVF was widely believed to have been behind the March 1999 murder of human-rights lawyer Rosemary Nelson. The murder was claimed by the Red Hand Defenders (RHD), suspected to be a flag of convenience for loyalist paramilitaries wishing to carry out attacks without breaching their parent organizations' cease-fires. Another incident in September 2001 that involved the killing of Martin O'Hagen, an investigative journalist, caused the British government to withdraw its recognition of the LVF (and the UDA/UFF) cease-fires. Although the RHD claimed responsibility for the murder, police forensic investigators discovered that the pistol O'Hagen had been shot with was the same one used in a previous LVF murder.

By the end of 1999 the LVF had become openly involved in another round of feuding with the UVF. Tension had built up between the two groups in Portadown, resulting in the UVF raiding an LVF bar and assaulting a number of LVF members, several of whom were badly beaten. In retaliation, the LVF murdered the UVF's regional commander, Richard Jameson. Jameson was a respected figure within his movement and the Protestant community, and thousands of supporters attended his funeral. The UVF subsequently drew up a hit list of those thought to have been responsible for Jameson's killing. In January 2000 two young men, one linked to the LVF, were abducted, beaten, and stabbed to death by a UVF gang in Tandragee. The UVF also tried but failed to kill the gunman who had assassinated Jameson. Members of Adair's UDA unit escorted the intended victim, who had survived the attack, out of Belfast, inflaming tensions between that group and the UVF. Hostility between the two groups turned into open conflict in August 2000, when a UDA parade turned into a violent confrontation with UVF supporters, and the two main loyalist paramilitary groupings embarked on an intensive bout of internecine violence and killing.

In June 2002, the LVF lost its second leader when Fulton was found hanging in Maghaberry prison; he was believed to have committed suicide. Fulton was replaced by his brother Gary, who was himself soon arrested. Robin King then assumed leadership and committed to repairing and restoring the damaged relationship between the LVF and Adair's Belfast UDA. At one point it appeared that the former might fully merge with the latter, but this was prevented by Adair's arrest and reimprisonment.

In 2004 and 2005, the LVF and UVF returned to fighting each other. The violence was so serious that the International Monitoring Commission resolved to issue a report dealing solely with the feud. Between May 2004 and August 2005 the UVF killed five individuals it judged to be associated with the LVF, with a further 38 attacks (including 17 attempted murders) on LVF members or associates. The UVF leadership sought to eliminate the LVF altogether, which caused the latter to issue a statement in October 2005 that it was "standing down" its military units. While the LVF does not appear to have actually disbanded, it was described in 2010 by the International Monitoring Commission as a "small organization without any political purpose; people historically linked to it were heavily involved in crime . . . and the proceeds of these crimes were for personal and not organizational use."

See also: Irish National Liberation Army (INLA); Red Hand Defenders (RHD); Ulster Defence Association (UDA)/Ulster Freedom Fighters (UFF); Ulster Volunteer Force (UVF)

Further Reading

"Call on LVF to Disband." *BBC News,* January 16, 2000. http://news.bbc.co.uk/2/hi/uk_news/northern_ireland/605553.stm.

Cusack, Jim, and Henry McDonald. *UVF: The Endgame.* Dublin: Poolberg, 2008.

"Loyalist Volunteer Force." *Jane's World Insurgency and Terrorism,* 2006.

"Politicians Assess Ceasefire End." *BBC News,* October 13, 2001. http://news.bbc.co.uk/2/hi/uk_news/northern_ireland/1596068.stm.

Sixth Report of the Independent Monitoring Commission. London: HMSO Stationery Office, September 2005.

Streeter, Michael. "UVF Disbands Unit Linked to Taxi Murder." *The Independent* (UK), August 3, 1996.

Taylor, Peter. *Loyalists.* London: Bloomsbury, 1999.

Twenty-Third Report of the Independent Monitoring Commission. London: HMSO Stationery Office, May 2010.

Greg Hannah

LUFTHANSA HIJACKING (1972)

On October 29, 1972, two Black September Organization (BSO) terrorists armed with revolvers and grenades hijacked Lufthansa Flight 615 after it departed the Beirut airport. The pair, Samir Arif El Shahed and Mahmoud Saleh, told the aircraft's captain they would blow up the plane unless the three BSO militants who had survived the September 5, 1972, Olympics attack in West Germany (also known as the Munich Massacre) were released from jail in a Munich prison. They ordered the captain, Walter Clausen, to divert to Nicosia, Cyprus.

The West German government initially responded that there was no plane immediately available to transport the three detained terrorists. The hijackers then offered an alternative solution, ordering the pilot to fly to Zagreb, Yugoslavia, where they would pick up their BSO colleagues. Bonn acceded and within hours flew the three militants to the designated transfer point, where they then joined the hijackers aboard the Lufthansa Boeing 727. The plane then departed for Tripoli, Libya, where they were greeted as heroes. The passengers and crew returned to Frankfurt, Germany, aboard a special flight the following day.

The return of the hostages was celebrated in the Middle East. But the Israelis were stunned. A Foreign Ministry spokesman vehemently denounced the decision, issuing a statement on October 29 that "every capitulation encourages the terrorists to continue their criminal acts." Golda Meir, the prime minister, decided that the release of the Munich killers could not go unanswered and required action. She immediately authorized Mossad to launch Operation Wrath of God (Mivtzan Elohim), and for the next 20 years Israeli agents were given the mandate to track down and assassinate all those connected with the Olympics attacks.

Of the three militants set free, two were subsequently killed by the Israelis. The third, Jamal al-Gashey, survived in hiding. He later gave an interview to the team of the Oscar-nominated documentary *One Day in September,* during which he claimed Bonn had entered into a prior agreement with the Popular Front for the Liberation of Palestine (PFLP) to release the trio to avoid further bloodshed in the country. Although Chancellor Willy Brandt strongly denied any such deal, Al-Gashey's allegations were supported by a range of senior German, Palestinian, and Israeli intelligence and political sources. Indeed, Ulrich Wegener, then a key aide of the interior minister and the founder of Germany's crack counterterrorist unit, Grenzschutzgruppe-9 (GSG-9), specifically claimed that following the Munich massacre, Bonn had instituted an unofficial policy of avoiding any confrontation with Palestinian groups.

See also: Black September Organization (BSO); Munich Olympic Games Massacre; Popular Front for the Liberation of Palestine (PFLP)

Further Reading

Dobson, Christopher. *Black September: Its Short, Violent History.* London: Robert Hale, 1975.
Klein, Aaron J. *Striking Back: The 1972 Munich Olympics Massacre and Israel's Deadly Response.* New York: Random House, 2005.
Reeve, Simon. *One Day in September: The Full Story of the 1972 Munich Olympics Massacre and the Israeli Revenge Operation "Wrath of God."* New York: Arcade, 2000.

Donna Bassett

LUFTHANSA HIJACKING (1977)

Since the early 1970s, the West German government had confronted a persistent terrorist threat from the Rote Armee Fraktion (RAF, or Red Army Faction). Although most of the group's leadership had been arrested by 1972, including Andreas Baader, Gudrun Ensslin, Ulrike Meinhof, and Jan-Carl Raspe, a second wave of RAF militants continued their actions. In 1977 these members hatched a plan with colleagues from Wadi Haddad's Popular Front for the Liberation of

Palestine—Special Operations Group (PFLP-SOG) to dramatically increase pressure on the West German government.

On October 13, 1977, Lufthansa Flight LH181 took off from Palma de Mallorca for Frankfurt in Germany. The crew consisted of Captain Jürgen Schumann, copilot Jurgen Vietor, and three stewardesses, with around 86 passengers. Within 30 minutes, four members of the PFLP-SOC hijacked the aircraft—two men, including the group's leader Zohair Yousif Akache, and two women, all of whom were armed with pistols and grenades. The passengers and crew were threatened and told that anyone who disobeyed the hijackers' commands would be shot; the attackers were distributed around the plane to enable easier control. The plane landed at Rome's Fiumicino Airport, where Akache, now referring to himself as Captain Martyr Mahmud, demanded the release of all RAF prisoners, two additional Palestinians, and a ransom of $15 million. An initial deadline was set for 8 A.M. on Sunday, October 16.

Because Italian government authorities were concerned at the prospect of a terrorist incident occurring on their territory, they agreed to refuel the plane and allowed it to leave. The jet flew first Cyprus before landing at the Bahrain airport in the early hours of October 14. Meanwhile, the German chancellor had formed a crisis cabinet, and, continuing a hard-line approach, Minister of State Hans-Jürgen Wischnewski contacted Colonel Ulrich Wegener, the head of the elite German intervention unit Grenzschutzgruppe-9 (GSG-9), to place the unit on standby. On the evening of October 13 a Lufthansa jet took off from Frankfurt containing government officials and officers from the Federal Criminal Police Office. Stopping briefly in Cologne to pick up 30 members of the GSG-9 in civilian clothes, the aircraft flew to Ankara, Turkey, where it remained in holding. By this time the hijacked plane had left Bahrain and been given permission to land in Dubai.

Despite the negotiations of the Dubai authorities, the situation on board the plane grew extremely tense, with Mahmud accusing the passengers and crew of being Jewish. He suffered violent mood swings, screaming abuse at one moment and demanding cake and champagne the next when he discovered it was the birthday of one stewardess. Tensions heightened when a generator providing power for air-conditioning failed, prompting suspicion on the part of Mahmud that a rescue plan was in the works. In response he threatened to shoot Captain Schumann.

On October 15, Minister of State Wischnewski and a psychologist named Wolfgang Salewski traveled to Dubai where they liaised with Colonel Wegener and a small GSG-9 reconnaissance team. The following day Major Alastair Morrison and Staff Sergeant Barry Davies of the British Special Air Service (SAS) joined them, following a request from the West German government for assistance. Despite the presence of such highly trained personnel, the Dubai authorities insisted that any rescue operation had to be carried out by their own forces. However, before such an option became necessary, Mahmud demanded that the jet be refueled and again took off, this time headed to Aden, where the plane was forced to make an emergency landing.

After the plane came to a stop Captain Schumann asked permission to check the exterior of the aircraft for any structural damage. Although Mahmud agreed, he soon became agitated at the amount of time the inspection was taking, and when Schumann returned, Mahmud shot him dead. Having demanded that the Yemenis refuel the aircraft, Vietor managed to take off and under Mahmud's orders flew to Mogadishu, Somalia, arriving on the morning of Monday, October 17.

Wischnewski, the GSG-9 team, and the two SAS troopers rapidly made their way to Mogadishu, where the minister of state sought permission to launch a rescue bid. This was granted, and Operation "Fire Magic" was initiated. Negotiators first opened a line of communication with Mahmud and successfully persuaded him to extend his latest deadline on the pretext that the RAF prisoners had been released and were being flown to Somalia. While these talks were going on, a small GSG-9 team crept up to the aircraft and, using sound detectors and image intensifiers, identified Mahmud and confirmed that he and another terrorist were in the cockpit.

At around 1:30 A.M. on the morning of October 18, the entry teams formed and approached the aircraft, where they silently placed ladders beside the fuselage and wings. At just past 2:00 A.M. Colonel Wegener gave the order to storm the plane, taking advantage of a huge fire that Somali troops had ignited to distract the terrorists. The two SAS men threw stun grenades over the cockpit and wings, causing deafening explosions and blinding light. At this moment the GSG-9 squad entered the aircraft through various doors. The rear team fatally shot one of the female hijackers almost immediately, injuring and capturing a second who had fled to a toilet. Mahmud and the other male terrorist were killed in the cockpit area. The whole assault was over in five minutes, and all remaining passengers and crew were released with only minor injuries.

See also: Popular Front for the Liberation of Palestine (PFLP); Rote Armee Fraktion (RAF)

Further Reading

Aust, Stefan. *The Baader-Meinhof Complex.* London: Bodley Head, 2008.

Harclerode, Peter. *Secret Soldiers: Special Forces in the War against Terrorism.* London: Cassell, 2002.

Merkl, Peter. "West German Left-Wing Terrorism." In Martha Crenshaw, ed., *Terrorism in Context.* University Park: Pennsylvania State University Press, 1995.

Scholzen, Reinhard, and Kerstin Froese. *GSG 9.* Stuttgart, Germany: Motorbuch, 2007.

Tophoven, Rolf. *GSG 9: Kommando gegen Terrorismus.* Koblenz, Germany: Wehr & Wissen, 1977.

Richard Warnes